The Secret Fidel Castro

Also by Servando González

BOOKS

Arte: realismo o realidad
Historia de las artes visuales
(with Armando Ledón)
Historia herética de la revolución fidelista
(published in Mexico as Fidel Castro para
herejes y otros invertebrados)
Observando

MULTIMEDIA

Real History of "The Horse": A HyperComic
How to Create Your Own Personal Intelligence Agency
The Riddle of the Swastika: A Study in Symbolism
Popol Vuh: An Interactive Text/Graphics Adventure
Hypertext for Beginners

INTERNET SITES

Castromania: The Fidel Watch
FAQs About Fidel Castro
Tyrant Aficionado
The Swastika and the Nazis
Memoirs of a Computer Heretic

The Secret Fidel Castro
Deconstructing the Symbol

Servando González

Spooks Books
An Imprint of InteliBooks *Publishers*

All rights reserved. Copyright © 2001 by Servando González

No part of this book may be reproduced or transmitted in any form or by any means, graphic, electronic or mechanical, including photocopying, recording, taping or by any information storage or retrieval system, without permission in writing from the publisher, except by a reviewer, who may quote short passages in a review.

Library of Congress Cataloging-in-Publication Data

González, Servando, 1935-

The secret Fidel Castro : deconstructing the symbol / Servando González.
p.   cm.

Includes bibliographical references and index.

ISBN 0-9711391-0-5 (hardcover) 0-9711391-1-3 (softcover)

1. Castro, Fidel, 1927-   —Psychology. 2. Castro, Fidel 1927-   —Mental health.
3. Cuba—History—1959-   I. Title.
F1788.22.C3 G68 2001
972.9106'4'092—dc21
Library of Congress Control Number 2001003119

Cover design: Damion Gordon - BTP Graphx
Cover illustration: Servando González

This book was printed in the United States of America
To order additional copies of this book, contact:

InteliBooks
www.InteliBooks.com
Orders@InteliBooks.com

This book is dedicated to Theodore Draper

Contents

Preface	xi
Acknowledgments	xiii
Introduction	xv
Do We Understand Fidel Castro?	xviii
An Unorthodox View of Fidel Castro	xxi

Part One: Deconstructing The Symbol

Chapter 1. Charisma . . . and Beyond   29

Castro's Powers of Fascination	31
Castro's Powers of Clairvoyance	43
Castro's Extraordinary Good Luck	49

Chapter 2. The Great Pulverizer   53

Fidel's Extraordinary Love for Nuclear Missiles	53
Castro's Attempts to Destroy New York . . . and Much More	56
Castro's Search for The Great Equalizer	59
Castro Goes Nuclear . . . Powered	62
Castro's Wet Dreams of Nuclear Armageddon	65
If Not With a Bang, Perhaps With a Whiff	71
Castro's Biological Weapons	73

Chapter 3. Castro's Manifest Destiny   76

Setting the Record Straight	78
I'll Kill 200,000 Gringos	82
Castro Follows his Course	85
Fidel's Thirst for Revenge	88
Self-provocation as a Foreign Policy Tool	89
Still, Americans Don't Get It	94

Chapter 4. A Caribbean Magnicide — 96

Castro's Version of the Kennedy Assassination — 101
Killing Presidents: Castro's Life-long Obsession — 105
Castro's Expertise in Political Assassination — 111
High-Tech Political Assassinations — 115
A Furiously Castro-hostile View of JFK's Assassination — 118
Was Fidel Castro the Hidden Hand? — 125

Chapter 5. Fidel's Sociolism — 132

The Cuban Economy Before Castro — 133
A Cuban Robber Baron — 136
Fidel's Happy, Good Life in His Proletarian Paradise — 139
A Corrupt Tyrant — 141
The Comandante's Reserves — 142
Fidel's Business Enterprises — 143
The Comandante's Other Revenue Sources — 146
Castro-Cuban Banking — 148
From Socialism to Sociolism — 149
Fidel's Cronies — 150
Castro Loves Cuban Art — 154

Part Two: Who is Fidel Castro? What is he?

Chapter 6. The Secret Fidel Castro — 161

The Maximum Leader — 162
Castro's Photographic Memory — 164
Castro's Uncommon Abilities — 165
The Dark Side of Fidel Castro — 171
Fidel The Procrastinator — 175
Castro's Mastery of Symbols — 178
A Man Driven by Envy — 179
The Misery Specialist — 183
Fidel's Epiphany — 186
Castro's Health Problems — 188
Fidel's Rages — 193
Castro's Innate Cruelty — 195

Castro's Twisted Mind	198
The Great Dissembler	203
Fidel's Lack of a Sense of Humor	207
The Cowman from Birán	208
Castro's Split Personality	212
Is Fidel Castro Crazy?	215
Is Fidel a Gay in the Closet?	216
Homosexuals in Fidel's Paradise	220
Is Fidel Castro a Racist?	223
A Closet Gringophile	227
King Fidel I	229

Chapter 7. Castroism: A Tropical Variety of Facism? 233

The Soviet Union and Latin America	234
The Cuban Communists and Fidel	236
Fidel's Short-lived Anticommunism	244
Fidel's Short-lived Humanism	246
Communist "Infiltration" Continues	248
Fidel Becomes a "Marxist"	249
Castro and the Catholic Church	252
Enter the Jesuits	255
The Opium of the People	259
A Man Called "The Horse"	260
Fidel's Links to Santería	261
Blood Offerings Disguised as Foreign Policy	267
The Babalawos Change Their Tune	268
Elián: Fidel's Eleggúa?	270
Castro and the anti-Communist Cuban Exiles	271
Fidel's Fascist Roots	274
A Caribbean Führer?	279
Is Castroism Fascism in Disguise?	284
What Really is Castroism?	295
The Castroist Cult	296
Fidel's True Ideology	299
The Man Behind the Symbol	303

Epilogue 306
Who is Fidel Castro? 307
What is He? 308
The Monster Next Door 309
The Boy Without a Name 316
What to do With Castro? 318
Castro and the Cuban "Revolution" 327

Afterword 331
A Sad Day for Fidel Castro? 331
Cuban Terrorists: In Miami or in Havana? 342
The U. S. Government's Strange Blindness 345

Appendixes
1. *Castro's Letter to Celia Sánchez* 354
2. *Castro's Letter to President Roosevelt* 356
3. *The Evaluation of Information* 361

Notes 363
Bibliography 463
Index 477

Preface

The Secret Fidel Castro: Deconstructing the Symbol, is not a history of the Cuban revolution but a study of Fidel Castro. Neither is it a biography of Fidel Castro, of whom many have been written, ranging from the excellent to the mediocre.

This book focuses on different aspects of Castro's personality which, for some reasons, have been either ignored or misrepresented. It originates from my own experiences in Cuba before and after Castro took power in 1959.

From 1959 to 1963 I was a political officer in the Cuban Army. As such I participated in the Bay of Pigs operation, the Cuban missile crisis, the massive anti-guerrilla actions in the Escambray mountains, and other important military operations. Also, on two occasions, in 1960 and in 1964, I had the opportunity of engaging in long conversations with Castro.

Though I was never part of the Castroist *nomenklatura* or a member of Castro's "communist" party, for some time I had the opportunity of moving within the high circles of the Castro government as a technocrat, specializing in educational technology and closed-circuit tv—the fad of the moment among the Castroist élite. In that capacity, in the mid-seventies I was an advisor to Raúl León Torras, President of the National Bank of Cuba, and to Dr. José Rivero Muñiz, Minister of Public Health. For a short period of time I was an advisor for Antonio Enrique Lussón, Minister of Transportation. I also provided advice on such subjects to Marcelo Fernández Font, Minister of Foreign Trade.

In addition, I had the opportunity of experiencing first hand most of the events I mention in this book, like the failed ten million ton sugar crop, the Mariel boatlift, and the planned, systematic destruction of Cuba and its people by Fidel Castro.

The reader will notice, however, that two important events in the history of the Cuban revolution, the Bay of Pigs and the Cuban missile crisis, are barely mentioned. There are two reasons for this. First, I am already working on two books dealing with these topics in detail. Second, as I explained above, this book is not a history of the Cuban revolution but a study of Fidel Castro, and I am not studying Castro's life as a linear process or one that is historically concluded.

On the other hand, every chapter of this book provides information which helps the reader understand the rest, therefore, it is better to read it in the order provided, avoiding the temptation to skip chapters. Secondly, I advise the reader not to miss the notes, because they provide as much information as the text itself. Finally, I would like to alert the reader that, like all studies on Fidel Castro, this book is a biased one.Therefore, I strongly recommend to read it with caution and skepticism, the way all history books should be read.

Acknowledgements

This book owes a great deal to a great many. I have been assisted in this study by a host of great men and women who have stood beside me and gone before me in this endeavor. These I do now gratefully acknowledge.

To the librarians of The Latin American Library at Tulane University, The Hoover Institution Library and Archives, The John F. Kennedy Library, The San Francisco State University Library, The University of San Francisco Library, and The University of Southern Alabama Library in Mobile.

To professor Isidoro Mauleón, for answering many questions about the Catholic Church and checking the accuracy of my Latin. To Carlota Caulfield and Jesús J. Barquet, for their critical readings and suggestions. To Franco González for his invaluable help in polishing my English and proofreading the manuscript.

To Robert Peters, Earl Nelson, Alejandro González Acosta, and Marcelo Fernández-Zayas, who greatly helped me to clarify my ideas through our long conversations about some of the subjects dealt with in this book.

To Neil Jensen, editor of *Sumeria*, who several years ago published two articles of mine which eventually grew to become chapters of this book which eventually grew to become chapters of this book.

To Greg Collins-Bosque, for editing a long time ago some manuscripts, parts of which are engrossing this book.

To my friend José Manuel Arias, who died a few years ago in Cuba, for his insightful observations on many aspects of Cuban society, politics and culture. Our frequent exchanges were so rich and varied that sometimes I cannot remember which ideas are his and which are mine.

To those whose names I cannot provide, because of their work in the shadow world of intelligence and espionage. All those who spoke with me have been promised anonymity in return for their secret thoughts, but I recognize my debt to them.

To Eduardo Corominas, Hans Filusch, Katsumi Ito, Alexander Hay, and many others who, unknowingly, helped me create the necessary conditions for writing this book.

To the United States of America and the American people, who accepted me as a citizen of this great nation and allowed me to express my controversial ideas without fear of reprisals or censorship. I hope that, faced with the choice, the American people will never make the wrong decision of renouncing freedom in exchange for promised security.

To all of these I wish to say thank you. But the responsibility for ideas expressed in this book is strictly my own. Thus, the views presented here do not necessarily represent the views of any of the persons or institutions mentioned above.

Introduction

Fidel Castro and the Cuban revolution have been the focus of a large number of excellent historical and scholarly books and papers. Among them, four books in particular stand out as masterpieces: the massive, *Cuba: the Pursuit of Freedom* by Hugh Thomas,[1] Theodore Draper's *Castro's Revolution: Myths and Realities*,[2] Andrés Suárez' *Cuba: Castroism and Communism, 1959-1966*,[3] and Maurice Halperin's *The Rise and Decline of Fidel Castro*.[4] There are numerous other books on the subject, most of them of an unusually high standard. It can even be argued that the work of such recognized orthodox scholars has rendered any subsequent efforts at researching the subject of Fidel Castro completely redundant.

The authors cited above have achieved deserved renown for their work. They have been fortunate, it may be said, in the intrinsic fascination of their subject matter, but then so has everyone who has attempted the task of studying and analyzing the Castro phenomenon. What distinguishes most of these scholars is, first, their enviable prose and, second, their acute power of analysis. There is even a third similarity among them: their methodology. Theirs is, above all, a method based upon rationality.[5] I am not talking here about their talent for original research and the integrity which moves them to check the accuracy of every source. I am referring more to the very nature of their approach, which consists of endeavoring to tackle their subject without previous preconceptions . . . well, sort of.

At some time it was fashionable among historians to invoke some ethereal "spirit of history." Today, even after the natural death of communism in most of the world, there is a school of Marxist historians that invokes the equally ethereal "spirit of economic forces" to explain historical events.[6] But the scholars I am referring to invoke none of these, and resolutely shun the temptation to impose upon their work an all embracing theory of history. Instead, they choose to present us with the bare facts, and from these facts they draw logical conclusions. No one, consequently, may criticize their writing for being "unscientific." Nor is there present in their books any element that a rational mind would automatically question and reject.

Yet, as Edward H. Carr pointed out in his excellent *What is History?*, the art of the historian does not merely consist of finding the facts, since everything that happens may be considered a fact, but in *selecting* the facts which, consciously or unconsciously, he believes are significant for his study. To some, therefore, the fact that, while attending grade school at the Colegio de Dolores in Santiago de Cuba, a 12-year-old Fidel Castro wrote a letter to President Roosevelt asking him for money and offering his help in locating some of Cuba's natural resources for U. S. exploitation, may be extremely important; to others, it is too trivial to be worth mentioning, save possibly as a curiosity in a footnote.

In other words, historians emphasize the facts they believe are important, while neglecting the ones they feel are not. This emphasis may be consciously exerted, as in the case of Marxist historians, who fit history into the preconceived pattern of economic relations, or unconsciously, as in the case of historians who are determined by the conviction that history is a rational process. Irrationalities and oddities, then, will be played down or forgotten. Therefore, everything depends on the facts which a historian selects from the infinite number that are available, and on the emphasis he gives to those facts, and the result is the pattern "seen" by the historian, which may be explicit or implicit in his narrative. Thus, there is no *objective* history, any more than there is no *objective* journalism.

I have a skeptic's attitude towards historical conclusions based on "facts." I firmly believe that there are no objective conclusions in history. All historical conclusions based on "facts" are impregnated with theories, which are contaminated with beliefs and political ideologies.

In the first place, historians usually differ about what they consider a fact. For example, most scholars of the Cuban missile crisis have accepted at face value the Kennedy administration's claims that the photographs provided by U-2 planes constituted hard, incontrovertible evidence that the Soviets were deploying strategic missiles in Cuba. But, as intelligence analysts know, photographic evidence alone is just an iconic sign pointing to a probable fact. In order for it to become true intelligence, that is, information that has been validated, it must be corroborated by information provided by other reliable sources, preferably by agents operating in the field and other independent sources.[7] Second, conclusions based on facts can differ not only because of the selection of the facts but also because of the way they are analyzed. Third, many historians seem to ignore that, particularly in recent history, some of the "facts" have been left in for the sole purpose of disinformation.[8] Finally, even though this book is full of new or less known facts about Castro, my major emphasis has been on the interpretation of the facts, including widely known ones.

Most intelligence services agree that the most difficult aspect of the intelligence business is not the collection of raw data, but its interpretation and transformation into usable intelligence. Many outsiders believe that intelligence consists mainly in stealing the bad guys' secrets. Most of the job of intelligence, however, consists in using your experience to evaluate the information you already know. Not all intelligence involves cloak and dagger spooks or high tech espionage. A vast amount of the information that later becomes intelligence proper comes from open sources—monitoring of foreign broadcasts, close reading of the press, attendance at commercial and scientific conferences, study of officially released statistics and, above all, books—all of which, added to the information from secret sources, becomes raw material for the production of intelligence.

Conscious of the pitfalls described above, in writing this book I have tried to use to some extent a new research methodology I have developed over the years for the study of contemporary or recent history. This methodology, which I call "historical tradecraft,"[9] is a combination of the research methodology of the historian with that of the intelligence analyst.[10] This is a new research and analysis tool, and I am still in the process of learning how to use it, therefore, some inconsistencies in its use may appear in this work. Also, though I see it as a promising tool, its effectiveness still needs to be evaluated.[11]

Finally, I warn the reader that he will find some amount of cynicism throughout these pages. In the first place, in writing this book I have used mainly the approach of an intelligence analyst, and cynicism is endemic in the intelligence field—a sort of *déformation professionnelle*. Secondly, cynicism is one of the main tools of the political satirist, and as a former writer of political satire I cannot take politicians too seriously.

Do We Understand Fidel Castro?

Some Western journalists and scholars, just after a few hours, and even minutes, of knowing Castro, claim to understand him almost completely. By contrast, most of his close associates admit that they don't know the "real" Castro. I remember a personal anecdote that illustrates the first case.

Some years ago, when I was a Visiting Scholar at the Hoover Institution, I was having lunch with professor Modesto Maidique at the faculty cafeteria at Stanford University. He invited to join us William Ratliff, a Senior Hoover Fellow who has written several excellent books and articles about the Cuban revolution. Soon after, the conversation changed to the subject of Castro and Cuba. When I told Ratliff that, while living in Cuba, I always had trouble trying to understand Castro and what was really going on in the country, he seemed surprised. "I've never had such a problem," he replied. "For me, Castro is very easy to understand."[12]

I was simply amazed by his assertion, because Herbert Matthews, who followed Castro closely since his Sierra Maestra days and also wrote several books and dozens of articles about him, only saw emotionality and irrationality in Castro. Finally, after spending innumerable hours with Castro and with people very close to him, Matthews had to admit in a letter to Theodore Draper that "Castro is an enigma."[13]

Over the years, rather than faltering, Matthews' opinions about the mystery of Castro's life grew stronger. In his biography of Castro, published seven years later, Matthews states, "He is always Fidel Castro, but Fidel is a baffling character who disguises himself so well and so often that he makes the real man elusive, mysterious, aloof, unreachable."[14]

In the same fashion, such a serious and accurate scholar as Hugh Thomas points out the intriguing characteristics of the revolution that took place in the 1950s in Cuba, one of the richest countries in Latin America, "where a Marxist regime had been established seemingly because of the will of a single man, himself a very untypical Marxist."[15] In an article he wrote that same year, Thomas calls the Castroist revolution, "One of the most perplexing mysteries of the mid-twentieth century."[16] Also, Theodore Draper, whose books show an uncommon insight on the subject, begins the first book he wrote about Castro with the questions: "Who is Fidel Castro? What is he?"[17] Even Georgie Anne Geyer, Castro's perceptive biographer, said that, even though from some point of view Castro is absolutely knowable, "we don't know him."[18]

Carlos Franqui, a former associate of Castro and editor of *Revolución*—the newspaper of the M-26-7 (*Movimiento 26 de Julio*, Castro's revolutionary organization) and for some years the official *Fidelista* newspaper—says that after the rebel army took over Havana in 1959, "as far as ideology was concerned, nothing was clear, and Fidel was the greatest enigma of all."[19] In his book about the Cuban missile crisis, professor Dinerstein asserts that "in presenting so many different facets to the public view, Castro creates the puzzle of who the real Castro is."[20] In the same fashion, Professor Michael Erisman, in an insightful analysis about Castro's foreign policy, claims that Castro "is undoubtedly one of the most intriguing figures of the twentieth century."[21]. More recently, Emilio Arco, a Cuban journalist in exile, writing about Castro, had to confess, "We are totally confused about Fidel Castro."[22]

I frankly believe that most of the distinguished scholars who claim to understand Castro perfectly well have never understood the true essence of Castro or his "revolution."[23] The pattern emerging from the works of most of the scholars that have studied the Castro phenomenon is a rational one in which everything is explained in terms that a rational mind can grasp. Unable to accept the irrationality of Castro's conduct, these scholars have created a rational and logical theory to explain Castro. But, in doing so, they have created a Fidel Castro that exists only in their rational minds and has nothing to do with the real, irrational one.

The remaining question is whether, after reading these and similar works, we understand the strange phenomenon called Fidel Castro. As you will see in this book, there are many unusual things about Castro, among them, his eidetic (photographic) memory, his uncanny ability to foretell events, his incredible good luck, his ability to mesmerize people, his extraordinary love for cows and dairy products, and his visceral hatred for Americans and for democratically elected presidents. Obviously, Fidel Castro is different—and not only because he is rich.

Despite the brilliance of the studies I have cited above, it is my conviction that these works alone do not ultimately enable us to fully understand either Castro himself or the changes he started in Cuba in 1959. After studying the mechanism by which Castro attained power, the uses to which he has put his power, his speeches, his writings and, above all, his actions, I hold that I am still baffled by a flood of unanswered questions.

Why did a small Caribbean country abruptly become an important player in world politics? How could a vulgar, filthy gangster,[24] so manifestly second-rate in matters of the intellect, achieved such unparalleled power in Cuba? How did he exert such a strong influence in other parts of the world?[25] Why did Cubans come to venerate Castro as a god? Why, after a long chain of failures, does he still exert a mystique that is conspicuously absent when we study Stalin, Mussolini or Perón? Why does one feel that the Castroist revolution stands for a radically different type of revolution from the Mexican, the French, the Russian, or the American ones? Most intriguing of all, what drives Fidel Castro, what motivates him, what makes him tick? What was his ultimate goal when he sent his troops to Africa in 1975? What were his true intentions when he promoted guerrilla subversion in Latin America and terrorism in the U.S. and Europe? What went on in his mind when he tried in 1962 to push the United States and the Soviet Union to a nuclear confrontation?

Most of the scholars on Castro have deluded themselves into thinking that he is just another Latin American tyrant seeking power and money. But Fidel Castro is nothing of the sort. Though he has amassed a large fortune and acquired great power, his ultimate goal goes beyond that. He has designated himself as Latin America's Messiah, who will destroy the evil colossus of the North. His doctrine is very simple: a shrewd blend of all Latin American aspirations, including seemingly conflicting ones, and a ruthless pragmatism devoid of any ethical or ideological considerations. He still believes that Cuba, under his rule, should be the foundation of a Latin American, Asian and African federation united against the United States. He has always intended to establish this federation by strict adherence to the war rule.

Notwithstanding the total failure of his policies in Cuba, Castro's doctrine still attracts people all around the world. The appeal of his doctrine lies in the following claims:

1. Its overt ultimate goal is to destroy the hated United States and its people, or, at least, to destroy the American way of life as we know it.[26] This aspect of Castro's doctrine has a strong appeal for America haters in the United States and abroad, and they are quite a few.
2. It will provide social justice for the oppressed Latin Americans, Asians, Africans and other peoples around the world for whom politics is an unchanging life of misery under a succession of U.S. ill-backed dictators. This aspect has many adherents among the intelligentsia and the naïve, illiterate and exploited masses in Third World countries, as well as among many opportunistic leftists and liberals in First World countries, particularly the U.S.

3. It will bring equality and social justice to oppressed American minorities, including women, hispanics, blacks, gays, and the like. Some leftist militants, like the Black Panthers and the American gays, failed to find facts substantiating Castro's words, but managed to keep the secret to themselves. Nevertheless, Castro's fiery speeches about the liberation of the "oppressed" masses are still heavenly music to the ears of all types of envious malcontents around the world.

Very little is known about the formative years of Castro's life, and he himself has gone to great lengths in his efforts to conceal or distort the little that is known. His long interviews with Brazilian priest Frei Betto and with Cuban journalist-in-exile Carlos Franqui, probably the only ones with whom he has talked at length about his early days, are a collection of half-truths and outright lies. A common disinformation technique used by Castro is that he usually presents important lies on a background of true but irrelevant details. Far from accepting them at face value, the job of the historian is to disregard the lies and try to assemble the minor details into relevant facts to form a meaningful picture of the man and his ideas. But, as Leo Tolstoy observed, most people can seldom accept the simplest and most obvious truth, particularly if it forces them to admit the falsity of conclusions which they explain to colleagues with great delight, which they have proudly taught to others, and which they have woven, thread by thread, into the fabric of their lives.

Biographies of Fidel Castro differ considerably. They do so in part because he has been notably successful in his efforts to deceive both himself and everybody seeking to know him. He has also been extremely successful in getting rid of the few people who knew about aspects of his life he doesn't want to be known. His reminiscences, and even most of his private letters, seem to have been designed more to hide than to reveal. Both consciously and unconsciously he lies about himself and his family. To his biographers he can appear considerate, reasonable and charming while, at the same time, he is concealing the dark side of a vicious, vindictive and crazed fanatic. As his Jesuit preceptors at the Belén School noticed, Fidel is a very good actor.

An Unorthodox View of Fidel Castro

I suggest that we stop accepting Castro's propaganda at face value and start searching for the real, secret Fidel Castro underneath his self-made cover. He has done everything to muddy the waters, but if we dig carefully enough we can still find nuggets of truth. But this is not an easy job. Like his CIA and KGB counterparts, Castro is a master in the subtle art of deception and disinformation.

To examine the life and particularly the mind of a person who has caused so much misery and destruction to mankind is not a pleasant task. Nor will it help, as many have done, to dismiss Castro with pejorative comments or oversimplifications. The combination of political genius, evil instincts, and inner compulsion that characterize Fidel Castro, though fortunately uncommon, is not unique. Castro belongs in the same class of men as Adolf Hitler, Charles Manson, and Jim Jones. For no apparent reason, and defying any rational explanation, people like them keep popping up in different parts of the world.

Since he was catapulted to the world stage in February 24, 1957, when Herbert Matthews' interview was published in *The New York Times*, Fidel Castro has been one of the most unpredictable and enigmatic leaders. Matthews himself, probably one of the Americans who knew him better, once said that "His is a character of such complexity, such contradictions, such emotionalism, such irrationality, such unpredictability that no one can really know him."[27] And added, "Fidel's actions are unpredictable, especially as he does not confide completely in anybody. His motives are not always clear."[28]

There is probably only one historical figure that may serve us as a guide in our study of Castro: Adolf Hitler. In the case of Hitler, similar questions as expressed above have resulted in a spate of books that furnish a strong contrast to the rationalistic works about Castro I have mentioned above. Among them there is an extraordinary book, *The Morning of the Magicians*, by Louis Pauwels and Jacques Bergier,[29] which made a profound impact on me when I read it more than thirty years ago. The book brings to light a vast number of facts, rumors,[30] coincidences and hypotheses, which unveil an irrational and evil Adolf Hitler as a mediumistic prophet with bizarre beliefs. Many people, however, still refuse to accept the irrefutable evidence.

As Vaclav Havel, the Czech playwright and essayist, expressed in clear terms,

> The civilization of the new age, having given up on the authority of myths, has surrendered to a large and dangerous illusion: the illusion that no higher and darker powers ever existed, either in the human conscious or in the mysterious universe. Today, the opinion prevails that everything can be "rationally explained," as they say. Nothing is obscure—and if it is, then we need only cast a ray of scientific light on it and it will cease to be so.[31]

In the case of Hitler there is an extensive bibliography dealing with this irrational aspect of the subject—of which recent books by Rosenbaum, Kershaw, Victor and Redlich[32] are the latest additions. In Castro's case, however, it is practically non-existent. I believe I pioneered this line of research about the irrationality of Castro's thought and actions in my *Historia herética de la revolución fidelista*, published in 1986.[33] Though a few authors have marginally mentioned this irrational aspect before, it was not until the early nineties that Georgie Annie Geyer's *Guerrilla Prince*,[34] and later Andres Oppenheimer's *Castro's Final Hour*,[35] gave some extended exposure to some aspects of Castro's irrational thinking.

Why have such superb scholars as those praised above never thought about seriously studying Castro's powers of clairvoyance or his ability to mesmerize people? It is probably because their outlook is a rational one, which forces them to overlook whatever strikes them as a collection of bizarre lunacies. Others may argue that there is precious little evidence to demonstrate Castro's passion for the bizarre. But the evidence is there, as I shall show, and this argues for the existence of a certain willful blindness among these scholars.

Orthodox historians seem determined to demonstrate that, however strange Castro might have acted at times, ultimately all the events of Castro's life conform to a rational pattern. As a matter of fact, most of the pro-Castro propaganda in the United States focuses on proving that, even though perhaps sometimes he has shown a strong hand, Castro is just another nationalistic, anti-American politician, not very different from many other Latin American ones, just trying to defend himself from the attacks of a big, imperialistic nation. As a heretical historian I categorically deny this and, at least just for the healthy sake of adding some cognitive dissonance to the discussion, emphasize the facts which upset that rational pattern.

One of the prime purposes of this book, and of the previous ones I have written about the subject, has been to select the available facts, and arrange them in such a pattern that the true nature of Castroism can be fully exposed and understood. Though many of these facts have been shunned or ignored by orthodox historians, I recognize that I owe them an enormous debt. I am greatly indebted too to the heretic historians, particularly the ones who have written about Adolf Hitler. As they previously did with the Führer, I have concentrated my efforts in exposing the darker side of Fidel Castro, and I venture the suggestion that, though far from being a definitive study on him, this work supplies a better insight into the subject than has hitherto been available.

When trying to understand the true nature of Castroism, one cannot avoid seeing the entire history of the decline and fall of Cuba and the systematic destruction of its values. If one confronts the question of Castro's role in Cuba's material and moral collapse, sees the implementation of the new values which accompanied the collapse, and notes their direct relation to Fidel Castro, one has to conclude that the two aspects are inextricably intertwined.

I believe that the life and career of Fidel Castro raises questions that cannot be answered by history or by psychohistory alone. Though I don't have answers to many of these questions, I am willing to expose the strange facts. To be sure, this book may disturb and even shock some readers, including some with widely different opinions about Fidel Castro. All I ask from them is to keep an open mind, and that they follow my arguments to their end with a minimum of emotional bias.

In writing this book I have made an effort to avoid the "either/or" trap, a pernicious thinking habit which grows out of the tendency to consider people or events as either good or bad, positive or negative. Human behavior is complex and demands complex explanations. The truth is that there are many different Castros. His most widely known persona is the symbolic, public one, as it has been portrayed in the official Cuban propaganda, in Castro-friendly biographies and histories of the Castro revolution, and in the American liberal media. But there are also many secret Castros, highly differents from the public one. By "deconstructing" different aspects of the life of the symbolic Fidel Castro I am trying to prove that all of them, the symbolic and the secret ones, are suspicious and, therefore, all answers are partial. A side effect of this approach is that, since each chapter has been designed to be read on its own merits, not only some of them overlap, but also some of the different analyses of the Castro phenomenon may appear contradictory among themselves. However, a close reading of the material will show that the contradictions have to do more with form than with content and, therefore, they do not fully exclude each other. The point I am trying to make is that, as in Virgilio Piñera's absurd play "Study in Black and White," between black and white, there is a very wide spectrum of . . . yellows![36] I hope the reader will not find this approach distracting or confusing.

Rendering a complex individual such as Fidel Castro is like putting together a large jigsaw puzzle, in which some of the pieces are still missing, and some of the pieces already in place were intentionally planted there with the sole purpose of misleading the casual observer and of obstructing the missing pieces from ever appearing.[37]

Theodore Draper, probably one of the American authors who better understood the essence of the Castro phenomenon since its very beginning, opened his 1962 book about the Cuban leader with the questions: "Who is Fidel Castro? What is he?"[38] Yet, more than forty years later and after dozens of books and hundreds of articles have been written about Castro, most people still don't know who or what he is. As a matter of fact, most of the studies about Castro have only added to the confusion instead of clarifying the enigma.

This book is my attempt to answer Draper's questions.

Servando González

PART ONE

Deconstructing the Symbol

Chapter 1

Charisma . . . and Beyond

> *"Fidel has the gift. I've seen it with my own eyes"*
> *"The gift?"*
> *"Yes, you know, like a wizard. He can make people dream crazy dreams. He could make them love him or make them scared for no reason. He can make them do lots of strange things. He's a devil!"*
>
> —Conversation between two Rebel Army soldiers overheard in Havana in 1959

"Charisma" is the word repeated over and over by most authors who have tried to provide an explanation for Castro's extraordinary control over the masses and isolated individuals. Herbert Matthews was probably the first who used the term in reference to Castro: "What Fidel had in overwhelming measure—was charisma, that magnetic, mystical quality which wins fanatical popular support."[1] Since Matthews defined Castro's powers this way, most of his biographers have used the word charisma to describe the source of his control over people. But, is Castro really charismatic? Is charisma the true source of his power?[2]

Charisma (literally the "gift of grace") is a term coined by sociologist Max Weber. It refers to the quality of leadership which appeals to non-rational motives. Weber defined charisma as "a certain quality of an individual personality by virtue of which he is considered extraordinary and treated as endowed with supernatural, superhuman, or exceptional powers or qualities."[3] Of all the specialized terms adopted by social scientists, "charisma" is probably not only the most thoroughly popularized, but also the most trivialized.

Weber originally borrowed the concept of charisma from Rudolf Sohm, a Strassburg jurist and church historian. According to Sohm, "The charisma is from God . . . and the service to which the charisma calls is a service imposed by God, and an office in the service of the church, and not of any other community."[4] Weber extended the concept to cover political as well as religious leaders, and secularized it when he described the term charisma as a relation between an individual and a group. It seems that Weber's idea of the charismatic leader also owed something to Nietzsche's notion of *Übermensh*, but Weber was a sociologist and was more concerned with the group that rallied to the leader's support than with the Nietzschean hero rejecting the masses and being rejected by them. Thus, Weber used the term charisma to characterize self-appointed leaders followed by people in distress who are in need of go behind a leader because they believe him to be extremely well qualified for his job.

According to Weber, the charismatic leader is always the creation of his followers. Charismatic authority is rooted in the belief system of the followers rather than in some transcendental characteristic of the leader. Miracles and revelations, heroic feats of valor and baffling success are characteristics of charismatic leaders. Failure, however, marks their ruin, says Weber, because the leader's image of infallibility cannot be maintained in the face of inevitable failures.

By its very nature, emphasizes Weber, the existence of charismatic authority is specifically unstable. If he fails, the charismatic leader may be deserted by his followers, because pure charisma does not know any "legitimacy" other than that coming from personal strength, that is, one which is constantly being proved. The charismatic leader gains and maintains authority solely by proving his strength in life. If he wants to be a prophet, he must perform miracles; if he wants to be a warlord, he must perform heroic deeds. Above all, his divine mission must "prove" itself in that those who faithfully surrender to him must fare well. If they do not fare well, he is obviously not the master sent by the gods.

Yet, Weber's assertion about the direct relationship between failure and ruin marking the fate of charismatic leaders clearly indicates that charisma is not the appropriate concept to explain Castro's almost total control over people. In the course of his long career as a leader Castro has faced big failures. The failure to produce a 10 million ton sugar harvest in 1969-70 and the Grenada affair are just two of the best known, but not the only ones. His dream of a victorious anti-American revolution in all of Latin America has vanished. In the last thirty years failure after failure has been piling up in front of his door. Nothing seems to work for Fidel Castro in the economic, social, military or political fields. It is not a secret that the Cuban people are not doing well under Castro's rule. Even his claimed achievements in education, health care and social justice are all but gone. There is virtually no fuel for public transportation, medicines are more scarce than ever before and life has turned unbearable for those who cannot get dollars. But, as a British scholar observed a few years ago, "There is still no sign that the regime is under any serious internal threat. Its resilience cannot be explained away simply by fear, superstition or state repression, nor indeed by Castro's statesmanship."[5] Surprisingly, the majority of the Cuban people are still under his total control.[6] Failure apparently has no effect upon his power.[7]

In Weber's view, the power of the charismatic leader rests in fact on the masses, the ones who project this power on him. In the case of Fidel Castro, however, his instant control over non-Cuban masses shows that the power resides fully on him, not on the masses. Therefore, it would be better to look somewhere else for another explanation to better describe the true nature of Castro's power, which definitely cannot be explained just by Weber's theory of charisma.

There is something, however, in which friends and foes alike seem to agree about, and it is the fact that Fidel Castro exerts a very strong influence upon most people, even upon some of his enemies.

Castro's Powers of Fascination

In a Harvard commencement speech, Mexican writer Carlos Fuentes mentioned the United States' refusal to discuss U.S.-Cuba relations with Castro, and asked: "Is Fidel Castro some sort of superior Machiavelli whom no *gringo* negotiator can meet at a bargain table without being bamboozled? I don't believe it."

I understand Mr. Fuentes' refusal to believe in Castro's powers of fascination, but I think that Mr. Fuentes is dead wrong. The record proves beyond any doubt that, with a few exceptions, everyone who has met Castro at a bargaining table has been bamboozled by his powers of fascination—including many tough *gringo* negotiators.

The original meaning of the word "fascination" is a reference to the power of casting a spell through looking. It is a usage that has survived to our times in relation to the ability of snakes to immobilize their prey through their gaze. The subject of fascination has interested writers and thinkers for centuries. In his insightful essay "Of Envy," published in 1625, Sir Francis Bacon wrote his reflections on the subject of fascination:

> There be none of the affections which have been noted to fascinate and to bewitch, but love and envy; they both have vehement witches, they frame themselves readily into imaginations and suggestions and they come easily into the eye, especially upon the presence of the objects which are the points that conduce to fascination, if any such be. We see likewise the Scripture calleth envy and evil eye . . .[8]

For lack of a better term, I am using the term "fascination" in an effort to describe as accurately as possible the strange phenomenon by which Castro exerts an extraordinary control over both single individuals and masses of people, though other terms have been used as well. Most of Castro's biographers have noticed the phenomenon, but there is no agreement among them about what to call it. For example, in her biography of Fidel Castro, Georgie Anne Geyer, mentions the word "spell" 10 times (pp. 38, 103, 108, 140, 212, 224, 240, 287, 241), and the word "magical" 5 times (pp. 207, 208, 279, 286, 329). Other terms she also uses are "personal hallucinatory power," (p. 254); "mystical," (p. 208); "sorcerer," (pp. 176, 297); "master illusionist," (p. 331); and "master political alchemist," (p. 332). She also mentions Castro's "mesmerizing techniques," (p. 337); "intuitive feelings," (pp. 226, 271); and "hyper-psychic level of intensity," (p. 159).[9]

Philip Bonsal, the last American Ambassador to Cuba before the two countries broke diplomatic relations in 1960, was also witness to Castro's strange powers. In a book he wrote about Cuba, he tells about the "mysterious force" that drives Castro (p. 56); about the way he weaves "his spells" (p. 57). He also tells how, when Castro spoke in private to a CIA officer for over an hour, the man "emerged in a state of ecstasy" about Castro's receptivity (p. 64); and how Castro exerts his form of personal, "hypnotic rule" over the Cuban people (p. 190).[10] In his report, the CIA officer described Castro as "a new spiritual leader of Latin American democratic and anti-dictator forces."[11]

In a book about Fidel, Juan Arcocha, a writer and former official in the Castro government who met Castro during his university days, says that Fidel always exerted a great "fascination" on him (pp. 17, 19), and mentions the "almost hypnotic" current emanating from the tv screens when Fidel is giving one of his speeches (p. 33).[12] Similarly, author Edwin Tetlow mentions Fidel's "hypnotic powers of persuasion."[13]

Similarly, CIA officer John Esterline, a seasoned intelligence officer then chief of station in Caracas, was highly impressed by Castro's charismatic powers when the Cuban leader visited Venezuela in 1959 and Esterline witnessed "the power of his charisma." According to Esterline, Castro was "something different, something more impressive . . . and definitely harder to handle than anyone had ever seen."[14] Many years later, on 31 May 1996, while attending a conference on the Bay of Pigs at the Arca Foundation's Musgrove conference center on St. Simons Island, Georgia, Esterline vividly recalled his impressions of Castro:

> It seemed to me that something like a chain reaction was occurring all over Latin America after Castro came to power. I saw—hell, anybody with eyes could see it—that a new and powerful force was at work in the hemisphere.[15]

Writing in the *CID* newspaper, two Cuban journalists expressed similar views. According to Roberto Lozano, "It is not by chance that it is *vox populi* in Cuba that Fidel Castro is a sorcerer."[16] In the same issue José M. Pou writes that "In his aberrant megalomania, Fidel Castro truly believes he is endowed with magical powers."[17]

The above terms used by Geyer, Bonsal and other authors and journalists are no exception. They are mentioned over and over to describe Castro's unexplainable powers and are repeatedly used by his biographers. No serious effort, however, has been made to clarify the use of those terms or to analyze the true source of Castro's power. Still, since the early sixties the Cuban people sensed Fidel Castro's special powers. As early as 1960 they began chanting: *Fidel, Fidel, ¿qué tiene Fidel, que los americanos no pueden con él?* (Fidel, Fidel, what does Fidel have, that the Americans can't handle him?)

It is a great mistake to believe, as some Cuban historians, government officials and Castro himself have tried to prove, that Agramonte, Céspedes, Maceo or Martí, the Cuban patriots who fought long wars against Spain, are the historical precursors of Fidel Castro. It is also erroneous to see in the fanatical enthusiasm which millions of Cubans still feel for Castro a continuation of the traditional veneration of Cubans for their patriots and founding fathers. The Castro phenomenon is of a totally different kind.

Does Fidel Castro possess what is commonly known as psychic or paranormal faculties? "Serious" scholars have never studied this aspect of Castro's personality, but the fact that he has extraordinary good luck, as well as his uncanny ability to "read" other peoples' minds and to exert a strong fascination upon them, has been recorded over and over.

For example, in 1961 Herbert Mathews observed that Fidel has a "magnetic personality," and his speech is "hypnotic in its repetitive rhythm."[18] Writing about Castro in 1964, Matthews also said that "He has enormous personal magnetism, so that he wins blind loyalty."[19] Matthews also observed that "One must listen to him; hear the hoarse, impassioned voice, feel the magnetism of his extraordinary personality. He is a spellbinder."[20]

Cuban writer Guillermo Cabrera Infante tells an interesting anecdote about his Argentinean colleague Julio Cortázar. According to Cabrera Infante, Cortázar told him his vivid recollection of the moment when he was granted an audience with Fidel Castro. Cortázar said that during the meeting Fidel put his hand on Julio's knee. "I felt the vibes," said Cortázar, "that told me that I was in the presence of a revolutionary."[21]

In an article he wrote for *Mother Jones* magazine, American film maker and writer Saul Landau described his impressions while he was in Cuba in 1988 filming an interview with Castro:

> As Fidel spoke, I allowed myself to listen closely and feel that peculiar sensation I experience in his presence, as if I am meeting with a force of nature, a man so filled with the energy of historical mission that he is almost of a different species. Power radiates from him, emitting acute awareness of his needs...[22]

Notable among the people who have fallen under Castro's spell are ex-Soviet ambassador and KGB officer Aleksandr Alekseev, Colombian Nobel Prize-winner Gabriel García Márquez,[23] former Head of U.S. Interests Office in Havana Wayne S. Smith, Italian publisher Giangiacomo Feltrinelli,[24] French philosophers Jean-Paul Sartre and Regis Debray, Senator George McGovern, UNESCO's director Federico Mayor, media mogul Ted Turner, former U.S. Secretary of State Robert S. McNamara, and a large group of the American liberal press and Hollywood stars who have met him.

Yet, Andres Oppenheimer, who visited Cuba in the early nineties, tells how, at least on one occasion, "Castro's semihypnotic speaking powers" failed to convince his audience.[25] Oppenheimer believes that, in his speeches, "Fidel had always established a quasi-magical connection with his listeners," but the connection is no longer there.[26] But Tad Szulc, one of the Castro-friendly biographers, is of a different opinion: "... it is untrue that nowadays Castro's speeches turn Cubans off. First, there still is a sense of fascination with him and his oratory..."[27] According to Szulc, Castro is still "mesmerizing" people.²⁸ I fully agree with Szulc that Castro's powers of fascination are still intact.

During a visit Castro made to New York in 1995 to deliver a speech at the United Nations, he was invited by *U.S. News and World Report* editor Mort Zuckerman to a lunch at his plush apartment on 5th Avenue. According to a witness, a mesmerized Zuckerman conferred on Fidel Castro "all the tenderness usually reserved to a family member." Mr. Zuckerman shared his beloved Fidel with a group of media stars who showered the Maximum Leader "with accolades and kisses (not those stylish little pecks, mind you, but warm embraces and sobering smacks)."²⁹ Among the kissers and embracers were Diane Sawyer, Barbara Walters, and John McLauglin, who confessed he was beginning to like Fidel. So, if Castro's powers of fascination lately are turning Cubans off, they are still turning some Americans on.

Earlier that year, a group of American journalists visited Castro in Cuba. Soon after he took his post at *Time* magazine in 1993, managing editor James R. Gainer felt a strong desire to have a meeting with Fidel. Finally, the meeting was arranged, and Gainer and a group of his associates visited Fidel in Havana. The historical photograph, shamelessly published in *Time* with the caption "Feasting with Fidel," shows a happy Castro surrounded by a group of mesmerized *gringos* displaying very stupid expressions. However, according to his body language as displayed in the photograph, Gainer himself seems to have been immune to Castro's powers of fascination.³⁰

In February, 1996, Fidel repeated his performance. Robert F. Kennedy Jr. and Michael Kennedy visited Cuba and had an interview with Fidel Castro to ask him to abandon his nuclear program and use alternative, ecologically safe sources of energy instead. The *New York Times* published an article about the visit and illustrated it with a revealing photograph. It shows Castro standing behind his desk and talking while he handles some pictures. Across his desk, the two Kennedy brothers and five more male members of the Kennedy entourage, attentively listen to Castro's words. While the expression of both Robert and Michael is one of distrust or reservation, the other five men seem to have fallen into a rapture of ecstasy. Saliva is about to dribble from their mouths half open in admiration while their gaze is fixed on Castro's eyes.³¹ Exactly the same mesmerized expression is present in the face of Time Warner's Gerald Levin in a photograph taken when he met Castro in Havana in 1995.³² Next year, UNESCO's director-general Federico Mayor visited Cuba and met Castro. A photograph of their meeting shows a mesmerized Mayor smiling in awe and love for Fidel.³³

In a recent exchange at the Harvard Law School a student confronted Ted Turner about some of his peculiar statements about Castro, among them "Fidel Castro is one hell of a guy." Turner's answer was, "Castro is a hell of a guy. Have you ever met him? You'd like him."[34] In late December, 1997, Ted Turner and Jane Fonda met with Castro as part of the couple's visit to CNN's office in Havana, the first U.S. news organization to open a Havana bureau since Castro expelled all of them in the early 1960s.[35] It is known that Turner is a frequent visitor to Cuba, where he goes hunting with the *Comandante en Jefe* and stays at one of Castro's mansions.

Among the latest additions to the long list of *gringos* who have fallen under Castro's spell are historian Arthur M. Schlesinger, Jr., Oakland Major Jerry Brown,[36] and Robert Reynolds, former CIA station chief in Miami in 1961. Schlesinger and Reynolds visited Cuba early this year to attend a conference on the Bay of Pigs organized by the Castro government and were instantly fascinated by Castro.[37]

Moreover, it seems that Fidel Castro's powers of fascination are not limited to humans. In the evening of January 8 1959, just a few hours after entering Havana commanding his victorious Rebel Army, Castro was giving one of his long speeches at Camp Columbia, former headquarters of Batista's army. The night fell and he kept speaking to his mesmerized audience. As he was finishing his speech, a pair of white doves suddenly came from nowhere to rest on his shoulders.[38]

The strange incident of the doves at Camp Columbia is well known, and has been graphically documented in many books. There is, however, another less known instance of it witnessed by Teresa Casuso, a former close friend of Castro, who told the story. It happened during Castro's visit to Washington D.C. in April, 1959. Castro was visiting the Lincoln Memorial and stood for some minutes in silent contemplation before Lincoln's statue. From a neighboring park a number of doves flew toward the monument, and one of them settled for a moment on Lincoln's hand. Then, it flew directly to Castro's shoulder, exactly as the one in Camp Columbia had done. Some Cuban photographers who had witnessed the previous occurrence were astounded. One of them told Casuso, "Look, I've got goose pimples—if I hadn't seen it I would never have believed it."[39]

Thirty years later, in 1989, Castro repeated his performance. As he was delivering his customary January speech in commemoration of the 30th anniversary of his revolution, a white dove came from nowhere and settled on his right shoulder. The photograph was published in a German newspaper.[40]

Since he was relatively young, Castro discovered his mesmerizing powers and put them to work for him. Some recorded incidents point in that direction. For example, in the midst of the Bogotazo riots of 1948, Castro and his friends were isolated in their hotel during a curfew, and were desperately trying to get to the Cuban embassy in order to get help to flee the country. Then, Castro ran into an Argentinean diplomat they had met a few days before, and persuaded him to drive them to the Cuban embassy (diplomatic cars being exempt from the curfew).[41] Just a few days before, Castro and his friends had been arrested by the Colombian secret police, but he managed to talk their way out. Szulc points out that apparently "[Castro's] talent for persuasion already was well developed, because they were released within a few hours."[42]

Szulc wrote that "Castro inspires widespread loyalty on the basis of human chemistry." "He is an unmatched persuader. He can and has convinced scores of men and women of varying backgrounds and temperaments to participate in military actions about which they are told nothing specific until the last moment (the assault on the Moncada barracks and the voyage of the *Granma* are cases in point)."[43]

When Castro and his men were doing time at the Presidio Modelo in Isle of Pines for the failed Moncada attack, they sent food from their cells to Castro's as a way to pass hidden messages. According to Pedro Miret, one of Castro's men who did time with him, a prisoner would cook a dish and had a guard take it over to Fidel's cell, together with a message hidden in the food. But on one occasion one of the guards discovered the ruse and threatened to blow the whistle. But Castro had a long conversation with him and not only convinced the man not to tell his superiors, but to help them pass the messages.[44]

Teresa Casuso wrote about him, "If Fidel were preparing a voyage to Mars, and you didn't want to go to Mars, keep away from him, because, otherwise, you would soon find yourself on the way to Mars."[45] She also said that against Castro's personal magnetism there is no possible resistance. It has caused many foreign writers and journalists interviewing him to be converted into rabid *fidelistas*.[46]

Examples about young Castro's power of persuasion abound. Eric Sevareid, for example, wrote this revealing anecdote for his column in the New York *Post*:

> The other night I sat in a Brazilian patio with a Cuban lawyer who had gone to school with Castro. He told me the story of a 16-year-old Fidel and the mountain:
> "So the professor said to me, you go and talk Fidel out of this crazy notion to climb the mountain. So I went to Fidel and in 30 minutes he had talked me into joining his expedition. So the two of us rode the train with Fidel for three, four hours. We got off at a village. 'Where is the mountain, Fidel?' we asked

him. 'This way,' he said, 'Just follow me.' So we walk, we walk, all night. In the morning there is no mountain."[47]

Interviewed by Georgie Anne Geyer, Carlos Bustillo, a participant in the Moncada attack, said that, "Fidel could convince any person to do anything." Another attacker, Gerardo Pérez, told her that "Fidel had this way of captivating people. Maybe it is the warmness of his speech."[48]

Ruby Hart Phillips, an American journalist in Havana, described the first time Castro addressed the Cuban masses from the Presidential Palace in Havana. "As he stood there with his rifle hung over his shoulder, his big voice rolling out over the crowd through a microphone, the magic of his personality was apparent."[49] Another journalist, describing the same event, tells how the crowd gazed up at the bearded figure on a balcony of the Presidential Palace "in hypnotized fascination."[50] Phillips also described how, when Castro wanted to get rid of President Urrutia, Fidel spoke over radio and television with the entire nation listening. "With his customary magic Castro worked his audience into a mob frenzy." As Castro went on with his verbal attack against the President, a crowd gathered around the Presidential palace yelling, "Out with Urrutia!"[51]

On September 28, 1960, Castro returned to Havana after visiting New York to attend the U.N. Assembly. Masses of people were waiting for him at the airport and all along the highway to the city, creating a human barrier to Castro's car. Waldo Frank, an American sympathetic to Castro, recorded the moment after the plane landed:

> Castro was rushed by his staff into a closed car where the people could not touch ... could scarcely see him. He objected and changed to an open jeep. Now, with the reverent reserve of a church procession the people stood, letting the jeep go forward.[52]

Castro repeated his performance during the riots Cubans call the *Habanazo* (named after the *Bogotazo* riots of 1948 in Bogotá, Colombia).

In the summer of 1994, thousands of Cubans congregated at Havana's Malecón avenue, close to the sea, apparently excited by the rumor that a flotilla of boats of Cuban exiles was on its way from Florida to pick up their relatives. Late in the morning the mass of people had grown close to 20,000 and expanded to the port, Prado Avenue, and some parts of the old section of the city.

In the afternoon, some police units tried to dissolve the group, asking them to go to their homes, but without success. Around 3 p.m., the police tried again, now resorting to violence, and were attacked with stones. Some people began shouting "Down with Fidel!," and "Freedom!, Freedom!" The police lost control, and the now infuriated mass of people took to the former American embassy, some 20 blocks away. At this time the group had turned into an uncontrollable mob, destroying store windows and fighting the police, ignoring the threats and warning shots. People from the nearby buildings joined the riot, throwing all kinds of heavy objects at the police. Notified of the inability of the police to control the rioters, Raúl Castro discussed with some senior Army officers the possibility of sending Army units with tanks to the streets.

But then, about five in the afternoon, Castro appeared on the streets riding a military jeep and, together with a few members of his personal detail and some senior government officials, confronted the rioters. As soon as they heard the news that Castro was on the streets, most of the rioters got rid of their improvised weapons, and changed their shouting to "Long live Fidel!" Others were saying "The old man has iron balls. Nobody can overthrow him!" A few minutes later the riot was over.[53]

It seems that, notwithstanding his long chain of failures, the feeling of reverence Castro generates is still strong. A young Cuban high-school student told Andres Oppenheimer in Havana in 1991 that most young people hate Fidel. "If he stepped down tomorrow, we would throw a big party." But then he added, "But if he walked into this room right now, I would melt."[54]

In 1996 Mike Garvey and Chuck Ryan, two Americans who fought with Castro in the Sierra Maestra, visited Cuba again after 27 years. Fidel received them like old friends and gave them warm embraces. After the visit Ryan said: "I love the man. I would die for the man today, right now, and I would have died for him in the mountains."[55]

On November 18, 1978, Guyana became the scene of unspeakable horror as Jim Jones led his followers into one of the worst suicide/mass murder in modern history.[56] In this unexplainable episode, Jones, a "charismatic" leader whose projects all ended in failure, convinced 900 of his followers to die for his cause.

In his closing speech at the Fourth Congress of his "Communist" Party in 1991, Castro expressed his belief that, "And if, in order to crush the revolution, they have to kill all the people, the people, behind its leaders and its Party, will be willing to die!"[57] It would be interesting to know how many Cubans would be willing to die ten years later for Fidel Castro? My guess is that today, even after the continued failures of his system, policies and ideas, many Cubans, probably a large percentage of the Cuban population, would be willing to die for Fidel Castro.

Castro's powers of fascination are not limited to the Cuban people. He has used them on foreign masses as well, as in Venezuela in 1959. Matthews observed that, "When he went to Caracas, Venezuela, a few weeks after his triumph, the tremendous popular emotions aroused frightened the Venezuelan Government."[58] Tad Szulc wrote about the uneasiness of President Betancourt during Castro's visit, mentioning Betancourt's confession that, if elections were held that day in Venezuela, Castro would win.[59] The phenomenon was repeated again when he visited the Soviet Union in 1963. Some Soviet officers privately commented that, since the death of Lenin, they had not seen any other person having such control over the Russian crowds like Castro.[60] This happened again when Castro traveled to Chile in 1971 to pay a visit to President Allende.

Similarly, the old, shrewd and ruthless Soviet bureaucrats were not immune to Castro's powers of fascination. Anastas Mikoyan, the Soviet deputy Prime Minister was the first to fall mesmerized by Castro. According to a report by Alekseev, Fidel charmed Mikoyan. "Yes, he is a genuine revolutionary. Completely like us," exclaimed the mesmerized Soviet leader. "I felt as if I had returned to my childhood."[61] The shrewd Armenian, considered the best horse trader in the Central Committee, became such a Castro advocate that many Cubans joked he was Fidel's agent in Russia.[62]

It was another Russian, however, the one who actually fell under Castro's spell and became his true agent in the Soviet Union. When Castro expelled Soviet Ambassador and senior GRU officer Sergei Kudryavtsev in early 1962 after a failed Soviet-sponsored *coup d'état* to overthrow Fidel, the Russians found themselves in the unprecedented situation of having to accept Castro's own candidate as Kudryavtsev's replacement. Castro's chosen man was Aleksandr Alekseev, the correspondent in Havana for Tass, the Soviet news agency.

But Alekseev, whose real name was Shitov, was actually a senior Soviet intelligence officer who eventually became the *rezident* (chief of office) of the KGB in Havana. As a Soviet intelligence officer, Alekseev had been previously deployed, under different covers, in France (1946-51), the Netherlands (1951-54), and finally in Argentina (1954- 58), where he polished both his proficiency in the Spanish language and in the mastering of tradecraft.[63] As a senior Soviet intelligence officer deployed in the field, Alekseev's main mission in Havana was to act as control to run self-recruited "agent" Fidel Castro.

Alekseev, however, proved to be incapable of running Castro, who was not only running himself but sometimes seemed to be the one actually running Alekseev.[64] Reports began piling up in KGB files informing that the Soviet intelligence officer had become Castro's personal friend. They had been seen drinking and womanizing together and it was evident that Alekseev had fallen under the spell of the Cuban leader.[65]

After Mikoyan and Alekseev, other Soviet citizens fell under Castro's powerful spell. Rumors I heard from fellow Army officers in Cuba in 1962, just after the Cuban missile crisis, claimed that Castro's mesmerizing powers had to do with the still unexplained shoot down of an American U-2 on the eastern part of Cuba by a Soviet surface-to-air missile. (See next chapter). According to the rumors, Castro himself asked the Soviet officer in charge to launch the missile. The officer, notwithstanding his knowledge that his action would be severely penalized, agreed with tears in his eyes by answering "Commander-in-Chief: at your orders!" Adding some credibility to the rumor is the fact that the phrase *"Comandante en Jefe: ¡Ordene!"* became a revolutionary slogan in Cuba just after the missile crisis. Another key to the possible veracity of the rumor is that, in a letter he wrote to Khrushchev, Castro himself mentioned that the news of the Soviet decision to withdraw the missiles brought tears to the eyes of countless Cuban and Soviet men "who were willing to die with supreme dignity."[66] Though the story is perhaps difficult to believe, Tad Szulc discovered during his research for his biography of Castro that "Cubans and foreigners without number have found it impossible to say no to Fidel."[67]

Proof that Castro's mesmerizing abilities are strong is that he used them to win a seemingly unapproachable Russian character. According to Ken Alibek, a Soviet Colonel who was in charge of developing bacteriological weapons for the Soviet Union, it was Premier Leonid Brezhnev the one who provided Castro with the necessary technology to produce bacteriological weapons. Alibek recalls that most Soviet officers were against providing Castro with the technology, but Brezhnev "was in love with Castro," and authorized the technology transfers.[68]

On April 13th, 1990, Gorbachev's envoy Leonid Abalkin arrived in Havana to discuss new economic terms with the Cubans. Abalkin, deputy chairman of the Soviet Union's Council of Ministers, was a reformist economist known for his drastic views about a substantial cut in Soviet aid to Cuba. But Castro gave him the royal treatment and the tough Abalkin inexplicably mellowed his attitude substantially. According to witnesses, Fidel never left Abalkin's side, using all his powers of persuasion to convince him that Cuba had great economic potential and a lot to offer the Soviet Union.

Abalkin's visit ended with the signing of a one-year trade protocol for 1990 that was incredibly better than the one the Russians had in mind. Yuri Pavlov, the Soviet Foreign Ministry's Latin American Department director at the time, had an explanation for what happened to Abalkin in Cuba: "Fidel charmed him. The agreement Abalkin came back with was seen by us as unrealistic."[69]

Soon after Castro approached the Soviets for the first time, Prime Minister Nikita Khrushchev had the opportunity to experience first hand Fidel's powers of fascination. Khrushchev met Castro for the first time in New York in September, 1960, when both leaders were visiting the United Nations. The Soviet Premier had invited Fidel to a dinner at the Soviet U.N. mission in New York. Castro, as usual, was a half hour late and kept Khrushchev waiting.[70] Witnesses to the incident report that Khrushchev was furious. But, as soon as Castro arrived, Khrushchev's mood changed and was all smiles. Apparently the Soviet leader was another victim of Fidel's powers of fascination.[71]

Khrushchev's first impression about Fidel was most likely not too different from the one Fidel made on other world leaders. After meeting Fidel for the first time Richard Nixon said that Castro had a compelling, intense glance, with sparkling black eyes, that radiated vitality. Adding, "He was intelligent, shrewd, at times eloquent."[72] The recently declassified full text of Nixon's memorandum of his conversation with Castro shows that, indeed, Castro made a strong impression on Nixon:

> The one fact we can be sure of is that Fidel Castro has those indefinable qualities which make him a leader of men. Whatever we may think of him, he is going to be a great factor in the development of Cuba and very possibly in Latin American affairs generally.[73]

Authors Frank Mankiewicz and Kirby Jones visited Cuba in 1975 to conduct an in-depth interview with Fidel Castro. Like many others, they were unable to resist Castro's spell. According to them, Castro is "one of the most charming and entertaining men either of us had ever met," adding that, "from the moment he looked you straight in the eye and spoke directly to every question, from the moment he first leaned eagerly forward to stress a point, his beard no more than six inches away, each of us knew we were in for a fascinating interview and an exciting experience."[74]

Ruby Hart Phillips, an American journalist and author who met Castro in early 1959 wrote, "He had undeniable charm. Everything he said sounded sincere and reasonable, but I found no warmth of personality nor sense of humor."[75] She also noticed that "Castro could play on the emotions of the people as a musician on the strings of his violin."[76] Author Daniel James, by no means a Castro sympathizer, wrote that, "Fidel Castro had hypnotized the Cuban people, including the anti-Communists, into thinking that to fight him was to fight the Revolution."[77]

Just a few days after the victory at the Bay of Pigs, Castro brought some of the prisoners to a tv program and confronted them. When Castro began talking most prisoners were openly defying him. But, as Castro continued talking about the benefits the revolution had brought to the Cuban people, many of the prisoners appeared to respond to his words. Finally, even before Castro advocated for clemency, the prisoners interrupted him several times by applause.[78] The anecdote explains why Carlos Franqui believes Castro possesses the power that turned people "from protagonists into obedient servants."[79]

Professor Maurice Halperin, who lived some years in Cuba, described Castro's first meeting with French agronomist André Voisin. After reading some of Voisin's books, Castro invited him to visit Cuba. The flight arrived at 2:00 a.m., and Castro was there to receive the professor. Voisin was dead tired after the long flight, but Castro began talking and talking until 6:00 a.m., and the professor later reported that his weariness and fatigue disappeared as if by magic.

Professor Voisin was not exaggerating. In close conversation, Fidel Castro "casts a hypnotic spell on his interlocutor, sitting close to him, transfixing him with his piercing eyes, gesticulating freely, occasionally patting his victim on the knee, with an incessant stream of flawless rhetoric from his mouth, and all the while totally oblivious to the passing of time and the lateness of the hour."[80]

Castro's Powers of Clairvoyance

Fidel Castro's life has always been bound up with prophesies, some of them strangely accurate. Probably the most widely known is the one made by Father Armando Llorente, who was Castro's Spanish language and public-speaking teacher as well as spiritual adviser at the Colegio de Belén. In 1959 Llorente told Jules Dubois "Fidel Castro is a man of destiny. Behind him is the hand of God. He has a mission to fulfill and he will fulfill it against all obstacles."[81] A year later, in July, 1960, Presbyterian minister Rafael Cepeda made a similar prophecy: "Fidel Castro is an instrument of God for the establishment of His reign among men."[82]

Llorente and Cepeda are not the only ones who have made prophecies about Castro. Some author claims that when Castro was a boy, a woman from the Congo told Fidel's mother that the lines on the boy's palm marked him with the destiny of a person who would change the world, and who would not die. The same source also tells of a prophecy made by Jean Baptiste Lavie, a French mystic who moved to Cuba in the early half of the 20th century and founded a retreat community known as "Los Letreros" near the city of Manzanillo, not far from the Sierra Maestra. La Vie prophesied, "Once Christ has appeared physically, he will establish his reign in Cuba."[83]

Even more intriguing are two extraordinary prophecies not many people know about. The first was made by Walter Blomquist, a Swedish mystic and scholar of occultism who moved to Havana in the late forties after living several years in Egypt. Some sources claim that, while Castro was fighting his guerrilla war against Batista's soldiers, Blomquist wrote an article, published in an important Cuban magazine, in which he told about a vision he had of two lines converging in the Sierra Maestra mountains. According to Blomquist an event that would happen in the Sierra Maestra would have global repercussions. Unfortunately, I have not been able to find documentary evidence about Blomquist's prediction. The other one, from my personal experience, has to do with a short story published in the early 1950s in *Más Allá*, a widely read science fiction magazine published in Argentina following the lines of *Beyond*, and American s.f. magazine. The story, which I personally read, took place in the early 21st century, and dealt with a world tyrant similar to George Orwell's Big Brother. The most amazing thing is that the place where the tyrant lived and the novel took action was a Caribbean island formerly called Cuba.[84]

When Fidel was attending Law school at the University of Havana, he used to visit his former high school, the Colegio de Belén. There he found a receptive ear in Mother Elizabeth Therese. One day, Fidel told her, "Mother: I will become the President of Cuba."[85]

On March 15, 1952, just a few days after Batista gave a *coup d'état* and took power in Cuba, Fidel Castro wrote him a prophetic letter. In it Castro told Batista that his coup of March 10 was going to bring graft and corruption, torture and death for many, and that the Cuban people would react by eventually overthrowing him.[86] His prophecy, to some extent self-fulfilled, proved to be extremely accurate.

In early 1953, preceding his departure for the Moncada attack, young lawyer Fidel Castro was sleeping at a different place every night to avoid detection by Batista's police. He moved around Havana avoiding any pattern or routine. His driver at the time was Teodulio Michel, an ex-soldier from Batista's army. Some of Castro's men had misgivings about Michel, but Fidel put his life in Michel's hands "based on his instinct." His "instinct" proved to be right.[87]

By mid 1953 Castro was actively conspiring against Batista and kept hiding from the police. But, in July 24, 1953, unexpectedly, Castro visited the secret police headquarters to inquire about a "client." He later told his friends he did so because once there he "would sense" if the police had suspicions about him.⁸⁸ His biographer Tad Szulc, for one, was convinced that "Fidel has a keenly developed sense of dangers facing him."⁸⁹

On December 2, 1956, Fidel Castro and a group of 81 men landed in the Oriente province of Cuba. The goal of the expedition was to fight President Batista. But just a few hours after the landing, Batista's Air Force planes bombed and strafed the group, killing 42 of the men. The rest, low on ammunition, without food and with a shortage of water, tried to escape to the nearby mountains. Castro found himself stranded with eight of his men. They marched for four days through sugar cane fields, nourishing themselves by sucking the raw cane dry. The next day, in one of the cane fields, Raúl Castro's party stumbled into Fidel's group. Despite the defeat, the fatigue, hunger and disillusionment, Fidel assured his men: "The days of the [Batista] dictatorship are numbered!"⁹⁰

The attack on the Moncada garrison is another good example of Castro's uncanny powers of foresight. The attack was amateurishly planned and incompetently executed. To a normal individual, its failure would have been the end of his political career. All that Castro had worked for now lay in ruins. He had nothing to look forward to except a trial for treason. But Castro, amazingly enough, still had boundless faith in his own mission.

Fidel felt that the Moncada failure was not the end, just the beginning of his struggle, and events were to prove him correct. He decided to use his trial as an excellent opportunity for political propaganda, which would be reported throughout the world, and hence enable him to create a legend. This was a plan that required the most brazen effrontery, but Castro carried it through, transforming the prisoner's dock in which he stood into an orator's podium. He treated his prosecutors with contempt, refuting their arguments and asserting the patriotic nature of his mission. By the time the judges were ready to pass sentence, Castro had obtained complete psychological ascendance over the courtroom. The trial for the Moncada attack was a sign of times to come. It showed the extraordinary personal magnetism, the powers of oratory and prophecy with which historians now have made us familiar.

Examples about Castro's strange intuition abound. When Ortodoxo Party leader Eddy Chibás committed suicide on 5 August, 1951, his casket was brought to the University of Havana for the students to pay their last respects to the dead politician. José (Pepe) Pardo Llada tells that, while they were carrying the casket down the University main stairs, Fidel approached him, suggesting they should bring the casket to the Presidential Palace and force President Carlos Prío Socarrás to resign.⁹¹

Pardo Llada though that it was a far-fetched idea and dismissed Fidel's suggestion, telling him "You're crazy, Fidel!". But Castro's intuition was right. Many years later President Prío admitted that, to avoid a bloodbath, he had planned to resign if the Ortodoxo leaders had asked for his resignation.[92]

Just a few months after the triumph of the revolution, Castro traveled to Buenos Aires to attend a session of the Economic Assembly of the Latin American states plus the United States. On May 2, 1959, Fidel made a long speech in which he made two proposals. In one of them he suggested that, in order to avoid problems in Latin America, the United States should aid the Latin American countries economically. According to Castro that would cost the Americans thirty billion dollars over a period of ten years. The second idea Castro presented to the meeting was the need for a Latin American common market.[93] Next month, in a speech at New York's Central Park during his first official visit to the U.S., Castro again raised his suggestion of an American "Marshall Plan" for all of Latin America in order to avoid the danger of communism.[94]

As expected, Fidel's suggestions were received with laughter and contempt. But, less than two years later, President Kennedy created his Alliance for Progress, pledging $10 billion for the first ten years. Later, President Johnson promised another $10 billion to continue the program. And less than ten years later, in the spring of 1967, a hemispheric conference was held in Uruguay where the decision was made for the creation of a Latin American common market. Incredibly, both of the apparently far-fetched suggestions Castro made eventually became a reality.

Many people close to Castro have been witnesses to evidences of his "sixth sense." For example, Castro's former interior minister Major Ramiro Valdés, one of the few men who has followed Fidel in many of his revolutionary activities, once told Szulc: "He can smell the dangers and the risks in the air . . . This Fidel is a sorcerer, a sorcerer . . ."[95]

Teresa Casuso told a strange story she heard from some who fought beside Castro in the Sierra Maestra. Going from one place to another in the middle of the forest Fidel would suddenly stop and say, "No, not through there." They would change direction and go by a round-about route, only to learn afterwards that near those places where Fidel had stopped—"as if struck by lightning," his comrades said—there had been enemy troops lying in ambush. This happened not once but several times.[96]

The fact has been recorded also by Castro's biographer Carlos Franqui. He tells how in several occasions Castro demonstrated his ability to foresee the movements, place and attack plans of Batista's army.[97] This ability proved to be extremely helpful in maintaining his position of leadership once he took power in Cuba in 1959.

Talking to Tad Szulc, Faustino Pérez, one of Castro's close associates during the early revolutionary days, said: ". . . what would actually happen afterwards was already clearly seen by Fidel."[98] After hearing so many anecdotes of Fidel's clairvoyant abilities, his biographer, Tad Szulc, had to admit that "One of Fidel's special gifts has been his ability, both instinctive and analytically intellectual, to predict the future moves of his adversaries."[99] Szulc, however, is wrong on one count: there is nothing analytically intellectual in Fidel's ability to foresee events; it is totally instinctive.

In his long fight against the Americans, Fidel Castro has always been one step ahead of their plans. For example, apparently for no reason at all, he placed the newly created National Revolutionary Militia on full alert on November, 1959.[100] A few days later, on December 16, 1959, Fidel Castro, addressing the Federation of Cuban Sugar Workers, warned that invasions by followers of Batista were inevitable in the coming year. He added that the civilian militia, which was then being formed and trained, would repel the invasion.[101] His forecast proved to be extremely accurate. It is difficult to explain, however, how he reached that conclusion, because it seems unlikely that at such an early time nobody in the American government had any plans or even had expressed any idea about invading Cuba. Previously classified documents later released by the CIA, show that plans for a Cuban invasion actually began four months later.

After an explosion destroyed a ship loaded with Belgian armaments on Havana's bay on March 4, 1960, Fidel called Alekseev to an impromptu meeting. During it, Fidel predicted that, following this action of sabotage, the U.S. would take the following steps:

1. The implementation of terrorist acts against him or his close associates.
2. A break in diplomatic relations.
3. The introduction of economic sanctions.
4. An overt attack.[102]

Again, all his predictions proved to be extremely accurate.

On December 31, 1960, Castro's newspaper *Revolución* came out with a banner headline in big, bold letters: "Yankee Invasion!" Inside, there was an alarmist article about an imminent American invasion of Cuba. That same night Castro went on tv to expand on *Revolución*'s article, which most likely had been written by Castro himself. According to Fidel, an invasion by Cuban exiles backed by U.S. marines would occur before President Eisenhower left the presidency on January 20.

One must keep in mind that Castro delivered this speech way before any indication that an actual American invasion had been planned. But, looking for a rational explanation, let's assume that, at least unofficially, some members of the U.S. government had made comments about the idea of an invasion of Cuba, and that Castro's moles had heard them and informed him. But what he said afterwards defies any rational explanation.

According to Castro, CIA Director Allen Dulles already had everything ready for an invasion. "The excuse would be the assertion that Cuba was allowing rocket pads to be constructed on its territory."[103] On the basis of this reasoning, Castro called for a general mobilization of Cuba's armed forces. Castro's words were very similar to a note addressed to the U.N. Security Council by Cuban Foreign Minister Raúl Roa. The note was delivered on December 31, 1960, more than sixteen months before the idea of deploying missiles in Cuba popped inside Khrushchev's mind.

In the same fashion, Castro apparently foresaw the exact place where the Bay of Pigs invaders were to land. Early in November 1960, six months before the invasion took place, Castro and Major Félix Duque had carefully inspected the Bay of Pigs area.[104]

Not all prophesies about Castro, however, have been favorable. There is an old legend that has been known for many years in Santiago de Cuba. It has to do with Antonio María Claret, a Catholic priest and scholar appointed archbishop of Santiago de Cuba in 1851 by Pius IX and declared venerable by Leo XIII in 1899.

According to the legend, the Virgin of the Charity, patron saint of Cuba, appeared to Father Claret during a visit he made to the Sierra Maestra mountains, and made a prophecy about the future of Cuba. The Virgin, said Claret, told him of a bold young man who would climb these same mountains with weapons in his hands, to descend victorious with a long beard, accompanied by many like him. Those young men would wear crucifixes and medals of saints, but would feel ashamed of it and stop wearing them.

Supported by most Cubans because of his initial good intentions, soon after he would become a tyrant, turning the country into a disastrous 40-year dictatorship. After this period of time, a short period of chaos would arrive, with some violence and bloodshed. Then, Cuba would rise to become an important country among the nations of the world.

Responding to the criticism of skeptics, the followers of Claret claim that, though they have found no written evidence of the prophecy among the saint's papers, the legend has been known and transmitted orally for many generations, way before Castro was born.[105]

Castro's Extraordinary Good Luck

Tad Szulc once observed that "Fidel's luck is a recurrent theme of his existence."[106] Fidel seems to believe that his true gift is what superstitious people call "a lucky star," wrote Teresa Casuso. Except for the Moncada disaster, his most absurd and hasty undertakings usually keep turning out well.[107]

On July 26, 1953, Castro miraculously escaped death on at least two occasions, first, when the army beat back the attack to the Moncada barracks and, second, when he was captured a few days later in the mountains.[108] After the failed attack, Castro and a small group of his men were in hiding in the hilly countryside, not far from Santiago de Cuba. Batista had ordered some of his trusted men in the Army to find Fidel and kill him immediately. The officer who was to be in charge of the operation was Lieutenant Luis Santiago Gamboa, a tough and merciless officer who would have killed Castro without the slightest hesitation. But Gamboa was in bed with flu and the operation was commanded by Lieutenant Pedro Manuel Sarría, a man of honor who took Castro alive and spared his life. Sarría later said that Castro's courage persuaded him to save Fidel's life.[109] But one can hardly call an act of courage Castro's precipitous escape from the scene leaving his men in the lurch.

When Castro was at the Boniato prison in Santiago awaiting trial for the Moncada attack, a plot was afoot to poison him. But Fidel sensed the danger, and for some weeks he ate only what was sent to him from his friends and relatives. Shortly after Castro's arrival at Boniato, Lieutenant Jesús Yanes Pelletier, the prison's military supervisor, was suddenly removed from his post. People rumored that it had been because he had refused to obey orders to poison Castro.[110]

During an incursion to a place called Caracas, at the Sierra Maestra mountains, a peasant named Eutimio Guerra, who earlier had acted as a guide, joined Castro and his guerrilla group. But Guerra had been previously captured by Batista's Army and had agreed, for a promise of $10,000 and an army rank, to kill Castro. A few days after joining the guerrilla group Guerra tried to accomplish his plan. The night was cold and he asked Castro for a blanket. Castro replied that they had none to spare, so they had better share the same one. So, Castro and his would be assassin, armed with a .45 pistol, lay down under the same blanket and Guerra spent the whole night fingering his pistol unable to make up his mind as to when to shoot.[111]

Cintio, a former guerrilla who fought close to Castro at the Sierra Maestra, told Ernesto Cardenal that Castro, "has often been close to death, but he had a kind of mysterious destiny, or providence, that always saved him." Once, when some farmers rebelled in the Escambray mountains, Castro went there to inspect the troops. One night, Cintio told Cardenal, Fidel left the camp alone to inspect the surroundings. As Castro reached a little stream and washed his face, a rebel farmer aimed his rifle at him, but he did not dare to kill Castro.

Later, the farmer was captured, and he told the story. Castro confronted the farmer and told him that the Revolution was made for them, "We have given them everything, and it's ridiculous that they should be fighting us now." The farmed answered, "All right, but I want to tell you that last night I had your life in my hands and I refused to kill you." He told how he had seen Castro at the stream when he was washing his face, and Castro realized that it was true. "And why didn't you kill me?," Fidel asked him. "Well, Fidel . . . because you were Fidel."[112] A few minutes later the farmer was executed by a firing squad.

In October, 1961, another unsuccessful attempt was made on the life of Fidel Castro. The attempt was set for the day of President Dorticós' return from a trip to Moscow and Peking. It was announced that Dorticós and Fidel would talk to the people from the northern terrace of the Presidential Palace. The conspirators had their weapons hidden in an apartment from which they dominated the terrace. Castro and Dorticós spoke on the given date but no attempt on Castro's life ever took place. Later that month, on October 23, after the attempt was discovered and the plotters apprehended, Castro explained it in detail and added: "I don't know why they did not shoot. They must have gotten nervous."[113]

In the early hours after his victory at the Bay of Pigs, Castro was inspecting the enemy positions and talking to the prisoners. There were so many of them and there was such confusion, that some of the prisoners still were carrying their weapons as they surrounded Fidel—the very man they had come to kill—to answer his questions. But none of them made the slightest attempt to shoot Castro.[114]

Franqui reports a similar incident,

> On the third day of fighting, I was in a jeep with Fidel and his escort. We had stopped somewhere along the front. Suddenly a group of invaders sprang out of a thicket in the swamp. They threw down their weapons and put their hands up. Fidel and the rest of us were shocked. One burst of machine-gun fire would have sent the lot of us to the next world.[115]

Franqui, who was very close to Fidel at the time, tells how, on one occasion, Fidel and President Dorticós were riding in a jeep on a secondary road not far from Havana. Suddenly, Fidel decided to do the driving and, after sending the driver to the back seat, moved with Dorticós to the front seats. A few minutes later a big tree fell on the back side of the jeep, seriously injuring the driver, but Fidel and Dorticós were unharmed.[116]

In the mid-forties, when Castro was a law school student involved in gangsterism at the University of Havana, he was challenged by a fellow student to fight out their differences in the early morning hours. Not knowing that several of his enemies had prepared an ambush to kill him, Fidel agreed to meet the contender at the University stadium, but apparently showed up late, after his enemies had left. "It was a miracle that I came out alive," he said, recalling the incident several years later.[117]

In 1949 a rival gang decided to assassinate Justo Fuentes and Fidel Castro. The attempt was set up for the time of the day both men usually left the radio station COCO where they hosted a daily program. But only Fuentes was killed, because Fidel did not show up at the station that day and escaped death.[118]

Similar incidents abound. One day in 1964 Castro stopped, as he often did, for a milkshake at the cafeteria at the Habana Libre (former Havana Hilton) hotel. The CIA knew of his habit, and had suborned a cafeteria employee to slip a cyanide capsule into Castro's milkshake. When Fidel came to the cafeteria and ordered the milkshake, the employee took the capsule out of the refrigerator, where he had kept it, to put it into the drink. But the capsule was frozen and it broke, and the man, who was very nervous, couldn't slip it into the milkshake.[119]

In a previous attempt, Castro's mistress Marita Lorenz was recruited by the CIA, who gave her some poison capsules to kill Castro. To hide the capsules, Marita buried them into a jar of cold cream. Before she met Castro that evening she sought to retrieve the capsules, but she discovered that they had been dissolved in the cold cream, and she disposed of the poisoned cream in the commode. Some time later, having learned of the plot, Castro asked Lorenz: "You couldn't kill me. You would never do that, would you?" She confessed to him that she could not have carried out the plan.[120]

On another occasion, while Castro was flying to Venezuela for the inauguration of president Carlos Andrés Suárez, one of Castro's bodyguards tried to assassinate him. The bodyguard, a tall, black man of proved courage, apparently had decided to kill Castro as soon as the plane landed in Caracas. He was sitting behind Castro, and carried a briefcase with an Uzi submachinegun and two hand grenades.

But the man became so nervous, and began sweating and trembling so much, that other people on the plane noticed it. Castro's physician, also on the plane, though the man was having a heart attack, and tried to take his pulse. But the man began crying, totally out of control, yelling that he was not guilty. He was taken into custody and sent back to Havana. The next day he was executed.[121]

There are many stories about how dozens of CIA-planned attempts to assassinate Castro ended in failure. In its investigations about the allegations, the Senate Committee, chaired by Senator Frank Church, found "concrete evidence" of eight murder plots involving the CIA against the Cuban leader. On the other hand, in August 1975, Castro complained to Senator George McGovern that the actual number was, in fact, twenty four.[122]

An explanation of the true source of Fidel Castro's strange powers of fascination, clairvoyance, and his extraordinary good luck is beyond the scope of this book. The fact remains that Castro's powers, as we have shown above, are quite different from the characteristics commonly associated with charisma. True charismatic personalities were John F. Kennedy, Mahatma Gandhi, Evita Perón, Winston Churchill, and Charles de Gaulle. But one cannot explain the powers of Adolf Hitler, Charlie Manson, Jim Jones or Fidel Castro by charisma alone. The extraordinary powers these men exerted over people go far beyond the powers associated with Weber's concept of charisma. Therefore, an alternative interpretation needs to be found to explain this power. I have not offered one because my intention was not to provide answers, but to show that the prevalent analyses of Castro's strange abilities have been approached from a narrow perspective, and that there are more questions in need of an answer than most people realize.

Chapter 2

The Great Pulverizer

> *The Soviet government has reached certain accords with the American government. But this does not mean that we have renounced the right to have the weapons we deem convenient and to take steps in international policy we deem convenient as a sovereign country.*
>
> — Fidel Castro. January 2, 1963

In an editorial piece for the *U.S. News and World Report*, its Editor-in-Chief, Mortimer B. Zuckerman, wrote: "For 33 years America has tried to pulverize Cuba's economy."[1] Granted, Mr. Zuckerman's assertion is true, and it is reprehensible that the United States, the most powerful nation on earth, has engaged in such behavior against a small, neighboring nation. But that story is old news, and it has been repeated over and over *ad nauseam*.

Instead, I would like to tell the reader about a less known story that American Liberals and mainstream media have managed to hide from the American public; a story about how for more than 40 years Fidel Castro has been carefully planning the pulverization of the whole United States of America, from sea to shining sea.

Fidel's Extraordinary Love for Nuclear Missiles

In December 1962, the Hearst-owned *San Francisco Chronicle* and *News Call Bulletin* published a UPI cable claiming that Ernesto "Ché" Guevara told a reporter in Havana that "to defend [himself] against aggression" Fidel Castro had planned a nuclear attack on key U.S. cities, including New York. Though the *Chronicle* buried the story on page 16, the *News Call Bulletin* ran a dramatic front-page headline in big, bold letters: "How Castro Plotted Atomic Attack on US!" The *Chronicle* added that "Secretary of State Dean Rusk called Guevara's remark about a nuclear attack 'just talk'."[2]

But Mr. Rusk was dead wrong. Guevara's remarks were not 'just talk.' In an interview Ché gave a few weeks after the crisis to Sam Russell, a British correspondent for the *Daily Worker*, Guevara said that if the missiles had been under Cuban control, they would had fired them off.[3]

Moreover, in an editorial he wrote during the missile crisis for *Verde Olivo*, the Cuban Armed Forces weekly magazine, Ché made his point even more clear, exhorting the Soviets to stand by their commitment to Cuba, no matter what the cost:

> What we contend is that we must walk by the path of liberation even when it may cost millions of atomic victims, because in the struggle to death between two systems the only thing that can be considered is the definitive victory of socialism or its retrogression under the nuclear victory of imperialist aggression.[4]

As in many other occasions, Guevara was acting as Castro's mouthpiece. It is a matter of public record that Fidel was extremely dissatisfied with the pacific solution of the Cuban missile crisis. The fact that nuclear war had been averted, and the Russians had allegedly received from the American government a pledge for the non-invasion of Cuba, was apparently not important for Castro. For him the kind of political solutions possible within the parameters of peaceful coexistence were not real solutions. They merely postponed what he believed was an inevitable final confrontation with American imperialism. As always, Castro was itching for a fight—in this case the definitive fight, a nuclear one.

Guevara's statement was written just a few weeks after the end of the Cuban missile crisis of 1962. A careful reading of Khrushchev's memoirs, however, shows that the Soviet Premier was fully aware of Castro's dreams of nuclear power and tried to use them to his advantage.[5] As a matter of fact, there are good reasons for believing that, in order to overcome Castro's initial reluctance to accept the deployment of strategic missiles on Cuban soil, Khrushchev enticed him by dangling a nuclear bait. Most likely the Soviet Premier suspected that Castro's secret plans would include an attempt to grab the Soviet nuclear missiles for his own use. That is why Khrushchev's plans were carefully laid down to avoid that possibility. Later developments proved Khrushchev was right.[6]

Castro's bellicose position during the crisis was revealed later by some of his closest associates. A year after the missile crisis, Ché Guevara wrote: "There can be no bargaining, no half measures, no partial guarantees of a country's stability. The victory must be total."[7] A month later, Raúl Castro, head of Cuba's armed forces, reiterated his brother's militant opposition to peaceful coexistence, saying, "We must never establish peaceful coexistence with our enemies."[8]

According to documents made public in Cuba in August, 1997, six years after the missile crisis, in a speech to the Central Committee of Cuba's Communist Party in 1968, Castro said he felt "an incredible love" for the nuclear missiles that brought on the crisis, and wanted to keep them even after the Soviets agreed to remove them. Castro admitted to laughing with his advisers even as the possibility of nuclear war loomed, as documents published by the French daily *Le Monde* show.[9]

Le Monde reported that Castro's account of the crisis was provided to the newspaper by Vincent Touze, a French academic and expert on the missile crisis. A few days after the crisis began, at the point when allegedly it had brought the two superpowers closer to a nuclear confrontation than at any other time during the Cold War, Soviet leader Nikita Khrushchev agreed to withdraw the missiles. Castro, who had little control over the situation, said he dearly wanted to keep the missiles, which he saw as a super weapon for any battle against the United States. "We defended these missiles with affection, with an incredible love. We were fighting for the first time almost on equal terms with an enemy that had threatened and provoked us unceasingly," Castro said in his report to the Central Committee of his "Communist" party.[10]

According to Cuban documents, when Soviet advisers came to Cuba in the summer of 1962 to discuss the installation of the missiles, Castro asked the Kremlin to deploy 1,000 missiles, and became upset when told that only about 40 would be installed. As the tension mounted and it appeared the Soviets would capitulate, Castro argued that a nuclear strike should be launched if the United States attacked Cuba.

"We didn't envisage lightly the idea we could disappear ... It was a very interesting fact because we were in the antechamber of the holocaust and we were telling jokes," the documents quoted Castro as saying. "Evidently, we knew that we were going to be made to play the role of death, but we were determined to play it," Castro told the Central Committee. Castro said Cuba had placed great faith in the Soviets but soon lost confidence in its ally. He said the Kremlin had botched the situation, which he called a "disaster."

Castro also said he had wanted to inform the United States about the missiles before reconnaissance planes spotted them, but was overruled by Khrushchev. He also professed to be shocked by the fact that they were not camouflaged, and suggested the Soviets had overlooked doing so on purpose. However, Castro admitted his government had been naïve, confessing that nobody in the Cuban leadership even knew what nuclear missiles looked like[11] although he accepted the weapons "without hesitation."[12]

In 1975 Castro told Senator George S. McGovern that, during the crisis, he would have taken a harder line than Khrushchev.[13] Recently declassified documents show that, on October 26, Castro demanded an assurance from Khrushchev that, if the U.S. invaded Cuba, the Soviet Union would launch a nuclear attack against the United States. In a clear reference to the use of nuclear weapons against the United States, Castro urged Khrushchev to consider the "elimination of such a danger," and added, "there is, I believe, no other choice."[14] But, apparently not happy with the Soviet Premier's non-committed answer to his plight, Castro took some specific steps to "help" Khrushchev push the button.

Castro's Attempts to Destroy New York . . . and Much More

On October 3, 1962, a few days before the onset of the crisis, Castro sent one of his trusted men to New York on a key mission. The man chosen for the job was Roberto Santiesteban Casanova, who had just been appointed to a minor post at the Cuban mission to the United Nations. His diplomatic passport identified him as an "attaché" to the Cuban mission. Santiesteban's professional field, however, was not diplomacy. Quite the contrary, he was an expert in terrorist techniques, just graduated from a highly secret school of terrorism and subversion, not far from Havana.

As soon as Santiesteban arrived in New York, he contacted the rest of his team, including José Gómez Abad and his wife Elsa, both attachés at the Cuban mission, and José García Orellana, a Cuban immigrant who ran a costume jewelry shop in Manhattan. FBI estimates of how many others were involved in the plot range from twenty-five to fifty people. The secret mission of the terrorist team was to accomplish Castro's orders to blow up a big portion of Manhattan, including the Statue of Liberty, Macy's department store, several subway stations, the 42nd street bus terminal and Grand Central station, as well as several refineries along the New Jersey shore, including the Humble Oil and Refining Company in Linden. To this effect they stored a huge cache of explosives at Garcia's shop.[15]

But the saboteurs' plan was too ambitious and included too many people, and soon the FBI got word of it and detained the main conspirators. Had their plan worked out the way it had been conceived, it would undoubtedly have ignited American public opinion and prompted retaliation against Cuba. Had it occurred during the tense days of the crisis it may have been taken for a Russian preemptive attack on the United States and may have triggered a spasm-like retaliatory strike on the Soviet Union, with unpredictable consequences. Fortunately, the plan failed. But Fidel Castro is a very resourceful man. After his failed attempt to create a provocation which may have brought a nuclear confrontation between the superpowers, Castro pulled another ace from his sleeve.

It is a well known fact that at the apex of the crisis, on October 27, 1962, an American U-2 spy plane was shot down on the eastern part of Cuba by a Soviet surface-to-air missile. Several explanations, some of them conflicting with each other, have been given to explain that bizarre event, but most people agree that the missile was fired in violation of orders from Khrushchev and the Soviet high command.

Following Castro's orders, and disregarding Soviet advice, in the morning of Saturday, October 27, antiaircraft batteries manned by the Cuban army began firing at American low-flying reconnaissance planes, damaging at least one. As Castro himself told Tad Szulc, "I am absolutely certain that if the low-level flights had been resumed we would have shot down one, two, or three of these planes... With so many batteries firing, we would have shot down some planes. I don't know whether this would have started nuclear war."[16] Though Cuban crews were operating anti-aircraft guns, the powerful surface-to-air missiles (SAMs) were under the Soviet's tight control, and the Cubans had no access to the bases and didn't know how to operate them. Nevertheless, at about 10:00 a.m. of that same Saturday morning, an American U-2 was shot down by a SAM fired from a battery at Los Angeles, near Banes, Oriente province.

Some years later, in 1989, Castro's double-agent Aleksandr Alekseev, former Soviet ambassador to Cuba and a senior KGB officer, said that the U-2 was shot down by a "trigger-happy Soviet air defense commander."[17] Alekseev's claim, however, is hard to believe. The Soviet military, and especially the Soviet air defense, has rigid standards and operating procedures. Its military doctrine and practice reflects a do-it-by-the-book attitude. No Soviet officer would give such an order unless he was out of his mind or forced to do it. Other explanations, therefore, seem to better fit the picture.

Carlos Franqui, former editor of *Revolución* now living in exile in Italy, and a close associate of Castro at the time, wrote some time ago that Castro himself told him he had personally pushed the button which launched the missile that shot down the U-2. According to Franqui, Fidel was eager for a nuclear confrontation between the USSR and the United States and had been growing restless as the crisis evolved. At one time, wrote Franqui, Fidel "went on to say that if he were in Moscow, he would send the government to the subway, which was supposed to be safe during a nuclear attack."

Franqui tells a bizarre version of the shoot down of the U-2 over Cuba. According to Franqui,

> One day, with a look of astuteness on his face I remembered from the guerrilla days, he said, "Now I'm going to find out if they'll invade or not, if this is for real or not." He said nothing more and drove his jeep to Pinar del Río.... Fidel went to one of the Russian rocket bases, where the Soviet generals took him on a tour of the installation. Just at that moment an American U-2 appeared on the radar screen, flying low over the island. Fidel asked how the Soviets would protect themselves in war if that had been an attack plane instead of a reconnaissance plane. The Russians showed him the ground-to-air missiles and said that all they would have to do would be to push a button and the plane would be blown out of the sky. "Which button?" "This one." Fidel pushed it and the rocket brought down the U-2.... The Russians were flabbergasted, but Fidel simply said, "Well, now we'll see if there's a war or not."[18]

Franqui's story, most likely based on hearsay, is hard to believe. First of all, the U-2 was not shot down in Pinar del Río, west of Havana, but in Oriente province, more than 500 miles east of Havana. Secondly, the type of surface-to-air missile fired by the Russians was an early-type model which requires more than simply pushing a button. Once fired, it has to be carefully guided by radar until it reaches its target. Therefore, the true story has to be, by force, a little more complicated. However, Franqui's account of the incident may contain at least one grain of truth.

According to Seymour Hersh, there is strong evidence that, on October 26, 1962, a Cuban army unit attacked and overran a Soviet-manned SAM base at Los Angeles, near Banes, in the Oriente province, killing many Soviets and seizing control of the site. Hersh based his article on information partly drawn from an interview with former Department of Defense analyst Daniel Ellsberg, who was himself citing classified material from a post-crisis study of the event. The speculation is based on an intercepted transmission from the Soviet base at Los Angeles indicating heavy fighting and casualties. Adrián Montoro, former director of Radio Havana Cuba, and Juan Antonio Rodríguez Menier, a senior Cuban intelligence officer who defected in 1987 and is now living in the U.S., seem to confirm Ellsberg's report.[19]

Though both Castro and the Russians have categorically denied that the attack took place, Raymond L. Garthoff, Special Assistant for Soviet bloc Political/Military Affairs in the State Department during the Kennedy administration, claims that, in fact, from October 28, the Cuban army *did* surround the Soviet missile bases for three days.[20] It is evident that, whatever really happened, Castro was trying to precipitate a nuclear confrontation between the Soviet Union and the United States.

Messages exchanged between Castro and Khrushchev on October 28, 1962, indicate that something very fishy happened that day. In his message the Soviet premier accused the Cuban leader of shooting down the American plane. Then, Khrushchev warned Castro that such steps "will be used by aggressors to their advantage, to further their aims." In his answer to Khrushchev Castro explained that he had mobilized his antiaircraft batteries "to support the position of the Soviet forces." Then, Castro added this cryptic remark: "The Soviet Forces Command can give you further detail on what happened with the plane that was shot down."[21]

The Cuban missile crisis was finally resolved in a pacific way, which apparently was not the way Castro envisioned. Evidence indicates that, since the crisis days, Dr. Strangelove Castro has been dreaming about pulverizing the United States, and he has taken strong steps to fulfill his cherished dream. And don't be misled by the relatively small size of the island of Cuba when compared with the United States. Rest assured that Castro is no small enemy. Herbert Matthews, who knew Castro well, once said, "He is the most dangerous enemy that the United States has ever had in the Western Hemisphere."[22]

Castro's Search for The Great Equalizer

Starting in the early 1960s, the Soviet Union under Khrushchev's guidance sought to moderate its relations with the United States. In the Soviet view, the threat of mutual annihilation in a nuclear war overshadowed the immediate conflict between the socialist and capitalist camps. At the 20th Congress of the Communist Party of the Soviet Union in 1956, the Soviets proclaimed their commitment to a new program of peaceful coexistence with the capitalist powers. Thereafter, they claimed, the struggle between Washington and Moscow would be a peaceful one, conducted solely in the political, economic, and social fields. Without ignoring the elements of duplicity involved in the new program, it seems that at the time the Soviets were sincerely convinced that in the long run their superior economic and social system would triumph, but that would be only *if* in the short run a nuclear conflagration could be averted.

But, to their utmost surprise, Castro openly disagreed. Although the Cubans were committed to avoiding nuclear war, reasoned the bearded leader, they would not allow its threat to weaken their determination to struggle against world imperialism. In Castro's view, the Third World countries could not afford to wait for the eventual triumph of socialism. Their life and death battles must be fought now.

As early as 1962, Castro began raising some highly critical questions about the Soviet commitment to peaceful coexistence. In a communiqué issued from Havana during the January 1962 meeting of the International Organization of Journalists, Castro outlined his dissenting view of peaceful coexistence:

> The policy of peaceful coexistence is coexistence between states. This does not mean coexistence of classes. This policy does not mean coexistence between exploitation and the exploited. It is impossible for peaceful coexistence to exist between the exploited masses of Latin America and the Yankee monopolies.... As long as imperialism exists, international class war will exist between the exploited masses and the monopolies.[23]

As history has shown once and again, Fidel Castro is a very stubborn person. After his failed attempts to spoil our day in 1962, he persisted in his goal, which became a sort of *idée fixe*. The first indication that he was still pursuing his own plans came when he surprised the Soviets again by rejecting the Limited Test Ban Treaty of 1963 and refusing to sign the Nuclear Non-Proliferation Treaty of 1968.

By 1967, Castro's criticism of peaceful coexistence had become strident and was no longer limited to philosophical considerations. In Castro's view, peaceful coexistence had become a primary issue of contention in the socialist's camp policy. The military struggle against imperialism should not be limited by concerns about peaceful coexistence.

It is interesting to note that, as it happens most of the time, for some strange reason Castro's views were very close to the views held by both the Soviet and American military-industrial-complexes, which saw Khrushchev's doctrine of pacific coexistence as a direct threat to their economic interests and, therefore, opposed it tooth and nail.

Following Castro's line, in May of that year Castro's own Cuban Communist Party issued the following statement:

> If the concept of peaceful coexistence between states with different social systems does not guarantee the integrity, sovereignty, and independence of all countries alike, large and small, it is essentially opposed to the premises of Proletarian Internationalism. What kind of peace are the Vietnamese enjoying? What kind of coexistence is the U. S. practicing in that country?[24]

In early 1968 the U.N. General Assembly opened discussions on a multilateral agreement to curb the spread of nuclear weapons. The discussions resulted in the Non-Proliferation Treaty. Since it was open for signature in 1968, 113 countries, including all the nuclear-weapons states, have signed the treaty. But, during the Non-Proliferation Treaty discussions, Cuban U.N. delegate Raúl Roa Kourí clearly expressed Castro's position when he asserted that "Cuba would never give up its inalienable right to defend itself using weapons of any kind, despite any international agreement."[25] In the same fashion, Castro had earlier refused to sign the Tlatelolco agreement of 1967.

Shortly after the missile crisis of October 1962, the heads of state of seven Latin American countries called for hemispheric consultations to create a nuclear-free zone in Latin America. The agreement was finally signed in Tlatelolco, Mexico, in February of 1967. Cuba was among the countries invited to participate, but the Castro government refused, stating that it would not participate in the negotiation of an agreement to denuclearize Latin America because the U.S. deployed nuclear weapons and maintained nuclear bases in Latin America.[26] Castro's posture in relation with the Tlatelolco agreement was in sharp contrast to the policy of the Soviet Union. In retrospect, it seems that his reticence to sign both agreements was not the product of a passing mood, but of a carefully designed plan directed at justifying the materialization of his nuclear dreams.

Juan Vivés, a former Cuban intelligence officer who defected to the West, claims that, for several years after the missile crisis, Castro tried unsuccessfully to build his own missile capable of carrying nuclear weapons. For the ultra secret project he recruited military engineers and professors from Cuban universities. The missile, a sort of primitive V-1 bomb similar to the one developed by the Nazis, would use a MiG-21 jet motor. The testing of the prototypes of the Cuban missile, called *libertadoras*, (liberators) was a series of failures, but in 1977 the project was still active. According to Vivés, Castro said that the missiles were not intended as offensive weapons, but they would be used against the U.S. in case of an American attack against Cuba.

Cuban nuclear capability at the time seemed remote, so Castro used to talk about using the missiles for bacteriological warfare.[27]

After his missile development projects ended in failure, Castro's nuclear dream was postponed, but not forgotten. In 1989 General Rafael del Pino Díaz, the highest ranking Cuban defector, said that at the time of the Grenada operation in 1983, Castro ordered Cuban MiG 23 pilots to program their computers to attack targets in Florida. Among the selected targets was the Turkey Point nuclear plant, which Castro said had the potential of producing a nuclear disaster larger than Chernobyl.[28] According to Gen. del Pino, Castro's words were: "I don't have nuclear bombs, but I can produce a nuclear explosion."[29]

In another interview, Gen. del Pino claimed that, in 1968, when a group of Cubans were authorized to recover a MiG 17 taken to the U. S. by a defector, Cuban agents secretly made detailed photographs of Homestead Air Force Base in Florida. The base, Gen. del Pino said, had been targeted for an air attack by Cuban planes. The intention of the attack, Castro told the Cuban Air Force officers, would be to provoke the United States into an even stronger action "so the Soviet Union would become involved."[30]

Castro Goes Nuclear . . . Powered

In December, 1971, Castro announced his intention to turn to nuclear power for electricity generation in Cuba. Since that date, two Soviet-designed VVER-440 nuclear reactors went under construction at Juraguá, not far from the city of Cienfuegos, in Cuba's southern coast, about 150 miles south of Key West. The Soviet VVER-440 reactors were known to be fatally flawed—poorly designed, made with defective materials and assembled incompetently, allowing for many unsafe welds in their critical cooling systems.[31]

But, keeping in mind Castro's previous attempts to have the bomb, this nuclear program raises new questions about the true nature of his nuclear ambitions. As professor Michael Mandelbaum has pointed out, it doesn't take a superpower to pose a nuclear threat. Any small, poor country with a few nuclear explosives and the means to deliver them could wreak terrible damage to the United States.[32] Castro's Cuba fits professor Mandelbaum's description. It is a small, poor country just ninety miles from Florida, that has been desperately trying to get nuclear capability and has the means to deliver its deadly radiation to the U.S. simply by allowing the wind to do the job.

In 1977 Castro was interviewed by Brazilian journalist Fernando Morais. In the course of the interview Morais brought up the subject of the nuclear plants being built in Cuba. Castro answered that, because Cuba lacks big rivers or lakes, in the future he plans to depend mostly on nuclear-generated power. But he ended the interview with this rather enigmatic remark: "And, in the future, all new power-generating units will have nuclear energy as their power source. That's the news I can give you. *For the present,* we don't plan to build an atomic bomb."[33] Perhaps Castro intended his last remark as a joke. Later developments in Cuba, however, indicate that Castro's words to Morais were not a joke, but rather a slip of the tongue.

Two years later, in an interview with Dan Rather on *CBS*, aired on September 30, 1979, Castro mentioned again his position regarding nuclear weapons. Responding to Rather's remark that some people in the United States believe "that Cuba is a nuclear pistol pointed at their heads," Castro answered: "We have no nuclear weapons," but added, "It is not that we don't have the right to: we don't relinquish that right."[34]

Cuban intelligence defector Juan Antonio Rodríguez Menier claims that he positively knows that Castro was been actively seeking the possibility of having nuclear weapons. The fact, according to Rodríguez Menier, was common knowledge among Cuban senior intelligence officers.[35] Menier's claims have been corroborated by other sources.

According to these sources, in the mid-1980s Castro began a highly secret nuclear-bomb research project. Most of the hard currency he needed for the project was coming from his involvement in the narcotics trade and perhaps explains one of the reasons why he decided to collaborate with the Latin American drug barons.[36]

Evidence seems to indicate that, notwithstanding Castro's reported outrage over the discovery that some of his senior officers were involved in drug trafficking, he was not alien to the operation. It has been known for years that the Castro government has been raking off huge payments from the Medellín drug cartel for providing a safe haven for trans-shipping their cargoes from Colombia to the United States. It has also been known that Castro's motivation was not limited to getting easy money. Flooding the U. S. with drugs has been a major objective of Castro for at least 30 years.[37]

Nuclear research, under the direction of Castro's eldest son, nuclear engineer Fidel Castro Díaz-Balart, was being conducted at two installations, one located between Jibacoa and Arroyo Bermejo beaches, on the north coast of Cuba, not far from Havana, and the other one in Las Villas province. Furthermore, the Cuban authorities never gave any indication as how they will dispose of the waste from the weapons-grade uranium they will use to power their 10-megawatt Soviet-designed research reactor. The reactor is similar to Iraq's Soviet-made IRT 10-megawatt research reactor, which was a key element of that nation's military nuclear program until it was bombed by U.S. planes during the Gulf War.

In 1982 Castro Díaz-Balart told an associate that they were very close to acquiring the necessary knowledge to produce a nuclear weapon. The facilities also were involved in research on nerve gases and bacteriological weapons that could be delivered to the U.S. by different ways. In the early 1990s Castro ordered another large nuclear research complex to be built at Pedro Pi, southeast of Havana. The facility occupies a seven-square-mile area and contains 27 buildings.[38] Moreover, as late as 1991, a U.S. Defense Intelligence Agency report indicated that Castro was still showing a strong interest in acquiring material capable of producing nuclear weapons.[39]

Strong concerns were raised at the time in the U.S. about safety standards at the Juraguá nuclear plant.[40] Nuclear power plants are prone to accidents and their normal operation is risky.[41] Among the main risks—aside from operation accidents—is the fact that some of the materials required for its operation, like plutonium and weapons-grade enriched uranium, could be used in building nuclear artifacts. But, given Castro's record of creating incidents, the main concern about the nuclear plant under construction in Cuba should not be limited only to the possibility of an accidental meltdown, but to an intentional explosion and subsequent radiation leaks from the Juraguá plant. It would be easier for Castro, and the results will be just the same, to resort to sabotaging his nuclear plant in Cuba's southern coast than bombing the American ones in Florida. Just a few minutes of cutting off the flow of coolant may result in a meltdown and release of deadly radioactivity.[42]

As soon as the Soviet authorities knew about the accident at Chernobyl they acted swiftly to mitigate its consequences, but not even their desperate efforts stopped radiation from spreading across most parts of Europe from the very start of the accident. Just a few days after, prevailing upper-level winds brought radiation to the Arabian Peninsula, Siberia and parts of Canada.[43]

Scientists at the U.S. National Oceanic and Atmospheric Administration told *NBC* reporters that a Chernobyl-like accident in Cuba would have catastrophic consequences for the United States: "The day after [a nuclear disaster in Cuba] could witness radioactive fallout stretch[ing] from Key West to Managua, Nicaragua. [By] day three, the cloud could cover Miami and Tampa, Florida. Within the first week, most of the Eastern seaboard, portions of Texas and Louisiana, plus all of Mexico might be at risk."[44]

If Chernobyl serves as an example, given the right weather conditions, a nuclear "accident" at the Juraguá plant will spoil the day to most people living in Florida, the East Coast and Southern states. A similar type of event in Cuba, a country without the resources and perhaps not even the willingness to fight the "accident," may result in even higher levels of radiation.

Gary Milhoun, a nuclear non-proliferation expert and former member of the Nuclear Regulatory Commission, pointed out that even a low-level contamination from a nuclear plant in Cuba will trigger an exodus in Florida that would disrupt most of the southern states.[45] Also, Juan Oro, a nuclear scientist who worked at the Center for Nuclear Investigation in Cuba, said that if a reactor explodes in Cuba, "Heavy isotopes can be released into the atmosphere . . . I can assure you that in highly dynamic atmospheric conditions, probably by the second day, it will be over Atlanta; by the sixth day it could be over places more farther to the North—not with lethal effects or even much less than that—but the ecological impact could be felt at a point near the Great Lakes."[46]

Castro's Wet Dreams of Nuclear Armageddon

In a speech delivered on October, 1991, to the Fourth Congress of his "Communist" party, Castro, in an address that sounded like an impassioned call to collective suicide, called on the Cuban people to prepare themselves for catastrophe, war and martyrdom.[47] Author Andres Oppenheimer observed that the words 'death' and 'blood' permeated Castro's rhetoric, as if he had already resigned himself to the inevitability of a tragic ending. Like a cornered animal, his eyes spilling rancor, he vowed to die—taking the Cuban people with him—rather than allow *La Revolución* to be sullied by Yankee imperialists. Cubans, Castro seems to believe, would redeem themselves only by dying in battle against their enemies.

And then Castro proceeded to recite what Cubans on the street soon would call "Fidel's Ode to Death":[48]

> We are invincible. Because if all members of the Politburo have to die, we will die, and we will not be weaker for it! If all members of the Central Committee have to die, we will die, and we will not be weaker for it! If all the delegates to the Congress have to die, all the delegates to the Congress will die, and we will not be weaker for it! . . . If all the members of the Party have to die, all the members of the Party will die, and we will not weaken! If all members of the Young Communist Union have to die, all the members of the Young Communist Union will die![49]

During this seemingly never-ending socio-economic crisis, which Castro euphemistically calls the "special period," he began chanting a new mantra for the weary Cuban populace: "Socialism or Death!" Apparently some Cubans want neither socialism nor death, because they have been taking to the ocean in inner tubes by the hundreds, trying to escape from Castro's madhouse and looking for other, less lethal options.

Evidence of strange activities in Cuba indicate that Fidel Castro has been toying with the idea of a nuclear holocaust and is preparing himself for the event. *Newsweek* reported in early 1992 that Castro has been building a massive network of underground tunnels and concrete shelters, allegedly to protect the Cuban people from U.S. bombs. Later inquiries brought out that, at least since 1981, more than 10,000 Cuban troops were working 24 hours a day digging an intricate network of concrete-reinforced tunnels and bunkers beneath Havana and other parts of the Island.[50] It is believed that some of these tunnels could house an entire division of troops, plus tanks and equipment.[51]

The construction of tunnels is still going on. As late as January, 1999, the newspaper *Tribuna de La Habana* reported positive advances in tunnel construction in Havana during the previous year. Castro's daughter Alina mentioned what has been a rumor running for many years in Cuba. Based on the fact that the tunnels have iron grills similar to jail cells, some people have speculated that their real purpose is to trap the people and kill them using poison gas.[52] As the Soviet army approached Berlin, Hitler ordered the floodgates to be opened and drowned thousands of German citizens who had taken refuge in the city's subway. Havana has no subway, so perhaps Castro is hurriedly building a makeshift one just in case.

There are indications, however, that Castro is not exactly preparing himself to survive, "some kind of final cataclysm," as *Newsweek* reported. Actually he is preparing to survive, or perhaps die, after a Castro-created cataclysm that will make Chernobyl look pale in comparison. That is, seemingly, his idea for a final solution to his "American problem."[53]

Signs that Castro has been preparing himself for a *Götterdämmerung* are clear for anyone to see.[54] Since the early nineties he has been consistently talking in his speeches about the ancient Numantians, who chose to die instead of being conquered, and ending his speeches exhorting the Cubans to "Socialism or Death!"[55] He has adopted an increasingly apocalyptic tone in public speeches. On several occasions Castro has told his audience that Cuba would better sink in the sea rather than return to the corrupt capitalist world.[56]

In its March 6, 1996, issue, the authoritative *Jane's Defence Weekly* published a short note under the headline: "Cuban special forces prepare for U.S. attack." The note tells how, since 1990, Cuban Special Forces troops (which are under the direct command of Castro himself) have been training for the possibility of an attack directed at some parts of the continental United States, most likely Florida. Intensive training courses have been underway, at least since 1990, under a program provided by Vietnam, at the Vietnam People's Army base at Hoa Binh, an inland town south-west of Hanoi.[57]

According to sources in Cuba, in the mid 1980's Castro created a special military school for an élite force of some 3,500 men in a region known as El Cacho, not far from the city of Los Palacios, in the Pinar del Rio province west of Havana. The training center is known as the Baraguá school, and was founded by the notorious de la Guardia twins following Castro's direct orders. Personnel attending the school specialize in commando attacks and infiltration. They are considered by experts to be a very professional group, with great potential to inflict damage to a country. They are between 20 and 35 years old, and speak fluent English.[58] The training operations of this military base were documented in 1997 by *NBC*, and shown as part of a special section of *NBC Nightly News*.

General Jose Luis Mesa is the military director in command of the school, and colonel Ramírez is the director of daily operations. Both men have experience in African wars, and Vietnam. Currently, the school has some Vietnamese advisors acting as professors. Because these men are trained in infiltration techniques and operations, they can be effectively used to carry bacteriological and chemical warfare to the United States.[59]

The information presented above may strike most Americans as insane. But one must never forget that we are dealing with an individual with a very peculiar mind set. Castro's plans, therefore, should be given serious consideration.

Contrary to what common logic may indicate, an attack on the United States by Castro's forces, would not necessarily be a suicidal one. Castro has shown, over and over, that the element of surprise is ever present in his plans. Florida is teeming with Castro's intelligence officers operating under cover, a fifth column who will create, in coordination with a military attack, chaos and panic, disrupting communications and taking control of vital centers in Florida. Also, it is safe to surmise that Castro's plans include his agents recruited among malcontent minorities in Florida, particularly blacks.[60] Liberty City, for example, may become a strong source of military support for Castro. If Castro is not stupid, and he has proved that he is not, a military attack by Cuban forces on Florida will be coordinated with riots and uprisings in many American cities where there is a strong anti-American sentiment among minorities. Most likely places for this to happen are Washington, D.C., New York, Chicago, Oakland and Los Angeles.

As crazy as it may sound, for many years Castro has dreamed about carrying out a fascist-like putsch to overthrow the President of the United States and becoming the head of the American government. Teresa Casuso, one of Castro's close associates until she defected in the early sixties, said that Castro believed at heart that his long speech at the U.N. denouncing American imperialism would galvanize Americans into action, provoking a Bogotazo-like spontaneous uprising, propelling him to the White House. Rufo López Fresquet, for a short time Castro's Minister of the Treasury, shared Casuso's opinion. According to López Fresquet, Fidel "is a megalomaniac" who told a group of friends after the Bay of Pigs invasion "that he will one day be sitting in the White House in Washington."[61]

As I will show in detail in Chapter 6 of this book, contrary to common belief, Fidel Castro is actually a closet Gringophile. He not only loves baseball and basketball, but American films—particularly cowboy films, in which the tall, lonely (sometimes bearded) hero defies superior forces, and wins, against all odds, in a last gunfight. It seems that, in true Hollywood fashion, Castro is preparing himself for a High Noon at the OK Corral. Like many Americans, Castro believes that there is nothing you cannot solve with a good shoot out. As Larry Rohter put it in an article for the *New York Times*, what Castro still needs is a good fight.[62]

In a speech delivered in October 1996 at the United Nations, Castro made a remark that perhaps passed unnoticed by many of the delegates. In an obvious reference to the U.S. embargo on Cuba, he said: "We lay claim to a world without ruthless blockades that cause the death of men, women, and children, youth and elders, *like noiseless atom bombs.*"[63]

During a visit he paid later to Harlem, he delivered a very similar message, using almost the same words: "As we were saying today at the United Nations, it's [the U.S. embargo] *like a noiseless atom bomb.*" The inference is very clear. If the U.S. has used atom bombs (the embargo) against Cuba, then Castro believes he has the right to defend himself in kind, using atom bombs against the United States.

After his visit to New York in 1996, Castro seemed to be in great spirits. But not for long. At the same time that some people in the American government were looking for ways to normalize the relations between the two countries, Castro ordered two small American civilian planes flying outside Cuba's territorial waters to be shot-down, just because he "felt humiliated."

Castro's behavior, though shocking, came as no surprise for people who really know him. In his book *The Fourth Floor*, Earl E. T. Smith, former U.S. ambassador to Cuba from 1957 until Castro took power in 1959, tells how he conducted intensive research into Castro's background and spent days talking to people who had known him closely from childhood. "It was the unanimous opinion of these people," writes Smith, "that Fidel was an unstable terrorist."[64]

Since he was very young Castro has been desperately craving for America's love and respect. A letter Fidel wrote when he was twelve years old to President Roosevelt is strong proof of it. (See Appendix 2) But, save for a short honeymoon in early 1959, the United States has given him neither love nor respect, which explains why he has been acting all these years like a scorned lover.

Over the years Castro has seen, time and again, how some Americans only respect force, particularly pulverizing force. As a matter of fact, the architects of American foreign policy match Castro on many counts—the United States was the first and only nation to use the atom bomb to pulverize human beings.[65] It makes sense, then, that Castro, a copycat of American foreign policy who desperately craves for American love and respect, wants to become a pulverizer himself. And, if his pulverizing plans become reality some day, I am convinced that many people in the U.S. are going to show a lot more respect for him.

Political scientists have discussed about what they call "crazy states."[66] Though several definitions have been given, the most accurate is that crazy states are the ones under the absolute control of crazy leaders. It is a big mistake, however, to think that just because the person controlling a state is a lunatic, he must be clumsy, erratic, or incompetent in carrying out his irrational goals. As Hitler's early history has proved, it is a big mistake to underestimate the power of leaders who profess the craziest of ends. A crazy leader can be both wise and cunning. Moreover, unbound by traditional moral or ethical restraint, he has a distinct advantage over his rational counterparts when he decides to choose his means.

As a crazy leader himself, Fidel Castro has always had an advantage. He is so utterly convinced of the righteousness of his ends that he lacks ordinary inhibiting scruples in choosing his means. He has never had any moral or ethical conflicts when matching means and ends. He has always considered the instrumental value of his means, not their moral value.

If Castro is not yet the greatest pulverizer—the honor still belongs to the United States, the country that pulverized Hiroshima, Nagasaki, and Tokyo—[67] it has not been for his lack of trying. Neither Hitler nor Stalin ever came as close as Castro to setting off a worldwide nuclear holocaust that would have made the horrors of WWII look pale in comparison. Contrary to the image most of the American media loves to portray, Fidel has never been an innocent bystander in the pulverizing business. Castro is old and sick, but he is not finished yet, and it is too early to tell his whole story. In 1961 Herbert Matthews called him "a prophet of doom."[68] He was right. As long as Castro is alive and in power in Cuba he will persist in his nuclear Armageddon dreams. Seemingly his grandiose plan is to go to the trash can of history with a big bang.

Like an ancient hero, Castro wants to go to his grave with human sacrifices. One of Castro's biographers, Georgie Anne Geyer, says that she has always believed that, "given his absolutist and apocalyptic personality, if he felt he was cornered or doomed, he would go down in an Armageddon end like Hitler in the bunker. It now looks as though that stage has begun."[69] Castro's own sister, Juana, said a long time ago that her brother's plans for Cuba are as sinister as Nero's for Rome.[70] Testifying before the House Committee on Un-American Activities, Juana Castro affirmed that "Fidel's feeling of hatred for this country cannot even be imagined by Americans. His intention, his obsession to destroy the U.S. is one of his main interests and objectives."[71]

Cuban writer Carlos Alberto Montaner provided one of the best characterizations of Fidel Castro. To Castro, says Montaner, "the world is like a gigantic video game, and his role is to destroy the nasty aliens to the last one."[72] His biographer Carlos Franqui sees Castro's revolution as an instrument of revenge against his enemies. But the revolution as revenge, says Franqui, destroys not only the enemy, but the country, its natural resources and its freedom.[73]

In October, 1992, it was unexpectedly announced that Castro's son had been fired from his post as Executive Secretary of the Cuban Atomic Energy Commission and as Director of the Cuban atomic energy program. The concise note, appeared in *Granma*, gave no reason for the demotion. Some have speculated that it had to do with the problems plaguing the construction of the Juraguá nuclear plant, but others believe that Castro fired his son because of his failure to produce the promised nuclear bomb.[74] Perhaps the rumors about the real reason for the firing of Fidelito Castro Díaz-Balart were true, because lately Fidel's plans for the final solution to his American problem seem to have taken a different course.

If Not With a Bang, Perhaps With a Whiff

Since the early 1980's Fidel Castro has been actively involved in the research and development of bacteriological warfare agents.[75] To reach his goal he has created several centers that do research and development in the areas of biotechnology, biomedicine, and related subjects. Within these centers, according to some engineers who have defected, there are special groups working on projects to develop CBW (Chemical, Biological, and Bacteriological Warfare) agents.

Some of the centers involved in this activity are: the Biotechnology Center, the Immunology Center, the Genetic Engineering Center, the Tropical Medicine Institute, the Finlay Institute, the Biocen, the Academy of Sciences, the Oceanographic Institute, the Biological Preparations Center, the Center for the Breeding of Laboratory Animals, the National Center for Animal and Plant Health, the Neuroscience Center, and *"La Fabriquita."*

Many Cuban engineers and scientists have been trained in former East Germany, Russia, North Korea, Iraq, Iran, Vietnam, and China. Since 1991, Castro has spent over $1.5 billion in instruments, equipment, and materials, apparently with very little commercial application because only a few vaccines against hepatitis and meningitis have been produced in these centers.

Under the cover of legitimate scientific work, the research groups work by sections and departments, with little connection among themselves. They have developed, among others, a paralyzing toxin which is now ready to be used. In 1992, the Institute of Oceanographic studies conducted an experiment with the Academy of Sciences to find which places in the Cuban coast were the best to let bottles and containers with cards inside reach the United States coast line fastest and most effectively. The cards said they were part of a scientific study of marine currents and asked finders to write down the exact time and location of the finding and send them to a government agency in Cuba. Their true goal, however, was to find where in Cuba it was best to throw containers with bacteriological material to reach the United States. Some of the bottles discovered in American waters have been found by or given to the U.S. Coast Guard.

Cuban scientists also have carried out studies on the propagation of microorganisms by means of fumigation with aircraft or microjets. They have tested the use of microjets on land and in the air. This same system could become the basis for the application of bacteriological weapons.

A few years ago the Castro government bought three expensive 10,000 RPM, high capacity centrifuges shielded against lethal agents, an important tool for the development of bacteriological agents.

These machines were installed, and are now in operation, at a facility located in East Havana, which Cuban General of the Army Raúl Castro with macabre humor affectionately calls *La Fabriquita* (the Little Factory). Though Raúl Castro calls the plant the Little Factory, the plant is huge, reportedly covering an area larger than two football fields.

There are strong suspicions that *La Fabriquita* could be engaged in producing an anthrax toxin like the one reportedly being developed by the Russians, according to the defense publication *Jane's*. Russia's new variant of the anthrax toxin is totally resistant to antibiotics and could cause a catastrophe.

Official government information claims that the little factory is devoted only to the production of livestock feed. However, according to information provided by a Cuban defector, the production of livestock feed is actually a cover the Cubans are using, because the plant's equipment is of little use to livestock.[76]

It is well known that Iraq's Saddam Hussein has a stock of anthrax, botulin, and other agents of germ warfare. Saddam and Fidel Castro are friendly allies, with Castro sending medical teams to Iraq ostensibly to show his friendship. Some experts speculate that the "medical teams" actually belong to Castro's CBW military units.

Anthrax, usually seen in livestock, can cause festering boils, with its victims dying in agony unless treated quickly—if an effective treatment can be found. This "if" raises the question as to whether the controversial anthrax vaccinations used by the U.S. Department of Defense for U.S. service people will immunize against the new strains of anthrax.

On 4 May 1997, *El Nuevo Herald* added to suspicions about Castro's experiments with bacteriological warfare, by reporting that Guillermo Cueto, identified as a former official of the U.S. Central Intelligence Agency, told reporters that various investigative centers linked to the medical branch of the Cuban Academy of Sciences have experimented with various types of marine toxins, ostensibly to obtain antidotes for diseases, but that they also could be early steps of programs for development of bacteriological weapons. "If Cuba," said Cueto, "is working on the extraction of microtoxins from the ocean or from terrestrial areas, one can guess that this concentration and specialization can be applied to bacteriological warfare."

Confidential sources in Cuba have reported that in July, 1999, some military units in Camagüey province received several containers of bacteriological weapons. The operation, conducted under extreme secrecy, was named "Palma Quemada" (burned palm tree) and directed by Lt. Colonel Desiderio Meléndez, of the Eastern Army headquarters, with the participation of Major Enrique de la Torre, Chief of Counterintelligence for the Camagüey province. The containers were moved to the La Soledad farm, in the San Martín hills near the town of Cascorro, where they were brought to their definitive destination, an underground storage in the farm.

Castro's Biological Weapons

Ken Alibek (the name adopted by Soviet Colonel Kanatjian Alibekov after he defected to the U.S.), a gifted doctor and a talented scientist, was first deputy director of the Soviet Union's main bioweapons directorate before defecting in 1992. Until his defection, Alibek was the head of Biopreparat, the largest biological warfare production complex in the world, at Stepnagorsk in what is now the Central Asian independent Republic of Kazakhstan, for many years one of the most closely guarded secrets in the Soviet Union's arsenal.

In an interview published a few weeks after the publication of his book *Biohazard*,[77] Alibek said he believes that Castro's bacteriological warfare program is at the same technological level of any European country, or even the United States. Alibek, who has lived in America for several years, is widely respected in the U.S. biological warfare community. Though he has no firsthand knowledge of Castro's programs, he heard some details about them from his boss, Maj. Gen. Yuri Kalinin.

Alibek mentioned that in 1990 Kalinin, deputy minister of the Soviet medical and microbiological industry, visited Cuba as a member of an official mission. Because of his job, he got in contact with the Cubans engaged in biotechnology. According to Alibek, Kalinin came back to Moscow convinced that the Cubans were actively engaged in a bacteriological warfare program.[78]

One of the things that caught Alibek's attention was that the Cubans were using the same cover stories the Soviet intelligence had developed for their own use, claiming their factories were producing single-cell bacteria for animal feed. "Maybe we were over-suspicious," said Alibek, "but we did not believe their stories. You have to understand that bio-weapons is one of the most sensitive topics in the world. No one shares this type of information, even with best friends. But in my personal opinion, I have no question Cuba is involved"[79]

Other sources seem to confirm Alibek's suspicions. Ex-Cuban intelligence Major Florentino Azpillaga, now living in exile after he defected in 1987 while visiting Prague, is probably the Cuban intelligence defector with the highest rank and credibility. Azpillaga, still under the protection of the U.S. government, told a reporter how in 1985 he delivered a parcel, sent by a Cuban intelligence officer in Japan, to a physician working at a secret biological weapons lab in a mansion at the Cubanacán section of Havana, the so-called *Polo Científico del Oeste* (West Scientific Pole).[80]

Azpillaga says that, on another occasion, he heard a secret recording of a speech by Fidel Castro, delivered to high-ranking intelligence officers, saying that, if Cuba was attacked or threatened by the U.S., he would use bacteriological warfare against the United States. According to Azpillaga, Castro's words were precise and concrete, leaving no doubts as to what his intentions and capabilities were. The recording was made around 1979-1981, and was so secret that even senior intelligence officers had to sign a document declaring that what they were going to hear was a state secret. Since that day, says Azpillaga, he and the rest of the senior Cuban intelligence officers, were convinced that Castro was working on a program of bacteriological warfare.[81]

Early in 1999, William Morrow published *Smokescreen*, a novel by Vincent Patrick, an engineer turned writer. The plot shows Fidel Castro threatening the American president by using biological weapons against the U.S. In the novel, Castro is willing to launch a bacteriological attack on the United States and kill 40 percent of its population.

After studying information about Castro's bacteriological developments for some time, Patrick reached the conclusion that such a plot would be very realistic. "As Ché was willing to die in Bolivia," says Patrick, "Fidel may well be willing to make a last raving attempt to save his revolution or destroy his enemy." Patrick is convinced both that Castro has bacteriological weapons and that he falls into the psychological profile of a person who would use these weapons.[82] After reading the information I have provided in this chapter and I will provide in the rest of this book, I think that most readers would agree with Patrick.

As soon as Castro began losing the military support of the Soviet Union and the Russians could no longer resupply him with conventional armaments, he began preparing for his coming war with the U.S. by focusing on the development of biological weapons—the poor man's nuclear weapons—which might be effective even without using his army.[83] Several observers believe Castro was sending a clear signal to the United States when in January 28, 1998, his speech carried the threat, "This lamb cannot ever be devoured, neither with airplanes, nor with smart bombs, because this lamb has more intelligence than you and in its blood there is and always will be poison for you!"

For many years Castro has been accusing the United States of spreading deadly diseases in Cuba. Knowing Castro's mind-set, and his penchant for projecting the blame on others as a self-justificatory mechanism, one may think that his accusations are just a product of his paranoid mind. But there is compelling evidence that, at least on one occasion in 1971, the CIA used biological warfare against Cuba in an effort to destabilize the Castro regime. In 1977 an unnamed intelligence source said he was given a sealed, unmarked container at Fort Gulich, containing African swine fever, a debilitating disease, for spreading in Cuba. Also, in 1981 Castro made the claim that an outbreak of hemorrhagic dengue fever in Cuba was the result of U.S. bacteriological warfare.[84] If, as it seems, his accusations are true, Castro has the perfect justification for using bacteriological warfare against the United States.[85] As the saying goes, even paranoids have enemies.

Is the U.S. government concerned about Castro's possible use of chemical or bacteriological weapons against the American people?[86] Apparently not. In mid 1997 the U.S. Senate ratified the Chemical Weapons Convention (CWC) treaty. Part of the treaty calls for the sharing of "defensive" chemical weapons manufacturing technology, including equipment, with other parties to the CWC. Castro's Cuba is among the countries which signed the CWC treaty and, consequently, will benefit from the sharing of know-how and manufacturing technology.

Fidel Castro is fully convinced that Americans are an infectious plague that must be eradicated in order to save planet earth. Contrary to his claims, Castro not only hates the U.S. government, but the American people as well, including (or perhaps particularly) the Americans who love and support him. His efforts to incite Khrushchev into firing nuclear missiles against the United States in 1962 is proof of this visceral hatred. Therefore, it makes sense that, as he tried to do during the Cuban missile crisis, he is willing to sacrifice the existence of the Cuban nation itself to reach his ultimate goal of purification of the world by the destruction of the American people.[87]

Castro's calls for nuclear disarmament are but the unconscious self-justifications of his twisted mind for his eventual use of nuclear or other weapons of mass destruction. Fortunately for Castro, he has found the ideal enemy in the United States, a country that has duly provided him with all the justifications he needs. Though very interested in disarming potential opponents through treaties against nuclear proliferation, the U.S. has never favored nuclear disarmament, nor has renounced to the first use of nuclear weapons. Moreover, it seems that some U.S. leaders are toying with the idea of developing small yield nuclear devices which will turn any military campaign into a nuclear war.[88] Moreover, Fidel Castro has repeatedly refused to renounce the use of land mines, the main cause of maiming and death of non-combatants, particularly children.[89]

Chapter 3

Castro's Manifest Destiny

> *"When this war is over, a much wider and bigger war will begin for me, the war I am going to wage against them. I realize that that is going to be my true destiny."*
>
> — Fidel Castro

In 1957 Herbert Matthews, a *New York Times* senior journalist and Latin American "expert," traveled to the Sierra Maestra mountains in Cuba's Oriente province to interview Fidel Castro. One of Matthews' questions during the interview dealt with the strong anti-imperialist tone of Castro's group. Castro answered: "You can be sure that we (Castro customarily uses the royal "we" instead of "I") have no animosity toward the United States and the American people."

But in January 27, 1959, less than a month after Batista left the country allowing for Castro's easy takeover of Cuba, Ché Guevara, in a talk he gave at the Nuestro Tiempo association in Havana, raised the specter of an American-backed attack on the revolution. "If we are attacked," he said, "the attack will be supported by a power that takes up almost an entire continent."[1] Then he suggested the necessity of creating a militia army to defend Cuba from the aggressors.

In September 1960, Castro openly voiced his anti-American feelings in a five-hour speech before the U.N. General Assembly in which he accused the United States of every conceivable evil. Just a few days before, Castro had staged the first part of his performance when he moved from his hotel in mid-town Manhattan to Harlem's

Theresa hotel, after a staged incident he used as a pretext to substantiate his false claims that the other hotel had discriminated against him.

By November 1960, less than two years after Castro took power, the relations between the two countries had turned sour. It was then that Ernesto "Ché" Guevara, once more acting as Castro's mouthpiece, formalized in a few words in an interview he gave to *Look* magazine the myth that became the guiding light for American liberals in the analysis of the causes of the Castro-U.S. problem:

> What lies ahead depends greatly on the United States. With the exception of our Agrarian Reform, which the people of Cuba desired and initiated themselves, all of our radical measures have been a direct response to direct aggressions by powerful monopolists, of which your country is a chief exponent. U.S. pressures on Cuba have made necessary the "radicalization" of the Revolution. To know how much further Cuba will go, it will be easier to ask the U.S. Government how far it plans to go.[2]

Since "Ché" Guevara enunciated the myth of the reactive revolution, it was immediately adopted and repeated over and over by Castro's supporters, among them Jean-Paul Sartre, Herbert Matthews, and C. Wright Mills. Castro's revolutionary measures, they claimed, including his embrace of "socialism," have always been reactive, as a response to American actions, but never proactive.[3] And even today, notwithstanding overwhelming evidence indicating that Castro actively chose his destiny as an enemy of the United States, there are still many people in the United States who seem to believe Guevara's myth of reactive anti-Americanism.

Moreover, apparently Guevara's myth was so powerful that he managed to convince not only the traditional Castro admirers, but also a few of his critics as well. Some of them, who claim that Castro betrayed his own revolution and sold it to Soviet Russia and communism, are convinced that he did so just because the United States forced him to do it.

Even John F. Kennedy at some time voiced the old fashioned argument that the Cuban tyrant was reluctantly pushed into his anti-American role by the failure of the U.S. Government to give Castro the economic aid he badly needed. According to Kennedy, Castro's behavior was justified because "We refused to help Cuba meet its desperate need for economic progress," and "We used the influence of our government to advance the interests and increase the profits of the private American companies which dominate the island's economy."[4]

In speech after speech, Castro himself has cleverly helped to perpetuate his image as an innocent victim of American imperialist perfidy. What Castro says, however, is invariably in strong contradiction with what he actually does. There is evidence that he chose his role as an enemy of the United States as a result of a pre-conceived idea—some have speculated it was the result of an early childhood psychic trauma—not as a reaction to American actions. The available record proves beyond any reasonable doubt that Castro's anti-American actions have always been pro-active, never reactive.

Granted, many world leaders viscerally hate the United States, and some of them have strong reasons for their feelings. What makes Fidel Castro unique, however, is that, among so many anti-American leaders, he was the only one who decided to risk the price of destroying the welfare of his country, and perhaps his own welfare, to settle his personal scores with the United States.[5] However, though he has not yet been successful in reaching his ultimate goal of destroying the United States, he has been totally successful in destroying his own country in the process.

Without exculpating the United States of the blame for some of the calamities of recent Cuban history, from the mysterious explosion of the U.S.S. *Maine* battleship in Havana's harbor in 1898, which was used as a pretext to steal the victory of the Cuban patriots over Spain, to the fall of Batista in 1958 after the U.S. retired its support to his government, the evidence shows that Fidel Castro has never been an innocent bystander, but the main actor creating one pretext after another to follow the course he had traced *a priori* for himself and his revolution. Furthermore, believing that his actions have always been unpremeditated responses to American acts does not take into consideration Castro's political Machiavellism. As Theodore Draper pointed out a long time ago, a revolutionary leader does not betray the fundamental character of his revolution just because some American oil companies refuse to refine Soviet oil or because the United States suspends a sugar quota he himself had called a "symbol of colonialism."[6] Probably the only thing French philosopher Jean-Paul Sartre was right about Castro was what he wrote in *France Soir*. "If the United States did not exist, Castro most probably would have to invent it."[7]

Setting the Record Straight

On January 5, 1959, still in Santiago de Cuba, Castro made one of his first speeches after Batista's departure. It contained a significant statement:

> This time it is Cuba's good fortune that the revolution will really take power. It will not be as in '98 [1898] when the

Americans arrived, took control of the situation, intervened at the last moment, and then would not even permit Calixto García, who had been fighting for thirty years, to enter Santiago.[8]

A few days later, on January 20, 1959, less than three weeks after Castro and his men arrived in Havana, *Revolución*, published an interview with Ernesto "Ché" Guevara. In his first-page interview, Guevara spoke bluntly about danger coming from the North. "Wall street," he said, "is dedicated to combat those people who are fighting for their liberty, and as with the case of the people of Guatemala, that same aggression is being planned against the people of Cuba." The analogy, however, was fallacious. The truth is that at that precise moment, "Wall Street" was literally besieging the Cuban Presidential Palace, almost begging for the opportunity to invest in a country that, mainly thanks to U.S. efforts, had just come under the control of Fidel Castro.

From the very beginning, the behavior of the United States Government *vis-à-vis* Castro's obvious anti-American feelings and actions was one of astonishment and confusion. The American Embassy in Havana was bending over backwards trying to ignore the insults and overlook the lies and deceit which were pouring forth every single day from Castro and his closest associates. Even more, Castro's baffling pronouncements regarding the future of the revolution created in Washington the idea that he was trying to reach a definite course under pressure from both left and right. But, if Fidel was not trying to confuse the Americans, he was very successful in doing so. He gave orders to take over the American owned Cuban Telephone Company in March, 1959, but when he visited the United States a month later he assured the members of the American Society of Newspaper Editors that he would welcome foreign investments in Cuba. He professed allegiance to democracy and a free press, but, less than a year after his promise, both were almost nonexistent in Cuba. Of course, at the time most people ignored the fact that Castro is an expert in saying one thing while doing exactly the opposite.

The available record shows that the United States had greeted the Cuban Revolution with caution but also with hope. In early 1958 the American Government stopped selling arms to Batista and throughout the rest of that year had moved gradually toward Castro's side. It is evident the Americans wanted Castro to win. One of the main indicators of the American Government's support for Castro was the fact that, breaking with all established diplomatic practices, it rushed to recognize the new revolutionary government in record-breaking time: provisional President Manuel Urrutia arrived in Havana on January 5th and his government was recognized by the United States on January 7th. The United States went even further: it was ready to give the Cuban government all the economic and financial aid it badly needed. But Castro ignored the American extended hand and secretly began seeking help from Moscow.

It is true that, since the very beginning, some Americans had reservations about Castro and the course of the Cuban revolution, but it is no less true that they were ready to support it. Granted, the American people, as well as the government in Washington, were revolted by the kangaroo courts and mass executions of Batista's men which began in mid-January, 1959, and continued all through March, reaching a total of about 400. Another source of irritation was the increasing attacks Castro himself was making against American companies and the U.S. government. Some voices in the States and in Cuba began raising the specter of communism. But, at least as far as late March, 1959, most of the American people and government were backing the Cuban Revolution and did not believe it was communist or controlled by the Cuban communists. It was then when the American Society of Newspaper Editors invited Castro to come to the U.S. to speak to its members and clarify his political position. Castro accepted the invitation.

Though the ostensible purpose of the trip was to speak before the ASNE, most people in Cuba and the United States, including close Castro advisors, believed that its real purpose was to offer Castro the opportunity for asking the American government for economic aid. As a matter of fact, during a televised interview on April 2, 1959, Castro told his Cuban audience that he was going to the United States, among other things, to obtain credits "that will defend Cuba and the Revolution."[9]

Upon Castro's arrival in the U.S., some reporters asked him if he was going to seek American aid. His surprising answer was a categoric no. Witnesses to the event, and shocked by Castro's answer, were some of the people in his own entourage, among them Felipe Pazos, President of the Cuban National Bank, and Finance Minister Rufo López Fresquet.[10]

López Fresquet, later told in detail about his startling experience:

> In respect to the visit of Castro and myself to the United States, I came with the idea of initiating negotiations for a loan and Dr. Castro expressly prohibited me from speaking about requesting loans. He was concerned about that when I had an appointment with Secretary Anderson the [United States] Secretary of the Treasury. Fidel at that moment was at a banquet and was speaking, and as I rose—he knew I was going to the appointment with Secretary Anderson—he stopped his speech and told me, 'Remember Rufo, I don't want you to discuss money.'[11]

In the conduct of U.S. diplomacy throughout the transformation of the Cuban revolution into Castro's own revolution one can feel a sort of bewilderment among the American diplomatic officers, with Nixon as one of the few exceptions. The State Department always acted as if it was at a loss to know how to deal with Fidel's unorthodox diplomatic behavior. His relentless hostility, his repeated charges of "imperialism" and "economic aggression" and his distortion of events in such a way as to accuse a country which had always been considered friendly was contrary to the accepted rules of diplomacy. This situation was completely new for Americans and apparently it took them by surprise.[12] One may guess that the American's surprise was in part because Fidel Castro was treating them exactly the same way some of them usually treat the rest of the world: with total contempt—something most Americans apparently believe is their exclusive privilege and would never expect from other people.

In order to put the blame of Castro's behavior on the errors of American diplomacy, some American liberals and pro-Castro apologists gave early support to "Ché" Guevara's myth that Washington's actions (or lack of them) forced Fidel Castro into Moscow's arms. Yet knowledgeable scholars of the Cuban revolution no longer take that theory seriously because there is no evidence to substantiate it. Even Herbert Matthews, by no means an anti-Castroist, observed that Fidel's, "basic, unending antagonism toward the 'Yankees' was always there."

Author Lionel Martin, an American journalist sympathetic to Fidel, was the first to expose to the American public the facsimile of a short letter Castro sent in June, 1958 (that is, six months before the triumph of the revolution) to Celia Sánchez, his secretary in the Sierra Maestra mountains.[13] The letter was prompted by a rocket attack by American-built jet fighters of Batista's air force on the house of Mario Sariol, a mountain villager who had collaborated with Castro's Rebel Army.

Fidel wrote:

Sierra Maestra
June 5 - 58

Celia: After seeing the rockets they shot at Mario's house, I've sworn that the Americans are going to pay dearly for what they are doing. When this war is over, a much wider and bigger war will begin for me, the war I am going to wage against them. I realize that that is going to be my true destiny.

Fidel

(See Appendix 1 for a facsimile of the letter.)

But Castro's note to Celia is not the earliest manifestation of his deep anti-American feelings. As early as 1956, when he was in Mexico preparing the Cuban invasion, Castro used to indoctrinate his men with anti-American ideas, a fact known to the Mexican secret police. Also, nearly all of his associations in Mexico were with persons or groups known for their strong anti-American views, like the Mexican communists, the Spanish Republican exiles (both communists and non-communists), the just defeated members of the Arbenz's Guatemalan government, and assorted Latin American Yankee-haters and red-lovers.[14]

Similarly, when Castro was in route to Havana for his triumphal entry into the capital, he warned the United States not to interfere in Cuba as it did in Guatemala five years before. "If you send the Marines," Fidel warned, "thousands of them will die on the beaches."[15]

I'll Kill 200,000 Gringos

Just seven days after he had arrived in Havana, on January 15, 1959, a strange incident took place which may show a glimpse of Castro's deep, hidden anti-American feelings. As he was emerging from an elevator into the lobby of the Havana Hilton Hotel somebody asked him about the criticism that the ongoing executions of Batista's Army officers had raised in the United States. Bob Pérez, a reporter from the Havana Post who was among the group says that the question blew Fidel's top. "If the Americans don't like what is happening in Cuba," said Fidel, "they can land the Marines and then there will be 200,000 gringos dead." Bob Pérez overheard Castro's angry remark and repeated it to some of his American colleagues. Bob's Spanish was perfect, so there is no doubt about what Fidel said. A journalist who listened to Pérez's story later commented that she was not totally surprised by Castro's statement, but by his use of the term *"gringo,"* a derogatory term used almost exclusively by Mexicans.[16]

But the above anecdote is not the only indication that Castro had his own secret agenda to deal with the Americans. Since January, 1959, a carefully prepared indoctrination campaign began in Oriente province to foment anti-Americanism. Mimeographed publications were issued in which a distorted, one-sided vision of Cuban-American relations was presented as true Cuban history.[17]

On January 23, 1959, Fidel visited Venezuela. Once there, he not only attacked the United States and proposed to "liberate" Puerto Rico, but he also had a bizarre conversation with President-elect Rómulo Betancourt. During it, he bluntly told the President that he was thinking of having a confrontation with the *"gringos."* He then asked Betancourt for a $300-million loan from Venezuela and support for his "master play against the *gringos*."[18]

One must keep in mind that this meeting with Betancourt took place within two weeks of Fidel arriving in Havana, and way before any direct confrontation with the United States had occurred. The use of the word *"gringo"* in both occasions is most significant, as Ms. R. Hart Phillips noticed. This derogatory term is an odd usage by Cubans, who normally call Americans *"americanos."* Hugh Thomas points out that the use of the term by Castro in these two particular occasions may presumably have been a calculated attempt to talk in the language of South Americans or Mexicans, perhaps trying to strike a sympathetic chord among them. Keeping in mind that, as his Jesuit teachers once noticed, Fidel Castro is a very good actor, Thomas' reasoning makes much sense.

Herbert Matthews mentions that Raúl Castro told him in 1967 that on January 8, 1959, the very day Castro's Rebel Army entered Havana, Fidel already had plans to buy 50,000 assault rifles and machine guns abroad.[19] Raúl's indiscretion proved to be true.

As early as February, 1959, long before any frictions between Castro and the United States appeared, Fidel Castro personally ordered Major Ricardo Lorié to travel to Belgium where he purchased $9 million in weapons. The purchase, made from the Belgian National Arms Factory, included 22,500 FN/FAL automatic rifles, 50 million rounds of ammunition, 70,000 anti-personal shells, anti-tank rifle grenades and 30,000 anti-tank grenades. It is evident that Castro was preparing himself for a long war, because he also had been trying to buy a whole arms factory from the Belgians.

According to Lorié, the rifles were issued serial numbers from 1 to 22,500. They also had the Cuban coat of arms engraved on them, probably made with the same dies used when Batista bought some FN/FAL rifles a few years earlier. Lorié reports that when Fidel learned of the engravings he got furious.

The fact is significant because on November 3, 1963, the Venezuelan Government discovered a three-ton arms-cache ready to be used by Castro-supported guerrilla units previously trained in Cuba. The Cuban coat of arms and the serial numbers of those arms show that they were part of the shipment bought by Lorié in Belgium in February 1959 following Castro's direct orders less than two months after he came to power in Cuba.[20]

On March 22, 1959, ex-president José Figueres of Costa Rica, who had been a friend and supporter of Castro, visited Cuba following an invitation of the Castro government. During his visit, Figueres was invited to speak at a mass meeting. During the meeting Castro and his men violently inveighed against the United States. Figueres made the mistake of defending the United States, while trying to lecture Castro on democracy. One of Castro's associates violently took the microphone from Figueres' hands, and replied attacking Figueres personally. Soon after, Castro joined in the attack, including in it President Betancourt of Venezuela. Next day, Figueres left Cuba in a hurry.[21]

Analyzing the behavior of the Cuban leaders during the first months of the revolution, author Adolf A. Berle, Jr., accurately observed that they "seemed as much interested in picking a quarrel with the United States as in effecting their social revolution." And he added, "Cuban politicians increasingly conceived themselves as divinely appointed leaders to carry on anti-United States activities throughout the entire hemisphere."[22]

In June, 1959, still long before any American action against his government had materialized, Castro sent to Mexico Maj. Ramiro Valdés, a senior officer in the Rebel Army and a man in whom he had total confidence, on a secret mission. Valdés' mission was to approach the Soviet ambassador in Mexico to explore the possibility of closer relations between Cuba and the Soviet Union.[23] Apparently Castro's logic for such a step was the old saying, "the enemy of my enemy is my friend," though one should not discount other secret reasons.

On July 26, 1960, Castro gave a speech on the commemoration of the anniversary of the attack on the Moncada garrisons, the first battle of his revolution. In his speech he expressed his commitment to the liberation of all of Latin America. To emphasize his point, he dramatically turned to the Sierra Maestra mountains, where he fought Batista's troops, and declared:

> Here, facing the unconquered mountain range, facing the Sierra Maestra, let us promise one another that we shall continue to make our fatherland an example that will change the Andes mountain range into the Sierra Maestra of all America. [24]

Though not holding the United States blameless with respect to the Castro-American differences, historian Robert F. Smith pointed out that Fidel was,

> ... blindly dedicated to a vision of the new Cuba... a fanatical idealist who never counted the costs of his action. This messianic self-righteousness produced an extremely hostile reaction to any hint of criticism or even neutralism. As a result he had heaped abuse on the United States and on Americans in Cuba which has provided ammunition for those Americans who look with disfavor on revolutions.[25]

Similarly, Lowry Nelson noticed that, in addition to the Cold War atmosphere in which Cuban-American discussions took place, there always was Castro's undeniable attitude of hostility toward the United States. Both factors made rational diplomatic exchanges virtually impossible.[26]

To be sure, Fidel Castro's anti-Americanism was not uncommon among many Cuban nationalist intellectuals and political leaders. Just a brief look at Cuba's history, particularly the Cuban-Spanish-American war (American textbooks call it the Spanish-American war, ignoring the Cuban patriot's 30-years of wars against Spain), shows that Cubans have enough reasons for harboring such feelings. But most Cubans were intelligent enough to distinguish between America and American politicians. A typical example of this attitude is found in the writings of Cuban patriot José Martí, a writer and poet who strongly opposed the nascent American imperialism, but harbored no anti-American feelings. But Fidel Castro's visceral anti-U.S. feelings go far beyond the understandable rational limits of political rivalry to a degree of bitterness which seems to indicate not only political, but very deep psychological roots as well. The fact that Fidel Castro is an appropriate patient for the psychiatrist's couch, as evidenced in most of his biographies, even the friendly ones, is perhaps sufficient reason for his hatred. A close reading of Castro's long interview with Frei Betto is enough to convince even the more skeptic that we are dealing with a very weird personality, to say the least.[27]

Castro Follows his Course

Describing his own conduct at the time of the German reoccupation of the Rhineland in 1936, Hitler used an extraordinary figure of speech: "I follow my course with the precision and security of a sleepwalker." Nothing as accurate to describe the behavior of Fidel Castro in his relations with the United States. With the precision and security of a sleepwalker he has followed the anti-American course he traced himself *a priori*. When the Americans did not provide him with incidents to justify his behavior, he has applied all his creative abilities to create the incidents himself.

One must bear in mind, however, that Castro has a very peculiar mind-set. It would be simplistic to think that his behavior is the product of a calculated effort to deceive others. It may actually be that the one he is actually deceiving is none other than himself.

A pathological mechanism which threatens all realistic and effective thinking is that of *projection*. The projection mechanism is best evidenced in the hostile and destructive person who accuses everybody else of being hostile and pictures himself as being innocent and victimized.[28] Yet, what is easily detected in individual cases is generally not seen when the same projection mechanism is shown by a nation's leader and supported by millions of his followers.

In the case of Fidel Castro, the result of this type of behavior manifests itself in the fact that, to him, the United States appears as the embodiment of all evil. He is not aware, however, that this is true to some extent because he has projected all the evil in himself onto the United States. Consequently, Castro considers himself as the embodiment of all good since the evil has been projected and transferred to his enemy. The result has been irrational indignation and hatred against the United States and the uncritical, narcissistic self-glorification of himself. This has created in Cuba a mood of common mania and shared passion of hate. But psychologists have found that love and hate are very closely related feelings.

This brings us to a hypothesis I developed some time ago. Perhaps the main reason why Fidel Castro has become an American nemesis is because at the bottom of his heart he is full of both admiration and envy for the Americans—to the point that he has unconsciously become a mirror image of the United States.

The record proves beyond any reasonable doubt that Fidel Castro chose his way as an enemy of the United States as a result of a pre-conceived idea, not as a reaction to American behavior. Some may believe that his anti-American feelings began after seeing Batista's planes attack a farmer's home with rockets made in America. Others may believe that the roots of his anti-American hatred run deep, going as far as his stay in Mexico while preparing himself for the Cuban invasion. Or probably they run even deeper, if we recall his behavior during the Bogotazo riots.

There is the possibility that his deep hatred began as a result of anti-American sentiments planted in his young mind by some Jesuit priests when he was a student at the Colegio de Belén in Havana. Any of these hypotheses may be true, but I believe that the roots of Castro's hatred for the United States come from even deeper regions of his convoluted mind. Perhaps it all began when he was a twelve-year-old student at the Colegio de Dolores in Santiago de Cuba, and he decided to write a letter to President Roosevelt *begging for money*. (For a facsimile of the letter see Appendix 2.) Unfortunately President Roosevelt didn't send him the "ten-dollar bill green American" he was asking for, and Fidel felt deeply humiliated.

There are many theories, none of them fully convincing, explaining the roots of Castro's hatred for Americans. But perhaps there is a clue. Another group of individuals Castro particularly hates is democratically elected presidents. Therefore, this strongly points to the possibility that President Roosevelt's negative response to his letter was the event that triggered Castro's life-long feelings of hatred and resentment against both Americans and democratically elected presidents.

As I mentioned above, in April 1959, just after having won his war against Batista, Castro visited the United States following an invitation by the American Association of Newspaper Editors. During the visit, a reporter asked him if he was going to ask the American government for money to help rebuild the Cuban economy after the war. An angry Castro answered that he was not a beggar. "We didn't come here for money," he said. And added, "Many come here to sell their souls. We want only sympathy and understanding.[29] Previously he had given a very similar answer to Pazos and López Fresquet when they asked him if he was going to ask the U.S. for economic help. Perhaps unwillingly, the reporter and his associates had reminded Castro of the humiliation he felt when, a long time ago, he actually begged for money to an American president who didn't send him the money.

Some authors still wonder about the true reasons of Castro's trip to the U.S. Some American liberals, senator John F. Kennedy among them, believed that, had Castro asked for help during his visit, or had the U.S. offered it, Castro might never have gone over to the Soviets to ask for support. The truth, however, is quite different. It is known that the American government as a whole was sympathetic to Castro and had plans to offer some economic help to the new-born Cuban revolution. But Castro was not interested at all. I have the feeling that the whole charade of his trip to the U.S. was an unconscious mechanism devised by Castro's twisted mind to prove to himself through a feat of convoluted reasoning that, despite the fact that he once begged Americans for money, he actually never begged Americans for money.

Anyway, trying to find the source of Castro's animosity against the United States may prove to be a total waste of time. Looking for rational causes to explain the behavior of such an irrational individual is an exercise in frustration.

During the rest of 1959 Castro seized every opportunity to openly ridicule the United States for everything bad that had happened in Cuba's past, from the American intervention in 1898 to the Mafia's control over Havana's casinos and American support for president Batista. Castro's vituperative attacks on the United States kept growing in frequency and intensity, culminating on November 1959, when he placed the newly created National Militia on full alert, waiting for an impending U.S. invasion that failed to materialize.

Fidel's Thirst for Revenge

During Castro's guerrilla war against Batista, a CIA officer, acting under a journalist's cover, visited the rebel leader at the Sierra Maestra mountains and spent several weeks there. Afterwards, he reported that Castro was an ego-maniac and emotionally unstable.[30] It seems that this early assessment of Castro's personality by the CIA officer was highly accurate. From the time he was a young boy, Castro was an emotionally unstable ego-maniac with a terrorist mind-set. It may well be that, when President Roosevelt refused to give him the money he had asked for, he damaged Castro's oversized ego and Fidel, as a result, became pathologically anti-American. One must bear in mind that Castro never forgets, particularly what he considers a humiliation—the worst offense to him.

One of Castro's main motivations in life is revenge. One of the very first things people discovered in early 1959 was, as Ruby Hart Phillips, the *New York Times* correspondent in Cuba put it, "the ruthlessness and vindictiveness of the new government." She also wrote that "What surprised me most was the vindictiveness of Castro and his fanatical followers. I had never considered this a characteristic of the Cuban people."[31] Ms. Phillips was right. Cubans are not a vindictive people. Proof of this is the generosity of Cubans toward the defeated Spaniards after the war. But Fidel Castro is not a typical Cuban.

Examples of Fidel Castro's vindictiveness abound. When he was at the Belén school, Castro had a heated argument, which ended in a brawl, with a classmate named Ramón Mestre. Some sources claim that the argument was the result of Mestre's desire to see a girl Fidel coveted.[32] Others claim that the fight was over money which Fidel owed Mestre and which Mestre wanted back. Many years later, when Castro took power in Cuba, Mestre was detained and accused of conspiring against the revolution and condemned to twenty years hard labor. The disproportionate harshness of the punishment in relation to the alleged crime made some people think that it was just Fidel's long memory craving for revenge.[33]

Jesús Conte Agüero, a former close friend of Castro says that, while Castro was in the Sierra Maestra mountains, he ordered the execution of a man called Evaristo Venereo on charges of "espionage." Venereo, it was later discovered, had been a lieutenant in the police force at the University of Havana while Fidel was a law student there, and on one occasion had tried to disarm Castro and take away his pistol. But the long memory of Fidel Castro caught up with poor Venereo in the Sierra Maestra and he, like many others, paid with his life for his mistake.[34]

Ruby Hart Phillips tells in detail what happened to Rafael del Pino Siero, an ex-friend of Castro. Del Pino, a naturalized American, was the pilot of a small Cessna plane which attempted to land on the Vía Blanca highway near Guanabo, east of Havana, to pick up two friends and smuggle them out of Cuba. But somebody had tipped the Cuban authorities and when the plane landed at dawn they opened fire and del Pino was captured. In the operation he was struck by several bullets, and was badly burned when the plane caught fire. Although del Pino had not participated actively against Castro, he was sentenced to thirty years in prison. Some relatives of del Pino tried to talk to Castro to let him back to the United States since he was so badly wounded and permanently crippled and was a former close friend of Fidel, but Castro did not want to listen to them.

If the name Rafael del Pino sounds familiar it is because he was the same del Pino who had accompanied Castro to Bogotá during the Bogotazo riots. Later, when he was in Mexico with Castro preparing the Cuban invasion, del Pino was accused of denouncing Castro and his group to the Mexican police. Though he managed to escape, and the accusation was never proved, he was apparently on Castro's black list, and Fidel never forgets.[35]

Self-provocation as a Foreign Policy Tool

During his long political career, Fidel Castro has been very resourceful and successful in provoking his enemies. The technique he uses over and over consists in making a move which provokes a desired hostile reaction, which he then uses to carry out an aggressive policy as if it were a defensive one. Examples of this behavior abound.

On October 21, 1959, Major Pedro Luis Díaz Lanz, former Chief of the Cuban Air Force who a few weeks before had defected to the United States, flew a plane over Havana dropping leaflets calling on Castro to eliminate communism from his government. Some anti-aircraft batteries from across the bay opened fire against the plane, the shrapnel causing injuries among the civilian population. Immediately radio stations began broadcasting that at least two planes had flown over Havana dropping bombs. The final toll was two dead and forty-five wounded.

The following morning *Revolución*, Castro's official newspaper, proclaimed that *two* planes from the United States had bombed the city and machine-gunned people on the streets The next night, October 23, Castro went on tv announcing that the "bombing of Havana" was a "graver incident" than Pearl Harbor or the sinking of the *Maine* battleship in Havana's harbor in 1898. He added that the planes took off from Florida and therefore the United States had either "consented" to the "bombing" or was "completely defenseless" if planes could take off without its knowledge. But, as we will see below, the "bombing" of Havana apparently awakened Castro's creativity.

On January 13, 1960, long before any like incident had occurred, the Castro-controlled Cuban press and Radio already was talking about planes coming from the United States to sabotage Cuban installations and burning canefields. Since the beginning of 1960, hardly a week passed that Castro did not refer to the overflight of small planes "based in Florida," sabotaging Cuban installations and burning canefields. He continually yelled that the United States not only was bombing Cuba, but allowing "counterrevolutionary elements" to fly from Florida and burn canefields with live phosphorus.

As a matter of fact, canefields *were* being burned in Cuba on a large scale. But, as Castro himself knew from his efforts when he was fighting Batista, canefields, particularly at that time of the year, are notoriously difficult to set on fire unless there are literally hundreds of people involved in the effort. Castro, of course, kept holding the United States responsible for the burnings, though of the three confirmed flights by small planes over Cuba, none had even the remotest capacity for burning canefields on the scale claimed by the Cuban government.

Then, in February, 1960, a Piper Comanche mysteriously exploded in mid-air over the España sugar mill in Las Villas province. Two dead Americans were pulled from the wreckage. Castro's newspaper *Revolución* identified the pilot as Robert Ellis Frost, claiming that he was connected with "the Pentagon." Other government newspapers published pictures of the wreckage of the plane, among headlines claiming "Yankee aggression." Castro's militia and Armed Forces were put on extreme alert, reservists were called up, and the eyes of the Cuban people were directed towards the criminal colossus of the North.

Next month, in March, another plane, a Piper Cub, flew over Cuba and was shot down. Immediately, the government radio and press took off on another thunderous propaganda clap. But it stopped as suddenly as it started. In this case the crew of the plane, American citizens Robert Shergalis and Harold Rundquist, escaped and eventually came back to the United States. It was known later that the small plane, damaged by rifle fire, landed on a small country road in Matanzas Province, not far from Havana. Tipped off by a telephone call, American Consul Hugh Kessler drove immediately to the spot, where he heard the whole story from the angry pilot and co-pilot. In a recorded interview made by Kessler, the two men told him that they had flown the plane over Cuba after having been paid to do so by Juan Orta, of the Office of Prime Minister Fidel Castro. Within a few minutes of recording their confessions, the men were whisked away by Castro's forces. As soon as they were brought in Havana, the propaganda clap was called off. The fact strongly indicates that Shergalis and Rundquist, as Robert Ellis Frost and his co-pilot before, were mercenaries who had been paid by Castro to sabotage Cuban canefields as self-provocations. Also, because dead men tell no tales, they were candidates to be murdered in cold blood. Most likely Ellis' plane had been sabotaged to explode in mid-air. Unfortunately for Castro, in the second case his plan failed.[36]

Unwittingly, Castro himself provided more evidence of his secret knowledge of the sabotaged plane. In a speech he delivered a few days later, he brought up the Robert Ellis Frost plane incident. In view of the recent history of aggression from the United States, said Castro, what is strange about dropping a "100-pound bomb" on a sugar mill? But the problem with Castro's allegations is that the bomb that killed Robert Ellis Frost and his co-pilot exploded in mid-air. Where did Castro come by the knowledge that is was actually a "100-pound bomb"? A good guess is that it came from his agents in Florida, the ones who booby-trapped the bomb to explode in the air.[37]

In October, 1960, the American Embassy in Havana sent a note of protest to the Castro government stating that it had received information that four or five American-made planes at the San Antonio de los Baños military airfield were being painted with U.S. military markings, including an American flag, on the fuselage.[38] Though Castro rejected the note in a lengthy and angry speech, in which he referred to the "criminal espionage activities of the United States Embassy," there are reasons to believe that he had been caught in the act while getting ready to stage another self-provocation.[39]

In the afternoon of March 4, 1960, a terrific explosion shook the whole city of Havana. People soon found out that the French freighter *La Coubre* had blown up in Havana harbor, killing 27 workers and injuring more than 300 people. Against all the provision of international requirements the ship had been unloading explosives and munitions within fifty yards of a densely populated area. The Cuban Government decreed a day of national mourning. Next day *Revolución's* headline in big, bold letters displayed a single word: Sabotage! The newspaper's editorial explicitly accused the United States of sabotaging the ship to prevent the Cubans from getting the arms and supplies. Though the editorial was not signed it evidenced the unmistakable soap-box style of Fidel Castro.

The cause of the explosion was never determined. Numerous explanations have been offered—ranging from high water temperature, men smoking while working, inexperience in unloading munitions (opinion supported later by some dock workers), to sabotage. But, as soon as Castro heard about the news of the explosion, he rushed to claim it was sabotage. It was his view that the explosion could not have been accidental—though he never offered evidence to support his charges.

In a speech on March 5, 1960, at a burial ceremony for the victims of the *La Coubre* explosion (later issued in pamphlet form by the Cuban Government under the title: "Sabotage of *La Coubre*") Castro voiced his suspicion. Aware that his Government would not have made a thorough investigation in just one day he was careful not to make direct charges:

> Functionaries of the United States Government have repeatedly tried to prevent our country from obtaining those arms. This is something they will not be able to deny. And this is a fact that demonstrates their interest in preventing us from acquiring these arms.
>
> It is among the interested parties that we must look for the parties responsible for the explosion. We are justified in believing that when, through diplomatic channels, they failed in their efforts to prevent the sale of these supplies, they might have tried other methods to prevent us from receiving them.
>
> We are not declaring that they did so. In order to make that statement, we would need material evidence, which we do not have. If we were in possession of such evidence, we would present it to the people of this country as well as to the whole world.
>
> But I do say that we have the right to think that those who have so far failed to achieve their purpose may well have tried to achieve it by other means. We have a right to think that the author of a crime must be sought among those who have motives. So it is among those with motives that we must look for those who brought about the toll of Cuban lives yesterday afternoon.

What Castro failed to mention in his speech was that, contrary to his claims, most of the cargo had already been unloaded before the ship exploded. The arms had been shipped by the Belgian Fabrique Nationale d'Armes de Guerre, also known as FN. The shipment consisted mainly of infantry rifles, sub-machine guns, and pistols. If you look carefully at photographs taken a year later, during the Bay of Pigs invasion, you will see hundreds of Castro's soldiers carrying FN/FAL and FAP rifles and Belgian-made Browning High Power 9 mm pistols. They were men from the Havana's Police Battalion, fully equipped with these excellent guns brought to the Island in the *La Coubre* shipment.

The guns, and a few Belgian-made UZI 9 mm submachine guns, were eventually issued to some units of Castro's militia. Later, when Russian equipment was fully adopted by the Cuban Army the FN guns were shelved, but some of them were used extensively by Cuban teams infiltrating in insurgency operations in foreign countries, like Venezuela, Nicaragua, Chile, and El Salvador.

In late 1975—fifteen years after the *La Coubre* explosion—thousands of Cuban reservists, this author among them, were trained in the mountains of Pinar del Río before being sent to Angola. The infantry weapons used for their training were the ever-faithful FAL and FAP rifles, still showing the engraving of the Cuban coat of arms. Hundred of thousands of Belgian-made cartridges were fired in those training exercises, and the officers encouraged the troops to shoot as much as possible, in order to get rid of those batches of ammunition that were getting old. The above mentioned evidence points to the fact that, contrary to Castro's claims, most of the *La Coubre* shipment had been unloaded before the ship exploded.

It seems, therefore, that Fidel Castro, a closet American admirer, used the explosion (either the product of an accident, internal sabotage, or of his own design) to create a commemorative American-style incident, such as "Remember the *Maine*," "Remember the *Lusitania*," "Remember Pearl Harbor," etc. His use of the *La Coubre* explosion as a propaganda tool to galvanize the Cuban people against the United States was a carbon copy of the use of the explosion of the *Maine* battleship to galvanize the American people against Spain.

Though since the very beginning the relations between the American government and Castro had been rapidly deteriorating, the final rupture was precipitated by Fidel Castro when in June 1960, he demanded that three American- and British-owned oil refineries in Cuba process Soviet crude oil. The companies refused, and their refineries were quickly confiscated by the Castro government. As a response, in July, the Eisenhower administration canceled the purchase of 700,000 tons that remained of Cuba's total 1960 sugar quota of about 3 million tons. Castro retaliated with a decree expropriating all business enterprises and properties wholly or partially owned by American citizens or companies. The expropriations took place in August and September. A few days later, President Eisenhower broke U.S. diplomatic relations with Cuba.

Still, Americans Don't Get It

Notwithstanding Castro's evident contempt toward the U.S., most Americans do not seem to understand that Castro cannot care less about the United States. This is best evidenced by the attempts of several administrations to reach an accommodation with Castro.

For example, in 1971 President Nixon hinted at a possible reconciliation. To his surprise, Castro's angered response was that "Normal relations with the imperialists would mean renouncing our elementary duties of solidarity with the revolutionary peoples . . . of Latin America."[40]

Three years later the U.S. attitude towards Cuba seemingly had softened, and the Ford administration began seeking a better understanding between the two countries. In November 1974, less than three months after Ford became president, secret talks between American officials and representatives of the Castro government took place, and the possibility of an improvement in relations was explored. On September 23, 1975, Assistant Secretary of State William D. Rogers openly mentioned the U.S. desire to improve relations with Cuba.

Then, when everything indicated that the two countries were moving toward better understanding, American intelligence discovered the first signs of Castro's involvement in Angola. On December 20, President Ford called a press conference, stating that "The action of the Cuban government in sending combat forces to Angola destroys any opportunity for improvement in relations with the United States."[41]

Two years later, in 1977, during the Carter administration, another effort was made to reach more normal U.S.-Cuba relations. On February 3, 1977, Secretary of State Cyrus Vance expressed U.S. willingness to begin a new cycle of discussions with the Castro government. On September, 1977, both countries opened interests offices as a first step for the normalization of diplomatic relations.

But then, on July 17, 1977, Somalian dictator Siad Barre invaded Ethiopia, and, soon after, Castro decided to militarily support the invasion. By January, 1978, several thousand Cuban troops, equipped with tanks and artillery, had joined the Somalis in their invasion of Ethiopia. Castro's decision cut short any American desire to improve relations with Cuba.

In early 1996, the Clinton administration took a series of steps toward a rapprochement with the Castro regime. Secret talks were held in Havana between Cuban government and Washington officials. Then, on February 24, 1996, Cuban MiGs shot down two unarmed American civilian planes over international waters, killing four Americans. The planes belonged to the Miami-based Brothers to the Rescue organization, an anti-Castro group providing help to rafters escaping from Cuba. The incident brought the rapprochement process to an abrupt halt.[42]

More recently, during the last months of 1998, the ever faithful liberals in the Clinton administration, who apparently didn't get it that Fidel Castro is not interested at all in improving relations with the U.S., tried again to win Fidel's love by unilaterally taking some measures directed at softening the conditions of the embargo. To everybody's surprise the reaction of the Castro government was outrage and criticism.[43] Finally Castro rejected the deal, allegedly because of the financial conditions attached. Clinton's aggressive and treasonous measures, Castro's officials claimed, were intended to undermine and attack the revolution. And so on and on, *ad nauseam*.

It seems that the Bush administration will soon be following the same steps. The fact that, notwithstanding overwhelming evidence that Castro is involved in terrorism and Cuba harbors terrorists, the Bush administration insists in looking the other way.

As we have seen above, Castro has always found the way to make every single one of his aggressive actions appear as a defensive step against American aggression. Forcing the Eisenhower administration to break diplomatic relations with Cuba, and keeping them that way, have been steps in Fidel Castro's long way towards accomplishing what he believes is his manifest destiny: to destroy the United States and assume himself America's self-imposed role as world policeman.

Chapter 4

A Caribbean Magnicide

> *Kennedy was trying to get Castro, but Castro got to him first. . . . It will come out someday!*
>
> —President Lyndon B. Johnson

Shortly after taking office in 1963, President Lyndon Baynes Johnson discovered that, as he graphically put it, "We had been operating a damned Murder Inc. in the Caribbean." According to what he told some close friends, LBJ suspected that President Kennedy's assassination may have been triggered by a vengeance-seeking Fidel Castro.[1]

Johnson had suspicions that John F. Kennedy's assassin had been "influenced or directed" by Fidel Castro, and his suspicions grew stronger with time. A few years after the Kennedy assassination, LBJ confided to his friend Howard K. Smith, "I will tell you something that will rock you. Kennedy was trying to get Castro, but Castro got to him first."[2]

A recent book about LBJ's White House tapes shows that Johnson suspected Castro had been an important player in President Kennedy's death. But, as he expressed in some secret tapes, if the U.S. had blamed Castro or the Russians, Americans would have demanded a retaliatory attack upon Cuba or the Soviet Union, initiating a war that would have killed 40 million Americans in the first hour.

According to the tapes, Johnson's suspicions that Fidel Castro was behind the assassination gained new force in February 1967. After listening to what his attorney general Ramsey Clark told him about the Kennedy administration's assassination attempts against Castro, LBJ said it was unbelievable that a president of the United States had engaged in such actions.[3]

Robert Kennedy apparently had similar suspicions. When, in January 1971, Jack Anderson broke the story of the anti-Castro plotting by the Kennedy brothers, he reported that Robert Kennedy was emotionally devastated after the President's assassination by the possibility that his efforts in trying to assassinate Castro may well have led to Castro assassinating his brother.[4]

In any event, President Johnson and Robert Kennedy were not alone in their suspicions about Castro's involvement in President Kennedy's assassination. It seems that some people at CIA shared their misgivings. John Karamessines, assistant to CIA Director Richard Helms, was quoted as saying that, "CIA feared that the Cubans were responsible for the assassination," which, if proved true, might lead to an international crisis that could literally mean the end of the world.[5] Also, among the many people who shared similar suspicions, was Chief Justice Earl Warren. He told some friends privately that he believed Castro was "one of the principal suspects" in the assassination.[6] Moreover, there is evidence that some senior intelligence officers in Cuba suspected that Castro had a direct participation in the assassination of President Kennedy.[7]

Another who had strong suspicions about Castro's role in the Kennedy assassination was Thomas Mann, former American Ambassador to Mexico. As he later expressed,

> Castro is the kind of person who would avenge himself in this way. He is the Latin type of extremist who reacts viscerally rather than intellectually and apparently without much regard for risks. His whole life story shows this.[8]

Senator Robert Morgan, a member of the Senate Intelligence Committee (the "Church Committee"), went a step further. He was not merely suspicious, but totally convinced that Castro was the assassin. According to Morgan, "There is no doubt in my mind that John Fitzgerald Kennedy was assassinated by Fidel Castro, or someone under his influence, in retaliation for our efforts to assassinate him."[9]

President Johnson and the rest of the people who had suspicions about Castro's role in the assassination were probably not too far off the mark, because Castro had strong reasons for revenge. The very same day that Kennedy was killed in Dallas, Desmond Fitzgerald, a senior CIA officer and a personal friend of Robert Kennedy, following orders from the U.S. Attorney General, was having a secret meeting with Rolando Cubela, a senior Cuban official, to discuss the assassination of Fidel Castro.[10]

Following President Kennedy's orders, the CIA always kept its efforts to assassinate Castro very quiet and hidden from the American public. After the assassination of President Kennedy, the CIA kept the records hidden from the Warren Commission as well. And the CIA's memory lapses before the Church Committee were remarkable, because spymaster Allen Dulles, then the Agency's Director, sat on the panel. Senator Richard Schweiker, who as a member of the Church Committee listened to all the witnesses on the subject, was puzzled by the CIA's forgetfulness, and raised the possibility that Kennedy had been killed in retaliation for his attempts to assassinate Castro.

But, strange bedfellows, both American liberals and the CIA have always been at pains in their efforts to hide the existence of any connections between Fidel Castro and the assassination of President John F. Kennedy. For example, in an article in which sixty different versions of the Kennedy assassination are mentioned and where all types of theories about the *who* and *why* are given, author Edward Jay Epstein, whose close CIA links have been suggested, mentions only one in which Castro appears implicated with the assassination. In this only case, it happens to be a theory proposed, of all people, by famous psychic Jeanne Dixon.[11]

In the same fashion, Russian author Igor Efimov gives a list of eight probable connections to the Kennedy assassination, and lists them in order of importance: 1. the Mafia; 2. LBJ; 3. J. Edgar Hoover; 4. right wing extremists; 5. anti-Castro Cubans; 6. the military-industrial complex; 7. Nikita Khrushchev; and 8. Fidel Castro.[12]

Likewise, sociologist David Simone, working on a study of the books dealing with the Kennedy assassination, compiled about six hundred titles and found that 20 percent of them blamed either a lone assassin or the media or the anti-Castro Cubans or the Russians. The other 80 percent blamed the CIA.[13] However, not a single book published at the time pointed to Fidel Castro as the instigator of the assassination.

Similarly, although there was a large amount of evidence pointing to the possibility of a Castro connection to the assassination of President Kennedy, the American investigative agencies, for some strange reason, choose to look the other way. The fact is explicitly mentioned in the Schweiker report,

> Despite knowledge of Oswald's apparent interest in pro-Castro and anti-Castro activities and top-level awareness of certain CIA assassination plots, the FBI made no special investigative effort into questions of possible Cuban government or Cuban exile involvement in the assassination independent of the Oswald investigation. . . . [This] failure to follow significant leads in the Cuba area is surprising. These leads raise significant questions.[14]

To some extent it is understandable that the CIA, President Johnson, and some other U.S. Government agencies, were apprehensive about the possibility of either a Kremlin or a Castro connection. Any link between Castro and the Kennedy assassination, they feared, might bring up a situation potentially as dangerous as the Cuban missile crisis.[15] It is more difficult, however, to understand the American liberals' interest in ignoring the possibility of any Castro-Kennedy connection. The only explanation is that they feared finding themselves in the end pointing a finger at their usual example of assassination attempts by the evil CIA, Fidel Castro himself.[16]

Some Castro-friendly authors have been making an extraordinary effort trying to prove that, far from hating Kennedy, at the time of the assassination Castro actually had begun an effort to seek an accommodation with the U.S.[17] A typical example of this type of argument is Peter Kornbluh's "JFK & Castro: The Secret Quest for Accommodation."[18] To support his thesis, Kornbluh brings a series of declassified documents showing that, unbeknownst to all but his brother and a few close advisors, President Kennedy had begun in 1963 a secret path towards a rapprochement with Castro. Kornbluh also offers some declassified documents proving that Castro had made some overtures in the same direction.

Apart from the inconsistencies between those documents and the actual behavior of Castro and the Kennedys, Kornbluh's article is too close for comfort to the official Castroist line developed by the Cuban intelligence services. Both Carlos Lechuga, a former Cuban ambassador to the U.N., and Fabián Escalante, a senior counterintelligence officer, have been producing this type of disinformation for many years.

In his article Kornbluh admits that "John F. Kennedy would seem the most unlikely of presidents to seek an accommodation with Fidel Castro." The reason for this, which Kornbluh seems to ignore, is because at the time of his alleged moves to rapprochement, JFK and his brother actually were aggressively planning the assassination of Fidel Castro, a fact that not even a thousand dubious declassified documents can deny.

Most of the arguments developed by these authors follow this line: After the Cuban missile crisis Kennedy made up his mind to tolerate Castro. Kennedy refused to invade Cuba, and was preparing to normalize relations with the Maximum Leader. During the Cuban missile crisis, the argument goes, President Kennedy reached an agreement with Soviet Premier Nikita Khrushchev which included his promise to stop the secret war against Cuba and the assassinations attempts against Castro.

But these arguments don't ring true. In the first place, there is no evidence that such an agreement between Kennedy and Khrushchev ever took place. Henry Kissinger, for one, once tried to find it when he was Secretary of State, but was not successful in his search. Other attempts to find the document have failed as well. Consequently, it is safe to surmise that it never existed. Secondly, there is strong evidence that after the Cuban missile crisis the Kennedys persisted in their anti-Castro policies. Close friends and associates have recorded the visceral hatred Kennedy and his brother felt for Castro before, during, and after the missile crisis. Ted Sorensen reported that, after the missile crisis, President Kennedy continued his efforts to isolate the Castro regime, and remained committed to "harass, disrupt and weaken Cuba politically and economically."[19]

A report by the CIA inspector general of August 25, 1967, stated,"We cannot overemphasize the extent to which responsible agency officers felt themselves subject to the Kennedy administration's severe pressures to do something about Castro and his regime."[20] Former CIA director Richard Helms shared the same opinion. Talking to Ronald Kessler, Helms said, "All I know is Jack Kennedy and his brother were bound to have us take on this effort [to get rid of Castro]."[21]

Notwithstanding Kennedy's claims after the Bay of Pigs' fiasco, he never "clipped the CIA wings." The fact was clearly expressed a few years later in a House Hearings report:

> Within a year of the Bay of Pigs, the CIA curiously and inexplicably began to grow, to branch out, to gather more and more responsibility for the "Cuban problem." The Company was given authority to help monitor Cuban wireless traffic; to observe its weather; to follow the Castro government's purchases abroad and its currency transactions; to move extraordinary numbers of clandestine field operatives in and out of Cuba; to acquire a support fleet of ships and aircraft in order to facilitate these secret agent movements; to advise, train, and help reorganize the police and security establishments of Latin countries which felt threatened by Castro guerrilla politics; to take a hand in U-2 overflights and sea-air Elint (Electronic Intelligence) operations aimed at tracing Cuban coastal defense communications on special devices; to pump . . . vast sums into political operations thought to be helpful in containing Castro . . .[22]

Through his efficient intelligence services, Castro was aware of these facts. He had, therefore, no reason to believe that the Kennedys had changed their minds about him so fast. Out of personal experience, Castro may have guessed that, as it happens with most politicians, President Kennedy's words for public consumption were in sharp contrast with his actions. But, even if the Kennedys had changed their minds; even if their hatred for Castro had suddenly and inexplicably turned into love, it would have made no difference at all, at least to Castro's vengeful, never forgetful eyes.

As his close friends have testified over and over, Castro is a very vindictive person. He never forgets a personal offense, real or imagined, particularly when he feels he has been humiliated. There is evidence that he felt deeply humiliated with the outcome of the missile crisis. Witnesses recall his furious tantrum when he got the news that Khrushchev and Kennedy had solved the crisis behind his back, fully ignoring him.

I had the opportunity of witnessing first hand Castro's rage when, a few days after the end of the crisis, Castro told a group of students at the University of Havana that Nikita Khrushchev was *"un maricón"* (a faggot), and John F. Kennedy *"un millonario come mierda y un hijo de puta"* (a shit-eating millionaire and a son of a bitch). Yet, Castro had enough reasons for feeling that Kennedy had tried to humiliate him. Sorensen recalls that some of the measures suggested by the Ex-Comm to President Kennedy, like low-level flights over Cuba, for example, were intended not only to improve reconnaissance but to harass and humiliate Castro.[23]

Teresa Casuso, one of Castro's sometime close associate, said that he has an overly proud nature. That is probably why, according to her, "Fidel never forgets a humiliation."[24] Herbert Matthews has written many times about this dark side of Castro's character. Matthews mentions how some pilots of Batista's Air Force had dropped bombs and machine-gunned Castro's guerrilla, arousing a "sense of bitterness that lead the unforgiving Fidel Castro to take a somewhat illegal vengeance later when some aviators went to trial." According to Matthews, Castro "is not a forgiving man."[25]

Castro's Version of the Kennedy Assassination

On November 22, 1963, Fidel Castro was engaged in a friendly conversation with French journalist Jean Daniel when the news came that President Kennedy had been assassinated. Daniel told the story in detail.

It was around 1:30 in the afternoon, Cuban time, wrote Daniel. We were having lunch in the living room of the modest summer residence which Fidel Castro owns on magnificent Varadero Beach, 120 kilometers from Havana. The phone rang, and an aide told Fidel that

President Dorticós had an urgent message for him. Fidel picked up the phone and I heard him say : *"¿Cómo? ¿Un atentado?"* (What? An attempted assassination?) Castro then turned and told Daniel that Kennedy had been shot in Dallas.

According to Daniel, Castro's initial reaction was of surprise and shock. He came back, wrote Daniel, sat down, and repeated three times the words: *"Es una mala noticia."* (That's bad news). Then, he asked Daniel, "But tell me, how many Presidents have there been in the United States? Thirty-six? And four of them have been assassinated. That's disturbing. Here in Cuba there has never been a President assassinated. You know, when we were in the Sierra, there were people (not in my group, but another) who wanted to kill Batista. They believed that they could put an end to the regime by cutting off his head. As for myself, I was always furiously hostile to such methods."[26]

Only three days earlier, in November 19th, *l'Express* had published Daniel's interview with Castro, in which the Cuban leader had said that, although he considered Kennedy was to blame for most of the Bay of Pigs incident, "I believe that in the last few months he has come to a better understanding of the situation and, in any case, I am convinced that anyone who might replace him would be worse." Daniel attributed to Castro the assertion that if peace in North and South America were to be won, "there must arise in the United States a man with the capacity to understand and to adapt himself to the explosive reality of Latin America." For Castro, Daniel pointed out,

> ...this man might, even now, be Kennedy. He still has the full opportunity of becoming, in the eyes of History, the greatest President of the United States—the one who would at last come to a recognition of the fact that there can be a coexistence between capitalists and socialists, even in the American hemisphere. He would then be even a greater President than Lincoln. I know that Khrushchev, for example, considers Kennedy a man with whom it is possible to have discussions. .. Other people tell me that, before discussions can take place, it will be necessary to await his second term. .. if you see him again, you can tell him that, if it helps him to win his re-election, I am ready to announce that [presidential candidate, senator Barry] Goldwater is a friend of mine![27]

Daniel had an interview scheduled to see Kennedy a short time after his return from Dallas. He already had had an interview with Kennedy on October 24th, before going directly to Havana to interview Castro. Daniel promised the Maximum Leader that he would go back to the United States to deliver Castro's confidential message to Kennedy before either interview were published.

Liberal journalists and scholars have interpreted Castro's message to Kennedy as an effort through non-diplomatic channels to explore the possibility of normalizing U.S.-Cuban relations. An affirmative response by the American president, they claim, would have paved the way to an eventual top-level meeting with Kennedy—a meeting much less likely to be held with his successor—one which might have stabilized the Castro Government, enabling it to channel funds and labor, now invested in national defense and weapons, to economic projects desperately needed by the Cuban people. That was not the right moment, they reason, Castro would have chosen to kill President Kennedy.

Between July and October of 1974, Frank Mankiewicz and Kirby Jones visited Cuba three times and recorded a series of interviews with Fidel Castro. In an introduction to the book they published later, the authors describe how, among dozens of requests from all three American tv networks and newspapers and many foreign countries, Castro rejected all others and selected them. It seems that Castro's intelligence officers did their homework, because the questions drawn up by Mankiewicz and Jones seem designed to allow him to show his best colors—not necessarily the true ones. In one of the interviews the subject of John F. Kennedy was brought up.

Contrary to what some people may think, Fidel Castro knows Americans very well. His answers to Mankiewicz and Jones mentioned all the nice things about Kennedy American liberals love to hear. In typical Castro fashion, like when he is trying to mesmerize his audience, he told Mankiewicz and Jones about Kennedy's courage and decisiveness, and how unpleasant it was for him to learn about the President's death.

Then, Castro approached the subject of the assassination and, after expressing some ideas that seem to have been taken directly from the Warren Commission report, he ended up by stating, categorically, "We have never believed in carrying out this type of activity of assassination of adversaries." Even during the early stages of your revolutionary fight,? he was asked. "Never. And our revolutionary background proves it."[28]

When Senator George McGovern visited Cuba in mid-1975, he again raised the question of Kennedy's assassination while he was talking to Castro during a long drive back to Havana from the provinces. McGovern recalls that Castro answered in disbelief: "We had troubles with the Kennedy administration, but it is monstrous even to contemplate that we might murder the head of state of any nation, to say nothing of being so foolish as to incur the wrath of a great power like the United States." Senator McGovern said that he was impressed by Castro's sincerity and rational, logical arguments.[29]

On April 3, 1978, some members of the House Select Committee on Assassinations traveled to Havana and managed to get an interview with Fidel Castro. In all, they spent more than four hours with the Cuban leader, in which many topics related and unrelated with the Kennedy assassination were discussed. Castro expressed his reaction to allegations of his complicity in the Kennedy assassination in this way:

> Who here could have operated and planned something so delicate as the death of the United States president? That was insane. From the ideological point of view, it was tremendous insanity. That would have been the most perfect pretext for the United States to invade our country, which is what I have tried to prevent for all these years.[30]

Though some members of the group were not fully satisfied with Castro's explanation, most of them agreed that what he had said made sense. But, by unconsciously applying the mirror image theory which implies that whatever makes sense to themselves must make sense to everybody, the members of the Committee made a big mistake. First of all, if something characterizes Castro's behavior it is his irrationality and lack of common sense. The fact has been extensively documented, mostly under a positive light, to explain some of Castro's successes. Secondly, contrary to his claims, the evidence shows that practically since he took power in Cuba in 1959, Fidel Castro has been actually trying, by any means available, to provoke the United States into invading Cuba. Finally, given Castro's long history of insanity and irrationality and the way his convoluted mind works, the fact that he so emphatically stated that it would have been insane for him to order the Kennedy assassination is in itself a strong indication that he may well have been involved in it.

The information given above summarizes most of the American scholars' and journalists' Castro-friendly version of Castro's version of the Kennedy assassination. As it happens most of the time, however, Castro's photographic memory functions selectively, because the available record by far contradicts his words. First of all, Castro never felt much respect for John F. Kennedy. In his speech to the U. N. General Assembly in 1960, Castro called Kennedy "an illiterate and ignorant millionaire," a characterization that perhaps was not too far off the mark.[31] In September 1963, just a few minutes after he expressed an unmistakable warning and threat to the lives of American leaders, Castro called President Kennedy, "the Batista of his time, and the most opportunistic American president of all times," and ended by calling Kennedy *"un cretino"* (an idiot). Secondly, just a little digging into his early history shows that Castro's claims that he has always been furiously hostile to the assassination of adversaries, including presidents, are in strong contradiction with the facts. Contrasting with the Kennedys, who were just *aficionados* in the art of political assassination, Castro has a lot of hands-on experience.

Killing Presidents: Castro's Life-long Obsession

It is possible, as his subsequent behavior seems to indicate, that his Jesuit preceptors may have introduced Fidel to the Theology of Father L'Amy, the guiding principle by which the Order gives its members the right to eliminate its adversaries.[32] But we know for sure that, as a student of the Jesuits at the Colegio de Belén in Havana, young Fidel Castro heard about the Compañía's principle of the legitimacy of assassinating tyrants and "to commit, without sin, acts which are considered criminal by the ignorant masses."[33] In his impassioned self-defense during the trial for the attack on the Moncada barracks, Castro mentioned how,

> No less a man than Juan Mariana, a Spanish Jesuit during the reign of Phillip II, asserts in his book, *De Rege et Regis Institutione*, that when a governor usurps power, or even if he were elected, when he governs in a tyrannical manner, it is licit for a private citizen to exercise tyrannicide, either directly or through subterfuge with the least possible disturbance.[34]

We cannot fully blame the Jesuits for Castro's behavior, but for some unknown reason killing presidents became one of his many obsessions, and he began aggressively pursuing it very early in his life. Hugh Thomas noticed Castro's "desire to carry out a student tradition of tyrannicide."[35] Unfortunately, as we will see below, Castro's deep hatred for democratically elected presidents misdirected whatever tyrannicidal desires he may have felt.

In 1947, when he was 21 years old, Castro joined a group of University students visiting President Grau San Martín, a democratic politician elected by popular vote, at the Presidential Palace. At some time during the visit, the President and the students moved close to one of the large, second floor windows facing the park. They were astonished when Castro suggested to some of them to kill the old President. "I have the formula," he whispered, "to take power at once and get rid of this old son-of-a-bitch once for all. Let's pick him up and throw him off the balcony. Once the President is dead, we'll proclaim the triumph of the student revolution and talk to the people on the radio."[36]

In the summer of that same year, Castro joined a group of adventurers who were planning an invasion of the Dominican Republic. The main element of their plan was the assassination of President Rafael L. Trujillo and a putsch to take control of the country. Castro participated in the weapons training at Cayo Confites, a small key on the coast of Oriente, and was ready for the action. Finally, the plot was discovered by the Cuban armed forces, who located the expeditionary group at the Nipe Bay, in the northern part of the Oriente province. Most of the participants were arrested, but Castro managed to escape, swimming across the bay while carrying a sub-machine gun and a pistol.[37]

On the occasion of the Ninth International Congress of the American States, a violent riot, known as the *Bogotazo*, destroyed most of the downtown part of the city of Bogotá, Colombia. The riot began in the early afternoon of April 9, 1948, when the leftist leader and presidential candidate Jorge Eliécer Gaitán was gunned down by a drifter who had once been an inmate of an insane asylum. The murder of Gaitán set off a frenzy of burning, looting and killing unparalleled in the history of Latin America. Some students of the University of Havana had arrived a few days before in Bogotá to attend an "anti-imperialist" student congress called to coincide with the Conference. There is evidence that the fares of most students attending the congress, including those of the delegation from the University of Havana, had been paid by Juan Domingo Perón, the Argentinean fascist dictator, who was anxious to create trouble for the United States in Latin America.[38] Prominent among the Cuban students attending the event were Rafael del Pino Siero and Fidel Castro.

Two of Castro's classmates, José Ovares and Alfredo Guevara (no relation to Ché Guevara), who also were in Bogotá with Castro and had joined the mob for some time, decided to get off the streets and return to their boarding house. At about 4 P.M., a mob shouting "¡A Palacio!" (to the [Presidential] Palace) swept by the boarding house. According to witnesses, Castro was in it, carrying a rifle and yelling hysterically that they were on their way to kill the Colombian President, Doctor Mariano Ospina Pérez. Fidel stopped and tried to persuade Ovares and Guevara to join him, but they refused.[39]

When Cuban Ortodoxo Party leader Eddy Chibás committed suicide on August 5, 1951, his casket was brought to the University of Havana, so the students would have the opportunity to show their respect for the dead politician. José (Pepe) Pardo Llada reports that, while they were carrying the casket down the University main stairs, Fidel approached him, saying: "Pepe, let's go to the [Presidential] Palace with the dead guy; we'll take power and you'll be the President and I'll be the Army Chief!"[40] The Cuban president was Carlos Prío

Socarrás. Pardo Llada does not mention if Castro told him how he planned to get rid of President Prío, but a previous similar incident may point to an answer.

In 1949, while Fidel was making arrangements for a trip to the U.S., he used to visit his friend Max Lesnick at his apartment on Morro Street, close to the Presidential palace. Lesnick told Tad Szulc that one day, while looking at the Presidential palace, Fidel grabbed a broomstick and, pointing it like a rifle to the north terrace of the place, said to Lesnick's grandmother: "You know, if Prío steps out on that terrace to make a speech, I could get him from here with a single bullet from a telescopic sight rifle . . ."[41]

On March of 1953 Fidel Castro and a group a conspirators concocted a plan to kill President Batista. Among the conspirators were Leonel Soto, Antonio Núñez Jiménez, Alfredo Guevara and Vicentina Antuña. In order to carry out their plan they had to wait for Batista to leave Havana, where he was always under a strong military protection. The opportunity came when President Batista decided to attend a meeting of Veterans of the Cuban Independence Wars to be held in Santiago de Cuba, Oriente.

Fidel and some of the conspirators obtained false documentation, army uniforms and official car plates and traveled to Santiago to wait for Batista's arrival. But Batista probably got word of the action, changed plans at the last moment and the assassination attempt didn't take place. The police had suspicions that Castro had been implicated on the attempt and he was detained, but he walked away because of lack of evidence.[42] There are rumors that Castro's attack on the Moncada barracks a few months later, on July 26, 1953, were to coincide with a visit President Batista had planned to make to Santiago. But, again, Batista canceled his visit at the last moment. There may be a grain of truth in the rumors, because the ruse Castro's men used to get the guards to open the gate for them was to yell: "Open the gate! The General [Batista] has arrived!"

On March 13, 1957, while Fidel Castro was in the Sierra Maestra mountains, a group of University students of the Directorio Revolucionario, headed by José Antonio Echeverría, stormed the Presidential Palace in Havana in an attempt to kill President Batista. The attackers failed to accomplish their goal and most of them were killed in the action or captured later. From his headquarters at the Sierra Maestra, Castro condemned the attack in the strongest terms. His condemnation was published in May 28, 1957, in *Bohemia*, the influential and widely read Cuban weekly magazine.

Castro-friendly historians and biographers have used his condemnation of the attempt on Batista's life as an example of Fidel's distaste for this type of action. The truth, however, is quite different. The Directorio Revolucionario was one among the many independent revolutionary organizations fighting Batista. Though the Directorio leaders had made an agreement with Castro in Mexico the previous summer, they knew about Castro's thirst for total power and had no love for him. To the Directorio leaders, Castro was more a rival than an ally. Had they accomplished their goal of killing Batista, Echeverría would have become a strong rival hero and revolutionary leader, and the Directorio would have taken control of the Cuban government, leaving Castro isolated and forgotten like a fool in the mountains. Castro's misgivings about the action, therefore, were not ethically, but politically motivated. Fidel suffers from a congenital dislike of competition. The attackers came within an ace of murdering Batista and perhaps of taking over the government. The true cause for Castro's condemnation of the attempt on Batista's life was only because somebody else, and not himself, would be the one to profit from the event.[43]

Castro's obsession with killing presidents didn't stop after he took power in Cuba in 1959. In April 26, just a few months after his victory over Batista's troops, Fidel sent a hit team of about eighty-four Cubans and Panamanians to Panama, to kill President Ernesto de la Guardia and spark a revolution. Within a few hours of landing, the invasion was crushed. Most observers agreed that the Castro government was behind the attack, but Castro denied the charges.[44]

The unsuccessful Panama expedition is a good clue to Castro's true political thinking. The Panamanian government was not a dictatorship, and its president had been elected by popular vote, therefore the attack had no ideological justification—that is, if Castro is really the leftist he claims to be. Moreover, adding insult to injury, at the time of the attack Castro was visiting Washington in an attempt to allay American fears of his totalitarian leanings.

Subsequently, both Castro and Ché Guevara denied official Cuban participation in the affair and condemned it as the work of "a group of adventurers headed by a *barbudo* [bearded guy] who had never been in the Sierra Maestra ... [who] managed to fire the enthusiasm of a group of boys to carry out the adventure." Guevara went further and claimed that the Cuban leadership had "worked with the Panamanian Government to destroy it."[45]

A few hours after landing in Panama and allegedly after having received an appeal from Castro to call off the expedition, the invaders surrendered to an Organization of American States investigating team. Though the Panamanian government never charged the Castro regime with responsibility for the invasion, most people believe Castro's hidden hand was behind it. The main reason for this is that the invasion followed Castro's *modus operandi* for that type of operation.

Just a month after the Panama affair, another group secretly departed from Cuba and headed for Costa Rica in an operation to kill Nicaraguan President/Dictator Luis Somoza. Somoza was a sworn enemy of Fidel Castro. On the first of June, 1959, two planes full of invaders left Costa Rica and headed for Nicaragua. They planned to coordinate their attack with the landing of several yachts filled with more armed revolutionaries. Somoza complained to the Organization of American States, and implied that the yachts had sailed from Cuba, but offered no evidence to support his charges. The invasion was suppressed in a few hours, and Castro denied any involvement in the attack.

Less than two weeks later, on June 14, 1959, Castro sent a similar group to the Dominican Republic to kill President Trujillo. Castro's hostility to Trujillo dated back to his days at the University of Havana, when, in 1947, he joined an expedition of several hundred men trying to assassinate Trujillo. Castro's hatred for Trujillo was intensified when the Dominican president gave political asylum to Batista and a large number of anti-Castro Cuban exiles.

Fidel Castro's personal involvement in this expedition is undeniable. On June 14, some 200 Dominican exiles who had been undergoing military training in Cuba, and ten Cubans, all commanded by one of Castro's Rebel Army officers, left Cuba in a plane and two small ships and headed for the northern coast of the Dominican Republic. Again, the plan followed Castro's *modus operandi*. It repeated the strategy followed in the landing of the yacht *Granma*. The guerrillas were to establish a *foco*—a small, armed, mobile guerrilla band—in the mountains while revolutionaries in the cities would rally mass demonstrations and strikes. But the invasion soon ended in total failure, and Trujillo's army soldiers left no survivors to tell the story.

However, in the case of the Dominican adventure, more than just suspicions points to Castro's involvement in personally preparing and arranging the operation. It seems that, in his enthusiasm, he forgot all prudence and made an appeal for open support to the invasion, which he hastened to disavow the next day.

On June 16, two days after the attack was launched, Castro appeared on tv and asked for support for the Dominican invaders.[46] But when Trujillo's government protested to the OAS, Castro recanted and denied his participation in the invasion. Making good use of his abilities as an unashamed dissembler, Fidel declared: "Our strategy is to repeal aggression, not to attack, but to defend ourselves and our territory."[47]

Both the Nicaraguan and Dominican operations ended in failure, and Castro denied that he personally had authorized the ventures. But, given Castro's propensity and his total control over Cuban events, one has to conclude that he was fully behind the attempts.[48]

Just a couple of months later, in mid-August, 1959, Castro struck again. This time an expeditionary force moved against Haiti. Its main goal was to assassinate François "Papa Doc" Duvalier, the dictatorial president of Haiti, another of Castro's preferred targets. According to official declarations of the Duvalier government, the invading force was composed of some thirty men, all of them Cubans. It was led by an Algerian who had served with Castro in the Sierra Maestra, and was financed by Louis Déjoie, a former Haitian senator and avowed enemy of Duvalier. The expedition had been organized by Ché Guevara, following Castro's direct orders.

Like the expeditions on Panama and Dominican Republic, the Haitian adventure ended in total disaster, and most of the attackers were killed. Castro never responded to or denied the Duvalier's government charges of his complicity in the affair.[49]

On July 26, 1960, in a speech commemorating the failed attack on the Moncada garrison in Santiago de Cuba, Fidel Castro declared his commitment to "liberate" the rest of Latin America.[50] What he didn't make clear, however, is that his technique to achieve that goal essentially consisted in the indiscriminate application of fascist-like putschist *coup d'états*, including the assassination of some democratically elected presidents of the target countries.

There is evidence that Castro tried to kill the democratically elected president of Panama, Roberto Chiari. According to an FBI report dated October 25, 1962, one of Castro's hit men, named Humberto Rodríguez Díaz, in complicity with a former Cuban ambassador to Panama, planned an attempt on the life of the Panamanian president.[51]

Later on, in the Spring of 1963, Castro shipped several tons of weapons and ammunition to a Venezuelan revolutionary underground.[52] Castro's obsession with killing President Rómulo Betancourt, who initially was his supporter, has been extensively documented.

It is highly revealing that Castro's actions against Venezuela were not directed against a tyrannical, undemocratic regime. On the contrary, they were directed at avoiding the establishment of democracy. The immediate goal of the Castro-backed revolutionaries was to disrupt the 1963 presidential elections. As Castro and the Venezuelan guerrillas saw it, if these elections were disrupted and the military provoked into seizing power, the democratic reform route would be completely discredited in Venezuela. But Betancourt and the democratic reformers were committed to holding the elections, and Castro lost interest.

That same year Bogotá's newspapers published reports that planes which had landed at Colombia's Guajira peninsula carrying a group of assassins from Cuba had been sent by Fidel Castro. Their mission was to kill President León Valencia and overthrow his government. The information was officially corroborated on October 17, 1963, by President León Valencia himself, who notified all diplomatic missions in Bogotá that he held Castro responsible for the action.

A few months later, on February 26, 1964, coinciding with a planned visit of President Valencia to Cali, another plot to kill him was uncovered. Next year President Valencia pointed to Castro as the instigator behind both assassination attempts.[53]

On July 19, 1979, Nicaraguan dictator Luis Somoza was overthrown by the Castro-backed *Frente Sandinista de Liberación Nacional* (FSLN, Sandinista Front for National Liberation), and fled the country to become a political exile in Paraguay. Just a few months later, Somoza and his bodyguards were assassinated on a street of Asunción by a Sandinista hit team using machine guns and bazookas. Some members of Castro's intelligence services boasted at the time that the assassination team had been trained in Cuba.[54]

Though most of Castro's early presidential assassination attempts failed to succeed, it would be a mistake to believe that they were just the lucubrations of a young, feverish mind. On the contrary, Fidel Castro had a lot of practical experience in the business of political assassination, and the evidence seems to indicate that sometimes he was successful—both in the attempt and in getting away with it.

Castro's Expertise in Political Assassination

In the Summer of 1947, while he was a law student at the University of Havana, Fidel Castro was accused of killing fellow student Leonel Gómez, his opponent for the nomination of president of the Law School Student Federation in the coming elections. But the judge decided there was not enough evidence and Castro was not indicted. In February 22, 1948, Manolo Castro (not related to Fidel), president of the University's Student Federation, was killed in a gangster-style shoot-out at a cinema not far from the University campus. Two days later Castro was detained on charges of murder, but he was set free after two days because of lack of evidence.

After he was set free for Manolo Castro's assassination, Fidel made an unexpected trip to Bogotá, Colombia. But just a few days after returning to Havana he was accused, on June 6, 1948, of murdering Oscar Fernández Caral, a sergeant in the University police. Before dying Caral named Fidel Castro as his killer. Charges against Fidel, however, were dismissed for lack of evidence. In 1949 Castro was arrested at the scene of a shoot out, and accused of killing Justo Fuentes, vice president of the University's Student Federation, and of Miguel Sáez, a bus driver. But, just a few hours later, he was set free, for lack of evidence.[55] It is important to point out that though Castro killed his opponents before several witnesses, they feared retaliation if they accused him of the crime.

It was widely known that, as a student, Castro always packed a Colt .45. As soon as he began attending law school at the University of Havana he created his own Nazi-like gang, and named it *"los Manicatos."* Afterwards he joined the MSR (Movimiento Social Revolucionario—Revolutionary Social Movement), and then switched to the rival faction, the UIR (*Unión Insurreccional Revolucionaria*—Revolutionary Insurrectional Union), over a quarrel with Rolando Masferrer, the MSR leader, who never held Fidel in high regard. Both organizations combined politics with sheer gangsterism. Luis Conte Agüero, at the time one of Castro's best friends, says that Fidel Castro has "the mentality of a gangster."[56] The UIR members would shoot it out with the police, with other students, and with almost anybody, over questions more of a purely personal nature than a political one. Fidel Castro found in the UIR his natural habitat.[57]

It was in the UIR in 1945 that Castro actually began his career as a professional gangster. The UIR initiated the scheme of leaving alongside its victims a note reading *"La justicia tarda, pero llega."* ("Justice is slow but sure."), and Castro made the slogan his own.[58] Ernst Halperin noticed the high frequency in which the word "justice" appears in Castro's speeches. It is not impossible, speculates Halperin, that this preoccupation of Castro's may have been born while he prepared those macabre notes.[59]

In November of 1957, while Castro was at the Sierra Maestra fighting his guerrilla war against Batista, a hit team executed the Holguín district commander, Colonel Fermín Cowley, a bloodthirsty member of Batista's army. The hit team in charge of the assassination attempt was composed of members of the Movimiento 26 de Julio, Castro's revolutionary organization, and the order for Cowley's assassination had been given by Castro himself.[60]

The most amazing thing about Castro's passion for gangsterism is that it didn't begin at the University of Havana when he joined the big league gangs. As soon as Fidel began attending high school at the Colegio de Belén, he organized a gang with four or five of his cronies and used it to harass his classmates. The Jesuit padres were terrorized. Never before had they experienced a student like Fidel Castro. One day a teacher expelled him from class for scuffling with another classmate. Fidel threatened the teacher, yelling: "I'm going to bring my gun." Nobody believed him, but a few minutes later he came back to the classroom brandishing a .45 pistol.

Another day he started a fist fight with Ramón Mestre, a classmate. But Mestre won, and the furious Fidel came back with this .45 pistol. Only the intervention of Father Larracea, who persuaded Fidel to give the pistol to him, saved Mestre. But now comes the most incredible thing. When Father Larracea persuaded him of the impropriety of his behavior, Fidel, in an act of repentance, went to his room again and came back with another .45 pistol which he gave to the amazed Father Larracea.[61]

During his long political life Fidel Castro has devoted much effort and time to get rid of his political adversaries, real or imagined, and he has been highly successful in his endeavors. There is circumstantial evidence pointing to the fact that he was the one who arranged the betrayal of Frank País, which paved the road for Fidel to become the undisputed leader of the 26th of July Movement. It also seems likely that Castro was behind the strange disappearance of Major Camilo Cienfuegos, a potential obstacle to Fidel's plans for achieving total power.

Airplane "accidents" have been extremely beneficial to Castro. On October, 1959, Fidel sent Army Chief Major Camilo Cienfuegos to Camagüey to detain Major Huber Matos. On his way back to Havana, Cienfuegos' plane disappeared forever without leaving a trace. Camilo Cienfuegos, one of the most colorful characters among the Rebel Army leaders, had fought courageously against Batista's troops. Camilo, rather than Ché Guevara, was responsible for the victory at the battle of Santa Clara. In January, 1959, Fidel appointed Camilo head of the Rebel Army, with Raúl Castro under his command as head of the army of Oriente province. Once in Havana, Camilo's charming personality quickly won him a wide popularity, perhaps too wide for Fidel's peace of mind.[62]

The cover-up surrounding the disappearance of Camilo Cienfuegos resulted in a long chain of mysterious deaths, among them Major Cristino Naranjo. A close friend of Major Cienfuegos and the officer in charge of the investigation surrounding his disappearance, Major Naranjo was "accidentally" killed by Major Manuel Beatón. A few weeks later, allegedly because he had rebelled against the Castro government, Beatón was captured and shot before he had the opportunity to talk. Beatón and Naranjo were not the only ones. Some other people related to the Cienfuegos' case committed suicide, among them one of his bodyguards and the person in charge of the control tower at Camagüey's airport, where Cienfuego's plane took off.

In late 1960, taking advantage of Major Ramiro Valdés' lack of experience, Osvaldo Sánchez, a senior PSP leader, almost managed, with the help of KGB operatives in Cuba, to displace de facto Valdés and Manuel Piñeiro from the direction of the DGI (General Directorate of Intelligence). From the very beginning the Russians made every effort to control the DGI and to mold it into their own image. The KGB was very active and managed to infiltrate into the DGI a large group of PSP members, headed by Osvaldo Sánchez.

But the Soviets made the mistake of underestimating Fidel's own abilities to hatch a plot. On January 9, 1961, Osvaldo Sánchez' Cessna plane was flying on a clear night along the north coast of the province of Matanzas when an anti-aircraft battery allegedly failed to properly identify his aircraft, and shot it down. Sánchez and his two PSP comrades were fatally injured in the mysterious accident. The Russians, though angry and suspicious, couldn't say or do anything, and were faced with the loss of their key man inside the DGI.

Another one who fell victim of Castro's intrigues was Ché Guevara. Recently surfaced information confirm suspicions that Castro, in cahoots with Bolivian Communist leaders, arranged the betrayal of Ché. According to Dariel Alarcón Ramírez ("Benigno"), one of Ché's trusted men, previous to Guevara's departure for Bolivia, Castro held a secret meeting with Mario Monje in Havana on December, 1966. Monje, secretary general of the pro-Soviet Bolivian Communist Party, was instrumental in Che's demise by denying the guerrilla any help and leaving them in total isolation. Benigno is convinced that Monje was following Castro's orders when he left Ché in the lurch.[63]

Many of Castro's close associates have died under mysterious circumstances. That is the case, i.e., of Alfredo Gamonal, a Spaniard raised in the Soviet Union which in the early sixties became the chief of Castro's security detail. There are reasons to believe, however, that Gamonal was a KGB operative. When the relations between Castro and the Soviets turned sour after the Cuban missile crisis, Gamonal allegedly died in a car accident in Santiago de Cuba.

On October 15, 1990, the Cuban press reported that René Rodríguez Cruz, President of the Cuban Committee of Solidarity with Vietnam had died of a heart attack. Rodríguez had been for many years the President of the Cuban Institute of Friendship with the Peoples, and was known to be a senior officer of the Cuban intelligence. He had no history of heart disease. Neither Fidel, nor Raúl, attended the burial ceremony. Apparently, Rodríguez knew too much.

In March 11, 1998, it was reported that Manuel Piñeiro Losada (Barbarroja) had died in a car accident after he lost control of his Soviet-made Lada and crashed against another car on his way back home after attending a reception at an embassy in Havana. People who knew him well, however, say that Piñeiro's car was not a Lada, but a Volga, always driven by his personal driver and bodyguard. For many years Piñeiro had been the chief of the America Department, mainly involved in intelligence and counterintelligence operations against the U.S.[64] Like Rodríguez, Piñeiro knew too much.

If one is to believe Walterio Carbonell, a former Cuban Ambassador to Morocco in the 1960s who was a close friend of Castro at the University of Havana, Castroist ambassadors double as assassins. According to Carbonell, Castro demanded from his ambassadors a personal oath to him stating that, in case he was assassinated by the CIA, his ambassadors in turn were to provide immediate retaliation by assassinating the American ambassadors in their respective countries.[65] Recent reports from Cuba seem to confirm Carbonell's claims.

On August 28, 1999, *Granma*, Castro's official newspaper, published a revealing article. More than 70 Cuban ambassadors from all around the world met in Havana with Castro for an unprecedented encounter. "You are a shock troop in the ideological world battle in which we are engaged," Castro told them.[66] Later during the meeting, Castro's new chancellor, Felipe Pérez Roque, stated that "Cuban ambassadors are not career diplomats, *but soldiers who would accomplish any mission assigned to them in this battle.*"[67] It is well known that, since the mid-seventies, most Cuban ambassadors and the personnel working in Cuban missions abroad are actually officers of the Cuban intelligence services operating under a diplomatic cover.

It seems that, over the years, the only noticeable difference between Fidel Castro, the University gangster, and Fidel Castro, the Maximum Leader, is that his assassination techniques have become more sophisticated.

High-Tech Political Assassinations

In an article published in *El Nuevo Herald*, Cuban writer in exile Carlos Alberto Montaner, writing from Spain, claimed that it is "very probable" that not only Jorge Más Canosa, the deceased head of the anti-Castro Cuban American National Foundation, but also Sebastián Arcos Bergnes and other anti-Castro activists have been assassinated by Fidel Castro by inoculation of lethal diseases.[68] Arcos, an important dissident in Castro's Cuba, died in Miami on November, 1997, after being allowed to leave a Cuban jail only when his cancer reached an irreversible stage. According to Montaner, Fidel Castro, like his close friend Saddam Hussein, has developed a great quantity of deadly viruses and bacteria to use against his political enemies.

Montaner wrote that the Castro jailers love to torture their prisoners and often boast about it to others imprisoned for political "crimes." On one occasion, his jailers told political prisoner Leonel Morejón Almagro, "We are going to put you in Sebastián's cell so you, too, can get cancer." When Arcos first became ill, the prison doctor told him the problem was nothing but bone fatigue. The pains he suffered gradually grew worse. Then Castro decided Arcos was beyond the possibility of cure but did not want him dying as a martyr inside a Cuban prison. So Arcos was allowed to go to Miami before the cancer killed him. Cancer is not a transmissible disease, therefore, some people speculate that the jailer's threats to Morejón indicate that something in the prison cell may have caused it.

Now comes the most scary story. Montaner says that, 19 years ago, a young Cuban biologist—whom Montaner identifies only as "David"—on a flight from Sofia, Bulgaria, to Cuba asked for political asylum in Spain. The next day after his defection, David approached the Spanish police and told his story, which was relayed to correspondents, including Montaner. Afterwards, Montaner obtained an interview with David.

David told Montaner that in Sofia he had been trained in the use of an effective technology to induce cancer in adversaries Castro wished to destroy with as little evidence as possible. He said they called it "the Bulgarian treatment." The simplest way was to plant a radioactive isotope in the chair in which the target regularly sits, or in an often-worn jacket, or in a sofa cushion or a mattress, or even in an automobile seat. After a few months, there was a great likelihood that a cancerous growth would develop with fatal results.[69]

Most hospitals have such radioactive isotopes which they ordinarily use to combat certain types of cancer. These isotopes consist of tiny metal fibers easily concealed. "The ideal way to cause a cancer is to plant the isotope and then leave the scene so as to be far away when the cancer is discovered," David told Montaner. Prompted by David's words, Montaner recalled some Castro allies and adversaries who died in unusual circumstances, among them: Major Aldo Vera, shot to death in a Puerto Rican street; Jose Elías de la Torriente, shot in Miami; Manuel Artime, political chief of the Bay of Pigs invaders, who died in exile at age 38 with his lungs mysteriously destroyed; Rafael García, disappeared at age 41; and Rolando Masferrer, blown up by a car bomb in Miami in 1975.[70]

Also, among the ones whose deaths many Cubans suspect may have been the result of Castro's high-tech foul play are, just to name a few: writer Virgilio Piñera, who allegedly died of a heart attack; American reporter Lisa Howard, who died of an overdose; writer Luis Rogelio (Wichy) Nogueras, who reportedly died of AIDS;[71] Jorge Más Canosa, Chair of the Cuban American National Foundation and a man Castro profoundly hated, who died in 1997 at age 58 from complications of lung cancer;[72] Rafael del Pino Siero, Castro's ex-friend and Bogotazo co-conspirator who allegedly died of a heart attack (or hanged himself, according to another version of the story) while in Castro's jail; Raúl Chirino, who reportedly committed suicide while was been interrogated by Castro himself; Beatriz and Laura Allende (daughter and sister of Chile's Salvador Allende), who allegedly committed suicide in Cuba; Onelio Pino, Captain of the yacht *Granma*, found dead in his garage under mysterious circumstances; and Castro's ex-Interior Minister and fellow drug smuggler General José Abrahantes, who reportedly died of a heart attack in a Cuban jail.[73]

In his biography about Ché Guevara, author Jon Lee Anderson tells an interesting story which, with the benefit of hindsight, becomes very significant. In 1974 Hilda Guevara, a very independent woman and Ché's only daughter with his first wife Hilda Gadea, left Cuba, and, after living a hippie-like life in several countries, ended up in Mexico where she married a Mexican guerrilla named Alberto. Afterwards they came to live in Cuba. But Alberto's continued conspiratorial activities against the Mexican government, Castro's all-time ally, forced Fidel to ask them to leave. Eventually Hilda divorced Alberto, and moved back to Cuba with her two sons, to work in various low-level government positions.

Though loyal to the revolution, Hilda was outspoken about what she believed were its defects, earning Castro's disapproval for her views and personal conduct. When one of her teenaged sons, a rock musician, became openly critical of Castro and his government, Hilda's position in Cuba became very difficult. It is known that, on several occasions, Castro commented to his close associates that Hilda was becoming a headache for him. Then, in 1995, Hilda suddenly died of cancer at the age of thirty-nine.[74] Was Ché's daughter one of Castro's high-tech assassination targets?

It is known that Castro's frequently resorts to unconscious projection mechanisms, accusing others of what actually are his intentions or deeds. Of lately he has been accusing different people of assassination by poisoning. For example, he accused exiled Cubans in the U.S. of poisoning a district judge who was substituted from the Elián's case after suffering a heart attack.[75] A few days later, he accused Elián Gonzalez' relatives of planning to purposely infect the boy so, once back in Cuba, he can transmit contagious diseases to Cuban leaders.[76] Sources close to Castro commented that the Comandante's latest hobby is a collection of particularly ugly, highly poisonous African snakes. They claim that Castro spends long hours watching his deadly pets, and proudly shows them to his terrorized visitors.

According to what we have seen above, sometimes Castro's photographic memory works selectively. His claims to Mankiewicz and Jones that "We have never believed in carrying out this type of activity of assassination of adversaries. Never.", are highly misleading.[77] Contrary to what he said to Jean Daniel when he heard the news of the Kennedy assassination, Fidel Castro's background actually shows that, far from being "furiously hostile" to political assassination, he actually has always been very fond of it.

A Furiously Castro-hostile View of JFK's Assassination

When Senator George McGovern took at face value Castro's answers to his questions, he was either too naïve, or just another victim of Castro's powers of fascination. Any intelligence analyst will agree that an evaluation of Fidel Castro's version of the Kennedy assassination would be close to E-4, that is, source unreliable and accuracy of the information doubtful. (See Appendix 3) Or perhaps McGovern was just another ignorant politician, because most of the information about Castro's president-killing inclinations has been available in the public record for many years for anyone to see.

The fact that the Kennedy brothers were out to get Castro has been extensively documented. Also, the evidence indicates that Castro knew all the time of the assassination attempts. On September 7, 1963, a few months before the Kennedy assassination, Castro referred to the assassination attempts against him in a speech, adding that Kennedy and his brother would take care of themselves, since they, too, might become targets.[78]

After Kennedy was killed in Dallas, the CIA engaged in an extraordinary cover-up operation. Though many facts pointed to a Castro connection, the CIA literally erased all links between Castro and the Kennedy assassination. Facts like Oswald's arrest in New Orleans while distributing pro-Castro pamphlets, his presentation on a New Orleans radio program defending Castro, and his visit to the Cuban consulate in Mexico City, were either ignored, interpreted as disinformation or treated as non-relevant. CIA counterintelligence Chief James J. Angleton even went to the point of calling Bill Sullivan of the FBI and rehearsing with him the misleading answers they would give to the Warren Commission investigators.[79]

Both Castro's reaction to the assassination and the American liberal media's explanation of the rationality of his position are in total contradiction with Castro's previous behavior. First of all, contrary to American wishful thinking, Castro never sought, nor has he ever been seeking (and probably will never seek), the normalization of his relations with the United States. A relatively recent incident, in which he ordered two civilian airplanes to be shot down, is further evidence of this. Castro's anti-American vendetta is his only *raison d'être*, so it doesn't make any sense that he was going to change precisely at that time. Secondly, the normalization of relations with the United States would have had no effect on the stabilization of the Castro regime, for the simple reason that the main destabilizing force in Cuba has never been the United States, but Castro himself. It doesn't make any sense either, as some have indicated, that the normalization of relations with the U.S. would have allowed Castro to channel funds and labor he was investing in weapons to economic projects desperately needed by the Cuban people. Living himself in opulence, Castro has never cared much for the desperate needs of the Cuban people. Investing in weapons and other means of mass destruction is his main hobby. No wonder Cubans call him, among many other nicknames, "*Armando Guerra,*" a common Hispanic name which is also a pun for "making war."

The answers to the question Who killed Kennedy?, range from the logical and probable to the incredible and the bizarre—with the Warren report theory of the lone madman placed at the incredible side of the spectrum. I am not going to try to provide here another answer to the enigma. As a matter of fact I think that the relevant question is not actually who killed Kennedy, but why nobody tried to kill him at least one year before.

If you read what has been published about both John and Robert Kennedy, even including the rosy stories written by court historians like Arthur Schlesinger and friends like Ben Bradlee and Ted Sorensen, you arrive at the conclusion that the Kennedy brothers were total jerks. There is abundant information available showing the total lack of respect for the rule of law prevailing in the Kennedy administration. As Henry Hurt pointed out, there was a wholesale abandonment of morality in Kennedy's Camelot, and it reached a point where murder was acceptable.[80]

Many people had enough reasons for wanting to kill President Kennedy. At the top of the list were the anti-Castro Cubans in the U.S.,[81] FBI's director J. Edgar Hoover, some important people at CIA,

Fidel Castro, the Mafia, and the South Vietnamese, just to mention a few. Anyway, it is possible that, thanks to whoever killed John F. Kennedy, this country was spared a return to monarchy, with the Kennedy-Camelot dynasty forever in power at the White House.

On the other hand, if the anti-Castro Cubans or the South Vietnamese did it, it cannot properly qualify as an assassination, but as the well deserved execution of a common criminal and a traitor.[82] In any case, the fact that both Kennedys, who spent so much time and effort planning assassinations, were themselves the targets of one, is a sort of crooked poetic justice. In a very direct way, President Johnson rightly expressed it when he confessed to Pierre Salinger: "Sometimes I think that, when you remember the assassination of Trujillo and the assassination of President Ngo Dinh Diem, what happened to Kennedy may have been divine retribution."[83]

On several occasions Fidel Castro has categorically denied any knowledge or participation in the Kennedy assassination, but the facts point to the contrary. For a long time there have been rumors in the media that, during his visit to the Cuban Consulate, Lee Harvey Oswald expressed his intentions to kill President Kennedy. Cuban Consulate employees Eusebio Azcue and Rubén Durán, the ones who talked to Oswald during his visit, claimed that they heard no such threat, and so the fact remains a mystery. But there is at least one important person who believed they were not telling the truth. Clarence Kelly, Hoover's replacement as FBI Director, believed that Oswald actually made such a threat.

The story of Oswald's visit to the Cuban Consulate in Mexico City has always been surrounded by mystery. The CIA claimed that it did not know that Oswald had visited the Cuban Consulate until after the assassination. An explanation given *a posteriori* by Richard Helms was that CIA denials were intended to protect the Agency's sources there. But some people believe the denial was actually intended to cover something even more troubling than the fact that the CIA knew about Oswald's threats to kill Kennedy.

FBI's Director J. Edgar Hoover told the Warren Commission that Castro mentioned Oswald's threat to a Bureau's source known by the code name "Solo," but this fact was withheld from the American public. Solo's file was released in early 1995 by the National Archives, and there are clues in it to suggest that "Solo" was probably Morris Childs. The file shows that Solo-Childs informed the FBI about Castro's knowledge of Oswald's threats.

Kelly is convinced that during his visit to the Cuban Consulate, Oswald "definitely offered to kill President Kennedy." He added that the "Solo" source in Cuba "verified that Oswald had offered to kill the American president." Kelly's use of the word "verified" instead of "discovered" seems to be hinting that the CIA knew about this and did not inform the FBI. Also, there are indications that, at some time before the assassination, the Cuban bureau at the CIA developed a keen operational interest in Oswald.[84]

But this is not the only disturbing fact linking Fidel Castro to the assassination of President Kennedy. On January 8, 1959, just a few days after Castro's victory over Batista's forces, Jack Ruby made a contact with Robert (Dick) McKeown, from Bashore, Texas, a gun-runner who had been supplying Castro with arms. A few weeks later, on February 1, Ruby met McKeown in Kemah, Texas, and offered him $25,000 for a personal introduction to Castro.

On April 27, 1959, after concluding his first trip to the United States following his victory, Castro traveled to Houston. Next day, he met with McKeown and offered him a post in the Cuban government. McKeown turned Castro's offer down.

On july 8, 1959, Castro ordered that an important CIA asset, Santos Trafficante, Jr., Florida numbers-racket boss and key man in the Lansky gambling empire in Havana, be detained and eventually expelled from Cuba. In the meanwhile, Trafficante was held in a jail not far from Havana. Some witnesses claim that Trafficante's conditions in Castro's jail were privileged.

On September 5, 1959, Jack Ruby flew to Havana where he spent several days. There is evidence that he visited Trafficante in his cell more than once. On September 12 Ruby flew again to Havana from Miami, returning the same day. U.S. Immigration and Naturalization records about Ruby's first visit to Havana are non-existent or missing, although they show that he did fly from Miami to Havana, and then from Havana to New Orleans on September 13.[85]

But there is more than meets the eye in the Castro-Trafficante connection. Some people, including some CIA officers, suspect that Castro had managed to turn Trafficante into his agent. It was Trafficante, then, the one who had been providing Castro with inside information about CIA-Mafia attempts to kill the Maximum Leader. There were rumors at the time among Cuban exiles in Miami, that when Castro ran the Mafia racketeers out of Cuba and seized the casinos, he put Trafficante in jail to cover up the fact that Trafficante was working for him.[86]

Even more, there is strong evidence that, in September of 1962, Trafficante hinted that Kennedy was going to be assassinated. In a conversation with José Alemán, a wealthy Cuban exile, Trafficante said, "Mark my words, this man Kennedy is in trouble and he will get what is coming to him." When Alemán suggested that Kennedy would probably get reelected, Trafficante replied, "No, José, he is going to be hit."[87] Some people interpreted this conversation as evidence that the Mafia was behind the president's assassination. However, if it is true, as evidence seems to indicate, that at the time Trafficante was in fact a Castro asset, Trafficante's words take on a totally different meaning.

Alemán was convinced that Trafficante had ties with Cubela, and that both Trafficante and Cubela were working for Castro. Though Alemán did not know at the time that Trafficante was the point man for the CIA's attempts to kill Castro, or that the CIA had recruited Rolando Cubela to do the job, he had a strong suspicion that Trafficante and Cubela were "linked", and that "something was wrong in some way." Alemán's suspicions were based mainly on the fact that he believed Cubela was a closet Castroist, and that Trafficante's *bolita* (numbers racket) revenues were used to pay off Castro's secret agent in the U. S.[88] Even though he was unaware of it, Alemán's suspicions had been expressed in a very similar way on a Federal Bureau of Narcotics memo dated July 21, 1961, reporting rumors that Castro had put Trafficante in jail merely "to make it appear that he had a personal dislike for Castro, when in fact Trafficante is an agent of Castro," and his "outlet for illegal contraband in the country." The memo went on to confirm Alemán's suspicions about the *bolita* scheme, stating that, "Fidel Castro has operatives in Miami making heavy bets with Santos Trafficante Jr.'s organization."[89]

On March 16, 1977, Santos Trafficante was summoned before the House Assassinations Committee and asked if he had known or discussed with anybody information that President Kennedy was going to be assassinated. Trafficante refused to answer, citing his Constitutional right to avoid self-incrimination.[90] He likewise remained silent when asked if he had been visited by Jack Ruby in Cuba in 1959. The Committee reported that there was "considerable evidence" that such an encounter "did take place."[91]

There are even more loose ends pointing to a Castro connection. First, there is information that on November 22, 1962, the very same day Kennedy was shot in Dallas at 12:30 p.m., a "mysterious passenger" departed from Mexico City to Havana after arriving from the United States in a highly irregular way. According to the Senate Committee report,

> On December 1, 1963, CIA received information that a November 22 Cubana Airlines flight from Mexico City to Cuba was delayed some five hours, from 6:00 p.m. to 11:00 p.m. E.S.T., awaiting an unidentified passenger. This unidentified passenger arrived at the airport in a twin-engine aircraft at 10:30 p.m. and boarded the Cubana Airlines plane without passing through customs, where he would have needed to identify him-

self by displaying a passport. The individual traveled to Cuba in the cockpit of the Cubana Airlines plane, thus again avoiding identification by the passengers.[92]

Moreover, in June, 1976, the Church Committee disclosed that CIA and FBI files relating to the assassination of President Kennedy contained references to the mysterious movements of a "pro-Castro Cuban-American" who flew to Cuba shortly after the events in Dallas.[93] According to the Senate Committee Report, at least one source told the CIA that this Cuban-American might have been involved in the assassination of President Kennedy. It is also believed that he was a member of the Tampa, Florida, branch of the Fair Play For Cuba Committee, to which Lee Oswald had once written. Evidence surfaced years later shows that the mysterious passenger was Miguel Casas Sáez, a close associate of Raúl Castro. Casas, who was fluent in Russian, had been in Dallas from early November to the 22nd.[94]

But apparently Casas was not the only Castro agent in Dallas the day of the assassination. James Johnston, a Washington lawyer who has studied the assassination in detail, wrote about the strange behavior of an alleged Cuban-American named Gilberto Policarpio López, a sort of Oswald's double. "Like Oswald," wrote Johnston, "he had recently applied for a Cuban visa but it had been denied. Like Oswald, he was living alone because of alleged marital problems. Like Oswald, he contacted with the Fair Play for Cuba Committee."[95] After getting a Mexican visa, López flew from Tampa to Texas on November 20th, and entered Mexico the day after the assassination. According to Johnston, López was the only passenger on board on a Cubana Airlines flight to Havana on November 27th.

But for some strange reasons the FBI failed to follow up on information received by CIA headquarters from its Mexico Station on December 3, 1963, about the suspicious activities of Casas and López. Though López' itinerary was confirmed by several sources, the FBI failed to investigate him. Even more, there is a March 20, 1964, memo from Mexico Station to the CIA Director, stating that one of their sources heard that "Gilberto López, U.S. citizen, was involved in President Kennedy's assassination."

Finally, there is the undeniable fact that Castro *did* threaten to kill President Kennedy. In an impromptu interview with Associate Press correspondent Daniel Harker while attending a reception at the Brazilian Embassy on September 7, 1963, Castro delivered a very clear warning to the Kennedy brothers. Talking about the attempts by the Kennedys to "get" him, he said that the members of the Kennedy administration would find themselves in danger if they persisted in their behavior, adding, "We are prepared to fight them and answer in kind.

United States leaders should think that if they are aiding terrorist plans to eliminate Cuban leaders, they themselves will not be safe." Castro's words to Harker, including his warning to the Kennedys, appeared on September 9, 1963, in the New Orleans *Times-Picayune*. The *New York Times* published the interview, but cautiously deleted the most important portion of Castro's warning. Fidel ended his message with a threatening note: "Let Kennedy and his brother Robert take care of themselves since they, too, can be the target of an attempt which will cause their death."

The timing of Castro's threat is revealing because it happened the very same day CIA headquarters was informed of the first attempt to recruit Rolando Cubela, a senior official in the Castro government, with the intention of inducing him to assassinate Castro. The operation is referred to in official CIA documents by its cryptograph, AM/LASH. But there is evidence indicating that Cubela was actually a double agent working for Castro.[96] Therefore, it seems that Castro knew of the CIA's plan, either through Cubela or through some other asset right in Langley.

Though many authors have tried to downplay or completely ignore the importance of Castro's words, there is evidence that his threat of reprisals against American leaders was considered serious enough as to trigger some reaction from the Kennedy Administration. The Special Group in the National Security Council, augmented by Attorney General Robert Kennedy and General Maxwell Taylor, which supervised the CIA's covert activities against Cuba, discussed Castro's words and designated a special committee to weigh the risks of continuing with their anti-Castro activities. The committee met on September 12 at the Department of State. According to a memorandum of the meeting, the members agreed that "there was a strong likelihood that Castro would retaliate in some way . . ." But they concluded that the specific possibility of "attacks against U.S. officials" was "unlikely."[97] It seems that, as it happens most of the time, they grossly underestimated Fidel Castro.

On October 7, just a few weeks after the incident at the Brazilian embassy, Castro repeated his threat. After delivering a long speech, Castro answered questions to foreign reporters. He accused the U.S. as the perpetrator of an undeclared war against Cuba, and blamed Kennedy for the responsibility. Then, in another direct threat, Castro stated emphatically, "They [the Kennedy administration] are our enemies, and we know how to be their enemies."[98]

To the above evidence I would like to add one from my own personal experience. The day Kennedy was assassinated I was working for one of the enterprises of the Cuban Ministry of Foreign Trade, after being released from active duty in the Army just a few months before. As soon as he heard the news of the assassination, Castro ordered a full mobilization of the Cuban armed forces, including the reserve and the militia. Half an hour after I heard the news on the radio I got a phone call from my reserve military unit ordering me to present myself immediately for active duty. Less than three hours later we were in the trenches, ready to fight an American invasion.[99]

With the benefit of hindsight now I see that some things were not quite right. When I arrived at my unit, about an hour after Castro ordered the mobilization, the trucks were ready, waiting to bring us to our positions. How had they managed to get the drivers, who were also reservists like myself, so quickly to the unit? Normally, giving the state of combat readiness of Cuban reserve units at the time, this type of mobilization normally would have taken no less than twelve hours to bring the men to the field. How come it worked so fast this time? When we reached our combat positions even the cooks were already there, apparently waiting for us to arrive. I have participated in many mobilizations before and after, and none of them worked as well as this one. But now a question comes to my mind. Was Castro aware that something would come up? Had the armed forces been put on alert beforehand for some upcoming military action?

Was Fidel Castro the Hidden Hand?

Historians believe in synchronicity and coincidences, intelligence officers don't. To any intelligence officer it would have seemed a strange coincidence that, just a few days before the Kennedy assassination, Castro had given, following his own suggestion, an interview to Jean Daniel. It was an even stranger coincidence that, at the very moment in which Kennedy was assassinated and a few hours after a senior CIA officer had a secret meeting with double agent Cubela to discuss Fidel's assassination, Castro was engaged in a friendly conversation with Daniel in which Castro said many rosy things about the American President.

The meeting with Daniel was very handy, because it allowed for Castro's friendly feelings toward Kennedy to be recorded for posterity by a respectable, easily verifiable independent source. But one must keep in mind that the Fidel Castro who told Daniel so many nice things about Kennedy, was the very same Fidel Castro who never lost an opportunity to berate the American president. He was also the one who, just a few weeks earlier, had threatened the Kennedys with retaliation in kind for their attempts to assassinate him.

The theory that Castro had absolutely nothing to do with the assassination of President Kennedy cannot stand a serious analysis.

Castro had the motive, the ability, the means, and the opportunity to have ordered the assassination of President Kennedy. Even more, like many experienced criminals, he was clever enough to create a perfect alibi, backed by a respectable, impartial witness.

In the first place, as I have shown above, Castro had sufficient motives to order President Kennedy's assassination. When the Church Committee developed the details of the Kennedy plots to kill Castro (which the Kennedy admirers disingenuously refer to as the CIA-Mafia plots), it established that Castro had ample reason to retaliate and seek the death of the American President. Even more, Kennedy had humiliated Castro, something that the Maximum Leader never takes easily or ever forgets.

Perhaps President Kennedy believed that Fidel Castro was just another Diem, easy to get rid of. But Fidel Castro was no Diem. Political assassination has never been alien to Castro, and his activities as a gangster at the University of Havana have been widely documented, as well as the fact that he is an expert in retaliating in kind.

Secondly, Castro had the ability to commit that type of crime. Very early in his political career he initiated himself in the art of political assassination, and has been practicing it for many years. Also, as I have shown above, he is very good at it, because he has never been caught. But, perhaps blinded by the arrogance of power that seems to emanate from the White House, President Kennedy failed to notice that he and his brother were amateur assassins dealing with a professional.

The fact that Castro is a professional assassin was acknowledged by a qualified colleague. Sam Giancana warned his associate Johnny Rosselli to be very careful with Castro because, "He's an assassin. He knows all the tricks."[100] But President Kennedy, like many others, ignored Castro's warning signs and paid with his life for his gross mistake.

Thirdly, Castro also had the means to carry out an assassination attempt on President Kennedy. The sophistication and efficiency of Castro's secret services and his network of agents operating freely among the thousands of Cubans in the United States has been documented. It would have been very easy for Castro to use his agents in place or infiltrate one or several hit teams into the United States to carry out his wet affairs.[101] It is well known that Castro's hit men were operating in the U.S. As UPI reporter Edward McCarthy revealed, at the moment President Kennedy was killed, four hit teams of Castro's assassins were actually in the United States.[102]

Finally, there is no doubt that Castro had the opportunity to order the assassination. We will never know, for sure, because there is no way we can check his whereabouts during the days prior to the assassination, but his threats were plain and clear.

But the fact that Castro had the motive, the ability, the means and the opportunity has been amply documented, though perhaps not to the extent it deserves.[103] What has remained unknown to the American public, however, is the fact that Fidel Castro always has shown a strong inclination to commit that particular type of crime.

We may safely surmise that, as a young student with the Jesuits, Castro was inculcated with the idea that killing presidents was right. In 1947 he tried to convince his friends to kill President Grau. That same year he actively conspired to kill Dominican Republic President Trujillo. In 1948 he was part of a mob marching to the Colombian Presidential Palace to kill President Ospina, and probably was involved in the assassination of presidential candidate Gaitán. In 1951 he tried to convince some friends to kill President Prío. In 1953 he participated in two different conspiracies to kill President Batista. In 1959 he tried to kill President la Guardia of Panama, Dominican Republic's President Trujillo, Nicaragua's President Somoza, and Haiti's President Duvalier. Later he tried to kill President Chiari of Panama and Venezuela's President Betancourt. In 1963, and again in 1964, he tried to kill President Valencia of Colombia. Also, there are strong suspicions that he was involved in the 1979 assassination of ex-President Somoza of Nicaragua by a Sandinista hit team. Moreover, there are suspicions that in 1976 he planned to assassinate both President Gerald Ford and his contender Ronald Reagan.[104]

Fidel Castro has always felt an irrational, visceral hatred for democratically elected presidents. It seems that these strong feelings have not tempered with age. Sources close to the Cuban leader have commented that, since late 2000, Castro has expressed in many occasions a strong hatred for presidents Francisco Flores of El Salvador, Vicente Fox of Mexico, Fernando de la Rúa of Argentina, and American president George W. Bush. Of lately, after the condemnation in Geneva of his regime's gross violations of human rights, the black list of presidents he wants to destroy has grown considerably. Costa Rica's President Miguel Angel Rodríguez, Panama's Mireya Moscoso, Guatemala's Alfonso Portillo, Uruguay's Jorge Batlle, and Canada's Prime Minister Jean Chrétien have been added to Castro's hit list. However, the same sources affirm that the main focus of Castro's hatred are President Vaclav Havel of the Czech Republic and Mexican Chancellor Jorge Castañeda.[105] Knowing of Castro's strong magnicidal inclinations and practical experience, one may guess that the lives of these people are in grave danger.[106]

Given his previous efforts to kill presidents, one can state without any shadow of a doubt that Castro not only had the motive, the ability, the means and the opportunity, but also the inclination to order such an incredible thing as the assassination of an American President. Moreover, given the fact that most people act consistently with their past conduct, one can safely assume that Castro at least was planning to assassinate President Kennedy. On the other hand, after knowing of John Kennedy's attempts to assassinate Castro, as well as the American president's role in the 1963 assassination of President Ngo Dinh Diem of South Vietnam, not to mention the assassinations of Trujillo and Patrice Lumumba,[107] one may well say that both Mafia capos, Castro and Kennedy, had a penchant for assassinating presidents. Castro, however, was by far the best.

As I mentioned above, like all professional criminals, Castro created a perfect alibi when he called Jean Daniel for an interview at exactly the time the assassination of President Kennedy was taking place. It is a common practice in intelligence business to use journalists as unwitting vehicles to pass disinformation. Castro's use of Jean Daniel is very similar to Kennedy's use of Tad Szulc, then a *New York Times* correspondent, when the President called Szulc to the White House on November 9, 1961, and asked him, "What would you think if I ordered Castro to be assassinated?" Szulc replied that he did not foresee Castro's killing necessarily leading to any change in Cuba, and that he did not think that the United States should be party to political assassinations. To this Kennedy replied, "I agree with you completely." And then he continued for several minutes stating that he and his brother felt "the United States for moral reasons should never be in a situation of having recourse to assassination."[108]

In a speech he gave on November 16 at the University of Washington, Kennedy elaborated upon the subject. He shamelessly declared, "We cannot, as a free nation, compete with our adversaries in tactics of terror, assassination, false promises, counterfeit mobs and crises." And that brings us to an interesting phenomenon that permeates American thinking of both the Right and the Left.

When President Kennedy told some friends that he was going to cut the CIA's wings, he was actually putting in practice a disinformation technique called "plausible denial." One has to be very naïve to believe even for a second that the CIA would try to kill a foreign leader without an express, or at least implied, order from the highest levels of the U.S. government—that is, from the President himself. Contrary to Church's claims, the CIA has never been a "rogue elephant." On the contrary, the CIA has always been the hidden arm of the American president, and Kennedy was using it to its fullest.

As Robert R. Simmons, a former staff director of the Senate Select Committee on Intelligence and a former CIA officer himself, put it bluntly: "What you had was an elephant taking orders from the White House," and added, "The president and his men were instructing the elephant."[109] Kennedy blamed the CIA for his own actions which caused the Bay of Pigs debacle, and promised that he was going to clip its wings, because one of the main functions of the CIA is to take the blame for the failures. What he actually did, however, was to reinforce the CIA's organization.

But, at the bottom of their minds, some Americans, Right and Left, cannot escape from their racist biases. Out of their white Anglo-Saxon superiority complex, they can easily accept the idea of President Kennedy using his cleverness and guile trying to assassinate Fidel Castro, but cannot understand how an "inferior" Cuban can be so bold and clever as to use the very same technique of plausible denial in ordering the assassination of the President of the United States. This simply goes beyond the limits of their narrow minds.

This superiority complex is so widespread than it also permeates the CIA. Talking to his officers after several Cuban double-agents were exposed, CIA's deputy director for operations Richard F. Stolz blamed his officers' sloppy performance on "ethnic egotism." According to him, it caused the ability of Latin Americans to be underestimated.[110]

The case of Senator McGovern asking Castro face to face if he had ordered the Kennedy assassination may be an example of naïvete or stupidity, but I don't think McGovern was naïve or stupid. Then, how can we explain such foolish behavior? As the Tower Commission Report stated, the disclosure of even the existence of a covert operation could have threatened its effectiveness and risked embarrassment to the government ordering it. As a result, there was strong pressure to withhold information, to limit knowledge of the operation to a minimum number of people and to deny it at all costs.[111] These techniques are known as need-to-know and plausible denial, and they have been used, and still are used, over and over by the American government and its intelligence agencies.

McGovern and others like him apparently believe that low, "inferior" races don't have the capacity for deception and guile that the superior Anglo-Saxon race has. E. Howard Hunt may have been capable of an assassination attempt, but not Fidel Castro. John F. Kennedy may have used the technique of plausible denial, but not Castro. It seems that McGovern was simply refusing to accept the possibility that a Latin American "rice-and-beans eater" had outfoxed and outmaneuvered some of the most powerful and clever men in Washington.

To McGovern's eyes, and to the eyes of most American liberals, Castro is a sort of Roussean *bon sauvage*, who is supposed to answer with the truth and nothing but the truth to any *gringo*'s questions. But McGovern apparently ignored that, as John F. Kennedy would have loved to put it in his earthy language, even "low-level" races have their fair share of high-level sons of bitches.

Fidel Castro, for one, has never been impressed by the Anglo-Saxons' superiority, particularly by their ability to deceive and lie. On the contrary, being a racist himself, Castro is fully convinced of the inferiority of the Anglo-Saxon race. He is known for bragging to members of his inner circle that *gringos* are too clean-cut, too naïve, too "*come mierdas*,"[112] (shit-eaters) to play the game of deception as well as Hispanics. For him, killing Kennedy may have been the ultimate high; his way to show the almighty Americans that a Hispanic could beat the *gringos* at their game in their home field.[113] It was, in fact, the ultimate way of humiliating an enemy; like an ancient warrior riding alone into an enemy camp and raping the chief's wife.[114]

It adds weight to the argument expressed above the fact that one of the things that characterizes Castro is that he has always treated Americans the very same way some Americans treat the rest of the world: with total arrogance and contempt. But Castro's behavior is so unusual that Americans seem unable to understand it. A key element to understand Castro's mindset is in a letter he wrote to President Roosevelt on November 6, 1940 (see Appendix 2). Castro's words are revealing: "I am twelve years old, I am a boy but I think very much I do not think that I am writing to the President of the United States." What Castro was trying to express in his broken English was simply that he didn't give a damn who President Roosevelt was; that, even though he was just a young Cuban student at a Catholic grade school, he felt himself as important as the President of the United States.

I would venture to say that, if Fidel ordered the assassination of President Kennedy, he actually may have been symbolically assassinating President Roosevelt, the very first American who humiliated him and deeply hurt his feelings by refusing to send him a "ten dollars bill green american." And one must keep in mind that it is very easy for Castro to feel humiliated and that he never forgets a humiliation. He told an American reporter that the main reason why he ordered his MiGs to shoot down two civilian planes of Brothers to the Rescue in March, 1996, was because the planes were dropping leaflets on Havana and, "it was so humiliating."[115]

I don't claim that the facts I have presented above prove beyond any reasonable doubt that Castro ordered the assassination of President Kennedy. Both Castro and Kennedy were aware that this type of criminal action is one of the most difficult to prove, and that is precisely why they resorted to it. Castro trusts nobody, and he works as secretly as he dares. In that way he can take risks, and cover them if he fails. He shares no information with his subordinates, who know nothing and only act on orders. He always keeps his plans from every one.

As in any intelligence report, however, you identify assumptions, search for facts, and leave it to others to arrive at the conclusions. What I want to point out is that, although there is no conclusive evidence, there is overwhelming circumstantial evidence indicating that, at least, the Castro connection to the assassination of President Kennedy is as valid as the CIA one—and, given the strange coincidence of interests between Castro and the CIA,[116] there is even the remote possibility that both of them may have been just different sides of the same coin . . . and not only because Jeanne Dixon got it psychically.

Chapter 5

Fidel's Sociolism

> *"Fidel screwed us with his communism, and now he's screwing us again with his capitalism."*
> — Overheard in Havana in 1999

> Fidel Castro- *A Trillion dollar bill? May I see it?*
> Homer Simpson- *Mr. Burns, I think we can trust the President of Cuba!*
> Burns- *Oh, all right.*—Hands Castro the trillion dollar bill— *Alright, now give it back!*
> Fidel Castro—Puts the bill in his pocket— *Give what back?*
> —The Simpsons

A few years after Fidel Castro took power in Cuba, Ramón Grau San Martín, a former Cuban president with a reputation for wit and corruption, told a friend, "Those honest kids," said Grau referring to Castro and his associates, "will manage with their honesty to accomplish what we, the traditional corrupt politicians, never were able to do: totally destroy this country." In retrospective, it seems that Grau was right, but just on one count. If it is true that Castro and his cronies have totally destroyed Cuba, it is no less true that they have proved to be more corrupt than all the politicians of the old school.[1]

According to Carlos Franqui, in the past there were many plantations in Cuba; now the whole Island has turned into a big plantation, and it belongs to Fidel Castro. "Who enjoys the fruits of the revolution, the houses of the rich, the luxuries of the rich? The *Comandante* and his court."[2]

The Cuban Economy Before Castro

American Liberals usually approach the issue of Third World revolution from a simplistic point of view: The real cause, they claim, is not external subversion but injustice, poverty and deprivation. If Latin America were not racked with injustice, they say, there would be no cause for revolution.

But liberals seem to ignore the cold hard facts. While economic and social conditions remained more or less the same in Latin America, since Fidel Castro came to power in Cuba in 1959 rebellious attempts in the region increased ten-fold. This may be just a matter of coincidence, but there are indications that such is not the case. Castro's direct efforts to create subversion and unrest in the region, beginning just a few days after he took power in Cuba in 1959, have been extensively documented in detail. On the other hand, no one can claim that injustice, poverty and deprivation in Latin America are now a thing of the past. But, since economic realities in Cuba after the fall of the Soviet Union forced Castro to reduce to a minimum his subversion attempts, the region, notwithstanding some isolated outbursts, no longer seems ripe for revolution. What happened then? The truth is that, though social injustice, poverty and deprivation are still there, Castro's subversive efforts almost disappeared, and with them the idea of a Latin American Castroist revolution.

Moreover, nobody can seriously deny that currently injustice, poverty and deprivation in Castro's Cuba is higher than in most Latin American countries. But, while many Latin American countries have seen their governments destabilized by Castro-backed guerrilla movements, the Castro government, free from Castro's own destabilizing efforts, has shown 42 years of continuous stability almost unprecedented in the region.

The most widely accepted theory explaining the Cuban revolution is that its main cause was the horrible economic condition in the Island. But there is something in these theories trying to explain *a posteriori* the causes of the Cuban revolution that do not ring true. Contrary to the view spread by Castro-friendly authors, when Fidel took power in Cuba the economic indexes for the Island were the highest in the world among the nonindustrial countries. Actually, in economic development Cuba was right behind the eight or ten leading industrial countries.

If one is to believe Jean-Paul Sartre, Cuba before 1959 was a vast sugar plantation, a Caribbean gulag where the American slave masters exploited an undernourished and sick people. According to the French philosopher's vision, Cuba was a country whose blood was been slowly sucked out by the American imperialist octopus.[3] The facts, however, show a very different picture.

Granted, the claim that Cuba from 1902 to 1934 was an American protectorate and economic colony is not a leftist exaggeration, but this situation changed dramatically after the end of WWII. According to estimates of the International Monetary Fund, in 1957 Cuba ranked fourth in per capita income among the 20 Latin American republics. In 1957, the average Cuban had an annual income of $361 annually. This compared with $409 annually for Argentina, $281 for Brazil, $234 for Mexico, and $88 for Paraguay. The average for Latin America as a whole was $284. The 1957 per capita income of Cuba was about one-sixth of the United States, 90% that of Italy, significantly higher than that of Japan, and six times that of India. All these estimates are in dollars of 1957 purchase power. In a 1956 report on Cuba, the U.S. Department of Commerce concluded that "Cuban national income has reached levels which give the Cuban people one of the highest standards of living in the Americas."[4]

Pre-Castro economic development in Cuba was sound, and it had been fast. Contrary to the image found in most American books sympathetic to Castro, the fact is that the Cuban economy experienced a constant boom during Batista's administration. The economy Castro inherited was a growing, not a declining one. And much of that growth was the direct result of American investment and of the development of export markets for the Cuban economy.

Around 1956 the Cuban economy under President Batista began an upward swing, and 1957—the year that Castro began fighting his guerrilla war in the mountains—was one of the best years for the Cuban economy since the creation of the Republic at the beginning of the century. During 1957 Cuba's economic activity reached the highest level registered since World War II, and the average income per capita soared to $400.00, one of the highest in Latin America.[5]

In terms of purchasing power, the average Cuban worker was one of the highest paid in the world. According to statistics published in 1958 by the International Labor Organization, from a comparative standpoint the American worker earned an average of $4.06 per diem, the Cuban worker earned $3.00 per diem, while the West German worker earned $2.73 per diem (approx 8% less than the Cuban worker). The statistics also show that the Cuban agricultural worker's average wage was 3 pesos (the Cuban peso was then at par with the U.S. dollar) for an 8 hour working day. But when these wages are adjusted to reflect their real value as determined by their purchasing power, we have the following results: United States: $4.06; Cuba: $3.00; Denmark: $2.86; West Germany: $2.73; Belgium: $2.70; France $1.74.

An author has pointed out how "In habits, in tastes, in attitudes, in other ways too numerous to fully appreciate, with consequences impossible to measure, Cubans participated daily in North American cultural transactions. They became like North Americans . . .,"[6] adding, "In almost every important way Cuba was integrated directly into North American marketing strategies."[7] The standard of living and mind-set of average Cubans was so close to their American neighbors, that the Island was used by American corporations as a testing ground for their products. Some of them, like Ajax, Fab, some beer brands, and other products, were launched in the Cuban market several months before their debut in the American one. In the mid-fifties, the leading American telecommunication companies used Cuba to test their new microwave technology and, upon leaving, left a network that in some aspects was better than any in the United States at the time.[8] The nickel refining plant under construction in Nipe bay, left unfinished when Castro nationalized it, was probably the most technologically advanced in the world.

On the other hand, while Americans exerted a considerable control over the Cuban economy, there was a growing trend toward more and more control by Cubans over their country's economy and resources. In 1959 most branches of the Cuban economy, probably with the exception of the railroad, power and telephone companies, and large sugar mills, were owned by Cubans. According to United Nations sources, in 1958 Cubans owned 86% of the total capital invested in the Island while foreign investments, having declined steadily since 1933, amounted to only 14%.

The sugar industry, the main Cuban source of income, presented a similar picture. Total sugar production by foreign interests had declined from 78% in 1939 to 38% in 1958. A similar decline in foreign influence was evidenced in bank deposits. Deposits in foreign banks of money earned in Cuba represented 83.2% of total deposits in 1939, but by 1955 they had declined to 38%.

To be sure, there were economic differences in Cuba, but they were not much different from the ones we find today in the U.S., Japan, or Germany. I would venture to say that, as a result of some characteristics of the Hispanic culture and Cuban character, those differences were less marked than in other countries.

According to Fidel Castro and his close associates, Batista was little more than a pimp, selling off their country to degenerate foreigners.[9] The truth, however, is that notwithstanding Batista's excesses and the graft and corruption prevalent among his close associates, when Castro took power in Cuba in 1959 the Island was experiencing an economic bonanza.

A Cuban Robber Baron

It may well be that, at least initially, Fidel Castro was a well intentioned social bandit,[10] a Cuban Robin Hood who stole from the rich to give to the poor—keeping a percentage in the process as a commission for covering the growing costs of his stealing services. The problem began when most of the Cuban rich left the Island and the ones who remained became poor. As Castro was forced to steal from the poor to give to the poor, his commission kept growing, and now it is probably close to 95 percent.

Closely following the steps of his unscrupulous father, who made his fortune by stealing sugar and moving fences under the cover of the night with the help of his buddies, Fidel Castro surrounded himself with a circle of cronies as corrupt as himself. Soon after he came to power, Castro accomplished two important things. First, he got rid of non-corrupt leaders like Huber Matos and Camilo Cienfuegos and, secondly, he began an accelerated process of stealing other people's money and property.

Forty-two years later, there is no doubt that his initial plan worked to perfection. Today, Cuba is practically the personal property of Fidel Castro and a small group of shamelessly corrupt feudal landlords. The economic system Fidel Castro has imposed in Cuba is a crony capitalism economy of systemic corruption which uses the overt application of state power as a tool to enrich the ruler and his cronies. Granted, throughout history, and particularly in Latin America, most political systems have served to benefit the rulers, but under Castro's crony capitalism, systemic corruption is more widespread and better organized in Cuba than ever before.

Government has been defined as a form of organization for the benefit of the governed. But what Castro has created in Cuba is an organization for the benefit of the governors—that is, organized crime.

One of the many myths still surrounding Fidel Castro is his utmost disdain for money and his honesty. "For those who do not know Cuban history," wrote Herbert Matthews, "it needs to be pointed out that the Castro regime is the first honest government that Cuba has ever had—honest in the sense that its leaders have not enriched themselves. Whatever the future brings, Cubans know that Fidel Castro has no money deposited in the United States or Switzerland . . ."[11] In the same fashion, Castro-friendly Edward Boorstein wrote: "One of the first consequences of the victory of the Revolution was the elimination of corruption from government. Corruption under Batista had been incredible. The revolutionaries immediately set about to establish absolute standards of honesty for public officials." And he added,

"The leaders of the Revolution set personal examples of austerity and dedication. 'The guerrilla soldier,' writes Major Guevara, 'should be an ascetic.'"[12] But, contrary to Matthews' predictions and Boorstein's claims, the future brought a very different reality to Cubans.

Castro, who allegedly earns a modest salary in Cuban pesos as Cuban President and has no other sources of income, has actually amassed an incredible personal fortune. The July 28, 1997, issue of *Forbes* magazine listed Fidel Castro as one of the richest people in the world, with a net worth of $1.4 billion. However, *Forbes'* estimate of the funds that Castro actually controls may be lower than his true worth. It merely assigned him 10 percent of an estimate of Cuba's gross domestic product. But the truth is that, in addition to controlling the Cuban economy, Castro possesses and personally controls international bank accounts and large amounts of gold and commodities, and has done so virtually from the very moment he grabbed power over the Island in 1959.

Fidel Castro claims that he doesn't care for money, but he has a stash of cash totalling several million dollars hidden away in banks in Zürich and other financial centers of the very Capitalist world he claims to despise. He has a private fleet of large yachts, helicopters, planes and luxury cars, and keeps stately homes in each of Cuba's 14 provinces. While the Cuban people struggle with housing shortages, Castro reserves hundreds of houses in Havana's Jaimanitas beach section for the use of his security guards and aides. While Castro demands austerity from the people and watching American tv is prohibited, he and his close associates buy foreign luxury items and use government satellite dishes to tune in to U.S. televised movies and sporting events.

Until recently, Castro had managed to push forward his image as a socialist Mr. Clean in contrast to the image of widespread corruption in Latin America and Cuba's previous history. Now it seems that Mr. Clean has dirty hands. When *Forbes* published its estimate of Castro's personal fortune, some foreign observers believed that the revelation placed him in a difficult position before the Cuban people, because it tarnished his image as a sworn enemy of capitalism, constantly asking the Cuban people for sacrifices and austerity in the name of socialism. But that was not the case. Perhaps Castro fooled some of his admirers in the U.S., but he never fooled the Cuban people. From the very beginning Cubans changed the name of the political system Castro imposed in Cuba from *socialismo* to *sociolismo* (from *"socio,"* Cuban slang for "buddy" or "crony"), a tropical version of crony capitalism.[13]

Contrary to the image portrayed by some of his biographers, who paint Castro as a young, idealistic lawyer fighting for the rights of the poor and humble, the truth is that Fidel Castro never had a job and never made any money from his work.[14] The first and only case he defended in court was the one in which he represented himself as a defendant for the failed attack to the Moncada garrisons in Santiago de Cuba. Before 1959, Castro had only three known sources of income: the money his father periodically sent him; the money he borrowed from his friends; and the money his wife, Mirtha Díaz-Balart, gave him.[15]

Under the pretext of creating in Cuba an egalitarian, just society, Castro seized private country clubs, beach resorts, and other recreational facilities and made them available to the lower classes of the Cuban population. Soon after, he also deprived the upper classes of most of their properties. Under the Agrarian Reform Law large tracts of land were divided and distributed among poor farmers . . . to be taken away from them a few years later under the Second Agrarian Reform Law. Today, in a veritable tourist apartheid, most Cubans are denied access to beaches, hotels, and resorts, reserved for dollar-carrying tourists and Castro's cronies.

Likewise, some big homes left vacant by the wealthy leaving the country in drones in the early years of the revolution were used as housing for students. But, contrary to government propaganda, not all mansions were turned into schools. Most high-ranking army officers appropriated the best mansions for their personal use. Later, when Castro found out that the number of available mansions was much larger than the number of his cronies, he created the so-called *"zonas congeladas"* ("frozen areas"); whole areas in the best sections of the cities, where luxurious mansions are kept closed waiting for a Castroist crony to take them in the future as a gift from the magnanimous *Comandante en Jefe*. But, while Fidel and his cronies have been enjoying stolen goods and properties from the very beginning, initially they did it with discretion, trying at the same time to maintain their public image of simple, busy public officials working hard for the revolutionary government and the betterment of the new society.

Since Castro openly embraced "socialism," in the mid-sixties, he began a campaign appealing to the revolutionary sentiments of the people, like "socialist emulation," patriotism, disdain of selfish competition and individualism—in other words, nonmaterialistic incentives. The main goal of the new society Castro had in mind was the creation of the "new man," fully imbued with collectivist, egalitarian, and non-materialistic values. This new man was to prefer moral incentives over material ones, and his work would be based on a socialist morality, or *conciencia* (consciousness), rather than on material rewards—like money, for example. The strict rationing, introduced in 1962 and still in place after 40 years, guaranteed all Cubans, regardless of their personal wealth, equal access to basic necessities . . . or so the Castroist government claimed.

Apparently, however, Castro and his cronies never followed the example they were teaching the masses. As early as 1974 professor Edward Gonzalez reported, "Most Cubans must subsist on their meager monthly quotas of food and clothing and must accept overcrowded or substandard housing and inadequate public facilities. In contrast, government and party officials enjoy privileges and amenities that simply are not available to the rest of the populace, such as supplementary rations, preferential treatment in housing, access to state vehicles, and special dining privileges."[16]

Still, for more than three decades Castro and his cronies, with the complicity of the American liberal mainstream media, managed to maintain their public facade as honest, self-sacrificing managers. But those idealistic times are gone now. The privileged *nomenklatura* does not care anymore about its public image, and there is a noticeable trend to concentrate wealth in the hands of Castro and a few of his cronies.

Fidel's Happy, Good Life in His Proletarian Paradise

Though rumors ran for years all around Cuba about Fidel and his cronies' enjoyment of the *dolce vita*, all the information available amounted to just that: rumors. Telltale signs, however, that Castro and his close friends were not affected by the food scarcities the Cuban people have been chronically suffering were evidenced in their health. By the mid-seventies most Cubans were showing in their skins, nails, and hair the effects of long years of poor diets, and were rapidly becoming a nation of very skinny, unhealthy people. But, contrary to the general trend, Fidel and his cronies were putting on weight and their skin was showing the healthy luster characteristic of fat pigs ready for the slaughterhouse.

As early as 1968, Luis Conte Agüero, once a close friend of Fidel, wrote that Castro already was a multimillionaire, with huge accounts in Swiss banks.[17] Rumors ran that some people had seen Celia Sánchez, Castro's trusted secretary and confidant, discreetly sneaking in and out of banks in Zürich's Banhoffstrasse.[18] According to some sources these funds were used to pay for Fidel's subversive activities all around the world. Others claimed, however, that the main purpose of the accounts was to provide Fidel and his close circle of cronies with luxury items—ranging from cars and electronic equipment to clothing and food—unavailable on the Island.[19] A fact that gives some credibility to the rumors is that, though Cuba's trade with Switzerland is almost nonexistent, the National Bank of Cuba keeps a relatively large office in Zürich.

It was not until 1990, however, that the cat was let out of the bag. In those days Fidel was enjoying his favorite form of entertainment: badmouthing Russia and its leaders on a daily basis. Then, Soviet journalist Alexei Novikov, a correspondent for *Konsomoslskaya Pravda*, (most Soviet "journalists" made money on the side moonlighting for the KGB) retaliated in kind by publishing a long article that brought to light a first glimpse at Fidel's corrupt lifestyle. Though articles critical about Cuba in general had been appearing in the Soviet press, this was the first one that went after Fidel himself. U.S. officials believe that the details of Fidel's personal life were leaked to Novikov by Soviet intelligence officers unfriendly to Castro who considered Russia should loosen its ties with the Castro government.

"Castro's private life," wrote Novikov, "like the rest of the Cuban party and government élite, is shrouded under an impenetrable veil of total secrecy. Like most secrets, however, with time they become known."[20] According to Novikov, Fidel has 32 stately mansions scattered throughout the Island. In Havana alone he has three bunkers where, if need be, he could hide together with his retinue of 57 generals.

The article pointed out that Castro has a personal guard of more than 9,700 men located throughout the Island, with 2,800 of them in Havana. When Castro travels to any of Cuba's provinces, additional units are deployed, enlarging his personal security to up to 28,000 of the best trained troops. When Castro decides to go bathing or sailing on one of his three luxurious yachts, "all naval forces in the area go on alert, and a special unit of more than 122 divers comb the sea inch by inch looking for underwater mines or booby traps disguised as fish."[21]

When Novikov's piece appeared in Moscow, it provoked a violent reaction in the official Cuban media. A few days after, Novikov was the victim of a suspicious "accident" and was forced to leave Cuba.

Novikov's report apparently touched a raw nerve in Cuban official circles. A Mexican television crew in Moscow made the mistake of reporting on the story and immediately the Castro government expelled from Cuba a crew from the same network that was on assignment in Havana.

More recently, perhaps to counteract the growing discontent among the Cuban population because of the privileges enjoyed by Castro and his cronies, the Cuban intelligence created a propaganda campaign to restore their egalitarian image. Part of it was Estela Bravo's 75-minute documentary, "Fidel: 40 Years of the Cuban Revolution and its Leader," showing a flattering image of the Maximum Leader and his family as living a very simple, austere life, almost like the rest of the Cubans.[22]

Nevertheless, as Norberto Fuentes, a corrupt Cuban intelligence officer and writer now in exile, pointed out, "I think that when this [Castro's rule] ends, most people in Cuba will be outraged by the relative comforts of the leadership," he added, "and most people in Miami will be surprised by their low level of life."[23]

A Corrupt Tyrant

Fidel Castro has done a very good job of keeping the inner workings of his government safe from prying eyes. Information about corruption at all levels, however, is becoming available, though in a fragmented way, as high Cuban government officials defect and freely report their experiences in Cuba and a new wave of independent journalists courageously fight repression in informing the world about Castro's real Cuba.

Most of the background information appearing below comes from Jesús M. Fernández, a senior official in the Castro government who left Cuba in May 1996 after holding important positions in the Cuban government, including Secretary of the Food Committee of the Cabinet and Secretary of the Foreign Exchange Commission of the Food Group.[24]

Fidel Castro has total, direct access to a very large amount of money. This money is referred to by the innermost circles of the Castro government as "the Comandante's reserves." It had its origin in 1959 in the famous "Fidel's checking account." From this account—which proved to be an administrative nightmare to Cuban fiscal authorities, because, as Castro hates capitalism and accounting, it was not subject to any type of control or budget—Fidel Castro draws funds as he pleases. These almost unlimited funds were used to satisfy all manner of needs and requests throughout the Island, instantly creating an image of himself as a powerful benefactor or sugar daddy.

Castro's lust for money was so intense that finally a special account was created in his name, not related to his official titles, so he can manage it personally without anyone's authorization or control. This account, which initially was in Cuban pesos, served as precedent for later creating a dollar account to finance international transactions, primarily of a political nature, but eventually it was also used for obtaining more personal items ranging from expensive food and clothing to all types of sophisticated electronic gadgets from the corrupt capitalist world, which Castro seems to love.

This dollar account was also used to finance subversion in other countries and propaganda activities such as the meeting of the Tricontinental Conference. Though the amounts involved are not known, the account was financed from state funds and from the forced exchange of dollars from Cuban workers at the American Naval Base in Guantánamo. So, before Castro began stealing the Soviets' money in large quantities, he managed to, indirectly, steal the American taxpayer's money through Guantánamo base.

In 1970 it became known that the proceeds from the sale of cattle to Canada—the intermediary for which was Merejo Curbelo, brother of the Minister of Agriculture, Major Raúl Curbelo, one of Fidel's cronies—were deposited in Castro's account. The magnitude of the sale has been estimated at between $5 million and $10 million. Sales of cattle have continued to this day and have included Venezuela as a buyer. The cattle come from another of Fidel Castro's personal exclusive reserves, which contains some 50,000 head of cattle.

The Comandante's Reserves

In 1970, Emilio Quesada Rey, one of Fidel's cronies since his days at the University of Havana, created an integrated system of reserves under Castro's exclusive control. These reserves consisted of automobiles, trucks, tractors, and other vehicles, and general construction equipment. By then, reserves of housing, also managed by Fidel Castro, were already in existence. From these reserves Castro assigned resources to government enterprises without any sort of plan and provided gifts to many of his cronies, both at home and abroad.

In 1976, the State Committee for the Provision of Technical Material was created under the direction of Provisions of the Central Planning Board (JUCEPLAN). Irma Sánchez, a member of the Central Planning Board, was placed in charge of the new committee as Minister-President. The new committee would become the most powerful organ of the Cuban government, since it centralized the control of the country's physical resources, with the exception of foodstuffs, clothing, and shoes. The resources it managed included equipment and machinery, petroleum, and construction and raw materials.[25]

The new committee considerably expanded the reserves personally controlled by Fidel Castro. By then, those at JUCEPLAN who knew of the reserves began calling them "the Comandante's reserves." The reserve of automobiles, for example, came to number 7,000 units, which were stored in the area of Managua, south of Havana. The reserve of trucks, which also numbered in the thousands, was kept in Albero, in the area of El Cotorro in the province of Havana. These reserves were administered by Castro separately from the central planning system, which he himself did not trust.

Ignoring the plans set down by JUCEPLAN, Castro kept assigning resources and equipment only to pet projects he personally initiated and directed. This system caused a great deal of irritation among the middle-level economic planners, and it generated friction and strong disputes among Vice Ministers of the Central Planning Board Luis Gutiérrez, Irma Sánchez, Emilio Quesada, Osvaldo Dorticós (in charge of the Central Planning Board), and Fidel Castro himself. But by then the lines that could have separated what was public property managed by Castro and what was his private property had been erased. All of Cuba became, de facto, the sole property of the only capitalist remaining in the supposed socialist Island: Fidel Castro.[26]

At the start of the war in Angola, in the mid-1970s, Castro's financial reserves were funded in part by monies from the Soviet Union and the rest of the Soviet block for financing Cuban military operations in that country. To this he added the hard currency he was receiving from British Shell in the form of payments to the Cuban Army for "protecting" the Shell's refineries in Cabinda from "saboteurs." Later, the war in Ethiopia became another important source of income for the *Comandante en Jefe*. It is known that Castro profited from his participation in the African wars by stealing large quantities of ivory, diamonds, precious wood and other natural resources. By the late 1970s, Castro was making good profits from the loot his mercenary army was sending back home.

During its military operations in Africa the Cuban armed forces accumulated large quantities of canned food for possible war contingency. These reserves were located in Cuba and were maintained at great cost to the country because of the need to renew them frequently to keep them fresh. As the dollar became king in Cuba after its legalization in 1993,[27] these reserves have been turned over to military personnel as compensation for their lack of access to dollars and because the food reserves cannot be maintained fresh as before given the current Cuban economic crisis. However, despite the food scarcities prevalent in Cuba, the canned food reserves have never been used to supply the severe alimentary needs of the civilian population—which Castro conveniently blames on the American embargo.

Fidel's Business Enterprises

In the early 1980s, the sources of funds for the Comandante's reserves were diversified. New enterprises under secret ownership were created by Castro to generate funds outside the planning system he himself had created to fool the Soviets. To all practical effects, these business enterprises are the private property of Fidel Castro. They also serve to launder drug money, a fact that became known during the process leading up to the execution of General Arnaldo Ochoa in 1989. The most important of these enterprises are the following:

1. The Corporation CIMEX; a conglomerate of export and import enterprises that currently has chains of stores in Cuba that only sell in dollars. The most important of these is the chain Panamericana. Part of CIMEX is the Treviso company, initially run by Colonel Tony de la Guardia, another close crony of Castro who was shot together with General Ochoa in 1989. Treviso sells tobacco products, shellfish, and construction materials. It also produces counterfeits of high quality goods, such as Chivas Regal whiskey and Levi's jeans. CIMEX is believed to generate a minimum of $50 million a year, possibly much more.

2. The now defunct Department MC (for *Moneda Convertible*, convertible money—hard currency), an operation fully controlled by the Interior Ministry. This was a secret operation allegedly designed to get around the U.S. embargo on Cuba, though it soon became another source of revenues for Fidel and his cronies. This department generated several million dollars a year, which was presented Mafia-Don-style to Castro on his birthday, every August 13. The largest amount known involved a "gift" of $10 million dollars, delivered in a suitcase full of bills by José Abrahantes during one of Castro's birthday parties in the 1980s. Part of this money came from drug trafficking operations.

3. Another important source of Castro's money is Cubanacán, a group of enterprises founded by Abraham Maciques, a Cuban "entrepreneur" who is also one of Fidel's closest cronies.[28] Cubanacán is the enterprise that opens the door to foreign investment in tourism. Like CIMEX, it has several chains of stores that sell only in dollars. Cubanacán controls approximately $600 million in foreign capital, primarily from business enterprises like Meliá, LTI International, TRIP, Delta International, Golden Tulip International, Cosmo World, and Super Club. It is estimated that Cubanacán currently contributes around $30 million a year to the "Comandante's reserves." El Palacio de Convenciones (The Conventions Palace) is another enterprise that contributes its net earnings to the Comandante's private account. Its earnings are generated by international events held there, many of a political nature. The earnings it generates are on the order of $3 million to $5 million a year.

4. Cubalse; another important enterprise, consists of a single store that was originally dedicated to selling to the diplomatic community. It is now open to any member of the general public who has access to dollars. Cubalse is the only store that always has beef, which it sells at monopoly prices because it comes from Castro's cattle reserve, the only provider in the Island. Cubalse's net earnings go to enrich the Comandante's reserves. It is estimated that it generates net earnings on the order of $30 million a year.

5. MediCuba; a foreign trade enterprise that sells abroad pharmaceutical products manufactured in the country, especially vaccines and antibiotics, generates an unknown amount of revenue that is estimated to be several million dollars. Another important source of MediCuba's hard currency earning is through the sale of placentae and other fetal tissue, important raw products in the production of skin collagen and other pharmaceutical products. Since Castro grabbed power in Cuba, the country has consistently shown one of the highest abortion rates in the world. One of the reasons why the Cuban government encourages abortion is because it profits by keeping the women's placentae.[29]

While the Cuban government is exporting vaccines, antibiotics and other drugs, Castro keeps blaming the U.S. blockade for their scarcity in Cuba. As expected, Fidel Castro is the principal investor in the biotechnology sector. He is kept informed of research on AIDS and other programs in this field.[30]

In 1995 the Castro government enacted Law 77 approving foreign investments. That law allowed foreigners to acquire real estate in Cuba. Soon after, the economic departments of MINFAR (Armed forces) and MININT (Internal security) began selling real estate in the Island to Cubans residing abroad, mostly in the United States. The properties for sale are the ones previously stolen from their legal owners.

The main sales pitch for real estate is directed towards Cuban exiles whose relatives live in crumbling houses. Cuban exiles with dollars can buy better houses and apartments in Cuba and the Cuban government will allow their relatives in the Island to move to the newly acquired property. This is a great business idea because, as it has happened before, sooner or later the properties will be stolen again from the new owners, ending up in Castro's hands to be put on sale again. Sometimes the money from these transactions is deposited directly in American banks in the U.S. and sometimes it is sent to Cuba. Some observers speculate that senior MINFAR and MININT officers fear the Castro government will fall very soon, so they are saving all the money they get their hands on for their eventual retirement abroad.

The Comandante's Other Revenue Sources

In addition to the earnings of the enterprises mentioned above, the Comandante's reserves are also supplied from other transactions, possibly the largest of which was the sale of rum factories and distilleries under the Havana Club name to a French firm. The initial sale price was estimated at $50 million, an amount that reportedly was deposited in its entirety in the Comandante's reserves. This transaction continues to generate earnings for the Comandante's account through commissions from the sale of Cuban rums and through the currency exchange from the salaries of Cuban workers.

For a government so anti-American and anti-capitalist, the U.S. dollar is unashamedly venerated in Cuba by both black marketeers and state owned enterprises in a way unknown to most countries around the world. But, though the dollar has become the most sought after currency on the Island, Cuban workers working for foreign firms in Cuba are not paid directly in dollars. Following instructions specified in their contracts, foreign firms operating in Cuba pay in dollars to some of Castro's personal enterprises which, in turn, pay the Cuban workers in devaluated pesos. For every dollar the Castro regime receives, it pays the poor Cuban worker the equivalent of five cents to the dollar while keeping the other 95 cents of the dollar to engross Fidel's Swiss bank accounts.

In the 1970s Castro discovered the potential of exploiting the highly qualified Cuban work-force, and created overseas civilian programs, mostly involving construction workers. This program drained the Cuban domestic economy at a moment it could least afford to export construction workers and supplies. Notwithstanding the negative effects on the Cuban economy, Castro continues with the program because it generates the hard currency he and his cronies highly desire. The initial program opened the door for exporting other types of Cuban qualified workers, mostly health and education professionals. The success of these programs has been frequently reported by the Cuban media in laudatory terms.

What the Cuban media has never mentioned, however, is that, as in the case of Cuban workers working for foreign firms in Cuba, the ones working abroad don't get their pay directly from their employers. While working abroad, Fidel's "internationalist" workers are actually under contracts with Castro's enterprises, who receive market price in hard currency for the work and in turn pay devaluated Cuban pesos to the workers.

Cubans working abroad have to sign a "Return-to-Cuba-Contract" in which they are forced to give 75 percent of the salaries received abroad to the Castro government. Before receiving a government authorization for working abroad, workers must prove that they have no ties to Cuban exiles or dissident groups in Cuba, have never solicited a U.S visa, and don't have family members abroad (because Castro does not want to lose the average $100 to $300 monthly per person that many Cuban exiles in the U.S. send to their relatives in Cuba). This way, the "Marxist" *Comandante*, in cahoots with his capitalist partners, steals the surplus value of the Cuban workers and keeps the lion's share of their money. A very creative brand of modern slavery on Fidel's Cuban plantation,[31] not very different from the system Fidel saw in operation at Angel Castro's Birán plantation. No wonder a joke running in Cuba in the late seventies explained that capitalism was a cruel economic system based on the merciless exploitation of man by man, while in Castro's sociolism it was the other way around.

The unexpected success of the Buenavista Social Club, thanks to the efforts of Ry Cooder and later because of the success of Wim Wenders' documentary film, apparently took the Castro government by surprise. The initial reaction was to launch a disinformation campaign, created by the Cuban intelligence services and propagated by its agents abroad, claiming that the Buenavista musicians were not the true representatives of the Cuban music, and spreading false rumors that while Cooder was making millions, he was paying pennies to the musicians. More recently, however, Castro and his sociolist gangsters have changed their tune. In order to keep the millions for themselves while paying pennies to the musicians, the Castro government is trying to enforce on them the same rules applying to other Cubans working abroad. Rumors running in musician's circles in Havana tell that most of them are not happy at all with these attempts to take the lion's share from their hard-earned money.

A Castro-friendly author rhetorically asks herself, if Cuba needs hard currency so badly why it has not expanded its exports? And she provides a sensible answer, "The Castro regime has been unusually successful at human resource development, to the extent that it can afford to export trained personnel. Also, *it can do so at low cost*."[32] Like the slave masters of old, Fidel Castro discovered the economic advantages of slavery and created his own brand of the peculiar institution.[33] Paradoxically, the very same Americans who praise the Underground Railroad and the courage of the runaway slaves, are the ones who despise the runaway Cuban slaves who have escaped from Castro's plantation.[34]

A considerable part of the net earnings of several foreign enterprises engaged in the growing of citrus also goes to the Comandante's reserves. Gross estimates place these contributions at no less than $10 to $15 million a year. One of the best known entrepreneurs in this sector is Max Marambio, ex-chief of Salvador Allende's personal guard, now one of Fidel's cronies. Another is Angel Domper, who is married to one of Ché (the incorruptible) Guevara's daughters. These Chilean businessmen are believed to be millionaires.

In his biography of Fidel Castro, Herbert Matthews claimed that "Fidel's contempt for money went so far that when he first came to power in 1959 he even grumbled because banks were charging interest."[35] It seems, however, that the passage of time has mellowed Fidel's initial distaste for usury. Of lately, an important source of income to the Comandante's reserves comes from loans that Capitalist Castro makes to the Cuban national economy using the very same funds he previously has stolen from it. Whenever there is a shortfall in the flow of foreign exchange—something that occurs frequently in the importation of food and oil—government officials in charge of payment submit requests for loans through Carlos Lage, Prime Minister of Cuba and a close crony of Fidel. If Lage passes on the request, Castro generally approves the loan, noting the date the loan is due and the interest to be paid. The interest is normally 10 percent, regardless of the amount of the loan.

Though these loans are kept secret, two specific transactions are known, one of $20 million and the other of $30 million, for imported foodstuffs, mostly cereals, and there have been other occasions involving the import of oil. Back in the days when the Soviet Union allowed Cuba to sell its oil surplus for dollars, part of the proceeds from this implicit subsidy were suspected of making their way into the Comandante's reserves. The reason for this suspicion is that it became an established custom at JUCEPLAN that the dollars from nonconventional exports would go to such reserves.

Castro-Cuban Banking

In 1984, the Castro government founded as part of CIMEX the Banco Financiero Internacional, the first Cuban financial institution with dollars operating with complete autonomy from the state system. The BFI operates as a private corporation whose owners are the Cuban government (that is, Fidel Castro) and some foreign investors who are suspected of acting as stand-ins for other persons. The apparent objective of this bank is to remove from the National Bank of Cuba operations that are intended to leave no trace. The main clients of this bank, which has 16 branches in Cuba and an unknown number abroad (there are branches in the United Kingdom and in Canada), are the same firms associated with the Comandante's reserves.

Another of the newly created financial institutions is the Banco de Inversiones, which makes loans to the Cuban government at high interest rates. It is run by Hector Rodríguez Llompart, ex-president of the National Bank of Cuba and known Castro-crony, and a Swiss-Israeli citizen only known as André. It is suspected that this bank's capital comes from the BFI. The operations of these two banks are so secretive that they give rise to many suspicions, including that they are involved in the laundering of drug money. A scandal involving the Grupo Oasis of Spain, which operated the tourist center at Cayo Largo, planted the seeds of this suspicion.

The Comandante's reserves also benefit from many of the foreign donations Cuba receives, including, for example, the World Food Program of the FAO, which made many donations of milk to Cuba between the 1970s and 1990s. The milk was intended for infants in the eastern provinces of Cuba, but was diverted instead to Nicaragua for political and profit purposes. Most donations made by Castro-loving American organizations and religious groups, like the notorious Pastors for Peace, also end up in the Comandante's reserves. On the other hand, some people in Cuba suspect that many of these groups are heavily (and illegally) subsidized by the *Comandante en Jefe*.

From Socialism to Sociolism

According to some specialists, the Cuban economy is currently undergoing a major institutional evolution, from a planned socialist economy to an openly full fledged fascist-like state-controlled Capitalist system. In the meantime, four economic subsystems have appeared. The first is Fidel Castro's flourishing crony capitalist economy, with his business enterprises, financial institutions, and virtually absolute control of the country's resources. The second subsystem, in partnership with Castro's economy, consists of the foreign enterprises, allowed to generate and repatriate earnings at the cost of helping Castro's own finances. The third system is the remains of the old planned socialist economy and public enterprises, including the sugar industry, still struggling for survival but in a general state of neglect and decay. The fourth system is the Cuban marginal private sector, consisting of those who are falling outside the other three systems (mainly the self-employed or black market operatives) and those who, though still working in the public sector, do not earn enough to make ends meet.

It appears that the first two subsystems are thriving, while the latter two are carrying the burdens imposed by predatory economics of the first two. In the aggregate, everything seems to indicate that the Cuban economy is in a free fall, with no visible solution, something similar to what happened to Zaire (now Congo) under Mobutu Sese Seko's crony capitalism.

To some people, the last straw in this high level system of corruption was the building of a private hospital for Castro's bodyguards in the Kohly district, at a cost of 20 million pesos. They call it the Personal Security Clinic, but everybody knows its patients are mostly Castro's cronies and their relatives. For "security reasons" the hospital is off limits to common Cubans.

Some years ago Castro also built an enormous hospital in the Siboney section of Havana at a cost of 200 million pesos, even with a helicopter landing-pad, something that no hospital in Cuba had. The hospital is called CIMEQ, which stands for Medical-Surgical Research Center.[36] The medical center is mostly intended for Castro and the top echelon élite and their families only. No ordinary person in Cuba has access to this hospital. Lately, is has been known that these and other hospitals forbidden to the Cuban public have been used in fomenting what is called "health tourism," which basically is offering medical services in Cuba to foreigners able to pay in dollars—another manifestation of Castro's apartheid.

A report from the U.S. Department of State in 1997 shows that the Cuban government exported the equivalent of 110 million U.S. dollars in medical supplies in 1994 alone. In 1995 the number increased to 125 million dollars. The same report estimates that, during this time, approximately seven thousand foreigners who took advantage of the so-called "health tourism" enriched the Comandante's reserves by approximately 25 million dollars.

Fidel's Cronies[37]

According to Castro-friendly authors, one of the main accomplishments of his revolution was the enactment of the Agrarian Reform Law, whose main goal allegedly was to destroy the semi-feudal system of latifundia and the semi-colonial economic structure American imperialism had imposed upon the Island. The new law was published in Cuba's *Gaceta Oficial* on June 3rd, 1959. Soon after, the large sugar plantations and cattle ranches were expropriated and became government "socialist" property. The landholders expropriated under the Agrarian Reform Law were never given the indemnity promised under Article 29 of the Law, which turned the expropriation into a confiscation.

Reading the letter of the Agrarian Reform Law one finds a reasonable piece of legislation directed to changing forever the endemic agricultural problems of Latin America—problems that Cuba actually never had. Article 1 proscribed latifundia, but generously allowed any farmer to own a maximum of 1,000 acres of land and made exceptions for cattlemen and certain sugar cane planters. Article 16 granted a peasant family of five the "vital minimum" of 66 acres of land. Article 29 conceded "the constitutional right of the landowners affected by this law to receive an indemnity for the expropriated property." Article 41 ordered the establishment of "centers of State aid equipped with machinery, implements, grain storage warehouses, transportation, experimental fields" and even provided for "maternity homes, first-aid stations, dispensaries" and the like.

Apparently, however, Castro and his cronies had a different interpretation of the Agrarian Reform Law. In the early seventies, a process began by which socialized state farms were given quietly to Fidel's cronies, mainly high-level retired FAR (Army) and MININT (security) officers[38] who, while passing off as Socialist administrators, act as true Capitalist landowners.

The *"fincas de los comandantes'"*(majors' estates), as they are unofficially called, are run under an autonomous administration, out of the state's central control. With free access to markets, no price controls, and without having to follow the regulations in place for private farmers, these estates have become excellent sources of revenue for Fidel's cronies. Contrary to private farmers, the comandantes are not forced to give up to seventy percent of their agricultural production to the government and are free from the high taxes imposed on small farmers for the selling of their products. The economic success of the "fincas de los comandantes," is sufficient proof that Castro is fully aware that the real cause for the failure of the Cuban economy is the limitations imposed by the Castroist government.

In a revealing study about the problems affecting the economies of third world countries, Peruvian economist Hernando de Soto shows that the main cause for economic failure is lack of the legal structures of ownership by the poor.[39] Castro's Cuba is an outstanding example of the truth of de Soto's theories.

In order to attract foreign investors, the Castro government has been making great effort in promising the investors that their property will be protected by law. But the Castro government has a long record of abuses against small Cuban entrepreneurs. According to de Soto, the main source of economic failure is precisely this lack of a rule of law that upholds private property and provides a framework for enterprise. Therefore, one has to conclude that the disastrous state of the Cuban economy,[40] which has brought malnutrition, disease and all sorts of calamities to the Cuban people, is by Castro's design and not by mistake or as a result of the U.S. embargo.

Contrary to Castro's claims, he has benefitted enormously with the U.S. embargo. Far for hurting him, the U.S. economic embargo has greatly helped Castro. Most people don't seem to realize that if the embargo is hurting the Cuban people it is because this was precisely its intended goal. According to the convoluted logic of the creators of the embargo, making the Cuban people suffer will eventually make them revolt and overthrow the Castro regime. Things, however, don't seem to work that way.

As a keen analyst of the embargo pointed out,

> First, the sanctions are an excuse for Castro to claim his regime is not the cause of any failure or suffering in Cuba. In that sense, I often wonder if the sanctions are not being imposed by closet supporters of Castro who know this is the only way to keep him over. Second, it's been known for a half century now that economic freedom leads to socio-political freedom. This is because the more prosperous someone can get, the more they desire socio-political freedoms, and the more independent they are of the government which might try to stop them." . . . "What kind of a monster would try to make the people of a country suffer in order to overthrow its leader? How many children should be starved to death, or suffer in some horrible way, so that a ruler we don't like is removed? Why hasn't it worked for the last thirty years? Why is the one country which has been hurt most, has the most suffering imposed through economic warfare, been the only to survive, as oppressive and Communist today as it was when it started? If Communism is so bad, then why would it need outside intervention to make the people suffer enough to revolt? The poorer the people of Cuba are, the more they suffer, the weaker they are and the less able they would ever be to overthrow their government. Tyrants have forever known to keep their people so weak they cannot resist. As it is, they are so impoverished that they depend even more on their government, no less. Who are the sanctions oppressing? Does Castro have less to eat? Are his living standards reduced? Hardly. The only people the sanctions are hurting are the very victims they claim to be trying to save.[41]

Another thing about the embargo that doesn't ring true is that it apparently refutes the philosophy the U.S. has been using towards other communist countries in the last years, namely, involving them in the global economy so that the Communist monopoly of power eventually erodes. It is currently used toward China, Vietnam, and even North Korea. On June 1, 2001, President Bush asked Congress to extend normal trade relations with China for another year, even after the incident involving the capture of a U.S. surveillance plane and its crew just a month before.[42] Why, therefore, not apply the same policy toward Cuba? Apparently, what is good for the Asian goose is not good for the Caribbean gander.

Writing about the right wing in Chile, Castro-friendly author James Petras affirms that "Throughout the nineteenth century, and for most of the first half of the twentieth, Chilean politics were strongly influenced by a conservative élite." Adding that "The landowning élite, which controlled agriculture through its ownership of the large farms *(fundos)*, formed the nucleus of the right-wing political organizations that dominated government. The large landowners' control over land, peasants, and law enforcement was the basis for rightist political power."[43] A better description of current affairs in Castro's Cuba can hardly be made. The only difference is that in Cuba these same things are the basis for leftist political power (that is, if we accept Castro's leftist claims at face value).

The new sociolist landowners of Castro's Cuba use plenty of free state resources, including all type of mechanical and transportation equipment, farm animals, and fodder. Currently there are dozens of these estates all along the Island. All these *fincas*, also called "residential estates," have excellent guest houses, but only the government *nomenklatura* has access to them. The work is mostly done by slave labor, in the form of inmates from neighboring state prisons, among them political prisoners—which Castro's Cuba has in large supply. The production of these farms fully fall outside state control, in a flagrant violation of the country's "socialist" laws.

The guest houses, several of which exist in every large city in Cuba, are located in beautiful areas, hidden from the prying eyes of the local population. Most of the guest houses, in which everything is free to the privileged, including the room, food and drinks, may be ranked five stars by international standards. They have been decorated in excellent taste by the best decorators and designers working for one of the many secret enterprises under the control of Celia Sánchez, Castro's private secretary and Minister of State. The furniture was designed by the same team, and built using the best Cuban precious woods.

In view of Castro's pretense at purity and the importance of his mission for building a new society in Cuba, it is extraordinary that he has been so careless about his associates. He has never restricted them in any way except at the times when he had to purge his organization of political enemies. At all other times, he has been liberal to a fault. The non-written law, and true necessary condition for the acceptance of membership in the inner circle of his "Communist" Party, his intelligence services, or any other important position in the Cuban government, has always been that the candidate be a *Fidelista*, unconditionally obedient and faithfully devoted to Castro. Regarding other things, it seems that the general attitude is: "Do anything you like but don't get caught at it." This attitude toward his associates, as the trial of Ochoa, Abrahantes, and the de la Guardia twins has shown in detail, certainly did not make for high moral or ethical standards in the Cuban government and Party.

Castro Loves Cuban Art[44]

Since 1959 thousands of works of art of the Cuban patrimony, many of them from private residences of Cuban families that had fled the country, were disposed of by prominent members of the Castroist élite. Most were taken to large warehouses in Avenida del Puerto and later sold abroad, mostly in Canada and Europe, for a considerable profit, through Cubartimpex, a foreign trade enterprise then headed by Heberto Padilla. An ex-employee of the Canadian shipping firm Kuehne & Nagel, says that in the mid-1960s he saw the packing lists describing the contents of boxes full of art objects stolen from Cuban families and shipped to Canada to be auctioned.[45]

The disappearance of Cuban national art began discreetly, in the form of "loans" of works of art from museums to decorate Castro's Palace of the Revolution and other places frequented by the *nomenklatura*. That way, invaluable archaeological pieces from the collections of the Montané Archaeological Museum at the University of Havana were taken on loan and disappeared forever. Similarly, many pieces from the Napoleonic Museum,[46] the Museum of Decorative Arts, the Museo Bacardí and many others have been quietly disappearing.

Between 1960 and 1970, approximately 30 million dollars in books, most from private libraries, but also from the Cuban National Library and similar institutions, were sold to western Europeans through East Berlin. There were also sales to dealers in Buenos Aires, Mexico City, Madrid and Barcelona. In Toronto and Montreal many auctions of Cuban rare books have taken place.

In mid-1996, Cuba's National Museum of Art (Museo de Bellas Artes) in Havana was closed, allegedly because of "building repairs." But Jesús Rosado Arredondo, head of registry, inventory and conservation at the Museum until November 1996, confirmed that its closing was part of an operation ordered by Castro in June 1996 and carried out by officers and personnel of the security forces of the Ministry of the Interior. During the operation, code-named "Operación Canasta," (Operation Basket) 50,000 paintings, sculptures and other works of art valued at $500 million dollars were removed and hidden in three buildings controlled by the security forces. Mr. Rosado presented lists and proofs of many works that vanished while he held his position at the museum. In the summer of 1997, Cuban National Heritage, an organization of the Cuban exile community monitoring the illegal sale of stolen Cuban works of art, issued a press release regarding the most recent attempts to dispose of the richest art collections of the Cuban nation. As it is customary, however, the American media has ignored their plea.

Last year, Eusebio Leal, the Historian of the City of Havana and a personal friend of Castro, spent several weeks in the U.S. Leal, an expert in Cuban colonial art, visited several American cities, among them New York, Washington D.C., and Miami. It is believed that Leal is in the business of selling Cuban works of art on behalf of the Castro government.[47]

The loss of important government documents stolen from Cuban archives has not been any less. Thousands of documents from the National Archives and the National Library have been systematically sold to dealers worldwide. The stamps and seals of these institutions are easily identifiable on books and documents, clearly indicating their place of origin. The most valuable rare books, illustrated with maps and engravings have disappeared from archives and libraries. In 1993 two copies of the invaluable *Libro de los ingenios*, illustrated by Laplante, mysteriously disappeared from the Palacio del Junco in the Matanzas Museum. Similar works, such as a rare edition of Miahle engravings, have disappeared from the library of the Sociedad Económica de Amigos del País. It is believed that the precious books have been sold abroad to enrich the Comandante's reserves.

Recently, Castro authorized the creation of *sociedades anónimas*; state companies turned over to private ownership by members of the Castroist *nomenklatura*. These companies operate fully outside even the pretense of a central government plan.[48] They run their own income and keep—after giving the *Comandante* his lion's share—whatever profits they generate. The only thing that makes them different from "normal" capitalist businesses, like the ones Castro expropriated in the early 1960s allegedly because they were exploiting the Cuban workers, is that the new Castroist enterprises exploit the Cuban workers a hundred times more.

Granted, before Fidel Castro Cuba knew of many corrupt politicians who stole the government's money. But, bad as it was, corruption in pre-Castro's Cuba pales in comparison with the way the Castroist Mafia has been systematically stealing everything that is not nailed down—and even quite a few things that were nailed down—from the one-day prosperous Caribbean island. By any standard, Castro and his cronies have redefined the terms graft and corruption in Latin America.

Just a glimpse at the sociolist system Fidel Castro has imposed on Cubans may explain why many capitalists love sociolism, a system where capitalists have all the rights—including the right of life and death—while the workers have none. The fact may also explain why the Council on Foreign Relations—a sort of crypto-communist party of the capitalists—has been always so friendly with Castro and is now frantically trying to save Castro's sociolism from its final debacle.[49]

On the other hand, notwithstanding the overwhelming evidence of widespread corruption in a Cuba where all capitalist vices have returned with a vengeance,[50] the American Left still mumbles about the marvels of free education and health, the absence of discrimination, prostitution,[51] gambling, government corruption, and unemployment, while praising Castro as the greatest example of honesty and unselfishness. The hypocrisy of the Left, liberation theologists included, proves that actually they have nothing against the exploitation of the poor by the rich and powerful, but only want themselves to be the rich and powerful exploiting the poor.

Now, believing that Fidel Castro's main goal in his 42-year reign in Cuba has been only his personal enrichment is to allow him a rational explanation he doesn't deserve. The truth is that, though he has amassed a large fortune, he doesn't care much for money. Castro still feels great admiration for the Jesuits, because, according to him, "The Jesuits were untouched by the profit motive."[52] Surrounded by luxury, Castro doesn't seem to have great appreciation for it. He told his biographer Carlos Franqui how the Jesuits formed people of character, and how he loved the Jesuits' Spartan style of life.[53]

The main purpose for Castro's amassing such an immense fortune has not been the enjoyment of the good things of life, but, first of all, to deprive Cubans from enjoying them (as I will show in Chapter 6, Castro's first motivation in life is envy) and, secondly, to finance anti-American revolution and terrorism all around the planet. There is strong evidence that the main reason for his involvement in drug trafficking was to obtain funds for subversion abroad, including the Cuban invasion of Angola.

The collapse of the Soviet Union and the end of its subsidies marked a period of relative calm in Castro's subversive activities abroad. A few years ago, however, he found a new source of revenue to finance his military adventures. Castro passed a law authorizing the use of dollars in Cuba, and opened the door for Cuban exiles to send ransom money to pay for the welfare of their relatives virtually kidnapped by Castro in Cuba.

Lately, large amounts of dollar remittances from exiled Cubans to relatives on the Island are playing an important role in helping some Cubans weather the current economic crisis. However, the remittances, combined with the foreign investment activity in Cuba, are offering Castro an excellent vehicle to hide money laundering activities. The United Nations Economic Commission for Latin America estimated that in 1996 about $80 million dollars were sent by Cuban exiles to their relatives in Cuba, most of which found its way into Castro's deep pockets. It is believed that the amount has been increasing every year. Cubans use this money basically to buy grossly overpriced food articles in government-controlled stores. These stores are part of Castro's personal enterprises, and their earnings engross the Comandante's reserves.

The infusion of money from anti-Castro exiles in the U.S. has become the main source of income for many Cubans in the Island who can only buy food and other essential items in dollar only stores.[54] This is becoming an extraordinary economic burden for the Cuban exile community abroad. Many of them are now deep into debt as the result of their periodical remittance of dollars to their starving relatives in Cuba. Therefore, Castro ruined not only the Cubans in Cuba, but now is in the process of ruining the Cubans abroad.

The new injection of money had an immediate effect on Castro's imperial dreams. Since early 1999, guerrilla activities and violent political turmoil are increasing again in Latin America.

PART TWO

Who is Fidel Castro? What is he?

Chapter 6

The Secret Fidel Castro

> *What good fortune for those in power that people don't think.*
> —Adolf Hitler

The available information obtained about any person's life sometimes poses almost insurmountable problems. While the most readily verifiable information may not be the most revealing, the most interesting may not be easily verifiable. Thus, we have many accurate accounts of what Castro *said*, which, most of the time, fully contradicts what he actually *did*. In addition, not many of his biographers have tried to find out *why* he said or did some of these things, because to do so might require going beyond narrative history to examine a different, more elusive type of fact.

The information on Fidel Castro which I will present in this chapter, roughly constitutes what an intelligence service calls a CPP, or Comprehensive Personality Profile—a personal file intelligence agencies keep on world leaders.[1] I have had no access to Castro's CPP at the CIA, nor the ones at the KGB or the Vatican, which presumably are very extensive,[2] but I have followed a similar methodology in assembling this one and, therefore, I assume it cannot be too different from Castro's dossiers kept at the secret KGB, Vatican,[3] or CIA archives. Every intelligence service, however, has its own biases and interests, just as I have my own. Therefore, the reader can safely assume that there that are aspects and information about Castro in those CPPs that don't appear in this one, just as some analyses and information appearing in the one I have created is missing in theirs.

As it happens with all CPPs, however, a bit of caution is required. Some of the information on which a CPP is based has been obtained through dubious sources and not all of it has been fully validated. (See Appendix 3) But, as intelligence services all around the world have learned over the years, even though a few particular details may not be fully verifiable or true, taken as a whole the material in a CPP usually gives a rather accurate picture of the person.[4]

An objection may be raised to this investigation, namely how one can study in detail a person without subjecting him to a close examination. The problem with Castro, as it was with Hitler, is that he is like a bright sun. The best way to study Fidel Castro is either indirectly or through very dark glasses. The force of his personality acts as a strong contaminant, distorting any analysis in which he is directly involved. Proof of this is that Georgie Anne Geyer, who didn't interview Castro or had his collaboration for her book on him,[5] wrote a biography of the Cuban leader far superior to the ones written by authors like Tad Szulc, who traveled several times to the Island and enjoyed Castro's full help and support.

Finally, the reader will notice that, though one of the longest in the book, this chapter has relatively fewer footnotes than the rest. One reason for this is that most of the facts to which this chapter refers have already been mentioned in detail in the previous chapters. The other reason is that some of the information I mention in this chapter comes mostly from direct verbal sources inside Cuba and, therefore, has never been published before except in the "invisible press".[6]

The Maximum Leader

Most people see Fidel Castro either as a great political leader or as a mentally disturbed and evil person. But this type of dichotomy has proved to be greatly inefficient in analyzing such a complex personality. To treat him solely as a rational statesman or as a paranoid tyrant is to misjudge the complexity of his personality and to misunderstand a great deal of his behavior.

Granted, the picture Castro and his propaganda machine has painted certainly does not seem very realistic. But, even ignoring the glorifying elements, Fidel Castro's life is like the wild dream of a superhero, right out of a comic book. Implausible as it may seem, however, there have been times when he has come close to such an exemplary model, winning both the fear and respect of his enemies and the praise and love of his close associates. So, let's first look at some of his remarkable qualities.

Fidel Castro's powers of concentration are uncommon, and he is able to master very complex problems in a relatively short time and break them into a few simple, fundamental ones, though sometimes his analyses prove to be simplistic, rudimentary and erroneous. Examples of his successes are his quick victory at the Bay of Pigs, and his effective planning of the initial phase of the Angolan invasion. Examples of his disastrous failures are his solutions to the problems of sugar cane production, cattle raising and coffee planting, just to name a few. But, disregarding the results, at such times when he is analyzing a problem Castro becomes a veritable monster for work and often strives for several days on end with little or no sleep.

During these periods of intense activity in which Castro is trying to solve a problem he is completely absorbed in the task confronting him. Discussion follows discussion with great speed and proficiency. His judgments are generally quick and decisive. He is impatient to get things done and expects everyone to apply himself with an ardor similar to his own. He is a very demanding boss, and expects great sacrifices from his associates.

At such times, however, he also becomes very human, showing an unusual degree of consideration toward others and even a certain tolerance of their weaknesses. During those periods he is usually in the best of spirits and jokes with everyone around him.[7]

Though he is not very good at solving economic problems, Castro can analyze a political or diplomatic problem brilliantly and respond to it with shattering effectiveness. He prides himself on this talent and has expressed it to many of his close associates.

Certainly, Castro has an enormous advantage over most people. He is not burdened with abstract theories, ideologies, or traditional points of view and has a peculiar notion of ethics and morals. He views the world as a place that exists only to serve him, and him alone. If he wants something, he takes it, without regard for its rightful owner. In his mind, it is his anyway, no matter the consequences for others.

Castro's mind is cold and implacable, and he knows neither pity nor remorse. He seldom hesitates to violate the rights of others to serve his own ends. This allows him to look at complex problems in a rather naïve and free-wheeling way and pick out the most important elements and apply them to the solution of the problem in question in a fairly simple and workable manner. To be sure, he never solves the entire problem in this way, but he is very good at manipulating the human elements involved. Since this is the part that interests him most, and the one that usually produces immediate results, his problem-solving ability has been rated very high and has won the admiration of his close associates from the earliest days of his political career.

Castro usually displays extraordinary boldness, courage and determination. He shows a great deal of initiative and is willing to assume full responsibility for the wisdom of the course he has mapped out. He is very persuasive and is able to muster and organize his people into an efficient, smooth-running unit. When he is in control, personal frictions among his associates disappear, at least for the time being, and everybody has but a single thought in mind: to do what Fidel wishes and make him happy.

The tremendous effect he produces on those he meets has been recorded over and over. He has an incredible talent for using one aspect of the personality of a person against the other, for spotting weaknesses, for creating confusion and appearing herein as the only source of leadership. He has a quick, simple but seemingly elaborated answer for everything. He is known for telling everyone to do their own thing, to be themselves, to show their own initiative, but his own strong personal magnetism, combined with a constant process of natural selection, attracts around him those without a personality of their own who crave the guidance of a leader. But, notwithstanding his constant speeches exhorting liberation and freedom, Castro's true goal is total control.

When he is engaged in his problem-solving mode, he usually works with great certainty and security and always gives the impression of having the situation entirely in hand. His staff has learned from past experience that when Castro is in one of these working moods he comes close to infallibility. This is particularly important when he needs the support of the people around him to carry through the project on which he is engaged. This may seem like an unwarranted statement, but, if our study is to be complete, we must appraise his strengths as well as his weaknesses. It can scarcely be denied that Castro has some extraordinary abilities to understand the psychology of the average man and use it to his advantage.

Castro's Photographic Memory

Fidel Castro has an extraordinary memory of the type called "eidetic"[8] or "photographic." This is not the type of memory anyone can develop through mnemonic or memorization exercises, but of a totally different type. At some time in his life, apparently when he was a teenager, Castro discovered his extraordinary faculty, and began boasting about it.[9]

Some of his sisters recall that, when he was a student, Fidel used to tear out the pages of the textbook he was reading and throw them away, and afterwards he could recite by heart the full content of the pages. He continued displaying this behavior when he attended law school at the University of Havana.[10] On meeting Fidel, French agricultural scientist André Voisin was surprised to hear Fidel recite, line by line, whole paragraphs of the books Voisin had written.

Alexandr Alekseev, one of the first Soviet officials to meet Castro in 1959, recalls that during their first meeting he was very much taken aback by Castro's ability to quote Marx, Engels and Lenin by heart. Alekseev's surprise was total, because the information he had been given in Moscow about Castro firmly stated that he was not a Communist and that his knowledge of Marxism was very limited.[11] What Alekseev ignored was that, in order to fool him as he has done with many others, the previous night Castro had spent several hours fast-reading whole chapters of books by Marx, Engels and Lenin. Next day, he parroted them back to Alekseev like a human tape recorder.

Castro has always been proud of his prodigious memory. Almost everyone who knows him is struck by his incredible retentive memory and the extraordinary range of his factual knowledge.[12] But, though he loves to give the impression that he is a voracious reader who has read hundreds of books, his speeches show only an amount of miscellaneous information without any true depth. The information he usually uses seems to have been collected largely from newspapers, magazines or book digests. Claiming to be a Marxist, his speeches reveal a total lack of understanding of Marxist theory and terminology.

When Castro is analyzing a problem, all kinds of facts and figures relevant to it flow from him without the slightest hesitation or effort, much to the amazement of those around. He can cite statistics on sugar-cane production, milk, eggs and ice cream. He can recite the name of each one of his cows and their individual milk production. He knows to the last detail every unit of the Cuban Army, including number of men, type of weapons, and ordnance.

He also uses his extensive mental archives as a defensive weapon to ward off displeasing arguments. During the guerrilla war in the Sierra Maestra he boasted about knowing how many bullets every single guerrilla had. When his officers resented his efforts to control from his headquarters in Havana the smallest details of the war in Angola, he frequently surprised senior Army officers by bringing out facts about their military units they themselves ignored, including how many crackers had been assigned to every soldier's rations.[13]

During his political career Castro has used his prodigious memory as a shield to protect his personality. It helped him to convince himself and others that he really is a person of great intellectual ability, in no way inferior to those who are better educated or trained.

Castro's Uncommon Abilities

Fidel Castro has been able, in one way or another, to discover and apply successfully some sociological and psychological principles, the relevance of which are still not wholly recognized, and has used them to his benefit. These principles might be briefly summarized as follows:

A born demagogue, with a demagogue's ability to appeal to the highest popular feelings and to exploit the lowest popular instincts, Castro likes to justify the most reprehensible acts as means to attain a higher goal by cloaking the elements of his program in an aura of nobility. Launched into one of his long speeches, he has the ability to identify with and express in simple but ardent language the deepest needs and sentiments of the average Cuban. His speeches seem carefully designed to appeal to the inner desires and fears of the people, fears lodged in their deepest subconscious minds. Characteristically, Castro knows how to touch the heart of the masses by simultaneously acknowledging their suffering and scapegoating the United States as the true and only source of all their problems.

To accomplish this, Castro has shown the capacity for learning from other organizations, even though he may be violently opposed to everything they believe or stand for. The use of terror, for example, he probably adopted from the Nazis; the use of sloganeering, from the Catholic Church;[14] the use of propaganda from the Soviet communists; the importance of public relations from the Americans, and so forth.

Castro has a "never-say-die" spirit which has allowed him to succeed when others have failed. After some of his severest setbacks—the disastrous attack on the Moncada barracks, the humiliation of the missile crisis, the failed ten million ton sugar crop—he was able to marshall his immediate associates and make plans for a "comeback." After the failure of the ten million ton sugar crop he coined the slogan *"A convertir el revés en victoria"* ("Let's turn this setback into a success"). Events that might have crushed most individuals, at least temporarily, seem to act as stimulants to greater efforts in Castro. Even in defeat, he has retained his hold on his inner circle.

For his indefatigability he draws on some basic rules of political engagement: never allow the public to cool off; never admit a fault or wrong; never concede that there may be some good in your enemy; never leave room for alternatives; never accept blame; concentrate on one enemy at a time and blame him for everything that may go wrong. People will believe a big lie more easily than a little one, and a lie repeated frequently enough will bring people sooner or later to believe it.[15] Fidel Castro is the first politician in the world to discover the extraordinarily persuasive powers of television and to use it as a propaganda tool—even more effectively than Hitler did with radio—to influence and control the masses for his personal benefit.[16]

The most powerful element in Castro's advent is his gift of radiating confidence in the future, and confidence in the principle "where there's a will, there's a way." This confidence is based on a fanatical faith in himself and in his mission, a faith that doubts, criticism, and even failure can scarcely touch. His self-confidence is the attribute that has assured him political superiority over so many highly cultured politicians who allowed themselves to be tormented by moral and ethical doubts.

One of Castro's strongest points is his firm belief that destiny itself singled him out to accomplish a great historical task, such that the complete dedication of his life is to realize its fulfillment. His convictions are so powerful that he believes he is sacrificing himself for a cause, and this quality makes his political program strongly appealing to others, persuading them to follow his example. His personal confidence is closely connected with his belief that he represents the true will of the Cuban people. At once his strength also represents his weakness, because his confidence in himself resists any criticism and borders on self-idolatry.

Castro recognizes the importance of conducting large meetings, rallies, and festivals, not only in terms of what they can accomplish in the way of evoking emotional responses but also as a venue for his participation in the total dramatic effect as main character and hero, and living symbol of the Cuban revolution. He values the importance of the masses in the success of any political movement. He appreciates the fact that the overwhelming majority of the people want to be led and are ready and willing to submit themselves to a true leader, provided he can win their respect and confidence. He has found an effective way to court the soul of both the Cuban lower and middle classes as well as the intellectuals and liberals abroad. He discovered the fact that the masses are as hungry for a sustaining political ideology in action as they are for their daily bread and appreciates their desire to sacrifice themselves on the altar of what they see as social improvement or spiritual values. He discovered that any political movement that does not satisfy this spiritual hunger in the masses will fail to mobilize their wholehearted support and is destined to fail. Related to this awareness is his recognition of the fundamental loneliness and feeling of isolation in people living under modern conditions and their craving to "belong" to an active group that carries a certain status, provides cohesiveness, and gives the individual a feeling of personal worth and belongingness. He is aware that his revolution brought meaning to the otherwise empty lives of many Cubans.

Castro ascribes cardinal importance to winning the support of the young people. He recognized the importance of early training and indoctrination, although in more recent years he seems to have lost the support of young Cubans as a whole. He has recognized the role of women in advancing the new movement and has lent lip service to the advancement of women in his revolution. But more fundamentally, he believes that the reactions of the masses as a whole may have deeply feminine characteristics, and, as the tough macho man he believes himself to be, he deals with the masses guided by this principle, throwing the sincerity of his feminism into doubt. But his ability to appeal to and arouse the sympathetic concern and protectiveness of his people by representing himself as the bearer of their burdens and their future has elicited the concern of his close associates, and many of them, particularly the women, feel tenderly and compassionately for him. They are always very careful not to inflict undue annoyance or suffering on the Maximum Leader. During the kangaroo trial that ended with the execution of Gen. Ochoa and other senior officers, Gen. Colomé Ibarra regretfully observed "how deep the events had hurt Fidel, how much damage they had inflicted on him, how much they had made him suffer."[17]

Though Fidel Castro sees political organizations as a means of attaining his personal goals, at the same time he appreciates the value underlying a political organization that allows him to have direct contact with each individual. Both the M-26-7, first, and later his "Communist" Party, were organized in that fashion. Castro has been able to elicit the confidence of the people largely because he has been able to convince his followers of his own self-confidence, and because he has managed to guess right on so many occasions in which everything seemed to contradict his decision. The success of his actions is almost uncanny, like his decision to send a large expeditionary force to Angola or his unexpected support of the Soviet invasion of Czechoslovakia.

As well, Castro's alleged charisma rests in his power to bewitch a large audience or a single individual, transforming rallies of the most varied individuals into a homogeneous pliable mass, putting that mass first into a kind of trance, and then producing in it a reaction close to a collective orgasm. Ché Guevara noticed Fidel's orgasmic relationship with the masses and described it masterly,

> At the great public mass meetings one can observe something like a counterpoint between two musical melodies whose vibrations provoke still newer notes. Fidel and the mass begin to vibrate together in a dialogue of growing intensity until they reach the climax in an abrupt conclusion culminating in our cry of struggle and victory.[18]

This extraordinary and uncanny power has been likened to the occult arts of the African medicine-man or the Asiatic Shaman.

Others have compared it to the sensitivity of a medium, and the magnetism of the hypnotist. Even today, after forty years of continuous failures, Castro still possesses enough flickering magnetism to convince many of those around him that the goals of his revolution might still be accomplished. The recent mass mobilizations in relation with the Elián González case is proof of the above.[19] That ability of mass hypnotism was Castro's first, and for a long time his only, political capital. The consciousness of his assured control of the masses, which he shared with no one, came gradually to be accompanied by a sense of political and intellectual superiority over all his rivals. It seems that at some point in his political career Castro realized that any rivalry was not just about the sharing of privileges in the new government, but about something he would not accept any rivalry about: his position as an all-powerful permanent dictator, uninhibited by any constitution or division of powers, without any limitations of collective leadership.

A key element of his success is his innate ability to surround himself with and maintain the personal allegiance of a group of devoted aides whom he fully controls and whose diverse talents he exploits to the fullest as they complement his own. But the essential source of his popularity with the Cuban people, which cuts across all classes, is the way he has discovered to establish this mass relationship primarily with his person, not with ideas or any ideology, such that he can change his ideas anytime he considers expedient without changing the relationship. The same applies to his close associates as well. Though some of them still claim to be Marxists, their first allegiance is to Castro.[20] None of them complained (though probably none of them believed him) when he "confessed" that he had been a Marxist all his life. Likewise, none of them would complain if someday Castro "confessed" that he has been a closet Jesuit all his life.

A phrase that was in continual use by Castro's followers during the early years of his revolution defines his relationship with the Cuban masses. Faced with the apparently unsolvable problems of their daily life, they said: "If Fidel only knew!"[21] The phrase suggests that their faith in Castro and their conversion to communism were two different things. The things people did not like about communism—and there were many—they instinctively tried to distanciate from Castro. This reasoning, however, is wrong. As Fidel Castro is fully responsible for the few constructive things his regime achieved, he is also responsible for the destructive ones.

Castro's skill at repudiating his own conscience when making political decisions has eliminated from him the force that usually checks and complicates the thoughts and decisions of other more socially responsible statesmen. He has therefore been able to take that course of action which seems the more expedient without pulling any punches. The result has been that he has frequently outwitted his adversaries and attained ends that would not have been as easily attained by a more normal course, helping to build up the myth of his infallibility and invincibility.

Equally important has been Castro's ability to persuade others around him to repudiate their individual consciences and allow him to assume that role and decree for these individuals what is right and wrong, permissible or impermissible, allowing him to use them freely like puppets in the attainment of his own ends. This opportunism has enabled him to make full use of terror to arouse the fears of the people, which he knows how to evaluate with an extraordinary precision.

Sometimes Castro's intelligence seems astonishing, and his miraculous political intuition, devoid of all moral sense, extraordinarily precise. Even in a very complex situation he knows exactly what is possible and what is not without caring about what is right, fair, or honest. Another peculiar characteristic of his character is the fact that he always responds to any real or perceived threat or aggression by raising the ante ten times more than what a normal person would consider an adequate response. This type of response not only surprises his enemies, but paralyzes them as well. His order to shoot down two civilian planes that allegedly had violated Cuban air space is a good example of this type of behavior.

Since his early days as a gangster apprentice at the University of Havana, Castro evidenced the traits of a born conspirator. He has an extraordinary ability to manipulate, confuse and disarm opponents, striking with lightning force at the moment they least expect. He is notorious for leading people to believe that he agrees with them entirely, without ever committing himself to their position. He is a master of the art of propaganda. He has a matchless instinct for taking advantage of every breeze, real or artificially created by himself, to raise a political whirlwind. As Gen. Ochoa's case proved, no official scandal is so petty that Castro cannot magnify it into a case of high treason and use it to his advantage.

These are some of Fidel Castro's outstanding talents and capacities. They allowed him to attain a position of unprecedented power in an incredibly short period of time, over a rarely used route, and to wield this power in a totally ruthless way. No other Cuban in a high government position or among his opponents, in Cuba or abroad, possesses these abilities in any comparable degree, and, consequently, they could not displace him in the minds of the Cuban masses.

His associates recognize Castro's political talent and admire and respect his extraordinary leadership qualities, particularly the strong, uncanny influence he has over people. In addition, they love him for his very human qualities when he is at his best and is engaged in some important undertaking. These are aspects of Castro's personality we should never lose sight of when evaluating his hold on his associates or on the Cuban people. There is a magnetic quality about him that, together with his past accomplishments, wins the allegiance of the people and seems to rob them of their critical ability to evaluate his failures. This is a bond that does not easily dissolve even in the face of unquestionable evidence that he is not always the successful leader he pretends to be.

The Dark Side of Fidel Castro

I have reviewed Castro's strengths and briefly portrayed his character when he is at his best. It is now time to look at the other side of his personality—the side that is known only to those who are on fairly intimate terms with him.

Most people, including most national leaders, show a capacity for growth. And, as they grow, their views, values and ideas change. But one of the most striking characteristics of Fidel Castro is that he is totally immune to change.[22] That is the reason why he has never matured. His character and personality were fixed at an early age, and have remained surprisingly unchanged with almost nothing new added to them. Though he has managed to hide it from the outside world, people close to Castro know of his immaturity and impulsivity. This is evidenced by his lack of tolerance for frustration and his inability to defer gratification.[23]

Today Castro is practically the same individual he was seventy years ago when he was a naughty farm boy at his father's Manacas estate near the town of Birán, not far from Mayarí, Oriente. At 75, though he pretends to be a grown-up, he is still the same spoiled brat who terrorized his classmates and teachers. A photograph of Fidel at the age of three, taken at his home in Birán, and a later one taken at the age of sixty-eight, shows exactly the same expression of hostility and arrogance evidenced by his pouting lower lip and the hardness of his dark, piercing eyes.[24]

The pursuit of other people's acceptance became Fidel's only way to find self-acceptance. For example, as a young student at the University of Havana, he distinguished himself from the rest of his classmates by always wearing dark suits and ties, a fact some people have interpreted as an effort to gain respectability.

But trying to gain respectability can hardly be considered a negative trait. In the case of Fidel Castro, however, the normal inborn tendencies for feeling powerless, deserted, ashamed, and guilty in relation to his parents was exacerbated by his being rejected by society because of his bastard origins. This resulted in a great amount of impotent rage and envy stored up and manifested later on in his destructively childish tendencies.[25] Though disguised as manly assertion, his temper tantrums are actually a manifestation of his lack of maturity.

From Angel, his father, Fidel inherited a trait of disloyalty, coldness, mistrust of others, and a tendency toward sly calculation. In his initial struggle against his father, the young Fidel Castro discovered that no holds were barred, and that the ends justify all means. Very early in life he put this theory into practice, with excellent results, when he threatened his father with burning their house after Angel refused to send Fidel to a school in Santiago de Cuba. In the Catholic schools of the Jesuit Fathers, first at the Colegio de Dolores in Santiago and later at the Colegio de Belén in Havana, he learnt that the right of the stronger prevails, contested at most by the right of the craftier.[26] Consequently, he has devoted his whole life to becoming stronger and craftier, and he has been successful to a great extent.

Much has been written by the Cuban propaganda machine about Fidel Castro's modest way of living. His personal life, however, shows that he is far from the ascetic he claims to be.

Castro's eating hours are chaotic and he has a Gargantuan appetite. His voracious appetite tempered as he grew old, but he used to eat great quantities of food whenever he felt hungry, sometimes eating while standing or moving around. His food is prepared in different ways by the best chefs in Cuba, and there are always large quantities and a great variety of food prepared in unusual ways ready for him. In relation to food, however, it seems he rather values quantity over quality. In addition, Castro consumes incredible quantities of pastries, chocolates and cookies in the course of a single day. All his vehicles carry a provision of candies for his personal consumption.

Contrary to common belief, Castro's personal tastes are not particularly inexpensive. Although his clothes are simple, mostly olive-green fatigues, they are made of the finest materials that can be procured and custom made by the best Cuban tailors. Usually he has an incredible number of each article of clothing, and he uses it for several days in a row, during which he usually doesn't take a bath, and then discards it. Normally his aides wait until he falls sleep to change his stinky clothes for fresh ones. Lately, particularly when he has traveled abroad, he dresses in expensive business suits.

When Fidel enrolled at the Colegio de Dolores in Santiago de Cuba, his personal hygiene was such that he soon got the nickname *bola de churre* (literally "grease ball"). He continued his untidy habits and refused to bathe, so the nickname stuck and followed him to the Jesuits' Colegio de Belén and later to the University of Havana. As a law school student he changed his dress from shirts and *guayaberas* to more formal suits and ties. But he seldom changed his underwear and he wore his suits and ties day after day until they literally fell off him.

Personal hygiene is extremely important to Cubans. There is probably no country in the world, perhaps with the exception of Japan, where personal cleanliness is more taken for granted.[27] An American author visiting the Island expressed his surprise when a Cuban beggar told him, "Please give me soap. Please do me this favor."[28] There are not many places around the world where one can find beggars asking for hygiene. In contrast, everybody who has come in close distance to Castro have felt his strong, repulsive body odor. The condition is particularly offensive in Cuba, where, particularly in the summer, most people *used to* take two or even three showers a day and use plenty of deodorant. I emphasized the words "used to," because now, after 40 years of Castroist rule, running water in Cuban cities is limited to a few minutes a day, and soap and deodorant are scarce commodities.[29] It seems that, willingly or unwillingly, Castro has managed to force his personal filthy habits upon the rest of the Cuban people.

In the hottest days of a Cuban summer, while everybody around him is wearing a cotton, short-sleeved, light shirt with an open collar, Castro usually wears a long-sleeved heavy shirt, and a heavy, long-sleeved bush jacket on top, buttoned up to his collar, and he doesn't seem to feel the heat or be sweating at all. Some people speculate that the reason Castro wears such heavy clothes in summer is because he suffers from chronic pleuritis, while others claim that the actual reason is to hide a bulletproof vest. But, even accepting that both reasons are true, and there are reasons to believe they are not, they don't explain why he does not seem to be affected at all by the intense heat.[30]

Castro has never been able to adjust to any regulated intellectual activity. He suffers from an all-embracing disorderliness. This has become less evident in time, but in the beginning it was apparent in everything he did. It was indeed so apparent that, since Castro was in the Sierra Maestra mountains fighting Batista, the main duty of Celia Sánchez, his personal secretary, was to keep track of him and, sometimes using a lot of personal persuasion and cajolery, see to it that he fulfilled his duties and obligations. The attempt, however, was only partially successful: Castro was always on the go but rarely on time. He is still rarely on time and frequently keeps important foreign leaders and diplomats, as well as his own staff, waiting for considerable periods of time. At their first meeting at the Soviet mission to the United Nations in New York, he kept an angry Nikita Khrushchev cooling his heels for more than half an hour when, as usual, Fidel was late for the appointment.[31]

Castro never had a steady job, therefore he never learned how to work steadily or keep a regular schedule. Indeed, he seems incapable of working at all. He dislikes desk work and seldom glances at the piles of reports that are placed on his desk daily. No matter how important these may be or how much his adjutants may urge him to give attention to a particular matter, he refuses to take them seriously unless it happens to be a project that interests him. On the whole, few reports interest him unless they deal with military affairs or political matters.

He has never been able to maintain any kind of personal working schedule. His hours are most irregular, and he may go to bed any time between midnight and seven o'clock in the morning and get up anywhere from nine o'clock in the morning to two in the afternoon. In later years the hours tended to get later, and it is unusual for him to go to bed before daybreak. The night, however, is not spent in working, as friendly biographers claim, but in viewing American films, watching sporting events on tv (mostly American baseball games), entertaining foreign personalities, or just sitting around chatting about inconsequential things with his staff.

A fact known only by his close associates is that, though he tries to hide it behind a cover of dynamism, Fidel Castro is an extremely lazy person. He sleeps long hours while everybody around him is forced to work. He spends hours and hours wasting his time in senseless activities which only serve to hide the fact that he is not doing anything useful.

He seldom sits in a cabinet meeting because they bore him. On several occasions, when sufficient pressure was brought to bear, he did pay attention for a short period of time, but got up abruptly in the middle of the session and left without apology. On the whole, he prefers to discuss cabinet matters with each member in person and then communicate his decision to the group as a whole.[32]

People close to Castro have noticed his hostility and contempt for the press. There is evidence of his early efforts to eliminate all free press in Cuba, something he achieved just a few months after he took power in 1959. This contrasts curiously with his avid interest for reading press reports from abroad.[33] But, though these foreign press reports are brought to him almost hourly, they seem to have no influence on his thinking, behavior or propaganda lines.

On the other hand, he has a passion for the latest news and for photographs of himself. If someone happens to enter his office with a foreign newspaper or magazine where Castro's photo appears, he will interrupt the most important meeting in order to scan through it. Very frequently he becomes so absorbed by the news or looking at his own photographs that he completely forgets the topic under discussion.

It is almost impossible for Castro to keep himself concentrated on one point. His quick mind runs away with the talk, or his attention is distracted by the sudden discovery of a newspaper and he stops to read it avidly, or he interrupts his aid's carefully prepared report with a long speech as though the aid was a large audience.

Castro has an unhealthy fixation with death. Beginning with a speech he gave on February 29, 1960, four days after the French ship *La Coubre* exploded in Havana's harbor, he ends his speeches with the slogan *"¡Patria o muerte!"* (Fatherland or death!).[34] The day before he embarked in the invasion of Cuba he told his comrades: "tomorrow we will be free or we will be martyrs." His war manifesto against the Batista dictatorship, dated March 12, 1958, ended with the phrase: "The whole nation is ready to become free or to perish."

Lately, after the collapse of the Soviet Union placed Cuba in a very difficult economic situation, his speeches have become even more necrophilic, and he added to them a new death slogan. During this seemingly never-ending socio-economic crisis, which Castro euphemistically calls the "special period," he began reciting a new mantra: "Socialism or death!"[35] In October, 1991, at his closing speech at the Fourth Congress of the Young Communists Union, Castro made a speech which some Cubans called "Fidel's Death Song," in which he almost predicted the death of his whole government.[36]

Fidel The Procrastinator

Fidel Castro is a procrastinator. His staff is usually in despair on account of this. He never takes their protests in this respect very seriously and usually brushes them aside stating that when the time is right, the matter will be settled one way or another.

Although Castro tries to present himself as a very decisive individual who never hesitates when he is confronted by a difficult situation, he is usually far from it. It is at these times that his procrastination becomes most marked. At such times it is almost impossible to get him to take action on anything. He stays very much by himself and is frequently almost inaccessible to his immediate staff. He often becomes depressed, is in bad humor, talks little, and prefers to read a magazine or watch television. His hesitation to act is not due to divergent views among his advisers. At such times he seldom pays very much attention to them and prefers not to discuss the matter.

A clear example of this procrastinating behavior was evidenced when, during 1961, he allowed the pro-Soviet PSP communists to take control of most of the government, ignoring the warning cries of his close associates. But, suddenly, he cracked down in a speech on March 26, 1962, and destroyed the PSP plans in a few hours. There has never been an explanation why Castro put up with this state of things as long as he did.

When he is immersed in the solution of a problem, what is known as the mastery of the material is quite unimportant to him. He quickly becomes impatient if the details of a problem are brought to him. He has always shown a strong dislike for experts and has little regard for their opinion.

On some occasions, in the middle of a problem, he has been known to leave Havana without a word and go to some of his private mansions around the Island, where he spends his time walking in the country or the beach entirely by himself. He recognizes nobody then. He wants to be alone. But usually he solves suddenly, at the very last minute, a situation that has become intolerable and dangerous only because of his vacillation and procrastination. It is during these periods of inactivity that Castro is waiting for his "inner voice" to guide him. He does not think the problem through in a normal way but waits until the solution comes to him as if by magic.

These periods of indecision may last from a few days to several weeks. If he is induced to talk about the problem during this time he becomes ill-natured and bad-tempered. When the solution has been "given" to him, however, he feels a great desire to express himself. He then calls in his adjutants, and they must sit and listen to him until he is finished, no matter what time it happens to be. On these occasions he does not want them to question him or even to understand him. It seems that he just wants to talk.

After this recital to his adjutants Castro calls in his advisers and the rest of the people involved in the problem, and informs them of his decision. When he has finished they are free to express their opinions. If Castro thinks that one of these opinions is worthwhile he will listen for a long time, but usually these opinions have little influence on his decision when this stage has been reached. Only if someone succeeds in introducing new factors is there any possibility of getting him to change his mind. If someone voices the opinion that the proposed plan is too difficult or onerous he becomes extremely angry and frequently says that he doesn't need people around him who have clever ideas of their own, but rather people who are clever in finding ways and means of carrying out *his* ideas.

As soon as he has the solution to a problem that has been haunting him, his mood changes very radically. He becomes again the Fidel Castro described at the beginning of this chapter. He is very cheerful, jokes all the time and does not give anybody an opportunity to speak, while he himself makes fun of everybody. This mood lasts throughout the period when necessary work has to be done. But, as soon as the requisite orders have been given to put the plan into execution, Castro seems to lose interest in it. He becomes perfectly calm, occupies himself with other matters, and sleeps unusually long hours.

This is a very fundamental trait of Castro's mind. He does not think things out in a logical and consistent fashion, gathering all available information pertinent to the problem, mapping out alternative courses of action, and then weighing the evidence pro and con for each of them before reaching a decision. His mental processes seem to operate in reverse. Instead of studying the problem, as an intellectual would do, he avoids it and occupies himself with other things until unconscious processes furnish him a solution.

When he thinks he has found the solution to the problem, he begins to look for facts that will prove it to be correct. In this process he is very clever, and by the time he presents it to his associates, it has the appearance of a rational judgment. Nevertheless, his thought processes proceed from the emotional to the factual instead of starting with the facts as an intellectual person normally does. It is this characteristic of his thinking process that makes it difficult for ordinary people to understand Castro or to predict his future actions. His behavior in this respect is that of an artist and not that of a statesman.

Castro has used this inspirational technique to determine his course of action. This technique, however, has its limitations. Probably the main one is that he becomes totally dependent on his inner guide, which makes for unpredictability on the one hand and rigidity on the other. The result is that he cannot modify his course of action in the face of unexpected developments or firm opposition. This rigidity of mental functioning is obvious even in ordinary everyday interviews. When an unexpected question is asked, he is completely at a loss. Castro wants things his own way and gets mad when he strikes firm opposition on solid ground.

This was evidenced recently during the 10th Iberoamerican Summit held in Panama, when Salvadorean president Francisco Flores not only rebutted Castro's allegations that El Salvador was protecting anti-Castro terrorists, but accused Castro of terrorist actions against El Salvador. Witnesses to the confrontation said that Castro lost control and began yelling like a crazy old lady, to the embarrassment of the chiefs of state attending the conference.[37]

Fidel Castro takes no advice and accepts no opposition. Anyone who gets in his way (or he *imagines* is getting in his way) is broken with complete ruthlessness, disregarding the person's previous history of faithful service to Fidel. Since the very beginning of his political career, Castro became very good at identifying potential enemies and swiftly taking them out of play while they are still unaware. When he decided to get rid of Gen. Abrahantes, he didn't send the Army to detain him, but Osmani Cienfuegos, Abrahantes' best friend. Osmany called Abrahantes and told him he was passing by early next morning to pick him up to go hunting. Once in Osmani's car, and away from Abrahantes' bodyguards, members of Castro's personal guard easily detained Abrahantes, who offered no resistance to the arrest.

In the same fashion, author Norberto Fuentes tells how his friend Colonel Tony de la Guardia, Castro's personal hit man, ignored all evidences and seemed to be totally unaware that Castro was planning to kill him.[38] As a boy in his father's farm at Birán, Fidel noticed how the man who was going to slaughter a pig kept the knife hidden from the animal until the very instant he was going to give the mortal stab. He learnt the lesson.

Castro is too single-minded and fanatical to feel gratitude or loyalty for people whose loyalty to him he feels has weakened, whatever they have done for him in the past. Frank País, Manuel Urrutia, Huber Matos, Camilo Cienfuegos, Ché Guevara, Arnaldo Ochoa, and many of his close associates, made the mistake of questioning his decisions, and paid dearly for their mistake.

Castro's Mastery of Symbols

In an age dominated by symbols, and particularly the symbols of language, Castro has demonstrated his knowledge of the immense power of language. He has shown great skill not only in the creation of verbal symbols but in the appropriation of traditional Cuban symbols as well. Castro has the skill to portray conflicting human feelings in vivid, tangible imagery that is comprehensible and moving even to simple, uneducated people. Therefore, in his long speeches he uses strong metaphors in the form of imagery, which, as Aristotle said, is the most powerful force on earth.

Similarly, Castro has created powerful verbal symbols for denigrating his opponents. He coined the word *"gusanos"* (worms) to designate his political opponents in Cuba and the United States. He used the term *"bandidos"* (bandits) to name the patriots fighting guerrilla warfare against him in the Escambray mountains. He coined the word *"contras"* (short from counter revolutionaries), used by Castro to designate people who actively opposed his regime and widely used later by the Sandinistas to denigrate the anti-Sandinista fighters. Amazingly, the term was also adopted by the anti-Sandinista guerrillas themselves and their sympathizers.

Like Hitler and the Nazis, Castro has appropriated old patriotic symbols. He found the way to draw on the traditions and history of the Cuban people and change them into oral symbols and slogans, like *"Socialismo o muerte"* or *"Los cien años de lucha,"* ("Socialism or Death," "The Hundred Years of Struggle"), storming the mind of the Cuban masses with these stereotyped, constantly repeated slogans.

Just after the failed attack on the Moncada barracks he called his group the "Generation of the Centenary," identifying it with the commemoration of José Martí's centenary and appropriating it for his own use. After he grabbed power in 1959 and needed to expand his revolution in order to neutralize the Rebel Army [39] and the M-26-7, he created the slogan *"El pueblo unido jamás será vencido,"* ("The people united will never be defeated") that soon after became the war cry of Leftist militants all around the world. After his victory at the Bay of Pigs in April, 1961, Castro added to his speeches the slogan *"Venceremos."* Almost immediately "We Shall Overcome" became the slogan of the American radical left.

By reference to those historical themes he evokes the deepest unconscious emotions of his audience. This constant repetition finally imprinted the desired ideas in the unconscious minds of the people. Most scholars and writers still don't understand why the unconscious mind is more intensely affected by great symbols and themes than by concrete facts, but the principle is extensively used by advertising companies. Similarly, very early in his political career Castro may have realized that enthusiastic political action does not occur if the people's emotions are not deeply involved. He also has a keen appreciation for the value of catchwords, dramatic phrases, and happy epigrams in penetrating the deeper levels of the psyche of the Cuban masses.

A Man Driven by Envy

Contrary to popular belief, far from been motivated by politics or ideology, most of Castro's actions have been motivated by envy. The case below illustrates the point.

By the mid-1980s the Cuban economy was in its normal state since Castro took power in the Island in 1959: in shambles. The only thing that seemed to be working was a pervasive black market economy. So, in order to get his piece of the pie, Fidel instituted his own version of a government black market and allowed farmers and artisans to sell the product of their hard work—after paying very high taxes to the state. But, by miracles of old, dirty Capitalism, the system worked. As a matter of fact, it worked so well that it stirred Fidel's anti-Capitalist soul. According to him, Cubans were filling their stomachs, but were becoming corrupt in the process.

So, by the late 1980s, Castro suddenly stopped the successful liberalization of the Cuban economy to prevent imaginative, hardworking farmers and artisans from becoming "too rich." Fidel, it was reported, was stunned by the fact that many people were making big money on the private farmers' markets that he himself had introduced in 1980 to stimulate production and reduce shortages. A few weeks after closing these markets he also stopped the recently created right to private home ownership. Fidel complained that homeowners were "getting rich" buying, selling, and trading houses. At the next congress of his "Communist" Party, he told the delegates: "No one is born a revolutionary. We must cultivate man's sense of shame."[40]

In the 1990s, the story repeated itself once more. In 1993 Castro legalized the U.S. dollar, and allowed people to go into certain small personal businesses. Almost overnight more than five thousand *paladares* (small restaurants in private homes) managed to serve a cheap, though varied menu. Some adventurous grass-roots entrepreneurs began offering home-delivered pizza (or at least something slightly resembling pizza) and steak sandwiches.

For the first time in their history since Castro took power in 1959, Cubans enjoyed the marvels of a makeshift free market economy competing against inefficient state enterprises. The new businessmen were happy, because they were making more in a day than others were making in a month of working for the government. Most Cubans were happy, because they were able to get in the market the products and services the government was unable to provide. But on April 11, 1994, allegedly after strong complaints from some hard-line government officials, Castro backpedalled again and issued a decree virtually eliminating all private business.[41]

Cubans, who know Castro very well, never believed that the reasons he gave for stopping the farmer's markets first and later private activities were the true ones. But they did not know his true reasons for taking this step. There is, however, an almost unknown incident that perhaps may give us a clue about the real, hidden motivation underlying Castro's actions.

In the mid sixties, Cuban Channel 6 began broadcasting a tv program that became an instant success: *Los galanes* (literally, the courtiers, or ladies' men). It was a sort of talk-show, targeted mostly at young women, having as guests the best good-looking actors from radio and tv. The popularity of those young actors skyrocketed. They were accosted by women in the studio and out in the streets.

Fidel Castro does not watch Cuban tv, therefore the program went on undisturbed for several weeks. But one day he heard about it, made some inquiries, and was told about its success. Instantly, he became furious and ordered the program to be taken off the air. No reasons were given for the suspension of the program, and just a small group of top executives at the tv station knew that the actual reason was Castro's direct order.

You may ask yourself why Castro stopped the program. He was not competing for an acting position. He is not a womanizer. Unlike the previously mentioned farmers or free market entrepreneurs, those actors were not making any money out of it. They were not being "corrupted by capitalism." But they had become the focus of the public's attention. They were loved by young women and admired by the public, and that made Fidel turn green with envy. In fact, if you want to know what really makes Fidel tick, what is the true motivation behind his actions, the answer is very simple: envy.[42]

The word "envy"[43] is derived from the Latin *invidia*, from the verb *invidere*, to see with intensity. Some negative emotions such as anger are believed to affect people through the eyes. Cartoonists have a very graphical way to express it, when they draw daggers coming from the eyes of a person to show hatred and envy. In many societies, particularly in Asia, staring at people is considered to be rude, and usually causes discomfort or provokes aggressive responses.

Some people's looks are supposed to be more harmful than others, and those who have been endowed with the evil eye are feared as bringers of bad luck and misfortune. But, though many negative emotions are linked to the evil eye, most people agree that envy is the most frequent emotion associated with it. Cuban poet and writer José Martí apparently believed it when he wrote that some people have "the envious eye of dwarves." And envy, which together with greed and jealousy comprise the three constituent elements of malice, is the most malevolent of all.

Greed is an insatiable desire to take for oneself what another possesses. A greedy person can admit that what he wants is good or valuable. In contrast, an envious person is not concerned with possessing, just with preventing others from doing it. For the envious or evil eyed, goodness must not be preserved, only attacked, spoiled, or destroyed.[44]

Jealousy, the other component of malice, is an emotion concerned with relationships. It has to do with rivalry with one person for the love of another. Jealousy consists both of a bitter hatred and a possessive love. But envy has nothing to do with love; it is pure malice. Envy has been defined as a disgruntled emotional state arising from the possessions of achievements of another, a spiteful wish that the other should lose them. The envious person begrudges others their personal or material assets, being more intent on their destruction than on their acquisition.

Envy is such a destructing vice that is was included among the seven principal faults or character flaws—the seven capital sins—to which almost every other vice can be traced. The Catholic Church defines envy as, "a sadness of mind that another should be better off than ourselves, as though we ourselves suffered because of another's fortune."[45]

Perhaps there was a grain of truth in Castro's assertion, "Money does not motivate me; material good does not motivate me."[46] Though he has accumulated large amounts of money and property, it seems that what Castro really enjoys is depriving other people of their money, their possessions, their freedom and their happiness. One of the things that makes him mad is other people's success. Like a Caribbean Aglaurus,[47] Fidel never smiles, except at the sight of someone else's troubles and hates the success of others because at its sight he pines away. One of the few things he really enjoys is to hurt, humiliate, and embarrass others, or to see them in humiliating and embarrassing situations.

Envious malice can be directed not only at an individual, but at a larger group including a nation or a whole culture. Castro is envious of almost everybody, particularly Americans. In the case of Fidel Castro, envy has been complicated by the presence of a twisted mind, and the combination has proved to be very dangerous. Luis Conte Agüero, once Castro's closest friend, observed that Fidel feels a strong resentment against people he suspect may be happier than he.[48]

The anecdote of *los galanes* mentioned above is not an isolated incident, but a characteristic of Castro's behavior. Before going any further, let me give another example. On May 30, 1959, just a few weeks after he took power in Cuba, the Castro Government announced a new tax law. It provided for a tax of 40 per cent on the profits of all foreign and domestic companies. Sales taxes were to go up to 20 per cent on such items as refrigerators, radios, and perfume, and 30 per cent on automobiles costing more than $3,000 and on luxury yachts. The government also announced a tax on society news. The person described in a society item in a newspaper was to pay $1.00 for each adjective used. Any mention of a title in connection with a Cuban citizen would cost him $100.00, and each column inch of a photograph would be $5.00 for a single person and $10.00 for a group.

At the time Cubans still had their sense of humor intact, therefore the reaction to the new tax law was shouts of laughter. There was still a free press in Cuba, which ridiculed the tax so much it was soon dropped. It was known later that the idea for such an insane tax law had come directly from Fidel Castro.

What is known of Castro's behavior strongly suggest that some of his apparently unexplainable actions, like, i.e., his utmost contempt for people in positions of power, his hatred for people who are economically solvent, his discomfort for other people's success, may have been motivated by envy.[49] Moreover, as envy has always been among the motives of those who accuse others of some crime and will distort the evidence to persuade themselves of the accused's guilt,[50] one may speculate that envy may be the true motivation behind Castro's deep hatred for the United States.

The Misery Specialist

I remember that, in the mid-sixties, a small group of writers and actors used to go to the Caballero funeral home in Havana's Vedado district to have a wee-hours cup of coffee after waiting in line for several hours (which had nothing to do with Cuban surrealism, but with coffee shortages). One of them, playwright Alfredo Pons, in order to help our waiting time go faster, developed, tongue-in-cheek, an interesting theory: the "misery specialists." Everywhere you go in this country, reasoned Pons, people treat you like dirt. Bus drivers, office clerks, restaurant waiters, hotel staff, deliberately do all kinds of things to make your life miserable, and they have become experts in their profession.[51] Therefore, continued Pons, there should be some special schools where they get their training in the misery trade. Graduates from those schools become certified "misery specialists," and they land good government jobs.

Pons and the rest of us loved the joke, and continued developing the concept for several weeks. But one day, almost unanimously, we arrived at the same conclusion. We were dead wrong. There were no such people as "misery specialists." As a matter of fact, there was only *one* misery specialist in Cuba: Fidel Castro! Now I am beginning to think that our conclusion was not far-fetched at all. Castro is a true misery specialist. Out of pure envy, he has always managed to destroy anything that gives the people around him any pleasure or makes them happy, from food for their stomachs to nourishment for their souls. One of his main purposes in life has been to inflict as much pain and suffering as possible on any people he can reach, and he has accomplished it to a remarkable extent.

Singer Carlos Puebla, a strong supporter of Castro, never guessed how right he was when he used to sing in the early 1960s: *"Se acabó la diversión / Llegó el Comandante y mandó a parar."* (The enjoyment has finished / The *Comandante* arrived and ordered a stop to it.)[52] Gabriel García Márquez commented that Fidel "is one of the rare Cubans who neither sings nor dances," adding that as soon as Fidel arrives to a party, "Inevitably the dancing is interrupted, the music stops, the dinner is put off."[53]

Carlos Franqui believes that,

> What Fidel has done is to impose in Cuba all the punishments he suffered as a boy in his Jesuit school: censure, separation of the sexes, discipline, thought control, a Spartan mentality. He hates culture, liberty, and any kind of literary or scientific brilliance. All sensuality, of course, is anathema to him.[54]

There are some indications that perhaps Franqui is not too off the mark. For example, in mid 1998, just a few years after Castro reluctantly gave orders to loosen some economic controls to allow the people to do limited business, he soon became envious of their economic success. In a long address to Cuba's National Assembly, aired by state television, Castro criticized the appearance of local "millionaires" in Cuban society, accusing them of amassing private wealth while state teachers, doctors and police had to survive on low salaries. He made clear he deeply disliked the socially divisive effects of the cautious, market-leaning economic reforms introduced by his government since 1993.[55]

Some of the new private entrepreneurs, Castro said, were earning as much as 1,000 U.S. dollars a month, equivalent to around 20,000 Cuban pesos, a small fortune by Cuban standards. (Cuban workers average about 20 to 40 U.S. dollars a month.) The idea that simple Cubans might be able to buy their own cars appeared distasteful to the ever envious Fidel. "If we start selling cars to all those who have dollars . . . [we will have] a whole class of rich people driving around Havana," he said.[56] Lately, Castro is blaming the enormous increase in street crime on the success of capitalist-style economic reforms. Consequently, he is seeking a crackdown on drug trafficking and criminals—and probably on state-approved market-oriented reforms.[57] On December, 2000, Carlos Lage, executive secretary of Castro's Council of Ministers, announced government plans to end most private economic activities by mid-2001.[58]

While the Cuban people lack adequate food supplies, Castro has been exporting food to finance his military adventures and terrorism abroad. Just a few years after Castro took power in Cuba, a strict system of food rationing was imposed, and is still in force. The daily diet to which most Cubans have been restricted for almost 40 years of rationing is not only inferior to the diet of the 1950s, but also to the nutritional ration normally allocated to slaves in the colonial Cuba of 1842. A final example will provide an indication that the true reason for food scarcities in Cuba is not the American embargo.

One can understand that, because of the embargo, Cubans cannot drink Coca-Cola or eat Burger King's hamburgers. But Cuba is a big Island with plenty of fertile soil, and a climate which supports four crops a year. Since the fifties, Cuba was self-sufficient in the production of basic foods for self-consumption, including beef, poultry, fish, vegetables, rice, beans, etc. Now, for the sake of argument, let's accept that because of the embargo Cuban farmers lack the adequate machinery, fertilizers, and the like to produce enough food. But how about fish? Cuba is a long, narrow island with miles and miles of sea coast where fish and seafood are varied and plentiful. Why, one may ask, Cubans don't fish to supplement their meager food rations? They don't fish because Fidel Castro strictly prohibits it, the same way he prohibits Cubans to engage in almost any productive activity he cannot fully control.

Just casting a fish hook on a line over the Malecón, Havana's promenade facing the sea, would allow a Cuban to bring home a red snapper and have a wonderful dinner for free. But, although that would make him and his family very happy, it would make Fidel Castro very angry, because other people's happiness is the worst offense to Cuba's misery specialist. Capturing seafood is particularly prohibited. A Cuban caught with a lobster goes straight to jail.

Some neighbors of the Castro family who were familiar with the Castro house in Birán say that it was indescribable filthy. Although there was a stream nearby, the Castros had no running water or toilets and they seldom washed or bathed. Visitors reported that chickens had the run of the dirty interior, sometimes roosting on the beds.[59] Gustavo Hevia, a friend of the Castros, related that on a visit he once made to the Birán estate to stay overnight a garden sprinkling can had been hung up for him in a corner of a room to serve as a shower. The only bed in the house which had sheets and a pillow case was his own.[60]

An American journalist who visited Cuba before 1959, wrote that "Havana was once the most cheerful city in the Americas, possibly the world. The colors blazing forth from the most delicious Spanish architecture anywhere, including Spain, made a tourist in pre-Castro Cuba feel that just looking around was worth the admission."[61] When he visited Havana again more than forty years later he only found deterioration and decrepit facades.[62] After forty-two years in power, Fidel Castro has turned Havana into a larger version of the Birán estate.

On December 9, 2000, the Castro government announced that it would cut phone communications between Cuba and the U.S. by December 16.[63] According to a brief note which appeared in Cuba's official newspaper *Granma*, the cause for the drastic measure was that U.S. companies had failed to pay a 10 percent surcharge that became effective at the end of October. But the timing for the cut gives an indication that perhaps the true motives are not exactly the ones stated in *Granma*.

In the first place, no one but Castro himself has the power in the Cuban government to order such a measure. Secondly, despite the Island's proximity to the U.S. the rate charging to callers to Cuba averaged 80 to 90 cents a minute, of which the companies were paying 60 cents a minute to the Castro government. Finally, Castro made a conscious decision to cut service during the Christmas holidays, one of the most important times of the year for families whose members have been apart for decades.

If one is to believe the arguments offered by Cuban officials, the rationale for the cut was simply money. But Cubans know better. Listening to their relatives' voices is a major source of happiness for Cuban families and friends on both sides of the Florida Straits, and this is something the misery specialist[64] cannot tolerate, even if it costs him money. No wonder Cubans have created a new nickname for Fidel Castro: *el castrasueños* (lit. the castrator of dreams).[65]

Fidel's Epiphany

A small parade organized by the Spanish embassy in Havana on January 6, 2001, celebrating the Epiphany, the day when, following the Hispanic tradition, the Three Wise Men bring gifts to the children, unleashed an unexpected virulent response in the government-controlled Cuban media. Even though the parade had been previously authorized by the government, Cuban tv and the press violently attacked the embassy personnel who, wearing the traditional costumes, distributed candies and small gifts to the children who attended the parade. Some of the press articles called the Spaniards "clowns," "good-for-nothings," "cheap kings," and all kinds of derogatory epithets. The celebration of the Epiphany was banned in Cuba just a few years after Castro took power in 1959.

The violent reaction surprised the Spanish diplomats. One of them commented that "The activity had been approved by the Cuban authorities," adding that, "there was absolutely no intention of creating an incident."[66]

Most Cubans were understandably confused about why such an insignificant event generated such an enormous response from the Castro government. Looking for a rational explanation some have tried to attribute it to the recent "battle of ideas," a kind of Cultural Revolution recently unleashed by the 75 year old Cuban tyrant. However, a small detail in the text of the attacks perhaps may be the key to a totally different explanation.

According to some of the attacks which appeared in the Cuban press, handing gifts to the Cuban children was just a way to "humiliate" them. The use of the word "humiliation" in the text is a strong clue pointing to the identity of the person who actually wrote the articles: Fidel Castro.

During a long conversation with the Brazilian priest Frei Betto, Fidel Castro made such revealing statements about an almost unknown incident of his early childhood that it is necessary to quote them in detail:

> *Castro*: January 6 was the Epiphany. We were told that the Three Wise Men, who had traveled to pay homage to Christ when he was born, came every year to bring children presents.
> I spent three Epiphanies with that family in Santiago de Cuba, Therefore, I must have been three at least two and a half years.
> *Betto*: So the capitalist Santa Claus never became popular in Cuba?
> *Castro*: No, never. We had the Three Wise Men: Caspar, Melchior and Balthazar. I can still remember the first letters I wrote them when I was five and asked them for everything—cars, trains, movie cameras, the works. I would write long letters to the Three Wise Men on January 3. Then I looked for some grass, and I put it under my bed with some water. The disappointment came later.
> *Betto*: What's that about the grass?
> *Castro*: Since the Three Wise Men rode camels, you had to provide them with some grass and water, which you put under your bed.
> Betto: All mixed up?

Castro: Either mixed up or the grass and water next to each other. You have to provide food and water for the camels, especially if you wanted the Three Wise Men to bring you lots of presents, everything you'd asked them for in your letter.

Betto: And what did the Three Wise Men eat?

Castro: Well, I don't know. Nobody remembered to leave food for the Three Wise Men. Maybe that's why they weren't very generous with me! The camels ate the grass and drank the water, but I got very few toys in exchange. I remember that my first present was a small cardboard trumpet; just the tip was made out of metal, something like aluminum. The trumpet was the size of a pencil.

For three consecutive years, I was given a trumpet; I should have become a musician! The second year's trumpet was half aluminum and half cardboard. The third time it was a trumpet with three small keys, made completely of aluminum.[67]

One of the most remarkable things about Castro's interview is his vivid description of the cheap toy trumpets he received. Undoubtedly they must have made such a strong impression that he was able to remember in detail, more than sixty years later, the exact form and material of the toy trumpets.

Seen through the light of Castro's words to Frei Betto, Castro's unprovoked, virulent attack on the well-intentioned Spaniards who dared to give gifts to the Cuban children takes a new meaning. Castro's reaction was not motivated by any political reasons, but by resentment and envy.[68] His convoluted mind could not accept the fact that the Three Wise Men, who didn't bring him the gifts he deserved when he was a child, were bringing gifts to the Cuban children. The Cuban children would therefore suffer the same misery he suffered as a child.

Castro's Health Problems

Castro suffers strong attacks of depression from time to time about which almost nothing has been written. During his years at the Belén School, he suffered from them a great deal. It is probably also true that he suffered from depression when he was at the Sierra Maestra fighting his guerrilla war against Batista.

After the death in 1980 of Celia Sánchez, Castro's personal secretary and confidant, he fell into a severe depression which lasted for some time. After Celia's death, he appeared strangely remote, preoccupied, even unaware of important things swirling around him.

The death of Celia Sánchez was a major crisis in Castro's life, and we can assume that it probably marked his worst depression. Undoubtedly he frequently has minor ones, during which he withdraws from his associates and broods by himself, or periods when he refuses to see anyone and is irritable and impatient with those around him. On the whole, however, it appears that the reports of Castro's depressions have been exaggerated. Not one of the people who has had close contact with him has any knowledge of his ever retiring to a sanatorium during such times and there are only unconfirmed reports that he ever sought psychiatric help.[69]

After she broke with Castro, Teresa Casuso, at some time one of Castro's close associates, told a tv reporter in New York that she believed Fidel was insane. Two psychiatrists are said to have had Fidel as a patient during the year following his victory. After moving to New York, one of them reported that she found nothing wrong with Castro. But then she also is said to have come unprofessionally under the spell of Castro's personality.[70]

In 1974, a book editor at the Editorial de Ciencia Sociales, a branch of the Cuban Book Institute, was discreetly given the task of hurriedly translating into Spanish [71] an obscure book entitled *La Folie de Jésus: son herédité, sa constitution, sa physiologie*, written by French author Charles Binet-Sangle. The book, published in 1908, dealt with children of alcoholics and their psychic traumas. Though the work was kept confidential, the translator somehow found out that the order for the job had come from Castro's office at the Revolution's Plaza. Once the book was translated, only three copies were printed.

One can safely surmise that the book was intended for Fidel Castro, who does not read French. No one can be certain, however, as to why Castro was so interested in reading Binet-Sangle's book. A good guess may be that he believed he was suffering from some type of real or imagined ailment common to the children of alcoholics. People suffering from that syndrome are known in the psychiatric literature as adult children of alcoholics (ACoA), and their behavior shows some similarities with Castro's.[72] Fidel has always feared he inherited some strange disease from his alcoholic father. It is known that, particularly after Fidel was born, his father Angel was drunk from morning to night.[73] Apparently his father's alcoholism marked Fidel's life.

Unknown even to most of his close associates, Fidel Castro has always been a hypochondriac.[74] Castro not only suffers from imaginary diseases, but from real ones as well. According to some sources in Cuba, a few years ago he had a scuffle with cancer, and is currently suffering from pulmonary problems, hypertension, and an uncommon brain disease called cerebral ischemia.[75]

Though the fact has been kept under an absolute veil of secrecy, it has come out that in 1990 Castro had parts of his colon removed to extirpate a malignant tumor. The operation was carried out at Cairo's University Hospital by Professor Ahmed Shafik, a specialist in gastro-intestinal diseases. According to Marcelo Fernández-Zayas, a Washington-based Cuban journalist and intelligence analyst in exile, Dr. Shafik admitted the fact during a telephone interview, adding that he had visited Cuba on five occasions. In the months preceding the operation Castro had lost more than fifty pounds.

Sources in Cuba claim that, around 1979 Col. Antonio de la Guardia, executed on Castro's orders in 1989, told some friends that while he was scuba diving with Castro, the Cuban leader had a serious respiratory problem. Other sources claim that Gen. Abelardo Colomé Ibarra told a similar version to his staff. The information tallies with the fact that in 1981 Castro suddenly stopped smoking his famous Cohiba cigars, and people meeting Castro in close environments were notified that they should not smoke.

Castro's pulmonary problems are not new. Since he was a teenager he became a heavy cigar smoker. In July, 1960, he had a severe attack of pneumonia and had to be hospitalized. After that he has had several less severe pulmonary infections.

Castro's health problems are not limited to colon cancer and pulmonary problems, but also affect his brain and heart. The first information about his brain problems came from a dubious source, but the fact that the Castro government made a great effort to discredit it indicates that the information might be true. Castro himself emphatically denied that he had any brain disease, but there is some information pointing to the contrary. For example, some people claim that during the trial of Gen. Arnaldo Ochoa in July, 1989, Castro suffered a short paralysis, first diagnosed as a cerebral embolism and later as a light cerebral ischemic attack. Castro's physicians also found symptoms of high hypertension. Though the patient rapidly recovered, his cardio-vascular problems persist.

Castro has a long history of brain problems. When he was about fifteen at the Belén School, he bet that he could ride a bicycle at top speed into a stone wall. He did so, and hit his head against the wall with such a force that he was unconscious for several days.[76] A few years later, when he was participating in an anti-government demonstration as a student at the University of Havana, he had a heated argument with a policeman, who hit Fidel on the head with his night stick. As a result Fidel had to be sent to a hospital. Next day a photo of Fidel, his head covered with bandages, appeared in many of Havana's newspapers. Some people claim that the bandages were just Fidel's theatrics, but a Cuban physician, who at the time was an intern at the School of Medicine's hospital, recalls that "Fidel was brought in with his scalp split open almost from his forward hairline to the nape of his neck.[77]

Some authors have speculated that, perhaps as a result of both incidents, Castro is affected with logorrhea, a rare disease characterized by excessive and often incoherent talkativeness.[78] There have been occasions when he became so unintelligible during one of his long speeches that he had to be pulled away from the microphone by his aids. When this has occurred, he has submitted with docility and seemed to be in a dazed state.

In the spring of 1990, during a meeting with some officials of the Ministry of Public Health in relation with an ongoing epidemic of polyneuritis, Castro had a heated discussion with Dr. Héctor Terry, deputy minister of hygiene and epidemiology. According to some witnesses, during the meeting Castro blamed the epidemic on Terry's poor job in relation with hygiene. Surprisingly, Terry, a highly qualified and respected professional, answered back, telling Castro that the real cause of the epidemic was the lack of adequate food for the people. Castro, a racist at heart, never expected such a response from a black person. Terry's answer provoked an irate explosion from Castro, during which he lost his speech and part of his face became paralyzed. Immediately, his staff helped him out of the room, and he never joined the meeting again. A few days after the incident Dr. Terry was fired.

At the time Castro was convinced that the old-style communists were going to kick Gorbachev out of the Kremlin. But the failed *coup d'état* of August, 1991, which eventually brought Yeltsin to power in Russia, was Castro's reality check. By the time he was under treatment for strong depression, and his constant attacks of paranoia had everybody around him on the edge. He had the looks of a sick person, and had suffered a paralysis of part of his body and face which forced him to undergo long rehabilitation therapy.[79]

In the summer of 1993 Castro traveled to Varadero beach, east of Havana, to attend the inauguration of a new hotel, a Cuban-Spanish joint venture. As he entered the reception area and was talking to some foreign journalists and visitors, he had a similar attack. Castro's security detail rapidly cleared the area of visitors, while he sat for more than 15 minutes trying to recover. Finally, his staff helped him get into his car and they left.

In April, 1994, Fidel received Frederick Chiluba, Zambia's president, on an official visit to the Island. Back at home, some of the president's aides mentioned at the University of Zambia, Lusaka, that during their visit, Castro had a partial face paralysis and had trouble speaking. Sources close to Lidia Castro, Fidel's half-sister, made comments that during April 12 to 16 she had been worried because her brother was very sick.

In 1996, Castro's aging looks and his failure to give his traditional 26 of July speech at the celebration of the attack on the Moncada garrison brought rumors of ill health and even accounts that he had died. But the rumors ceased in October when he delivered a seven-hour speech before the Communist Party Congress.

Though he still looked like a man who has lost weight, Castro was intellectually active. He was again giving long speeches, and his health seemed to have improved. American intelligence analysts apparently agreed. In June 12, 1997, two months before Castro turned 71, CIA Director George Tenet told the U.S. Congress that Cuban President Fidel Castro was relatively fit. "Unless he suffers a health crisis, he is likely to be in power a year from now."[80]

In November 1999, after four hours of a long speech in which he furiously attacked some dissident leaders in Cuba, Castro suddenly had to stop and run to the bathroom. "Put some music on or something," he said to the surprised tv producers who for some time were unable to do anything, "I'll be back in a moment." Castro's urgency may be a symptom of incontinence caused by an enlarged prostate, a common ailment affecting old men. Some people watching Castro on tv that night observed that during his long speech he lost his line of thought several times. An evident symptom of senility was when he referred to former Interior Minister, Gen. José Abrahantes, as *"el compañero Abrahantes"* (comrade Abrahantes), apparently forgetting that Abrahantes had died a few months earlier in one of Castro's jails.

However, by mid 2000, when Castro reached 74, he looked fully revitalized and full of energy, physically and politically. Some people believe that the source of Castro's new found energy was none other than his fight with the Cubans in exile because of the Elián González case. The case brought back Castro's abilities as a political agitator, planning strategies, leading mass mobilizations, writing press releases, denouncing Washington's policies on long tv speeches, and even showing signs of modernization, like marching to mass meetings wearing sneakers and using a cell phone. Even some of his much younger close collaborators were having trouble following the *Comandante*'s steps.

But Castro seems to have another explanation for the phenomenon of his newly acquired vitality. Last April, Castro met in Havana Illinois Governor George Ryan, and the Cuban leader told him he is taking a special medicine to stay young. He even gave Ryan some of the pills he said keep him youthful. Back in Illinois, Ryan asked somebody at a lab to check the pills out, and they found a component they cannot identify.[81]

However, in mid-June, while he was giving a televised speech, Castro's prodigious memory faltered when he mentioned Cuba's 5 provinces, which he soon after corrected to 6. (Castro himself changed some years ago the number of provinces from 6 to 14). The video showed Castro getting very frustrated when he was unable to read his own speech notes. Also, his mouth began showing ticks on both sides and he began mumbling to himself. At one point saliva dribbled from his mouth.[82]

A few days later, on June 23, while he was giving a speech at El Cotorro, a small town south of Havana, Castro slumped forward with his head on the microphones and passed out. He was quickly whisked away by his bodyguards. A few minutes later he came back to the podium and told the surprised audience that he had fainted because of the heat, but he was okay.[83] According to sources in Havana, some Western diplomats were not surprised, claiming they had already notified their countries about Castro's rapidly deteriorating health.[84] Some physicians in Florida speculate that Castro's problems may be the result of another attack of cerebral ischemia.[85]

Fidel's Rages

Almost every author who has written about Castro has mentioned his rages. These are well known to all of his associates, and they have learned to fear them. The descriptions of his behavior during these rages vary considerably. The more extreme descriptions claim that at the climax his face turns purple, he stomps on the floor and kicks the walls. Probably one of his best known rages is the one he threw when he knew about Khrushchev's unilateral decision to dismantle the missile bases in 1962. Ché Guevara told some friends that, when Castro heard the news, he threw one of his worst rages, kicking the wall so forcefully that he broke a mirror.

Teresa Casuso has described in detail some of Fidel's temper tantrums. One day, during his first visit to the United States after the fall of Batista, Castro agreed to be interviewed in "domestic relaxation" for an American tv channel. The producer brought a whole wardrobe of civilian clothes for Fidel, but none of the suits was large enough, and he had none of his own. Finally Castro agreed to wear a pair of pajamas. But the program producer brought a fine dressing gown for Castro to use over his pajamas. Casuso tells that the temper tantrum he flew into when he saw the dressing gown (he said it was too luxurious for him) was of epic quality. He suddenly shut himself up in a room and furiously threw himself on the bed. Nobody dared to go in and talk to him. Finally, Casuso entered the room and sat on the edge of the bed. She talked to him softly, but firmly, as one talks to an obstinate child. Casuso remembers that Castro was lying face down, in a perfect rage, his head buried in pillows. Finally, Casuso convinced him to appear wearing his own pajamas. As soon as he came under the lights, the rage was gone and he changed into a reasonable person.[86]

Casuso tells about another of Castro's rages she witnessed. "Suddenly Fidel started emitting frightful yells, clutched his head, and threw himself face down upon the bed in an absolute loss of self-control. Using the strongest possible language, he screamed hysterically that he be left alone, and kicked furiously."[87]

Other people who have seen Castro during his rages, testify that, during them, his behavior turns extremely violent and shows an almost total lack of emotional control. In the worst rages he undoubtedly acts like a spoiled child who cannot have his own way and bangs his fists on the tables and walls. He scolds and shouts and stammers, his face turns purple and, on some occasions, foaming saliva gathers in the corners of his mouth.

It is wrong to believe, however, that these rages occur only when he is crossed on major issues. On the contrary, very insignificant matters might trigger this reaction. In general they are brought on whenever anyone contradicts him, when there is unpleasant news for which he might feel responsible, when there is any skepticism concerning his judgment, or when a situation arises in which his infallibility might be challenged or belittled. There is a tacit understanding among his staff not to tell him bad news—not to mention things which are not as he believes them to be. They know that the slightest difficulty or obstacle could make him scream with rage.

Fidel Castro is a manipulator. His relationship with other people is always based on exploitation. He believes he is perfect, and he will readily exploit friends, associates and acquaintances in order to promote his perfection.[88] Castro lives in an unreal world he has created himself, in which he is the only perfect and pure creature, surrounded by all kinds of evil people. When one of the people around him is unable to change reality according to his wishes, the supremacy of his perfection is threatened, and he reacts violently. A typical example of this was when, during one of his tantrums, he fired sugar industry minister Orlando Borrego when Borrego dared to express his doubts that the ten million ton sugar harvest quota of 1970 would be attained. Just a few months after Borrego was fired Castro was forced to publicly accept the fact that the goal was not reached, but he never apologized to Borrego or reappointed him to his previous position.

When exploitation fails, Castro turns to a tantrum to intimidate the person who is pushing reality upon him. Castro's tantrums are the walls that keep him isolated from the real world, keeping him happy and secure in his world of fantasy. Unfortunately, they isolate him from close contact with others.

Many people close to him believe that these rages are just play acting. There is probably some truth to this point of view since Castro's first reaction to an unpleasant situation is not indignation, as one would ordinarily expect, but rage. Similarly, when he has finished there is no aftermath. He immediately cools down and begins to talk about other matters in a perfectly calm tone of voice as though nothing had happened. Occasionally he will look around sheepishly, as if to see if anyone is laughing, and then proceeds with other matters, without the slightest trace of resentment.

Some of his closest associates think that he induces these rages consciously to frighten those about him. Some of them believe that they are a technique by which he can throw his entire entourage into confusion by well-timed fits of rage and thus make them more submissive. Rage and abuse have always been among the favorite weapons in his armory.

It is not the purpose of this analysis to enter into a detailed discussion concerning the nature and purpose of the rages. It is sufficient, for the present time, to realize that his associates are well aware that Castro can and does behave in this way. It is a part of the Castro they know and are forced to deal with. I may point out, however, that these rages do not seem to be conscious acting since it is almost impossible for an actor actually to turn purple in the face unless he really is in an emotional state.

Castro's Innate Cruelty

During a party *U.S. News and World Report* editor Mortimer Zuckerman gave honoring Castro's visit to New York in 1995, David Asman, a journalist writing for the *Wall Street Journal* noticed that Castro has "the eyes of a killer shark. There's no emotion behind them."[89] Though in his early days, being the good actor he is, Fidel managed to put some life into his eyes, they now reflect his inner hatred, rancor and envy. Truly, they are the eyes of a killer. Like some fascists, Castro looks at people "with the gaze of the coffin maker."[90] "I meet people who I immediately know are going to die young," he told one of his *Playboy* interviewers.[91]

Since his early childhood Fidel Castro exhibited a total contempt for life, which, as he grew older, extended to human life as well. Actually, the destruction of human beings in great numbers seems to be one of Fidel's true private pleasures. He has an extraordinary ability for using, abusing and destroying people. The cases of Frank País, Camilo Cienfuegos, Ché Guevara, Arnaldo Ochoa, Tony de la Guardia, José Abrahantes, and hundreds like them, prove that Castro uses people as a means to an end and then discards them, whether the end be business, war, or even what he may call love. The real problem with Fidel Castro is that he cannot meet his fellow man naturally, on an equal level; he can only do him violence, or himself suffer violence.

He was not yet ten when he enjoyed killing his mother's chickens with a .22 rifle. A few years later, when Fidel was in Santiago de Cuba attending Colegio Dolores, he got sick and had his appendix removed. After surgery he had to spend several weeks in the hospital. His main distraction while he was there, as Fidel told his biographer Carlos Franqui, was capturing lizards and "operating" on them with a razor. As expected, all of them died. Fidel then told Franqui how he enjoyed watching how the ants, who came by the hundreds, carried the dead lizards to their anthills. The amazing fact is not what he did as a young boy—this type of cruel behavior is not uncommon among some children—but that he remembered it so vividly after so may years.[92]

Georgie Anne Geyer, Castro's insightful biographer, tells two stories she heard from persons who were eye witnesses to Fidel's cruelty. According to one of them, Rolando Amador, one day Fidel was hunting near the sea and shot an albatross. Then, apparently not happy with his feat, he dragged the dying poor bird back to town and, as a joke, threw it through a friend's kitchen window, terrifying the people there.[93]

On another occasion, he was riding in a car with two friends and, as he saw some cows near the highway, Fidel asked them to stop. He got out of the car, drew the .45 pistol he always carried, and began shooting at the poor animals. Asked by his friends why he was doing such a thing, he answered that he was target practicing.

Many animal control officers believe that there is a close link between cruelty toward animals and violence toward humans. People who show no compassion for animals, they think, often have little regard for their fellow humans. Psychologist Mitchell Rosen believes that any sadistic act against an animal by a child "is a red flag of severe illness." Based on studies by FBI profilers, Rosen says that some of the most notorious serial killers in history started by killing animals. "If a child continues to torture an animal after the animal yelps, it shows detachment and lack of empathy and compassion, which would be eventually transferred to humans."[94]

During his whole life Castro has shown a total indifference to the death and suffering of others. As I mentioned above, Castro's biographer Carlos Franqui rightly pointed out that power is Fidel's orgasm. But it seems that Castro's lust for power is not an end by itself, but just a means to carry on with impunity the enjoyment of his true passion: killing people. As Cuba's Maximum Leader, he is intoxicated with his God-like power over life and death, and fully enjoys exercising it to the hilt. Apparently he believes that life is cheap and, consequently, he shows a total indifference to death.

During the early guerrilla days at the Sierra Maestra mountains, one of the guerrilla men, a seventeen year old poor, uneducated farmer, was caught stealing a can of condensed milk and a few cigars from another man's backpack. Castro had passed stiff penalties for people caught stealing, and the poor boy, after being found guilty, was sentenced to death. Because of the boy's young age, and the low value of the things stolen, the officer who acted as a judge asked for Castro's authorization in order to proceed with the execution. Most of the men expected that Castro was going to spare the boy's life. But that was not Castro's way of looking at things. According to witnesses, Castro said coldly: "We must shoot him, to give an example."[95] A few minutes later, the boy was executed.

There is certainly the streak of the sadist in him. A few weeks after he grabbed power in Cuba, dozens of captured officers of the former Cuban constitutional army who had been fighting Castro's rebels in the mountains were prosecuted. Though some of the officers had in fact committed serious crimes, the judicial process was highly irregular, where most of the evidence was hearsay and "witnesses" expressed their feelings of hatred, most of them not based on facts. As expected, most of the suspects were found guilty and given a death sentence. Castro ordered the executions to be filmed and the films to be aired on tv and shown on movie theaters. For several months the Cuban people contemplated in the screens the grim spectacle of brains blown off and smiling Castroist officers giving the *coup de grace* to convulsing, dying men.

When Major Humberto Sorí Marín, a close friend of Castro who had an active role in the fight against Batista, turned against his regime, Fidel sent his men to capture him. Sorí Marín was shot in the leg before he was captured. Sent to jail, Castro ordered him to be executed. Marín's mother called Fidel and asked him to spare her son's life, and Castro promised her to do so. The next day Marín was shot against the wall by a firing squad. Because of Sorí Marín's wounds, he was dragged to a pole and fastened to it before being shot. What gives a sense of Fidel's cruelty is that, during the whole event, Castro was present, watching his friend's horrible death.[96]

In February 1961, Major William Morgan, an American who won his rank fighting Batista in the Escambray mountains, faced

Castro's shooting squad. Morgan had been accused of treason after a failed operation against the Dominican Republic. The final moments of Morgan's life, at 2:30 a.m., have been described in detail by his fellow inmate John Martino. It is worth quoting him in detail:

> As his hands were being tied behind his back, an unidentified voice in the shadows of the lights beamed on Morgan shouted: "Kneel and beg for your life!" Morgan shouted back: "I kneel for no man!" But it was a sharp shooter, not a firing squad, that killed him. First, a bullet was put through one knee, then one through the other. As Morgan crashed to the ground cursing the Communists, the same unidentified voice from the shadows exulted: "There! You see, we made you kneel!" The rifleman put another bullet through one of Morgan's shoulders. He took his time putting a bullet through the other, prolonging the agony of his victim. Then, a captain walked up to Morgan and emptied a clip from his Tommy gun into his chest.[97]

Martino adds that both Fidel and Raúl Castro were there, enjoying their ex-friend's last minutes of agony.

Since Castro took power in Cuba, prisons have mushroomed all over the Island. Torture, both physical and mental, is a standard practice, and dissidents are commonly sent to jail or to psychiatric institutions. The number of people killed by the Castro government, both directly by firing squad or by Castro's military, and indirectly while trying to flee the country, is in the tens of thousands. People who have lost their lives thanks to Castro's actions in Africa, Latin America, and other parts of the world, including the United States, probably number several hundred thousands.

On the other hand, we should not measure Castro's crimes by bloodletting alone. To measure the real depth of Castro's crimes we must think about the broken homes, the destroyed lives, the humiliations, the sadness of exile, the many Castro-created misfortunes which have fallen upon a formerly happy people.

Castro's Twisted Mind

Fidel Castro is a very vindictive person. While apparently compassionate and even generous with family and friends, he becomes filled with vindictive rage at anyone—including close friends—he believes stand in the way of his personal agenda. Accordingly, Castro could be charming or brutal, generous or savage. When brutality is called for, he could act with force and decisiveness. He would not shrink from cruelty.

Castro never forgets a personal offense, real or imagined. For him one of the worst offenses is when he feels he has been humiliated, and apparently he feels humiliated very often for the most varied reasons. Jesús Conte Agüero, a former close friend of Fidel, says that he saw written on the margin of a page of José Martí's *Poesías Completas* belonging to Fidel, "I prefer to die riddled with bullets than to live humiliated."[98]

The sense of humiliation is extremely strong in Fidel Castro. Like many easily humiliated people, Castro is likely to become upset by actions and events that most people either don't notice or see as too unimportant to merit any emotional involvement.

Any person familiar with Castro's speeches may testify that the word "humiliation," is a mantra he repeats over and over. And when he feels humiliated he will do everything to recover his self-esteem, including engaging in risky or heroic deeds, like the Moncada attack, or acts of sheer *bravado*, like shooting down a U-2 plane during the Cuban missile crisis. This complicated mechanism of psychological survival explains the irrationality of most of Castro's policy decisions.

Evidence indicates that most of the time Castro makes policy choices not for political, but for psychotherapeutic reasons. The incident in which he ordered two unarmed civilian planes of the Miami-based Brothers to the Rescue organization to be shot down by his MiG fighters is an example of the above. According to Castro he did so because the planes were violating Cuban air space and he felt "humiliated."

Another personal trait of Fidel Castro is his sadistic tendencies, evidenced by the fact that he is stimulated only by the helpless, never by those whom he perceives as strong. Above all, he sees everything in terms of control. He does not seem to get any pleasure when he has the opportunity to inflict a wound on an enemy in a fight between equals, because in this situation the infliction of the wound is not an expression of control. For Castro there is only one admirable quality, and that is power. He admires, loves, and submits to those who have power, and he despises and tries to control those who are powerless and cannot fight.

A recent proof of the above was Castro's reaction to U.S. Secretary of State Colin Powell's praising words claiming that Castro has done "some good things for his people."[99] Castro's immediate response was blasting Powell, calling him "the commander-in-chief of Latin American lackeys."[100]

Some psychologists who have analyzed Castro's behavior say they recognize in him the symptoms of a paranoid personality. Castro, they say, slips easily from his real life of ease, power and satisfaction to a world made up systematically of illusions and projections of his personal conflicts, which he ascribes to hostilities arising outside himself. Those who can please him by playing his game, by accepting as real his delusions and the imagined hostility of others, as Celia Sánchez did, can manipulate Fidel to some extent, though they realize that living close to Fidel Castro is a dangerous game. Paraphrasing a poem by José Martí, his brother Raúl once referred to Fidel as "a star that shines and kills."

There are many other aspects of Castro's personality, as it is known to his close associates, that do not fit into the picture of the Maximum Leader as it is presented to the Cuban people. A few of the more important of these merit mention. Castro is represented as a man of great courage, with nerves of steel who is always in complete control of every situation. Nevertheless, he often runs away from an unpleasant, unexpected, or difficult situation.

Several occasions have been reported when he has not carried through his own plans because he feared opposition. Furthermore, many may wonder about the necessity of the extreme precautions that are taken for his safety, most of which are carefully concealed from the common Cubans. When Castro gives a speech at a public meeting he looks for all the world like an extremely brave man as he stands up and salutes, oblivious to the many times that, according to his claims, his enemies have tried to assassinate him. But the Cuban people don't know of the tremendous number of secret service and security men who constantly mingle with the crowds in addition to the guards hiding in the surrounding buildings and lining the streets through which he is to pass. Neither do they know of all the precautions taken at his office at the Central Committee.

When he plans to visit a place and it is announced in the press, several thousand troops from his personal guard are sent in weeks in advance to set up machine-gun nests and antiaircraft batteries in the hills immediately adjoining. When he travels unannounced around the Island he is accompanied by more than 1, 200, SS-like special operations troops. This *Führerbegleit-kommando*, Fidel's hand-picked personal guard, is more heavily armed than an emperor's guard.

In relation to the claims of his great courage there are some opinions on the contrary. Some of the survivors from the attack to the Moncada barracks in 1953 claim that Fidel got cold feet and fled the scene, abandoning his men during the action. The fact is that he and his brother Raúl escaped unharmed, and nobody saw them anymore after the actual fight began. Photographs taken during his Sierra Maestra days, show that Castro's weapon of choice was a powerful rifle with a telescopic sight, a weapon which allows its user to keep a long distance from the enemy. Even more, notwithstanding claims on the contrary, there is no evidence that he participated in any important battle against the forces of president Batista.

Particularly noticeable is Castro's inability to cope with unexpected situations. I will refer to two incidents, among many others, that illustrate this behavior:

In the evening of July 17, 1959, Castro went on the air to bring about the first overthrow of a chief of state by means of television. He called President Urrutia almost everything in the book, including a traitor to his country. While he was talking, somebody suggested bringing a crew to the Presidential Palace to ask President Urrutia to reply to Castro's accusation. The information reached Castro when he was still speaking and he suffered an extraordinary transformation. Fright reflected on his face, a swift look of panic that took everyone present by surprise. Evidently his plans had not called for President Urrutia replying to him live from the Palace, and he was horrified at the possibility.[101]

On another occasion, in early 1960, Castro went on television to accuse the United States of crimes against the Cuban revolution. During the course of his speech he violently attacked the American ambassador, as well as the Spanish ambassador, Juan Pablo de Lojendio, allegedly for helping counter-revolutionaries in Cuba. But Lojendio, who by chance was watching Castro on tv, got furious, drove to the station and stormed into the studio interrupting him and demanding the microphone to answer in kind. Some witnesses to the confrontation report that Castro was taken aback, completely lost his composure and looked wildly about him in the manner of a small boy caught stealing the cookie jar. Finally Castro's bodyguards forcefully removed Lojendio from the studio. It took several minutes for Castro to recover his composure and continue his speech.

Sometimes Castro becomes nervous and tends to lose his composure when he has to meet foreign journalists. Being a genius of propaganda he knows the power of the press in influencing public opinion and he always provides the foreign press (he totally ignores the Cuban press) with choice seats at all public ceremonies. When it comes to interviews, however, he feels himself on the defensive and insists that the questions be submitted in advance. When the interview takes place he is able to maintain considerable poise because he has his answers prepared. Even then he gives no opportunity to ask for further clarification because he immediately launches into a lengthy dissertation. When this is finished, the interview is over.

Castro is also terrified when he is called upon to speak to an audience he cannot fully control, like foreign intellectuals or any group in which he feels opposition or the possibility of criticism. During a visit he made to the Dominican Republic early in 1999, he left a press conference in a hurry after he discovered that one of the journalists was from the exile press in Miami.[102]

Castro's adjustment to people in general is very poor. He is not really on intimate terms with any of his associates. On the whole, he always maintains a considerable distance from other people. Even in his intimate and cozy moments, there is no attitude of familiarity towards him on the part of his staff. There is always a certain distance about him, that subtle quality of aloofness. He lives in the midst of many men and yet he lives alone. Many years of loneliness have cut him off from seeking refuge in people who really care about him. The reason for that is that Fidel Castro doesn't *really* care about anyone but himself. He is extremely selfish. The people around him are always afraid of him, but under his total control.

It is well-known that he cannot carry on a normal conversation or discussion with people. Even if only one person is present he must do all the talking. His manner of speech soon loses any conversational qualities it might have had and takes on all the characteristics of a lecture and may easily develop into a tirade. He simply forgets his companions and behaves as though he were addressing a multitude. He talks *to* people, but never *with* people.

Castro's extreme talkativeness does not only appear in connection with political matters. Even when he is alone with his adjutants or immediate staff and tries to be friendly he is unable to enter into a give-and-take conversation. At times he seems to want to get closer to people and relates personal experiences, such as "When I was in Mexico," or "When I was in the Sierra Maestra." But under these circumstances, too, he insists on doing all the talking and always repeats the same stories over and over again in exactly the same form, almost as though he had memorized them. His close associates have all heard them dozens of times, but this does not deter him from repeating them again with great enthusiasm. Nothing but the most superficial aspects of these experiences is ever touched upon. It seems as though he is unable to give more of himself than that.

When two or more people are present, even when they are some of Castro's close associates, there is no general exchange, no true conversation. Either Castro talks and they listen silent, or they talk among themselves and Castro sits silent. He does not seem to be annoyed at all when members of his own circle talk to each other unless, of course, he feels like doing the talking himself. But ordinarily he seems to enjoy listening to others while he makes believe that he is thinking or paying attention to something else. Nevertheless, people close to him know that he overhears everything that is being said and often uses it later on. However, he never gives credit to the person from whom he has learned it but simply passes it off as his own idea. He has always been a *poseur*.

Some members of his intimate circle quietly complain that if you try to tell Fidel anything, about any imaginable subject, you will find out that he "knows" everything already. Though he sometimes does what his advisers suggest, at first he laughs in their faces, and later does the very thing as if it were all his own idea and creation. He doesn't even seem to be aware of how dishonest he is. Another of his tricks that drives people and particularly his associates to distraction is his capacity of forgetting selectively. All his closest associates know how he can say something one day and a few days later say the opposite, completely oblivious of his earlier statement. When they show their dismay and call his attention to the inconsistency, he flies off into a rage and demands to know if the other person thinks he is a liar.

The Great Dissembler

Many people ignore that, notwithstanding his constant claims for truthfulness, Fidel Castro *is* a consummate liar, and a very convincing one. Over the years, he has proved to be a master of saying one thing while having in mind something totally different.

Author K. S. Karol reports an interesting anecdote about how he met Castro. On the occasion of Castro's visit to New York in 1960 to address the U.N. General Assembly, a group of Castro admirers, among them Henri Cartier-Bresson, I. F. Stone and Karol himself, met Castro, who told them about his speech the next day. Castro complained that the United States government was waging a perfidious war against Cuba, just because Cubans wanted their independence from the United States. According to Karol, "He was speaking in a low voice, as if his words were meant for us alone, with obvious sincerity and great conviction."[103] What Karol and his friends didn't know was that Fidel Castro has learnt to lie not only with words, but with facial expressions and body language as well.

Fidel Castro is a compulsive, delusionary pathological liar. He lies not only for political reasons about things of cardinal importance, but also gratuitously, over matters of little relevance. But, as it happens with most compulsive liars, he has a strong concern about keeping his image of a sincere, truthful person. Like many pathological liars, Fidel has the utter conviction that everybody around him is a liar.[104]

Just a few days after he was let free from the prison in Isle of Pines, he published an article in *Bohemia* entitled *"Mientes, Chaviano"* ("You Lie, Chaviano"); a vituperous attack on the colonel in command in Santiago during his assault on the Moncada Barracks.[105] While he was in Mexico preparing for the invasion of Cuba he wrote an article in which he angrily denounced the Cuban Embassy in Mexico for giving out false information about him. He titled the article *"Basta ya de mentiras"* ("Enough of Lies"). One of his first speeches after his rise to power had as a main theme the phrase: *"Nos casaron con la mentira y nos obligaron a vivir con ella."* ("They married us to a lie and forced us to live with it.") In his speeches, Castro keeps hammering his love for truth.

In a speech he made at Céspedes Park in Santiago de Cuba, he said: "To tell the truth is the first duty of all revolutionaries; to fool the people always brings the worse consequences . . . That is why I want to continue the system of always telling the people the truth."[106] In another speech, on January 8th, he stated: "To tell the truth is the duty of every revolutionary."[107] But, after the fall of Batista, and just a few months before he grabbed total power in Cuba, the ever truthful Fidel said: "I should add that, personally, I am not interested in power nor do I envisage assuming it at any time."[108] In 1987 Fidel told Frei Betto, "As I told you, I detest lies, and I've never lied—not to the people or to anyone else, because anybody who lies is degrading himself, lowering himself, prostituting himself, demoralizing himself."[109] During his long interview with *Playboy* magazine, he claimed four times that he has never told a lie.[110]

Like many policemen and lawyers, Castro is very adept at lying. He exudes friendship and trust while being duplicitous. Since he was very young, he discovered that he had been endowed with the liar's best gift: he could absolutely convince himself that he is telling the truth, convince his own respiratory system, and eventually come to believe it wholly. Matthews once said that Fidel passionately believes every word he says. In fact, Castro believes his lies. He has shaped the politics, culture, and the whole life of the Cuban nation with lies that soon after became official truths as reflected in the laws of the land.

When Castro is lying through his teeth, he doesn't swallow or tremble, he doesn't breathe raspily, or touch his mouth. He has no difficulty meeting anyone's eyes, his pupils do not get small and faraway, his face color does not change, his face is perfectly passive. His voice is calm, earnest, under control, his throat is unfilled with phlegm, his heart beats dully.

If you look carefully at him when he is lying—and he does it most of the time—you will not find any of the telltale signs of the liar: a strained neck, a furrowed brow or a false smile. His face is totally free from anxiety, fear, mistrust or nervousness.[111] But, even for a professional liar like Fidel, lying is not an easy task. Some intelligence analysts have observed that when he lowers his voice, looks you in the eye and speaks slowly with sincerity and conviction, it is an unmistakable sign that he is lying. Another sign is that, perhaps unconsciously, when Castro is lying he reverts to the drooling accent characteristic of his native Oriente province.

One of Castro's political assets is his ability to convince many different people that each of them alone enjoys his special confidence. Sooner or later they find they have been deceived, for Fidel gives his confidence and trust to nobody. This basic distrust for others was developed at an early age, during his infancy at Angel Castro's Birán estate.

It seems that Castro is very proud of his ability to lie without being detected. As he told his biographer Carlos Franqui, when Fidel was attending a Catholic school in Santiago de Cuba he was getting very low grades, so he devised a clever trick to fool his parents. He lied to his teachers and told them he had lost his gradebook, and another one was given to him. "From then on," Fidel confessed to Franqui, "I would put my grades in the new book and take that one home to be signed—with very good grades in it, of course. The other notebook, the one they put the real marks in at school, I signed myself and returned to school."[112]

As he became a political leader, his distrust for others grew to the point that he became an expert in concealing his thoughts even from his closest advisers. And when he suspects that someone might be penetrating his defenses, he reinforces them through deliberate disinformation. This quality of distrust, aloofness and impenetrability has been of considerable political advantage to him. In his rise to power it helped him play to perfection the role of the inaccessible and infallible Maximum Leader operating in a realm far removed from petty political or personal squabbles.

As good as he is avoiding having his outer shell penetrated, he is an expert in penetrating other people's defenses. Moreover, he possesses the odd, chameleon-like ability of absorbing *your* personality, of becoming *you*, and so in effect entering your subconscious as he grinds you down with furious and direct eye contact, smothering, ass-kissing charm, and a bandit's utter ruthlessness. The ones who become the focus of Castro's attention usually fall in love with him at first sight. In these moments Castro becomes an actor, a salesman, a therapist, and, above all, a friend. He is quick with a handshake and a smile, tossing off a friendly confidence and effortlessly lending an understanding ear. Immediately he becomes the kind of individual you like, and whose admiration you would like to earn in return. He is the kind of person you just want to talk to. While he is playing his charmer's role to the hilt he is carefully watching his interlocutor's face looking for signs that the other person is a liar—signs he always believes he has found, thus reinforcing his need to protect himself from liars by lying.

Fidel Castro has not only that weird psycho's gift of utter conviction, but also the ability of convincing other people about anything he wants. He is a very good salesman. He managed to convince the anti-Castro exiles that he is a Communist, convinced his close associates that he is not a Communist, and convinced the Left that he is a leftist. He convinced both friends and enemies that he is against the American embargo. He convinced the Soviet leaders that his theory of exporting revolution was better than their theory of pacific coexistence—with disastrous results for the Soviet Union. He convinced the Jesuits and other Catholic "revolutionaries" that he agrees with Liberation Theology. He is now trying to convince his Muslim terrorist friends that he is an admirer of the Muslim faith. I have no doubts that he will succeed in his endeavors.

Stanislavsky's customary critique for bad acting, "I don't believe you!," would never have applied to Fidel Castro. His teachers and schoolmates at the Colegio de Belén apparently had a similar view in mind when they wrote about him in the school's year book when Fidel graduated in 1945: "He has good timber, and the actor in him will not be lacking."[113]

However, at least once, Castro made the mistake of leaving written evidence that he is a liar. In 1954, he wrote a revealing letter to Melba Hernández, one of the women who participated in the assault of the Moncada garrisons and a close Castro associate. In it Fidel advised her that, in order to outfox their opponents, she must use, "Much guile and smiles for everyone . . . defend our points of view without creating problems. There will be ample time later to squash all the cockroaches together."[114]

Castro is not only a good liar, he is also a shameless one. When he visited New York in 1996 to give a speech at the U.N. General Assembly, he paid an impromptu visit to the CBS studios, where he talked to his good friend Dan Rather and others. Just before he left, Mike Wallace asked him a difficult question. "More than thirty years ago you came to New York to speak at the U.N. and, before leaving, you said you were going back to Cuba to restore democracy and to call for free elections. What happened?" To which Castro unabashedly answered: "¡Eso fue hace mucho tiempo!" ("That was a long time ago!") and, smiling, left the studio accompanied by his bodyguards.

In fact, in the Sierra Maestra manifesto published in July, 1957, Castro specifically promised that within a year after his provisional government took power there would be general elections, and he gave "absolute guarantee" that his government would grant individual and political rights specified in the 1940 Constitution. But, as Castro said, that was a long time ago.

More recently, he visited the Dominican Republic to attend a summit of Caribbean leaders. The meeting's joint declaration included a provision to "reaffirm our commitment to preserve, consolidate and strengthen democracy, political pluralism and a state of law as the privileged backdrop that allows respect, defense and promotion of human rights."[115] Castro signed it without batting an eyelash.

A perfunctory reading of Castro's speeches shows dozens of instances in which he has admitted a posteriori that he has lied. An analyst of Castro's political behavior pointed out that "the Cuban dictator is a liar who confesses the truth—retroactively."[116] The fact explains why, writing about Castro's unbroken record of deceit, Cuban exile Mario Lazo, called Fidel Castro "the great dissembler."[117]

Fidel's Lack of a Sense of Humor

Although Castro almost invariably introduces a few humorous elements into his speeches and gives the impression of considerable wit, he lacks any real sense of humor.[118] He can never take a joke on himself. Though he enjoys laughing at others, he rarely does so at himself.[119] He is incapable of purifying his gloomy self with self-irony and humor. He is extremely sensitive to ridicule. He takes himself very seriously and will flare up in a temperamental rage at the least impingement by act or attitude on the dignity and holiness of the Maximum Leader.

The following incident gives an idea about Castro's lack of a sense of humor. In early February, 1959, *Zig-Zag*, the humorous Cuban weekly newspaper, tried to show through its cartoons that the Castro movement, like virtually every Cuban political movement before, was being high jacked by political hacks. It is pertinent to add that *Zig-Zag* enjoyed a well earned reputation for letting the air out of gassy politicians. Its full front page cartoons were brilliant, and even President Batista, often the butt of *Zig-Zag's* satire, let it pass with a smile. In this instance, the full-page cartoon showed Castro marching along, followed by a group of his *barbudos* and a multitude of civilians wearing derby hats. Derby hats are known in Cuba as *bombines*, an appellation for political turncoats, professional flatterers who follow every government in power.

But Castro's unexpected reaction was an explosion of rage. Next day, while giving a speech, he accused *Zig-Zag* of employing "cowardly writers," who, he alleged, had pictured him as "consorting with *bombines*." "Don't ever," threatened an angry Castro, "portray me in the company of *bombines*." His threat proved not to be an empty one. A few months later he banned *Zig-Zag*, which that way won the dubious honor of becoming the first member of the Cuban free press in the long list of the ones destroyed by Fidel Castro.

After the banning of *Zig-Zag*, just a few humor publications have appeared in Castro's Cuba, among them *Palante* and *Dedeté*. But political satire in these publications is mostly devoted to ridiculing the "Yankee imperialists" and other Castro opponents. Caricatures of the Maximum Leader have been conspicuously absent from their pages. But, despite overwhelming government vigilance, the ever-irreverent Cubans keep making jokes of Castro and his cronies behind their backs.[120]

In 1987, however, a caricaturist known as Ajubel published probably the only caricature of Castro appeared in the Cuban state-controlled press. It depicted a gigantic Fidel walking through a field of desks and bureaucrats, destroying them with his feet. It was supposed to be a depiction of Castro fighting the government bureaucracy. After approval from the Ministry of Culture, the caricature was published in *Dedeté*. But, almost immediately, the whole edition of *Dedeté* was confiscated and destroyed when somebody realized that Ajubel's caricature could be easily interpreted as Fidel destroying the whole country. Ajubel now lives in exile in Spain.[121]

The Cowman From Birán

All his life Fidel has shown a strange attraction for cows, milk and dairy products. He loves ice cream and consumes extraordinary quantities of it.[122] Most of the time he prefers to drink milk instead of water. This may sound normal to an American reader, but it is very uncommon in the Hispanic culture, where adults, though commonly consume plenty of dairy products, rarely drink milk.

Since he was very young, Fidel Castro has shown an abnormal fixation with cows, milk and dairy products. Many visitors have been surprised to find that Fidel knows all his cows by name.[123] Author Fred Ward tells an interesting anecdote about Castro's intimate knowledge of his cows. At some time Castro moved Enrique Oltulski, who had been the Cuban Minister of Communications, to a new position in charge of cattle-raising operations in the province of Pinar del Río. Eager to please Fidel, Oltulski made the mistake of taking, without Castro's authorization, some of Fidel's cows in Pinar del Río and moving them to another place. But a few days later Fidel drove out to one of his farms and began looking for some of the cows he recognized and knew by name. Castro walked around for a while and soon realized that something was wrong. Then, he called the manager and asked him about the cows. The man, a bit scared, told him that Oltulski had taken them. That made Fidel mad. He threw one of his tantrums and, not having Oltulski at hand, wrote him a note that began: "Enrique, you think that you have the biggest balls in this country, but you don't. There is someone in the country with even bigger balls."[124] The manager was amazed by Fidel's ability to recognize by name most of the 1500 cows at the farm.

All the milk and dairy products Castro consumes come from some Holstein cows he owns. Castro's cows live in air conditioned stables, and enjoy better living conditions than most average Cubans. They are under the protection of a special military unit, to avoid any tampering with the milk.[125]

Examples of Fidel's strange fixation with cows and milk abound. Just after departing for Santiago de Cuba to initiate the attack on the Moncada garrison, Castro joined his men at the Siboney farm. On his way to the farm, he stopped and bought three big canteens full of milk. Later, while he unveiled the details of his plan to his men, Melba Hernández and Haydée Santamaría, the only two female members of the group, walked among the men giving them glasses full of milk.[126]

After he took power in Cuba, Castro focused his attention on milk production, cattle-raising and genetic experimentation. Among other things, he wanted to create a new variety of cow, a mix of Cebú and Holstein. Cebú is a meat-producing cattle with strong resistance to tropical climates, while Holstein is a milk-producing type with high milk production, but low resistance to heat. The new breed was expected to produce both meat and milk.

Castro called the new hybrid races F-1s, F-2s or F-3s according to the breed, in which the "F" was supposed to stand for "family," but some people believed it stood for "Fidel." Castro claimed that no cow in the world would produce as much milk as "his" cows.[127] But, after years of experimentation, the F-1 cows did not produce more milk or more meat, nor were they resistant to the Cuban tropical climate. Tens of millions of dollars were wasted in air-conditioned facilities for this type of cattle.

Nevertheless, Castro's genetic experiments continued for years. One prize bull, *Rosafé*, became a sort of Cuban national hero and his feats of masculine prowess were followed with interest in the official press. A cow called *Ubre Blanca* (White Udders), which produced a high milk output, reached even higher levels in the rank of revolutionary heroes. But Ubre Blanca's high milk output was the result of chemical stimulation, which ended up by affecting her health. She died young, and it was a terrible loss for the *Comandante en Jefe*.

When Ubre Blanca died, the whole country stopped, closely following the drama developing at the highest levels of the Cuban government. A sad and sorrowful Castro gave orders to bury her with military honors. Flags were lowered to half mast. A gigantic picture of Ubre Blanca was placed on the facade of the National Library, facing Castro's office. Laureate poet Pablo Armando Fernández wrote a moving poem to Fidel's favorite cow, and ever faithful singers Silvio Rodríguez and Pablo Milanés composed sweet songs in her honor.[128] Following Castro's orders, her cadaver was embalmed and saved for posterity to be shown to visitors at the Museum of the Revolution, like a Cuban bovine Lenin. Later, Castro commissioned a sculptor to make a statue of the wonder cow.

The statue of Ubre Blanca was placed at the entrance of the milk farm Los Naranjos, near Caimito, in Havana province. Los Naranjos was created in 1961 by Castro himself as one of his pet projects or "special plans."[129] Los Naranjos was one of the main centers devoted to testing Castro's genetic theories. For his dubious accomplishments in genetic research, Castro was officially given the title of Father of Cuban Genetics, becoming the official Cuban Lysenko.[130] Photos of Castro in his office show several statuettes of his cows stacked between the books on the shelves.

One of the latest attempts at the genetic manipulation of cows by the Father of Cuban Genetics occurred in the early 1980s, when Castro had an idea to solve both the problem of production and distribution of milk. The solution, according to Fidel, was the creation of a family "pet cow" which would produce one gallon of milk every day. Though the idea provoked shouts of laughter behind the Comandante's back, Castro took it very seriously. He gave detailed instructions to the Center for Biotechnology and Genetics, then led by Manuel Limonta, for the genetic design of his mini-cow. He even surprised the scientist at the center when, during one of the Center's scientific meetings, he unexpectedly showed up and explained to the embarrassed scientists his plans for the creation of the necessary equipment needed for every family to feed its pet cow.[131]

Before Castro took power in Cuba there was relatively little use for milk on the Island, and only the large cities provided a market for fresh milk. Most of the milk was processed into butter, cheese, or condensed and evaporated milk. But Castro changed everything and forced his love for milk upon the Cuban people. Matthews noticed that "Fidel has made Cubans into a milk-drinking people."[132]

And he put a great effort into forcing upon Cubans not only his love for milk, but also for yogurt and cheese. In the late sixties he created the Coppelia brand of ice cream, and a gigantic ice cream parlor with the same name, probably the largest in the world, was built in 23rd and L streets in the heart of the Vedado section of Havana. Coppelia's dairy plant goal was to produce more ice cream flavors than the big American brands. Consequently, he bought the best dairy machinery in Holland and Sweden, to produce ice cream, yogurt and cheese. Of course, as it happens most of the time, his grandiose plans ended up in a total failure. The yogurt and cheese factories are all but gone, and the Coppelia ice cream parlor, most of the time offering its customers just one or two different flavors after an endless wait in long lines, stands as a silent monument to Castro's economic incompetence—or madness.

It seems that Castro's obsession with milk and cows began when he was very young. Probably the most intriguing aspects of Castro's love affair with milk were revealed by Fidel himself in interviews with his biographer Carlos Franqui and in a long interview with Brazilian priest Frei Betto, later published in book form under the title *Fidel and Religion*. Though Fidel is never candid about anything, and he has been particularly careful in muddying the waters about his past, a careful reading between the lines of these interviews yields unexpected results.

In a recorded interview with Franqui, Castro told him about his early days in his father's farm at Birán: "My house was a two-story, big, wooden house on top of wood stilts. It was a Spanish-type house. Cattle was kept below. They milked the cows under the house."[133]

In the interview with Frei Betto, Castro tells about his origins at his father's *finca* in Birán, near Mayarí, in the province of Oriente, and he repeats almost verbatim the story he told Franqui. According to Castro, the family house was built on stilts, more than six feet high. "When I was young—about three, four, five or maybe six years old—the cows used to sleep under the house. There were from 20 to 30 of them, and they were rounded up at dusk and driven to the house, where they slept below. They were milked there, and some were tied to the stilts."[134] Later in the interview he mentions his favorite subject again. "When I was a child, the cows were kept under the house. Later, they were moved to somewhere else."[135]

Jorge Edwards, a Chilean writer and diplomat in Havana, tells an interesting anecdote of a trip with Castro in which they visited one of Fidel's milk farms. For lunch,

> . . . a soldier, who apparently was a man of confidence to the Commander in Chief, placed on the table cold cuts, sausages, and big white beer mugs, similar to the ones used in German beer halls. Instead of beer to fill the mugs, the soldier placed on the table several bottles of milk, with different labels to differentiate them. Fidel was asking which cow was the milk from—the cows had delicate feminine names like María Rosa, Clarisa, María Gracia—but he pretended to know the cow just by tasting her milk. 'Ah, this one,' he exclaimed: 'This one tastes like almonds!' and he passed us the jugs to taste the milk, until there was a total confusion. It was impossible to determine to which cow—Clara, Florinda, or María Gloria—the milk had come from, and, to top it off, in some jugs the milk from different cows had been mixed up.[136]

Carlos Franqui, mentioned the strange phenomenon that happens when Fidel moves to a different house. When that happens, Franqui wrote, he finally makes it his own, "by bringing in cows and farm equipment."[137] When, in the mid-sixties, Havana was the host of France's *Salon de mai*, an avant-garde sample of world art, visitors enjoyed a surrealist work not mentioned in the exhibition's catalog. Close to works by Matta, Picasso, Lam, Siqueiros, and other masters, was a large cage containing several live cows, Castro's personal contribution to the exhibition.

Castro's Split Personality

Some psychologists believe that the condition known as "borderline personality" is the one that best describes Fidel Castro's behavioral patterns. But, like with all mental disorders, it is impossible to fit all of his behavior into that description.

Generally speaking, borderline personalities are those affecting people who, while mentally ill, can still function in some areas with great effectiveness. Their pathology differs from neurosis and is less severe than psychosis. Actually, the name comes because they occupy an area on the borderline between the two.[138]

Borderline individuals characteristically show paranoid tendencies. They distrust everybody and are highly suspicious of other people's intentions. They consider themselves "especially privileged persons" and fantasize about their "magical omnipotence." They are convinced that they have a right to exploit others for their own gratification. Most of them show an unconscious impulse for self-destruction.

Patients suffering from borderline personality disorders tend to be infantile, selfish and narcissistic.[139] They often display a contradiction between an inflated concept of themselves and an inordinate need for tribute from others. Typically, while they express fantasies of omnipotence, their behavior may also reveal deep-seated uncertainty, self-doubt, and insecurity.

One of the most basic characteristics of borderline personalities is the one known as "splitting of the ego." Individuals affected by this disorder show dramatically opposed personality traits: they are cruel and kind, sentimental and hard, creative and destructive; they swing violently between excessive manifestations of love and wild outbursts of hate. It often appears as if there were in each individual two distinct selves, equally strong, completely separated from each other.

Foreign journalists and visitors to the Island often describe Castro as an amiable, self-controlled, kind individual, full of generosity and capable of enthusiasm for beauty and greatness. But others tell of a cruel, unjust, capricious, self-pitying and vulgar man.

A plausible explanation for such an apparently contradictory evaluation of Castro's character is that, even contradictory among themselves, both types of descriptions give a fairly accurate picture of the personality of Fidel Castro.[140] In studying Castro's behavior one discovers a man who is so deeply divided that he often appears torn between opposing qualities: omnipotent and vulnerable, sophisticated and vulgar, creative and destructive, pragmatic and fanatical, brave and cowardly, rigid and flexible, cruel and generous. An author pointed out that there is a considerable discrepancy between Castro as he is known to the Cuban people and foreign press and visitors and Castro as he is known to his associates, but few, if any, foreigners have had a glimpse at the maximum leader who at one moment inflicts humiliation, and at the next offers flattery and comradeship.[141]

The splitting of the individual's personality appears to be not only a defect of the ego, but also an active and very powerful defense mechanism.[142] This feeling of being split apart seems to have plagued Castro throughout his life. Hence the endless assertions about his iron will and his compulsion to master and control others. In fact, Castroism, the political system he created in Cuba, is basically a system for dominating other people.

Going further in their analyses, some researchers believe that Castro, like most individuals suffering from borderline personality, characteristically reinforces his splitting through introjection and projection: the good is introjected by him and the bad is projected unto others. During his life Castro has introjected and claimed as his own all the attributes he considers good: intelligence, creativity, courage, honesty, iron will, toughness, masculinity, even sainthood. He has projected all the bad onto others, especially Americans: treachery, dishonesty, softness, stupidity, cowardice, hesitation, femininity and evil. This projection mechanism produced in Castro a terrifying view of the world as an irreconcilable split between good and bad, with the evil forces, present in others, constantly conspiring against the good, symbolized by himself. As a consequence, he feels compelled to fight and destroy the encircling and ubiquitous enemy before it destroys him.

While the split world Castro has created in his mind is dangerous and is constantly threatening him, it has served as an important therapeutic defense mechanism. It has enabled him to externalize a conflict which, if left bottled within him, can lead to mental disintegration and collapse. The hypothesis that Castro is suffering from borderline personality helps to explain why, according to some specialists, though he may have experienced psychotic episodes, he never crossed over the border into full-blow psychosis. He managed to project and externalize his own neuroses, rationalize them, and proclaim them officially as a governmental policy and world view.

Though Fidel Castro's distorted view of the world bears very little relationship to the external reality, it closely corresponds to his own psychic needs. In this respect, his fantasies are not unlike those of thousands of other mentally disturbed people. What makes Castro different is that, instead of seeking psychological treatment, he managed to obtain the enormous political power which allowed him to transform his private fantasies into objective reality.[143]

His political ideas cast Castro as the heroic leader called by destiny to save Cuba, Latin America, Africa, and perhaps the rest of the world, from American imperialism. His political theory institutionalizes distrust and hatred. It preaches aggressive warfare. It exalts brutality and demands total obedience to himself.

Nevertheless, it appears that, notwithstanding Castro's excesses, most of his associates have a deep allegiance to him personally and are quite ready to forgive or ignore his shortcomings. In many cases it seems as though his associates are quite oblivious to the contradictory traits in his character—to them he is still the Maximum Leader and they live for the increasingly shorter and infrequent moments when he actually plays this role.

In recent years, however, confidential information coming from Cuba reveals that people close to Castro are extremely concerned and frightened.[144] They have noticed that the Maximum Leader has become alarmingly erratic. Some of them, particularly among the military and the intelligence services, are convinced that Castro is mad and constitutes a danger to them, their families and their country. There are rumors that Castro is undergoing psychiatric treatment and taking medication. Some psychiatrists in Cuba believe that Castro is a psychotic and megalomaniac. The fact that Castro is actively seeking the development of bacteriological weapons and other means of mass destruction gives some basis for the uneasiness of his close associates.

Is Fidel Castro Crazy?

One of the many nicknames Fidel had since an early age was *"el loco Fidel"* (crazy Fidel). The descriptive nickname followed him to the Colegio de Belén, and later to the University of Havana.

There is no doubt that Fidel Castro's personality lends itself freely to the psycho-analytical vocabulary. In fact, psycho-analytical studies of Castro agree on the important point that, already early in life, he showed strong paranoid symptoms. Excessive aggression and obsessional reactions are among the most important of these. Documented facts about Castro's private early life lead to the hypothesis that these manifestations were connected with a series of unsolved oedipal conflicts, his repressed hatred towards his father in particular. Angel Castro's violent character, his drinking addiction and his philandering, is the evidence supporting this hypothesis.

Luis Conte Agüero, at some time one of Castro's closest friends, tells a revealing story he heard from Lina Ruz, Fidel's mother. When Fidel was a young boy, sometimes his mother became upset as a result of some wrongdoing. When she threatened him with corporal punishment, he used to lower his pants, offering his buttocks to the spanking.[145]

The formative years of Castro's life show a strange coincidence of events possibly leading to frustration and insecurity. His father's authoritarian and violent behavior created a permanent threat to Castro's expectations of tender, loving feelings. The jealousy and scorn of his stepbrothers created an additional source of insecurity. Later conditions in his life, like his troubles at the schools he attended in Santiago de Cuba, came to foster this first layer of insecurity. The ideas he holds as an adult, the feelings he displays and the prejudices he fanatically defends, are but elaborate shields he uses as protection from himself.

This frustrated need for security in Castro's personality manifests itself in several ways. One of the most characteristic is his strong need for self-assertion, indicating his need to prove to everybody and himself his self-confidence. Thus, his aggressiveness, his thirst for adventure, his "iron will-power," are but different dimensions of his need for self-demonstration—as when he crashed his bicycle against a wall at Belén high school or when he attacked the Moncada barracks. On the fantasy level, his projection of himself as the providential leader of all Cubans, and of all Latin Americans and the "humiliated masses of the world," is rooted in the same basic insecurity.

Sources in Cuba reveal that currently most Cubans strongly believe that the mental health of the Maximum Leader is severely impaired.[146] Apparently they are not alone. Recent reports revealed that in early 2000 the U.S. State Department asked the CIA to update Castro's psychological profile.[147] The request came after Castro's behavior turned more weird than what is considered normal for him. Proof of this, some sources claim, are three incoherent letters he wrote to Canada's Prime Minister in relation with a Cuban diplomat expelled from Canada over charges of espionage. There is also a four page letter he wrote to U.S. representative Jim Macdermott, offering an almost unintelligible explanation for his decision about not attending an international conference in Seattle. Another indication that Castro is losing his marbles is some exceptionally long articles he wrote for *Granma* in which he suggested that Cubans in exile had poisoned district judge William Hoeveler, which had to be substituted in the Elián González trial after suffering a heart attack.[148]

Miami's Cuban psychiatrist Lino Fernández, who has been closely following Castro's behavior for many years, thinks that the Cuban leader's verbal expression and concentration are faltering. His growing irritability and bursts of anger make Fernández believe that Castro's mental health is quickly deteriorating.[149] According to witnesses, Castro's speeches have become more incoherent than normal, his digressions longer and farther away from the subject. His verbal attacks on his enemies, particularly after the condemnation of his regime's human rights record in Geneva last April, have turned harsher and more personal.

Is Fidel a Gay in the Closet?

Another characteristic of Castro's fundamental insecurity is his deep desire to be accepted and loved, not only by his followers, but also by his enemies. In Castro, this is a compensation for his repressed desire for belongingness, and may very well be seen as another form of self-assurance. This characteristic explains Castro's identification with the Cuban masses and his particular need for "loyalty." Castro's demand for absolute loyalty in his close associates reaches the point where it comes close to an homoerotic relationship. This explains why his relations with some of his close associates sometimes resemble a strange love affair.

Based on Fidel's repression of a tender tie with his mother, some psychiatrists have speculated that Fidel Castro is a man of markedly pre-genital or immature personality structure in which libido organization followed a sado-masochistic pattern, resulting in a homosexual relation to a harsh and ambivalently loved and hated father figure. This theory may explain Fidel's sadism towards symbols of the displaced bad portion of this father figure, his increased secondary or "defensive" narcissism and his tendencies toward hypochondriacal and schizoid features.

Some authors have suggested that homosexuality is a regression to the infantile, oral stage, where milk plays an important role, as it has played in Castro's life:

> In some way the penis becomes the symbol for the maternal breast, and hence homosexual behavior comes about. For example, in sucking the semen from the penis one is symbolically taking milk from the breast. Alternatively, taking the penis either orally or anally is taking over the 'masculine' strength of the donor, undoing one's own castration, and fitting oneself to the battles of the world again.[150]

Some of the psychologists who studied Castro in the early sixties, believe that in these unsolved oedipal conflicts lies the source of a series of other personality traits such as his emotional attachment to men (as opposed to women)—which may be interpreted as latent homosexuality—his strong revulsion from acts he considered obscene or lewd, and his strong fixation on his mother.

At any rate, a word of caution is in order. Any attempt to find a psychiatrically based explanation of Fidel Castro's actions inevitably falls short of his true nature. As professor Frederick Crews has pointed out, psychiatric explanations of a person's behavior are so open-ended, and the connections usually so far-fetched, that almost everything can be explained as a cause for anything.[151]

For a long time, however, there has been some rumors and speculation about the possibility that Castro is actually a gay in the closet. Allen Ginsberg, for one, was convinced that Fidel has had at least some homosexual experiences. Though the available information tends to negate the fact, the truth is that, during all his life, homosexuals have been attracted to Castro and he has accepted them into his inner circle. Names like Alfredo Guevara, Celia Sánchez, Melba Hernández, and his own brother Raúl come to mind.

Fidel's special appeal to homosexuals is widely known and has been extensively documented. During his early days as a law student in the University of Havana a group of known homosexuals made up some of his closest friends. The most prominent of these friends, and the one closest to Fidel, was Alfredo Guevara (no relation to Ché Guevara). Guevara traveled with Fidel to Colombia in 1948, was with him during the Bogotazo, and has been holding important positions in the Castro government since 1959.

When Fidel was attending Belén, most of his classmates treated him as a country bumpkin. He did not dance well. His clothes hung loosely on his lanky frame. Paradoxically, the girls loved him for all of that, but he never seemed to be interested in them.[152]

At Belén he was always in the company of other boys. He showed interest in attractive young women, especially foreigners, but he was never comfortable with them. His first marriage fell apart because he preferred the life of politics and male companionship to staying at home with his young, beautiful wife.[153] At the same time, it seems that he sincerely loathed the effete *maricones* (faggots) of Havana's Vedado district, the artists and poets he believed posed a threat to a man's true sexuality and to society.[154]

Evidence indicates that, over the years, Castro's lack of interest in women has not changed. His attitude toward women is close to licentious, with thinly disguised disrespect and hostility. Though he has had several wives and lovers, apparently he uses women only for propagation purposes. Proof of this is the great number of children he has fathered through countless women as if spreading his divine seed. At any rate, when Castro has any heterosexual sex, it seems it is not for the pleasure of it. Carlos Franqui claims that some women with whom Castro has had sex, call him "*mal palo*" (literally "lousy fuck"). He makes love, they say, as if he was peeing, with his boots on, fast and without any intimacy, with his bodyguards listening behind the door.[155]

Though there is no direct evidence that Fidel is a homosexual, some of his actions seem a little odd, such as his efforts to impose strict heterosexual discipline in the 26th of July Movement. When Fidel's group was in Mexico preparing for the invasion, heterosexual abstinence was enforced, sometimes with angry protests from some Movement members.

Fidel's aversion for heterosexual love is not new. In a recorded interview, Castro told his biographer Carlos Franqui that, when he was visiting Princeton University in 1948, he was incensed after seeing coed dormitories, where students of both sexes were kissing each other and showing their affection in public. According to Fidel's own words, that vision produced in him "an impression of total licentiousness."[156]

Among the attackers of the Moncada barracks and later in the guerrilla war in the Sierra Maestra, homosexuals were Fidel's closest associates. None of them—his brother Raúl, Celia Sánchez, Armando Hart, Melba Hernández, Haydée Santamaría or José Martínez Páez—came from the "exploited masses," but were members of a small élite segment of Cuban society; pro-American, well educated and affluent. None of them—perhaps with the exception of Alfredo Guevara—were known for their communist faith or had been members of the Cuban Communist Party. When Fidel Castro began to emerge as a political leader they were attracted by Fidel's personal magnetism and drifted to his side. Almost overnight they became fanatical radicals of Fidelismo and active leaders in his revolution.

Some observers have noticed that Castro manages to develop and maintain a sort of homoerotic relationship of dominance/submissiveness with some of his close associates and friends. Examples in case are Ché Guevara and novelist Gabriel García Márquez.[157] Though the relationship may be more homoerotic than fully homosexual, it seems very close to it. Author Paul Bethel noticed that, lacking manliness, some men are attracted like flies to Castro's virile image.[158] Indeed, the homoerotic connection between Castro and some type of men is undeniable. On seeing Fidel, Abbie Hoffman wrote that when Castro stood erect, he was "like a penis coming to life."[159]

According to Carlos Alberto Montaner, Fidel Castro *conquered* Ché Guevara, and that "strange politico-erotic relation, so frequent in the Cuban mad-house, always presided the relationship between the two men."[160] According to Montaner, another one who fell under Castro's homoerotic spell was Regis Debray, the French intellectual and guerrilla *aficionado*. It was only when he was back in Paris, safe from the Maximum Leader's "virile seduction," that he recovered his mental lucidity and wrote some revealing books about Cuba.[161] There are some, however, who apparently never recovered.

Prominent among the people who always had suspicions about Fidel's true sexual orientation were the Cuban Communists. They had always despised Fidel, believing he was totally crazy, and considering him effeminate. Esmeril (a pseudonym), a journalist writing a column under his byline for *Hoy*, the Cuban Communist Party official newspaper, repeatedly called him *"el casto Fidel"* ("Fidel the chaste"), an injurious remark with homosexual connotations created after the name of a film in vogue in Cuba at the time.[162]

To be sure, Castro's associates know that in respect to women Castro is far from the ascetic he would like to have the Cuban people believe. None of them, however, with the possible exception of his personal adjutants, know the true nature of his sexual activities. This has led to a great deal of conjecture. There are some who believe that his heterosexual sex life is perfectly normal but restricted. Others, that he is immune from such temptations and that nothing happens when he is alone with women. Others believe that he is either a homosexual or has homosexual inclinations, and that his profound, visceral hatred for effeminate homosexuals is an indication of Fidel's hidden or latent homosexuality.

Homosexuals in Fidel's Paradise

As an author observed, Fidel Castro has long assigned the United States the same universal malevolence which Hitler arrogated to the Jews.[163] However, not having many Americans at hand, Castro displaced his hatred toward other social groups, among them effeminate homosexuals. This brings to mind a joke that was popular in Cuba in the mid 1960s. People used to ask, "Why is Fidel persecuting homosexuals?" The answer was, "Because there are not enough Jews in Cuba."[164]

Poet Armando Valladares, who spent long years in prison in Cuba, believes that "there have been few examples of repression of homosexuals in history as virulent as in Cuba."[165] Also, Duncan Green, author of a book on Latin America, writes that Cuba is particularly repressive toward homosexuals, and "imposes a maximum 20 years sentence for public expression of homosexuality."[166] The anti-homosexual nature of the Castro regime has been documented in detail by authors Allen Young and Dennis Altman,[167] among others.

Even Castro-friendly Herbert Matthews, who visited Cuba several times and moved freely among senior officers of the Castro government, once commented that "There seems to be an unusually strong emotional aversion to homosexuals in Cuba—which Castro shares."[168] In 1963 Castro approved Operation P, so called because of a big, black "P" (for *prostitutas, pederastas, proxenetas*—prostitutes, pederasts, pimps) painted on the uniform of the inmates. Operation P was a massive dragnet which began with a nation-wide census of effeminate homosexuals.[169]

Operation P was the first step leading to the creation of the UMAPs (Military Units to Help Production), an euphemism for concentration camps for effeminate homosexuals and other "deviates." Some of the "deviations" were being a Jehovah's Witness, wearing tight blue jeans, listening to The Beatles' records, or wearing the hair "too long."[170] UMAP inmates were under a regime of hard labor and subject to verbal and physical abuse, including open attacks and homosexual harassment from their butch, *macho* jailers.

In his short novel *Arturo, la estrella más brillante*,[171] Reinaldo Arenas exposed in stark detail the mental and physical torture suffered by Cuban effeminate homosexuals interned at the UMAPs. The merciless persecution of effeminate homosexuals in Cuba has also been documented in *Conducta impropia* (Conduct Unbecoming), a documentary film by Néstor Almendros and Orlando Jiménez Leal, which has been shown in many parts of the world, except Cuba.[172] An interesting detail is that the gates of the UMAPs displayed the sign *"El trabajo libera"* (Work makes you free). The Nazi counterpart, displayed at the gates of many concentration camps, was *"Arbeit Macht Frei"* (Work makes you free).[173]

In the hands of the Castro government, Operation P and the UMAPs became a tool to destroy all political opposition. Apparently, Castro's definition of "deviate," was any person opposing his government. Consequently, the government security and police forces began "outing" not only true closet homosexuals, but accusing government opponents of being homosexuals and sending them to the UMAPs. It is interesting to note that the "outing" technique was not new. It was used before by the Nazis in Germany.

Operation P apparently went too far, and it ultimately irritated the population. Generally, although most Cubans had no objection to making fun of effeminate homosexuals, they were strongly against imprisoning or harassing them. The popular condemnation of Operation P was so strong, that some senior government officials called for a meeting to discuss the issue with Castro and President Dorticós. During the meeting, which took place at the Presidential palace, some people, including some senior old-line Communists, raised objections about the harsh treatment of homosexuals. The main supporter of Operation P was gay Raúl Castro. He bragged about the success of the operation, while his entourage, formed by Ramiro Valdés, Isidoro Malmierca, Manuel Piñeiro and José Abrahantes, laughed heartily.

By mid-1965 the battle against effeminate homosexuals intensified, as the Castro government unleashed a fierce campaign against them. More and more homosexuals were forcefully drafted into the UMAPs. Intellectuals were especially persecuted, and there was a severe purge at the University of Havana. This brought a protest from the Union of Cuban Writers and Artists (UNEAC), which had strong repercussions abroad. The international repercussions to the protest lead to the eventual dissolution of the UMAPs in 1967, but it did not end the harassment and ill-treatment of homosexuals.[174] In typical Castro fashion, the attack on homosexuals continues, but it is now disguised as AIDS treatment and control.

Castro's response to the AIDS crisis in Cuba was mandatory nation-wide testing with forced incarceration of anyone who tested positive for the HIV virus. A special police force sporting purple berets was created both to guard the concentration camps/sanatoria and to capture the ones who attempted escape or refused to be interned in the camps. Many Cubans have witnessed how AIDS patients who have escaped from the sanatoria are chased like mad dogs, captured, and sent back to the camps.

American gay ideologues contend that mandatory AIDS testing is a form of discrimination against gays that is akin to the discrimination suffered by segregated blacks in the American South.[175] But, though American gays are aware of mandatory AIDS testing in Cuba, for some strange reason criticism against the Castro government in the gay press is conspicuously nonexistent.

Dr. Jorge Pérez, a Cuban physician and AIDS specialist, now in exile in Spain, reported a horrible story in Madrid's newspaper *ABC*.[176] According to Dr. Pérez, in the 1980s the Cuban government aired ads on tv portraying the AIDS sanatoria as if they were five star hotels, with air conditioning, color tv, swimming pools, and excellent food. The goal of the ads was to get volunteers for Nazi-like experiments on AIDS vaccines and treatment which, if successful, would mean plenty of hard currency for the Castro government. The response was overwhelming, and the volunteers were interned in a center near Santiago de las Vegas, in Havana province, where they were inoculated with the AIDS virus. But, according to Dr. Pérez, the strain used was particularly strong, and ninety percent of the people who volunteered died within a few years.

In a letter dated 14 September, 1992, which was smuggled out of a Cuban prison by a group of political prisoners and published on the Web, it was reported that a number of prisoners infected with AIDS rioted on 19 August, demanding better food and medical attention. Apparently the cause for the riots was that, two months earlier, a prisoner with AIDS sent to this area had his food ration cut in half and the diet recommended by doctors withdrawn. He died three weeks later. Prison guards attacked the rioters using rubber batons, wooden sticks, and other blunt instruments, and a large group of them suffered severe injuries. Several of the prisoners suffering from AIDS were transferred to the maximum security area of the prison.[177]

Castro has a long tradition of imprisoning effeminate homosexuals and transsexuals as "undesirables." Imprisonment is often based on mere suspicion or rumor. A few years ago it was reported that some young people in Cuba were purposely injecting themselves with HIV infected blood so they could be sent to the sanatoria and avoid forced labor and police harassment. The fact was exposed in the film *Bitter Sugar*.

Some Castro-friendly American authors claim that the UMAPs were just a short-lived and rapidly corrected deviation in the course of the Castroist revolution. But a relatively recent incident shows that this is not the case. On September, 1997, profiting from the recently acquired sense of relative freedom which began with Cuba's opening to tourism, a group of Cuban and foreign homosexuals were having a party at a discotheque known as El Periquitón, in Havana's La Ceiba section. Just after midnight the place was cordoned by more than 60 police officers and 30 squad cars. The police arrested more than 500 effeminate homosexuals, lesbians, and prostitutes and sent them to jail. Among the detainees were Jean Paul Gautier, a famous French modiste, the Spanish film director Pedro Almodóvar and transsexual Bibi Anderson.[178]

The next day the group of foreign homosexuals was allowed to leave the country in a hurry. Nothing was reported about the Cuban ones. According to the Cuban Penal Code, open manifestation of homosexuality is a crime punishable with up to a year in prison. Transvestites and effeminate homosexuals are commonly arrested, charged with public scandal and sentenced to three months in prison and/or a 500 pesos fine.

After the incident, the International Lesbian and Gay Association sent a bland letter of complaint to the Castro government, but no answer was ever received. Though widely reported in Europe, the incident passed almost unmentioned in the American media.

Is Fidel Castro a Racist?

Most people seem to ignore the fact that, before Castro came to power, Cuba was one of the most racially integrated nations in the world, with a socio-cultural system relatively free of racial discrimination. As Professor Richard R. Fagen pointed out, "Batista's Cuba exhibited a greater degree of national integration than did Mexico after 50 years of 'integrative revolution.'"[179]

Though racial biases were far from non-existent, Cuba was almost free of institutional racism. Racial relations among Cubans were very different from the ones currently existing in the U.S. Proof of this is that Fulgencio Batista, a dark skinned mulatto, found his way to top political positions in Cuba—though not to high society—and eventually became president of the country by popular vote. Further proof of the above is that the Cuban equivalent to U.S. Veterans Day is the 7th of December, the anniversary of the death in combat of General Antonio Maceo y Grajales—whose tactics were studied in important military academics around the world. Also, probably one of the most important women in Cuban history is Mariana Grajales, Maceo's mother, who sent her sons to fight the Spaniards. The Maceos were black. Moreover, among the delegates to the convention to approve the first Constitution of Cuba in 1901 were two prominent blacks, Martín Morúa Delgado and Juan Gualberto Gómez. A list of prominent black men and women in Cuba's history in the field of politics, law, science, journalism, literature and education, not to mention music and sports, could fill hundreds of pages.[180]

Since Castro assumed power in 1959 he has been claiming that his regime brought an end to racial discrimination in Cuba. However, if one is to believe what Castro does, as opposed to what he says, the evidence strongly indicates that he does not have a high appreciation for what he considers the "lower," dark-skinned races.[181]

There is evidence that at least part of his hatred and contempt for President Batista was racially motivated. Fulgencio Batista's humble origins and his mixed blood (half black, and probably Cuban Indian) was a motive of scorn among some of his opponents—most of them members of the Cuban wealthy and aristocratic classes, including Fidel Castro. As an interesting detail one might add that Fidel's racial slurs about Batista (he usually referred to the Cuban President as *"negro de mierda"*—shitty nigger) had a sympathetic echo among CIA officers under diplomatic cover at the American Embassy in Havana who were sympathetic with Castro and strongly despised the Cuban president.

Some people claim that perhaps Fidel learnt his racial biases from his father Angel and his mother Lina (Angel's second wife).[182] Angel and Lina ruled their largely black cane cutters at the Birán estate by gun law, unmercifully killing the bold ones who stepped too far out of line. The Castros never ventured into the field without their guns, and the local military post, a corporal and two soldiers, slept on Angel's land, ate his food and received a small monthly stipend from him.[183] Another reason for Fidel's racism may be that María Argote,[184] Angel Castro's first wife—a woman Fidel deeply hated—was a dark-skinned mulatta.[185]

A few years ago Dr. Antonio Castro Soto del Valle, an orthopedic surgeon and one of the five sons of Fidel Castro with his common-law wife Dalia Soto del Valle, unexpectedly married a black Cuban woman. When they heard the news, consternation erupted in Fidel Castro's family.[186]

Contrary to Fidel's political demagoguery, the fact is that, even though blacks constitute a large segment of the Cuban population, only 15 blacks hold seats in the 150-member Central Committee of Castro's "Communist" Party, and only six of the 24-member Politburo are black.[187] A simple look at Castro's ministers and generals, shows a group of old white men.[188] Amazingly, the Cuban government's official Web site provides strong evidence of the sexual and racial discrimination prevalent in the Castro government. A list of the 52 most senior members of the Castro government shows only four women and three blacks. The Cuban government's official statistics available in the site show that the Cuban population is 37 percent caucasian, 62 percent black, and 1 percent asian.[189]

It is extremely revealing that not a single one of the many Army officers involved in the "drug trafficking" case of 1989, all of them men close to Castro's inner circle, was black.[190] As a matter of fact, blacks have had a larger representation in most, if not all, previous Cuban governments than in Castro's. However, a notable exception to the small presence of blacks in the Castro government is found in the Cuban army.

Photographs of Cuban army units show close to 90 percent of black *soldiers*. But officers, particularly high ranking senior officers, are 95 percent white. Evidently Castro, like the leaders of many imperialist nations, uses racial minorities as cannon fodder. Most Cuban soldiers among the several thousands killed in Angola were black. (Though the Castro government has never provided any figures, analysts estimate Cuban casualties in Africa to number between 4,000 and 7,000.) Another fact that makes one wonder about Castro's professed love for blacks (he visits Harlem every time he comes to the U.S.), is that of lately American blacks are seemingly not welcome in Cuba. But this was not the case at the beginning of his revolution.

Since the very first day he took power in Cuba, Fidel Castro planned to use American black radicals to spearhead his revolution inside the United States. As early as September 1960, while he was visiting the U.S. to deliver a speech at the U.N. General Assembly Castro staged an incident and used it as a pretext for moving from his hotel in midtown Manhattan to the Hotel Theresa.

Located in the heart of Harlem, the Theresa was in an area known as the center of black nationalism. Down the street from the Theresa was Lewis Michaux's African Memorial Book Store, the biggest black nationalist book store in the country. Around the corner was the Harlem Labor Center, a black militant organization. Within a few blocks from the hotel were located the offices of several black nationalist publications and organizations, including the Black Muslims. During his stay at the Theresa, Castro met several times with Malcolm X and other black leaders. Some authors claim that the so-called "Black Revolution" was actually a creation of Fidel Castro, carefully planned and directed from Cuba.[191]

In the early sixties some American black leaders, among them Huey Newton, Stokely Carmichael, Rap Brown, Bobby Seal, Eldridge Cleaver, and Robert F. Williams, were routinely visiting Havana to experience first hand the marvels of a society free of racial discrimination. Some of them received urban guerrilla and terrorist training in Cuba. It is not a coincidence that in the summer of 1967, while the Organization of Latin American Solidarity was gathering in Havana, riots were erupting in many American cities.[192] Detailed instruction for methods of urban warfare, later applied in Watts, Detroit, Newark and other riot scenes, had appeared in *The Crusader*, a Cuban-financed newsletter mailed from Canada to the U.S.[193] Copies of Ché Guevara's manual on guerrilla warfare were sold by the thousands in book stores frequented by black nationalists, such as Vaughan's in Detroit, Robin's in Philadelphia, and Michaux's in New York.

Eventually, however, the relations between Castro and the American black radicals went sour. By mid 1969, some Black Panther leaders visiting Cuba, including Eldridge Cleaver, complained of harassment and even arrests from Cuban authorities.[194] Finally, after some bold attempts at controlling the American black revolutionary movements in the late 1960s, the honeymoon between Castro and the black militants was over. Now, perhaps with the exception of Louis Farrakhan, no American black is using Castro's Cuba anymore as an example of a racism-free society.[195]

In early 1999, William Lee Brent, one of the few American black militants still living in Cuba, told *Salon* magazine about widespread racial discrimination in Castro's Cuba. Brent is a 65-year-old Black Panther and air pirate who took refuge in Cuba thirty years ago to avoid American justice. Currently he lives a precarious life in Havana with his wife of 23 years, journalist and fellow radical Jane McManus, making a living by doing odd translating and teaching jobs. Brent says that Cuban blacks lack a sense of identity as blacks and continue to face discrimination—something he feels every time he walks into certain buildings with Jane, who is white, at his side. "They wave me right in and they ask him for his ID," Jane says.[196]

In the mid-sixties some Cuban intellectuals, among them Walterio Carbonell, a Marxist sociologist and a friend of Castro from their days at the University of Havana, and Nancy Morejón, a young poet, tried to create a Cuban version of the black liberation movement. It was a sort of a makeshift mixture of Black Power with a touch of Aimée Cesaire's *negritude* theories. As soon as Castro's secret police got word of it they were detained. Morejón quickly realized her ideological "mistake" and promised to reform. Carbonell, who sincerely believed that there were too many whites in high places in Fidel's "non-racist" society, persisted in his ideas and was given a two year hard-labor sentence in one of Castro's gulags.[197]

One of the outcomes of the expansion of tourism in Cuba has been an increase in racial discrimination. Almost all of the employees at the new hotels catering to dollar-carrying tourists are white, and the Castroist police use racial profiling to stop and question young blacks on the streets, particularly near the areas where foreign tourists concentrate.[198]

Though some "progressive" American blacks keep visiting Castro's Cuba to enjoy the marvels of a racism-free society,[199] it seems that Cuban blacks know better. Almost 40 percent of the Cubans who escaped during the Mariel boatlift in 1980 were black.[200] Since then, blacks have continued to escape from the Island in great numbers. So much for Fidel Castro's non-racist Cuban society.

A Closet Gringophile

Fidel Castro loves to portray himself as the archenemy of the United States. In speech after speech he berates Yankee imperialism as the ultimate evil—which probably explains why American liberals and leftists love him so much. However, if you pay more attention to what Castro *does* rather than what he *says* the picture changes considerably. For example, author Georgie Anne Geyer, who has been studying Castro for many years, noted that most women with whom Castro has been romantically involved, including his first wife Mirtha Díaz-Balart,[201] the daughter of a lawyer who had the United Fruit among his clients, are upper-class, americanized, English-speaking, and blond.[202] Naty Revuelta, the mother of Castro's daughter Alina, worked for an American oil company and for the American Embassy. In a country where the mulatta is the canon of feminine beauty, none of Castro's known women have been dark-skinned. So, it seems that Fidel's idea of feminine beauty has been dictated more by Hollywood than by Havana.[203]

By all standards, Fidel Castro is not the typical anti-American, to say the least. Contrary to extended belief, the available evidence shows that Fidel, like most of the anti-Castro Cubans in the U.S., is an admirer of the American way of life. He is totally obsessed with the U.S. His friend García Márquez reports that "the country he knows most about, after Cuba, is the United States."[204] During Mikhail Gorbachev's visit to Cuba in April, 1989, the Soviet Premier unsuccessfully tried to convince Castro to improve his relations with the U.S. An angry Castro kept yelling over and over, "I know the Yankees!, I know the Yankees!"[205]

Like many Americans, Castro's favorite sports are baseball and basketball. While living in Queens in 1946, he was an aspiring pitcher in the New York Giants farm system and was even offered a contract, which he strangely turned down, allegedly because of his new political and study interests.

As Castro told Dan Rather in an interview, during his guerrilla days at the Sierra Maestra he stopped the war for three days in order to listen to the American baseball games on the radio. The revelation was so amazing that Rather asked him again in disbelief, "Listening to the [New York] Yankees games?" To which Fidel answered proudly, "Yes!, Yes! The Yankees games!"[206]

The only films he seems to enjoy are American movies, particularly the ones about gangsters and cowboys. At some time in the early 1940s, before his "Bogotazo" adventure, he became so infatuated with American films that he traveled to California where he managed to get a job as an extra at the Metro Goldwin studios at Culver City. He appeared at least in two films, *Bathing Beauty* (1944), starring Esther Williams and Red Skelton, and *Holiday in Mexico* (1946), starring Walter Pidgeon and Ilona Massey. Both films were directed by George Sidney and included music by Xavier Cugat and his orchestra.[207]

When he was just twelve years old, while attending the Colegio Dolores in Santiago de Cuba, Fidel wrote a bizarre letter to President Franklin D. Roosevelt. In it, he not only expressed his admiration for him and asked the American President for money (an early vice),[208] but also offered his services to the Americans to better locate Cuba's mineral resources. (See Appendix 2 for a facsimile of the letter). Thus, at that early age, the spoiled brat who now calls himself "anti-imperialist" was already volunteering to become an agent of the "American imperialists" in helping them locate the natural resources of his country to better exploit them.

Though Castro has always managed to enlist a group of followers, he actually has been rather socially isolated, with no close relationships to other people. His interests are confined to politics, sports, handguns and electronic gadgets. People close to him may testify that Castro loves big American cars and all types of American-made gadgets and products. Many photographs have been published of him enjoying a Coke like a little child, or fascinated by a Polaroid camera.[209] When he married Mirtha, they followed the americanized usage of the Cuban middle-class and traveled to the United States for their honeymoon—to which President Batista, who was a friend of Fidel's father, contributed with a wedding gift of a thousand dollars.

On the other hand, people close to him testify that Fidel shows a seemingly true visceral hatred for the United States. Fidel Castro despises America, he has a burning hatred for Americans as people, and would do anything to destroy America. A proof of it is that he tried to push Nikita Khrushchev into launching nuclear missiles against the U.S. during the crisis of 1962. Why does Castro love everything American and, at the same time, hate it? What is the cause for this love-hate relationship? The answer is perhaps very simple: he envies America and Americans.

To Castro, being American symbolizes what he always wanted to be and was never able to attain. He envies Americans and, because of that, he hates Americans and would like to destroy them. Of course, many people around the world envy Americans, but in the case of Fidel Castro, envy is an extra component of a disturbed mind, and that is a very unstable, explosive and dangerous combination, particularly in a man with such pulverizing power in his hands.

History has shown that trying to deal with Castro in non-confrontational terms is a waste of time. He interprets good will and politeness as a sign of weakness. The only language he understands is force—which, by the way, is an accurate term to describe American foreign policy since the end of the 19th century. And that brings us again to the subjects of gringophilia and envy.

A brief analysis of the Cuban foreign policy since 1959 shows that it is a mirror image of the American one. Castro envies America's strength and use of force as a means to get results. He envies American imperialism. As a matter of fact, most Americans don't realize, and don't even seem to understand, that Castro has always treated them exactly the same way the U.S. usually treats the rest of the world: with total contempt. As political science scholar Jorge Dominguez pointed out, "Cuba is a small country, but it has a big country's foreign policy."[210] The fact was also noted by professor Irving Louis Horowitz, who observed that, ". . . at least with respect to participation in the affairs of other nations, Cuba scores higher than any nation in the Western hemisphere other than the United States."[211]

Both scholars are absolutely right. Cuba's foreign policy under 42 years of Castro's rule has been a carbon copy of the American foreign policy, with imperialistic wars, military intervention, support of corrupt tyrants, covert action, political assassination, development of weapons of mass destruction, and the like. Castro's envy of America has turned him into a copycat of the U.S. Unfortunately, he has copied only the worst aspects of America, the ones he seems to love from the bottom of his heart.

King Fidel I

Many people have noticed that Castro customarily uses the royal "we" instead of "I" in his speeches. Some Castro-friendly people claim that he does so as a way of deemphasizing the importance of his personality while giving more importance to the collective leadership of his Communist party. But there are indications that Castro actually believes he is Cuba's king.

Like the absolutist monarchs of ancient times, Castro is convinced that he was born to possess all and command all. Notwithstanding his claims of being a Marxist, he acts as if his power came from God such that no one should question it. Like French King Louis XIV, Castro rules Cuba like an absolute monarch, keeping the whole power of the state in his own hands. There is no system of checks to limit his power. There is no better description of Castro's government than *"L'état, c'est moi."* [212]

An old friend of Castro who lives abroad and visited him a few years ago, told the following anecdote.[213] He was talking to Castro while they were moving around in the building where Castro has his offices. Then, out of the blue, came this servant, with his eyes fixed on the ground in the most servile attitude, who began carefully polishing Castro's shoes with a piece of cloth while Castro kept moving, totally ignoring the servant as if he were a piece of furniture. Other people have reported that, after Castro finishes eating, a servant comes and cleans his beard (he is a sloppy eater), while Castro keeps talking totally ignoring the servant.[214]

The image of Castro portrayed in most of the American liberal media is one of a democratic leader—perhaps a little too authoritarian—in power because of the will of his people, and governing the Island collegially. But this image is far from the truth. Dariel (Benigno) Alarcón Ramírez, a survivor of Ché's guerrilla in Bolivia now in exile in France, gives us a revealing view of how things really work in Fidel's kingdom.

During a high-level meeting at the Political Bureau of the party, just after the end of Soviet subsidies and the implementation of the "special period," Castro talked extensively about the grim future of Cuba's economy, and how to prepare the population for the coming hard times. Some of those present expressed their opinions, all of them just carefully paraphrasing Castro's words. Then, to everybody's surprise, Juan Almeida, a senior member of the Political Bureau and an old associate of Castro since the Moncada attack, expressed a dissenting view, and criticized him for most of the problems. Almeida, one of the few blacks in the high hierarchy of Castro's "Communist" Party, went to the point of saying that most of the problems were the result of Castro's whims.

"Shut your mouth, you shit-eater," yelled Castro in anger. "Right now you are under arrest!" That marked the end of the meeting. A few minutes later Almeida was detained and sent to his home under domiciliary arrest.[215]

On another occasion, in 1968, also during a meeting of the Political Bureau, with President Dorticós in attendance, Castro talked about his plans for a massive intervention of all the small businesses still in private hands. Some of those present expressed their concerns about the wisdom of such measure, and talked freely about it. Finally, somebody suggested a vote. Castro, apparently convinced that everybody was going to approve, authorized the vote. But, to his utmost surprise, the majority voted against his plans.

As soon as he knew the results of the vote, Castro threw one of his tantrums, yelling and stomping the floor, his face red with anger. Finally, he smashed his fist on the table and yelled: "Out of my balls we are going to do everything exactly as I say!"[216] Next day, Castro announced during a speech the beginning of the massive intervention of small businesses. Eventually, his unilateral decision proved to be a disastrous one.

Members of Castro's close circle of associates treat him with the respect deserving of a monarch, and Castro is always looking for signs of disrespect to punish the offenders. It is not a coincidence that most of the people who have fallen from grace are the same ones who made the mistake of believing they were Castro's friends and could deal with him accordingly. General Ochoa used to call Castro "The Horse" behind his back.[217] Tony de la Guardia, for many years one of the men closest to Castro, used to fall asleep during meetings with Castro, and sometimes walked out without asking his permission. He openly called Castro "Number One."[218] Both of them ended their lives facing Castro's firing squads.

Though the system of public health in Cuba has lately deteriorated to levels close to that of the poorest countries in the world, it is true that at some time, during the 1960s and 1970s, it became a model of public health. On close examination, however, there are reasons to believe that Castro's reasons for improving public health in Cuba were not guided by altruistic motives.

Since the advent of Castro's era, Cubans are not citizens any more, but subjects of an absolute monarch. Cubans belong to the state, and, as such, are Castro's private property. He has total power of life and death over them. He decides what they read, what they hear, what they eat, how they dress, where and how they live. As farmers take good care of their chickens and their cows, because they are their private property, Castro is interested in keeping his human property in good health. Slave masters were known for their concern for their slaves' health, because sickness would surely lower the value of their human property.[219]

Like a modern slave master, Castro is selling the work force of his slaves to foreign investors in Cuba, who are not only exempt from the normal labor codes, but who pay him market prices in dollars while he pays his subjects low salaries in devaluated Cuban pesos.

Evidence indicates, however, that Cuban slaves in the 19th century were better fed than Castro's subjects. A comparison between the average caloric content of a slave's daily food intake and what an average Cuban can buy with his meager salary in Castro's Cuba shows that, though both diets lack variety and flavor, the slaves were by far better fed.[220]

Chapter 7

Castroism: A Tropical Variety of Fascism?

Je sui Marxiste, tendence Groucho.
—Graffiti in a Paris subway station

During a long televised speech on December 2, 1961, Fidel Castro announced to the world that he was a Marxist-Leninist and would remain so until the last day of his life. Both Castro supporters in Cuba, and anti-Castro exiles in the U.S., uncritically accepted Fidel's claims at face value. But Herbert Matthews, the *New York Times* journalist who first interviewed him at the Sierra Maestra mountains, knew better. Asked a few days later about Castro's confession of Marxist faith, Matthews told a gathering of his colleagues at the Overseas Press Club in New York that he didn't believe Castro; that the Communist label didn't fit him. "Today Castro may believe he is a Communist," he said, "but tomorrow he may believe something else."[1]

Matthews, who closely followed Castro's actions and political career since his guerrilla days, was right. As a matter of fact, there is nothing in Castro's political life or speeches that allow us to conclude that Marx's or Lenin's works have influenced his ideas or political behavior in any way. And Matthew's views on Castro are not an isolated case. Many people seem to share his views.

Free lance photographer Andrew St. George, a CIA asset acting under a journalist's cover, visited Castro at the Sierra Maestra mountain and remained with the guerrilla for two or three weeks. Upon returning to Washington he expressed his opinion that Castro was an ego-maniac and emotionally unstable individual, but not a Communist.[2] Similarly, a senior CIA officer, General C. P. Cabell,

Deputy Director of Central Intelligence, testifying before the Internal Security Sub-Committee of the U.S. Senate, expressed CIA's opinion that, "We believe Castro is not a member of the Communist Party, and does not consider himself a Communist."[3] Apparently Matthews, St. George, and Cabell were not alone. Neither the Soviets, nor the Cuban Communists, true experts in communism, ever believed Castro was one of them.

The Soviet Union and Latin America

Moscow's strategies in Latin America during the war years, prior to Fidel's take-over of Cuba and before his rapprochement with the Soviet Union, were restrained and cautious. The reason for this behavior was dictated by the weakness of their puppet Communist parties in Latin America and the lack of an industrial proletariat, a necessary condition—according to Marxist dogma—for the development of revolutionary movements. It seems unlikely that Stalin would have been excited about the possibility of a Communist experiment in Latin America. Good relations with the United States were surely favored by the Russians over any Communist advances in Mexico, Cuba, Argentina or Chile.

The Soviet Union was relatively weak in those days. Therefore, recognition by the United States as an equal power in world politics, access to American technology and industrial equipment, and American help in World War II, were much more important to Moscow than relatively minor Communist successes in a geographical area in which Washington had long ago asserted a predominant interest and influence.[4]

When a highly volatile revolutionary situation developed in Mexico in the 1930s, the Soviets gave the local Communists no support to fight for political control on their own. In tune with this policy, during all those years the activities of Latin American Communist parties were reported without too much interest in the Soviet Press. The tiny American Communist Party was suffered by the American people as a bothersome fact of life, like pollution and taxes, but a Communist state in the Americas, reasoned the Russians, would surely have touched a too sensitive nerve in the American body.

Of course, the Soviets knew of the growing wave of anti American feelings among Latin American members of the intelligentsia, and the chronic social and economic problems of the continent, but they continued to follow their cautious policy even after the end of World War II, despite the Cold War and the rapidly changing power structure in Latin America.

For example, on November 7, 1933, coinciding with the anniversary of the Bolshevik revolution in Russia, the Cuban Communists attempted a small revolution of their own and managed to establish a "Soviet" of farmers and workers in Oriente province, in the eastern part of Cuba. Peasants seized the land they had been working, and a mini-Communist regime backed by a militia of "red guards" took control. This Communist experiment lasted for several months, but ended in failure. The Soviet leaders were not pleased at all.

Paradoxically, it was Fulgencio Batista—the dictator overthrown by Fidel Castro—who in his first term in the presidency gave legal status to the Cuban Communists. Initially, Batista authorized the Communists to found a newspaper called *Noticias de Hoy*, which began publication in May, 1938, and some months later, in September, legalized the Communist party for the first time in the history of the country.

In the coming years the Communists advanced in Cuba like never before. In the elections of 1940 ten Communists were elected to the Chamber of Deputies, and a Communist was elected major of Santiago de Cuba, the second largest city of the Island. During WW II the collaboration between Batista and the Communists became closer, and the dictator, as a way of payment for their support, appointed a few Communists to his Cabinet in 1943. Moreover, Batista permitted the Communists to infiltrate the labor movement and take control over the most important labor unions and gain some power in the Ministry of Labor.[5] Thus, a cohesive and skilled Communist nucleus existed in Cuba prior to 1959, but they were apparently happy with their meager gains and never showed much enthusiasm to the idea of taking political power in Cuba by means of democratic elections and much less in a revolutionary way by armed violence.

As late as 1954 the overthrow of president Jacobo Arbenz's communist-friendly government in Guatemala, largely CIA's dirty work, brought only a weak reaction from Moscow. This prudence and restraint, however, began to disappear after Soviet space successes shocked the world in 1957 and Nikita S. Khrushchev launched his aggressive campaign of "Sputnik diplomacy" on a global scale. But even then Latin America was not considered a prime target, or "ripe for revolution." Rather, Moscow set out to expand Soviet presence in the area by attempting to project an image of international respectability; an image of the Soviet Union as a great power possessing a well-developed industrial base with advanced technology capable of accomplishing great feats in space and willing—through the development of traditional trade and cultural relations—to share these accomplishments with other nations peacefully. Through his newly formulated doctrine of "pacific coexistence," Khrushchev sought to "demonstrate before the world the superiority of communism over capitalism."[6]

An analysis of the Soviet policy toward Latin America during most of this period shows several trends. First of all, the area was not top priority for the Soviets, though they had stood ready to take advantage to any favorable development. Second, until 1960 they had had only modest success in their attempts. The turn of events in Cuba gave them an opportunity to extend Soviet influence, but it was not clear that they wanted to assume the responsibilities—either economic or political—thrown upon them by an unexpected event such as Castro's revolution.[7]

All in all, before 1959 Soviet objectives in Latin America had been twofold. On the one hand, the Kremlin short-term political objectives had been to increase the number of countries extending diplomatic recognition to the USSR and to increase its trade with the countries of the area. On the other hand, and sometimes conflicting with the former, the Russians longer-run objectives had remained what they have always been: to gain, under the name of the Marxist ideology, influence and control on the Latin American republics of the hemisphere.

Soviet success in achieving diplomatic recognition had changed considerably over the last four decades. In the 1920s Mexico and Uruguay became the first Latin American countries to recognize the Soviet Union. Colombia followed in 1935, but subsequently Mexico and Uruguay severed relations; thus at the outbreak of World War II Colombia was the only Latin American country maintaining diplomatic relations with the USSR. But the wartime alliance of the Western nations with the Soviet Union persuaded a relatively large number of Latin American countries to extend their recognition—Cuba in 1942; Nicaragua, Chile and Costa Rica in 1944; Bolivia, Brazil, the Dominican Republic, Ecuador, Guatemala and Venezuela in 1945; and Argentina in 1946.[8]

But the beginning of the Cold War reversed this trend again. On the charges, most likely true, that Soviet diplomats were meddling in the internal politics of the nations to which they were accredited, several countries broke off relations with the Soviet Union.[9] By early 1958 the USSR had legations only in Argentina, Brazil, Bolivia and Mexico, plus a commercial legation in Uruguay and a consulate general in Colombia.[10]

The Cuban Communists and Fidel

The pro-Soviet Cuban Communist Party had languished in apathy for a long time in the usual Latin American Communist fashion, without showing too much enthusiasm for the idea of gaining political control in Cuba. In mid 1958, with Fidel already in the Sierra Maestra mountains, the Cuban Communists made secret contact with him. Though at that moment Castro's forces consisted of no more than a few hundred men and he was far from attaining victory, Batista's days seemed to be numbered and Fidel was becoming—with the help of the American media—the symbol of resistance against Batista's dictatorship. Under such circumstances a closer alliance with the man who represented a major fighting force against Batista was in order. Bearing in mind the strict discipline of the pro-Soviet Cuban Communist party, one must assume that this alliance was authorized and maybe suggested by Moscow, especially at that time of Soviet alliances with nationalistic movements and leaders such as Nasser in Egypt, Sukarno in Indonesia, Nkrumah in Ghana, Sekou Touré in Guinea and the FNL in Algeria. One way or another, it is certain that Moscow gave the green light and from mid-1958 on the Cuban Communists reluctantly began supporting Fidel.

One can only guess the actual role of the Cuban Communist Party (or PSP, *Partido Socialista Popular*, the name adopted by the Party since 1944)[11] during Fidel's struggle against Batista. But the real fact is that the *ñángaras* (Cuban nickname for the local Communists) never were among Fidel's best friends. In fact Fidel's first clash with the Cuban Communists began as early as 1944, during his last high school year at the Colegio de Belén.

As a young student, Fidel used Belén as a tribune to attack an educational proposal, popularly known as the Marinello Law,[12] the creation of Juan Marinello, the president of the Partido Socialista Popular and a Communist senator, implying that Marinello's plan was conceived following Soviet Russia's or Nazi Germany's lines. The true motive for Fidel's attack was that, if approved by Congress, the proposal would negatively affect private education in Cuba, including the Colegio de Belén. Although Fidel was but a high school student at the time, the Communists took exception to his words and retaliated with a vicious attack on the young Fidel in the pages of *Hoy*, the Communist Party official newspaper. They called Fidel a *"come gofio"* (sucker).

Aside from the Communists personal distaste for Castro, their attitude must be seen as a direct result of their blind adherence to the Soviet brand of doctrinaire communism. For this reason they must have been the first to be surprised by the triumph of a revolution accomplished without the guidance of the sacrosanct Communist party.

When Fidel and his men attacked the Moncada garrison in Santiago de Cuba on July 26, 1953, some senior PSP leaders were in Santiago, allegedly attending a sort of semi-clandestine meeting. As soon as Batista knew of the attack he blamed the usual suspects: the Communists. However, when Batista accused them of being responsible for the incident, the PSP leaders explained that they had been in Santiago just by chance, for the sole purpose of celebrating the birthday party of Blas Roca, one of the members of the PSP's political bureau and founder of the Party.[13] Then, they denounced Fidel Castro and strongly criticized him for the attack. One of the PSP's senior leaders, Joaquín Ordoqui, distinguished himself above the rest by his virulent verbal abuse of Fidel.

Indeed Castro's attack on the Moncada had serious repercussions for the Cuban Communists. Batista suppressed their publications immediately after the attack, and the party itself was subsequently outlawed. As a result, the Cuban Communists became even more resentful of Castro, and the PSP issued a statement—published in the *Daily Worker*, and circulated clandestinely in Cuba because *Hoy*, the party's newspaper, had been banished—stating:

> We oppose the actions of Santiago de Cuba and Bayamo.[14] The putschist methods which were used are characteristic of bourgeois groups. This is an adventurous attempt to conquer military bases. The heroism manifested by the participants is wrong and unproductive; at its root are mistaken bourgeois conceptions . . .
> The whole country knows who organized, directed, and led the actions against the barracks. The line of the PSP and the mass movement has been and is: Fight against the Batista tyranny and then unmask the putschists and adventurers of the bourgeois opposition who act against the interests of the people! The PSP considers it necessary to bring the masses together in a united front against the government so as to find a democratic way out of the Cuban situation, to resurrect the constitution of 1940, to secure civil liberties, hold general elections and form a government of the national democratic front. In its fight the PSP bases its support on the masses and condemns the putschist adventurism which is directed against the fight of the masses and against the democratic solution which the people desire.[15]

The Communists' distrust of Fidel was more than justified. Though he had some acquaintances among the Communists at Havana University, Castro had never been a Communist himself. Moreover, it seems that the animosity was mutual. In 1956 Fidel was mixed up in a controversy over the accusation that he was a Communist, as a result of an article which appeared in *Bohemia*, a leading Cuban magazine, written by Luis Dam, a Spanish Republican in exile. The Mexican police, affirmed Dam, had proof that Fidel was a member of the Communist party.[16]

Fidel quickly replied in the next issue of *Bohemia* with an impassioned article he titled "No more lies!" He wrote:

> Naturally the accusation of my being a Communist was absurd in the eyes of all who knew my public path in Cuba, without any kind of ties with the Communist Party. I totally denounce Mr. Luis Dam's report where he says, 'Incidentally, the Federal Security Police affirms that Fidel is a member of the Communist Party.' Captain Gutiérrez Barros himself read me the report forwarded to the President of Mexico after a week of minute investigation; among its observations it was categorically affirmed that we had no ties whatsoever with Communist organizations. An abstract of the report was published in all newspapers. I have before me *Excelsior* of June 26, page 8, column 6, paragraph 5, where it reads as follows: 'The Federal Bureau of Security emphasized that the 26th of July group has no Communist ties nor receives help from the Communists.'

Fidel continued his attack accusing the Batista government of plotting against him and also reminding the Cuban communists of their past collaboration with the Cuban dictator.

> Besides, the intrigue is ridiculous and without the least foundation because I have been a militant in only one political party, and that is the one founded by Eduardo Chibás. What moral authority, on the other hand, does Mr. Batista have to speak of communism, when he was the Communist Party presidential candidate in the elections of 1940, if his electoral posters took shelter under the hammer and the sickle, if his pictures beside Blas Roca and Lázaro Peña are still around, if half a dozen of his present ministers and trusted collaborators were well-known members of the Communist Party?[17]

Fidel's remarks about the Communists' past collaboration with Batista was the worse attack they could receive. And even worse was Fidel's slanderous suggestion that they were still collaborating with Batista. As Theodore Draper rightly points out, it is really very hard to believe that a Communist would justify himself in such a bizarre way.[18]

Therefore, one cannot blame the Communists for criticizing Fidel in such strong terms. Notwithstanding theories to the contrary, there is a great deal of evidence pointing to the fact that Fidel Castro never was a Communist. For example, Javier Felipe Pazos, who met Fidel in the Sierra Maestra mountains, expresses his total disbelief in the theory that Castro was a Communist and that the revolution was a Communist conspiracy from the beginning.[19]

According to Carlos Franqui, not even Ché Guevara considered Fidel to be a Communist at the time of the Sierra Maestra struggle. In a letter Ché wrote in 1957, he asserted that he considered Fidel's movement motivated by the eagerness of the bourgeoisie to free itself from the economic chains of imperialism. And Ché added that he always considered Fidel to be "an authentic left-wing bourgeois leader, although his figure is glorified by personal qualities of extraordinary brilliance that set him far above his class."[20] Franqui points out that neither the ideas not the language of *History Will Absolve Me*—Castro's political manifesto at the Moncada trial—reveals a clandestine communism.[21] Totally missing from *History Will Absolve Me* is the central idea of Marxism: the notion of the self-emancipation of the working class under the guidance of its vanguard, the Communist party.

Some senior U.S. intelligence officers agree with Franqui. According to a 900 page declassified report released on March 27, 1982, soon after Fidel Castro's rise to power in 1959, Allen Dulles, the Director of Central Intelligence, told a Senate committee at a secret briefing on January 16, 1959, that the Cuban leader did not have any Communist affiliations. "We do not think that Castro himself has any Communist leanings," Mr. Dulles said, "We do not believe Castro is in the pay of or working for the Communists."[22]

The fact is that, contrary to many allegations, very few of Fidel's followers were active members of the Cuban Communist Party. While still in the Sierra Maestra, Castro actually expressed strong democratic and anti-Communist opinions in an interview with Andrew S. George.[23]

After Castro unexpectedly announced in 1961 that he always had been a Marxist at heart, some authors have tried to prove Fidel's point *a posteriori*, though some of them with different intentions. Author Lionel Martin claims that the Moncada leadership nucleus studied Marxism together, and draws a circle of Marxist ideology around various leaders of the 26th of July Movement who themselves had had some Marxist education and were involved with the Communists.[24]

Another author, Nathaniel Weyl, wrote about Castro's allegedly early recruitment by an international Communist conspiracy, and stresses Castro's student involvement with radical politics.[25] There is, however, no solid evidence to support this view, and Hugh Thomas' opinion is that Castro was "in no way a Marxist in 1953."[26]

Contrasting with the above claims that Castro was a crypto-Communist, Ramón Eduardo Ruiz points out that, if Castro was a Communist from the beginning, he did not have to hide his supposedly Communist background. Instead, he could have become a convert just after he came to power following Cuban precedent. The history of the Island is colored with the case histories of Julio Antonio Mella, Carlos Baliño and Rubén Martínez Villena, who later in their political careers turned Communists. Castro could easily have walked in their footsteps. However, as the Island's pre-1958 history illustrates, the Cubans had never put much emphasis on their ability to keep political secrets. If young Castro was a Communist before his victory in 1959, says Ruiz, the story was the best-kept secret in a land notorious for rumors and gossip.[27]

The bitterness between Fidel and the Communists did not end with the Moncada attack, and continued throughout his struggle against Batista. The Communists did not approve of Fidel's *Granma* expedition in 1956. Their position was stated in a letter addressed to the 26th of July Movement (also known as M-26-7)—of which Fidel was an important leader, but not the main one—which expressed their "radical disagreement with the tactics and plans" of Fidel Castro. They also insisted that the armed action was the wrong tactic, and complained that the 26th of July Movement had not yet taken a strong stand against "imperialist domination."

The Cuban Communists maintained their anti-Castro position for the next five years after the Moncada attack, and they were not invited to the first negotiations about forming a united front against Batista in 1957. When such an agreement was reached the following year, five months before the overthrow of the dictator, the PSP still wasn't there.[28]

Former President Carlos Prío Socarrás affirms that the Cuban Communists never had much faith in what Castro was to do in Cuba. During the two years of Castro's war, says Prío, the 26th of July Movement never received a single bullet nor a single *peso* from the Cuban Communists.[29]

In July of 1958, from the Sierra Maestra, Fidel made some startling statements to Jules Dubois, an American journalist. Some of Fidel's remarks were so tilted to the right that a group of young radicals from Santiago de Cuba dropped out of the 26th of July Movement because of the conservatism of Fidel's words. Franqui says that in fact Fidel's statements were so reactionary they were suspicious.[30] After the *Granma* landing and during the initial phase of Fidel's war against

Batista, *Carta Semanal*, a semi-clandestine weekly publication of the PSP frequently launched both open criticism and veiled attacks on Fidel. As late as October, 1956, the *Carta Semanal* referred to the Moncada attack as a "dangerous and sterile" action.[31] But by February, 1958, the Communists made a quick about-face and adopted a dual policy of supporting simultaneously both "the armed struggle in the countryside and the unarmed, civil struggle in the cities." It was at that time that they ordered a few of their members to join Fidel's forces in the Sierra Maestra.

In April, 1958, Castro called for a general strike, an event he thought would have a decisive outcome in the struggle, but instead resulted in a total failure.[32] The PSP leadership did not openly oppose the strike, but predicted its failure, and distanced itself from it as soon as it became clear that the strike had failed. Carlos Rafael Rodríguez, a prominent PSP leader, went to the point of telling French journalist Claude Julien he hoped these futile actions would teach Castro a lesson. The failure would make him realize, said Rodríguez, that unless he entered a broad coalition with the liberals and toned down his anti-American propaganda, he didn't have a chance by himself. Later, in a letter to the same journalist, Rodríguez explained that the Communists did not feel that "there were sufficient forces in Cuba to bring down Batista and create a progressive anti-imperialist government."[33]

The first negotiations between the PSP and Castro's rebels in the Sierra Maestra mountains did not occur until late in the summer of 1958 after the defeat of Batista's counteroffensive, during the height of the guerrilla war. Not much is known about the negotiations, because neither of the two sides has published any documentary material about it. The only certain thing is that Carlos Rafael Rodríguez went to the Sierra Maestra in July and that further emissaries followed him in the Fall. But, according to the testimony of the Communists, no binding arrangement was reached before Castro's victory.[34] By mid-1958, however, the PSP began to collaborate with Castro's M-26-7. This cooperation meant a change in attitude on the part of the PSP leaders, not Castro's embrace of the PSP. After PSP leaders Carlos Rafael Rodríguez and Osvaldo Sánchez visited the Sierra Maestra in May, PSP militants increasingly joined the Rebel Army. They collaborated with the M-26-7 in the cities, and even established their own guerrilla group in the Escambray Mountains in northern Las Villas Province, near the city of Yaguajay.[35] Though some Fidelistas and some Communists had worked before 1958 for such alliance, it could not have been reached before because a very important part of the M-26-7 was militantly anti-Communist.

Only a short time before Castro entered Havana in January, 1959, the Cuban Communists and those few Soviet officials who watched Latin American affairs did not expect Castro to win. Both the Russian and Cuban Communists were not ready for the coming of Castro to power and even less prepared for the radicalization of the Cuban revolution and its rapid conversion into a Socialist revolution. But by the end of 1958 Fidel had become such a real force in the struggle against Batista that the Communists were reluctantly forced to accept him as the true leader and to cautiously try to find a place in his shadow. Yet, when the guerrillas headed by Castro entered Havana on January 8, 1959, and a coalition government was established following the lines of the Caracas Pact of July 20, 1958, the PSP was not represented in this coalition government.

On January 10, 1959, K. E. Voroshilov, in the name of the Soviet Union, officially recognized the new government of Cuba.[36] But the Castro government did not reciprocate. Still Cuba established no official relations with the Soviet Union.

When Castro took the office of prime minister on February 16, 1959, the PSP was disappointed again. They were neither included in the new government nor were they permitted to expand their control in the labor unions. In fact, during the first six months of the new regime, little trace of the Communists was detectable in the revolutionary coalition, and known Communists had no official posts in either the primary or secondary echelons of government.[37]

Granted, after the triumph of the revolution on January 2, 1959, only one of the old political parties, the PSP, had been allowed to operate legally and officially. But the Communists were not in a pleasant position. They had no representation in the new formed government, and it was evident that Fidel Castro and most of his people mistrusted them and felt some bitterness toward them. Some Communists even feared that a public rupture between Fidel and the Communists was in the immediate offing.[38]

In a speech before Eduardo Chibás' grave on January 16, 1959, Fidel emphatically denied that he was a Communist. To make things worse, on May 21 he gave a speech in which he still held an openly anti-Communist position:

> Our revolution is neither capitalist nor Communist . . . What matters to us, who are attached to a Humanist doctrine, is the people, and we mobilize all our energies for the good of the majority. We want to free mankind of every dogma; we want to make the economy and society free without terrorizing or forcing anyone. Today's world situation confronts us with the choice between capitalism which starves people and communism which solves their economic problems but suppresses

their freedoms which are dear to them ... Capitalism sacrifices the human being, communism with its totalitarian conceptions sacrifices human rights. We agree neither with the one nor the other ... Our revolution is not red but olive green. It bears the color of the rebel army from the Sierra Maestra.[39]

The Communists were justifiably incensed, and did not let Castro's attacks on communism go unanswered. Aníbal Escalante, a senior PSP leader, accused Fidel of "ideological confusion." Subsequent polemics between the Communist and anti-Communist members of the M-26-7 were openly conducted in the pages of *Hoy*, the PSP newspaper, and *Revolución*, the official M-26-7 newspaper, during all the spring and summer months of 1959.

On May 25-28, 1959, the PSP had a plenary session of its central committee, and its conclusions were openly critical of the politics followed by Fidel:

We are a small country that lies in the immediate vicinity of the U.S. The imperialist influence has deformed our economy; we are therefore dependent on imports when it comes to feeding our people. In view of these circumstances, all leftist-extremist tendencies and all excessive measures on the part of the Revolution, all attempts to ignore the realities and the concrete difficulties facing Cuba have to be sharply opposed.[40]

Seemingly concerned about Fidel's intentions, the PSP also asked from the revolutionary leaders a profound revolutionary consciousness, a great firmness of conviction, and an invincible determination (which apparently they doubted Fidel had), as well as a great flexibility and skill in tactics.[41]

Not only the relations between Fidel and the Cuban Communists was strained. In foreign policy too, Castro continued to hold the Soviet Union at arms length. At the end of January Roberto Agramonte, foreign minister of the Cuban revolutionary government, declared that relations with Russia remained unchanged, that is, they were nonexistent. Writing in *Hoy*, Carlos Rafael Rodríguez, the main PSP ideologue, strongly criticized the Castro government for not having diplomatic relations with the Soviet Union.[42]

Fidel's Short-lived Anti-Communism

The available record proves that the Cuban Communists never trusted Fidel.[43] As a matter of fact they were so cautious that in January 1959, after Castro's triumph, they sent a letter to President Urrutia in which they simply called for the restoration of the "democratic-bourgeois" Constitution of 1940 and for a few minor agrarian reforms. But at no time did they ever attempt, either before or after Fidel's victory, to force him into a more radical posture, and, paradoxically, in almost all PSP publications they made an effort—obviously following Moscow's suggestions—to moderate the revolutionary ardor of Fidel and his men to avoid a confrontation with the United States. This moderate behavior was in line with the prevailing strategy of the Soviet Union at the time.

In the first months of 1959, after Fidel's victory over Batista, Nikita Khrushchev was already working in the preparatory phase of his carefully planned visit to the United States. What he desired most was to see all Communist parties throughout the world promoting his newly created concept of pacific coexistence. Of course, there was nothing intrinsically wrong in the PSP's participation in a patriotic struggle to rid Cuba of a corrupt tyrant. But the last thing Khrushchev wanted at the time was for the Cuban Communists to undertake a revolutionary course that might give the Americans a motive to doubt his good intentions. For Khrushchev Castro was just another case of a bourgeois nationalistic leader with a radical posture and confused ideas who eventually would seek an accommodation with the United States. Both the Soviet and the PSP leaders feared that if Castro followed Arbenz's example, he would share his fate. Therefore, the Cuban Communists' caution was more than justified.

Following with their line of prudence, on February 27, 1959, the Communists adopted a mild program proposing an agrarian reform in which cooperatives were cautiously relegated to the last place. But then, on May 17, less than three months later, Fidel made cooperatives the most important point of his proposal for an agrarian reform—which was immediately approved and implemented. This action left the Communists totally confused. Fidel's revolutionary program in the Sierra Maestra never went beyond the overthrow of Batista's dictatorship and the formation of a corruption-free democratic government. Consequently, the Communists were very surprised by what they considered to be Fidel's reckless behavior.

In fact the Agrarian Reform Law dictated by Fidel was much farther reaching than anybody previously expected. The Communists were against such radical change because they did not feel Cuba was ready. Blas Roca, the PSP's Secretary General, felt himself compelled to declare, ". . . the measures adopted by the revolutionary government and its laws are not of a Communist character. There is not a single Communist in the government, although the Communists render it wholehearted support and uphold it against counter-revolutionary attacks."[44]

In the Spring of 1959 the internal political situation in Cuba was still unclear, but it was evident that the old PSP Communists were gaining new positions at the expense of Castro's 26th of July Movement. But, though at that time they had already made great advances, the Communists had run into strong resistance in Fidel's Rebel Army ranks and especially within his cabinet, whose anti-Communist members were so upset they were expressing their views in the open. By that time the 26th of July Movement had split into two well-defined pro- and anti-Communist factions.

Fidel's Short-lived Humanism

During his visit to the U.S. in April, 1959, Castro was very careful to disassociate himself from communism, to which he opposed a foggy doctrine he called "humanism." At a press conference held on April 20 at the National Press Club in Washington, he said: "We are against all kinds of dictatorships, whether of a man, or of a country, or a class, or an oligarchy, or by the military. That is why we are against communism."[45] Then, during a speech in New York on April 24, Castro, while continuing with his anti-Communist line, suddenly came up with a totally new idea: "Neither bread without liberty, nor liberty without bread; neither dictatorships of man nor classes; the government of the people without oligarchies; liberty with bread and without terror: that is humanism."[46]

A few days later, talking to American congressmen in the Senate Foreign relations Committee, a relaxed, amiable and assured Castro declared: "The 26th of July Movement is not a Communist movement. Its members are Roman Catholics mostly."[47] Answering questions from newspaper reporters Castro stated that neither he nor his brother Raúl nor Raúl's wife was a Communist and that if there were any Communists in his government, and he knew of none, they had no influence. When questioned on his stand in the Cold War, he said that his heart was with the West. Cuba, he said, would honor its membership in the Rio Treaty of 1947, by which 18 Latin American countries and the United States pledged themselves to defend any state in the Western hemisphere against aggression.[48] Back at home, the Cuban Communists understandably became quite nervous.

Just after his visit to the U.S., when Fidel was paying an official visit to Canada, he said in a speech in Montreal, "We believe that there should not be bread without liberty, but neither should there be liberty without bread. We call that humanism."[49]

Castro had never tried to give his M-26-7 a distinctive doctrine or ideology, therefore he took even his closest associates by surprise when he suddenly began talking about this doctrine called humanism. Though Castro never expanded on the subject, for him, "humanism" seemed to be a kind of third way; an alternative to both communism and capitalism.[50]

After Castro's speeches in the United States and Canada with references to his new "humanist" doctrine, some members of the M-26-7 hurriedly began parroting the new slogan, brandishing it against the Communists. The PSP finally decided to fight back and Aníbal Escalante, one of the party ideologues, criticized Castro's "humanism," labelling it "ideological confusion."[51] It was the second time Escalante criticized Fidel for his ideological confusion. But soon after his trip to the U.S., Fidel stopped talking about "humanism" and the term was never used again. Fidel's "humanist" phase—apparently surged, like most of his plans, on the spur of the moment—had a short life-span of about three months.

Some scholars have tried to find out the source for Castro's short-lived humanist phase, but with no success. It seems that Fidel's humanism had nothing in common with secular humanist philosophy, nor with the Socialist Humanism doctrine developed by some Marxist philosophers, like Louis Althusser. Likewise, there is no evidence that Castro's humanism was inspired by the ideas of Jacques Maritain, a French Liberal Catholic philosopher who, in the 1930s, wrote *Integral Humanism*, a very influential book in the long history of humanism.

Some people have mentioned the possibility that when Castro mentioned 'humanism' he had in mind a so-called "humanist movement" that appeared in Cuba in the mid-fifties founded by Rubén Darío Rumbaut, a well-known Cuban psychiatrist and intellectual.[52] This movement had its origins as an offshoot of the Catholic left apparently paving the way for a Cuban Christian Democratic Party. But the "humanist movement" never had any political importance, and soon disappeared from the Cuban political panorama. Nobody knows if Castro's "humanism" was inspired by Rumbaut's humanist movement, though Rumbaut recalls that, after Castro left prison in May, 1955, Castro visited him to talk about humanism.[53]

Anybody trying to find a rational connection between any of Castro's claims of ideological commitment and any particular ideology is bound to have a difficult time. Having been endowed with an amazing photographic memory, Castro's mind works like a Xerox machine gone berserk, creating instant *collages* of bits and pieces which if examined separately are fully realistic, but when seen together as a whole create a totally surrealistic picture.

Communist "Infiltration" Continues

When Fidel returned to Cuba on May, 1959, from a trip to South America, he found widespread discontent and dissention among his own people against Communist "infiltration." The problem had reached such proportions that the issue had been exposed to the public by *Revolución*, where an ongoing dispute between the Communists and their critics was being published. Finally, Fidel moved to rebuff the Communists and bluntly and angrily again dissociated himself from the Communist party and its ideas and programmes.

In an effort to settle things, Fidel made a major speech on May 8 in which he tried to convince the Cubans that he was not a Communist. On May 21 he said publicly:

> The tremendous problem faced by the world is that it has been placed in a position where it must choose between capitalism, which starves people, and communism, which resolves economic problems, but suppresses the liberties so cherished by man. Both Cubans and Latin Americans cherish and foster a revolution that may meet their material needs without sacrificing those liberties.[54]

Following the same lines, Ché Guevara addressed a letter in June to the influential magazine *Bohemia* in which he declared that although he hated anti-communism, he had never been a Communist. "If I were a Communist," he claimed, "I would not hesitate to shout it from the rooftops."[55]

When some of his people from the M-26-7 approached him to protest against the schemes and advances of the PSP, Fidel feigned surprise, blamed Raúl or Ché Guevara or broke out into a tirade against the PSP Communists. But in practice he did nothing to intervene against the PSP, and those who complained soon found themselves out of favor with Castro himself.[56]

After his unexpected victory over Batista in January, 1959, Castro was given even more coverage in the American press and was hailed in the United States as the hero who brought an end to a corrupt and backward Latin American dictatorship. But nothing went beyond such sympathy of the public and a statement of approval from the United States government. Apparently there was the unstated assumption that Castro would become a democratic Latin American leader, in the style of Costa Rica's José Figueres, and little thought seems to have been given either to the social and political character of his government, or to the long-range implications of such a dramatic change. Apparently the Americans were unaware of the increasing anti-American feelings developing in Castro's Cuba. The logical reaction when they finally discovered it, was a growing anti-Castro sentiment in the United States. Similarly, in Cuba anti-Americanism soon became the *leit-motiv* of Castro's propaganda, while at the same time the non-Communist leaders in the new government were being politically and physically eliminated.

On July 16, 1959, *Revolución* brought the dramatic news that Fidel had resigned his premiership. In his customary way of not revealing his plans in advance to anyone, Fidel's resignation surprised even his closest associates. That evening he explained on tv the reasons for his resignation by furiously accusing President Manuel Urrutia of holding anti-Communist ideas to the point of treason. As he was speaking on tv the populace "spontaneously" rushed to the presidential palace and forced Urrutia to resign. After this incident Raúl, Ché Guevara and others managed to "convince" Fidel to change his mind and remain in his post. Then, Fidel handed over the presidency to Osvaldo Dorticós, a former Cuban aristocrat and a faithful puppet.[57]

But things continued deteriorating to the point that, on October 20, 1959, Fidel had to send Major Camilo Cienfuegos, one of the Rebel Army's most popular leaders after Fidel himself, to detain Huber Matos, a highly respected Rebel Army major and 26th of July Movement member in charge of Camagüey province, accusing him of plotting against the government. Matos' only guilt actually was that he had tendered his resignation as a result of his concern about Communists having taken command of key government posts and in the Rebel Army ranks.

The detention of Huber Matos brought on a major government crisis. As a result of Fidel's order to detain Matos, Manuel Ray and Faustino Pérez, both Cabinet members, also tendered their resignations in protest. On November 26 a wide-ranging ministerial reshuffle was carried out. In the same month Fidel placed Ché Guevara in charge of the National Bank, replacing Felipe Pazos.

On December 14, after a Stalinist-type show-trial in which Fidel himself provided "evidence" for the prosecution, Huber Matos was sentenced to twenty years hard labor. From then on anti-communism became a serious political crime in Fidel's Caribbean paradise. With the imprisonment of Huber Matos Fidel made it clear that his previous guarantees of political freedom would not be honored. Contrary to his claims during his short-lived "humanist" period, living in Castro's Cuba would soon mean neither bread nor freedom.

Fidel Becomes a "Marxist"

During 1960 Castro continued raising the PSP Communists to more powerful positions and protecting them on the grounds that loyalty to the revolution and unity were the two main needs of the country. By late 1959, the Cuban delegation to the United Nations had begun to separate itself from the Latin American "bloc" in order to pursue a "neutral" line that corresponded more often than not with that of the Communist countries. By December, Secretary of State Christian Herter was complaining of the difficulty of even communicating with the Cuban government, let alone doing anything to alleviate the existing "unhappy" relations.[58] From that time on the events in Cuba's convoluted political life began developing at a vertiginous speed.

In a speech after the air attack which initiated the Bay of Pigs invasion, Fidel proclaimed for the first time that the Cuban revolution was a democratic socialist one. Even with the qualifier word "democratic" attached to the word socialist, the term created shock and confusion in Moscow.

Finally, on December 2, 1961, Fidel went to the point of delivering the famous speech in which, after admitting his bourgeois prejudices, he declared that he always had been a Marxist-Leninist at heart.[59] Fidel began his speech at about midnight on December 1 and finished speaking at 5:00 a.m. on December 2. Author Loree Wilkerson, who wrote probably the best analysis of Castro's speech, observed that Fidel's self-analysis in this speech presents the picture of a man desperately trying to modify his past so that it would conform to the present.[60]

Castro's confession of Marxist faith was received with surprise by the Soviet leadership and with extreme suspicion by the Soviet intelligence analysts in charge of Cuba. Their suspicion was understandable, because an evaluation of Castro's claims may have produced something close to an E-5 (that is, source unreliable, accuracy of information improbable. See Appendix 3, The Evaluation of Information). Evidently, Fidel Castro was trying to create for himself, *a posteriori*, what in intelligence parlance is known as a "legend," a false biography or cover story, supplied mostly to illegals and sleepers,[61] enabling them to live undetected within a foreign country under a false identity. The Soviets were not alone in their misgivings about Castro's claims. Fidel's non-Communist affiliation had been so widely accepted in international circles that his speech caused a sensation abroad.[62]

In January, 1962, Fidel confessed to a French journalist that, even though he had never read beyond page 370 of the first volume of Marx's *Capital*, he had always been a Marxist. Hugh Thomas said that Castro must be therefore the first Marxist-Leninist leader who had scarcely read any of the works of the Master and who scarcely allowed more than a few words and few expressions taken from Marxism to enter his vocabulary.[63] Thomas' remark is highly accurate. An analysis of Castro's speeches shows that, while giving lip service to Marxism, true Marxist terminology and concepts are totally absent from them.

By the end of 1960 apparently Fidel had decided to make a fusion with the Communists. (Perhaps instead of a fusion we may call it more properly an absorption). But though his decision was not officially exposed until the Summer of 1961, it seems reasonable to think that he began his drift toward the capture of the Communists in the very beginning of 1959, because all the internal crisis in his regime that year were related with his rapprochement with the Communists.

Finally, after his insincerely humble admission of ideological underdevelopment and his tribute to the old PSP leaders, Fidel pledged allegiance to the "collective leadership" of the new party he had in mind, product of the fusion of the PSP and the 26th of July Movement but almost completely in the hands of the old PSP party (or so the Communists believed). After this sudden change of their leader's ideology the members of the 26th of July Movement divided themselves into two well defined groups: those who expressed their discontent in various ways, and those who, in typical Cuban turncoat fashion, claimed to have been Marxists all the time without knowing it, and paid allegiance to the old PSP Communists—whom they suspected were actually in Fidel's hands.

By the end of 1961 the campaign on behalf of communism was led by Fidel himself and in Cuba it became a political crime to express any critical opinion against the PSP. Faster than a speeding bullet, Fidel had metamorphosed himself from anti-Communist into non-Communist; from non-Communist into anti- anti-Communist; and from anti- anti-Communist into Communist, before the astonished eyes not only of the Cuban and American anti-Communists, but of the Cuban and Soviet Communists as well.

The rest of the story of Castro's "communism" is well known, and I am not going to repeat it here. With the benefit of hindsight, however, it seems that the main reason for Castro's confession of Marxist faith was to sugarcoat the pill he wanted the Soviets to swallow. Proof of it is that after the disappearance of the Soviet Union, references to Marxism in his speeches are more and more close to zero, and Marxism as official ideology of his revolution has seen a dramatic decline. Marxism is no longer a subject of study at Cuban universities, and the few professors of Marxist studies who complained about it have been quietly separated from their teaching duties, expelled from Castro's "Communist" party, and ostracized. Paradoxically, Castro's "communism" currently seems to be stronger in the minds of most anti-Castro exiles in Miami than it is in Havana.

Castro and the Catholic Church

Since the beginning of his struggle against Batista, the Catholic Church was one of Castro's most loyal allies. A large number of Catholics and many priests became active members of the M-26-7. Father Guillermo Sardiñas was one of the first Catholic priests to climb the Sierra Maestra and join the guerrillas and became, with the authorization of the bishop of Havana, chaplain of Fidel's Rebel Army. Another priest, Father Chelala, became treasurer to the M-26-7 in Holguín. The Movement's national treasurer, Enrique Canto, was a leading Catholic.[64]

Among the many things the Cuban Communists felt uneasy about was Castro's close ties with both the United States and the Catholic Church. As late as January, 1959, the Cuban Communists not only were calling Fidel a "rebel" and a "petit bourgeois," but also a "man of the Church."[65] The Cuban Communists never forgot that Enrique Pérez Serantes, bishop of Santiago de Cuba and a close friend of Fidel's father, Angel, had played a key role in saving Fidel's life after the unsuccessful attack on the Moncada garrisons in 1953. But the Communists were not the only ones who saw Castro as a man of the Church. While Fidel was in the Sierra Maestra, the correspondent of the *Times* in Havana reported that Fidel was a devout Catholic.[66] Moreover, Fidel himself publicly said on repeated occasions that he was a Catholic and an anti-Communist.

Even at the time when American public opinion was outraged by the kangaroo courts and the killing of prisoners by firing squad, Father Ignacio Biaín, editor of *La Quincena*, the leading Church magazine, justified Castro's revolutionary tribunals.[67] By the end of 1959, though most Catholics had begun to feel uneasy about Castro, Father Biaín kept praising the revolution in the pages of his journal. Since the beginning of the guerrilla war against Batista, *La Quincena* had adopted a strong anti-Batista posture. It is known that the auxiliary bishop of Havana was a supporter of Castro and that most of the Catholic secular clergy opposed Batista.

By mid 1960, however, the relations between Castro and the Cuban Church had turned into mutual hostility. On the other hand, it is worth noting that the Castro government never broke diplomatic relations with the Holy See, and there was never any thought of breaking diplomatic relations on either side. Luis Amado-Blanco, a devout practicing Catholic, was for long years the Cuban Ambassador to the Holy See, and was the only "Communist" diplomat present throughout the Ecumenical Council sessions.

Monsignor Cesare Zacchi, for more than ten years the Papal Nuncio in Havana, was known to be very close to Castro and other Cuban leaders. Zacchi went to the point of urging Cuban Catholics to participate in voluntary work and join official organizations and unions. He also advised young Catholics to participate in the revolutionary process as members of the Communist Youth, and he seized every opportunity to emphasize the need for a greater liberalization of the Church.[68] In an interview that appeared in the Mexican newspaper *Excelsior*, Zacchi expressed his belief that while Castro declared himself to be a Marxist, Zacchi considered him ethically a Christian.[69]

Castro and Zacchi had a very close friendship that went far beyond diplomatic courtesy. It is known that they went scuba-diving together on several occasions, and that Castro frequently invited him to private parties. While Castro was wining and dining his close friend, anti-Castro Catholics were being shot by firing squads after shouting "Long live Christ the King!" As a recognition for Zacchi's good job in Cuba, the pope ordained him bishop in 1967. As expected, Fidel made an official visit to the Nunciate to celebrate the occasion with his friend.

Contrasting with the Mexican revolution, where the revolutionaries were anticlerical as well as antireligious, Fidel Castro is a pragmatical politician who, in principle, is not against any particular ideology. He doesn't care much about what people think or what they are. He opposes only the ones who, for any reason, are against him. While Mexican revolutionaries were in conflict with the Catholic Church, Castro has never been against the Church, just against some priests, and only for political reasons.

Herbert Matthews rightly wrote that he has never seen or heard Castro do or say anything against religion—an astonishing fact Matthews considered one of the aberrant characteristics of Castro's communism. According to Matthews, Castro expelled about a hundred and forty Spanish priests from Cuba in 1960-1961, but just for political, not religious reasons.[70] Save for a few mean actions during the very first years, the truth is that Castro has taken more measures against the Jehovah's Witnesses than against the Catholic Church. Accordingly, the Holy See's attitude towards Castro has always been either friendly or non-confrontational. For example, during a visit to the Island in 1974, mons. Agostino Casaroli, at the time the Holy See's Secretary of Public Affairs, was reported saying that "Catholics living in Cuba are happy under the socialist system."[71]

But news coming from Cuba tell about growing intolerance and persecution towards Catholics. According to a report, a recently passed law suspends diplomas or degrees of professionals who enter a seminar or religious order. Apparently the new law was directed against a number of medical doctors who joined Jesuit and Franciscan communities. Under the new law, these physicians will be barred from practicing their profession.[72] The fact may be wrongly interpreted as a sign that the relations between Castro and the Catholic Church are deteriorating, but this is not the case. While it is true that Catholics are harassed in Cuba, the relations between the Castro government and the Holy See continue to be good. On October 19, 2000, during the 55th Session of the U.N. General Assembly, archbishop Renato Martino, the Holy See's Permanent Observer to the U.N., took Castro's side and strongly condemned the "use of coercive economic measures against the social development of a nation and its people."[73]

The friendliness of some members of the Church hierarchy toward the Castro regime is in sharp contrast with their attitude towards escaping victims of Castro. Dr. Ana Rodríguez, a physician who spent long years as a political prisoner in Castro's prisons, wrote a book after leaving the Island, *Diary of a Survivor*,[74] in which she tells a revealing story.

On one occasion, she and two other women managed to escape from one of Castro's concentration camps for political prisoners. After two months in hiding, terrorized by the massive police manhunt and lacking food and shelter, they decided to approach the Catholic Church. They visited the Havana archdiocese and explained their desperate situation to Archbishop Mons. Fernando Azcárate, and asked him for help. "Get out of here immediately!," yelled an angry Azcárate. "You are outlaws who have escaped from justice! Get out of here before I do my citizen's duty and call the police!" So much for human sensitivity at the Cuban Catholic Church.[75]

In the mid-eighties Castro began a carefully planned process of rapprochement with some sectors the Catholic Church,[76] which culminated with the Pope's visit to Cuba in 1998.[77] In February, 1983, Castro was invited to participate in the Cuban Episcopal Conference meeting, in which he told the bishops, "I am prepared to help the process of rapprochement between the Church and State in Cuba as much as possible."[78] In 1985 Castro was visited in Havana by a delegation of the U.S. Roman Catholic bishops. According to his biographer Tad Szulc, Castro had a marvelous time dazzling the mesmerized bishops with his familiarity with theology and liturgy.[79]

On March 13th, 1998, Cardinal Bernard Law of Boston stated in a speech that, in the last years, Fidel Castro has been a promoter, rather than an obstacle to freedom of religion in Cuba. Coming from such an important figure in the Catholic hierarchy, such a statement gives an idea of how far the process of accommodation between Castro and some rebel factions in the Catholic Church has advanced.

A close reading of Castro's long interview with Frei Betto, a disinformation exercise published under the title *Fidel y la religión*, now translated into several languages, shows in detail Castro's view that he and the rebel factions in the Catholic Church have many points of agreement. If one is to believe Castro, Church missionaries, like Castro's internationalists, are fighters against poverty. Like the Church, Castro claims, he has chosen the option of the poor. He firmly believes that "if the Church were to create a state in line with those principles, it would organize a state like ours."[80] Recent events, like the growing support of the Opus Dei to the Castro regime, indicate that, at least to some extent, some of the high hierarchy of the Catholic Church seems to agree with the Cuban tyrant.

Enter the Jesuits

As I have mentioned over and over throughout this book, in the field of intelligence and espionage things are seldom as they seem. To what extent, one may ask, have most of the characteristics of the Castro revolution not been Marxist-, as Castro claims, but Jesuit-inspired? To what extent was Castro's attack on the Moncada barracks, which the Cuban Communists qualified as a "putschist attempt," not Marxist-, but Jesuit-inspired? To what extent was the failed Nicaraguan revolution not a Castro-Soviet, but a Castro-Jesuit joint operation?

A close analysis of Castro's theory of internationalism, which he claims was Marxist-inspired, does not seem too different from the Jesuits' doctrine of ultramontanism, their practical affirmation of universalism.[81] Moreover, Castro's totalitarian control over Cuba is similar to Loyola's idea that Catholic unity cannot be achieved without a total submission to the Pope.[82] The Jesuits wanted to impose this monarchical absolutism not only upon the Church, but on civil society as well. To them, sovereigns were just temporal representatives of the Pope, the true head of Christianity. As long as those monarchs were entirely docile to the Pope, the Jesuits were their most faithful supporters. But, if any of these princes rebelled, they found in the Jesuits their worst enemies. This does not seem too different from Castro's view of his relations with Latin America.

The term *compañero*, used by Fidel Castro and adopted by his followers to address their fellow Castroists, has been erroneously translated as "comrade," a word with obvious communist connotations. But *compañero*, companion, was actually the term chosen by Ignatius Loyola to refer to his fellow Jesuit members of the *Compañía*, to emphasize the fact that all of them were companions in the struggle for attaining their religious goal.

Few people seem to have noticed the many similarities between Jesuitism and Castroism. Evidence indicates, however, that the "socialist" state Fidel Castro has created in Cuba is not very different from the one the Jesuits created at the beginning of the 17th century in Paraguay, where the Guaraní Indians of the region were indoctrinated and forced to live a regimented life under a strict discipline. The Jesuit state ignored personal liberties of any type. The natives could not dispose of their time and person freely, and all property belonged to the state. But, if one is to believe Jesuit ideologues, the natives were very happy for having free education, health and a steady job.

The Jesuit priests governed over the indians with a strong hand, punishing the smallest deviations from the code of behavior they had imposed upon them. Penitence, fasting, public whipping, and prison were commonly used to keep the "happy" indians in line.[83] They kept the indians isolated from the outside world; traders were barred from entering and had to transact all business from hostels at an appropriate distance. The picture described above closely resembles the society Fidel Castro has created in Cuba. May it be that Castro, like the Jesuits in Paraguay, has been all these years trying to create in Cuba the ideal theocratic society?[84]

Like in Castro's Cuba, the Jesuit socialist experiment ended in total failure. Lacking incentive, the indians lost all interest in their work. As Castro blames the Cubans for his failures, the Jesuits blamed the indians for their lack of success. According to the Jesuits, the indians were lazy, greedy, and narrow minded. According to Castro, Cubans are lazy, greedy, and lack "socialist consciousness." In the Jesuit paradise the harvest was left to rot in the fields, implements were abandoned and deteriorated, and the herds went unattended and died. A few years after the beginning of the experiment, hunger was so widespread that it was not uncommon for workers in the field to unyoke an ox and kill it on the spot, light a fire with the wood of the plough, and cook and eat the meat until none was left.[85] A better description of current conditions in Castro's Cuba can scarcely be made.[86]

In 1750, Spain and Portugal signed a treaty fixing the boundaries in America. By this treaty, Spain gave Portugal the rights over a vast territory east of the Uruguay river, the area where the Jesuits had established their socialist state. Accordingly, the Jesuits were ordered to retreat with their indians to the Spanish side of the new frontier. But, instead of complying, the Jesuits armed their Guaraní Indians and started a long guerrilla war against Portugal. Finally, after many years of struggle, they remained masters of the land, which was given back to Spain.[87] May it be, one may ask, that Castro's guerrilla warfare against Batista was not inspired by Mao, as Ché Guevara claimed, but by the Jesuits?

The socialist-totalitarian organization of the *Compañía* is so attractive to totalitarian-minded leaders that some of them have copied it successfully. Heinrich Himmler chose to model his *Schutzstaffel* organization (the infamous SS) following the principles of the Jesuit order. The service statutes and spiritual exercises prescribed by Ignatius Loyola formed a pattern which Himmler assiduously copied. As in the Jesuit Order, absolute obedience was the SS's supreme rule. Each and every order from a superior had to be accepted by subordinates without a question or mental reservations, *perinde ac cadaver* (like a corpse).[88]

Responding to criticism for the lack of democratic freedoms in Cuba, Castro has answered by claiming that, on the contrary, the regime he has imposed upon the Cuban people is an example of true democracy. One may wonder, then, if the "democracy" Castro chose to create in Cuba was modelled after the Jesuits' idea of democracy within the Order.[89]

Of late, after the Pope visited Cuba in 1998, the relations between the Castro government and some sectors of the Church (but not the Cuban Catholics) are reaching new heights. In December 1998, the Political Bureau of Castro's "Communist" Party published a declaration stating that Cuba may well become a social laboratory for a *sui generis* experiment on the convergence of communism and catholicism (actually Castro's version of communism and the renegade Jesuits' version of Catholicism), which would bring back to life the seemingly forgotten dreams of liberation theologists.

Among the new apologists of Castro is Cardinal Jaime Ortega, Havana's Archbishop, and Mons. Carlos Manuel de Céspedes, Vicar of the Archdiocese of Havana. Both Ortega and Céspedes seize every occasion to propagandize the achievements of the Castroist revolution in matters of public education, public health and social justice.[90] Most Cuban Catholics, however, seem to disagree with their religious leaders' idyllic vision of things in Castro's Cuba.

Some Catholic leaders have become the most acerbic critics of authoritarian regimes in Latin America. One of the most well known, Archbishop Oscar Romero of El Salvador, made an emotional appeal to the government at Sunday mass the day before he was assassinated: "The Church, defender of the rights of God, of the law of God, and of the dignity of each human being, cannot remain silent in the presence of such abominations."[91]

Unfortunately, the Cuban Church has remained silent in the presence of Castro's abominations, and Cuban Catholics are still waiting for their own Archbishop Romero to appear. It seems, however, that they are going to wait for a long time. For some unexplainable reason, the Catholic Church's revolutionaries, who cannot remain silent in the presence of abominations committed by the Right, prefer to remain silent before abominations committed by the Fascist Left.

The attitude of the pro-Castro faction of the Cuban Catholic Church exposes in its stark nakedness the hypocrisy of the liberation theologians and their followers. Allegedly, they are opposed to a Catholic Church as the religion of the landowners and the wealthy, and they prefer to exert the "option of the poor." But in Cuba, where a small group of recently created wealthy landowners have pushed most of the people into poverty,[92] instead of exerting the option of the poor they have chosen to protect the interests of the landowners and the wealthy, that is, Castro and his cronies.

As the Orthodox theologian John Meyerdorff pointed out,

> Christianity has suffered enough because it identified itself with power, with the state, with money, with the establishment. Many of us rightly want to disengage it from these embarrassing allies. But in order to win its true freedom the Church must become itself again, and not simply change camps.[93]

A document posted on the Internet on January 16, 1999, gives a pretty good idea of the state of confusion prevalent in Catholic anti-Castro circles in the U.S. *vis-à-vis* Fidel's rapprochement with the rebel faction of Catholic Church. The document, titled *"¿Por qué abren sus brazos al tirano, y se los cierran al pueblo cubano?"* ("Why do they open their arms to the tyrant and close them to the Cuban people?"), was posted by Grupo No-Castro, an anti-Castro organization that has been very active in the Web since mid-1998. It refers mostly to another Internet document, *"1999: La causa de la libertad de Cuba y el destierro cubano en la mayor encrucijada de su historia"* ("1999: The Cause for Cuba's Liberation, and Cuban Exile in the Greatest Crossroads of its History."), posted on the Web on January 11, 1999, and published in Miami's *Diario Las Américas* on January 17. It was written by the *Comisión de Estudios por la Libertad de Cuba* (Commission for the Study of Cuban Liberation), a Miami-based anti-Castro organization, and signed by hundreds of prominent Catholic anti-Castro exiles who are desperately trying to show the Vatican that its policy toward Castro is wrong.

The document expresses strong criticism for world leaders who, according to the Cuban exiles, have misinterpreted the Pope's message of opening to Cuba as an encouragement to deal with the Castro government. The authors of the document also respectfully disapprove of the message the Pope sent to Castro on January 1, 1999, in which he referred to the 1st of January, the anniversary of Castro's victory over Batista, as "Cuba's national festivity."

More recently, Armando Valladares, a Catholic poet and former political prisoner in Castro's gulag, wrote an article in which he expresses his "deep perplexity" about statements made by archbishop Renato Martino, the Holy See's observer on the United Nations, on October 19, during the 55th session.[94] Referring to Castro's Cuba, Martino strongly condemned the "use of coercive economic measures against a nation and its people."[95]

Those Cuban exiles apparently forget that the Holy See is not only the visible head of the Catholic Church, but also a powerful state with varied global interests. Contrary to most states, however, the Holy See has no armed forces, so it has to rely heavily on its intelligence services, mostly composed of Jesuits, in pursuing its political goals.[96] Changes in the Church, however, prove once more that intelligence services are a very dangerous two-edged sword.

Has Castro managed to fool the rebel faction of the Catholic Church? Most likely not, but it seems that, like many others before, they have plans to turn Castro into a puppet and use him to reach their goals. For some strange reason, Fidel Castro has always exerted a great appeal over people who believe they can use him to their advantage because they are more clever than him. But anybody who tries to use Castro should be aware that everybody who has tried to use him, sooner or later has paid dearly for the mistake. A good example is what happened to Nikita Khrushchev and other Soviet leaders after him.

Though nobody can blame Castro alone for the fall of the Soviet Union, it is an unquestionable fact that he contributed to some extent to its demise. It is known that the Reagan administration relentlessly pursued a secret plan to bring about the bankruptcy of the Soviet Union by creating a false image of heavy spending by the American military, which in turn provoked a similar attempt from their Soviet counterparts.[97] Added to the heavy spending in their military development, the Soviets had the extra burden of having to financially support Castro's ever-crumbling economy, which by 1982 was running close to $11 million per day, and they were paying four times the world price for Cuban sugar. By the mid-eighties, Castro's debt to the Soviet Union had reached $9 billion, without counting the value of the military aid. The amount of money they were dumping into the Cuban black hole, added to the cost of the increased investment in armaments, proved to be too high a bill for the Soviets to foot.[98]

The Opium of the People

Lately, some Catholic authorities have been asking themselves to what extent the Castro regime has encouraged the expansion of Santería to the detriment of the traditional Western religions, particularly Catholicism. One reason for their concern is that, according to them, the practice of Santería may not only provide the people with a valve to dissipate the high level of tension so common in Castro's Cuba, but may also contribute to creating an ideological confusion in the minds of the people which directly affects the expansion of what they consider the "true religion."

As a matter of fact, since the early nineties the Castro government not only has been tolerating but also promoting Santería to some extent. Some visitors to Cuba have noticed that many government officials openly display Santería necklaces and bracelets. Monsignor Jaime Ortega commented that one might think that the Castro government has substituted Santería for its official atheist ideology.

Farfetched as it may seem, probably Ortega was not far from the truth, though perhaps not exactly the one he had in mind. French reporter Janette Habel, who visited Cuba in 1997 on an assignment from the French newspaper *Le Monde Diplomatique*, claims that the Castro government has been toying with the idea of using religion as a palliative against increased social tensions in the Island.[99]

While she was researching in Cuba for her article, Habel found an amazing piece of information on a confidential publication of the Central Committee of Castro's "Communist" Party. According to Habel, "Some [Cuban] leaders believe that religious incentives could be used to channel social tensions." According to them, faced with the frustrations and insecurity the present economic and social crisis is causing, "religion could be used as a valid solution."

Catholic leaders in Cuba, among them Monsignor Emilio Aranguren Echevarría, Secretary of the Cuban Episcopal Conference, believe that the religious incentives mentioned in the article are none other than the ones found in Santería, because that type of "pagan belief" doesn't bother the Castro regime, to the extent that it does not oppose the Cuban socialist state.

It may be, however, that these Catholic leaders have not fathomed Castro's capacity for improvisation. Information coming from Cuba still shows a growing rapprochement between Castro and some segments of the Catholic Church. Though nobody in Cuba believes any more that Castro is a true Marxist, it seems that, at least, he agrees with Marx's dictum that religion is the opium of the people.[100]

A Man Called "The Horse"

Some authors claim that Castro's nickname, "The Horse," was first heard at the Sierra Maestra mountains, where Fidel was fighting a guerrilla war against president Batista's troops. According to this version, Castro's ability to march for hours without stopping or giving signs of being tired earned him the nickname.[101] But Carlos Franqui, who was Castro's close associate during the Sierra Maestra days, has a different story. According to Franqui, the nickname was the creation of Beny Moré.[102] It was past midnight, says Franqui, and the popular musician was singing at a party when, unexpectedly, Castro showed up. When he saw Fidel approaching, Beny yelled: "Hey, guys! Here comes The Horse!"[103]

When the people at the party heard Beny they cried out: "The Horse! The Horse! The Horse!" When Castro heard the people calling him "The Horse," he was furious and threw one of his famous tantrums. But the nickname stuck, and, after some time, he got used to it and ended up by accepting the nickname as a sign of the people's affection. Anyway, Castro has always considered himself number one in everything, and the horse is the number one in the Chinese charade or *chifa*, a very popular game in Cuba among the lower classes.

Perhaps the nickname made sense to him, because the horse is one of the most accepted symbols of masculine virility and, particularly in a *machista* society like Castro's Cuba, Fidel has always wanted to be the number one *macho* man. One of the few authors who has noticed this *machista* aspect of Castro's personality is Carlos Alberto Montaner. Fidel Castro, says Montaner, sees himself as a *supermacho* exercising a lover's control over the country he has conquered.[104]

Nevertheless, though Franqui's story about Beny Moré is probably true, a more esoteric explanation of Castro's nickname may be found in Fidel's links to Santería, a religion rooted in the beliefs of a large part of the Cuban people.

Fidel's Links to Santería

Though it has now become fashionable to mention Castro's links to Santería, very few scholars mentioned the connections during the sixties and seventies. One of them is Hans-Albert Sleger, a German scholar. In one of his essays, Sleger affirms that the identification of Castro with Shangó's horse ties his charisma to Cuban syncretism.[105] In 1972 Sleger wrote another essay on the same subject, in which he mentions "charisma backed by Santería" as an element of Castro's power.[106] In 1986 I analyzed in some detail Castro's links to Santería in my *Historia herética de la revolución fidelista*.[107] In 1989 it was the subject of Nelson P. Valdés' article "La Cachita y el Ché: Patron Saints of Revolutionary Cuba."[108] More recently, Georgie Anne Geyer and Andres Oppen— heimer have studied in some detail Fidel's Santería connections in their books about Castro.

But, as I said above, these studies are the exception in the enormous bibliography about Castro. However, notwithstanding the scholars' lack of interest in the subject, many people in Cuba are convinced that Santería played an important role in Batista's downfall and in Castro's victory.

According to them, the first signs that Batista's power was eroding came after the nearly successful attack by a group of university students on the Presidential Palace on March 13, 1957, where the dictator's life was seriously threatened. Just a few days before the attack, special Santería sessions had taken place on Batista's behalf all around the Island. Some people who attended them, got the impression that it seemed as if the "saints" no longer were protecting President Batista. Soon after the sessions ended, rumors began circulating that the "saints" were abandoning the General, and some santeros began turning their eyes to Fidel Castro and his guerrilla fighters in the Sierra Maestra.[109] Those people believe that it was actually at that time that Fidel Castro became "The Horse."

An event of great religious significance in the practice of Santería happens when the deity, also known as *orisha* or *santo*, takes possession of an adept, who then is referred to as the *horse*. Georgie A. Geyer observed that a better description of what Fidel has been doing to the Cuban people could scarcely be found.[110] There are some occasions in which the adept (or horse) falls into a seizure during the ceremony. It is said, then, that he is possessed by the saint or orisha, who is literally mounting him.

In the symbology of Santería, horse-riding is a metaphor for possession by a *loa*, or spiritual entity. The person possessed is referred to as the horse, and the loa is the rider who "mounts" him. Santería thinking does not envisage possession by a loa just in terms of trance or shamanism; the material world, including human bodies, is seen as inanimate and purposeless without such a possession or infusion at all levels.[111]

Horses also appear in the Yoruba mythology, as in the story of the curse that fell upon the kingdom of the thunder God Shangó (Changó), one of Yoruba's many children, when his servants imprisoned Obatalá (who was in his human disguise), after accusing him of stealing a horse he was feeding out of pity. After that, the crops withered, the lakes dried, the women became sterile, and Shangó became impotent. When Shangó realized his mistake, he apologized to Obatalá and set him free. After that, the curse was lifted. Shangó was a great horseman, usually depicted riding a horse.[112]

Some people have also seen connections between Santería and *Granma*, the yacht that brought Castro and his men from Mexico for the invasion of Cuba. The name *Granma* was probably just a coincidence—the yacht already had that name when Fidel bought it from an old American couple living in Mexico. But some people claim that the true significance of the yacht was that is had been named after the Gran Ma, a mysterious pagan goddess. The story may not be true, and may perhaps just be the creation of someone who knew that Fidel and some of his close associates were actively involved in Santería. What doesn't seem to be the product of a coincidence, however, is the date Fidel chose for the arrival of the *Granma* in Cuba.

Castro's plans were to arrive in Cuba in time to coordinate his military actions with an uprising in Santiago commanded by M-26-7 leader Frank País. But, as it happens most of the time, Fidel's plans didn't coincide with the stubborn reality. As the official story goes, Fidel had estimated the voyage would take five days, and he sent a coded message to Frank País, that the *Granma* would arrive on November 30 at a deserted beach in Oriente called Playa las Coloradas. But strong winds delayed the *Granma* in the high seas, and the Santiago uprising so carefully planned by Frank País for the 30th of November was drowned in blood. Instead of the planned five days, the journey took seven, and the *Granma* ran aground in a mangrove swamp, not far from the coast. The invaders had to abandon it, leaving behind their weapons, ammunition, and food. As soon as they landed they were unmercifully harassed by Batista's air, land, and sea forces. Most of them were easily captured, a few were killed, and only a handful of men, among them Fidel, Raúl, and "Ché" Guevara, managed to survive, escaping to the nearby Sierra Maestra mountains.

But, as a matter of fact, Santiago santeros didn't expect their "saint" to arrive in Cuba on December 2, the day Fidel actually arrived, but on the 3rd of December, the eve of the anniversary of Changó, the Santería god of war. It could not have been a coincidence, therefore, that Fidel had precisely chosen that day to arrive in Cuba on a war footing. According to those views, the *Granma* was not delayed two days, as the official story goes, but in fact it arrived too early.[113]

Evidence of Castro's Santería connections abound. When he was in the Sierra Maestra mountains Castro used to wear two watches. The fact has been recorded in multiple photographs of Castro at the time. To reporters who asked him the reasons for his unusual behavior, he answered that it was just to have a spare watch, just in case the other got broken. Other sources, however, claim that the real reason is that Fidel is an initiated *olocha*, and one of the "wristwatches" was in fact a device to conceal his *resguardo* (protection), an initiation bracelet which adepts must wear at all times.

There are some unconfirmed rumors that Castro is in fact a Santería initiate. Migene González-Whippler, an author who has published several books about Santería, tells an interesting anecdote, told to her by a Cuban Santera now living in New York. The woman claims that, a long time ago in Cuba, she attended a Santería grand ritual in which Fidel was immersed in a bathtub full of blood from sacrificed animals. This ritual would protect him against harm and give him total control against his enemies.[114] Another source claims that Castro was consecrated at an early age to Ayaguna, an African deity—one of the 16 types of manifestations of Obatalá—which had miraculously saved him from certain death at the age of six. The consecration was performed at the Birán estate by a servant at the Castro's home, a black woman from Congo and a santera of the Palo Mayombe cult.[115] Castro's daughter Alina Fernández mentions that both Fidel's mother, Lina, and his grandmother, Dominga, were involved in Santería.[116]

By mid-1958 most of the Cuban people profoundly hated the Batista regime. By that time the santeros from Regla and Guanabacoa, two small seafaring towns Southeast of Havana, had joined their Santiago colleagues in their prophecy of Batista's downfall. They were fully convinced that Batista's days were counted after they got word that Fidel was wearing a *resguardo* prepared by his godmother Celia Sánchez, a powerful santera and a daughter of Yemayá.

When Batista abandoned the country in the early hours of January 1st, 1959, Cuban santeros interpreted the event as an auspicious sign: The revolution was won the day of San Manuel, a holy day of the Orishas. Fidel Castro, therefore, was an *"elegido,"* a man chosen by the Gods.

In January, 1959, Castro and his guerrillas arrived in Havana. Many of them were sporting Santería necklaces and bracelets, made out of colorful beads. Though largely ignored by the American media, the fact did not escape the attention of Santería believers throughout the Island. Santería necklaces are colorful and have a precise color symbolism. Red and black beads, for example, are the colors of Eleggúa. All white beads are the ones of Obatalá; red and white are Changó's; blue and crystal beads are Yemayá's; and red and yellow beads are the colors of Ochún. The color of the beads may vary, depending on the aspect or "path" of the orisha.

Colors have an important symbolism in Santería. To Santería adepts, the red-and-black colors of the Movimiento 26 de julio (26th of July Movement, M-26-7) banner had a special meaning: they are also the colors of Eleggúa, the God of Destiny, the one who opens and closes the doors to happiness and disgrace. In many Cuban homes a glass full of water devoted to Eleggúa is kept behind the main door as a talisman of good luck. When Fidel's *barbudos* entered Havana in triumph carrying the M-26-7 flags many interpreted it as a signal that Eleggúa was protecting Fidel Castro.[117]

In the evening of January 8 1959, just a few hours after entering Havana commanding his victorious Rebel Army, Castro was giving one of his long speeches at Camp Columbia, former headquarters of Batista's army. Night fell and he kept speaking to his mesmerized audience. As he was finishing his speech, a pair of white doves suddenly came from nowhere to rest on his shoulders. This astounding symbolism was not lost for his audience, and touched off explosive shouts of "Fi-del! Fi-del! Fi-del!"[118]

To Santería believers, doves are symbols of Obatalá, the Son of God. Obatalá is the God who shaped the human body, and rules the mind, thoughts and dreams. The doves perched on Fidel's shoulder were a clear sign that Fidel had been chosen by the Santería Gods to guide and protect the people of Cuba.[119]

Though the fact that Fidel is a Santería initiated "saint" has never been fully confirmed, it seems that he firmly believes in his sainthood. In his long interview with Frei Betto, Fidel, while talking about the origin of his name, said: "April 24 was my saint's day, because there's a saint named Fidel. *There was another saint before me, I want you to know.*"[120]

One may guess that Fidel's claims of sainthood to Frei Betto were made tongue-in-cheek, but nine years later, in an interview with Dan Rather, Fidel mentions the subject again, this time very seriously. As usual, in order to make his interview appear as if it were an impartial one,[121] Rather resorted to a known media trick. Close to the end of the long interview, of which all the questions to Fidel had been approved in advance as is customary practice in Cuba, Rather asked him a "difficult" one. Castro's answer is so revealing that it is worth quoting it in detail:

> Rather: There are people in my country who said to me 'Dan Rather, you've been fooled. That when the history of Fidel Castro is written, that it would be like Stalin was in the Soviet Union.'[sic]
> Castro: (feigning surprise) That much?
> Rather: Yes, that's what they say.
> Castro: Like Stalin in the Soviet Union?
> Rather: That's what they say. Now, is there a chance—any chance—that history's judgment is going to be anywhere near that?
> Castro: Not even one-hundredth near that. Absolutely zero. Zero! . . . And perhaps one day somebody will come up to you and say that they have tried to fool you *by comparing me to Stalin and not by comparing me to a saint*—because none of us are saints. But, in the po-

litical terms we are talking here, now, *I can tell you that I have the integrity and firmness that saints have.*[122]

There is strong evidence showing that both Celia Sánchez, Castro's personal secretary and confidant, and Dr. René Vallejo, Castro's physician, were *santeros*.

René Vallejo, a physician from Manzanillo, Oriente, became very close to Castro since the Sierra Maestra days. After the triumph of the rebels in 1959 Castro appointed Vallejo Minister of Public Health. A few years later Vallejo ceased to have any important government position, but remained Castro's personal physician and was very close to him.

Celia Sánchez Manduley, an eccentric woman from Pilón, Oriente, was probably the second most powerful person in Cuba until her death. Though probably she was initially romantically involved with Castro, actually she was not Fidel's lover, as many believed, but his godmother in the Santería religion. Celia was an *Iyalocha*, a priestess devoted to Obatalá. Some people claim that it was Celia who initiated Fidel in the practice of Santería. Celia became Fidel's *madrina* (godmother) after Fidel was initiated as a *santo*.

An anonymous source claims that a woman known as "Isadora," a santera daughter of a politician from the city of Pinar del Río, created the *resguardos* for both Celia and Fidel. According to "Isadora," the *resguardos* had been made with human bones from Africa, and "nourished" in human blood.

Celia Sánchez died in 1980. As a member of the higher hierarchy of the Cuban government, her casket was placed in state at the Martí monument in the Revolution square. But, when the funeral procession left the monument for the Colón cemetery, the people were not allowed to accompany it, as the tradition indicates. All live tv coverage stopped, and the casket virtually disappeared for a period of time much longer than usually required for the short trip to the cemetery. Once it reappeared at the cemetery, and the casket was ready for burial, everybody was required to leave the grounds, and the actual burial was performed in secrecy, under heavy vigilance by a few selected armed guards. Rumors ran that in both instances the corpse was undergoing the ceremonies required in the Santería religion for the burial of an Iyalocha. All of these happened in a country run by a self-proclaimed Marxist, Leninist, and atheist. No wonder Cuba under Castro has turned into a country of total cynics.

Blood Offerings Disguised as Foreign Policy

In late 1975 Castro sent troops to Angola, and Cuba became deeply involved in Africa, providing military and technical assistance to several African revolutionary leaders, including the infamous Idi Amin, a bloodthirsty tyrant. Castro also began a new revolutionary effort in Latin America, particularly in Nicaragua, El Salvador, Suriname and Grenada. But economic and political conditions continued deteriorating in Cuba. In mid-1980 125,000 Cubans escaped from the Island through the port of Mariel, west of Havana, in one of the largest mass exodus of modern times.

At the time, some santeros in Miami believed that Eleggua had turned his back to Castro because he was involved in black magic, sending thousand of Cubans to die in African and Latin American wars as a blood offering to placate the evil spirits. They claimed that Castro was under the control of an *eshú*, or demon. This particular eshú is very bad; he lives in darkness and is always planning how to do evil things to people.

According to some santeros, The Horse was *pikuti*, that is, under punishment by the gods. Also, Changó, the god who most seemed to protect Castro, and Oggún, who had him as his favorite son, both were very angry with Fidel. But, according to them, Castro's worst enemy is Ochún, the lady saint of Cuba. Ochún is the owner of bellies, that's why Castro fears eating any food offered by a woman. Castro, santeros claim, knows that most *bilongos* (witchcraft) enter through the mouth in the form of innocent-looking, tasty food.

Some years ago a Miami magazine published an almost unknown photograph of Fidel Castro during a trip he took to several African countries in the mid-1970s. The photograph, taken while he was visiting Guinea, shows Castro not wearing his customary olive green uniform, but a white one. Santería priests customarily sport white clothes and shoes. And when an adept is in the process of preparing himself for the initiation rituals he is supposed to dress in white all the time.[123] At the time Santería adepts in Cuba were openly claiming that Fidel had become a "saint."

Some claim that, while Castro was visiting his friend, Nigerian leader Sékou Touré, he was initiated in another African cult. Castro returned to Cuba with a number of "prendas" (power objects), provided by Nigerian shamans. Some of these "prendas" were made of such elements as the skulls of criminals, violent individuals or persons who died violent deaths, and they had been "harvested" from cemeteries.

There are other indications that Fidel Castro's involvement in Africa was not only politically motivated. In 1987, Nigerian religious leader Alaiyeluwa Oba Okunade Sijuwade Olobuse II—the great Oni of Ifá of the babalawos—was invited by Castro for a five-day visit to Cuba. The Yoruba Pope, accompanied by several of his wives, appeared at official meetings in Havana clad in a white robe, topped with a white, pearl-covered fez. His visit was portrayed in the Cuban media as a major international event, and a foreign relations victory for the Castro government.[124] Some people, however, interpreted the visit under a totally different light.

According to some Santería adepts, in December 1986 the Ifá Oracle, on its annual predictions for the new year, had stated that Castro would die unless the Oni of Ifá traveled to Cuba and kissed the ground, and the main purpose of Castro's hurried invitation was to allow the Oni to do just that. According to witnesses present at Havana's José Martí airport, as soon as the great Oni of Ifá arrived, he kissed the Cuban soil.[125]

Just recently scholars have begun to accept the fact, always widely known in Cuba, that Castro's Angolan adventure was not Soviet motivated, but fully his own idea. According to some analysts, between 7,000 to 9,000 Cubans died in military actions in Africa. May it be, as some santeros claim, that Castro's motivation was not only military or political, but religious? Was he symbolically sacrificing his soldiers at the altar of some blood-thirsty African god? Could it be that Castro, like primitive peoples all over the world and many modern-day black magicians, believes in the value of human sacrifice? The subject may be an interesting one for further research and study.

The Babalawos Change Their Tune

On July 14, 1989, the Castro government reported the executions on the wall of Cuban Army General Arnaldo Ochoa and intelligence officer Colonel Antonio (Tony) de la Guardia, and the sentencing to long prison terms of other Cuban officials on charges of treason and international drug trafficking, among them Patricio de la Guardia, Tony's twin brother. Col. Tony de la Guardia, a senior officer in the Cuban intelligence, was for many years one of Castro's closest friends.

As Castro's personal hit-man, Tony de la Guardia had a direct participation in the assassination of dozens of Castro's enemies, mostly abroad. He was also in charge of delicate special operations, including smuggling computers and other high-tech gadgets used by the feared Ministerio del Interior in its repressive actions against the cuban people. Tony used to spend most of his time abroad, sometimes even sneaking into the U.S. In a country where possessing a disposable razor constitutes a privilege, Tony de la Guardia had access to the most advanced technology money can buy. He was also one of Castro's key men in the narcotics business.

General Ochoa, Castro's personal friend who had loyally served him for more than three decades, was a farmer who fought the guerrilla war against Batista in the mountains of Oriente. After the victory in 1959, he studied in the USSR and graduated with honors from the Frunze Military Academy and later lead Cuban army forces in Angola in victorious battles against the powerful South African army.

Ochoa, the Cuban army officer most decorated with medals won in battle, was very popular among Army troops and war veterans. In a country where government corruption, privileges and excesses go rampant, Ochoa reputedly lived an average citizen's life, always lending a helping hand to war veterans. Maybe his popularity in the Army ranks was too much for Castro's comfort and may have played a key role in his fateful death. But, like Huber Matos, Camilo Cienfuegos, "Ché" Guevara, and many others before him, Ochoa discovered the hard way that with friends like Fidel you don't need any enemies.

Evidence indicates that, notwithstanding Castro's reported outrage over the discovery that some of his senior officers were involved in drug trafficking, the whole operation was not alien to him. It has been known for years that the Castro government has been raking off huge payments from the Medellín drug cartel for providing a safe haven for transshipping their cargoes from Colombia to the United States. It has also been known that Castro's motivation was not limited to easy money. Flooding the U.S. with drugs has been a major objective of Castro for more than 30 years.[126]

At the time of the trial of General Ochoa and the de la Guardia twins, Cuban babalawos began claiming that the Orishas were forecasting a dark future for Fidel Castro. All along the Island, particularly after the execution of one of the de la Guardia twins, babalawos said that the Gods were no longer supporting the Cuban leader. There is no greater sin in Santería, they claimed, than the separation of twin brothers, because *jimaguas* (twins) are considered messengers of the Gods and carriers of good luck. The killing of Col. Tony de la Guardia, the santería priests warned, was an affront to the Gods, and they would seek revenge. Nevertheless, to this day the Orishas' forecasts about Fidel Castro's demise have failed to materialize, and apparently the babalawos seem to have toned down their interpretation of the Orishas' signs.

Elián: Fidel's Elegguá?

The sad story of Elián González, the 6-year-old Cuban boy who arrived at American shores on Thanksgiving Day, 1999, is too well known to repeat it here. There are some angles to the story, however, that are not known in the U.S.

A puzzling aspect of the Elián González story is Castro's motives for having paralyzed the Island with mass demonstrations asking for the boy's return to Cuba. Apart from the obvious political gains, the whole act does not ring true, because Cubans positively know that Castro does not care much for anybody but himself, much less for this obscure boy. However, if one is to believe an anonymous document clandestinely circulating in Cuba, allegedly written by a MININT officer, Castro's real motive is linked to Santería.

According to the document, during 1999 Castro was passing through a dark period, with failure after failure piling up in front of his doorstep. In order to know the cause of his problems, he had sought the help of the best Cuban santeros. When he asked advise about his upcoming trip to Seattle, where Castro feared he may be arrested as it happened to Pinochet in London, the four coconut shells fell displaying the combination called Okana Oyeyun, all of them black, which meant a very bad omen. As a result, Castro canceled the trip.

Many babalawos, iyalochas and olúas were brought in order to ask the saints what was going on.[127] The four coconut shells were cast again and again, and the lecture was always bad. The santero priests asked the saints: Oggún, Ochosí, Obatalá, Changó, Yemayá, Ochún, and Orunmila, and all of them gave an answer, with the exception of Elegguá. It was Elegguá, the lord of the roads, the one Fidel most needed, because he was looking for a clear path. But Elegguá refused to manifest himself, and the answer kept coming as Okana Oyekun, which also means death. Then, Castro heard the news about the boy miraculously saved by dolphins and rescued from the sea without sunburns. Apparently Fidel thought he had found the cause of his problems.

Elegguá is a naughty boy, spoiled by the gods, who is always the first to eat. Elegguá is the one who clears the paths. The person who loses Elegguá's favors is in big trouble, because nothing will come right for him. According to santeros, Elegguá was born from a mother who had trouble conceiving him. One night, while walking with her back to the full moon, she sat under a coconut tree, and a coconut dropped in front of her. The coconut had a strange luminosity, and she drank its water. After that she became pregnant, and Elegguá was born. It is known that Elián's mother had several miscarriages before conceiving the boy. The sign was clear: the boy was Castro's Elegguá, who had abandoned Castro taking his good luck with him, and he needed the boy badly in order to restore his good luck. The fact perhaps explains Castro's apparently irrational behavior in the Elián Gonzalez' case.[128]

Castro and the anti-Communist Cuban Exiles

In their confrontation with the man who was taking the political and economical control of Cuba from their hands, the Cuban oligarchs, most of them in exile in Florida, tried desperately to find an ideological position to justify their opposition to Castro—without admitting that the main reason was simply because he had stolen their properties and kicked them out of Cuba.[129] But Castro, the good-for-nothing son of a wealthy landlord who made a fortune exploiting the poor and serving the interests of the United Fruit Company, was one of them. Proof of this is that, as customary with members of the Cuban oligarchy, Angel Castro sent his son to be educated by the Jesuits at Havana's exclusive Colegio de Belén. Thus, if the anti-Castro Cubans were to attack Fidel for what he really was, they might end up in the awkward position of attacking themselves. Therefore, they resorted to the fallacious argument that Castro was a Communist. The result was that, instead of becoming anti-Castroists, which common sense seemed to indicate, most Cuban exiles became anti-Communists. They were unable to realize that, by claiming that Castro was a Communist, which clearly he was not, they were unwittingly cooperating with the Communists by placing them in a position of revolutionary vanguard which they had never occupied before in Latin America.

Even more paradoxical is the lack of consistency of the exiles in their ideological position against the Cuban tyrant. The Cuban anti-Communists have always claimed that Castro is a dissembler and a liar, which many people fully agree. When Castro claimed that "Cuba is a democratic country," the exiles said "He's lying." When Castro said, "education in Cuba is free," they repeated, "He's lying." "Medical care and medicines are free in Cuba," said Castro. "He's a liar," they rebutted. "We have eradicated gambling, prostitution and drugs from Cuba," he said. "He's not telling the truth," they said. And so on and on. But then, one day, out of the blue, Fidel Castro, the great dissembler and liar, said: "I am a Marxist and a Communist and I will be so until the last day of my life," and all his enemies in Miami yelled with a single voice: "Look, he's telling the truth. He's a Marxist. He's a Communist." In their rush to hide Fidel's true colors, they accepted without reservations a Castroist definition of Castroism. They implicitly accepted the liar's words in an important ideological area in which they should never have accepted his ideas without serious analysis. A counterintelligence officer would say that they were captivated by the enemy's propaganda.

The anti-Castro exiles have based their analysis of Castroism on what they wish to believe, not on what the actual facts indicate. They want to believe that Castro is a Communist, therefore they have built an entire ideological infrastructure to support that belief. They fell for one of the oldest rules of intelligence deception operations: If you are willing to be deceived, you will be. Yet, we should not blame them. We have to understand that it is very difficult indeed to accept, as Pogo (Walter Kelly) did, that "We have seen the enemy, and he is us."[130]

On the other hand, adding to the ideological confusion prevalent among Cuban exiles, there is the documented fact that Castro's intelligence services have successfully penetrated most of the anti-Castro organizations in the U.S.[131] An axiom of intelligence work is never to accept something as it appears. Given a particular fact, the intelligence analyst should look for its inverse, because in the world of intelligence and espionage things are often not what they seem. As a rule, the more vociferously anti-Castrocommunist a Cuban in exile is, and the more foam in the mouth he shows, the higher the possibility that he is actually a member of Castro's intelligence services. But, blinded by their justified hatred for Castro, the Cuban exiles have been an easy target for Castro's penetration and disinformation efforts. Using Lyndon Johnson's earthy vernacular about the ExComm members during the Cuban missile crisis, I would say that, in their fight against Castro, most Cuban exiles have proved to have "more balls than brains." For them, a careful reading of Sun Tzu's classic is in order.[132]

We will probably never be able to determine the extent to which the virulent anti-communism of the anti-Castro exiles has been self-generated or artificially planted by Castro through his intelligence services, though, most likely, it is the result of both factors. A rule of intelligence and espionage is that disinformation cannot be generated in a vacuum, but must be based on the target's expectations. Usually, intelligence services use disinformation to fully convince the target of something about which he is already half-convinced. In the case of the anti-Castro exiles in the U.S., the target was ripe for disinformation.

But the problem with accepting the image of Castro's self-portrait as a Communist has more implications than just ideological ones. First of all, it is an image concocted by the Great Dissembler himself to blow a smoke screen behind which he could hide his true face. But the Cuban and Soviet Communists, real experts in communism, never believed even for an instant that Castro was, or may some day would turn into, a Communist. Their association was a shotgun marriage, with Castro holding the shotgun, consummated because the Soviets believed they were going to profit from the association. But, like many others, the Russians were to find out very soon that it is not easy to get any profit from Fidel Castro.

Secondly, the reduction of the Castroist problem to the communism/anti-communism equation allowed for the oversimplification of a very complex phenomenon. The proof that it has never been a good idea is that, after more than forty years, Castro is still in power in Cuba and the anti-Communist Cuban exiles are still in the U.S., concocting elaborate plans to overthrow him.

Moreover, and because they are basically anti-Communists, not anti-Castroists, these Cuban exiles failed to notice the strong disagreements between Castro and the Soviet Union—the Soviets unsuccessfully tried to overthrow Castro in 1962, in 1968, and probably were planning it again in 1998—and apparently never thought of using those differences to their advantage. By the way, it has not been easy for the Cuban exiles to explain how, after the collapse of communism in the Soviet Union, Castro, the alleged Soviet puppet, is still alive and well and in power in Cuba.

Finally, and even more important from an ethical point of view, the focusing of the anti-Communist exiles' hatred on Castro's alleged communism, not on Castro himself, opened a very disturbing door: If some day, one may ask, Castro decides to change into a Capitalist tyrant, returning to the community of Western nations and giving back the stolen properties to their previous owners, will all the differences between Fidel Castro and the anti-Communist exiles be automatically solved? It seems that, if the only reason for hating Castro is not because he is a bloodthirsty tyrant, but just because he is a Communist, a simple solution to the problem will always be at hand. This seems to indicate that, according to the available evidence, the differences between most anti-Communist Cuban exiles and Fidel Castro is based more on politics than on ethics. The fact perhaps explains why the Cuban community in the United States, so eager to condemn Castro's human rights abuses, has never been known for condemning human rights violations by the American government, at home or abroad.[133]

The attitude of the anti-Castro exiles in the U.S. is exactly the reverse of the one exhibited by American Leftists and Liberals. Always ready to condemn human rights violations by the American government, they have shown a callous insensitivity for Castro's human rights violations in Cuba.[134]

Fidel's Fascist Roots

In his long political career, Castro has proved to be the great destroyer of organizations. First, he used his Rebel Army to destroy the M-26-7. Then, he used the newly created militia, "controlled" by the Communists, to destroy the Rebel Army. Finally, he regained control over the Army and the militia and created his own "Communist" Party to destroy the real one. The members of the old Communist Party who joined Castro's new "Communist" Party were guaranteed their political survival. The ones who refused ended up in exile, in jail, or facing Castro's firing squads.

Like most corrupt politicians Fidel Castro is an opportunist. Prominent among his goals in life are political survival and power. Evidence indicates that, though giving lip service to Marxism and communism, Castro has never committed himself to any existing movement or ideology, at least not to the point of being hampered by any truths to defend. Since he is uncommitted, he has always been open-minded enough to see which things work and why, thus giving him a clear advantage over his adversaries who have all been committed to something or other.

What, then, are Castro's ideals, his *raison d'être?* It is hard to say, but we do have some clues. Castro has always been a dreamer, and he has never considered himself a politician. One reason for his inability to succeed in any field before he became the Maximum Leader, was his dispersed interests. He has always been the great *dilettante*, vehemently against specializing in any particular field. His talents are more of a supervising kind. No wonder he was successful when he entered politics. It was a made-to-measure job for him. Politicians usually know nothing except the outlines of their party program, but they have their own ideas as to how it should be brought about. In the case of Castro, however, if one digs enough for an underlying political ideology, we will find that his thought and actions are closer to fascism than to any other ideology.

Fidel Alejandro Castro Ruz was born on August 13, 1927, at 2 a.m., in Birán, a small village founded by the United Fruit Company near Mayarí, close to Nipe Bay, on the north coast of the province of Oriente. He spent his first years at the Manacas estate, owned by his father, Angel Castro, near Birán.[135]

When Fidel reached school age his parents sent him to Santiago de Cuba, the capital of Oriente province, to study at the LaSalle School, operated by the Christian Brothers. After a short period of time he was transferred to the Dolores School, operated by the Jesuits. In 1942, after finishing grade school, he was sent to Belén High School in Havana, also operated by the Jesuits.

At Belén Fidel stood out as an athlete, an indefatigable speaker and a good student—perhaps not too brilliant, but with a photographic memory. Some of his ex-classmates claim that at Belén Fidel fell under the influence of fathers Armando Llorente and Alberto de Castro (no relation to Fidel). Both priests, like most of the Spanish *padres* in Cuba, were staunch supporters of Francisco Franco's Falange,[136] a Spanish brand of fascism, and harbored strong anti-American feelings. They passed on to their young disciples at Belén their enthusiasm for their anti-American cause.

Father Alberto de Castro, who taught Latin American history, expounded on some of his ideas. According to him, the independence of Latin America had been frustrated because the adoption of materialistic Anglo-Saxon values and traditions had supplanted Spanish cultural domination. He emphasized how Franco had liberated Spain from both Anglo-Saxon materialism and Communist Marxist-Leninism. De Castro emphasized that those having the truth, which is revealed by God, had the duty to defend it against all errors. He rejected compromise and called for the purification of society.

Young Fidel apparently was captivated by the teachings of his Jesuit tutors, and particularly by Father de Castro's ideas.[137] It is known that Fidel read most of the works of José Antonio Primo de Rivera, founder of the Spanish Falange. José Pardo Llada, a radio commentator and politician who at some time was close to Castro, said that Fidel had Primo de Rivera's complete works at his camp in the Sierra Maestra.[138] It is also known that Fidel was fascinated by Primo de Rivera's speeches—some claim that Castro knew many of the speeches by heart—and by de Rivera's image of a wealthy man who left everything and went to fight for what he believed in.

Fidel's classmates at Belén testify that he was an admirer of other fascist leaders, including Hitler, Mussolini, and Perón. Among Castro's preferred reading was an eight-volume collection of Mussolini's speeches.[139] Also, Castro told a friend that he had learned many things about propaganda by studying Hitler's *Mein Kampf*, which he also knew by heart. Some friends recall that young Fidel had pinned on one of his room's walls a large map of Europe, where he happily marked the victorious advances of the Wehrmacht's panzers. Carlos Rafael Rodríguez, a former senior member of the original Cuban Communist Party who later became a Castro follower, seems to confirm the stories. Talking to one of Castro's biographers, Rodríguez told him that he recalls an article about Castro published in the conservative newspaper *Diario de la Marina* when Castro was at Belén. The article mentions Castro "speaking about fascism in a favorable way."[140]

Father de Castro had founded at Belén an elitist secret society named *Convivio*, through which he attracted young students with leadership qualities. It is safe to surmise that Father de Castro was actually a talent spotter[141] for the Vatican's intelligence services. Like their CIA and KGB counterparts, the Jesuits know the advantages of the early recruitment of agents[142] and agents of influence[143] from the ranks of their highly impressionable students. Most, if not all, students at the Colegio de Belén came from the Cuban upper classes, and many of them eventually would end up occupying high positions in the Cuban economy, press, armed forces and government.

Fidel Castro soon became one of *Convivio's* more active members. In 1943 Father de Castro and his disciples of *Convivio* signed a pact in which they swore to fight for a united Hispanic America, large, united, and opposed to the treacherous Anglo-Saxons' control over the New World.[144]

Dr. José Ignacio Rasco, Fidel's schoolmate at Belén, recalls that on one occasion, during an academic discussion, Fidel defended, as a thesis, the necessity of a good dictator in lieu of democracy. Fidel believed that, in the specific instance of Cuba, problems would remain unresolved unless a strong hand took hold of the Island, since democracy had proved incapable of solving its problems.[145]

The Cuban communists, and through them the Soviets, must have known Fidel's ideas regarding class struggle, which explains why they never trusted Fidel or considered him one of their own. Theodore Draper published a letter Castro wrote his friend Luis Conte Agüero on August 14, 1954. In it Fidel tells him about his goal "to organize the men of the 26th of July and to unite into an unbreakable body all the fighters."[146] Though Draper uses the word *body* in his translation into English, the actual word used by Castro in the Spanish original is *"haz."* *Haces* (the plural of *haz*), is Spanish for *fasces*, the very Latin word after which fascism was named.[147]

Fidel believed that, instead of an organized proletarian struggle, leadership alone could provide the catalyst that would mobilize the masses behind the revolution. In a letter to Conte Agüero Castro emphasizes the two conditions he considers more important for his movement to achieve. They are "discipline" and "leadership," especially the latter. Castro's axiom, *"La jefatura es básica,"* ("Leadership is basic") repeated several times in his articles, letters and speeches,[148] is more closely related to the Nazi *führerprinzip* than to any known Marxist principle.

The leadership principle is an integral part of all fascist systems. Contrary to what we saw in most communist countries, the personality of the leaders plays a crucial role in all fascist regimes. As Walter Laqueur rightly points out, "leadership as an institution and a symbol has been an essential part of fascism and one of its specific characteristics, in contrast with earlier forms of dictatorship, such as military rule."[149]

Though not all fascist leaders have been charismatic, the personality of the leader has always played an important role in fascist regimes. It is symptomatic, though, that the two most known fascist movements in the history of mankind are precisely the ones lead by charismatic leaders: Mussolini and Hitler. By contrast, the idea of the charismatic leader is totally absent from Marxist thought. Not even in the times of Stalin or Mao were they called "charismatic." On the contrary, Marxists and Communists have always deemphasized the role of the individual, placing more importance in the role of the masses. Even more, Castro's visceral hatred of capitalism, one of the alleged proofs of his Communist leanings, is no evidence that he was either a leftist or a Marxist, because Fascists are also known to attack capitalism and foreign imperialism.[150]

In 1948 Fidel Castro attended a student congress in Bogotá, Colombia. The congress had been called to coincide with the Ninth Inter-American Conference, backed by the United States, which had as a primary objective the creation of the Organization of American States. But the assassination of Colombian leader Jorge Eliécer Gaitán triggered a violent revolt, later known as the *Bogotazo*, that destroyed most of the city and triggered a long violent period in Colombia's history that caused thousand of deaths. There is evidence that Castro joined the revolt.[151] What is less known is that the student congress had been sponsored and financed by Argentinean Fascist leader Juan Domingo Perón. It is highly unlikely that Castro ignored the fact that the money for his trip to Colombia came from Perón's pockets.[152]

There are more indications of Castro's strong fascist proclivities. For example, Fidel's last words in his own defense at the Moncada trial, "Condemn me, never mind, History will absolve me," were too evocative of Hitler's final words in his own defense at the trial for the frustrated 1923 beer-hall putsch to pass unnoticed to the Cuban Communists.[153]

The colors appearing on the 26th of July Movement's banner were red, black, and white. This is very unusual because, though red and white are colors present in the Cuban flag, black is absent from all of Cuban national symbols. Hugh Thomas believes that Castro unconsciously got the idea from the colors of the anarchist flag.[154] But red, black and white are also the colors of the Nazi swastika flag. This may be just the product of a coincidence, but when it is seen together with other information it takes on a very specific meaning.

The first militia units, created at Havana's University, wore dark shirts resembling those of the Nazis.[155] There were some early mass rallies at the University where torches were burnt. The similarities with the Nazi Storm Troopers became so blatantly evident that the University militia soon changed its uniforms to more conventional ones. But, rather than new, the University's militia and their dark shirts was actually an old dream of Fidel Castro. On January 27, 1953, on the eve of the centennial of José Martí's birth, a large group of Fidel's followers showed up at the University. Then, they descended the large staircase marching shoulder to shoulder and carrying torches in an impressive Nazi-like parade.[156]

When Castro was in Mexico preparing for his invasion of Cuba, he was denounced to the Mexican secret police, who detained some of the revolutionaries and searched their house. Among the things the Mexican police came across was a copy of Hitler's *Mein Kampf*, which allegedly Castro always kept at hand.[157]

An American journalist and author found out that Castro "reportedly read Marx, and Hitler's *Mein Kampf*, during his University days and was greatly influenced by both."[158] Also, Mario Llerena, a prominent member of the M-26-7, claims that many people have seen in Fidel the characteristics of a Fascist dictator, and that he often heard it said that one of Fidel's favorite books was *Mein Kampf*.[159] Evidence shows that Castro was in fact very familiar with Hitler's ideas.

For example, Hitler was called "the Führer" (the chief) by his close followers. Among his intimate circle Fidel is called *"el jefe"* (the chief).[160] Hitler used to defile his enemies calling them vermin. Castro calls his opponents *"gusanos,"* literally "worms."[161] Castro used the term *"bandidos"* (bandits) for the patriots fighting guerrilla warfare against him in the Escambray mountains. A Special Instruction of the German Oberkommado, dated August 23, 1942, ordered that, for psychological reasons, the term "partisan" should not be used. "Bandit" was the appropriate term for guerrillas fighting the Nazis. It makes sense that Fidel, an avid reader of Nazi literature, copied the use of these terms from the Nazis.

Over and over the Cuban people have been recorded chanting rhythmically *"Fi-del!, Fi-del! Fi-del!,"* at rallies and mass meetings.[162] The chanting closely resembles the Nazi *"Zieg-Heil!, Zieg-Heil!, Zieg-Heil!"* and the *"Du-ce!, Du-ce!, Du-ce!"* cheers of Mussolini's Fascist thugs. A common slogan in Hitler's Germany was: "The Führer orders, let us obey!," very similar to the Italian Fascist motto *"Credere, Obedire, Combattere!"* ("Believe, Obey, Fight!"). Its Castroist counterpart is: *"Comandante en jefe: ¡Ordene!"* ("Commander-in-Chief, give us your orders!"). Evidently, there are too many similarities to be just the product of coincidences.

It was in vogue among Cuban intellectuals, particularly during the pre-war and war years, to play with the totalitarian theories espoused by the then powerful members of the Rome-Berlin-Tokyo

Axis. It was only after WW II, when Fidel Castro was a student at the University of Havana, that the ideas of communism began gaining popularity in Cuba, though fascism still attracted a large number of the Cuban intelligentsia.

Fidel evidenced from his early days a strong totalitarian bent. In April, 1948, he took a trip to Colombia together with his friend Rafael del Pino Siero. Once in Colombia Fidel lectured at the University in Bogotá on the techniques of the *coup d'état*.[163] Knowing Fidel's mentality and his craving for absolute personal power, it is easy to conclude that it was just a matter of political pragmatism as to which of the two ideologies, fascism or communism, would best serve his purposes. Dr. Raúl Chibás, a long time political associate of Castro, said that he believed Fidel was just "utilizing communism as the most appropriate system for reaching the objectives of one-man government." Totalitarian communism, Chibás believed, was useful for establishing Fidel's one-man rule in Cuba. "Twenty-five years ago it could have been Nazism or fascism."[164]

It was revealed that at the time Castro took power in Cuba some people at the U.S. State Department were convinced that Castro was going to follow a Fascist path. The reasons for such belief were that Castro's leadership style was closer to that of the Spanish dictatorship than to that of Marxists. Other reasons were the similarities between his techniques and those of the Nazis and of Mussolini. Those techniques emphasized national socialism and mass mobilization, exactly the same techniques Castro was using.[165]

A close analysis of Castro's strategy since the early days of the revolution shows that it resembles fascism more than Marxism,[166] and from the very beginning the Cuban Communists noticed the similarities. After Castro attacked the Moncada garrison in 1953 they criticized the action and labeled its participants as "putschists" and "petty bourgeois," terms that in Communist parlance mean Fascist. Moreover, the revolutionary movement led by Fidel was never defined by the Cuban Communists as Marxist or Marxist-Leninist, but "petty bourgeois" and "nationalist," a common description used by Marxists to portray fascism. The Cuban Communists, who were true experts in ideological matters, always saw Castro as a Fascist, that is why they labelled the attack on the Moncada barracks a "putschist attempt." History has proved that they were absolutely right.

A Caribbean Führer?

In a speech delivered in Santiago de Cuba in early 1959, Castro denounced the "ill-intentioned" American press and advanced the idea of a Latin American international news service, "written in our own language." Immediately he began recruiting reporters and by the beginning of March, 1959, the *Prensa Latina* news service, totally under his control, went into operation. Curiously, Castro's idea resembled very closely, even in name, a similar one another Latin American Fascist dictator had many years earlier. That dictator was none other than Juan Domingo Perón who created *Agencia Latina*, a news service which would faithfully carry on the propaganda work of his regime. The analogy between the names and the purpose of the two news agencies becomes even more striking when one discovers that Castro's appointee as director of *Prensa Latina* was Jorge Ricardo Masetti, a close friend of Ché Guevara who had been a member of Perón's *Agencia Latina*.[167]

The strange affinity between Nazism and Castroism was noticed not only by the Cuban communists, but also by the Trostkyists. As early as April, 1961, *The Militant,* a Trostkyist magazine, published an article by Trent Hatter entitled "Danger Signals in Cuba," in which the author pointed out the similarities between Hitler and Castro.[168] Despite Fidel's later rhetorical attempts to make the rebellion seem a poor man's revolt, the truth is that it was in fact largely a petty bourgeois phenomenon. Actually, Castro's rebellion was opposed by most Cuban blacks, who filled Batista's army, and by the majority of the urban poor and rural masses who watched apathetically from the sidelines.

It is clear that neither "Yankee imperialism" nor economic conditions were responsible for Fidel's alleged turn to "communism." Adding still further to the mystery and complexity of the enigma was the fact that the Cuban Communist party never really opposed Batista. On the contrary, they opposed all of the anti-Batista movements, including that of Fidel Castro. How could Cuba become a Communist state when the Communists opposed the revolution that produced that state? If Fidel was a Communist, why had the Communist party initially made such a contemptuous estimate of his military operations? If he was a Communist, why did a CIA officer, testifying before a congressional subcommittee, declare that the available evidence did not warrant such a conclusion?

There is circumstantial evidence indicating that the main motive behind Castro's claims of a Marxist affiliation was neither because he believed in Marxism nor because he had drawn his support from embittered peasants and workers—middle class disgust was, in fact, Batista's worst problem—but because it was the only path Fidel knew would allow him to exercise forever the unlimited power he had suddenly achieved. Fidel's history, however, shows that he was temperamentally more akin to fascism than to communism.[169] But fascism, particularly after the defeat of Nazi Germany, was not fashionable any more. As Professor Paul Seabury observed, "Under different circumstances of international conflict a movement as Castro's in Cuba might well have simply been an anti-American Fascist one. Castro's philosophy of revolutionary activism bears closer resemblance to Mussolini's than to Lenin's."[170]

The decision to declare his revolution Marxist was Fidel's trick to fool friends and enemies alike. Fearing the loss of the power he had obtained, he grabbed the only path which seemed likely to preserve his leadership forever and also deal with the problems it would create.

In February 1959, Castro passed a decree named the "Fundamental Law of the Revolution." The decree not only canceled all constitutional rights, but also invested legislative power in the cabinet—the equivalent of Hitler's Enabling Law. Immediately after, Castro took over as Prime Minister, banning the President from Cabinet meetings.

By mid 1959 the exodus of Cubans fleeing the country was picking up momentum. Day after day hundreds of Cubans—small children, elderly people, and young and middle-aged couples—lined up at the counters of airline companies with flights from Havana. Their personal luggage included children's tricycles, blankets, photographs of their loved ones, their table silver and virtually everything of value that was movable, including jewels and gold watches. In dramatic scenes resembling the early flight of Jews from Nazi Germany, Castro's G-2 officers at the airport seized all their properties. The value of watches and wedding rings was assessed by the agents at the airport, and often those agents would take for themselves those watches and rings on the spot.[171]

In the first months of 1962 opposition to the Castro regime became widely extended in Cuba. Wholesale roundups by government troops became commonplace. Though Castro graduated from the University of Havana's law school, he never believed in the rule of law, but in the rule of men. Within months of taking power he turned Cuba's entire judicial system upside down. As in Hitler's Germany, *Führergewalt*—Führer power—soon became the absolute law of the land, and Castro's every maniacal whim was immediately translated into codes and regulations.

In mid-1962 Castro created the "mobile military tribunals," an extermination technique which made all Batista's crimes look pale in comparison. Panel and covered trucks traveled around the countryside conducting on-the-spot trials. Three or five members of a summary military court were dispatched to an area where a disturbance had been reported. Infractions, under the blanket charge of "enemies of the state," ranged from refusing to attend school or "volunteer" to cut sugar cane, to speaking against the Castro regime. The trials took only a few minutes, and most of the accused were executed on the spot. In many cases, caskets had been delivered beforehand and the "judges" served as the firing squad. The lucky ones not shot were condemned to 30 years hard labor.[172]

By early 1964 Castro had created a large system of mass detention, with 57 prisons and 18 concentration camps, holding an estimate of 100,000 political prisoners in a state of servitude to the tyrant.[173] Though many people believe that, contrary to other totalitarian tyrants, it has not been customary for Castro to indulge in vengeful and arbitrary brutalities, a quite different image emerges from the facts. While he has denied that prisoners in his jails are tortured or given inhuman treatment, released and escaped political prisoners have extensively testified to the contrary.[174]

By early 1980, widespread repression in Cuba had reached intolerable levels. In April, 1980, out of desperation, a group of Cuban families seeking freedom hijacked a city bus, and, after crashing it against the wall of the Peruvian Embassy in Havana, tried to gain access to the embassy through the hole in the wall. The Cuban soldiers surrounding the compound opened fire and killed several of them, including young children and women. The ones who managed to sneak in asked for political asylum. A few hours later, an angry Fidel appeared on tv and verbally abused the Cubans who had taken refuge in the embassy with insults ranging from *"gusanos"* to "scum" and "CIA agents." He ended his speech by yelling, *"No los queremos aquí. ¡Todo el que quiera irse, que se vaya!"* ("We don't want them here. Everyone who wants to leave, should leave!") Next day Castro's words were reproduced in big, bold letters in the first page of newspapers. But apparently most Cubans took his advice too literally. The resulting gigantic wave of Cuban fleeing the Island came to be known as the Mariel boatlift.[175]

Concerned about the spectacle of thousands of Cubans legally leaving the Island, Castro back pedalled. He began calling the desperate Cubans "scum" and claimed that they were criminals. Soon after, he conceived the so called *"actos de repudio"* (repudiation acts) to physically and psychologically harass the Cubans planning to leave the country following his own suggestion. A detailed description of the "repudiation acts" is out of the scope of this book, but it is enough to say that they were a re-enactment of the persecution of the Jews in the early days of Nazi Germany.[176] Finally, in a cynical attempt to taint the exiles, he conceived the evil idea of mixing in mental patients released from institutions and hard-core criminals from the Island's prisons into the mass of refugees. Though these criminal elements totalled less than 5% of the over 125,000 Cubans who entered the U.S., they managed to give a bad name to the refugees. Very soon, *"marielito"* became a synonym in the U.S. for a ruthless criminal, like the one immortalized in Al Pacino's film *Scarface*.

Apparently the behavior of his mobs in the "repudiation acts" inspired Castro for the creation of another of his Fascist abominations, the infamous *Brigadas de Acción Rápida* (Fast Action Brigades), groups of government-sponsored gangs of thugs and common criminals, apparently inspired by Mussolini's street fighters, the *squadristi*.[177] The *Brigadas* were Castro's invention for the brutal repression of Cuban dissidents. Probably the action that best typifies the *Brigadas'* heroic actions is their treatment of dissident poet María Elena Cruz Varela.

In 1989, Varela won Cuba's National Award for Poetry, a prize awarded by the Union of Cuban Writers. But in 1991, as Varela's dissident posture became widely known, the Union expelled her from its ranks. That same year, *Criterio Alternativo*, a group of Cuban intellectuals led by Varela, published a manifesto denouncing the Castro government and calling for democratic and economic reforms. A few days later some members of a *Brigada* broke into her apartment and dragged her downstairs into the street, where they cursed and beat her. Then, they attempted to force her to eat a copy of her manifesto. Finally, the police, who had witnessed the whole event without intervening to stop it, arrested Varela and sent her to prison for two years. In any event, physical aggression against defenseless women, as in the Varela case, is a common occurrence in Castro's Cuba.

In November of 1988, two Spanish women, María Paz Martínez Nieto, president of ASOPAZCO (*Asociación por la Paz Continental*—Association for Continental Peace), and Dr. Loyola del Palacio, a Spanish senator, traveled to Cuba with a group of human rights activists and reporters to see for themselves allegations of violations of human rights by the Castro government. Soon after their arrival in Havana's international airport they were detained by Cuban immigration authorities and held incommunicado. A few hours later, a group of about thirty Cuban Army soldiers, under the command of General Fabián Escalante, a senior officer of Castro's military intelligence, appeared on the scene and physically attacked the visitors, including the women. Afterwards they were kept in detention, without any medical attention, until they were sent back to Spain on the next plane.[178]

Another Fascist-inspired abomination created by Fidel Castro in Cuba is the *Comités de Defensa de la Revolución* (CDRs, Committees for the Defense of the Revolution), groups of government informers organized in every city block to spy on their fellow citizens. Lacking originality, Castro got his inspiration for the CDRs right from the *blockwarts*, a very similar institution created by Hitler in Nazi Germany.[179]

It seems that, though it has taken some time, more and more people in Cuba have become aware of the similarities of Castroism and Nazism. In 1986, the government's official newspaper *Granma* published on its first page a photograph of Castro attending a meeting of the feared MININT (*Ministerio del Interior*, Castro's secret police). The photo depicted Fidel with his right hand raised in a typical "Nazi" salute. Behind him the word *"ario"* (Spanish for "Aryan") appeared written on a banner on the wall, captured by an astute photographer who purposely had framed the four last letters of the word *"revolucionario"* to appear on the photograph. Just a few copies of the newspaper reached the streets before the authorities discovered the subterfuge and confiscated and destroyed the whole edition.[180] Afterwards, a severe purge was carried out at *Granma*, and several journalists and photographers ended up in Castro's jails.

Is Castroism Fascism in Disguise?

What most anti-Batista fighters had in mind when they fought the Cuban dictator was only to get rid of him and bring the Island back to normalcy under the guidelines of the Cuban Constitution. But Castro's secret plans were quite different. His goal was not only the total transformation of Cuba but also the creation of a "new man,"—an old Fascist idea.[181] Such a profound, dramatic change would not be possible by any amount of superficial social tinkering. His goal was not a return to democracy, but the total destruction of what he saw as an oppressive social system. The system that Fidel Castro established in Cuba and which unfortunately so many Cubans were so eager to embrace, began with an idea and ended in the system of concentration camps. It was the "total state." The term, from which the adjective "totalitarian" derives, was coined by Benito Mussolini.

Castro's idea of "total state" implied the concentration of power in the state and the concentration of state power in his own hands, at the expense of individual liberty. In principle, Castro's revolution does not represent a new approach to government; it is the continuation of the political absolutism which has characterized most of human history, evidenced by absolute monarchies, oligarchies, theocracies, dictatorships and tyrannies. But, although some Latin American dictators often preached the unlimited power of the state, most of them proved to be unable or unwilling to enforce that power. As a rule, citizens of such countries, including Cuba under Batista, enjoyed a kind of partial "freedom" which, if not a freedom-on-principle, was at least freedom-by-default.

Castroism, however, is a different, virulent form of statism only present in totalitarian regimes. Even the freedom-by-default is absent in Castro's Cuba. His regime has shown many characteristics typical of fascist regimes, among them, an extraordinary efficiency in dominating its subjects, the all-encompassing character of its coercion, a complete mass regimentation on a scale involving millions of people, and the systematic slaughter of the citizens by its own government, all of which are without parallel in the recent history of Latin America, including the worst crimes committed in Argentina, Chile or El Salvador. The fact that the Castro-friendly mainstream American media does not report most of Castro's crimes does not mean that these crimes are not happening.

Castroism shares with other totalitarian regimes the idea of the infinite pliability of human beings, which explains its emphasis on education as a long-range arm of propaganda. Also, the constant rejection of the present for the sake of grandiose schemes of social reconstruction and human remodeling, like the New Man, the Island of Youth, etc., provided the basis for the expansion of Castro's totalitarian power to all segments of Cuban society.

It was Castro's determination to achieve total change that brought political terror in Cuba. Change, even for the better, always entails opposition. In a free society, total, drastic change cannot occur, because it brings forward massive resistance by a variety of groups and interests. In Castro's totalitarian society opposition was prevented from developing and growing by the imposition of total terror which eventually engulfed every Cuban citizen.

Fascists see opponents as enemies they have to eliminate. This explains the apparition of concentration camps in all Fascist societies. Concentration camps are not a distortion of the Fascist regime, but they are at its very core. Fascist regimes cannot exist without a system of concentration camps to "re-educate" and annihilate opponents. In the concentration and slave labor camps the Fascist regimes seek to destroy the legal and moral person in human beings and to deprive them of the last residue of individuality. Since Castro took power in Cuba in 1959 a pervasive system of prisons and concentration camps has mushroomed all across the Island.[182]

Data released by the Cuban American National Foundation shows that Castro's Cuba currently has a penal population totalling no less than 289,000 men, women and children in 241 prisons and concentration camps distributed throughout the Island. In the last 37 years, 54,000 people have died for political reasons in Cuba—among them 12,486 executed by firing squads. In 1986 39,200 women were rotting in 27 prisons and 56,500 minors had been confined in 73 prisons. Some analysts believe that today those numbers are higher.

Amnesty International believes that there are some 600 confirmed political prisoners of conscience in Cuba, but other groups estimate that the number is probably close to 3,000. Among them are those who have received sentences for political offenses and those who are in jail serving time for non-political offenses but whose sentences were politically motivated. These prisoners, according to Amnesty International, have been jailed solely for having peacefully exercised their right to freedom of expression, association and assembly, or for trying to leave the country.

According to representatives of the Cuban Council, an organization that monitors human rights abuses in Cuba, the Island presently has one of the largest prison populations in the world, for a country of 11 million inhabitants. The estimates of the Council match closely those given by the Cuban American National Foundation regarding prisoners of all types. In a document distributed through the Web, Rodolfo González, of the Cuban Council Support Group, stated that "Spain, to cite an example, has in its jails about 40,000 inmates and is considered the country with the largest prison population among European countries. However, Spain has 40 million inhabitants. Cuba, with only 11 million inhabitants, has in its jails more than 275,000 inmates, almost equal to the prison population of the whole of Europe."[183] When looking at the high number of inmates in Castro's prisons one most keep in mind that, as soon as he took power in Cuba, Castro implemented the capital sentence, which is applied liberally and fast. Generally the death sentence is executed in less than 24 hours. The use of the death sentence is an effective way of reducing the number of people incarcerated.

Amnesty International, the U.N. Human Rights Commission, the OAS, and numerous organizations have received innumerable reports about systematic use of torture in Castro's jails. Normally torture is not carried out using electric shocks but with other techniques learned from the KGB. When a person is detained, it is quite common to deprive him of sleep. Another torture consists of confining the prisoner to a cell with the floor covered with a few centimeters of water whilst a strong draught of cold air keeps the prisoner frozen. The single light bulb in the cell is turned on and off arbitrarily, so as to distort the prisoner's sense of time. The idea is to force him to sign a confession without marking his body.

The main detention center where torture is carried out is known as Villa Marista, in Havana, and the "technical" director of this specialty is Colonel Blanco Oropesa, but there are similar centers in other provinces. Once sentenced and imprisoned, the blows are frequent. When they are punished, it is not unusual to place the prisoners in coffin-like cells called *"gavetas,"* (drawers) in which they cannot move. They are kept like that for weeks at a time. Predictably, the food is inadequate, to the extent that diseases like beriberi, pellagra, scurvy, and tuberculosis, occur frequently and are common causes of death among inmates.[184]

Another characteristic Castroism shares with fascist regimes is its violent passion for unanimity. Since Castro is convinced that history has shown that he is right, he expects others to agree with him, thereby vindicating the correctness of his historical insight. This passion for unanimity makes Castro insist on the complete agreement of the entire population under his control with any measure the regime imposes on them. This agreement, which in Cuba has found expression in periodical coerced elections and plebiscites, must not be passive. On the contrary, Castro expects an enthusiastic political behavior from the captive Cuban people. Cubans must always show to the world that they are in the grip of passion, the passion of self-assertion and self-realization. When that enthusiasm and passion fails to materialize, the Maximum Leader gets very upset.

Two cardinal characteristics of the fascist mentality are the direct result of its rejection of reason and intellect and their replacement by the will and spirit. The first is the lack of importance of theory, and the second is the idea that politics and society are just a stage for permanent revolution and war.[185] It is not theory what mobilizes fascists, but the will of the leader.[186] Despite Castro's early unsuccessful attempts at disguising his nationalism under a cover of Marxist theory (which he totally ignores), his main tool for mobilizing the masses has always been his personal will.

The similarities between Fascist and Communist regimes have been documented elsewhere, but contrary to Communist movements, which draw their supporters mostly from the working classes, fascist movements, like Castro's revolution, draw their followers disproportionally from the middle classes. In Communist regimes, the emphasis is on the concept of class; in fascist regimes, like Castro's Cuba, the emphasis is on the nation and the state.

Contrary to Marxists leaders, who try to identify with the proletariat and whose alleged goal is the emancipation of the workers from bourgeois exploitation, Castro's alleged main goal has been the emancipation of the cuban *people* from the bourgeois nations, mainly the U.S. A short time after his seizure of power in Cuba he coined the slogan "El pueblo unido jamás será vencido," ("The people united will never be defeated"). Like Castroism, fascist "socialism" is socialism for the people, and not just for the proletariat.[187] By cleverly dissolving class into nation, Castro transformed the agent of the revolution from the proletariat to the nation. That way, the Cuban proletariat was removed from its position as the subject of history and supplanted with the nation.[188]

When Castro took power in Cuba in 1959 the Island had one of the strongest working classes of Latin America organized into powerful unions, some of them controlled by the Communists, who used them to foment class division. One of the first things that Castro did, to the utmost surprise of most of his non-Communist followers, and to the surprise of the Communists as well, was to unify all unions into a single one, and give its control to the Communists. The old style Communists' victory, however, proved to be a phyrric one. Instead of an organization fighting for the rights of the Cuban workers, the new unified union was an organization of the totality of the Cuban people, without class distinctions. A few months later the new unified workers' union became just another tool in Castro's hands, without any effective power to fight neither for the rights of the Cuban workers nor for the rights of the Cuban people as a whole.

Marxists see society divided into classes engaged in internal struggle, but Castroism sees it as the struggle of a state, a people, and a nation against other states, other people, and other nations. But, as it happened in other fascist states, the goal of Castroism, as it has become evident in Cuba, was never the emancipation of the Cuban working class (strong, by all standards, when Castro seized power in Cuba in 1959) but the taming of the masses.[189] Actually, Castroism has tamed the Cuban working class, depriving it of all its rights and privileges conquered after long years of struggle. As such, it has revealed itself as a tool in the service of the worst type of capitalism. No wonder Cuba has lately become a haven for unscrupulous capitalists who enthusiastically have joined Castro in the exploitation of the Cuban workers.[190]

While communism is strictly an atheistic ideology, fascism shares with Castroism its vaguely deistic inclination. Hitler and Mussolini looked for an accommodation with organized religion on condition that the Church accepted their fascist states as its political overlord and supported them.[191] Castro would not have any objections to an accommodation with the Catholic Church, providing that the Church accept him as the maximum leader and support him. The knowledge of this fact is one of the reasons why the top leaders of the Catholic Church have always seen Castro as a Fascist rather than a Communist.

The main reason for the clashes between Castro and the Catholic Church is because Castroism is itself a secular religion with a sense of messianic mission, and could not tolerate the activities of a rival religion. The ultimate goal of Castroism is to dominate all aspects of the Cubans' life. It therefore resents any time they devote to non-Castroist religious activities.

Both communist and fascist regimes rely heavily on propaganda to provide legitimacy to power. But propaganda in communist societies relies more on ideological indoctrination than emotional issues. Castroism shares with fascist regimes its use of symbols and rites and its appeal to emotion rather than ideology.

There is still another basic difference between the two systems that must be pointed out. Contrary to Communists, fascist leaders of all shades, including Fidel Castro, glorify war.[192] One of the main characteristics the Castro revolution shares with fascist totalitarian regimes is its immanent violence, which turns inward as well as outward and manifests itself in a constant state of preparation for war.

The Fascist view of war contrasts sharply with the Communist view. For the Communist, war is primarily the struggle of classes rather than of nations. But this class-war, which culminates in revolution, is not a goal in itself. Indeed, although communism rejects the possibility of peace between communism and capitalism, it envisions a peaceful Communist world order. The Communist readiness to prepare for war is explained because they view Capitalist man as a class-bound being, motivated only by economic interest. But this bellicosity will disappear, they claim, when the world revolution is consummated after capitalism is abolished from the face of the earth. Therefore, war is a necessary means to the end the Communist strives for, but, at least in theory, it is not an end in itself.

Fascists, however, have a different view of war. The glorification of war and the warrior, and the worship of military technique and the aims of destruction for the sake of it, stands at the center of the Fascist view of man. This glorification is a direct result of the ideological importance of the collective commanding a total dedication of the individual. As Mussolini expressed it,

> Fascism ... believes neither in the possibility nor the utility of perpetual peace ... War alone brings up to its highest tension all human energy and puts the stamp of nobility upon the peoples who have the courage to meet it. All other trials are substitutes, which never really put men into the position where they have to make the great decision—the alternative of life and death.[193]

Ché Guevara's letter to the Tricontinental Conference in Havana in 1966, asking for the creation of "Two, three ... many Vietnams," is a message of hatred and war only found in Fascist, not Communist, literature. As Guevara crudely put it, ". . . hatred is an element of the struggle, a relentless hatred of the enemy impelling us over and beyond the natural limitations that man is heir to and transforming him into an effective, violent, selective and cold killing machine."[194] Ché's description of the perfect guerrilla fighter is a very accurate description of Himmler's SS troops.

Castro created in Cuba the second largest armed forces in the Americas, second only to that of the United States. Since he came to power in 1959, the whole Cuban society and economy has been in a constant state of preparation for war. The preparation for military service begins early in the life of the Cuban citizen, and extends to old age. The degree of militarization of the Cuban society is unknown in the rest of Latin America, even under the toughest authoritarian dictatorships. Not even the Soviet Union, except during war periods, has ever been close to the total degree of militarization found in Cuba. That degree of total militarization is found only in fascist regimes, and had its maximum expression in Nazi Germany.

The glorification of war as an end in itself and the total contempt for international law and order has characterized the Castro regime since its very beginning. This glorification of war in Castro's Cuba is just the continuation of Castro's own life of constant military adventures, terrorist actions, and violence.

Nothing evidences more the fascist ideology of Castroism than Castro's activities in foreign affairs. Just a few weeks before he took power in Cuba, Castro launched military incursions against Santo Domingo, Panama, Venezuela and other countries. Since then, he has had an active role in subversive activities in Latin America, Africa, North America and Europe.

It was not a coincidence that Ché Guevara, who in his younger days had been a follower and admirer of Juan Domingo Perón, was the one who developed the fascist scheme he called the *foco* theory of revolution—later popularized by Regis Debray in his tract *Revolución en la revolución*.[195] According to this revolutionary theory small bands of armed élite men should launch guerilla attacks in the countryside, acting as the "detonator" to the masses to spontaneously rise up to overthrow the old regime, and put the "heroic guerilla" in power.

Professor Irving Louis Horowitz rightly pointed out that, at an ideological level, the *foco* theory of the revolution "represents the transformation of guerrillas into *gorilas*, into advocates of the total militarization of Latin America. This seems to incorporate Rightist doctrine into a Leftist framework."[196] The fact was also noticed by professor A. James Gregor. In a book he wrote about fascism, he observed that, "The relationship between what Debray calls 'revolutionary nationalism or Fidelism' and fascism is far more intimate than contemporary radicals are prepared to admit." And added, "The political commitments with which Castro came to power were all but indistinguishable in style and content from the original programmatic commitments of Mussolini in 1922."[197]

Guevara's *foco* theory, which was to a great extent the theoretical expression of Castro's ideas, claimed that the building of the new society depends on "enlightened" rulers with the interests of the masses at heart.[198] The Castroist élite, who view themselves as among the most enlightened "saviors" of the masses of all time, believed they could impose their wishes on society. The Castroist line was never accepted by most Communist parties in Latin America. But it had great appeal among many revolutionary-minded people, particularly the American leftist petty-bourgeoisie and intelligentsia, which shares Castro's deep hatred and contempt for the lower classes and whose most cherished dream is an American-dominated techno-fascist world.

Actually, the Castro-Guevara "foco" theory was nothing but a thinly disguised fascist scheme that goes contrary to the Communist theory of revolution, which is based on the conscious and organized struggle of the masses under the guidance of a Communist party—under Moscow's control. That was the reason why the Soviet Communists and their Latin American clients always viewed Ché Guevara's actions with extreme suspicion. It also explains why the Bolivian Communist party didn't help Guevara, and was instrumental in his demise.

Fidel Castro shares with most fascist leaders a strong love for action per se, as well as a total dislike for intellectuals. In a talk he gave in the early sixties during a meeting with some Cuban writers and artists, he insisted on his ignorance of the things that preoccupied his audience—problems of form and the intellectual's attitude towards the revolution—and maintained that he had come to the discussion as a ruler and as a revolutionary, and not as an intellectual.[199] And it seems that Castro is proud of it. "I am not an intellectual," he told Jacques Arnault, "I am a man of revolutionary action."[200]

The code of behavior of fascist regimes stresses violence and lies in all aspects of human relations, within the fascist nation and between nations. Contrary to the democratic point of view, in which politics is seen as the mechanism through which social conflicts of interest are peacefully adjusted through compromise, the fascist view is that politics is a friend-enemy relation. In the democratic way of thinking, the antithesis to the friend is the opponent, who is potentially tomorrow's government. In the fascist view there are no opponents, only enemies. Because the fascist sees all opponents as enemies, and enemies represent evil incarnate, the only solution is total annihilation. A recent example of this way of thinking is Castro's treatment of previously friendly countries who voted in Geneva condemning his human rights' violations. Even countries like Mexico, who abstained from voting, didn't escape the ire of the Cuban Fascist tyrant.

It was very easy for Castro to fool the amateur anti-Communist[201] exiles in Florida, because they were ripe for disinformation. But, notwithstanding his repeated claims of Marxist ideology, Castro never fooled the three main world experts on communism: the Communists themselves, the CIA, and the Catholic Church. None of them, perhaps for different reasons, ever saw Castro as a Marxist or a Communist.[202]

Most people find it difficult to accept the fact that a leader whose methods, symbolism and ideology resembles fascism could not be a rightist. However, though most people believe that fascism is, by definition, a political manifestation of the right, this is not totally true. The Nazis, for example, considered themselves Socialists, defenders of the German lower classes and enemies of capitalism.[203]

The close resemblance between Castroism and fascism may explain why Georgie Anne Geyer pointed out that Fidel Castro has created "the first fascist left regime in history."[204] The idea, however, was not new. As early as 1978, Hugh Thomas wrote:

> Fascist techniques were used so much during the early days of the Cuban revolution in 1959 and 1960 that, indeed, that useful term "fascist left" might have been coined to apply to it. Castro's cult of heroic leadership, of endless struggle, of exalted nationalism had characterized all fascist movements in Europe. The emotional oratory, the carefully staged mass meetings, the deliberate exacerbation of tension before the "leader" spoke, the banners, and the mob intimidation—all these Castroist techniques recalled the days of Nazism.[205]

In a previous book Thomas expressed the similarities between Castroism and fascism so clearly that it is useful to quote him in detail:

> It is tempting to compare the distinctive colouring which Castro has given to Cuban communism with fascism; there is Castro's evident belief, with Chibás but also with Mosley or Hitler, that political power lies in 'the response of a large audience to a stirring speech'. There is the willingness of large sections of the population, including intelligent and humane people, to surrender their individuality to Castro as men did

to Fascist leaders. There is the persistent elevation of the principle of violence and the appeals to martial reactions in the regime's propaganda; and there is the cult of leadership, the emphasis on physical fitness in the education system, and the continual denigration of bourgeois democracies. The very statements of Guevara's in *Socialism and Man* which defines the drives of Cuban socialism shares with fascism, as with expressionism, 'the urge to recapture the "whole man" who seems atomized and alienated by society', a man who could not find himself among the 'commonplaces of bourgeois democracy', as Guevara put it. The 'New Man,' held to be typified by Guevara, a hero, and man of action, will and character, would have been admired by French fascists such as Brasillach or Drieu or by D'Annunzio, of the wild demagogic epoch of the Republic of the Fiume, who himself has seemed to at least one commentator to have been Castro's intellectual precursor. Castro's moralizing and his desire to break with all material aims reflects fascism regenerationism; and his presentation of himself as the thoughtful and benevolent father resembles Mussolini. In fact, of course, the fascist revolutions of the 1930s cannot be understood (any more than Castro's can) if observed wholly negatively, or if it is forgotten that even the Nazi revolution 'satisfied a deeply felt need for activism combined with identification [with] . . . a classless society'. Fascism was a heresy of the international socialist movement and several fascist leaders had once been men of the Left: it is possible to imagine Castro moving in time (or, more probably, at a certain time) from extreme Left to what passes for extreme Right.[206]

But there is a well known ideologue of the Castroist revolution who perceived the true nature of Castroism much earlier than Geyer and Thomas. In January 1960, just a year after Castro's seizure of power in Cuba, Ché Guevara provided a concise definition of the ideology of the Castroist revolution: "Se podría esquematizar llamándole 'nacionalismo de la izquierda.'" ("As an oversimplification it may be called a 'left-wing nationalist' one.").[207] As a follower of Perón, Ché was never fooled by Fidel's Marxist claims.

However, probably the earliest mention of Castro's true ideology was made by his brother-in-law, Rafael Díaz-Balart. During a farsighted speech to the Cuban Congress on May, 1955, representative Díaz-Balart expressed his opposition to a law approving an amnesty for Fidel Castro and his followers imprisoned for their participation in the attack on the Moncada garrison:

They don't want peace. They don't want any type of national solution, nor democracy, neither elections nor fraternizing. Fidel Castro and his group only want a single thing: power, but total power which will allow them to destroy all traces of the Constitution and the law in Cuba to impose the most cruel, barbaric tyranny; a tyranny which will show the people the true meaning of what is a tyranny; an unscrupulous, criminal totalitarian regime which will be very difficult to overthrow at least in twenty years. Because *Fidel Castro is nothing but a Fascist psychopath*, who, once in power, and only because fascism was defeated during WWII, would pact with the forces of international communism. And communism would give Fidel the pseudo-ideological cover to assassinate, steal, and violate with impunity all rights, and such destroying all the spiritual, historic, moral and judicial legacy of our Republic.[208]

Of late, more and more people are arriving at a similar conclusion. José Fernández González, a Spanish businessman who lived in Cuba for more than fifteen years doing business with the Castro government, finally discovered that Castro's "socialism" is just fascism with another name, and exposed it in great detail in a book he wrote in 1996.[209] Also, Rogelio Saunders, a Cuban poet and writer living in Havana, wrote an interesting article in which, though apparently referring to fascism in general, actually gives an accurate description of the Castroist regime.[210]

Even some of Castro's own intelligence officers in charge of disinformation activities cannot avoid the same conclusion. Jesús Arboleya, a member of the Cuban intelligence services under cover as a professor of the University of Havana, pointed out that "The Cuban revolution is a project of social justice that found its viability in anti-imperialist nationalism."[211] And Arboleya's conclusion apparently was not a mistake, because a few pages below he mentions again "the nationalist and anti-imperialist orientation adopted by the revolution,..."[212] No mention of communism or Marxism is found in Arboleya's definition of Castro's revolution.

Although Mussolini's fascism and Franco's falange were definitively rightist regimes, the Nazi's position on the political spectrum is not totally clear, and some of their policies were to some extent leftist oriented. One must keep in mind that, before it seized power in the German state, the National Socialist German Workers Party was a left-wing, revolutionary movement which had sprouted out of the Bohemian gutters. Some authors see the popular fascist movements of Juan Domingo Perón in Argentina and Getulio Vargas in Brazil, as "A Fascism which is essentially progressive and almost a forerunner of Castroism, and which has gone further to the left than the respective *Caudillos* intended."²¹³ The idea that Castro created the first leftist fascist regime in the history of mankind is open to debate. What nobody can deny is that, if he actually did so, it was the first fascist regime disguised under cover of Marxism.²¹⁴

So much for Fidel Castro's Marxism and communism. In conclusion, it seems that, contrary to his unsupported Marxist claims, the Maximum Leader is but a Fascist of the Nazi type, and will remain so until the last day of his life.

Or maybe not.

What Really is Castroism?

People who have seen Castro merely as a nationalist, anti-American political leader have totally missed the true meaning of Castroism. Even though Fidel Castro has profited from organizational and political techniques copied from other political and religious organizations, like the communists and the fascists, among others, Castroism's emphasis in the creation of a new man with a new consciousness, indicates that, basically, Castroism is a religious cult.

As we have seen above, Castro's true ideology is an enigma that has confused not only most of the scholars who have attempted to decipher it but Castro's close associates and opponents as well. The fact that he has been so clever in hiding his true beliefs and ideological allegiances, planting false clues to disorient both enemies and friends, is one of the reasons why he has been so successful.

There is ample evidence pointing to the fact that, contrary to common belief, Fidel Castro never was, has never been, and will never be a Marxist, or a Communist. Moreover, it seems that he is not even a true Fascist. The relationship Fidel Castro has established with the Cuban people and with his associates is with his person, not with ideas or with any particular ideology,²¹⁵ so he could change his ideas without changing this relationship. As Herbert Matthews observed,

> Early in the revolution I suggested that Castro picked up movements and ideas as one would garments, putting them on, taking them off, throwing them away, placing them in the wardrobe—but that in all cases the wearer was the same Fidel Castro.²¹⁶

Furthermore, given the peculiar characteristics of his mindset, it is very difficult to believe that, during his whole life, Fidel Castro has been nothing else but a fanatic Castroist. The reason for the close resemblance between Castroism and Nazism is because Nazism was actually a cult, and some modern cults are secretly inspired on Nazism. On the other hand, if I were forced to pigeonhole Fidel Castro ideologically, which is not easy to do, I would say that he is a sort of renegade Jesuit[217] who attained power and is keeping it using fascist tactics.[218]

The Castroist Cult

The term *cult* comes from the Latin word *cultus*, which literally means to worship or show reverence to something. The most widely accepted definition of the term is that a cult is a group of people basing their belief upon the world view of a leader. As we have seen above, Castroism, like Nazism, strongly evidences most of the characteristics of a cult.

Scholars of cults classify them into Western, Eastern, and New Age cults. Cults appeal to the people's basic emotional need for love and for a meaningful direction in life. Individuals who experience an identity crisis or have emotional problems are particularly susceptible to fall under the influence of a cult. Cults relieve people from the burden of having to make decisions in their lives. Most cults tell their followers what to believe, how to behave and what to think, and emphasize dependence upon the group leader for their emotional stability.

One of the main characteristics of cults is the existence of central leader figures who consider themselves messengers of God with unique access to the almighty. This strong leadership puts the cult follower in a position of total dependence upon the cult for belief, support, behavior and lifestyle. As a rule, the more dramatic the claims of the cult leader, the more possibility of a tragic conclusion.[219]

Like Adolf Hitler, Charles Manson, Jim Jones, Sun Myung Moon, David Koresh, and Daisaku Ikeda,[220] Fidel Castro created a personal cult with a fanatical group of followers. Granted, Castroism has never claimed to be a cult, and many of its followers are decent people who were deceived into believing that Castroism was a socio-political movement fighting morally and materially to improve the human condition. But very early into its evolution, Castroism turned from a political movement in search of social and political justice into a paranoid and abusive, all-embracing totalitarian cult[221] which deliberately activated the religious impulse in the Cuban people.

With the benefit of hindsight, it becomes evident that this cult element was central to the initial indoctrination process; it focused on "eternal truths" which adepts must never forget. Cardinal among them was the evil role of American "imperialism" in the modern world. These "eternal truths" were purveyed and reinforced trough the endless repetition of slogans (¡Patria o muerte! ¡Venceremos!), choruses (!Fidel, Fidel, ¿qué tiene Fidel?, que los americanos no pueden con él!), and symbols (gigantic photos of Ché-Guevara-as-saint in the background). This liturgical element has always been present in the mass meetings in which the setting played a vital part, focusing on the leader who will direct the masses' enthusiasm into the proper "eternal" channels.

Once in power, Fidel Castro developed a set of professed beliefs which—though he used different terms like humanism, socialism, and Marxism to label them—were quite similar to Jim Jones' "apostolic socialism" in its negation of the Christian God and its deification of social justice and worshipping of the redemptive powers of socialism. One could plausibly argue that ultimately Castroism is not based on social, economic, or political principles, but on religious or magical principles.

As it happens with most cults, at the center of the Castroist church is its spiritual leader and guru: Fidel Castro. The Maximum Leader is the absolute judge of what is good and bad in Cuba. He determines to the smallest detail how his followers may live and assesses the depth and sincerity of their faith. Because he is totally convinced that he is divinely inspired, he is not open to questions nor will he participate in any reasonable debate. Anyone who makes the mistake of challenging his divine leadership is immediately declared guilty of lacking the essential faith necessary to be a true member of his cult. The ones he considers are not true believers or have lost their faith are rapidly eliminated.

Castroism not only evidences certain characteristics typical of most cults, but the effects it has had upon its followers are also similar to the ones caused by cults. In the Castroist cult debate is discouraged and unquestioning obedience praised, and followers have learnt to suppress their critical thinking. True Castroists do not weigh, evaluate, or question the accuracy of the information they receive from Castro himself or through the different Castro-controlled media. The true believers accept it, even if most of it makes little or no sense at all.

In exchange for this, the members of the Castroist cult become members of the spiritual élite. They are special. They are the chosen ones. They are more advanced than normal people, and have a higher awareness of the social problems affecting the world. They have reached a higher level of *conciencia revolucionaria* (revolutionary consciousness).

Castro, the all-powerful, infallible cult leader, demands and gets from his followers a blind obedience which he uses as he sees fit.

His followers must obey him, and would die for him, if he so decides.[222] Photos of the crowd attending the early mass meetings show faces stamped with a vacuous enthralled stupefaction, a mindless beatitude similar to the faces at a fundamentalist church meeting. Chanting the mantra *Fi-del!, Fi-del!, Fi-del!*, people intoxicated themselves into a state of rapture and ecstasy. What one witnessed at Castro's early mass meetings was, and still is to some extent after all these years, a phenomenon similar to the "alteration of consciousness" psychologists generally associate with a mystical experience.

The first signs of the emergence of the Castroist cult appeared early, while Castro was preparing his followers at the *granjita Siboney* in the outskirts of Santiago de Cuba, for the attack on the Moncada garrisons. A cult-like atmosphere was enforced upon the would be attackers. They were totally isolated from the outside world, kept under constant surveillance, brainwashed, and strict heterosexual abstinence was enforced. Not even Castro's closest associates knew about his true plans for the attack; they were kept in the dark until the very last moment as to what type of action they were supposed to perform. Georgie Anne Geyer observed that Castro's followers were "a collection of marginalized Cubans who, as if sleepwalking, obeyed unquestioningly everything Fidel commanded."[223]

The second manifestation appeared while Castro and his men were in Mexico preparing themselves for the *Granma* invasion. Again, strict heterosexual abstinence was enforced, and the participants were kept isolated. No drinking was allowed. Curfew was at midnight, every night. None of them had a clear idea about what Fidel's plans were, and the participants were subjected to constant brainwashing and indoctrination.[224]

The phenomenon repeated itself in the Sierra Maestra mountains, with the difference that isolation was not possible because of the requirements of fighting a guerrilla war. After the war was won, Castroism began functioning as a cult in power, now extending the brainwashing and isolation techniques to the whole Cuban population.[225] The New Man that Castro claimed to be creating in Cuba was not very different from the typical cult member: a life of total sacrifice for the leader and the future, and total devotion for the cause of destroying the evil enemy.

Like most cult leaders, Castro maintains a luxurious life-style while his followers suffer poverty as a sacrifice for their beliefs. Those who accept sacrifices and obediently follow Castro will be rewarded some day in a future that every day seems farther away. In most cults, members are expected to donate up to 80 percent of their income through thites, fees, and gifts. Similarly, the Castroist cult takes up to 95% of the income of the Cuban citizens.

Fidel Castro maintains his power by acting like the worst kind of tyrannical father—the Angel Castro of all Cubans. Members of the Castroist cult desperately want his approval even if they are terribly afraid of him. He throws a temper tantrum and yells at a cult member who has done something he does not like, accusing him of undermining his authority. This is conceived to throw his followers off-balance and keep them under control. Accordingly, much of his fury is reserved for those who challenge him. But, as anyone who shows any sign of independence is beaten down, the ones who manage to always agree with him are fine.

Closely following the characteristics of all major cults, Castroism believes in the coming battle between the forces of evil, personified by the U.S., and the forces of good, personified by Castro himself and his true believers. Since the very first day he seized power in Cuba in 1959 he has been preparing himself and his chosen people for this final Armageddon.

Fidel's True Ideology

Henry Kissinger once pointed out the fact that leaders who have run the risks of revolutionary struggle are not likely to favor a system of government which makes them dispensable. Indeed the attraction of communism for many leaders is not Marxism-Leninism itself but the legitimacy for authoritarian rule which it provides.[226] If Castro had openly adopted fascism as his ideology, liberal shock and outrage would have been immediate. The memories of Nazi horrors would have been more than enough to provoke a strong negative reaction. But his adoption of Communist symbolism not only failed to horrify liberals; it actually attracted their support. To most liberals the symbols of communism, even after more than sixty years of terror, mass murder, totalitarianism and aggression,[227] still mean good intentions. It is true, they claim, that Communist regimes have made some "mistakes", but it is not because they are intrinsically evil—as Nazism was—but because the encircling and aggression from the West turned them into over-defensive regimes.

As Marc Thiessen pointed out in a review of *The Black Book of Communism*,

> The same week that Pinochet was arrested in London, Cuban dictator Fidel Castro was in Portugal clicking glasses with heads of state at the InterAmerican summit. His crimes, too, are well documented in the *Black Book*: "From 1959 through the late 1990, more than 100,000 Cubans experienced life in

one of [Castro's] camps [or] prisons ... [and b]etween 15,000 and 17,000 people were shot." Yet Pinochet (who relinquished power and left Chile a prosperous, thriving, free-market democracy) is held prisoner, while Castro is free, feted by world leaders.[228]

Castro's major motivation in life, since adolescence, has been his drive for absolute personal power. His biographer Carlos Franqui rightly pointed out that power is Fidel's orgasm. Granted, many politicians love power—President John F. Kennedy once remarked that he wanted to be President "because that's where the real power is." But in the case of Fidel Castro, his lust for power knows no limits; everything is subordinate to it.

Castro controls power undreamed of by most of the greatest conquerors and rulers of the past. And like them, the more power he gets, the more he wants. He seems totally absorbed by the pursuit and exercise of power. If politics is the business of the world, for Castro power is its reward. Yet he has paid a price. Insightful observers have noticed that the Maximum Leader's emotions seem to have been self-anesthetized.

It is very difficult for Fidel Castro to delegate any power. He is possessed by such a love for total power that he cannot share it even with his most loyal subordinates—not even with his brother Raúl. One has to get at him directly if something has to be done in Cuba. As he rarely settles down anywhere for any length of time, his ministers and head of departments always have trouble getting in touch with him. The result is often frustration and chaos.

Fidel cannot accept any sharing of authority, any subjection of his will to any individual or body of people. This drive for power is the only constant element in his makeup, though sometimes he has tried to hide it behind some revolutionary philosophy like communism or Marxism. Castro believes in nothing but power and action, not as the means to reach an objective, but as goals in life.

Everything in Cuba centers around Fidel Castro. He is responsible for the course of events in Cuba to an incredible degree, which sometimes has included not only national and foreign policy, but also the color schools and public buildings are painted, and the length of men's hair and women's skirts. Even more, Castro's aim is to control not only the bodies of all Cubans, but also their minds.

Fidel Castro is subordinate to no legal or institutional structure. He holds his job at his own pleasure. He uses his absolute power over other people's lives as a tool to strike terror into everyone around him, and make them feel insecure. They know that Castro will do anything, including killing his own people, to cling to power. As I have shown above, he has gotten rid of many of his most loyal supporters on grounds that they had gained a degree of influence and public recognition that he perceived as a threat to him personally. He knows that terror is his best weapon, and he uses it without remorse. In fact, the concept of remorse is completely alien to him—he does not seem to understand the meaning of the word.

The longest survivors in the Castroist hierarchy have been those who, like Chomy Miyar and Pepín Naranjo, have proved completely servile, remained faceless and, strange as it may seem, shown a degree of incompetence. As the case of the once highly successful de la Guardia twins shows, Castro sees initiative and competence in others as a potential threat. As well as being a vicious, ruthless psychopath, Castro is paranoid. He sees plots and conspiracies wherever he looks. As writer and former Castroist insider Norberto Fuentes puts it, Fidel *"está persuadido de que todo el mundo quiere 'echárselo',"* ("is convinced that everybody wants to kill him .")[229] Yet, one must keep in mind that even paranoids have enemies.

Though Fidel Castro has used Nazism rather than communism as the blueprint for the system he has created in Cuba, that does not mean he is a typical Fascist. Being a Fascist, like being a Communist or an Anarchist, implies commitment and enthusiasm for an idea outside the limits of personal advancement, material gain or power control. It implies zeal on behalf of a cause, dedication to an idea, likes and dislikes expressed with ideological fervor. But, disregarding what he *says*, Castro has shown his total impermeability to ideological concerns as well as his contempt for people excessively moved by ideas—like Ché Guevara, for example. On the other hand, Castro's personal secretary Celia Sánchez, a woman known for her anti-communist feelings but blindly loyal to Castro, never had any problems and for many years was the second most powerful person in Cuba.

Granted, Castroism as a movement is the product of doctrinaire ideas, and doctrinaire elements play an important part in it, but the most important constituent of Castroism is the connection between what is considered as Castroist doctrine and the two elements that characterize it, namely, the irrationality of the passions it arouses on the one side, and Castro's leading personality on the other. Therefore, a sharp distinction must be made between this genuinely irrational revolutionary passion, which affects not only the masses but the low echelon leaders as well, and the very deliberate, utterly cold and calculating pursuit of power and dominance by Castro. In Castro's Cuba, the doctrine is just an instrument for the control of the masses and nothing else. The leader and the revolutionary élite stand above the doctrine, which is meant for the masses, and Castro makes use of it as a way to accomplish his purposes of personal, total control.

Senior Castroist leaders know that the overt doctrine of Castroism has only symbolic value, something used to stir the masses' imagination, to divert their minds from other things, to brainwash and discipline them. The Castroist doctrine is just a cover for realities which must not be "given away" to the masses. That explains why Castro is so upset about the idea of even a limited free press in Cuba. The allegiance and faith in the revolutionary program and official Castroist philosophy are for the masses. The Castroist gutter élite has no commitment to any philosophy or ethical standard. Its only obligation is its absolute loyalty to Castro, and he is perhaps the only one who knows what his true allegiance is. Only understanding this distinction between Castro, the élite, and the masses one can understand many inconsistencies that leave the outsider perplexed.

The inner strength of Castroism lies in its constant activity and in embarking on any adventure so long as it keeps things moving. Castroism is pure and simple action; dynamics *in vacuo*, revolution at a variable tempo, ready to be changed at any moment. Though it does not base its policy on a doctrine, it pursues it with the aid of a philosophy.

Originally, the Castroist cult developed out of the need to provide the masses with the necessary myth which would give them the required energy for action. The main consideration in the creation of Castroism was its power to influence the masses by suggestion, to instill in them the sense of duty and obedience. The great paradox of the Castroist *meme*[230] is that its lack of principle is one of the main sources of its effectiveness.[231]

Fidel Castro has shown an extraordinary ability for temporarily appropriating different ideologies as a cover for his true, secret allegiances and goals. After the demise of the Soviet Union and the total bankruptcy of Marxism, he is looking for a new cover, like a snake shedding its skin. It seems that the new ideological cover he is looking for is liberation theology.

This may not be difficult at all. Contrary to Jesuit claims, liberation theology is *not* Marxist-, much less Leninist-inspired. Liberation theology is actually a sort of Castroism in disguise, that is, neo-Nazism.[232] No wonder Fidel Castro has become the *de facto* Pope of the rebel faction[233] inside the Catholic Church, and Havana the new place of pilgrimage for liberation theologists.

Like the demagogues in the Catholic Church, Fidel has seized every opportunity for praising his concern for the poor. Farfetched as it may seem, perhaps Fidel Castro may develop a mutually rewarding symbiotic relationship with the Church. The Church allegedly has chosen to make the poor the very reason for its existence, and, as the Cuban example shows, Fidel Castro has been creating the poor, the raw material for the Church's work, by the millions.[234]

By appropriating for lip-service the ideas of genuine political and social élites, Fidel Castro has succeeded to this day in deceiving not only his enemies but his supporters as well, masking the true fact that Castroism brought to power in Cuba a primitive, vulgar gutter élite[235] under the cover of social and national legitimate goals. But the best kept secret of the Castroist élite is their lack of principle and doctrine. No allegiance to any sort of doctrine, but total allegiance to Fidel and the simple fact of having fought for their power, merited membership in the actual élite.
Though the naïve, idealistic element among the Rebel Army was quickly purged very soon after the revolutionary triumph in 1959, the subtle and far more effectual element, the Castroist gutter élite under the Maximum Leader's direct protection, has remained. This Castroist élite is the one which has kept alive the revolutionary spirit, in spite of all announcements of the end of the revolution. Castro cannot abandon this dynamic élite, because doing so would mean abandoning himself. And the question of how long can a state, a nation, a society, endure without disintegrating under a corrupt, inept governing gutter élite devoid of all ethic and principles has found an answer in Castro's Cuba: a very long time.[236]

The Man Behind the Symbol

Since the very beginning of his "anti-Yankee" revolution, Fidel Castro became the undisputed mentor and symbol of the American and Latin American Left—Communist parties not included. The American leftists and other fellow-travelers and America-haters, as well as their mirror images around the world, created an image of Fidel Castro as a nationalistic leader who had the guts to stand firm in the face of American imperialism.

Today, all of Castro's grandiose plans have failed catastrophically. After forty-two years of furious anti-Americanism, the Cuban peso is virtually worthless and the U.S. dollar is king in Cuba. Admiration for the American way of life, in previous times found almost exclusively among the middle classes, has become an obsession in all sectors of the Cuban population. After forty-two years of official Yankee hatred (Castro calls all Americans "Yankees"), independent journalists in Cuba have reported the growing presence of people wearing N.Y. Yankees baseball caps, bought for $30.00 on the black market—the equivalent of a month's salary for most Cubans.

But the American Left, faced with the unavoidable fact that they cannot talk any more about the marvels of free education and health, or the absence of discrimination, prostitution, gambling, government corruption and unemployment, in a Cuba where all Capitalist vices have returned with a vengeance, still holds onto the only remaining reason for their undiminished love for Castro: his radical anti-American posture. To them Fidel Castro is the very symbol of anti-Americanism. But the Fidel Castro they have created exists only in their imagination, a fact that Castro has always been aware of and has used on his own behalf. No wonder in Castro's inner circle his leftist supporters, particularly the American ones, are called *come mierdas* (literally "shit eaters").

The evidence indicates that Fidel Castro's claims of anti-Americanism have been highly exaggerated. As a matter of fact, and for different reasons that are difficult to understand, he always ends up, one way or another, playing the American card. You don't need to be a rocket scientist to realize that Fidel Castro is probably the best thing that ever happened to the American military-industrial-academic complex.[237]

The American military-industrial-academic complex craves for war, revolutions and low-intensity international conflicts, and Dr. Castro has been giving them precisely that medicine for many long profitable years. One can safely assume that, when Ché Guevara sent his famous message to the Tricontinental Conference in Havana, asking for the creation of "two, three, . . . many Vietnams," many presidents and CEOs of arms manufacturing American corporations and their friends in the Pentagon became extremely excited about their bright economic future.[238] If one stops listening to Castro's rhetoric and looks closely at his actions, the unavoidable conclusion is that he may well qualify for the dubious honor of being one of the most pro-American leaders of all times in Latin America; a strong benefactor of the interests of the American corporations he claims to hate.[239]

Yet, notwithstanding the extraordinary evidence on the contrary, the anti-Communist Cuban exiles in the U.S. still hold to the only remaining reason for their hatred of Castro: his alleged anti-Americanism and Communist affiliation. To them Fidel Castro is the very symbol of all the evils of communism. But, as in the case of the American Left, the Fidel Castro they have created exists only in their imagination. This perhaps explains why for more than forty years he has proved to be immune to the Cuban exiles' attempts to get rid of him.

It would be a sad paradox that, after the end of Castro's reign of error and terror, his virulent anti-Americanism may bring what Cuban patriot José Martí feared the most; that Cuba would become a colony of the United States.[240] I can only hope this will never happen, because it will be a bad thing not only for Cuba, but for the United States as well.

Epilogue

> *Whoever fights monsters should see to it that in the process he does not become a monster himself. When you look long into the abyss, the abyss also looks into you.*
>
> —Friedrich Nietzsche

In a letter to Bill Clinton dated March 13, 1996, writer Alice Walker, after telling the President how she loved Cuba and its people, including Fidel, asked Clinton to speak to Fidel Castro face to face. "[Fidel] is not the monster he has been portrayed," she claimed.[1] Well, I fully agree with Ms. Walker. Fidel Castro is not the monster he has been portrayed in the American *conservative* media; he is much worse.[2]

As I wrote above in the Introduction, I am very skeptical about historical objectivity. Historians, like scientists, politicians, journalists, intelligence analysts, postmodernists, and almost everybody else, consciously or unconsciously select the facts that back their preconceived ideas and biases and tend not to see the ones that refute them. But, contrary to other common liars, historians base their lies on the interpretation of facts they don't fabricate out of the blue. That is why they carefully select the facts supporting their preconceived ideas while ignore the ones that do not fit. This explains why it is not uncommon to find two totally opposing views of the same historical event written by two different "serious" scholars.[3]

But there are limits to the historian's ability to tinker with the facts: some conclusions, no matter how hard you try, are not compatible with the data, while others are.[4] Even the most biased historian will avoid conclusions that fail the test when subjected to critical analysis. Although historical truth may never be more than tentative, it still exists in the sense that certain conclusions fit the facts better than others. In the case of Fidel Castro, there is an overwhelming number of facts I have carefully selected to support the preconceived, biased arguments I have expressed in this book. Without disregarding my obvious biases, these facts cannot be ignored.

Who is Fidel Castro?

Castro regards himself as a great man. In some sense, and from a certain perspective, he is right. It would be foolish to think that anyone who has exerted such a strong influence in the course of world events is of ordinary stature. For most people, however, the expression "great man," has positive connotations, denoting some valuable human qualities one cannot find in the Cuban tyrant. In fact, there is no aspect of Cuba or the world that one can consider better off after having been touched by Fidel Castro's influence.

But greatness can be either positive or negative. Men like Stalin or Hitler undoubtedly towered above their fellows. Hence, Castro's greatness, which has been almost entirely negative, has to be measured in terms of the disastrous consequences of his policies and the magnitude of his crimes.

I believe, though, that in writing this book I am still falling short of the real dimension of Fidel Castro. Hitler's crimes were exposed very soon after the end of the war because he lost it, while it took more than thirty years after Stalin's death to have, thanks mainly to Solzhenitsyn and a few others, a first glimpse at his crimes. If most of Castro's crimes are still unknown, it is because he is still alive and in power, and because all his life he has been a master of deception and disinformation.[5]

When I mention his crimes I am not talking about crimes he has committed with his own hands. Like Hitler, Stalin, Mao, and others like them, Castro just gives the orders, while his henchmen commit the atrocities. On the other hand, Castro is perhaps one of the leaders of the modern, "civilized" world who has taken more lives with his own hands. This began in his early days at the Birán estate when he began shooting at farm animals for fun, and continued after he became a gangster-student at the University of Havana when he began killing human beings for fun and for profit. Castro's total lack of respect for the sanctity of human life continues to this day.[6]

Nevertheless, even in Cuba, some people refuse to see the truth behind Castro's mask. In this they are not different from the ones who today still deny that the Holocaust ever happened. They are not different from the ones who denied that Stalin killed millions of Soviet citizens by deliberately planned famine and by sending them to the gulags. They are not different from the ones who still deny that Mao killed millions of Chinese citizens, or that some Middle East and African dictators have had thousands of their own citizens shot. As A. M. Rosenthal has pointed out, atrocity in the 20th-century was not only slow to become internationally known, it was also quickly denied.

After Castro's death, some of the missing parts of the puzzle will appear and the world will be horrified.[7] I say *some* of the missing parts of the puzzle because I know that there are people in the United States who will try at all costs to keep some embarrassing information about Castro from surfacing and will do everything to hide or destroy the evidence.[8] It happened in Nazi Germany after Hitler's defeat, and it will happen again in Cuba.

But, notwithstanding the attempts to destroy the evidence, some of the horrifying facts will be known, and they will reveal a system as revolting as its worst critics have been charging for many long years. Then, there will be no more excuses for loving Fidel.

It is not merely Castro's genius for murder and destruction which makes him equal to any evil figure in history. What marks Castro as particularly evil is his extraordinary ability to corrupt anybody who does not actively oppose him.[9] Both Miguel Angel Quevedo, editor of the magazine *Bohemia* and an early Castro supporter, and Haydée Santamaría, one of Fidel's closest collaborators since the Moncada days, discovered Castro's evil too late, and committed suicide rather than continue living with their moral shame.

At any rate, Castro himself denies those crimes, and he is very convincing. After Fidel talked to him for the first time, author K. S. Karol's impression was, "he is so charming! When he looks you in the eye and speaks in such a low voice with obvious sincerity and conviction, as if his words were meant for you alone, you realize that he cannot tell a lie."[10] But, very soon after, Karol, like many others, was to discover the hard way that Fidel *can* tell a lie.

What is He?

In his famous meditation on American literature, D. H. Lawrence discussed the duality of the human mind. While the upper consciousness tells *Love and produce! Love and produce!*, the devilish under-consciousness hums *Destroy! destroy! destroy!*[11] In the case of Fidel Castro, the strong hum of the under-consciousness has totally silenced the voice of the upper consciousness. After forty years of total power in Cuba as national Prophet and Messiah, what has Castro achieved? He has achieved unprecedented personal wealth and power. What has he done with this wealth and power? He has destroyed.

Despite the possibility that Castro had been initially motivated by good intentions, a very questionable possibility indeed, one cannot judge politicians, particularly the ones who have achieved power, by their intentions alone. The unavoidable fact is that by the late eighties it became obvious that, despite all his millions, his power, and his will, Fidel Castro had not succeeded in anything positive he claimed he tried to accomplish. He is a King Midas with crossed cables.[12] As a Cuban told an American writer visiting the Island, "Cuba has all the ingredients of paradise, but Fidel doesn't know how to cook."[13]

As early as 1964, even Castro-friendly author Herbert Matthews had to admit, "Castro is by no means a model to be blindly admired or copied; he is not a good person by normal moral standards. If he has done some good, he has done much harm."[14] Matthews had no idea at the time how much harm Fidel Castro was going to do during his long life.

The Monster Next Door

My answer to Theodore Draper's questions, "Who is Fidel Castro? What is he?,"[15] is very simple. Fidel Castro is a monster, and he is evil.[16]

When I affirm that Castro is evil I don't have in mind St. Agustine's idea of evil as *privatio boni*, or deprivation of the good, but evil as the *opposite* of good. Malevolence, a characteristic of evil persons, is evidenced when one's actions cause others to suffer unnecessary, avoidable suffering.[17] Consequently, if malevolence "is the *deliberate* infliction of cruel, painful suffering on another living being,"[18] the available record indicates that Fidel Castro is a malevolent, evil person.[19]

Fidel Castro himself seems to agree that at least some of his crimes were not necessary. In a book proposal for *History Will Absolve Me: The Autobiography of Fidel Castro*, which circulated in the 1997 Frankfurt Book Fair, Castro candidly confessed that "In our youthful exuberance and sense of righteousness, of knowing that our end was a noble one—we were unjust, we took measures not because they helped the cause of the Revolution, but because they satisfied a human impulse to punish."[20]

I stated in the Preface that this was a book about Fidel Castro. This, however, is true only to some extent. After reading this book I think that most readers would agree with me that, though it uses Castro as an example, this book is actually about human evil.

Psychiatrist M. Scott Peck points out to lying as the main characteristic of evil people; this is why he named his book about evil *People of the Lie*. Peck defines evil as the use of political power—that is, the imposition of one's will upon others by overt or covert coercion—to destroy others in order to preserve the integrity of one's own sick self and avoid spiritual growth.[21] He also sees evil as a kind of immaturity, as the inability of the child to grow out of narcissism.[22] Peck's definition of evil describes extremely well Castro's personality and behavior.

As I have shown above, Fidel Castro's life has always been bound up with prophesies, some of them strangely accurate. Probably the best known is the one made by Father Antonio Llorente, Castro's teacher and spiritual adviser at the Colegio de Belén. "Fidel Castro is a man of destiny," prophesied Llorente. "Behind him is the hand of God. He has a mission to fulfill and he will fulfill it against all obstacles."[23] In this particular case, however, it seems that Father Llorente was slightly confused about whose hand was behind Fidel Castro.

The May 3, 1999, issue of *Time* magazine included an extensive special report on the Littleton, Colorado school massacre. The title of the report was "The Monsters Next Door." After reading the report, however, one has to conclude that, though the title was appropriate, there is still a question lingering in the back of one's mind: Why?

Some scientists have tried to answer that question. Motivated by the increase of violence in American public schools, the National School Safety Center, a nonprofit organization funded by the Department of Education and Justice, created a test with questions about warning signs that could indicate the potential for violence by young people.[24] The questions are based on statistics of school-associated violent deaths in the United States from July 1992 to the present. The questions must be answered *yes* or *no*.

Using the NSSC data as a guide, *MSNBC* created an on-line interactive quiz available on the Internet.[25] Based on known, documented facts about Castro's early life, I retroactively applied the on-line test to Fidel Castro, entering information about him from the time he was a student at the grade school in Birán, at Catholic schools in Santiago de Cuba, and at the Jesuit Colegio de Belén high school in Havana. I also included information of his life as a Law student at the University of Havana. Below are the questions of the Warning Signs quiz and the answers I have provided to it. The results of the hypothetical test are both revealing and disturbing:

Q1. The student has a history of tantrums and uncontrollable angry outbursts.
A **Yes**. Fidel's tantrums and uncontrollable an-

gry outbursts began when he was a small child at the Birán estate and have continued throughout most of his adult life.[26]

Q2. He has threatened or attempted suicide.
A No. There is no evidence that Castro has ever threatened or attempted suicide. However, his fixation with death, and his eminently necrophilic discourse, may be interpreted as veiled suicide threats.

Q3. He characteristically resorts to name calling, cursing or abusive language.
A Yes. Castro's use of abusive language, cursing and name calling during his infancy and most of his adult life has been extensively documented.

Q4. The student habitually makes violent threats when angry.
A Yes. Some of his classmates at Belén reported his violent threats to other classmates.[27] This behavior continued when he was a student at the University of Havana. Though he became more cautious after he took power in 1959, his threats against foreign leaders, President Kennedy among them, have been amply documented.

Q5. The student has previously brought a weapon to school.
A Yes. He began bringing guns to school as soon as he began attending the Belén high school.[28] He continued doing so as a student at the University of Havana.[29]

Q6. The student has a background of serious disciplinary problems at school and in the community.
A Yes. Fidel had serious disciplinary problems at the first school he attended at Birán. He shamelessly told his biographer Carlos Franqui how he verbally, and sometimes physically harassed his teacher,[30] and how he

sneaked into the school during a weekend and vandalized it.[31] His disciplinary problems continued when he was attending Catholic schools in Santiago de Cuba. According to his own words, while attending the Colegio Dolores, he physically attacked one of his teachers, a LaSallian brother.[32]

Q7. The student has a background of drug, alcohol or other substance abuse.
A **No**. None of this has been documented.

Q8. He is on the fringe of his peer group with few or no close friends.
A **Yes**. At the schools he attended in Birán and Santiago he was a solitary student. Later, when he began attending Belén, he created a small gang to harass other students, though he had few close friends.

Q9. The student is preoccupied with weapons, explosives or other incendiary devices.
A **Yes**. It has been documented that, while he was a boy at Birán, Fidel threatened his parents with burning down the house.[33] It was at Birán where his life-long preoccupation with guns and explosive devices began.

Q10. He has previously been truant, suspended, or expelled from school.
A **Yes**. Fidel was a truant while attending school at Birán, and though he was never expelled, he was suspended several times because of his unruly behavior.[34] He maintained this type of behavior at the schools he attended in Santiago de Cuba and later at the Belén School in Havana.

Q11. He displays cruelty to animals.
A **Yes**. Fidel's cruelty to animals began at an early age. He used to shoot at his mother's chickens at the Birán estate. As an adolescent, there are numerous anecdotes telling about his cruelty to animals.[35]

Q12.	The student has little or no supervision and support from parents or a caring adult.
A	**Yes**. He grew up mostly by himself, with little supervision or support from his parents. The animosity between him and his father is well known. At an early age he was sent to live with some family friends in Santiago. Castro himself has told some of his biographers how he suffered because of the mistreatment he received from these people.
Q13.	He has witnessed or been a victim of abuse or neglect in the home.
A	**Yes**. Though it has not been documented that he was the victim of abuse, it is known that he was neglected by his parents.[36]
Q14.	The student has been bullied and/or bullies or intimidates peer or younger children.
A	**Yes**. He was the school bully at the schools he attended in Birán, Santiago and Havana. As soon as he began attending Belén, he created a gang to harass other students. At the University of Havana he joined some gangs and harassed and physically attacked other students and some university staff and professors as well. There is circumstantial evidence proving that he personally killed or participated in the killing of several university students and employees.
Q15.	He tends to blame others for difficulties or problems he causes himself.
A	**Yes**. He habitually blames others for his difficulties and problems, and never recognizes his own mistakes. This behavior has continued during his adult life.
Q16.	The student consistently prefers tv shows, movies or music expressing violent themes and acts.
A	**Yes**. Castro was born before tv and before Hollywood created such jewels as *Natural*

Born Killers and *Pulp Fiction*. He was also born way before children were exposed to the violence of video games. It seems, however, that he created in his mind his own version of violent video games. According to his own recollection, he used to invent violent action games and, using little scraps and tiny balls of paper arranged on a playing board, create military battles, in which there was destruction, mayhem, and blood. Like most video game fans, he became addicted to his war games. "I played this game of war for hours at a time," he told his biographer Franqui.[37]

Q17. He prefers reading materials dealing with violent themes, rituals and abuse.
A No. There is no evidence of any of this.

Q18. He reflects anger, frustration and the dark side of life in school essays or writing projects.
A No. There is no reference to any of the above. However, his predilection for themes related to destruction, violence and death is evidenced in most of his early writings and throughout his speeches.

Q19. The student is involved with a gang or an antisocial group on the fringe of peer acceptance.
A Yes. It has been extensively documented that, as soon as he joined Belén, he formed his own gang and began harassing other students. The Jesuit *padres* were terrorized. They had never seen a student like Fidel Castro.[38] He continued his involvement with gangs when he became a Law student at the University of Havana.[39]

Q20. He is often depressed and/or has significant mood swings.
A Yes. His mood swings and depression bouts have been documented.[40]

Sixteen questions out of twenty are answered in the affirmative.[41] The answers to two of the questions are unknown, though there is some indication that they may also be positive. Only two of them are definitely answered in the negative. Moreover, like the monsters who carried out the Colorado school massacre, young Fidel Castro was an avid reader of Nazi literature.

According to the creators of the Warning Signs quiz, a youngster with the characteristics mentioned above is,

> a "ticking time bomb." The child and his immediate family are at risk. They should get some help immediately. They must seek support from law enforcement, social and health services, parenting classes and the family court or other youth-serving professionals.

I would like to venture the theory that Fidel Castro's attack on the Moncada barracks in 1953 was but his own version of what some American kids are doing today. Writer Camille Paglia described the attack on Columbine High as a "cruel, abortive, self-destructive act by bourgeois screw-ups who hated their meaningless lives."[42] One cannot find a better definition of Castro and his friends' attack on the Moncada barracks.[43] As a matter of fact, Paglia's words closely resemble the evaluation the Cuban communists made of the attack.

Though nobody is to blame for the creation of the evil monster but the monster himself,[44] it is evident that the Jesuit *padres* at the Colegio de Belén committed a gross dereliction of their religious duty when, rather than detecting and neutralizing the evil creature they had in their hands, they encouraged and nurtured Fidel's dark side.[45]

Moreover, it seems that the Jesuits' efforts in nurturing the monster were not by mistake, but by design. Argentinean journalist Alfredo Muñoz Unsaín, for many years Havana's correspondent for France Press Agency, tells a quite revealing story. When father Pedro de Arrupe visited Cuba in the early 1980s, Muñoz Unsaín talked to him on several occasions. On one of them, recalls the reporter, the Black Pope gave him the classic Jesuit spiel, ending by saying that he was very pleased with the work of the Jesuits in Latin America, particularly of the many important disciples they had developed who later reached prominent positions in all walks of life. "Well, I guess you are not proud of all of them," retorted Unsaín, and added, "Don't forget that Fidel Castro was one of your disciples." To which Arrupe, in the classic Jesuit manner, answered by using a question to respond another one, "And what makes you think that we are not proud of Fidel Castro?"[46]

The Boy Without a Name

Developmental psychologist Erik Erikson suggested that the root of the totalitarian personality must be found in early childhood. Most historians, however, seem to ignore the simple fact that all individuals, including totalitarian tyrants, were once children.[47]

In an interview Castro gave in 1985 to Brazilian priest Frei Betto, Fidel offered some previously unknown information about his childhood that perhaps may serve as a clue to understand the true cause of his destructive, evil behavior. After asking Fidel a few questions about the place where he was born, Betto asked Castro if he was baptized at Birán.

> Betto - Were you baptized there?
> Castro - No; I was baptized in Santiago de Cuba, several years after I was born.
> Betto - How old were you then?
> Castro - I think I was around five or six. I was one of the last children in my family to be baptized. . . As a rule, everybody there had been baptized. I remember that those who hadn't been baptized were called Jews. I couldn't understand what the term *Jew* meant—I'm referring to the time when I was four or five years old. I knew it was a very noisy, dark-colored bird, and every time somebody said, "He's a Jew," I thought they were talking about that bird. Those were my first impressions. Anyone who hadn't been baptized was a "Jew."[48]

The fact that he was five or six years old and had not been yet baptized seems to have caused a profound impression on Castro, because a few moments later during the course of the interview he brings the subject up again:

> I remained unbaptized, and I remember that people called me a Jew. They used to say, "he's a Jew." I was four or five and was already being criticized, for people were saying I was a Jew. I didn't know the meaning of the word *Jew*, but there was no doubt that it had a negative connotation, that it was something disgraceful. It was all because I hadn't been baptized, and I wasn't really to blame for that.[49]

Betto does not follow up on the subject, and the question of why Castro had not been baptized remained unanswered. But the fact is that it was a very strange thing in the Cuba of the 1920s to find a child born of Catholic parents who had not been baptized at such an advanced age. That anomaly cannot be explained just because of the remoteness of the place, because, just a few moments before, Castro himself told Betto that, though there was no church close to the farm, a priest visited the area once a year to baptize the children. What Castro selectively forgets to tell Betto is that the problem had nothing to do with the inaccessibility of the place, but with a fact that Castro is at pains to hide: his bastard origins.

Fidel Alejandro Castro Ruz was the result of an extramarital affair of Angel Castro with his housemaid, Lina Ruz. Fidel was born in a small shack Angel had built for Lina, just a few feet behind the main house,[50] while Angel's legitimate wife was still living in the farm. Angel kept his two houses and his two wives, and other children from Lina were born after Fidel. The boy's legal situation was kept in limbo for many years, and it was not resolved until after Angel's first wife died and he married Lina. That explains why several times Fidel was refused admission to Santiago's Catholic schools when his family tried to enroll him.

But the fact that Fidel was a bastard was not the real impediment for not being baptized. Though it may not be the norm, bastard sons were not uncommon in the Cuban countryside, particularly at the beginning of the century. The real problem was that Fidel was not only a bastard, but also the product of a bigamous relationship, a practice strictly condemned by the Catholic Church and Cuban society at large.

Then, perhaps lulled by the late night hour and by Frei Betto's placid stare,[51] Castro tells the Brazilian priest the most amazing revelation:

> Castro - Yet, when I tell you why I'm called Fidel, you'll laugh. You'll see that the origin of the name isn't so idyllic. I had no name of my own. I was called Fidel because of somebody who was going to be my godfather.[52]

Yes, you have not read wrong. Castro is telling Frei Betto that he was five or six years old *and he still had no name of his own*. Which not only means that he had not been baptized, but that his birth had not been officially registered in the civil or the Church's records. And being a five-year-old boy without having a name of his own is an anomaly that, by force, must have had a profound negative impact in any child's life.

What type of problems; what extraordinary situation may have existed to cause a five-year-old boy not to be given a name? What feelings of rejection, abandonment and humiliation may such a child have suffered after being so ignored, so despised, to the point of not having been given a name? One can only imagine the resentment and hatred such a child may have felt against a family and a society which denied him even the right of having his own name. Most likely such a situation provoked in him feelings of hatred and resentment so strong as to accompany him for his whole life; feelings of hatred and resentment that neither total power nor immense riches have been able to erase; feelings of hatred and resentment against society and mankind, the ones he blames for his misfortune, which unconsciously have pushed him through his whole life seeking the punishment and destruction of all that he considers responsible for his pain—even risking his own destruction.

More than thirty years ago, my friend José Manuel Arias, a keen observer of Cuban events, made an accurate analysis of Castro's Cuba. According to Arias, the Cuban problem was not economic, social, or political; but a psychiatric one.

Thought it seems true that some conditions found in infancy are the cause of an individual's behavior, this makes him no less responsible for his actions. In the case of Fidel Castro, his destructive behavior may be explained because of the hatred he felt for his alcoholic, abusive father; the fact that he was a bastard son; the rage against other kids who called him a "Jew"; the humiliation he felt when President Roosevelt denied him the money he asked for; the whack to his head when he crashed his bicycle at Belén, etcetera, etcetera. You may add things to this list almost *ad infinitum*.

But, while it is true that some events in the childhood of a person may be the cause for evil behavior, it is no less true that not all abused children eventually turn into evil adults. Therefore, one must admit the existence of pure, conscious evil, an idea developed in detail by Berel Lang, Erich Fromm, M. Scott Peck and a few other scholars, studied in detail in Ron Rosenbaum's recent book on Adolf Hitler,[53] and shown in films like *The Silence of the Lambs* and *Seven*.

In his long self-defense speech at the trial for the assault on the Moncada barracks, Fidel Castro called President Batista "*Monstrum horrendum.*" Actually, there is no other term that better describes Fidel Castro. His political trajectory proves once more that power that is not balanced with compassion and humility easily turns into evil.

What to do With Castro?

After having read the previous chapters of this book some readers may still think that comparing Fidel Castro with Adolf Hitler is not only unfair, but far-fetched. Granted, the human cost of Hitler's madness was close to forty million dead, while Castro has been directly responsible only for a hundred thousand. But the reasoning is fallacious. In the first place, evil cannot be measured by the number of deaths alone. Some American snipers in Vietnam killed more people than Jeffrey Dahmer,[54] but they cannot be properly called evil while Dahmer evidently was. Secondly, and this is even more important, one must keep in mind that while Hitler is dead Castro is still alive, and he does not mind how many have to die, so long as he takes revenge against the world. He still has the desire, the capability, and the means to cause mayhem and destruction in the United States on a magnitude never seen before in the history of this country, and such becoming one of the greatest mass murderers in modern history.

In a fascinating book about Adolf Hitler, George Victor arrived at a controversial conclusion:

> Three blunders by Hitler are often cited as causing Germany's defeat—letting the British forces escape Dunkirk, not invading England, and invading the Soviet Union. These decisions were not blunders, however, for Hitler's goals were not what they seemed. The decisions were calculated risks taken to further a secret goal—the launching of the Holocaust—which was more important to Hitler than military victory. Although they led to disaster, from his viewpoint they were right decisions, because they enabled him to carry out the Holocaust. His conduct of the war, costing forty million lives, is extreme when viewed as an event in geopolitics and militarism. But when understood as a cover for getting rid of Europe's Jews, it is even more chilling.[55]

I fully agree with Victor. In the same fashion, Castro's secret goal has always been the destruction of the United States. Most of his political and military actions have been a cover for the consummation of his ultimate dream: getting rid of the Americans—Castro's Jews.

In his book about the 1989 events culminating with the death by firing squad of Gen. Arnaldo Ochoa and Col. Antonio de la Guardia, Norberto Fuentes mentions an old dream of Fidel Castro: the creation of the proper conditions to be the first to drop bombs in the U.S. territory so the yankees will suffer in their own home the same he suffered when Batista's planes were bombing he and his men in the Sierra Maestra.

Castro's remarks are a direct reference to his June, 1958, letter to Celia Sánchez. (See Appendix 1). But it will be a mistake to believe that the bombing of a farmer's home by Batista's planes using American-made rockets is the true cause for Castro's deep hatred for Americans. There is evidence that Castro does not care much for anybody except himself, less for some obscure, poor farmer in the Sierra Maestra. Therefore there should be more profound reasons for the irrational, inexhaustible hatred he feels for the United States and its people.

As I mentioned above, noted psychologist Erik Erikson believes that the causes of many manifestations of irrational behavior are to be found in early childhood.[56] Therefore the true reasons for Castro's hatred for Americans must be found in his early childhood at the Birán ranch in the Oriente Province. It is known that Fidel profoundly hated his father Angel, and Angel had close working relations with the Americans at the United Fruit's and the West Indies Sugar Company's plantations in Oriente. There is the possibility that Fidel displaced the hatred he felt for his father to the Americans who did business with Angel and provided for part of his fortune.

Hugh Thomas pointed out that the area where Fidel was born and raised had a strong American presence. Four American companies operated there: the United Fruit, the Dumois-Nipe Company, the Spanish-American Iron Company, and the Cuba Railroad Company. There were American schools and hospitals in the area, and the United Fruit's employees had swimming pools, a polo club, and a social club.[57] Some people believe that one of the sources for Fidel's anti-American hatred was motivated because, as a bastard, he was not allowed to participate in the parties at the United Fruit's American Club in Banes.[58]

Another explanation may be found in the letter a 12-year-old Fidel wrote to President Roosevelt asking for money and offering his help in locating some of Cuba's natural resources. (See Appendix 2). Unfortunately President Roosevelt didn't sent the money Fidel requested, and that may have deeply humiliated him.

In an essay about the Cuban missile crisis, a Cuban intelligence defector mentioned the fact that, contrary to Soviet claims, the Cuban intelligence found no evidence that the U.S. was preparing for an invasion of Cuba, nor that it had plans to invade the Island.[59] Surprisingly, Castro ignored his own intelligence officers and sided with the Soviets. Castro was totally sure that the U.S. was ready to invade Cuba. What most people ignore, is that, for forty long years, Fidel Castro has been preparing himself and waiting for an American invasion of Cuba. Not only waiting, it seems, but longing for the American invasion that will fulfill his prophecy.

During a five-hour speech on the occasion of commemorating the 40th anniversary of his revolution, Castro brought up again the subject of a U.S. invasion of Cuba. Talking about some anti-Castro organizations in the U.S., Castro claimed, in a typical freudian projection mechanism, that they "dream about a war confrontation" between Cuba and the U.S., adding that "their hatred is such, that they would like to see our motherland suffering a demolishing *genocidal* attack similar to the one suffered by the Serbian people."[60]

More recently, National Assembly President Ricardo Alarcón, one of the non-entities Castro surrounds himself with, declared in a lengthy proclamation that "the economic blockade imposed by the United States of America on Cuba constitutes an act of genocide."[61] Likewise, the word "genocide" keeps popping up in Castro's speeches in his references to the U.S.

One must keep in mind that the monster next door has an irrational hatred for the United States. Following Castro's reasoning one can arrive at the conclusion that, if it were true, as he claims, that the U.S. has been committing genocidal actions against Cuba, then Castro would be morally justified to commit genocidal actions against the U.S. It seems that, as it happens all the time, Castro's twisted mind has found a good excuse to justify his evil plans.

According to Norberto Fuentes, Castro's plans for a Cuban military attack on the U.S. territory were laid down a long time ago and are still operative.[62] Fuentes tells how Carlos Aldana, at the time Castro's main ideologue, had been commissioned to write down the ethical principles justifying a devastating Cuban attack on the U.S territory.[63] Recent information obtained from the "Wasp Network," a net of Cuban spies captured in Florida, indicate that Castro is still actively planning the destruction of America.[64]

For more than forty years, Castro has been itching for a fight, and there is evidence that now he has the poor man's great equalizer: bacteriological weapons of mass destruction. Even more frightening is the fact that everything indicates that he is willing to use them; he is just waiting for a good pretext.

Some anti-Castro exiles in the U.S. apparently have never put to rest their dreams of overthrowing Fidel Castro by force. What they apparently fail to realize, however, is that, once more, willingly or unwillingly, they are playing into Castro's hands.[65] A typical example from which they should learn is the case of Brothers to the Rescue.

Created by anti-Castro exiles in Florida, Brothers to the Rescue is an organization whose main purpose is to help the U.S. Coast Guard locate stray rafters escaping from Cuba and save them from the sea. As such, Brothers to the Rescue has contributed to saving the life of many desperate Cubans risking their lives to escape from totalitarian tyranny. Theirs is a commendable humanitarian effort, and every decent human being in this planet should be thankful to them.

But, at some time during their job, Brothers to the Rescue took a fateful step: they went beyond their humanitarian activities and used their planes to drop anti-Castro leaflets in Cuban territory. Granted, they never violated any law. They dropped the leaflets outside Cuban territorial waters, with the hope that some of them would be carried to land by the wind, as they actually did. But, what was the result of their reckless action? Did the Cuban people rebel against Castro and overthrow him? No. Far from hurting Castro, Brothers to the Rescue gave him the perfect excuse to commit another crime: he ordered his MiG fighters to shoot down two of the Brothers to the Rescue civilian planes.[66]

Another example was the passing of the Helms-Burton Law (officially called the Cuban Liberty and Democratic Solidarity Law) signed by President Clinton in 1996, allegedly to punish Castro for shooting down the Brothers to the Rescue planes. Castro's response was swift. He passed the Anti-Helms-Burton Law (officially called the Reaffirmation Law of Cuban Dignity and Sovereignty). While the Helms-Burton Law accomplished nothing, the Anti-Helms-Burton law increased the levels of intolerance, censorship and repression in the Island.

More recently, Senate Foreign Relations Chairman Jesse Helms, apparently not happy with his dubious anti-Castro achievements, has proposed legislation to send $100 million in U.S. government aid to the Cuban people and back democratic change on the island. Called the Cuban Solidarity Act, the proposed bill would authorize direct flights to deliver the aid, and order the U.S. government to step its support for dissident groups in Cuba.[67] But most dissident groups in Cuba fear that, rather from helping them, the "help" will damage their struggle for political freedom in the Island.[68] Castro seems to agree. He called the Helms initiative, "An excellent plan. The more mistakes they make," Castro said, "the weaker the U.S. position and the better for us."[69]

An easy way for the anti-Castro exiles in the U.S. to get rid of the Cuban tyrant would be to convince the American people that Castro is a Communist, then trick the U.S. into invading Cuba and let the Americans do the dirty job.[70] That is, more or less, what they have been trying to do for many years without much success. The plan, however, in not only unethical but also risky. In the first place, a full fledged U.S. invasion of Cuba would make Castro very happy. That is exactly what he has been preparing for during all these years. Secondly, even with all the U.S. military force it will not be an easy task to defeat Castro. He has some surprises of his own to counteract this kind of action.

Since early 1962 Castro developed a plan, at the time codenamed Operation Boomerang, by which in the case of a direct U.S.

attack on Cuba he was going to bring the war back to American soil. This would include not only direct action by Cuban special forces, most likely to targets in Florida, but also suicidal air raids to targets as far as Washington D.C., including some nuclear power plants in the East coast. In the meantime, Castro's agents in the U.S. would carry out their part of the plan, which include sabotage and bombings of civilian and military targets, like government buildings, tunnels, bridges, airports, and so forth.[71] To all this Castro now has added the capability for cyberwar, disrupting computer networks and the internet, and bacteriological warfare. Not a very encouraging scenario.

My personal advice to those still dreaming of Castro's demise by violent means is very simple: unless you have nuclear weapons, and are willing to use them against him destroying half of Cuba in the process, leave Castro alone. Don't touch him with a ten-foot pole. Another reason for leaving Castro unmolested is that one cannot successfully fight evil with evil.[72] Since the death of Celia Sánchez, probably the only person who brought out the best in Castro, all constraints to his dark side have disappeared. This alone should make people think twice before making any violent anti-Castro moves.

After Castro killed Ochoa, de la Guardia, Abrahantes, and several others of his close associates, everybody around him is scared, including members of his intelligence services and the feared Ministerio del Interior. They have realized, probably too late, that Castro is as efficient killing his friends as he is killing his enemies. That explains why, since Ochoa's death, the defections among members of the Cuban intelligence services have increased ten-fold.

Most anti-Castro Cubans seem not to understand that the true battle they are engaged in is not against Fidel Castro, but against evil. In the closing sequence of *Conducta Impropia*, playwright René Ariza, who suffered harassment, persecution and prison in Cuba, pointed out that the real fight is not against Castro, but ultimately against the Castro we all carry inside.[73] Thefore, the fight should not be *against* the evil in Fidel Castro, but *for* the good in ourselves.[74] "Whoever fights monsters should see to it that in the process he does not becomes a monster himself," warned Nietzsche.[75] If destroying Castro requires becoming an evil monster like him, it would be the ultimate proof that he has won the final battle for the soul of the Cuban people.[76]

Probably the best strategy to deal with Castro is the Vatican's time-proved *romanità*. Romanità is based on a single principle: *Cunctando regitur mundus*, which essentially means that if you can outwait all, you can rule all.[77] Cubans in exile and in the Island have been waiting for the death of Castro for more than forty long years. It is much better for them to keep patiently waiting, and see Castro die someday peacefully alone, than provoke him into an Armageddon which would bring his destruction together with the lives of several million innocent human beings. This would be a price too high to pay for Castro's life.

On the other hand, even if all anti-Castro Cubans were to follow my humble advice—which I am sure they will not—I don't think that leaving Castro alone would pacify him. On the contrary, an attitude of total indifference from the part of his enemies may well turn to be the greatest humiliation to him. And humiliating Castro has proved to be extremely unhealthy. Therefore, the anti-Castro Cubans are facing a very delicate, no-win situation which they can only turn around by acting with extreme prudence and intelligence—a very difficult task indeed having so many of Castro's *agent provocateurs* infiltrated in their ranks.

Some people in the U.S. are concerned about Castro's Cuba. According to Richard Nuccio, who served as President Clinton's special adviser for Cuban policy in 1995 and 1996, the United States should go a long way toward improving relations with Castro without lifting its economic embargo. This may include remaking its policy toward Cuba and encouraging some limited foreign investment on the Island.

Talking at an academic seminar on Cuban policy at Georgetown University, Nuccio expressed his opinion that without a change in policy, relations between the two countries could become volatile. He also said he is worried about the possibility of a military confrontation with Castro. "I believe Castro would rather take us down with him than be the Gorbachev of Cuba," he said. "I don't want to find out where the breaking point is."[78]

Though Nuccio's words will surely make many anti-Castro Cubans furious, I think that after reading this book[79] many readers would agree with me that any time and effort devoted to pacify the naughty boy from Birán is worth trying. The problem with Castro, however, is that he is actually not fighting the enemies he sees as evil, but the evil in himself he has projected unto his enemies. Therefore, as history has proved once and again, any approach to Castro, even a sincerely friendly one, is bound to provoke a negative response from him.[80]

There are strong reasons to be concerned about Castro's future actions. As I have shown above, Castro has always been very creative in fulfilling his prophesies through self-provocations. In mid-1999, professor Brian Latell, an ex-CIA officer expert in Cuban affairs, warned about the possibility of Castro creating a Mao-inspired Cultural Revolution in Cuba or taking a fateful action against the U.S.[81] Recent news from Cuba seem to indicate that at least part of Latell's prediction has materialized and Fidel's Cultural Revolution has already began.

During an unusual interview on Cuban tv in the evening of January 4, 2001, Raúl Castro advised the American "imperialists" that it would be better for them to normalize diplomatic relations with Cuba while Fidel is still alive than in the future.[82] Most analysts of Cuban politics are totally confused about the meaning of Raúl's words. Why does he believe that it would be easier to normalize relations now than after Fidel's death?[83] Apparently Castro is concerned that he is getting old and perhaps may die before seeing the United States destroyed and humiliated.

As I have mentioned above, on several occasions Fidel Castro has referred to the U.S. embargo on Cuba as a genocidal action, and he compared it to "noiseless atom bombs." Therefore, he has all the justification he needs to retaliate in kind. Under this light Raúl's words could be interpreted not as an advice, but as an ultimatum. Either the U.S. unconditionally stops the embargo and normalizes relations with the Castro government while Fidel is still alive, or else. Perhaps Castro sees himself as a Samson, and wants to bring down the temple burying himself along with the Philistines in the ruins of a bacteriological Armageddon. That many Cuban people will die does not matter to him. If he can hurt the U.S. badly he will be covered in glory. If he can hurt America he will be the ultimate winner. Dead or alive, he would have won the final battle against America.

Recently, both Fidel and Raúl have been making cryptic references to the massive use of "mines" against the U.S.[84] Castro can also cause heavy damage to the U.S. by resorting to "asymmetric war," a new military term originating in technology and cybernetics. According to military specialists, asymmetric war is a very effective military response of an inferior force against the military and civil infrastructures of a superior force. Asymmetric war is not fought in the traditional battlefields, but against computer networks in commercial aviation, banks, power grids, telephones and transportation, and using weapons like bio-terrorism. Sources in Cuba report that Castro has been preparing for many years to wage asymmetric war, and has all the necessary human and technical means to do it.[85] Testifying to a senatorial subcommittee, Thomas Wilson, Director of the Defense Intelligence Agency, expressed his belief that Cuba is well equipped to wage a technological war attacking the U.S. computer networks.[86]

Secretary of State Colin Powell's recent statement claiming that Castro is "no longer the threat he was," reflects either his total ignorance on the subject or shows that he has privileged secret information on it.[87] Granted, I can understand that there may be some good reasons explaining why Secretary Powell is confused about Castro's capabilities and intentions as a potential threat to the U.S.[88] One of them may be that, being a Cold Warrior of the old school, Powell is not familiar with the new theories of asymmetric war. But I think that his words have more to do with his poorly disguised liberal feelings than with his lack of knowledge.

In 1961, Senator J. William Fulbright wrote a memo to President Kennedy which included a phrase that became famous, "The Castro regime is a thorn in the flesh, but it is not a dagger in the heart."[89] 40 years later, however, there are strong reasons to believe that the Castro regime is not a thorn in the flesh, but a poisonous dagger pointing to the heart of the United States. As Cuban writer Guillermo Cabrera Infante pointed out quoting an old Chinese proverb, "the most dangerous part of the dragon is its tail."[90]

Castro and the Cuban "Revolution"[91]

In an essay I mentioned above, "Evil in a Rational Age," Vaclav Havel observed how most people, including most "serious" authors, share the opinion that everything can be rationally explained. To them nothing is obscure—and, if it is by chance, then the only thing we need to do is to cast a ray of scientific light on it and it will cease to be so.

But, as Havel pointed out, this is simply not true. To this day, for example, it is difficult to understand how one of the greatest civilized nations of the Western world fell to the fascination of a ridiculous clown named Adolf Hitler and, in the name of his crazy theories, ravaged nations and killed millions of innocent human beings.

Mass insanity has nothing in common with any form of rationality, but power, money and success are excellent catalysts for the production of explanations of the unexplainable. Had Charles Manson's plans been successful and he were residing today in the White House instead of San Quentin, we would surely have now hundreds of volumes written by "serious" scholars entrenched in prestigious research universities and non-profit foundations explaining with unbeatable logic the rational causes of the second American Revolution[92]—of which, just by sheer luck, we were spared.[93]

Long articles and profound papers and books have been written explaining the causes of the Cuban "revolution." The causes, according to these prestigious scholars, range from resentment against the U.S. for its policy on Cuba, to underdevelopment, poverty and class struggle. The problem with these theories is that all of them have been formulated *a posteriori*.

A typical example of the above is a State Department White Paper on Cuba released on April 1961. Largely written by Harvard historian Arthur M. Schlesinger, Jr., it tried to find logical causes for the revolt against Batista. According to Schlesinger, "The character of the Batista regime made a violent reaction almost inevitable. The rapacity of the leadership, the corruption of the government, the brutality of the police, the regime's indifference to the needs of the people for education, medical care, housing, for social justice and economic opportunity—all these, in Cuba and elsewhere, constitute an open invitation to revolution."[94]

Schlesinger's argument, however, is false. The words he used to describe conditions in Cuba during the Batista regime, while not totally true about Batista's Cuba, can be used, without changing a single word, to accurately describe the conditions in Castro's Cuba, particularly during the last fifteen years. But not even the most virulent anti-Castroist expects an internal revolution against the Castro regime to happen in the foreseeable future.

Had someone in January 1959 uttered a prophecy accurately describing what was going to happen in Cuba in the next forty years, he would surely have been a good candidate for the lunatic asylum. Had someone in January 1959 written a political-fiction novel describing the career of someone like Fidel Castro, he would have been dismissed by most publishers as a hopeless fool. Any way you try to find rational causes for the Cuban "revolution" you end up by realizing that the causes are totally inadequate to account for the enormous size of its effects.

It is wrong to conclude, as some historians have done, that the Castroist "revolution" grew inevitably from the Cuban past.[95] On the contrary, Castroism is an anomaly, an aberration that has no real substantive connection to the history of Cuba. If one thing is certain about the Castroist "revolution" it is its essential lack of historical precedent. Except for a few, short periods in Cuban history, Cubans have not been ultra-nationalistic or anti-American,[96] and have never had any imperial dreams. Almost any country in Latin America in the forties and fifties had more potential for harboring an anti-American revolution than Cuba.[97] Nor was the Castroist "revolution" needed because of Cuba's economic conditions before the Castro takeover.[98] As I have shown in some chapters of this book, Cuba's level of development in the pre-Castro era, particularly during the Batista administration, was among the highest in Latin America, and one of the highest of all the non-industrialized world.[99]

Never before have Cubans approved totalitarianism. As a matter of fact, most Cubans fought Batista's authoritarianism because they preferred the ideals of democracy and freedom. The unorthodox truth is that the Castroist "revolution," the way we now know it, had no real causes at all and was neither needed nor sought by the Cuban people, nor by the Cuban communists, nor by the people fighting Batista in the cities and in the mountains. Thus, it was not a matter of Castro cynically exploiting anti-American sentiments because the Cuban people were ripe to respond to his appeal. The rabid anti-Americanism that pervades Castro's thinking has no outside sources, but comes from deep irrational sources within Castro himself.[100] In fact, though Castro believes he is fighting the "evil" Americans, he is actually fighting the demons inside his head. In an interview in the Mexican magazine *La Jornada*, writer Norberto Fuentes said that "Fidel Castro is the leader of the counter-revolution."[101] In other words, Fidel Castro is his worst enemy.

In the *Ethics* Aristotle wrote, "Men start revolutionary changes for reasons connected with their private lives." In the case of the Cuban revolution that assertion is absolutely true. The causes of the Castroist "revolution" are to be found only in the mind of Fidel Castro. They lie in the intimate psychology of Castro's social and moral failure. For most individuals, living with moral failure is hard to accept, mostly because of the rebuke of their conscience. Habitual moral failure, like the ever present one in Castro's life, can be faced only by placating one's conscience through rationalization.[102]

Very early in life, Castro became a master in rationalization, convincing himself that everybody was wrong and his hidden desires of power and revenge were right. He cleverly advanced the reality of his desires over the reality of the moral order to which his desires should have been subordinated. In his mind he replaced the reality of moral order with his ideas and wishes. Finally, fully convinced that bad was good, he put all his evil talents to changing the world according to his vision. The result of this convoluted thinking is the Cuban revolution—or, to better express it, the Castroist revolution. Bizarre as it may seem, this is the only theory that fully explains the strange phenomenon that has intrigued so many bright minds.

Probably the only thing about the Castroist revolution on which most scholars agree is that it shows some features that are unusually puzzling. More than thirty years ago Hugh Thomas pointed out the intriguing characteristics of the revolution that took place in Cuba, "one of the richest countries in Latin America, where a Marxist regime had been established seemingly because of the will of a single man, himself a very untypical Marxist."[103]

Thomas is not the only one puzzled by the Castro phenomenon. "It is too early to say with finality just why a revolution of the nature and extent of that in Cuba should have come to that country rather than to any of half a dozen others in Latin America," wrote Russell H. Fitzgibbon in 1961. "Why did Castro's rebellion break out and why did it succeed?," asked Stanislav Andreski; "How had such a dismaying situation come about?," asked John Fagg; "no one can say precisely why a radical upheaval engulfed the island in 1959," commented Ramón E. Ruiz; "Just why this profound tragedy has come to afflict the Cuban people . . . will always remain a matter of dispute," wrote Frank Tannenbaum.[104]

The reason why Castro has confused almost everybody who has tried to make sense of his actions is because he has covered his tracks with a communist ideological mask. But Castroism has never been a political movement. Like Hitler's Nazism, Castroism is a religious cult with deep roots in the occult. Castro is not a political leader, but a cult leader.

Notwithstanding claims on the contrary, there is not a single shred of evidence proving that Fidel Castro's push for Castroism came as the result of pressure from below, such as the Cuban masses, or from above, either from the United States, as Castro himself has tried to make us believe, or from the Soviet Union, as most anti-Castroist Cubans in exile claim. A dispassionate analysis of the Castroist "revolution" shows that there were no real, objective reasons for it. Like a Caribbean Pallas Athena, it sprang, fully formed, armed and uttering her war cry, out of the head of Fidel Alejandro Castro Ruz.[105] After analyzing the facts, the unavoidable conclusion is that the Castroist "revolution" *is* Fidel Castro, and Fidel Castro is . . . well, Fidel Castro *is* Fidel Castro!

Many people have predicted what will happen to the Cuban revolution after the death of Fidel Castro. Let me add a prediction of my own: Nothing! If we are lucky, and Fidel's destructive dreams don't come true, nothing will happen to the Cuban revolution. In the first place, because there was never a revolution in Cuba. Secondly, because after the death of the Caribbean cult leader, none of his associates has what is needed to become the next cult leader of Castroism.

Fidel Castro is enshrined in the Cuban constitution as president for life. To oppose him is not only counterrevolutionary, but also unconstitutional. Castro is both head of the government and head of the state as well as first secretary of his "Communist" Party, commander-in-chief of the armed forces, and head of dozens of other organizations that probably only he can remember. All power is concentrated in his hands and he imposes his personal will on every important decision in Cuba. With Castro now in his mid-seventies and showing growing symptoms of poor mental and physical health, succession is becoming an increasingly pressing question.

Castro himself is fully aware that nobody can substitute him. The pyramid of power he has created in Cuba is a truncated one, with Castro at the very top, an empty second tier, and a few third rank bureaucrats—among them Raúl, his brother and designated successor, Ricardo Alarcón, Carlos Lage, Felipe Pérez Roque, and a few others—fighting among themselves for the leftovers of power.[106] This chaotic situation is not the product of bureaucratic mistakes but of Castro's careful design. He has deliberately brought about a situation in which the different high-level officials in the government have been ranged alongside and against one another, without defined boundaries, in competition, and overlapping—and only he himself stands at the very top of all of them. When any of his close associates has had the misfortune of getting dangerously close to the second row, as it happened to Frank País, Camilo Cienfuegos, Osvaldo Sánchez, Ché Guevara and, more recently, Arnaldo Ochoa, their lives have been dramatically shortened. Consequently, none of the third rank bureaucrats will be able to fit into Castro's boots.[107]

After the death of the evil Caribbean Pied Piper,[108] the Cuban people will wake up from their long incantation with the feeling that they had a bad dream. Then, the Cuban "revolution" will simply extinguish itself and disappear without a sequel, and Cuba will return to normalcy—whatever that means.[109]

Many years ago, when he was a Law student at the University of Havana, Fidel Castro told a friend that his main ambition in life was to have a page in Cuban history. Well, he may not have a full page dedicated to him, but it is likely that he will get at least one sentence. Fifty years from now, Cuban history textbooks will show a very short mention of Fidel Castro as "a corrupt, bloodthirsty tyrant and envious millionaire who lived in the times of Celia Cruz."[110]

Afterword

*T*he *Secret Fidel Castro Castro: Deconstructing the Symbol*, was written before the tragic events of September 11th. The book was scheduled to appear in October, 2001, and some uncorrected copies for reviewers had already been printed before September 11th. After serious consideration I decided to stop the publishing process to include some relevant information about the possibility of a Castro connection with these events. The core for this Afterword is an article I published on several Internet sites, including *Pravda* online, English edition (*Pravda* online has nothing to do with the printed *Pravda*, still under the control of the Russian Communists).

A Sad Day for Fidel Castro?

Tuesday, September 11, 2001, was a very sad day for Fidel Castro.

In his book about the 1989 events culminating with the death by firing squad of Gen. Arnaldo Ochoa and Col. Antonio de la Guardia, Norberto Fuentes, a Cuban intelligence officer under a writer's cover, at some time very close to the highest levels of the Castro government, mentions an old dream of Fidel Castro: to be the first to drop bombs in the U.S. so the Yankees (Castro calls all Americans "Yankees") will suffer in their own home the same he suffered when Batista's planes were bombing Castro and his men in the Sierra Maestra.[1] Castro's words were a direct reference to a short letter he sent to Celia Sánchez, his secretary in the Sierra Maestra mountains.

During the Cuban missile crisis, Castro did his best to spoil our day by pushing the Soviet Union and the United States into a nuclear Armageddon which would have killed at least 25 percent of the population of the United States and the Soviet Union. He not only tried to convince Khruschev to fire the missiles, but was also planning to blow up several portions of Manhattan to make the Americans believe that they were under a nuclear attack and provoke them to retaliate with a nuclear salvo against the Soviet Union. When everything failed, the resourceful Fidel shot down an American U-2 plane over Cuba, in another effort to push the U.S. into invading the island and kill Soviet soldiers as a way to force Nikita Khruschev into a nuclear retaliation. After the crisis was over, he began a secret plan to create his home-made missiles using modified MiG 21 planes. According to some of his associates, his plans were to use the missiles to deliver nuclear or bacteriological weapons to the U.S. territory.

As I explained above, the Juraguá nuclear plant, which he tried for many years to build near the city of Cienfuegos, was just a cover whose real objective was to produce fissionable material to create nuclear bombs. In 1982 Fidel Castro Díaz-Balart, Castro's son in charge of the nuclear program, told an associate that they were very close to acquiring the necessary knowledge to produce a nuclear weapon. Other facilities were also involved in research on nerve gases and bacteriological weapons that could be delivered to the U.S. by different ways. But Castro's son failed to deliver the nuclear goods, and Castro fired him.

After his missile development projects ended in failure, Castro's nuclear dream was postponed, but not forgotten. In 1989 General Rafael del Pino Díaz, the highest ranking Cuban defector, said that at the time of the Grenada operation in 1983, Castro ordered Cuban MiG 23 pilots to program their computers to attack targets in Florida. Among the selected targets was the Turkey Point nuclear plant South of Miami, which Castro said had the potential of producing a nuclear disaster larger than Chernobyl. According to Gen. del Pino, Castro's words were: "I don't have nuclear bombs, but I can produce a nuclear explosion."

In a forthcoming book, *Inside Castro's Bunker*, General del Pino expands on the subject. According to del Pino, Castro's initial plans were to destroy Homestead Air Force Base, but then decided to destroy Turkey Point instead. Castro's words, says del Pino, were:

> I want to do something that they will remember for the rest of their lives and then, when we are gone, history will remind them that we were the only ones who made them pay dearly for their imperialistic arrogance around the world.[2]

On July 1980, while he was visiting Nicaragua to celebrate the Sandinista takeover,[3] Castro bragged,

> We have agents of absolute confidence all over the United States who are ready to undertake whatever actions are necessary at the time of our choosing. The Yankees can-

not even begin to imagine the capabilities we have in their country. You all read about the riots in Miami . . . We can accomplish things that would make the riots in Florida look like a sunshower.[4]

When Castro realized that making missiles or nuclear bombs was not an easy task, he began developing bacteriological weapons—the poor man's nuclear weapons. Sice the late 1980s, sources inside and outside Cuba have insistently mentioned that Castro himself has put a strong emphasis in developing an ambitious program capable of producing nuclear, chemical and biological weapons of mass destruction.[5]

In his book *Biohazard*, Ken Alibek, who was first deputy director of the Soviet Union's main bioweapons directorate before defecting to the U.S. in 1992, wrote that he is convinced that Castro is developing bacteriological weapons. On January 28, 1998, during a virulent anti-American speech, Castro's words carried an obvious threat, "This lamb cannot ever be devoured, neither with airplanes, nor with smart bombs, because this lamb has more intelligence than you and in its blood there is and always will be poison for you!"[6]

Apparently, however, Fidel's good Arab friends, showing a total lack of respect and consideration for the Cuban tyrant, beat him to it. It seems that Castro has mellowed with age, and the Arab terrorists took the initiative and won the big honor of being the first to drop bombs in the United States. Knowing the hatred Castro has always felt for America and the Americans, one may safely surmise that on September 11th Castro had a very sad day. Now he will die some day without being remembered as the one who first attacked the Americans in their own soil.

Or perhaps not.

As we saw above in this book, many people who know Castro well see him as an unstable terrorist. As a matter of fact, Castro's terrorist activities began while he was still at the Sierra Maestra mountains, when, following his orders, his brother Raúl kidnapped several marines and civilians from the Guantánamo Naval Base and used them as hostages to obtain concessions from the U.S. government.[7] Once in power he began supporting all kinds of terrorist groups, particularly anti-American ones, and created the America Department, an organization whose main objective was supporting anti-American terrorist activites in Latin America and the U.S.[8]

In 1966 Castro, as chief coordinator of international terrorism, hosted in Havana the Tricontinental Conference, a Cuba-based international organization for promoting revolution, particularly by violent means, including terrorism. More than 500 representatives from virtually every terrorist group in the world attended the conference. A secretariat to the organization was created at the America Department, to select what groups to support and to promote subversion and terrorism. The MININT created several training camps, where would-be terrorists were trained in urban guerrilla warfare, kidnappings, assassinations, and other types of terrorist activities.

Many terrorist groups received their training there, among them the Uruguayan Tupamaros, the Argentinean Montoneros and ERP, the Colombian FARC, M-19, and ELN, the Chilean MIR and Frente Patriótico Manuel Rodríguez, the Peruvian MRTA (Tupac Amaru Revolutionary Movement, who attacked the U.S. Embassy in Lima in 1984 and the residence of the U.S. Ambassador in 1985), the Basque ETA (which has a General Headquarters in Havana), the Irish IRA, and the Sandinista, Guatemalan and Salvadoran guerrillas. Moreover, Castro also supported American terrorist groups like the Weathermen, the Porto Rican FALN (Armed Forces of National Liberation), who between 1974 and 1985 organized 120 terrorist bombings in the U.S., and the Macheteros,[9] responsible for highjacking a Wells Fargo armored truck in Connecticut in September 1983 and robbing $7.2 million—some of which found its way to Havana. Both the FALN and the Macheteros were organized by Castro's intelligence services and some of its members received their terrorist training in Cuba.[10]

It has been extensively documented that members of the Black Panther organization were trained in Cuba in terrorist operations. In the mid-seventies the CIA reported that close to 300 Palestinians were undergoing training in Cuban camps. It is known also that Ilich Ramírez Sánchez, the infamous "Carlos, the Jackal," attended the Tricontinental Conference in Havana in 1966 and was trained in Cuba in urban guerrilla tactics, explosives, sabotage, and other terrorist activities.[11] It is highly revealing that when several Ibero-American heads of state attending the 2000 Ibero-American Summit in Panamá passed a resolution condemning ETA's terrorist acts, Fidel Castro refused to sign it.[12]

Since late 2000, Castro has been working frantically creating a strong alliance of anti-American Muslim countries. Visits to Cuba of Muslim leaders of all levels, as well as visits of members of the Castroist government to anti-American Muslim countries, have increased considerably. In July of 2001, Hojjatoleslam Hajj Seyed Hassan Khamenei, grandson of Iran's Ayatollah Khomenei—leader and founder of the Islamic republic of Iran—visited Cuba for the celebration of the triumph of Fidel's revolution.[13] According to official Cuban reports, Fidel Castro himself, accompanied by his distinguished guest, led the combative march of 1.2 million Cubans along Havana's sea side Malecón avenue. Apart from celebrating another anniversary of the victory of Castro's revolution, the event main purpose was to make three key demands to the U.S.: an end to the blockade (Castro's jargon for the embargo), the release of the five Castro spies detained in a Miami jail, and *the end of U.S. acts of terrorism against Cuba*.[14]

In May of 2001 Castro made a long trip visiting several anti-American Muslim countries, among them Algeria, Iran, Malaysia, Qatar, Syria and Libya.[15] Iran, Libya, and Syria, together with Cuba, Iraq, North Korea and Sudan, have been listed since 1993 in the U.S. Department of State yearly report "Patterns of Global Terrorism." According to the report,

> Cuba continued to provide safe haven to several terrorists and U.S. fugitives in 1999. A number of Basque ETA terrorists who gained sanctuary in Cuba some years ago continued to live on the island, as did several U.S. terrorist fugitives.
> Havana also maintained ties to other states sponsors of terrorism and Latin American insurgents. Colombia's two largest terrorist organizations, the Revolutionary Armed Forces of Colombia and the National Liberation Army (ELN), both maintained a permanent presence on the island. In late 1999, Cuba hosted a series of meetings between Colombian Government officials and ELN leaders.[16]

In Algeria, Castro was received by Algerian President Abdelaziz Bouteflika. One source close to the Cuban delegation commented privately that the official communiqués always gave the impression that more things were actually discussed in the exchanges with "an old friend of many revolutionary conspiracies" than it were reported in the press. Political analysts in Havana mentioned the possibility that, despite what was said publicly in Algiers, the two leaders examined topics related to the Cuban interest in strengthening the Non-Aligned Movement and the so-called Group of 77, as the official Cuban press affirmed in evaluating the tour, and also about how to stop the worldwide spread of United States influence.

Upon his arrival in Iran, the second stage of his journey, Castro was prodigal in praising Iranian Islamism. Afterwards, he made an emphatic declaration: "I have not come to speak of trade, but of politics and of culture." Observers noted attentively an affirmation by the president Mohammed Khatami: "The cooperation between Iran and Cuba will be able to confront the hegemony and the injustice of the great arrogance [of the United States]." Speaking at Tehran University on May 10, 2001, Castro vowed that "the imperialist king will finally fall."[17]

During Castro's meeting with Iranian Supreme leader Ayatollah Ali Khamenei, the Iranian leader proposed an "Irano-Cuban cooperation" against the U.S. Referring to "U.S. hegemony," Khamenei said that Tehran considers the "American regime as an arrogant power, seeking a unipolar world, to which we seriously object."[18]

"The U.S. is weak and extremely vulnerable today," Khamenei stressed, adding that "U.S. grandeur can be broken, and if this takes place, it will be a service rendered to mankind and even the American people," adding that their resistance against U.S. hegemony "is based on our Islamic beliefs, since in Islam resistance against injustice is considered a value."[19]

For his part, Castro said that he was not "afraid of America, and the Cuban nation, 40 years after its revolution, is now stronger than ever." "Iran and Cuba," Castro added, "in cooperation with each other, can bring America to its knees. The U.S. regime is very weak, and we are witnessing this weakness from close up."[20]

One of the existing Cuban-Iranian cooperation agreements refers to the area of scientific investigation and vaccine production technology—a common cover for the secret production of bacteriological agents—in a high-technology laboratory now nearing completion in Iran. But there is probably more than meets the eye in the Cuban-Iranian agreement. According to José de la Fuente, a Cuban scientist now living in the U.S., this technology, used to manufacture lifesaving medical products, can be easily adapted to produce lethal agents for biowarfare, like anthrax bacteria or the smallpox virus. Many steps in the fermentation process that produces vaccines and other medicines are similar to the ones used to manufacture biochemical weapons.[21]

According to the U.S. Department of State Background Note on Iran available on the Dept. of State web site, "Iran remains a significant sponsor of terrorism." The Note also added,

> The U.S. Government defines five areas of objectionable Iranian behavior: Iranian efforts to acquire nuclear weapons and other weapons of mass destruction, its involvement in international terrorism, its support for violent opposition to the Arab-Israeli peace process, its threats and subversive activities against its neighbors, and its dismal human rights record.[22]

Iran is one of the most active sponsors of terrorism in the world. At least until September, 2001, there was no evidence that Iranian anti-American policy had changed, and Iran continues to provide support to several terrorist organizations and to assassinate dissidents abroad.

In his visit to Qatar, Castro was received by the Sheik Hamad bin Kalifa Al-Thani, the emir of Qatar, who had visited Cuba last September. From Qatar, Castro flew to Damascus, responding to an invitation by Syrian leader Bashar al-Assad, who received him at the airport. It was reported that, while in Syria, Castro held private and official talks with his Syrian counterpart, in which they examined how to strenghten bilateral ties.[23] During his visit, Castro again publicly praised the importance of Islamism in the modern world. In his visit to Libya, the next step of his trip, Castro was received by Colonel Muammar al-Qaddafi, who gave his friend Fidel a tour of the house the Americans bombarded in 1986. After visiting the house, Castro mentioned that, as in his own case, the U.S. has used explosives, *biological weapons* and every means possible to destroy Qadaffi, but has failed.[24]

But, before visiting Syria and Qatar, Castro made a stop in Quala Lumpur, Malaysia, to pay a visit to his friend Mahatir Mohamad, whom he praised as an "excellent leader." During his visit to Malaysia, Castro repeated his new-coined mantra that he is a "great admirer of [the Islamic] religion." In Kuala Lumpur Castro and his large entourage visited the famous Petronas twin towers. With its 88 floors, the Petronas twin towers are considered the tallest buildings in the world. During his long visit to the towers, Castro said that he "felt closer to heaven." Castro's visit to the Petronas seemed the most innocuous of his activities during his tour. However, after the attack on the World Trade Center's twin towers Castro's apparently innocent visit to the Petronas twin towers takes on a totally different meaning.

The engineers who built the World Trade Center were shocked by the way the towers collapsed. They had calculated that the WTC towers would have been able to withstand the direct crash of a big commercial plane. But, just a few minutes after the suicide planes crashed against the towers, they collapsed like card castles. Undoubtedly, the suicide bombers were familiar with the structure of the buildings, and knew exactly where to crash their planes to cause maximum structural damage. Short of a computer simulation model, only a close inspection of the WTC towers, or of a building with similar characteristics, would have allowed them to discover the weak points in the building's structure. Did Fidel Castro bring with him some of his highly trained army demolition engineers to study the structure of the Petronas towers? Did he pass the information on to the men who perpetrated the attack to the WTC? Is Castro directly or indirectly involved in the September 11th terrorist attacks on the American people? These are questions that should be investigated.

In an article for *WorldNetDaily*, Toby Westerman mentions a conversation he had, on condition of anonimity, with a former intelligence officer for the Lebanese army now living in the U.S. In his report, the officer, which he refers to simply as Jack, cited Cuba as a "fertilizer ingredient" for Islamic terrorism.[25] Probably there is more than a grain of truth in Jack's remarks. As a matter of fact, Castro loves playing the "catalizer" (or fertilizer) role, and he has played it to perfection in innumerable occassions. He has been the catalizer in the creation of anti-American guerrillas in Latin America. Without his expert intervention neither the Sandinistas in Nicaragua nor the New Jewel Movement in Grenada would have achieved power. His hidden catalizer hand has also being present in the work of many terrorist groups in Europe and the U.S.

As I mentioned above in this book, it has been documented that on several occassions Castro has used his uncanny fascination abilities to persuade people to do the most incredible things, like convincing a group of poorly armed Cubans to attack a military garrison or persuading a Soviet army officer to shoot down an American U-2 plane. In his trip to several Islamic countries in early 2001, he mentioned several times his appreciation of the Islamic religion. During his visit to Kuala Lumpur, he even claimed that lately he had become more rational about the role of religion in people's lives. Referring to his previous visit to Iran, Castro said that women were accorded better treatment in some Islamic nations than in the West. "In the West," continued Castro, "women are regarded as a commodity and an object of business. I think of Western women as those who have been asphyxiated because of the way they're treated."[26]

One may safely surmise that, the same way Castro surprised Alexeev with his "deep knowledge" of Marxism, and the Catholic bishops with his "deep knowledge" of theology and liturgy, he now surprised his Islamic hosts with his "deep knowledge" of Islam. Apparently, Castro's photographic memory is still in good shape, and he keeps using it to dupe the fools and recruit them as proxies to do his dirty work. Cuban dictator Fulgencio Batista was right in his suspicions that Fidel Castro is an *agent provocateur*.

In a news story of March 4, 2000, the *Associated Press* reported that a young Afghan who was trained in the mountains of the province of Kunar, in the northeast of Afghanistan, said he had seen there some men from Chechnia, Sudan, Libya, Iraq, North Korea, and Cuba. According to the young Afghan, the North Koreans had brought chemical weapons, which were deposited in caves.

Just a few days after the terrorist attack on American soil, the government of Great Cayman informed in an official communiqué dated September 16, 2001, that three Afghan nationals had been detained after entering the country, allegedly by plane, with false Pakistani passports. Actually, the Afghans had arrived by ship from Cuba.

After the arrest, the Cayman government released a letter from boat captain Byron Barnett, which had been sent to Radio Cayman 13 days before the September 11 attack, foretelling the coming events. According to Barnett, he overheard the three men while they were talking to another individual. Barnett was convinced that the men were plotting terrorist attacks on the U.S. using commercial airline planes.[27]

In an interview with reporters from the Al-Jazeera tv station, based in Qatar, Castro emphatically declared that he was not ready for a reconciliation with the U.S. As a matter of fact, continued Castro, "I will never reconciliate myself with the Capitalist system."

During a five-hour speech on the occasion of commemorating the 40th anniversary of his revolution, Castro brought up again the subject of a U.S. invasion of Cuba. Talking about some anti-Castro organizations in the U.S., Castro claimed, in a typical Freudian projection mechanism, that they "dream about a war confrontation" between Cuba and the U.S., adding that "their hatred is such, that they would like to see our motherland suffering a demolishing *genocidal* attack similar to the one suffered by the Serbian people."

More recently, National Assembly President Ricardo Alarcón declared in a lengthy proclamation that "the economic blockade imposed by the United States of America on Cuba constitutes an act of genocide." Likewise, the word "genocide" keeps popping up in Castro's speeches in his references to the U.S.

When an epidemic of dengue fever broke out in Cuba in the mid-seventies, affecting 350,000 people, among them this writer, Castro immediately claimed Cuba was under a U.S. biological attack.[28] When Soviet General Lebedenski and a team of military scientists visited Cuba, Castro asked him to analyze the strain to verify his suspicions. The Soviet scientists found no evidence of this, and suspected that it was a natural outbreak, because the strain happened to be Cuban, not American.[29] Perhaps Castro, following the CIA's example, was testing his biological weapons on the Cuban people.[30]

As I mentioned above in this book, the Mariel boatlift of 1980 was not Castro's knee-jerk reaction after an incident at the Peruvian Embassy, but a psy-op carefully planned way in advance by his intelligence services following his instructions. A few days after the massive exodus began, however, Castro ordered to mix in mental patients released from institutions and hard-core criminals from the Island's prisons into the mass of refugees. This order took by surprise even high-rank officers of his intelligence apparatus.

Some people have found a strange coincidence that the AIDS epidemic appeared in the U.S. after the Mariel exodus, particularly knowing that as many as twenty thousand of the Cubans who were part of the boatlift were homosexuals. Researchers at the University of Miami subsequently confirmed that some of them were infected with AIDS before they entered the U.S.[31]

As journalist John Crewdson pointed out,

> The fact that HIV was present in Cuba at least as early 1980 raises new questions about when and how AIDS arrived in the U.S. and how it was transmitted so rapidly through the homosexual population. Equally intriguing is how HIV found its way to a closed society like Cuba at a time when it was barely present in the U.S.[32]

Crewdson advances two theories to explain the strange phenomenom. One is that AIDS was brought to the Island by Cuban soldiers coming back from the war in Angola. Another theory is that the disease was artificially created in Castro's secret bioweapon labs and innoculated to the men forcefully mixed in among the people who legitimately were leaving the Island. It is significant that, for whatever reasons, by 1988 only 174 Cubans in Cuba had been reported positive for HIV, while it had caused more then 200,000 fatalities in the U.S.

In July, 2001, a strange news circulated in the Internet, but was totally ignored by the mainstream American media. According to some reports, Lucius Walker, one of the leaders of the Castro-freindly Pastors for Peace, a political organization under a religious cover, was trying to bring several tons of an unlicensed Cuban-made bio-chemical known as Biorat, a strong rat poison, allegedly to fight rat infestation in American ghettos.[33] Biorat, a product of Labiofam, one of Castro's biological labs, combines salmonella, some phage and lysine negative into a meal of biological components. According to some experts, Biorat was invented in the Soviet Union in the 1920s. Reports from people who have visited Cuba recently tell of a widespread rat infestation in most cities, particularly Havana. One wonders, if the Castro government, the producer of Biorat, has not been able to stop the rat infestation in Cuba, why getting this potentially harmful bio product from them?

In their book *America the Vulnerable*, Joseph Douglass and Neil Livingstone informed that Russian instructors at Cuban chemical warfare schools in the 1980s boasted that Castro was prepared to kill tens of millions of Americans with toxins he had stockpiled.[34] One must keep in mind that the monster next door has an irrational hatred for the United States. Following Castro's reasoning one can arrive at the conclusion that, if it were true, as he claims, that the U.S. has been committing genocidal actions against Cuba, then Castro would be morally justified to commit genocidal actions against the U.S. It seems that, as it happens all the time, Castro's twisted mind has found a good excuse to justify his evil plans.

Norberto Fuentes mentioned that Castro's plans for a Cuban military attack on the U.S. territory were laid down many years ago and as late as 1999 were still operative. Fuentes tells how Carlos Aldana, at the time Castro's main ideologue, was writing down the ethical principles justifying a devastating Cuban attack on U.S territory.[35] Recent information obtained from the "Wasp Network," a net of Cuban spies captured in Florida, indicates that Castro is still actively planning the destruction of America.

It is useful to remember that, in an unusual interview on Cuban tv in the evening of January 4, 2001, Raúl Castro advised the American "imperialists" that it would be better for them to normalize diplomatic relations with Cuba while Fidel was still alive than in the future. Most analysts of Cuban politics were confused about the true meaning of Raúl's words. Why does he believe that it would be easier to normalize relations now than after Fidel's death? Apparently Castro was concerned that he was getting old and perhaps would die before bringing America to its knees, destroyed and humiliated.

As I have mentioned above, on several occasions Fidel Castro has referred to the U.S. embargo on Cuba as a genocidal action. This can only mean that he already has found the right pretext he needs to retaliate in kind. Under this light Raúl's words should not be interpreted as an advice, but as an ultimatum: either the U.S. unconditionally stops the embargo and normalizes relations with the Castro government while Fidel is still alive, or he will retaliate in kind.

Since late 2000, subtle signals emanating from Havana made evident for anyone with eyes to see, that Castro was up to something big. As we have shown above in this book, the magnitude of Castro's thirst for revenge against the United States and the American people is not in any way constricted by any moral bounds. For people closely observing Castro's actions the only questions were what? where? and when? One may wonder if the September 11 atttacks were the materialization of Raúl Castro's ultimatum. Giving substance to this suspicion is the fact that destroying Manhattan is an old dream of Castro. In October, 1962, Cuban agents, following Castro's direct order, were planning to blow several portions of Manhattan, including Macy's department store, the Statue of Liberty, several subway stations, the 42nd street bus terminal, and Grand Central station. Only the FBI's quick intervention avoided the catastrophe.

Cuban Terrorists: In Miami, or in Havana?

Just a few hours after the attack on September 11, 2001, many anti-Castro Cubans in the U.S. and abroad began raising questions, mainly in articles published on the Web, about Castros' involvement in terrorism. Actually, articles about Castro's terrorist activities written by anti-Castro Cubans are not new; they have been appearing on the Web for many years. After the September attack they just increased in volume and provided fresh information, mostly based on articles that appeared in the Cuban press, particularly its Web sites.

Obviously, the anti-Castro Cubans were trying to influence public opinion by reminding the American public of Castro's terrorist activities and that Cuba has been for many years in the U.S. Department of State's list of countries who are involved in or support terrorism. Immediately, Castro counter-attacked in his typical style by unleashing a campaign whose main goal was to accuse the anti-Castro Cubans in the U.S. of being the true terrorists. A few days later, some Castro-admirers in the U.S mainstream media and the academia joined the campaign following similar lines. The first one was an article dated September 25 by Sue Anne Pressley, a staff writer for the *Washington Post*, entitled "Among Miami's Cuban Americans, Terrorism is a Familiar Story. Tactics Used by—and against—Castro still Stir Debate in Exile."[36]

In her article, Pressley paints a grim picture of Miami as a city where American democracy has been conspicuously absent. Quoting several Cubans who express their personal opinion, and bringing as main proof the case of the 1976 Cuban airliner, she attempts to build a case against the anti-Castro Cubans in Miami. The case, though not easy to prove in court, is easier to prove in a newspaper article. As a matter of fact, the American mainstream media, who controls public opinion, has been for many years visceraly against the anti-Castro Cubans in Miami. An extreme example of this is that, after the abduction of Elián González by one of Janet Reno's SWAT teams, left wing pundit Alexander Cockburn wrote an article headlined "Just Nuke Miami," in which he stated,

> There is a sound case to be made for dropping a tactical nuclear weapon on the Cuban section of Miami. The move would be applauded heartily by most Americans. Alas, Operation Good Riddance would require the sort of political courage sadly lacking in Washington these days.[37]

As usual, Cockburn's example of hate speech of the worst kind passed unnoticed to the pro-Castro anti-hate-speech crowd. But it would be a mistake to take Cockburn's word as a joke. I am convinced that cardinal among Castro's plans for the destruction of America is the destruction of the Cuban-American community in Florida.

On the other hand, I don't blame any American who may end up accepting Pressley's picture of the anti-Castro Cubans as terrorists. As a matter of fact, for many years, perhaps under the influence of the media barrage, I was close to accept that picture. However, after many years of research for writing this book I discovered a quite different picture. If anything, far from being vicious terrorists, one can only accuse the anti-Castro Cubans in Miami of being extremely naïve: Castro has played most of them like a violin, and they have fallen for every trick and every trap the Cuban tyrant has set up for them.

As I analized earlier in this book, most of the terrorist actions allegedly committed by the U.S. government and by anti-Castro Cubans in the U.S. against Castro, from the burning of canefields to all types of sabotages, were committed, directly or indirectly, by people paid by Castro himself. It has been extensively documented that Castro's secret agents have penetrated most, if not all, anti-Castro organization in the U.S. How come, one may ask, the anti-Castro organizations have been able to commit acts of terrorism against Castro, when Castro has had his agents infiltrated in these organizations? How come they have not alerted him of the impending terrorist acts? The reason is because Castro needs the terrorist actions to justify his counteractions. Even more, there is evidence that most of the terrorist actions commited by anti-Castro Cubans have been instigated by Castroist *agent provocateurs* in their midst—the case of the Brothers to the Rescue actions, which ended in the downing of the planes by Castro's MiGs, is an example of that.

Even the events surrounding the bombing of the Cuban airliner, the most heinous terrorist act allegedly committed by anti-Castro Cubans, are not totally clear. As I mentioned above in this book, there is circumstancial evidence that at least the Cuban government knew that the plane was going to be blown, but they allowed the passengers, with a notable exception, to board the plane and die.

But the campaign directed at putting the blame on terrorism on the anti-Castro Cubans didn't end with Pressley's article. On September 28, a press release, following similar lines, was circulated by a group of 16 pro-Castro U.S. policy organizations which publicly questioned the inclusion of Cuba among the U.S. government's list of terrorist states.[38] The statement mentioned Castro's reiterated willingness to cooperate with all countries in the total eradication of terrorism. The press release advanced a new argument—most likely the concoction of the disinformation department of Castro's intelligence services—expressing the notion that, "while there are no convincing reasons to keep Cuba on the list of terrorist states, it is best left on because it would offend elements of the Cuban-American community."[39] To be sure, removing Castro's Cuba from the list of terrorist nations will offend the anti-Castro Cubans in the U.S., and they have enough reasons to be offended if this happens some day. But such an action will also offend the intelligence of the educated American public.

Two weeks after the press release mentioned above circulated, Mr. Wayne Smith and other author made a personal contribution to the pro-Castro side, trying to prove that the true terrorists are not in Cuba, but in Miami. In this article, Smith told his readers that since the September 11 attack,

> ... there has been a concerted effort on the part of hard-line Cuban exiles in Miami and their political allies in Washington to describe Cuba as part of an international terrorist network and to suggest that the United States must act against Castro as part of its reponse to the September 11 attacks.[40]

Mr. Smith's claims, however, are only partially true. It is true that, through their articles, the anti-Castro Cubans have been pressing the U.S. government to put its wallet where its mouth is, that is, to act against Castro. As a matter of fact, not acting against Castro's Cuba, who has been for many years in official U.S. government's lists of nations involved in terrorism, will detract credibility to the U.S. anti-terrorist actions. It is not true, however that the Cuban's effort was a "concerted" one. Far from that, if something characterizes the anti-Castro community in Miami is its total lack of organization. Contrary to the pro-Castro American Left, the Cubans in the U.S. have taken democracy seriously, and it is evident that there is more freedom of expression and diversity of opinions among the Cuban exile community than among the totalitarian-minded American Left.

Nor is it true that the anti-Castro Cubans have any "political allies in Washington." If something has become evident, particularly after the Elián González case and now because of the Cubans' effort to point to Castro's terrorist actions, it is that the Cuban community is mostly isolated, with not many friends in Washington and even less friends in the U.S. mainstream media. Proof of it is that Cockburn's "nuke Miami"article passed unchallenged by the supposedly "hard-line Cuban exiles in Miami and their political allies in Washington."

Smith's arguments are based on a fallacious principle: he accepts Castro's words at face value, while ignores Castro's actions. For example, among Smith's "proofs" that Castro is against terrorism are "his specific reactions to the terrorist attacks on America."[41] He also adds the fact that the Cuban government immediately condemned the terrorist attacks on the United States and offered "its sincere condolences to the American people for the distressing and unjustifiable loss of human lives.'"[42] But, as I have shown in this book, this is part of Castro's *modus operandi,* closely resembling his reaction to the news of the assassination of President John F. Kennedy.

Smith also mentions a September 15th rally in Havana dedicated to condemning the attacks on American people and Castro saying, "the territory of Cuba will never be used for terrorist actions against the American people."[43] But, as we have seen in this book, the Great Dissembler's words do not carry much weight, because most of his actions are in strong contradiction with his words.

Smith points out that "the U.S. Interest Section in Havana was one of the few U.S. diplomatic missions not to close as a precautionary measure immediately after the September 11 attacks. No terrorist threats to Americans in Havana!"[44] The fact, however, comes as no surprise to Cubans in Cuba. Contrary to common lore, the U.S. diplomatic mission in Havana has always been extremely friendly to the Cuban tyrant—a fact that Mr. Smith does not ignore, because he was an important part of this friendship during his days as an American diplomat in Havana. It is known that Smith's close friendship with Castro began when he was in charge of the U.S. Interests Section in Havana. The fact perhaps explains why during his tenure Cubans who approached the Interests Section, desperately trying to obtain visas to flee the country, were treated like dirt—something I experienced first hand.

As expected, Mr. Smith criticizes the anti-Castro Cubans for trying to advance "their own narrow anti-Castro agenda, when U.S. foreign policy most requires cooperation with all nations willing to work with us in the struggle against terrorism."[45] The problem with Mr. Smith's arguments is not only that he is a tainted source, too close for comfort to terrorist Castro, but also because his arguments follow too closely the arguments concocted by Castro himself and promoted by his intelligence services. During a short interview on Cuban tv on June 19, 2001, Castro referred 3 times to the anti-Castro Cubans in Miami as "the Miami terrorist mob."[46] Therefore, one has to conclude that the "terrorists-in-Miami" propaganda theme, now advanced by Pressley, Smith, *et al,* was created in Havana way in advance—perhaps as a counteraction to the events to come.

The U.S. Government's Strange Blindness

The record ponts to overwhelming evidence that Fidel Castro has developed bacteriological warfare agents and other means of mass destruction and is willing to use them against the United States. Now, is the U.S. government going to investigate the possibility that Castro has been connected to the September 11 tragic events? I suggest that you don't hold your breath. For reasons difficult to understand, Fidel Castro has proved to be an untouchable to the American government. Therefore, one may safely predict that the U.S. government is not going to investigate the Castro connection to the September 11 attacks, the same way it never investigated the Castro connection to the Kennedy assassination despite the fact that most of the incriminating evidence pointed to Castro. Further proof of it is that, despite overwhelming evidence about Castro's capabilities and intentions, Secretary of State Colin Powell recently claimed that Castro is "no longer the threat he was."[47]

Soon after the September 11th attack, President George W. Bush declared that the U.S. government was going to go not only after the terrorists but after the countries who harbor them. Well, since Fidel Castro grabbed power in Cuba in 1959 with the help of the American government and media, he has been harboring all types of anti-American terrorists. For forty long years, Castro has been openly promoting anti-American guerrilla subversion in Latin America and terrorism in the U.S. and Europe.

It is useful to remember Castro's cryptical references to the use of "mines" against the U.S., and that his plans to cause heavy damage to the U.S. waging "asymmetric war" are still active. As we have seen, Castro has both the capability and the willingness to wage asymmetric war against American commercial aviation, banks, power grids, telephones and transportation, and to use weapons like conventional terrorism and bio-terrorism against the U.S. Moreover, there are strong indications that Castro has been preparing for many years to wage asymmetric war, and has all the necessary human and technical means to do it. However, no serious actions have been taken or, as we will see, will be taken by the U.S. government to punish or at least investigate Castro for his threats and actions against the American people.

The unavoidable fact is that, despite overwhelming evidence pointing to Fidel Castro as a terrorist and Castro's Cuba as a country involved in terrorism and harboring terrorists, for some unknown reasons the U.S. government continues ignoring the evidence. The fact was pointed out by Judicial Watch, a Washington, D.C., public interest firm that investigates government abuse and corruption.[48] According to Judicial Watch,

> while the United States government continues to ignore that Cuba is an imminent threat to this country, more and more evidence surfaces that dictator Fidel Castro is in fact

a tremendous danger that government officials can no longer afford to ignore. Castro's cozy relationship with Iran, strong ties to some of the world's deadliest terrorists groups and biotechnology manufacturing plants along with his well-documented hatred of America, should be enough to consider him dangerous. Additionally, more and more evidence has recently been uncovered that Castro is in fact a threat to national security. Yet, the Bush administration, which early on expressed an interest to soften the U.S. embargo agaist Cuba, continues to ignore the facts.[49]

Judicial Watch was not the only organization expressing its dissappointment with the Bush administration's attitute towards the Castro regime. Just a few weeks after the September 11 events, Congressman Robert Menendez of New Jersey presented Secretary of State Colin Powell with information regarding recent events directly implicating Castro in bioterrorist activities. He also added some interesting questions, among them, about the U.S. government knowledge of three suspected Afghan nationals arrested in the Cayman Islands with fake passports after transit to Cuba.

Menendez also mentioned the Cuban spy Ana Belén Montes,[50] who had an important position at the Pentagon,[51] and the kind of classified information she had been providing the Cuban intelligence services. He also told Powell of how the Cuban spies recently convicted in Florida provided Castro with information about strategic military centers in the U.S and other important government officers, including detailed information about the U.S. mail system. Finally, Menendez reminded Powell of Castro's recent visit to Iran and the close scientific relations between Iran and Cuba. Powells' incredible response was that "With respect to your comments about Cuba, I'm not familiar with most of the items you mentioned," adding that ". . . I don't know that we have seen any linkages that would cause us to believe the the events of September 11 in any way trace back to Havana, but I'm sure our intelligence agencies are keeping their antennae up."[52]

It is hard to believe, however, that Mr. Powell could be that ignorant about Castro's blatant anti-American activites in the recent months, including his recent approaches to anti-American Muslim leaders involved in terrorism, openly conspiring with them to commit anti-American actions. Castro's words during his visit to Iran early this year, widely quoted in the media, cannot be more threatening: "Iran and Cuba, in cooperation with each other, can bring America to its knees." Adding insult to injury, instead of taking a serious stand against Castro's threatening words and actions against America, only a few days after the terrorist attack on New York and Washington, D.C., the U.S. government contacted Castro, an unrepentant anti-American terrorist, for his support. As expected, the Great Dissembler promised the U.S. government to help the Americans in their fight against terrorism.

There are more clues pointing to a possible Castro connection with the current terrorist conspiracy against the U.S. It has surfaced that during the days following the September 11 attack, Montes sent repeated messages to her Cuban intelligence handlers.[53] Intelligence sources also found that within hours after the attack Castro placed his armed forces in extreme alert, apparently expecting American retaliation—exactly as he did after the Kennedy assassination.

Apparenlty related with the above was the unexpected Russian decision of closing their electronic spy facilities at Lourdes, south of Havana. It seems that some Russian officials were highly concerned about a repetition of the Cuban missile crisis of 1962, with Castro dragging Russia into an unwanted confrontation with the U.S. Some observers believe that the main motive for the Russian's concern was a not publicized incident recorded by the Federal Communications Commission in 1999 in which Cuban electronic warfare specialists broke into New York's air-traffic control system by simulating U.S. Air Force flight codes. The signals, which seriously threatened to disrupt air traffic, were traced to a 1,500 kilowatt trasmitter operating west of Havana.[54]

Some analysts believe that Castro's new alignment with Islam fundamentalists could go beyond anti-American declarations. It has been reported that U.S. law-enforcement agencies suspect that Castro may have given planning and logistic support to the terrorist groups reponsible for the September 11 attacks. [55]

The sudden occurrence of some cases of anthrax in the U.S. began with the infection and eventual death of a photo editor of the *Sun*, a supermarket tabloid[56] published by American Media, and the infection of five more employees. This was the beginning of a series of reports of people contaminated by anthrax spores in letters that had been sent to The *New York Times* and *NBC*. After this, the possibility that the U.S. would be under a biological attack is not a theory any more.

The fact that the contaminated letters were posted from a post office in St. Petersbourg, Florida, and that Mohamed Atta, the leader of the hijackers, lived within 3 miles of the American Media offices established the possibility of a connection to Osama Bin Laden. There is another suspect, however, that has been ignored by the American intelligence agencies: Fidel Castro.[57] Given Castro's installed capabilities for the production of biological weapons, some people asked a simple question: "Why should anyone go to the trouble of producing anthrax and then risk shipping it half way round the world when their good pal in Cuba, a mere 90 miles from the Florida coast, can provide him with all he needs at a moment's notice?"[58] Moreover, rumors running in intelligence circles in Cuba claim that Castro has been in personal contact with Bin Laden. This contacts involve not only links of the DGI (Castro's secret service) with Bin Laden's terrorist network, which engages in terrorism and cocaine smuggling, but also financial transactions the nature of which are apparently unknown outside Castro and Bin Laden's inner circle.

Though Tom Ridge, the chief of the recently created Homeland Security, initially reported that the anthrax used in the attacks was not weaponized, apparently this is not true. According to Dr. Byron Weeks, a former Air Force doctor and retired colonel specialized in biowarfare and infectious diseases, the anthrax used in the attack on U.S. soil was weaponized.[59] Even more, contrary to official U.S. government agencies statements, this weaponized form of anthrax could have been easily aerosolized.[60]

According to Dr. Weeks, "the weaponized anthrax used in the attacks indicates the people behind these attacks are capable of much more significant attacks and could have easily killed tens of thousands, or more, if they had chosen to."[61] Dr. Weeks believes that the current attacks have all the fingerprints of a nation-state. Even though it is relatively easy to produce a homegrown biological agent like anthrax, it would yield a wet form, hard to use as a biowarfare weapon. But the anthrax used in the U.S. is a highly processed form of dry anthrax, only produced in sophisticated biowarfare labs with highly sophisticated high-speed centrifuges shielded against lethal agents.

After the attacks, some U.S. government officials mentioned that only three countries in the world have the installed technology to successfully weaponize anthrax: the U.S., Russia, and Iraq. But this is also not true. As I explained in detail above in this book, Castro's Cuba has the technology to weaponize anthrax, and has been experimenting with it for many long years. Therefore, if we discard the U.S. and Russia as the producers of the anthrax employed in the attacks, the two remaining suspects are Hussein's Iraq and Castro's Cuba.

The fact that Fidel Castro, a terrorist and sworn enemy of the U.S., has the technology for weaponizing anthrax[62] is very disturbing, particularly under the present cirmcumstances. Even more disturbing is the fact that, unknown to the majority of the American people, Cuban commercial planes routinely fly over the U.S. territory almost every single day, and it would be extremely easy to aerosolize weaponized anthrax spores from a plane flying over the U.S. in a biological warfare attack as lethal as a nuclear one.

It seems that, after more than thirty years of prohibition, the Federal Aviation Administration, apparently following Clinton's orders, lifted in 1998 the ban against Cuban planes flying over U.S. airspace while going to and from Canada. Since then, Cuban planes are now permitted to fly two paths, one over land on the U.S. east coast, and other offshore over the Atlantic Ocean near the U.S. coastline.[63]

Nevertheless, despite overwhelming evidence pointing to Castro, since mid-1990s, the U.S. government, both during the Clinton and Bush administrations, has been making an extraordinary effort in downplaying Castro's capabilities and intentions for waging asymmetric war against the U.S. On May, 1998, the Pentagon released an unclassified version of a Defense Intelligence Agency[64] assessment of the threat to U.S. national security posed by Cuba, produced in response to a request from Congress. According to people who read it, the report concluded that "Cuba does not pose a significant military threat to the U.S. or to other countries in the region."[65] When the report was leaked to reporters, and news of it appeared on the press, it precipitated a public outcry, and prompted a postponement of the study's final submission, pending a personal review of its content by Secretary of Defense William Cohen.

After reading the report, Secretary Cohen wrote a letter to Senate Armed Services Committee Chairman Strom Thurmond, expressing, among other things, that

> While the assessment notes that the direct conventional threat by the Cuban military has decreased, I remain concerned about the use of Cuba as a base for intelligence activities directed against the United States, the potential threat that Cuba may pose to neighboring islands, Castro's continued dictatorship that represses the Cuban people's desire for political and economic freedom, and the potential instability that could accompany the end of his regime depending on the circumstances under which Castro departs.[66]

Moreover, Secretary Cohen raised his concern "about Cuba's potential to develop and produce biological agents, given its biotechnology infrastructure. . ."

The asymmetric threats posed by the Castro regime had been the focus of two Symposia sponsored by the William J. Casey Institute of the Center for Security Policy on 12 and 13 March, 1997. In a summary of these meetings, which adressed "Vital U.S. Security Interests in Cuba," the Institute captured important insights of the participants, including the dangers to millions of Americans from the controversial Cuban nuclear plant at Juraguá, and Cuba's potential biological weapons capabilities.[67]

The attitude of the United States government vis-à-vis Fidel Castro, through a long parade of Republican and Democrat administrations, shows that, for reasons that we ignore, American leaders simply don't want to see what cannot be more evident. Despite claims on the contrary, the Bush administration is clearly showing that it is no exception to the unwritten rule.[68] I hope they have good reasons for doing this.

Just a few hours after the September 11 events, President Bush expressed his conviction that there were no neutral grounds in this struggle, and those who harbor terrorists share the guilt for the acts they commit. Under the Bush doctrine, a regime that harbors or support terrorists will be regarded as hostile to the United States.[69] It is hard to understand, however, why Castro's Cuba, which fully falls into this category, has been totally left out of the picture.

At any rate, some day both the Cuban and the American people are going to discover the true reasons for the U.S. government's lack of interest in confronting Castro's openly belligerent anti-American words and actions. When that happens, and you can rest assured that it will happen some day, I have the feeling that the Cuban people, and a large portion of the American people as well, are not going to be happy at all.

Appendixes

Appendix 1
Castro's Letter to Celia Sánchez

Sierra Maestra
junio -58

Celia:

When I saw the rockets they dropped on Mario's house, I swore to myself that the Americans are going to pay dearly for what they are doing. When this war is over, a much wider and bigger war will begin for me: the war that I am going to launch against them. I realize that that is going to be my true destiny.

Fidel.

The Spanish original of this letter was first published in *Bohemia*, (Havana) May 18, 1973, and was printed in English for the first time in *Granma Weekly Review*, (Havana) August 27, 1967. See also Ramon L. Bonachea and Nelson P.Valdés, *Revolutionary Struggle, 1947-1959* (Cambridge, Mass.: The MIT Press, 1972), p. 379.

Though the letter was dated June 5, 1958, it was not widely known about until 1967, when a greatly enlarged reproduction of it was hung at the La Rampa Art Gallery in Havana, during a conference of the Organization of Latin American Solidarity (OLAS). Next year, author

Lionel Martin published a facsimile of the letter in his book *The Early Fidel* (Seacaucus, N. J.: Lyle Stuart, 1978), pp. 209-210.

The Mario mentioned in the note was a peasant in the Sierra Maestra mountains, in Cuba's Oriente province. The rockets that destroyed his house came from one of Batista's planes, but they had been made in the United States.

Appendix 2
Castro's Letter to President Roosevelt

COLEGIO DE DOLORES
APARTADO 1
SANTIAGO DE CUBA

Santiago de Cuba.
Nov 6 1940.
Mr. Franklin Roosevelt,
President of the United
States.

My good friend Roosvelt:
I don't know very English, but I know as much as write to you.
I like to hear the radio, and I am very happy, because I heard in it, that you will be President for a new (período.)
I am twelve years old.
I am a boy but I think very much but I do not think that I am writing to the

President of the United States.
If you like, give me a ten dollars bill green american, in the letter, because never, I have not seen a ten dollars bill green american and I would like to have one of them.
My address is:
    Sr. Fidel Castro
    Colegio de Dolores
        Santiago de Cuba
            Oriente. Cuba.
I don't know very English but I know very much Spanish and I suppose you don't know very Spanish but you know very English because you are American but I am not American.

(Thank you very much)
Good by. Your friend,

Fidel Castro

If you want iron to make your sheaps ships I will show to you the bigest (minas) of iron of the land. They are in Mayarí. Oriente Cuba.

*Colegio de Dolores
Apartado 1
Santiago de Cuba*

*Santiago de Cuba.
Nov 6, 1940.
Mr. Franklin Roosevelt,
President of the United
States.*

My good friend, Roosevelt:

I don't know very English, but I know as much as write to you.

I like to hear the radio, and I am very happy, because I heard in it, that you will be President for a new (período) [term].

I am twelve years old. I am a boy but I think very much but I do not think that I am writing to the President of the United States.

If you like, give me a ten dollar bill green american, in the letter, because never, I have not seen a ten dollars bill green american and I would like to have one of them.

My address is:

*Sr. Fidel Castro
Colegio de Dolores
Santiago de Cuba
Oriente, Cuba.*

*I don't know very English
but I know very much
Spanish and I suppose
you don't know very Spa-
nish but you know very
English because you
are American but I am
not American.*

*(Thank you very much)
Good by, your friend,*

*F. Castro
Fidel Castro*

*If you want iron to make
your ~~sheaps~~ ships I will
show to you the bigest
(minas) [mines] of iron of the land.
They are in Mayarí. Oriente,
Cuba.*

The letter was found among the retained files of the American Embassy at Havana, and is now housed in the records of the foreign service posts of the Department of State, National Archives, Washington, D.C., record group 84.

A facsimile of the letter was published in the *American Archivist* (Vol. 50, Spring 1987, pp. 284-288), whose Editor, Bill Burck, kindly sent me a photocopy.

Many years later, in an interview with Frei Betto, Castro seized the opportunity to criticize the Unted States for their intervention in Cuba, "It intervened more than once and seized our best land, *our mines*, our trade, our finances and our economy." Perhaps at the bottom of his twisted mind Fidel was unconsciously criticizing himself for the time when he offered the American interventionists the Cuban mines to exploit them at their leisure.

Castro criticizing American intervention in Frei Betto, *Fidel and Religion* (New York: Simon and Schuster, 1987), p. 148 (emphasis added).

Appendix 3
The Evaluation of Information

The evaluation of information, also known as appraisal, deals with the analysis of a piece of information in terms of credibility, reliability, pertinency, accuracy, and the use of an item of information, an intelligence product, or the performance of an intelligence system. The evaluation of information is accomplished at several stages within the intelligence cycle with progressively different contexts.

The evaluation or appraisal of items of information is indicated by a conventional letter-number system.

Reliability of the Source	Accuracy of Information
A Completely reliable	1 Confirmed by other reliable sources
B Usually reliable	2 Probably true
C Fairly reliable	3 Possibly true
D Not usually reliable	4 Doubtful
E Unreliable	5 Improbable
F Reliability cannot be judged	6 Accuracy cannot be judged

The evaluation simultaneously concerns with both the credibility of the information itself—a process involving a check against information already in hand and an educated guess as to the accuracy of the new information—and the reliability of the source. The two aspects cannot be totally separated from each other. The authoritativeness of the source, which may not necessarily coincide with its reliability, can never be ignored, though it is sometimes overrated in the light of the credibility of the information, something that has to do with the expectations of the people involved in the evaluation process. People, however, including intelligence analysts, tend to believe what they suspect or expect to be true.

It must be emphasized that both evaluations should be entirely independent of each other, and they are indicated in accordance with the system shown above. Thus, information judged to be "probably true" received from a source considered to be "usually reliable" is designated "B2".

The question of what is authoritative and what is not is very relative. A highly authoritative source may produce credible information, but the intelligence officer must always ask himself the question "Why?" The higher the authoritativeness of the source, the higher the possibility that it may be biased or had been compromised and, therefore, the higher the danger of disinformation. Highly authoritative sources from totalitarian governments may not always tell the truth, to say the least, but highly authoritative sources from democratic countries may not be very reliable either. There is evidence that the CIA has been involved in recruiting scholars at the most prestigious American universities, and journalists in the most influential American media. Also, there is suspicion that the KGB, the Mossad, and even the Cuban intelligence services, among others, have done a good job penetrating American universities and media.

From the point of view of intelligence, a stolen document is often more valuable than a gratuitously conveyed secret from whatever source, since it diminishes, though not totally eliminates, the risk of deliberately misleading information. The "why?", however, applies not only to the danger of planted disinformation. It must also be asked of the source whose *bona fides* is beyond question. The danger here is of an intelligence service believing what it wants to believe—a problem that has affected all the world's intelligence services at one time or another. The problem of the bias of the evaluator is one that is unavoidable in intelligence; it extends even to information of fullest credibility from the most reliable sources.

Bias in evaluation can never be fully overcome in an intelligence service and, more importantly, in high government circles, and it can only be compounded by creating evaluators to evaluate the evaluators. Within the intelligence establishment, the only effective safeguard lies in the individual competence and quality of its members as well as their intellectual honesty and personal courage to face pressures from above.

One must always bear in mind that no source can ever be regarded as infallible, and no single bit of information can ever be regarded as totally accurate. Whatever the case, the chances for error, misinterpretation, misunderstanding and deceit are too high to blindly trust any information.

Oliver-North-style superpatriots, doctrinaire partisans, court historians, bureaucratic climbers, intelligence defectors, people of provincial outlook—all are potential dangers to sound information evaluation. Perspective, perspicacity, worldliness, a soundly philosophical outlook, the knowledge of history and perhaps a bit of skepticism and a sense of humor—these are the individual qualities which minimize error in the interpretation and evaluation of information.

Notes

Introduction

1 New York: Harper & Row, 1971. Thomas was probably the first scholar who mentioned Castro's fascist inclinations.
2 New York: Praeger, 1962.
3 Cambridge, Mass.: The M.I.T. Press, 1967.
4 Berkeley: University of California Press, 1972.
5 Maurice Halperin, however, had to admit that, at least in relation to some events which allowed for Castro's advent to power, one can find ". . . those strange quirks of fate that are the despair of the historian who looks for a rational explanation of the course of human events." See *op. cit.*, p. 28.
6 But, the sole existence of a phenomenon such as Fidel Castro proves that historical materialism has always been on the wrong track.
7 For a strong criticism of the prevalent theories about the presence of strategic missiles and their nuclear warheads in Cuba in 1962 see Servando González, "A Missile is a Missile is a Missile: A Semiological Analysis of Some Aspects of the Cuban Missile Crisis," *Sumeria*, http://www.sumeria.net/politics/amissile.html, August 2000.
8 An excellent example is Bobby Kennedy's efforts to produce a totally disingenuous memo in order to leave a paper track proving that, contrary to his actions, he actually opposed the ongoing assassination attempts on Castro. See, Gus Russo, *Live by the Sword* (Baltimore: Bancroft Press, 1998), pp. 72-73.
9 Tradecraft: The methods and techniques of the intelligence and espionage business, in other words, its *modus operandi*. According to CIA veteran William Hood, tradecraft, though mysterious to outsiders, is just a "little more than a compound of common sense, experience, and certain almost universally accepted security practices . . ." *Mole* (New York: Ballantine Books, 1982), p. xiv.

10 The goal of the historian and the intelligence analyst is basically the same: to search for facts and establish the truth. Their approach, however, is totally different. Give a historian a paper with information on it and he will do three things: check it for accuracy; evaluate its place in the context of his own knowledge of its subject matter; and try to exploit it for producing a finished paper or book.

Now give the same paper to an intelligence analyst. He will do four things, but quite different ones. First, he will examine it to verify that the document is not a falsification and that its source is the one it purports to be; second, he will try to know if its source has disseminated it wittingly or unwittingly, and, if unwittingly, if its source knows the fact that the document has been compromised; third, he will attempt to find, guess, or intuit the source's real motives for disseminating it; and, finally, he will try to use it—by divulging it, or by not divulging it—to influence somebody, either his employers or his employees.

As such, the historian is trained to react *ad causam*, the intelligence analyst *ad hominem*. The historian focuses on subject matter and its relevance to understanding recorded events, the intelligence analyst focuses on people and their motives.

Historians usually ignore evidence that contradicts their preconceptions. They just line up events that fit the pattern of their prejudices. However, when intelligence analysts find evidence that contradicts their preconceptions, they assume it is enemy deception until it has been corroborated and proved beyond any reasonable doubt.

Some cognitive theories state that there are two different ways by which human beings process information: the data-driven way and the theory-driven way. The first is (or, ideally, should be) the historian's approach, the second is the intelligence analyst's. The research methodology I have used in this book is a fusion of the two approaches but with an emphasis on the theory-driven one. The result is this new approach I call *historical tradecraft*.

11 Since biblical times, intelligence, counterintelligence, espionage and counterespionage play an extraordinarily important role in historical events. For unknown reasons, however, few historians seem to bother looking at these aspects.

12 In the prologue to a book Ratliff published a few years later, John R. Silber advances the same thesis: "Even today, the press continues to treat Fidel Castro as something of a mystery." "In reality, there is nothing mysterious about Castro. The questions have been answered. He can be explained much more easily than other leaders." See William E. Ratliff, ed., *The Selling of Fidel Castro* (New Brunswick: Transaction Books, 1987), vii.

13 Matthews letter in Theodore Draper *Castro's Revolution* (New

York: Praeger, 1962), p. 196.

14 *Fidel Castro* (New York: Simon and Schuster, 1969) p. 354.

15 Foreword to Mario Llerena, *The Unsuspected Revolution* (Ithaca, New York: Cornell University Press, 1978), p. 11.

16 "The U.S. and Castro, 1959-1962," *American Heritage*, Vol. 29 No. 6 (October/November, 1978), p. 27.

17 *Castro's Revolution: Myths and Realities* (New York: Praeger, 1962), p. 3.

18 "Castro: The 'Knowable' Dictator," in *The Cuban Revolution at Thirty*, Proceedings from a conference sponsored by the Cuban American National Foundation, Washington, D.C., January 10, 1989, p. 31.

19 Carlos Franqui, *Family Portrait with Fidel* (New York: Random House, 1984), p. 22.

20 Herbert S. Dinerstein, *The Making of a Missile Crisis* (Baltimore, Md.: Johns Hopkins University Press, 1976), p. 24.

21 Erisman on Castro in *Cuba's International Relations* (Boulder, Colorado: Westview Press, 1985), p. xiii.

22 "¿Contra quién luchamos?", *El Bohemio News* (San Francisco), July 29, 1998, p. 2.

23 As I mentioned above, I have the greatest respect for Dr. Ratliff and most of the scholars who have studied the Cuban revolution. My point, however, is that their own rigorous academic training has acted as a barrier for their full understanding of such an irrational person as Fidel Castro. Proof of it is that during the last thirty years most academic studies on Castro have consistently predicted his downfall—a totally rational and logical conclusion. But Castro's downfall has never materialized, and he always manages to surprise everybody by pulling a card from his sleeve. Anyway, nobody can blame these bright scholars for having been deceived by Fidel Castro. He managed to deceive even his closest friends and associates, including Frank País, Ché Guevara, Camilo Cienfuegos, Haydée Santamaría, Tony de la Guardia and many others.

On the other hand, it is interesting to see that the best portraits of Castro have been made by authors like Luis Conte Agüero, José Pardo Llada, Carlos Franqui, Juan Arcocha, Carlos Alberto Montaner, and Georgie Anne Geyer, who are not involved in the academic field—with Hugh Thomas as a notable exception. Similarly, notwithstanding the high level of academic studies on Adolf Hitler, British historian H. R. Trevor-Roper believes, and I fully agree, that one of the best sources to understand Hitler and his motives still is Hermann Rauschning's *The Revolution of Nihilism* (New York: Alliance Book Corporation, 1939), a sensationalistic and vulgar book written by an ex-Nazi.

The authors I have mentioned above portray Castro as a wild, ideologically confused, obsessively ambitious, and envious man craving revenge against a world he hates. Unfortunately, most scholars, particularly the Castro-friendly ones, have dismissed this characterization as the result of the authors' bitterness at what they consider the betrayal of the original democratic goal of the revolution.

24 When in his early twenties Castro was a Law student at the University of Havana, he already had gained a reputation as a gangster and merciless assassin to the point that, unbeknown to him, he became the model for the character of a gangster in at least two stories. It is rumored that Ernest Hemingway based the character of the assassin for his short story *The Shot* on young Castro. Also, Venezuelan writer exiled in Cuba Rómulo Gallegos claimed that he got his inspiration on Fidel Castro for the creation of Justo Rigores, "El Caudillo," one of the turbulent gangsters of his novel *La brizna de paja en el viento* (A Bit of Straw in the Wind). The fact is mentioned in Carlos Alberto Montaner, *Journey to the Heart of Cuba: Life as Fidel Castro* (New York: Algora, 2001), p. 16.

25 From the mid-1970s to the end of the 1980s, over 300,000 cuban troops served abroad, and Castro provided training in Cuba to 20,000 foreigners. See Jorge I. Dominguez, "Cuba as a Superpower: Havana and Moscow, 1979," National Security Archives, *Bulletin*, www.gwu.edu/~nsarchiv/CWIHP/BULLETINS/b8-9a16.htm.

26 Testifying before a House Committee in June, 1965, Fidel's older sister, Juana Castro Ruz, said that "Fidel's feelings of hatred for this country cannot even be imagined by Americans. His intention, his obsession to destroy the U.S. is one of his main interests and objectives." Report of Committee of Un-American Activities, House of Representatives, June 1965.

27 *The Cuban Story* (New York: George Brazillier, 1961), p. 149.

28 *Ibid.*, pp. 161-162.

29 New York: Avon, 1960.

30 One of the principles of intelligence work is not to leave any isolated fact or rumor unexamined, no matter how groundless it may seem.

31 "Evil in a Rational Age," from "Thriller," in the June/July, 1985, issue of the *Idler*, a magazine published in Toronto. Reproduced in *Harper's*, October 1985, p. 17. See also Andrew Delbanco, *The Death of Satan: How Americans Have Lost Their Sense of Evil* (New York: Farrar, Straus and Giroux, 1995).

32 Ron Rosenbaum, *Explaining Hitler: The Search for the Origins of His Evil* (New York: Random House, 1998); Ian Kershaw, *Hitler, 1889-1936: Hubris* (New York: W. W. Norton, 1999); George Victor, *Hitler:*

The Pathology of Evil (Washington, D.C.: Brassey's, 1998); Fritz Redlich, *Hitler: Diagnosis of a Destructive Prophet* (New York: Oxford University Press, 1999).

33 San Francisco: El Gato Tuerto, 1986.

34 Boston: Little, Brown and Company, 1991.

35 New York: Simon and Schuster, 1992.

36 Piñera's play (trans. Jesús J. Barquet), in *Horizontes*, Ponce (P.R.), Vol 39 No. 77, 1977, pp. 132-143. According to some scholars, Piñera was writing absurd stories and plays many years before Ionesco.

37 Lately, a group of scholars, mostly American, have, wittingly of unwittingly, joined Castro in his job of avoiding the true history of his regime to be known. Most of the books written by American scholars in the last ten years about the Cuban missile crisis and the Bay of Pigs follow that pattern.

38 *Castro's Revolution: Myths and Realities* (New York: Praeger, 1962), p. 3. On April, 1999, I had the pleasure of talking to Mr. Draper over the phone. He was 88 years old and still writing.

Chapter 1: Charisma . . . and Beyond

1 *The Cuban Story* (New York: George Brazillier, 1961), p. 59. Apparently the CIA agreed with Matthews. Among the failed attempts to eliminate Castro was a plot to get his beard to fall off by having a CIA agent dust his shoes with thalium, a radioactive substance, on the ground that his success lay in his charisma and his charisma lay in his beard.

2 For studies on Castro's charisma, see Ward M. Morton, *Castro as a Charismatic Hero* (Lawrence, Kansas: Center for Latin American Studies, University of Kansas, 1965); Richard Fagen, "Charismatic Authority and the Leadership of Fidel Castro," in Bonachea and Valdés, *Cuba in Revolution* (Garden City, New York: Anchor Books, 1972); and Edward González, *Cuba Under Castro: The Limits of Charisma* (Boston: Houghton Mifflin, 1974).

However, even though the American mass media played an important role in the creation of the Castroist myth, surrounding Castro with a mysterious aura and treating him as a film star, Castro's abilities, as we will see below, cannot be explained by Wolpert's concept of "pseudo-charisma;" a false charisma artificially created by the manipulation of techniques of mass persuasion. See, Jeremiah F. Wolpert, "Toward a Sociology of Authority," in Alvin W. Gouldner, ed., *Studies in Leadership* (New York: Harper and Brothers, 1956).

3 Max Weber, *Economy and Society: An Outline of Interpretive Sociol-*

ogy, 3 vols., 4th ed., edited by Guenther Roth and Claus Wittic (New York: Irvington, 1948), Vol. I, p. 241.

4 Rudolf Sohm, *Kirchenrecht* (Leipzig: Dunker and Hombolt, 1892), vol. I, p. 26.

5 Sebastian Balfour, *Castro*, second edition (London: Longman, 1995), p. ix.

6 A possible explanation for this behavior may be that most of the Cuban people had succumbed to what scholars of hostage-taking events know as the "Stockholm syndrome"—they had identified with their captor and transferred their trust to him.

7 Louis A. Pérez, Jr., observed that, even after the difficult times of the nineties, "Fidel Castro retained considerably moral authority among vast numbers of Cubans and commanded mass support and loyalty," adding that the support was not all the result of repression. See, *Cuba: Between Reform and Revolution, second edition* (New York: Oxford University Press, 1995), pp. 396-397.

8 Francis Bacon, "Of Envy," in *The Essays of Counsels, Civil and Moral* (Oxford: 1890).

9 *Guerrilla Prince* (Boston: Little, Brown & Company, 1991).

10 *Cuba, Castro, and the United States* (Pittsburgh: University of Pittsburgh Press, 1971).

11 CIA memorandum, 8 May 1959, declassified June 1998.

12 *Fidel Castro en rompecabezas* (Madrid: Ediciones R, 1973).

13 *Eye on Cuba* (New York: Hartcourt, Brace & World, 1966), p. 103.

14 Esterline impressions in Peter Kornbluh, ed., *Bay of Pigs Declassified* (New York: The Free Press, 1998), pp. 6-7.

15 *Ibid.*, p. 7. Conference proceedings in James G. Blight and Peter Kornbluh, *Politics of Illusion: The Bay of Pigs Invasion Reexamined* (New York: Houghton Mifflin, 1965).

16 "Que el conjuro se desvanezca," in *CID*, No. 41 (November of 1988), p. 22.

17 "Fidel Castro y la locura de los números," *Ibid.*, p. 22.

18 *The Cuban Story* (New York: George Brazillier, 1961), pp. 167-168.

19 *Cuba* (New York: Macmillan, 1964), p. 105.

20 *Revolution in Cuba* (Hew York: Scribner's, 1975), p. 127.

21 Andrew Graham-Yool, *After the Despots* (London: Bloomsbury, 1991), p. 194.

22 *Mother Jones*, July-August 1989, quoted in Jacobo Timerman, *Cuba: A Journey* (New York: Alfred A. Knopf, 1990), p. 47.

23 In a study about García Márquez' literary work, Cuban writer in exile César Leante offers some interesting insights about García Márquez' irrational relationship with Castro, see *Gabriel García Márquez,*

el hechicero (Madrid: Pliegos, 1996).

24 It seems, however, that eventually Feltrinelli was put off by Castro's intolerance and virulent homophobia. The fact is revealed in Feltrinelli's recently published biography written by his son Carlo. See, Gina Montaner, "El millonario que quería revolución," *El Nuevo Herald*, May 29, 2001.

25 Andres Oppenheimer, *Castro's Final Hour* (New York: Simon & Schuster, 1992), p. 21.

26 *Op. cit.*, p. 407.

27 Tad Szulc, *Fidel: A Critical Portrait* (New York: William Morrow, 1986), p. 41.

28 *Ibid.*, p. 468.

29 David Asman, "I've been to a Marvelous Party," The *Wall Street Journal*, November 3, 1995, A-14.

30 *Time*, February 20, 1995.

31 Larry Rohter, "A Kennedy-Castro Talk Touched by History," The *New York Times*, February 19, 1996, p. A-1.

32 *Time*, October 23, 1995, p. 4.

33 *U. S. News and World Report*, April 8, 1996.

34 Myles Kantor, "Ted Turner, Moral Moron," *FrontPage* magazine, April 4, 2001.

35 David Rubinger, "Ted Turner Meets With Fidel Castro as Part of 'Courtesy Visit' to Havana," Atlanta Business Chronicle, January 9, 1998.

36 Carl Limbacher, "Jerry Brown: Castro Grooming Elián as Successor," *NewsMax.com*, July 2, 2001.

37 Ronald Radosh, "Human Rights and Foreign Policy: How to Deal with the Totalitarian Remnant," *FrontPageMagazine.com*, March 27, 2001. Radosh described the reunion as "a love fest between Castro and a group of Americans," where "As usual, the American guests quickly fell under the dictator's spell."

38 Szulc, *op. cit.*, pp. 469-70.

39 Teresa Casuso, *Cuba and Castro* (New York: Random House, 1961), p. 138.

40 Hanspeter Bürgin, "Am Heldendenkmal Fidel Castro darf nicht gekratz werden," *Tages-Anzeiger*, January 10, 1989, p. 4.

41 Szulc, *op. cit.*, p. 180.

42 *Ibid.*, p. 175.

43 *Ibid.*, p. 46.

44 *Ibid.*, p. 312.

45 Casuso quoted in Herbert Matthews, *The Cuban Story* (New York: George Brazillier, 1961), p. 146.

46 Teresa Casuso, *Cuba and Castro* (New York: Random House, 1961),

p. 138.

47 New York *Post*, May 15, 1961.

48 Geyer, *op. cit.*, p. 107.

49 *The Cuban Dilemma* (New York: Ivan Obolensky, 1962), p. 15.

50 Paul D. Bethel, *The Losers* (New Rochelle, N.Y.: Arlington House, 1969), p. 124.

51 R. Hart Phillips, *op. cit.*, p. 102.

52 *Cuba: Prophetic Island* (New York: Marzani & Munzell, 1961), p. 60.

53 Homero Campa and Orlando Pérez, *Cuba: los años duros* (Barcelona: Plaza y Janés, 1997). There is, however, another quite different version of the event. According to Dariel (Benigno) Alarcón, before Castro appeared, members of Castro's armed forces, disguised as civilians, had infiltrated the rioters. These were the ones who actually backed Castro. See *Memorias de un soldado cubano* (Barcelona: Tusquets, 1997), p. 306.

54 Oppenheimer, *op. cit.*, p. 272.

55 "The Last Revolutionary," and interview with Dan Rather, CBS, July 19, 1996.

56 Larry D. Hatfield, "Days of Darkness. Utopian Nightmare," *San Francisco Examiner*, November 8, 1998, p. 1.

57 *Granma International*, October 20, 1991.

58 Matthews, *op. cit.*, p. 152.

59 Betancourt's statement in Tad Szulc, "Exporting the Cuban Revolution," in John Plank, ed., *Cuba and the United States* (Washington, D.C.: Brookings Institution, 1967), p. 78.

60 Castro does not speak Russian, therefore, his power has nothing to do with language.

61 Aleksandr Fursenko and Timothy Naftali, *"One Hell of a Gamble"* (New York: W.W. Norton & Company, 1997), p. 39.

62 C. Wright Mills, *Listen Yankee* (New York: Ballantine, 1960), p. 102.

63 John Barron, *KGB* (London: Corgi, 1974), p. 534.

64 Eventually, Alekseev was recruited by Castro and, wittingly or unwittingly, became a double agent. The term "double agent" is used by intelligence officers with two different meanings. In its first meaning, a double agent is an agent working for an intelligence service who begins working for an enemy, rival or friendly service, both of which may be aware of the double contacts, and provides information about each service to the other. This was the case, i. e., of Panama's Jaime Noriega as an agent of both the CIA and Castro.

In its second meaning, a double agent is an agent working for an intelligence service who begins working for an enemy, rival or friendly service and provides information of one service about the other and, wittingly or unwittingly, is manipulated by one service against the other. (Also called a "turned" or "doubled" agent.) This seems to be the case of Alekseev.

65 Arkady N. Shevchenko, *Breaking with Moscow* (New York: Ballantine, 1985), p. 187.

66 Fidel Castro's letter to Nikita S. Khrushchev, October 31, 1962, Folio 3, List 65, File 907, pp. 137-137, reproduced in James G. Blight *et al.*, *Cuba on the Brink* (New York: Pantheon, 1993), pp. 489-91.

67 Szulc, *op. cit.*, p. 46.

68 Roberto Fabricio, "Las instalaciones cubanas de biotecnología 'están llenas de zonas cerradas y secretas'" *El Nuevo Herald*, June 20 1999.

69 Oppenheimer, *op. cit.*, pp. 236-237.

70 Carlos Franqui, *op. cit,*, p. 86.

71 Vladislav Zubok and Constantine Pleshakov, *Inside the Kremlin's Cold War* (Cambridge, Mass.: Harvard University Press, 1996), p. 207.

72 Philip Bonsal, *Cuba, Castro, and the United States* (Pittsburgh: University of Pittsburgh Press, 1971), pp. 283-284.

73 Rough Draft of Summary of Conversation Between Vice President and Fidel Castro, April 25, 1959.

74 *With Fidel* (New York: Ballantine, 1975), p. 9.

75 R. Hart Phillips, *op. cit.*, p. 28.

76 R. Hart Phillips, *op. cit.*, p. 30.

77 *Cuba: First Soviet Satellite in the Americas* (New York: Avon, 1961), p. 151.

78 *Family Portrait with Fidel* (New York: Random House, 1984), p. 125; see also Richard Eder, "Castro Tells Jailed Rebels He Will Suggest Clemency," the *New York Times*, 28 April 1961, p. 2.

79 Franqui, *Ibid.*, p. 79.

80 Maurice Halperin, *The Taming of Fidel Castro* (Berkeley: University of California Press, 1981), p. 136.

81 Jules Dubois, *Fidel Castro: Rebel, Liberator or Dictator?* (Indianapolis: Bobbs-Merrill, 1959), p. 145.

"82Fidel Castro y el Reino de Dios," *Bohemia*, 17 July 1960. Cepeda, however, was not the first to compare Castro to Christ. Just a few days after Castro took Havana in 1959, the American photographer Lester Cole took a photograph of an angelic, young, white, tall, bearded Fidel Castro looking at the camera full of sincerity and humility. The photo, published in some of the most important Cuban magazines, instantly became the symbol of the Christ-like aura that hung over him. A few months later, on August 30, 1959, the widely read *Bohemia* magazine published a *Playboy*-like centerfold of a drawing by Luis

Rey depicting a Christ-like Castro. The picture was an instant success, and it ended up framed and hung in a special place in many Cuban homes.

83 See Rafael A. Lara, "Fidel Castro and Cuba's Secret Societies," *Power Games*, www.inexplicata.com/samizdat/paranormal/power_games.html.

84 A few days after I wrote the above lines, and after extensive unsuccessful research trying to find the exact reference to this story, I found an internet site in Argentina which listed the index of all articles and stories appeared in the issues of *Más Allá*. According to my (45 year old) recollection, the name of the story was "El día del control total," but such title does not appear among the ones listed on the site. I have contacted the site's webmaster to see if I can get their help to find the story, but I am still waiting for an answer. Anyway, I vividly remember having read the story.

85 Luis Conte Agüero, *Fidel Castro: Psiquiatría y política* (Mexico: Editorial Jus, 1968), p. 89.

86 Dubois, *op. cit.*, p. 26. It seems, however, that what was true for Batista is not true for Castro. Castroism has brought graft and corruption, torture and death for many, but the Cuban people has never tried to overthrow him.

87 Tad Szulc, *op. cit.*, pp. 248-249.

88 *Ibid.*, pp. 252-253.

89 *Ibid.*, p. 291.

90 Dubois, *op. cit.*, p. 144.

91 Carlos Franqui, *Vida, aventuras y desastres de un hombre llamado Castro* (Barcelona: Planeta, 1988), p. 12.

92 *Ibid.*, pp. 12-13.

93 Herbert Matthews, *Fidel Castro* (New York: Simon and Schuster, 1969), pp. 166-167.

94 *Hispanic American Report*, Vol XII, No. 4, 1959, p. 205.

95 Szulc, *op. cit.*, pp. 291-292.

96 Casuso, *op.cit.*, p. 137.

97 Franqui *op. cit.*, p. 115-116.

98 Szulc, *op. cit.*, p. 33.

99 *Ibid.*, pp. 161-162.

100 Carla Anne Robbins, *The Cuban Threat* (New York: MacGraw-Hill, 1983), p. 16.

101 R. Hart Phillips, *op. cit.*, p. 138.

102 Aleksandr Fursenko and Timothy Naftali, *"One Hell of a Gamble"* (New York: W.W. Norton & Company, 1997), p. 41. On the other hand, a paranoid counter-intelligence officer (some degree of paranoia is necessary condition for becoming a counterintelligence officer) would

assume that Fidel's predictions may have not been based on clairvoyance, but on more mundane abilities, i.e., that either Castro had penetrated the American intelligence services or that they were willingly providing him with inside information.

103 *Revolución*, January 2, 1961.

104 Peter Wyden, *The Bay of Pigs* (New York: Simon and Schuster, 1979), p. 104.

105 Monike de Motas, ¿Las profecías orales también pueden cumplirse? (*CubaNet*, November 19, 1998).

106 Szulc, *op. cit.*, p. 23.

107 Casuso, *op.cit.* p. 189.

108 Szulc, *op. cit.*, p. 43.

109 *Ibid.*, pp. 46, 276.

110 *Ibid.*, p. 291. Like many others who have saved Castro's life, Pelletier ended up in Castro's jails.

111 Thomas, *Cuba: The Pursuit of Freedom* (New York: Harper and Row, 1971), pp. 916-917.

112 Ernesto Cardenal, *In Cuba* (New York: New Directions, 1974), pp. 130-131.

113 Andrés Suárez, *Cuba: Castroism and Communism, 1959-1966* (Cambridge, Mass.: The MIT Press, 1967), p. 138.

114 Szulc, *op. cit.*, 1986, 554; the story is told also in Franqui *op. cit.*, p. 401.

115 Carlos Franqui, *Family Portrait with Fidel* (New York: Random House, 1984), pp. 124-125.

116 Carlos Franqui, *Vida, aventuras y desastres de un hombre llamado Castro* (Barcelona: Planeta, 1988), p. 400.

117 "Fidel Castro visitó la universidad," *Diario de la Marina*, January 14, 1959, pp. 1, 9b.

118 Thomas, *op.cit.*, p. 817.

119 Szulc, *op. cit.*, p. 600.

120 Mark Lane, *Plausible Denial* (New York: Thunder's Mouth, 1991), p. 290.

121 Dariel (Benigno) Alarcón Ramírez, *Memorias de un soldado cubano* (Barcelona: Tusquets, 1997), pp. 284-285.

122 Due to the fact that at least some of the most known alleged attempts on Castro's life may have failed not because of his extremely good luck, but because of other reasons, I have not mentioned them. I, for one, take those Castro-CIA assassination stories with a grain of salt. And, as I will repeat over and over in this book, in the world of intelligence and espionage things are seldom as they seem.

Chapter 2: The Great Pulverizer

1 "Let's Start Talking to Castro," *U.S. News and World Report*, May 15, 1995, p. 106.

2 U.S. Senate, Committee of the Judiciary, Subcommittee to Investigate the Administration of Internal Security Act, "Castro's Network in the United States," Hearing, 88th Congress, First Session, Part 6, February 8, 1963.

3 *Che Guevara* (New York: Grove Press, 1997), p. 545.

4 *Verde Olivo*, December 22, 1968. An interesting detail is that, though Guevara wrote the editorial in 1962, it was not published until 1968, when the Cuban-Soviet differences over armed struggle had finally come out in the open.

5 Servando González, "Bomba y Paranoia," *Observando*, Segunda Edición (San Francisco: El Gato Tuerto, 1986), pp. 53-54.

6 An unexpected outcome of the end of the Cold War is that the liars from both sides (that is, intelligence officers) have joined efforts with a group of naïve (or compromised) scholars to disinform the public. Among these disinformation efforts are the claims that nuclear warheads were actually in the Island, and that more were bound for Cuba in Soviet ships.

But CIA reports at the time consistently denied the presence of nuclear warheads in Cuba. Also, American planes, flying low over the missile sites and Soviet ships, never detected any of the radiation that would be expected to emanate from nuclear warheads.

The main force behind a concerted effort to prove that nuclear warheads were in Cuba is Robert Strange McNamara, a known CIA foe (according to declassified documents, the CIA never found proof of the presence of nuclear warheads on the island), whose main goal has been to justify his absurd—or criminal—policies as Secretary of Defense during the Kennedy administration and later. Recently, McNamara has found support for his theories from none other than his former executive action target, Fidel Castro, and from a group of Russians, among them, Sergei Mikoyan, an old KGB hand, and Aleksandr Alekseev, a KGB officer who, wittingly or unwittingly, was recruited as a double agent by Castro.

It is very difficult to believe, however, that nuclear warheads were on Cuban soil, and even more incredible that Russian officers in Cuba had been authorized to use them without further consultation with Moscow. Such an action would have been tantamount to mass suicide, since a single nuclear warhead fired by Russian troops in Cuba would had been equivalent to a declaration of nuclear war between the United States and the Soviet Union and would have brought a devastating nuclear salvo against the Soviet Union. One must bear in mind, however, that McNamara, Castro, and the ex-KGB operatives who have been trying to pass this disinformation are very questionable sources of intelligence. (See Appendix 3)

The problem some people have with accepting the fact that there were no nuclear warheads on Cuban soil, or on their way to the island, is that it blows away all the grand theories developed and supported by the American establishment and tacitly accepted by the ex-Soviets. As CIA's legendary chief of counterintelligence James Jesus Angleton used to say, "The past telescopes into the present."

For a fascinating and extremely well annotated transcription of the discussions this group of professional liars (I am not using here the word "liars" in a pejorative sense, but only to indicate that, as expected from seasoned intelligence professionals, lying and disinformation are essential aspects of their trade and their professional training) held in Havana in January 1992, see James G. Blight, Bruce J. Allyn and David A. Welch, *Cuba on the Brink: Castro, the Missile Crisis, and the Soviet Collapse* (New York: Pantheon, 1993). For probably one of the most foolish rendering of the events leading to the crisis, written by two authors totally ignorant of both espionage and Cuban affairs, see Aleksandr Fursenko and Timothy Naftali, *"One Hell of a Gamble"* (New York: W. W. Norton, 1997). For a strong, well documented criticism of Blight and Welch's views on the crisis see Mark Kramer, "Tactical Nuclear Weapons, Soviet Command Authority, and the Cuban Missile Crisis," *Cold War International History Project Bulletin* 3 (Fall 1993). The Cuban missile crisis will be the subject of my forthcoming book: *The Nuclear Deception: Nikita Khrushchev and the Cuban Missile Crisis.*

7 *Granma Weekly Review*, December 22, 1963.

8 Andrés Suárez, *Cuba: Castroism and Communism, 1959-66* (Boston: MIT Press, 1967), p. 94.

9 *Le Monde*, November 24, 1997; also in "Castro Fond of Missiles," *AP* report, August 16, 1997.

10 *Le Monde*, November 24, 1997.

11 For a controversial analysis of the missiles in Cuba see Servando González, "A Missile is a Missile is a Missile," *Sumeria*, http://www.sumeria.net/politics/amissile.html. See also, Servando González, "Thirteen Lies (and Perhaps a Single Truth)," *LewRockwell.com*, http://www.lewrockwell.com/orig/gonzalez1.html.

12 *Ibid.*

13 U.S. Senate, Committee on Foreign Relations, "Cuban Realities: May 1975," a Report by Senator George S. McGovern to the Committee on Foreign Relations, August 1975, p. 14.

14 Dino A. Brugioni, *Eyeball To Eyeball* (New York: Random House, 1991), p. 461. Castro's letter to Khrushchev of October 26 is part of a set of documents obtained by the Cold War International History Project, Woodrow Wilson International Center, Harvard Collection.

15 Andrew Tully, *White Tie and Dagger* (New York: Pocket Books, 1968), pp. 74-78. Tully mistakenly believes the plot was a Soviet idea, but it was Castro's. The plot is also reported in Andres Oppenheimer, *Castro's Final Hour* (New York: Simon and Schuster, 1992).

16 Daniel Ellsberg, "The Day Castro Almost Started World War III," The *New York Times*, October 31, 1987, p. A7.

17 Dino A. Brugioni, *op. cit.*, pp. 462, 463.

18 Franqui, *Family Portrait With Fidel* (New York: Vintage, 1984), p. 193.

19 Seymour Hersh, "Was Castro Out of Control in 1962?" in the *Washington Post*, October 11, 1987; Adrián Montoro, "Moscow Was Caught Between Cuba and U.S.," the *New York Times*, November 17, 1987; Rodríguez Menier in personal communication to the author, December 20, 1994. Menier claims he heard the story from Gen. José Abrahantes.

20 James Blight and David Welch, *On the Brink* (New York: Hill and Wang, 1989), p. 56.

21 The messages exchanged between Castro and Khrushchev were published by the Cuban government in 1990 and copies of them exist at the Kennedy Library. Soviet sources have verified the accuracy of the messages.

22 *Cuba* (New York: Macmillan, 1964), p. 105.

23 Andrés Suárez, *Cuba: Castroism and Communism, 1959-66* (Boston: MIT Press, 1967), p. 144.

24 *Granma Weekly Review*, May 21, 1967.

25 *Granma*, May 14, 1968, p. 4.

26 Fidel Castro "Cuba no firma desnuclearización mientras E.U. sea una amenaza atómica," *Revolución*, August 27, 1965, pp. 1-2.

27 Juan Vivés, *Los amos de Cuba* (Buenos Aires: Emecé Editores, 1982), pp. 181-182.

28 Ernesto Betancourt, *"Is Castro Planning a Preemptive Strike Against the U.S.?"* (Washington, D.C., 1996), p. 4.

29 Jeanne Kirkpatrick, "Is a stubborn Castro testing U.S. defenses?," the *Miami Herald*, March 31, 1991, p. 3C.

30 Joseph B. Treaster, "Defecting General Says Cuba Has Plan to Raid Base in the U.S. if It Is Attacked," the *New York Times*, October 11, 1987.

31 Frank Gaffney, Jr., "With Help From Russia, Cuba Poses Nuclear Threat," *Insight*, December 14, 1995, p. 20.

32 "Lessons of the Next Nuclear War," *Foreign Affairs*, Vol. 74, No. 2 (March/April 1995), p. 308.

33 *La Isla: Cuba y los cubanos hoy, (segunda edición)* (México, D.F.: Editorial Abril, 1978), p. 169, (emphasis added).

34 Castro's *CBS* interview with Dan Rather published in *Granma*, October 7, 1979.

35 *Cuba por dentro* (Miami: Ediciones Universal, 1994), pp. 84, 150.

36 Joseph Barron, "Castro, Cocaine and the A-Bomb Connection," *Reader's Digest*, March 1990, pp. 69-70.

37 For an interesting compilation of articles that appeared in the American press about the subject, see The Cuban-American National Foundation, *Castro's Narcotics Trade* (Washington, D.C.: The Cuban-American Foundation, Inc., 1983).

38 Eric Ehrmann, "Cuba's Nuclear Safety Struggle," the *Journal of Commerce*, July 5, 1991.

39 Eric Ehrmann, "Cuba Joins Nuclear Renegades," *The Journal of Commerce*, November 26, 1991.

40 Thomas F. Berg, "Cuban Nuclear Plant Assailed for Safety Flaws," *Public Utilities Fortnightly*, July 15, 1991, p. 32.

41 Bennet Ramberg, "Learning From Chernobyl," *Foreign Affairs*, Vol. 65, No. 2 (Winter 1986-87), p. 304.

42 *Ibid.*, p. 308.

43 *Ibid.*, p. 311.

44 Frank Gaffney, Jr., *op. cit.*, p. 21.

45 Associated Press release, "Nuclear power in Cuba makes experts uneasy," *The Times Picayune*, May 29, 1991, p. B-8.

46 Juan Oro quoted in *ibid.*

47 *Granma International*, October 20, 1991.

48 Andres Oppenheimer, *Castro's Final Hour*. (New York: Simon and Schuster, 1992), pp. 399-400.

49 *Ibid.*

50 Following a Cuban usage in Spanish, I have capitalized the word *Island* when it stands for Cuba.

51 "Running Against Fidel," *Newsweek*, March 9, 1992.

52 Alina Fernández, *Castro's Daughter* (New York: St. Martin's Press, 1998), p. 194.

53 "Tunnel Vision," *Newsweek*, February 24, 1992, p. 4.

54 Oppenheimer, *op. cit*, p. 20.

55 "Running Against Fidel," *Newsweek*, March 9, 1992.

56 For a revealing view of how Cuba is currently sinking fast into the corrupt sociolist world, see Chapter 5, Fidel's Sociolism.

57 Jim Hampton, "Is Castro ready to attack Florida?," the *Miami Herald*, March 24, 1996.

58 A few days after Castro ordered the detention of his close friend and Interior Minister José Abrahantes, rumors ran that the true reason was because Abrahantes was conspiring to overthrow Castro. According to the rumors Castro had found that Abrahantes was keeping a heavily guarded, secret warehouse full of U.S. Army uniforms and American-made infantry weapons. It doesn't make sense, however, that Castro ignored the existence of the warehouse. Therefore, a more likely explanation would be that the uniforms and weapons were to be used by Castro's English speaking infiltration teams in the event of a Cuban attack on the U.S.

59 Manuel Cereijo, "Castro: A Threat to the Security of the United States," InfoNewsAg@aol.com, 11 April 1999.

60 American black leaders has been highly successful in hiding Castro's racism from the American black masses. (See Chapter 6)

61 Rufo López Fresquet, *My 14 Months With Castro* (New York: World Publishing Co., 1966), p. 187.

62 "What Castro Still Needs Is a Good Fight," The *New York Times*, March 3, 1996, p. E-5.

63 Jarvis Tyner, "Fidel Castro cheered at Harlem meeting," *People's Week World*, October 28, 1996 [on the Internet], (emphasis added).

64 *The Fourth Floor* (New York, Random House, 1962), p. 29.

65 It seems that in his Strangelovian affection for the bomb Fidel Castro found a twin soul in some Amerrican politicians. On December 9, 1982, the U.N. General Assembly voted on three resolutions concerning the nuclear issue. Two of them would ban testing nuclear weapons. The U.S. opposed both of them. See Eric Pace, "U.N., in 3 Votes, Asks Ban on Nuclear Arms Tests," the *New York Times*, December 10, 1982.

One of the most disturbing aspects of the U.S. as a superpower is its insistence in being the major stockpiler of nuclear weapons. It is believed that the U.S. keeps between 12,000 to 15,000 nuclear devices of different types, from small megatonnage back-pack bombs to large, several megaton warheads. In December 1977 the U.S. declared again that nuclear weapons would remain the cornerstone of its defense policy, with nuclear weapons on permanent alert. The U.S. will also retain the option of first use and massive retaliation against threats of chemical and biochemical weapons. This attitude goes against the Nuclear Non-Proliferation Treaty of 1970, to which the U.S. is a party, requiring that nuclear powers "pursue negotiations in good faith on effective measures relating to cessation of the nuclear arms race at an early date and to nuclear disarmament, and on a treaty on general and complete disarmament under strict and effective international control."

However, instead of beginning disarmament negotiations with other nuclear powers, the U.S. has consistently pursued negotiations for a comprehensive test ban treaty, whose main goal is to prevent other nations from developing nuclear weapons. During a meeting of the Non-Proliferation Treaty Preparatory Committee, held at Geneva, Switzerland, in May 1998, the U.S. blocked a proposal to discuss nuclear disarmament. It was after that action that India decided to test nuclear weapons.

As a superpower, the United States has consistently attempted to deny other nations access to nuclear weapons while continuing tests as part of a program involved in the design of new nuclear weapons. In 1998 the U.S. Congress appropriated $4.5 billion to pay for this program. Writing in the November-December issue of the *Bulletin of the Atomic Scientists*, William Arkin asserted that "a wide variety of new nuclear weapons are under development in the United States . . . in a secret mode."

This behavior presents some dangerous risks. One of them is that it encourages American enemies like Castro to develop other terrorist weapons, like chemical and biological ones. The most dangerous aspect for the U.S., however, is not physical, but ethical and moral. As Jonathan Schell put it in the February 2, 1999, issue of *The Nation*, "Rudimentary moral principle taught that we must never, even in 'retaliation,' threaten to kill millions of innocent people, but nuclear strategy required us to do so. Common sense rebelled against offering up every person in our country as a hostage to a hostile power and seizing every person on the territory of that power as a counter-hostage, meanwhile placing the whole arrangement on a hairtrigger."

66 Charles Krauthammer, "How to deal with Countries Gone Mad," *Time*, September 21, 1987, p. 82. In a recent article she wrote for the *National Review* ("Target America," February 22, 1999, pp. 28), Jeane Kirkpatrick calls them "rogue states." Of course, she includes Cuba among them.

67 On the night of 9-10 March 300 American B-29s dropped several tons of incendiary bombs on Tokyo, killing 83,000 and injuring 102,000. Paul Johnson, *Modern Times* (New York: Harper and Row, 1983), pp. 403-404. Moreover, it seems that, like Castro, some American politicians have never renounced their "right" to pulverize other people. See, i.e., William Drozdiak, "U.S. Bomber 'Pulverizes' Serbian Troops. Hundreds Killed in Raid, Sources Say," the *San Francisco Chronicle*, June 19, 1999, p. A8.

68 Herbert Matthews, *The Cuban Story* (New York: George Brazillier, 1961), p. 172.

69 Georgie Anne Geyer, "Anti-Reforms are evidence the Cuban

revolution is over," *Mobile Press Register*, June 6, 1994, 13-A.

70 Jesús Conte Agüero, *Fidel Castro: Psiquiatría y Política* (Mexico, D.F.,: Editorial Jus, 1968), p. 105.

71 Report of the Committee of Un-American Activities, House of Representatives, June 1965.

72 *Fidel Castro y la revolución cubana* (Madrid: Playor, 1983), p. 117.

73 *Vida, aventuras y desastres de un hombre llamado Castro* (Barcelona: Planeta, 1988), pp. 82-83.

74 The possibility that Castro fired his son because of his failure to produce a nuclear device was suggested by Juan Antonio Rodríguez Menier in private communication with the author, August, 1996. Also, José Fernández González reports that Baudilio Castellanos told him that Fidelito told his father he wanted to quit because the whole plan was crazy. See, *Cuba: del socialismo al fascismo* (San Juan, P.R.: First Book Publishing, 1996), p. 166. Apparently Castro got mad and fired Fidelito.

75 According to a source, "Castro initiated his chemical-weapons program in 1981 when Soviet technicians built a plant to produce tricothecen, the main component of 'yellow rain,' in an underground tunnel complex at Quimonor in Matanzas province." see Martin Arostegui, "Fidel Castro's Deadly Secret: Five BioChem Warfare Labs," *Insight*, July 20, 1998.

76 Jonathan T. Stride, "Who Will Check Out Fidel Castro's New Chemical/Biological Weapons Plant in East Havana?," (*CubaNews*, 18 January 1999, via Internet).

77 (New York: Random House, 1999).

78 Juan O. Tamayo, "U.S. skeptical of report on Cuban biological weapons," *The Miami Herald*, June 23, 1999.

79 *Ibid*.

80 Roberto Fabricio, "Ex oficial cubano confirma la posesión de armas bacteriológicas," *El Nuevo Herald*, 12 July, 1999.

81 *Ibid*.

82 Roberto Fabricio, "Tiene visos de verdad la novela sobre un arma bacteriológica de Cuba contra EU," *El Nuevo Herald*, 21 June 1999.

83 The fact perhaps explains why Castro didn't object to Russian President Vladimir Putin's suggestion to stop working on the Juraguá plant. See EFE Agency, "Castro desiste de completar el reactor nuclear de Juraguá," *El Nuevo Herald*, December 19, 2000.

84 Jeanne McDarmott, *The Killing Fields* (New York: Arbor House, 1987), pp. 155-156, 245.

85 As a matter of fact, Castro has a strong justification for doing so. It is known that in 1962 a CIA officer acting under cover asked James Donovan, an attorney who was negotiating with Castro the release of the Bay of Pigs prisoners, to deliver a diving suit to Castro as a present.

Unknown to Donovan, the CIA had contaminated the suit with a deadly fungus and a pathogenic bacillus. The plot failed when Donovan, probably smelling a rat, bought himself a diving suit and gave it to Castro as a genuine present. See Technical Services Division: Church Committee, *Interim Report*.

86 Because it cannot distinguish between combatants and non-combatants, all biological warfare is, by definition, unethical. Political leaders should keep in mind that any country involved in the creation of bacteriological warfare agents becomes itself fair game for biological warfare attacks.

87 Some scientists fear the possibility that the smallpox virus can be resurrected as a biological weapon, and this is a motive of concern at some levels of the U.S. government. Smallpox was eradicated since 1979, therefore vaccination against it was not considered necessary any more and labs stopped producing the vaccine. Because the smallpox virus is highly contagious, a small amount released in heavily populated areas in the U.S. would be sufficient to kill millions of Americans. See John Grauerholz, "A New Defense For an Old Enemy," *Insight*, November 13, 2000, p. 25.

88 See Martin Butcher and Theresa Hitchens, "Unleashing 'Mini-Nukes' Will Bring Dire Consequences," the *San Francisco Chronicle*, September 21, 2000, p. A-27.

89 See Chalmers Johnson, "When Might Makes Wrong," the *San Francisco Chronicle*, October 8, 2000, p. 6-1. On Castro's willingness to continue using land mines see France Press Agency, "Castro la emprende contra Jean Chrétien," *El Nuevo Herald*, April 27, 2001.

Chapter 3: Castro's Manifest Destiny

1 Fidel Castro, *La revolución cubana*, selection, Prologue, and notes by Gregorio Selser (Buenos Aires: Palestra, 1967), pp. 427 ff.

2 *Look*, November 1960.

3 Typical of this approach is, i. e., Lynn Darrell Bender's *The Politics of Hostility: Castro's Revolution and United States Policy* (Hato Rey, P. R.: Inter American University Press, 1975).

4 Victor Lasky, *JFK: The Man and the Myth* (New Rochelle, N.Y.: Arlington House, 1965), p. 447.

5 The fact was noticed by Mark Falcoff. See his "How to Think about Cuban-American Relations," in Irving Louis Horowitz, (ed.), *Cuban Communism, Fifth Edition* (New Brunswick, N.J.: Transaction Books, 1984), p. 543. While keeping the essence of his analysis, I have slightly modified the way he expressed it.

6 *Castro's Revolution: Myths and Realities* (New York, Praeger, 1962), p. 105.

7 For an interesting analysis of how struggling groups actually *need* enemies, see Lewis A. Coser, *The Functions of Social Conflict* (New York: The Free Press, 1956), pp. 104-110.

8 *Hoy*, January 6, 1959.

9 *Ibid.*, p. 122.

10 Daniel James, *Cuba: First Soviet Satellite in the Americas* (New York: Avon, 1961), p. 123.

11 *Ibid.*, pp. 125-126.

12 Lowry Nelson, *Cuba: The Measure of a Revolution* (Minneapolis: University of Minnesota Press, 1972), pp. 33-34.

13 Lionel Martin, *The Early Fidel: Roots of Castro's Communism* (Seacaucus, N.J.: Lyle Stuart, 1978), pp. 209-210.

14 Daniel James, *op. cit.*, p. 265.

15 Castro warning the United States in Samuel Shapiro, "Cuba: A Dissenting Report," *The New Republic*, september 12, 1960, p. 11.

16 R. Hart Phillips, *The Cuban Dilemma* (New York: Ivan Obolensky, 1962), p. 28; also in *Time*, January 19, 1959.

17 Fermín Peinado, *Beware Yankee: The Revolution in Cuba* (Miami: [n. e.], 1964), p. 35.

18 For a detailed account of the Castro-Betancourt meeting see Jay Mallin, *Fortress Cuba* (Chicago: Henry Regnery, 1965), pp. 73-74; also Hugh Thomas, *Cuba: The Pursuit of Freedom* (New York: Harper & Row, 1971), p. 1090; and Paul D. Bethel, *The Losers* (New Rochelle, N.Y.: Arlington House, 1969), pp. 132-133. Also, Betancourt himself talks about the incident at length in an article he published in *The Reporter* on August 13, 1964, and filled out the information about the loan in an article in *Cuadernos* (Paris), December 1964.

19 Herbert Matthews, *Fidel Castro* (New York: Simon and Schuster, 1969), p. 200.

20 Paul D. Bethel, *The Losers* (New Rochelle, N.Y.: Arlington House, 1969), p. 131. Some years later, an unknown variant of the FN/FAL assault rifle with a hole in its side appeared in service with some anti-government guerrillas in El Salvador. The hole, slightly larger than a 25-cent piece, had been cut through the right side of the upper receiver's magazine well. A close analysis revealed that its only purpose was removing the Cuban coat-of-arms marked underneath with the legend: *Ejército de Cuba* (Cuban Army). Unfortunately, Castro's gun experts forgot to remove the serial numbers. Reference to holes in Cuban rifles in Peter G. Kokalis, "The Cuban Connection," *Soldier of Fortune*, September 1983, p. 66.

21 Adolf A. Berle, Jr., "The Cuban Crisis," *Foreign Affairs*, Vol. 39,

No. I (October, 1960), pp. 44-45; see also Hugh Thomas, *Cuba: The Pursuit of Freedom* (New York: Harper & Row, 1971), p. 1204.

22 Adolf A. Berle, Jr., *op. cit.*, p. 47.

23 Daniel James, "Castro Unmasked," *Global Affairs* 2 (Summer 1987), 168-69.

24 *Revolución*, July 27, 1960.

25 *What Happened in Cuba* (New York: Twayne, 1963), p. 182.

26 Lowry Nelson, *Cuba: The Measure of a Revolution* (Minneapolis: University of Minnesota Press, 1972), p. 22.

27 Frei Betto, *Fidel and Religion* (New York: Simon and Schuster, 1987), pp. 91-153; see also Servando González, "¿Milagro en La Habana?", *Mariel*, Año 1, Vol. 4, 1988.

28 Erich Fromm, *May Man Prevail?* (New York: Anchor, 1961), p. 21.

29 The *New York Times*, April 21, 1959.

30 CIA officer visiting Castro at the Sierra Maestra in Mario Lazo, *Dagger in the Heart* (New York: Twin Circle, 1968), p. 248.

31 R. Hart Phillips, *op. cit.*, p. 15, 23.

32 José Domingo Cabús, *Castro ante la historia* (Mexico, D.F.: Editores Mexicanos Unidos, 1963), p. 25.

33 Carlos Franqui, *Vida, aventuras y desastres de un hombre llamado Castro* (Barcelona: Planeta, 1988), p. 36.

34 Daniel James, *op. cit.*, p. 82.

35 R. Hart Phillips, *op. cit.*, pp. 132-133. There is the possibility, however, that del Pino's alleged treason was not the only reason why Castro wanted him to rote in a Cuban jail. Perhaps del Pino knew too much about Castro's true role in the Bogotazo.

36 Paul D. Bethel, *The Losers* (New Rochelle, N.Y.: Arlington House, 1969), pp. 226-229; also in Luis Conte Agüero, *Fidel Castro: Psiquiatría y Política* (Mexico, D.F.: Editorial Jus, 1968), p. 104; and in Ruby H. Phillips, *op.cit.*, pp. 181-182.

37 Paul D. Bethel, *op.cit.*, p. 231.

38 Ruby H. Phillips, *op.cit.*, p. 260.

39 *Ibid.*, p. 260. Planes have been the vehicle of choice for Castro's self-provocation exercises. I heard in Havana some years ago an interesting rumor about the Cubana de Aviación airliner allegedly sabotaged by anti-Castro terrorist Luis Posada Carriles in 1973, killing all people on board, including the Cuban Olympic fencing team. According to the rumor, Beatriz Márquez, a Cuban singer in vogue at the time, was on a tour in Venezuela and was scheduled to fly back to Cuba in that plane. But, at the very last moment, she allegedly changed her mind and decided to cancel her flight. The plane took off with the rest of the passengers and was blown out of the sky. Everybody aboard

the plane died. Beatriz Márquez was very lucky, and her last moment decision saved her from a sure death.

But Beatriz Márquez was probably not only lucky. Her husband was a senior officer of Fidel Castro's personal security team, and she had very good contacts at the highest levels of the Castro government. Some people in Cuba believe that, though the Castro government perhaps was not directly involved in the terrorist action, they knew the plane was doomed, and they saved Ms. Márquez' life. The rest of the people in the plane, including the team of young Olympic fencers, were expendable. Revolutions need martyrs, and Castro has never been shy in committing terrorist actions in order to provide martyrs for his revolution.

40 *Granma Weekly Review*, May 2, 1971. Also, Editorial, "No Ping-Pong for Castro," *The New York Times*, April 21, 1971.

41 "Toward Improved United States-Cuban Relations," a report of a special study mission to Cuba, printed for the use of the Committee on International Relations, May 23, 1977, p. 63.

42 See David Rieff, "Cuba Refrozen," *Foreign Affairs*, July/August 1996, pp. 62-76.

43 See Ellis Cose, "Castro no cede un ápice. Fidel no le ve mucho valor a una iniciativa de EEUU," *Newsweek en Español*, January 20, 1999, p. 17. See also, AFP, "El régimen castrista rechaza las medidas de EEUU para flexibilizar el embargo," *La Razón*, January 10, 1999.

Chapter 4: A Caribbean Magnicide

1 Leo Janos, the *Atlantic*, June 1973.

2 The Washington *Star*, June 25, 1976.

3 Michael R. Beschloss, *Taking Charge: The Johnson White House Tapes, 1963-1964* (New York, Simon and Schuster, 1997).

4 The *Washington Post*, July 27, 1975; see also G. Robert Blakey and Richard N. Billings, *The Plot to Kill the President*. (New York: Times Books, 1981), p. 140.

5 Daniel Schorr, "The Assassins," the *New York Review of Books*, October 13, 1977.

6 The *Washington Post*, November 25, 1983; also in G. Robert Blakey and Richard N. Billings, *op. cit.*, pp. 137, 176.

7 See, i.e., Norberto Fuentes, *Dulces guerreros cubanos* (Barcelona: Seix Barral, 1999), p. 275.

8 Anthony Summers, *Conspiracy* (New York: McGraw-Hills, 1980), p. 441.

9 *Human Events*, 24 July, 1979, pp. 13-15.

10 *Alleged Assassination Plots Involving Foreign Leaders,* U.S. Senate, November 20, 1975, 94th Congress, 1st Session, pp. 86-90.

11 Edward Jay Epstein, "Sixty Versions of the Kennedy Assassination," in Harold Haynes (ed.), *Smiling Through the Apocalypse* (New York: McCall, 1969), p. 486.

12 *Who Killed President Kennedy?* (Moscow: Terra Publishing House, 1991).

13 Michael Parentis, *Dirty Truths* (San Francisco: City Lights, 1996), p. 158.

14 U.S. Senate Select Committee to Study Governmental Operations with Respect to Intelligence Activities, *Final Report, Book Five, The Investigation of the Assassination of President John F. Kennedy: Performance of the Intelligence Agencies,* 94th Congress, 2nd sess., 1976, pp. 4, 60.

15 My personal opinion is that their fears were totally unfounded. Had the U.S. proved beyond any reasonable doubt that Castro had been involved in the Kennedy assassination, the Soviets either would have remained silent, or would have joined the Americans in their condemnation. There is the possibility, however that the alleged fears were actually a cover to avoid a thorough investigation of the Castro connection which may have brought up very damaging information about some people in the CIA and other branches of the American government.

16 As it is difficult to understand the American liberals' love for Fidel Castro, it is also difficult to understand their love for John F. Kennedy. It was Kennedy who invented the non-existent missile gap to boost the fortunes of the military-industrial-academic complex. He was personally involved in political assassination. He created the Green Berets and introduced the dirty game of counterinsurgency. Camelot, Kennedy's bright and shining moment, was a post-mortem concoction of Theodore H. White and Jacqueline Kennedy. Actually, the bright and shining moment never existed. It was a fiction. Far from being a liberal, Kennedy was a very conservative and even reactionary individual.

17 See, i.e., Peter Kornbluh and James Blight, "Our Secret Dialogue With Castro: A Hidden History," *The New York Times Review of Books,* October 6, 1994. For a detailed account of how this alleged accommodation never took place see Carlos Ripoll, "Kennedy y Castro: el abrazo imposible," www.eddosrios.org/obras/politica/kennedy.htm.

18 *Cigar Aficionado,* September-October, 1999.

19 Ted Sorensen, *Kennedy* (New York: Bantam, 1965), p. 814.

20 Ronald Kessler, *Inside the CIA* (New York: Pocket Books, 1992), p. 53.

21 *Ibid.*, p. 83.

22 U.S. House of Representatives, 95th Congress, 2nd. sess., Appendix to Hearings Before the Select Committee on Assassinations, *Anti-Castro Activities and Organizations*, Washington, D.C., Vol. X, March 1979, p. 11.

23 Sorensen, *op. cit.*, p. 802.

24 *Cuba and Castro* (New York: Random House, 1961), p. 187.

25 *Revolution in Cuba* (New York: Scribner's, 1975), pp. 114, 409.

26 "When Castro Heard the News," The *New Republic*, Vol, 149, No. 23 (December 7, 1963), pp. 7-9.

27 Castro's *l'Express* interview with Daniel in Thomas G. Buchanan, *Who Killed Kennedy?* (New York: MacFadden, 1965), pp. 15-16.

28 Frank Mankiewicz and Kirby Jones, *With Fidel* (New York: Ballantine, 1975), pp. 140-148.

29 Robert Sam Anson, *"They've Killed the President!"* (New York: Bantam, 1975), pp. 264-265.

30 Blakey and Billings, *op. cit.*, pp. 145-146.

31 Speech to the U.N. General Assembly, September 26, 1960, reproduced in Martin Kenner and James Petras, eds., *Fidel Castro Speaks* (New York: Grove Press, 1969), p. 30.

32 Edmond Paris, *The Secret History of the Jesuits* (Chino, California: Chick Publications, 1975), p. 65.

33 H. Boehmer, *Les Jesuits*. (Paris: Armand Collin, 1910), pp. 238-241.

34 Fidel Castro, *History Will Absolve Me* (New York: Center for Cuban Studies, n. d.), p. 62

35 Hugh Thomas, *Cuba: The Pursuit of Freedom* (New York: Harper & Row, 1971), p. 819.

36 Carlos Franqui, *Vida, aventuras y desastres de un hombre llamado Castro* (Barcelona: Planeta, 1988), pp. 69-70; see also Georgie Annie Geyer, *Guerrilla Prince* (Boston: Little, Brown and Company, 1991), p. 49.

37 Thomas, *op. cit.*, p. 812.

38 *Ibid.*, p. 814.

39 Mario Lazo, *Dagger in the Heart* (New York: Twin Circle 1968), p. 144; also in Jules Dubois, *Fidel Castro* (New York: Bobbs-Merrill, 1959), pp. 19-23.

40 Franqui, *op. cit.*, p. 12.

41 Tad Szulc, *Fidel: A Critical Portrait* (New York: William Morrow, 1986), p. 191.

42 José Domingo Cabús, *Castro ante la historia* (Mexico, D.F.: Editores Mexicanos Unidos, 1963), pp. 133-135.

43 Herbert Matthews, *Revolution in Cuba* (New York: Scribner's,

1975), p. 89.

44 Tad Szulc, "Exporting the Cuban Revolution," in John Plank, ed., *Cuba and the United States* (Washington, D.C.: Brookings Institution, 1967), p. 79.

45 Richard Gott, *Guerrilla Movements in Latin America* (New York: Anchor Books, 1972), p. 13.

46 *Hoy*, June 16 and 17, 1959.

47 Andrés Suárez, *Cuba: Castroism and Communism, 1959-66* (Boston: MIT Press, 1967), p. 68.

48 Mario Lazo, *op. cit.*, p. 195.

49 Geoffrey Warner, "Latin America," in Geoffrey Barraclough, ed., *Survey of International Affairs 1959-1960* (London: Oxford University Press, 1964), pp. 478-479.

50 Quoted in Andrés Suárez, *op. cit.*, p. 94.

51 FBI report of agent William Stevens, File # 105-655, 24 October 1962, in Gus Russo, *Live by the Sword* (Baltimore: Bancroft Press, 1998), p. 223.

52 "Communist Activities in Latin America," *Report of the Subcommittee on Inter-American Affairs*, U. S. House of Representatives Committee on Foreign Affairs (July 1967), p. 7.

53 Paul D. Bethel, *The Losers* (New Rochelle, N.Y.: Arlington House,1969), pp. 424-425.

54 Recently surfaced confidential information from secret sources in Cuba seem to confirm their claims. Apparently, the notorious Ilich Sánchez Ramírez (aka "Carlos" and "the Jackal") was one of Fidel's hit men, and had an active role in the assassination of Somoza. When Carlos had his operations center in Paris in the 1960s, he received Cuban logistic and economic support. His Cuban handler was Armando Pérez Orta, an officer of the Cuban intelligence services operating under the pseudonym "Archimedes."

55 Daniel James, *Cuba: The First Soviet Satellite in the Americas* (New York: Avon, 1961), pp. 32-33; also in Nathaniel Weyl, *Red Star Over Cuba* (New York : Hillman/MacFadden, 1961), pp. 57-60, 64-65. Like Hillary Rotham and Bill Clinton, Castro is very good at concealing and destroying evidence.

56 *Los dos rostros de Fidel Castro* (Mexico, D. F.: Editorial Jus, 1960), p. 222.

57 *Ibid.*, p. 227.

58 Andrés Suárez, *op. cit.*, 14.

59 Ernst Halperin, "Castroism—Challenge to Latin American Communism," *Problems of Communism*, Vol. XII, No. 5 (September-October 1963).

60 Robert Taber, *M-26: Biography of a Revolution* (New York, Lyle

Stuart, 1961), p. 187. In a recent book, *Dulces guerreros cubanos* (Barcelona: Seix Barral, 1999), Cuban writer Norberto Fuentes deals in detail with aspects of the military career of Colonel Tony de la Guardia, probably the best of Castro's hit men who ended up facing a firing squad. But, while he was still Castro's hit man, he boasted of having assassinated, following Castro's direct orders, more than forty of Fidel's real and imagined enemies, mostly abroad, some of them in the U.S.

61 José D. Cabús, *Castro ante la historia* (Mexico: Editores Mexicanos Unidos, 1963), pp. 24-25.

62 Rufo López Fresquet, *My 14 Months with Castro* (Cleveland, Ohio: World Publishing, Co., 1966), p. 66; see also Manuel Urrutia Lleó, *Fidel Castro and Company, Inc.* (New York: Praeger, 1964), pp. 80-82.

63 *Memorias de un soldado cubano. Vida y muerte de la Revolución* (Barcelona: Tusquets, 1997).

64 Piñeiro attended Columbia University from 1953 to 1955, where he met Lorna Nell Bursdall, a professional dancer. They got married in June 1955. After Castro's take over in 1959 Piñeiro was appointed Deputy Minister of the Ministerio del Interior and chief of its DGI. In 1966 he took training courses in the secret arts in the Soviet Union. As chief of the America Department he had total control over the Cuban Ministry of Foreign Relations, which acted more as a cover for intelligence operations than as a true ministry in charge of diplomacy. In the 1970s Piñeiro was instrumental in the creation of a clandestine printing shop in Panama for the production of counterfeit American dollars. He was the one who, in August 23, 1985, planned the theft of a Wells Fargo truck in West Hartford, Connecticut, by the Puerto Rican group Los Macheteros, where 7 million dollars were stolen. Most of the money found its way to Cuba. Piñeiro had direct participation in drug trafficking operations against the U.S.

65 *The Miami Herald*, October 23, 1975. Like many friends of Castro, Carbonell ended up in prison.

66 "Desde la Isla. Tropa de choque." *El Nuevo Herald*, 29 August 1999. (emphasis added).

67 *Ibid.*, (emphasis added).

68 "El tratamiento búlgaro" in *El Nuevo Herald*, December 28, 1997.

69 *Ibid.* Since the technology for artificially inducing prostate cancer is cheap and easily available, a paranoid counterintelligence officer will see with extreme suspicion the sudden discovery of the disease on a previously healthy person, particularly if that person was a mayor obstacle in the advancement of the political career of an unscrupulous individual.

70 *Ibid.*

71 According to Reinaldo Arenas, Nogueras "died under suspi-

cious circumstances, it being unclear whether from AIDS or at the hands of Castro's police," *Before the Night Falls* (New York: Penguin,1993), p. 89.

72 There is evidence that the Cuban intelligence services, through its agents in the U.S., was extremely interested in Más Canosa's health. See Rui Ferreira, "La red informó a Cuba sobre la salud de Más," *El Nuevo Herald*, December 22, 2000. Andrei Codrescu reported that some Cuban *babalawos*, believe Castro killed Más Canosa with a magic spell he learned during a visit to Nigeria. See *Ay, Cuba!* (New York: St. Martins Press, 1999), p. 68.

73 While Abrahantes was still in prison, ex-Cuban intelligence officer in exile Juan Antonio Rodríguez Menier accurately predicted that, because of Abrahantes' knowledge of some secret aspects of Castro's life, he was a good candidate for a "heart attack." See *Cuba por dentro* (Miami: Ediciones Universal, 1993), p. 32.

74 *Ché Guevara. A Revolutionary Life* (New York: Grove Press, 1997), p. 752.

75 Juan O. Tamayo, "Preocupa a E.U. la siquis de Castro," *El Nuevo Herald*, March 4, 2000.

76 Pablo Alfonso, "Conducta de Castro inquieta a siquiatras," *El Nuevo Herald*, March 28, 2000.

77 Frank Mankiewicz and Kirby Jones, *With Fidel* (New York: Ballantine, 1975), pp. 140-148.

78 Harry R. Haldeman, *The Ends of Power* (New York: Times Books, 1978), p. 39.

79 *Ibid*.

80 *Reasonable Doubt* (New York: Holt, Rinehart and Winston, 1985), p. 324.

81 Documents declassified in 1985 show that, despite all claims to the contrary, it was President Kennedy himself who was the one and only responsible for the treasonous decisions and actions which lead to the defeat of the Cuban invaders at the Bay of Pigs and caused the death of 117 of them. See Jack Skelly, "Ducking the Blame at the Bay of Pigs," *Insight* (www.insightmag.com) Vol. 15, No. 15, April 26, 1999. See also Grayston L. Lynch, *Decision for Disaster: Betrayal at the Bay of Pigs* (Washington: Brassey's, 1998), pp. 155-156.

82 This is the moral of the story of Guy Russo's *Live by the Sword* (Baltimore: Bancroft Press, 1998). It seems, however, that the Bible's wisdom does not always work. In the case of Fidel Castro, he has been living by the sword for more than sixty years, but it does not seem likely that he will die by the sword.

83 Arthur M. Schlesinger, Jr., *Robert Kennedy and His Times* (London: Future, 1979), p. 700.

84 John Newman, *Oswald and the CIA* (New York: Carroll & Graf, 1985), pp. 427-430.

85 Seth Cantor, *The Ruby Cover-Up* (New York: Zebra, 1978), pp. 249-252.

86 *Ibid.*, pp. 261-262.

87 George Crile III, "The Mafia, the CIA, and Castro," the *Washington Post*, May 16, 1976, C4.

88 Mark Riebling, *Wedge* (New York: Knopf, 1994), p. 171.

89 *Ibid.*, pp. 171-172.

90 *The New York Times*, March 17, 1977, A23.

91 House Assassinations Committee Report, 173, and House Assassinations Committee, *Hearings*, Vol. 5, 345-48, 373-77.

92 *Alleged Assassination Plots Involving Foreign Leaders*, U.S. Senate, November 20, 1975, 94th Congress, 1st Session, pp. 60-61; also blind memo, 12/2/63, CIA FOIA #1384-491-B.

93 *Alleged Assassination Plots Involving Foreign Leaders*, U.S. Senate, November 20, 1975, 94th Congress, 1st Session, pp. 60-61.

94 Henry Hurt, *Reasonable Doubt* (New York: Holt, Rinehart and Winston, 1985), pp. 421-422.

95 James Johnston, "Did Cuba Murder JFK?" *The Washington Post*, November 19, 1989, p. D-5.

96 Grayston Lynch, a former CIA agent in Florida, told Gus Russo, "The AM/LASH plot was known to Castro. We believed Cubela was a double agent." See *Live by the Sword* (Baltimore: Bancroft Press, 1998), p. 242.

97 A memorandum of the meeting of the Special Committee concluding that an attack was unlikely was furnished to the Select Committee of the United States Senate to Study Government Operations, which published parts of it in its final report in 1976.

98 *The New York Times*, October 8, 1963.

99 In August 1997, almost 34 years after the assassination of president Kennedy, the Assassination Records board, a special committee appointed by Congress to facilitate the release of records on the incident, released 84 formerly classified documents of the National Security Agency (NSA). The NSA's specializes in "signals intelligence"— the global interception, collection and analysis of telephone and radio conversations. Some of the released intercepts refer to defensive measures immediately ordered by Castro. According to some documents, the very day Kennedy was killed Cuban military units hit the trenches on Cuba's northern coast, waiting for an American invasion. In a speech broadcast on Cuban radio and tv on November 23, Castro said that JFK's death "may have very negative repercussions with regard to the interests of our country." Moreover, an intercepted message a Euro-

pean intelligence officer cabled home from Havana: "Although it was only the third time I had witnessed a speech by Fidel, I got the impression that on this occasion he was frightened, if not terrified." See *Foreign Broadcast Information Service*, "Report on Cuban Propaganda - No 12: Havana's Response to the Death of President kennedy and Comment on the New Administration," December 31, 1963; George Lander, Jr., "Castro 'Frightened' After JFK Killing," *The Washington Post*, August 20, 1997, p. A9; Neil A. Lewis, "Documents Indicate Cuban Forces Were Put on Alert After Kennedy Assassination," *The New York Times*, August 20, 1997.

100 Giancana's evaluation of Castro in Roselli's deposition to the Church Committee, quoted in Gus Russo, *op. cit.*, p. 523, n. 19.

101 Wet Affairs (*mokrie dela*), KGB euphemism for assassination.

102 Edward McCarthy, *Working Press*, pp. 9-19, quoted in Gus Russo, *op. cit.*, p. 228. See also Lucia Newman, "In Rare Admission, Castro Says Cuba has Dispatched Spies Across U.S.," *CNN*, October 20, 1998.

103 A notable exception is Gus Russo's *Live by the Sword* (Baltimore: Bancroft Press, 1998). Russo's book brings out a wealth of new information that cannot be ignored.

104 According to a U.S. Justice Department source, the FBI and the CIA were investigating the possibility that Castro was plotting to use his agents in the U.S. to kill both President Ford and his Republican presidential contender Ronald Reagan in August, 1976. An FBI informer told the Bureau that San Francisco Bay Area radicals of the Emiliano Zapata terrorist group, in coordination with Andrés Gómez, a Castro agent, had plans to kill both men. See Daryl Lempke, "Cuban Spy Link to Ford, Reagan Death Plot Probed," *The Los Angeles Times*, March 19, 1976.

105 Probably it works against Havel and Castañeda the fact that they are also intellectuals, and Castro hates intellectuals as much as he hates democratically elected presidents.

106 Since his regime was condemned at the U.N. Human Rights Commission in Geneva, Castro has been uttering strong epithets, accusations and even veiled threats against the leaders of the countries that voted against him. See "Castro insulta y se aísla del continente," *El Nuevo Herald*, April 29, 2001.

107 For revealing details about John F. Kennedy's involvement in political assassination see Seymour Hersh, *The Dark Side of Camelot* (New York: Little, Brown and Company, 1997), particularly Chapter 13, Executive Action. Like Castro, John F. Kennedy was never worried about the ethical or moral issues involving political assassination, only about how to do it without getting caught.

108 Senate Select Committee to Study Governmental Operations

with Respect to Intelligence Activities, *Alleged Assassination Plots Involving Foreign Leaders: An Interim Report*, 94th Congress, 1st sess., November 20, 1975, 138.

109 Ronald Kessler, *Inside the CIA* (New York: Pocket Books, 1992), p. 87.

110 *Ibid.*, p. 46.

111 John Tower et al, *The Tower Commission Report*, New York: Bantam/Times, 1987, p. 15.

112 In a book proposal for his autobiography circulated at the Frankfurt Fair in 1997, Castro expressed his opinion that "McNamara was an idiot—and still is! And Robert Kennedy was a complete fool." See Arthur Allen, "Ché and Diana: The Shocking Untold Story," *Salon*, October 14, 1997, www.salon.com/media/1997/10/14castro.html.

113 An interesting detail is that, soon after the Kennedy assassination, CIA closed the AM/LASH operation. See Gus Russo, *Live by the Sword* (Baltimore: Bancroft Press, 1998), p. 304. History shows that most Americans admire force, act by force and only respect force. In that sense, by giving them a taste of their own medicine, Fidel Castro proved that he is more American than most Americans.

114 The descriptive image is from Nelson Demille, *The Lion's Game* (New York: Warner Books, 2000), p.253.

115 Kevin Fedarko, "This Cold War Is Back," *Time*, March 11, 1996, p. 37.

116 Out of unavoidable oversimplification, people always refer to actions taken by intelligence services as "the CIA knew," "the KGB acted," "the Mossad believed," etc., forgetting that intelligence services are not homogeneous entities. Due to the application of the need-to-know and compartmentation principles, a common characteristic of intelligence services is that the right hand doesn't know what the left hand is doing, and vice versa. Therefore, when one says "the CIA knew," it actually means "some people at the CIA knew." In the case of critical operations, as in the case of assassination attempts on a foreign leader, it is likely that most people at CIA, including very senior officers, were left out in the dark about the operation. On the other hand, there is some evidence that, since the sixties, the CIA has been not only teeming with liberals but it has had some crypto-leftists among its ranks. Contrary to what most people think, Castro has always had many secret admirers among CIA officers. Some CIA defectors, like Philip Agee, are notoriously pro-Castro. The strange coincidence of interests between Castro and the CIA will be the subject of my next book, *Fidel Castro Supermole: Walking Back the Cat in the Cuban Operation*.

Chapter 5: Fidel's Sociolism

1 For a succinct analysis of how Castro has destroyed the Cuban economy see Peter Brimelow, "The Cost of Castro," *Forbes*, March 23, 1998, p. 80; on how Castro's own mismanagement, not external agents like the U.S. embargo, has destroyed Cuba's economy see Modesto Maidique, "Fidel's Plantation," *The Stanford Magazine*, Winter 1983, pp. 27-32.

An analysis of Cuba's economic performance throughout the past decade shows that it has been the worst in Latin America. While most countries have experienced some growth, the Cuban economy diminished by 4.2 percent annually between 1991 and 1997, performing below the level of Haiti. See "Cuba's economy in the 1990s," the *Miami Herald*, March 21, 1999.

2 *Family Portrait with Fidel* (New York: Random House, 1984), p. 170.

3 *Sartre on Cuba* (New York: Ballantine, 1961).

4 U.S. Department of Commerce, *Investment in Cuba*. (Washington D.C.: Government Printing Office, 1956), p. 184.

5 Department of Economic and Social Affairs, *Economic Survey of Latin America 1957* (New York: United Nations, 1959), p. 177.

6 Louis A. Pérez, Jr., *On Becoming Cuban* (Chapel Hill: University of North Carolina Press, 1999), p. 53. Pérez's book studies in detail the growing similarities between the American and the Cuban culture and society.

7 *Ibid*, p. 307.

8 K. S. Karol, *Guerrillas in Power* (New York: Hill and Wang, 1970), p. 324.

9 Jon Lee Anderson, *Ché Guevara* (New York: Grove Press, 1997), p. 170.

10 The term "social bandit" is from Eric Hobsbawn, *Bandits* (London: Weidenfeld and Nicholson, 2000).

11 *Fidel Castro* (New York: Simon and Schuster, 1969), p. 34.

12 Edward Boorstein, *The Economic Transformation of Cuba* (New York: Modern Reader, 1968), p. 39.

13 Mentions of *"sociolismo"* in Carlos Franqui, *Family Portrait with Fidel* (New York: Random House, 1984), pp. 171-172; also in *General del Pino Speaks: An Insight into Élite Corruption and Military Dissention in Castro's Cuba*. Washington, D.C.: The Cuban American National Foundation, 1987, 20. See also Francisco León, "Socialism and *Sociolismo*; Social Actors and Economic Change in 1990s Cuba," in Miguel Centeno and Mauricio Font, eds., *Toward a New Cuba? Legacies*

of a Revolution (Boulder: Lynne Rienner, 1997), pp. 39-52. For a detailed analysis of Castro's sociolism see Juan Clark, "Igualdad y privilegio en la revolución de Castro," in *The Cuban Center for Cultural and Strategic Studies*, 40 años de revolución, 1999, www.cubancenter.org/uploads/40years08.html. Professor Clark sees Castro's sociolism as a form of feudalism.

14 Some people believe that the main reason for Castro's lack of clients when he tried to work as a lawyer was that he never really studied any law text. It was common knowledge at the University of Havana that he got his grades either by buying them from corrupt professors or by coercing them at gun point.

15 Castro's wife Mirtha was the daughter of a rich Cuban linked to the government of Fulgencio Batista, whom Castro allegedly hated. It is known that, when he married Mirtha, Batista sent them a thousand dollars as a wedding present.

16 *Cuba Under Castro* (Boston: Houghton Mifflin, 1974), p. 10.

17 *Fidel Castro: Psiquiatría y política* (Editorial Jus: Mexico, 1968), p. 8.

18 Juan Vivés, *Los amos de Cuba* (Buenos Aires: Emecé Editores, 1982), p. 300.

19 This was the time when the Rolex became the identifying sign of the Castroist nomenklatura.

20 Miguel Bas, "Intimidades de Castro," *Diario Las Américas*, October 20, 1990, 1; see also Associated Press report, "Castro has wife, 5 sons, 32 houses, Soviets claim," *The Times Picayune*, October 27, 1990.

21 *Ibid.*

22 Juan O. Tamayo, "Castro's Family: Fidel's Private Life with his Wife and Sons is so Secret than Even the CIA is Left to Wonder," *The Miami Herald*, October 8, 2000; see also Marie Sanz, "Film Offers Glimpse of Castro's Life," *The Miami Herald*, March 21, 200. Many people in Cuba suspect that Estela Bravo, a Leni Riefenstahl without talent, has been for many years an asset of the Cuban intelligence services. The subject of most of Bravo's propaganda films has been the denigration of the anti-Castro exiles in the U.S. The fact that two of Bravo's children recently joined the Cuban exile community in Florida apparently has not tempered her pro-Castro propaganda activities.

23 *Ibid.*

24 Information supplied by Jesus M. Fernández reported in a special edition of *Cuba Monthly Economic Report*, (August 1997), published on the Internet.

25 The source for much of the background information on this section is a report of the same name published in a special edition of the *Cuba Monthly Economic Report*, (August 1997), published on the Internet.

26 Like most anti-Castro Cubans in the U.S., Castro hates communism.

27 See Marc Cooper, "For Sale: Used Marxism," *Harper's*, March 1995, pp. 54-66; see also, "L'île du dollar roi," *Le Figaro*, December 12, 2000, p. 4.

28 Maciques, a truculent character out of a B gangster movie, is perhaps one of the most hated and feared men among Castro's inner circle. A shark among sharks, Maciques is known for stealing property from foreigners and Cubans through coercion and extortion. For many years director of the Conventions Palace and later appointed by Castro director of the all-powerful Cubanacán Corporation, Maciques has been the object of hundreds of accusations by his colleagues, but his close friendship with Castro guarantees his immunity. For a description of some of Maciques' activities see José Fernández González, *Cuba: del socialismo al fascismo* (San Juan, P.R.: First Book Publishing, 1996).

29 A note appeared in *Granma* after Castro visited his friend President Hugo Chávez in Venezuela in late 2000, informed that a commercial agreement had been signed between the two countries by which Venezuela will export oil to Cuba in exchange for, among other things, human organs. It is known that Cuba is a big exporter of human blood, and sources in Cuba affirm that its main source is the Cuban prisons. Now Castro apparently has added human organs to his export list. A single dead body of a young, healthy person can yield more than $200,000 in products for tissue and organ banks. (See Associated Press, "Big Profits in Human Donated Organs," *The San Francisco Chronicle*, January 14, 2001, p. A19). As the practice grows in Cuba, this may become a strong incentive for the Castro government to continue killing Cuban citizens.

30 Jesús Hernández Cuéllar, "Castro exporta medicinas," *Contacto*, June 1988.

31 One wonders if, as the Jews and other slave workers demanded reparation from the companies who exploited them during World War II, the Cuban workers will some day demand reparation from the companies who, in complicity with the Castro government, are now exploiting them. The Cuban-American National Foundation believes it can be done, and is already pioneering a new legal strategy to hold foreign investors who do business with the illegitimate Castro government liable for violations of international and U.S. labor laws. See Tom Carter, "Outside Investors Face 'Slave Labor' Suit," *The Washington Times*, April 9, 2001.

32 Susan Eckstein, "Cuban Internationalism," in Sandor Halebsky and John M. Kirk, eds., *Cuba: Twenty-Five Years of Revolution, 1959-1984*

(New York: Praeger, 1985), pp. 382-383 (emphasis added).

33 By the 1830s, most southerners had persuaded themselves that slavery was not only good for the masters, but for the slaves as well. "Compare the life of the slave with that of the northern free worker," they urged. "Did slaves ever have to worry about where their next meal was coming from? Did anyone ever see a slave begging in the South? Sick slaves were cared for by their masters. Old slaves were certain of support as long as they lived and a decent burial when death finally came." See John A. Garraty, *The Story of America: Beginnings to 1914* (Orlando, FL: Holt, Rinehart and Winston, 1991), p. 461. Just substituting "Cuban" for "slave," and "Castro government" for "masters" throughout the text, you will see how close it resembles the argument used by Castro and his American leftist and liberal friends in their justification for neo-slavery in Cuba.

34 Some Castro-friendly scholars and journalists have made for years an effort to convince the American public that the Cubans escaping from the Island are not real exiles, but economic immigrants, not very different from the Mexicans or Haitians. A recent incident, however, indicates that this is not the case.

On Christmas Eve, 2000, British authorities found two bodies who had dropped from a British Airways plane who arrived from Havana. The post-mortem examination showed that the two young men were stowaways who died of cold and lack of oxygen after they manage to hide themselves in the wheel compartment of the plane. (See Yves Colon, "2 Bodies Found in Britain Believed to be Jet Stowaways from Cuba," *The Miami Herald*, December 29, 2000).

However, a few days later it was reported that the two Cuban teenagers, Alberto Vázquez, 17, and Maikel Fonseca, 16, were *Camilitos*, that is, students of the élite Camilo Cienfuegos Military Academy, where the privileged members of the Castroist nomenklatura send their children to become Castro's New Men. Apparently Castro himself was shocked with the news, because he visited the school and had thoroughly interrogated another student, Yassel Díaz, who apparently was part of the escape plan. Yassel's father, Col. Juan Tomás Díaz, attended the meeting. (See Associated Press, "Fuerte interrogatorio de Castro a un joven," *El Nuevo Herald*, January 14, 2001).

The teenagers who died while attempting to escape from the Island were not poor Cubans looking for a better economic future, but the children of the Cuban *nouveau riche*. Therefore, they were not looking for the good things of capitalism, which they had in abundance in Cuba, but for freedom. But Fidel Castro doesn't seem to understand that even the children of the rich and the privileged would better face death than remaining in the inferno he has created in Cuba. As usual,

Fidel blamed the U.S. for the death of the two boys.

35 *Fidel Castro* (New York: Simon and Schuster, 1969), p. 35.

36 *General del Pino Speaks: An Insight into Élite Corruption and Military Dissention in Castro's Cuba*. Washington, D.C.:The Cuban American National Foundation, 1987, p. 48.

37 For this section I am borrowing extensively from the article "Las Fincas de los Comandantes," by Juan Carlos Céspedes, Agencia de Prensa Libre Oriental, published in *Carta de Cuba*, Summer of 1997, and distributed in the Internet by CubaNet.

38 According to General del Pino, the highest ranking Cuban officer that has defected, a major at the MININT can be compared to a general in the Army in terms of privileges, sinecures, life style and all the corruption involved." See *op. cit.*, p. 31.

39 Hernando de Soto, *The Mystery of Capital* (New York: Basic Books, 2000).

40 Cuba's economy under Castro is way beyond recovery, with a demoralized working class begging desperately for dollars, little industry other than tourism, years of poor sugar harvest, and more than $11 billion in debt.

41 Kaz Vorpal, "Does the Cuban Embargo Hurt Castro or Help Him?," http://smart.net/~kaz/cuba.html.

42 "Bush Asks Congress to Reward Chinese Regime With Trade," *NewsMax.com Wires*, June 2, 2001, www.newsmax.com/archives/articles/2001/6/1/172453.shtml.

43 *Politics and Social Force in Chilean Development* (Berkeley: University of California Press, 1969), p. 73.

44 For this section I have relied mostly on Alberto Bustamante's "Art Lost: Cuban Artistic Patrimony and Its Restitution," *Contacto*, August, 1998.

45 Agustín Blázquez, "Levanten el embargo moral II," (Internet Document), February 12, 1999.

46 See Luis Aguilar León, "El saqueo del patrimonio cubano," *El Nuevo Herald*, November 22, 1998.

47 Marcelo Fernandez-Zayas, "Intelligence Report from Washington - 01112000," wpais@cais.com.

48 See, Mark Detroit, "The Imperialist Helms-Burton Law and the Myth of Cuban Socialism," *Communist Voice*, Vol. 2, No. 5 (October 1, 1996).

49 See, i.e, the report by the Council on Foreign Relations, *U.S.-Cuban Relations in the 21st Century: A Follow-on Report* (New York: Council on Foreign Relations, 2001). The document can only be described as a frantic, desperate effort to avoid the final demise of the crumbling Castroist tyranny. See also, Miguel A. Faría, "Cuba and the Council on

Foreign Relations," *NewsMax.com*, February 15, 2001.

50 For a revealing view of the magnitude of the corruption Castro's crony capitalism has brought to Cuba, see Frank Smith, "Gays, Catholics and transvestites find their places in the new Cuba," *SALON NewsReal*, January 4, 1999. See also Cooper, *op. cit.*

51 A permanent exhibition at Havana's Museum of the Revolution, still blames the prostitution that allegedly flourished before Castro's takeover on capitalist decadence and the harsh choices it forced upon young Cuban women. No explanation is offered for the widespread prostitution currently flourishing in decadent sociolist Cuba, and its negative impact on young Cuban women and men who get into prostitution because they don't have any other choice.

52 Frei Betto, *Fidel and Religion* (New York: Simon and Schuster, 1987), p. 126.

53 Carlos Franqui, *Diary of the Cuban Revolution* (New York: Viking, 1980), p. 8. Though any study of Castro's life is teeming with contradictions, his claims of love for a Spartan life may not be totally unfounded. A technician who visited in the mid-seventies one of Fidel's many places, on Vedado's 11th Street, facing Celia Sánchez offices, told me that Castro's living quarters were Spartan indeed. He described Castro's bedroom as long and narrow, just a few feet wider than his bed, which my informant said was a sort of "hospital bed." The room he described had no windows, no pictures on the walls and a small bookcase with books and American magazines. It looked more like a prison or a monk's cell than a true bedroom.

54 The fact is so blatant that it became the subject of an scholarly paper by Pablo Monreal, a top level Cuban economist member of the Castroist *nomenklatura*. The paper, entitled "Las remesas familiares en la economía cubana," was published in Germany in 1999. Professor Monreal is the president of the Cuban *Centro Internacional de Investigaciones Económicas* (International Center for Economic Research).

Chapter 6. The Secret Fidel Castro

1 The creation and updating of CPPs is a key part of an intelligence services' activities. For example, CIA's core mission is to provide the nation's leaders with reliable information about world events and personalities, and most of the information about personalities comes from their CPPs. Every time new information is added to a CPP, it is carefully checked against the already existing information, looking for anomalies and inconsistencies.

2 A CPP usually begins by recording the main physical characteristics of the individual, like height, weight, skin and eye color, etc. It also shows any false identities or aliases on record ("Alejandro," and "Alex" in the case of Fidel Castro), as well as languages spoken and countries the person has visited or has resided. Particularly important are dark areas, like when the person has disappeared from public view for a period of time. A CPP lists everything known about the individual involved: every professional fact, every personal foible, every rumor that has ever reached the agents' ears. Though Fidel Castro has erected a very efficient barrier around himself, and information about leaders of totalitarian societies is not easy to obtain, there are bits and pieces from the press, defectors, and other sources. The role of the intelligence analyst is to put these pieces together and come to some conclusion about the future actions of a foreign leader if they are consistent with his past behavior.

3 As I mentioned above, the Holy See runs an efficient intelligence service, probably the best in the world.

4 In preparing Castro's CPP, I have drawn extensively from two studies about Adolf Hitler: Walter C. Langer, *The Mind of Adolf Hitler: The Secret Wartime Report* (New York: Signet, 1972); and Robert G. L. Waite, *The Psychopathic God: Adolf Hitler* (New York: Signet, 1977). Dr. Langer's book, written during the war in 1943 for the OSS (Office of Strategic Services, the forerunner of the CIA), is a CPP of Hitler written from a psychological point of view. Kept secret for many years, it was not published until the early seventies. Waite's book follows closely the path taken by Langer, but with the hindsight provided by his access to a wealth of documentation that was unavailable to Langer.

I have been able to use the above mentioned studies as a pattern for my work only because of the strange similarities existing between Fidel Castro and Adolf Hitler. Granted, there is evidence that, before taking power in Cuba, Castro had read some of Hitler's books and speeches and that, thanks to Fidel's photographic memory, he repeated them in detail in some of his speeches. Phrases like *"Jamás capitularemos,"* (We will never capitulate) and *"La Historia me absolverá,"* (History will absolve me) are too close to Hitler's words to be the product of a coincidence. But there are other aspects of this similarity that defy a rational explanation.

Both Hitler and Fidel are born at the periphery of their respective countries and raised under the iron rule of an authoritarian father they profoundly hate. Both attend Catholic schools and are mediocre and troublesome students. The two of them are endowed with a photographic memory. At some time in their adolescent years they feel that they have been touched by the hand of Destiny to play an extraordinary role in the history of their countries. Both suffer accidents that keep them unconscious for several days. Both Hitler and Castro attempt to grab political power through a *coup d'état*, fail, and are sent to jail. During the trial they take upon themselves their own defense, changing their roles from accused to prosecutor and denounce the government they had tried to overthrow. Both are found guilty and sent to prison where, under privileged conditions and surrounded by a group of their loyal followers, write their memoirs. Both Hitler and Castro master the art of oratory evidenced in long, mesmerizing speeches. Both of them survive innumerable assassination attempts, and are fully convinced that all of them have failed because of divine intervention.

One may expand this uncanny parallel almost *ad infinitum*. By some coincidence that defies any rational explanation, Fidel Castro's life looks like a carbon copy of Adolf Hitler's, including the fact that, as it happened to Hitler during his last days, lately Castro is suffering sporadic attacks of a type of aphasia that paralyzes part of his body and face.

5 Brian Lamb, "Interview with Georgie Anne Geyer," Booknotes, *C-SPAN*, aired on March 10, 1991.

6 Over the time, a new phenomenon has appeared in Cuba which some people have come to call the "invisible press." In a speech he gave on April 19, 1976, Fidel Castro himself referred to the phenomenon, mentioning how the Cuban people had come to know everything about the war in Angola without anything having been published in the Cuban press. But the "invisible press" kept working actively after the end of the Angolan war, mostly reporting about the widespread corruption at all levels of the Castro government, with an emphasis on Castro's secret life.

7 Castro's problem-solving process described in Gabriel García Márquez, "A Personal Portrait of Fidel," in *Fidel Castro, My Early Years* (New York: Ocean Press, 1998), p. 18.

8 The term *eidetic* (virtually identical or duplicative) was coined by the German psychologist E. R. Jaensch. Eidetic memory is a rare, still scientifically unexplained phenomenon, usually appearing in early age in a very small percent of the population and tending to decline with age. See Ian M. L. Hunter, *Memory* (Baltimore: Penguin, 1966), pp. 195-204.

9 Apparently, Castro's photographic memory suddenly appeared when he was a student at the Colegio de Belén high school in Havana. It was at Belén where he suddenly changed from a mediocre student to an excellent one, consistently obtaining high grades in all subjects. Though there is no clear information about the cause for this sudden

change, it seems that Castro's eidetic memory suddenly appeared after he hit his head against a wall at Belén and was unconscious for several days. Similarly, Hitler's eidetic memory seems to have appeared after he was unconscious for several days as the result of a gas attack when he was a soldier in WWI.

10 Daniel James, *Cuba: The First Soviet Satellite in the Americas* (New York: Avon, 1961), p. 31.

11 *America Latina*, October-November, 1984.

12 In one occasion I had a private meeting with Castro and we talked for a few hours. At the end of our conversation he asked me some personal questions. Three years later we met again by chance and, to my surprise, Castro not only recognized me immediately but continued the conversation as if we had just taken a short break.

13 Pablo Alfonso, "El Comandante no tuvo quien le dijera," *El Nuevo Herald*, December 17, 2000.

14 Castro's slogan about culture in the early 1960s: "Within the revolution, everything; outside the revolution, nothing." is but his tropical version of the Church's *"Extra ecclesiam nulla salus."*

15 The way he managed the whole Elián González affair is an excellent example of the effectivity of a frequently repeated big lie.

16 On the other hand, Fidel Castro, like most politicians around the world, was taken by surprise with the sudden power the Internet has brings to the people. His immediate reaction was banning it, if not by law, by practice. The Castro government has created so many obstacles and restrictions to access the Web that only government organizations and officials can access it freely. It is true that most governments fear the Web, a medium they cannot control, but totalitarian governments fear it even more.

17 Juan Benemelis and Melvin Mañón, *Juicio a Fidel* (Santo Domingo: Taller, 1990), p. 32.

18 "Notes on Man and Socialism in Cuba," in George Lavan, ed., *Ché Guevara Speaks* (New York: Grove Press, 1967), p. 125.

19 According to dissident poet and journalist Raúl Rivero, president of Cuba Press, an independent press agency, Elián's case awakened true nationalist feelings among the majority of Cubans, even among many who are not Castro supporters. Of course, part of the support was the result of both official political pressures and outright coercion—some people were fired because they refused to attend the mass rallies—but most of the support seemed to be spontaneous and genuine. See, Roberto Fabricio, "Lo que busca Castro," *El Nuevo Herald* (January 16, 2000).

20 Juan Benemelis and Melvin Mañón, *op. cit.*, p. 155.

21 During the third congress of Castro's "Communist" Party, Carlos

Aldana, at the time a leading member of the Central Committee and a Castro protégé, clearly expressed this idea when he said to the Congress, "In no small number of meetings and assemblies during these past months I have heard people regret the fact that once again it has been comrade Fidel who has had to confront the deviations and mistaken policies." See *Granma*, December 1, 1986.

22 As an expert in Cuban affairs put it, "Cuba continues to be led by someone 'who dresses the same, who thinks the same, who dreams the same' as when he came down from the Sierra Maestra on January 1, 1959," see Richard E. Nuccio, "Cuba: The Current Situation," in *Cuba in Transition* (Miami: Association for the Study of the Cuban Economy, 1999), p. 14.

23 This may explain Castro's demonological interpretation of the evil forces—mostly personified by the U.S.—which he believes are conspiring against him. Some child psychologists see this behavior as a typical characteristic of adolescent attitude and perspective.

24 Photograph of Fidel at age three in Wendy Gimbel, *Havana Dreams* (New York: Knopf, 1998), p. 118; photo of Fidel at age sixty-eight in Adam Kufeld, *Cuba* (New York: W. W. Norton, 1994), p. 81. A very similar photo, taken by Maurice Cohn Band in 1991 at a ceremony where Castro was honoring troops returning from Angola, appears in Don E. Beyer, *Castro!* (New York, Franklin Watts, 1993), p. 16 top (illustrations).

25 For an interesting theory about how the roots of totalitarianism are to be found in early childhood see Erik Erikson, *Identity, Youth and Crisis* (New York: W.W. Norton, 1968), pp. 74-90.

26 Their moral "flexibility"—manifested by their idea that a noble end justifies the use of sordid and base means—as well as their propensity for careerism have provided grounds for the accusations of hypocrisy and duplicity that are made against the Jesuits. English Prime Minister William Gladstone called them "the deadliest foes that mental and moral liberty have ever known."

27 I am convinced that the main reason why most Cubans hated the Russians so much was not because they were communists, but because most of the ones in Cuba stunk like hell.

28 Christopher Hunt, *Waiting for Fidel* (New York: Houghton Mifflin, 1997).

29 For a vivid description of the scarcity of running water, soap, deodorant and other similar products for personal hygiene affect Cubans, see Manuel Vázquez Portal, "Los días del agua," *CubaNet Weekly* (Internet), February 4, 1999. See also, Daína Chaviano, *El hombre, la hembra y el hambre* (Barcelona: Planeta, 1998).

30 Rumors that his bush jacket has a portable cooling unit are part

of the mythology surrounding Castro.

31 Carlos Franqui, *Family Portrait with Fidel* (New York:Random House, 1984), p. 86.

32 The first time Castro met the full assembly of the State Council, created in 1975, was in 1989. Usually he deals with its executive committee of five members. See Juan Benemelis and Melvin Mañón, *op. cit.*, p. 31, n. 18.

33 Sources in Cuba inform that Castro has become addicted to the Internet. According to the reports, the Cuban leader spends many hours every day surfing the Web, glued to his personal computer in his mansion in Havana's exclusive Siboney district. Castro's recent interest in the Web and the discovery of its possibilities apparently motivated his recent claims that he wants to turn Cuba into the most educated country in the world. It seems, however, that while Castro enjoys surfing the Web most Cubans are not that lucky. Computers in Cuba, even the cheapest models, are beyond the reach of the ordinary citizen. Moreover, Castro apparently is not happy with the freedom of information the Web provides to the people, and sees it as a threat to his government's information monopoly. Therefore, Internet connections in Cuba are prohibited without government authorization. Only 40,000 government officials and foreigners in a country of 11 million people have been authorized to link up to the Net. Nevertheless, Cubans are very resourceful, and a new type of nerdy rebels has emerged: the *"informáticos,"* a sort of Internet guerrilla composed mostly of young male professionals. Bypassing all government efforts these Cuban hackers manage to get connected at least several minutes every day, and they in turn serve as a source of fresh outside information in a country whose government has sought to suppress the free flow of information since its very beginning in 1959. For information about the "informáticos" see Scott Wilson, "Web of Resistance Rises in Cuba," *Washington Post Foreign Service*, December 26, 2000, p. a01.)

34 Andrés Suárez, *Cuba: Castroism and Communism, 1959-1966*. Cambridge, Mass.: The M.I.T. Press, 1967, 87; for full text of the *La Coubre* speech see *Hoy*, March 6, 1960.

35 "Running Against Fidel," *Newsweek*, March 9, 1992.

36 Andres Oppenheimer, *Castro's Final Hour*. New York: Simon and Schuster, 1992, 399-400; also in *Granma International*, October 20, 1991.

37 Associated Press, "Fuerte crítica de Castro a Flores, México y España," *El Nuevo Herald*, November 26, 2000.

38 Norberto Fuentes, *Dulces guerreros cubanos* (Barcelona: Seix Barral, 1999), p. 119.

39 The Rebel Army was merely Castro's instrument for his seizure of power, as his "Communist" Party was the instrument for the con-

solidation of his newly acquired power. Once he reached his goals the instruments lost all value for him and were either destroyed or deprived of any real political importance. For a Fidel-friendly view of Castro's manipulation of symbols see C. Fred Hudson, "Continuity and Evolution of Revolutionary Symbolism in Verde Olivo," in Sandor Halebsky and John M. Kirk, *Cuba: Twenty-Five Years of Revolution, 1959-1984* (New York: Praeger, 1985), pp. 233-250.

40 Joseph Treaster, "To Cure 'Capitalist Vice,' Cuba Applies Austerity," *The International Herald Tribune*, 9 February, 1987, 13, 17.

41 Marc Cooper, "For Sale: Used Marxism," *Harper's*, March 1995, p. 65.

42 More than two years after I wrote this section about envy as Castro's main motivation in life, I found an article by Carlos Alberto Montaner in which he arrives at a similar conclusion. See "Castro y la medalla de la envidia," *El Nuevo Herald*, August 8, 1999.

Also, the back cover of a recent book by Montaner shows a photo of Castro which may give us another clue to Castro's peculiar mind. The photograph, taken in 1955, shows a young Fidel Castro with a thin mustache. Castro dedicated it to Montaner's father, Ernesto Montaner, a journalist and member of the Ortodoxo Party. But this is no ordinary photograph. In the first place, the dedication appears on the front of the photo, not on the back, as it was customary in Cuba. Secondly, it follows the style commonly used by Armand (the photographer of the stars), or Rembrandt Studios, and it is the typical photo used by actors to give to their fans. Therefore, it seems that Fidel considered himself a famous actor. Most likely he saw *los galanes* as competition to his acting career, and we know that Fidel Castro cannot accept any kind of competition. See, Carlos Alberto Montaner, *Journey to the Heart of Cuba: Life as Fidel Castro* (New York: Algora, 2001).

43 Though envy has played a key role in human affairs and it has been observed in almost every culture in the planet, it is remarkable how few works have studied it. For an excellent study on the subject of envy, see Helmut Schoeck, *Envy: A Theory of Social Behaviour* (New York: Hartcourt, Brace and World, 1969). Another book containing several interesting papers on envy is Peter Salovey, ed., *The Psychology of Jealousy and Envy* (New York: The Guilford Press, 1991). See also the study by William L. Davidson, "Envy and Emulation," in James Hastings, ed., *Encyclopedia of Religion and Ethics*, Vol. V (New York: Scribner & Clark, 1912).

44 Joseph H. Berke, *The Tyranny of Malice* (New York: Summit Books, 1988), 13-14.

45 Leo J. Trese, *The Faith Explained* (Manila: Sinag-Tala Publishers, 1983), p. 60.

46 "Playboy Interview: Fidel Castro," *Playboy*, August, 1985.

47 Daughter of Cecrops whose heart was infected by Envy's venom.

48 Luis Conte Agüero, *Fidel Castro: Psiquiatría y política* (Mexico: Editorial Jus, 1968), 15.

49 On his exhaustive study of envy Helmut Schoeck devotes a whole chapter to the analysis of crimes of envy, see *op. cit.*, pp. 106-115.

50 Schoeck, *op. cit.*, p. 110.

51 It seems that, thirty years later, rather than improving, things have deteriorated even more. See, i.e., Claudia Márquez Linares, "Un socialismo para siempre, por favor," *Grupo Decoro - Cuba News*, June 1, 2001, www.cubanet.org/CNews/y01/jun01/o4a9.htm.

52 The Germans have a word for this impulse to take pleasure in the misfortune of others: *Schadenfreude*.

53 "A Personal Portrait of Fidel," in *Fidel Castro, My Early Years* (New York: Ocean Press, 1998), p. 15.

54 *Ibid.*, p. 170.

55 Pascal Fletcher, "Castro blasts Cuba's home-grown 'millionaires,'" *Reuters*, July 23, 1998.

56 *Ibid*. One must keep in mind that the goal of the envious is not acquiring or enjoying things, but depriving other people from doing so. Therefore, what really makes Castro happy is not that he rides a bullet-proof Mercedes 560 SEL, but that no other person in Cuba can ride even a cheap recent model car. Proof of the above is that just he possibility that the U.S. and a large part of the world may suffer an economic recession made Castro very happy. In an apocalyptic speech in the town of San José de las Lajas, not far from Havana, Castro predicted that, sooner than later, "a deep crisis will bring the ruin of most of the world's nations." See, "Apocalíptico discurso sobre E.U. y el futuro mundial," *El Nuevo Herald*, January 28, 2001.

57 "Castro seeks crackdown on street crime, drug trafficking." *The Philadelphia Inquirer*, January 8, 1999.

58 Oscar Espinosa Chepe, "¿Fin del cuentapropismo?" *CubaNet News*, December 23, 2000, http://www.cubanet.org/CNews/y00/dec00/22a6.htm.

59 Mario Lazo, *Dagger in the Heart* (New York:Twin Circle,1968), pp. 113-114.

60 *Ibid*.

61 Barry Farber, "Castro's Catastrophe: A Visit to Today's Cuba," *NewsMax.com*, January 9, 2001, http://newsmax.com/archives/articles/2001/1/9/205349.shtml.

62 *Ibid*.

63 "Holiday Hang-up: Cuba to Cut Phone Connection with U.S.,"

The Miami Herald, December 9, 2000.

64 Of course, Fidel Castro is not the only misery specialist in the world. Ward Connerly, the University of California regent who led the fight to end racial preferences in that state, believes that, "people like Jesse Jackson and others don't want blacks to enjoy life in America. They want them to be miserable." (Robert Stacy McCain, "How the democrats Made Loving Dixie a Hate Crime," *The Washington Times*, January 16, 2001). The fact perhaps explains the strong admiration Mr. Jackson feels for his Cuban colleague in the misery trade.

65 The nickname is mentioned in *Cubamor*, a revealing and touching film directed by Joshua Bee Alafia with script by Abel Robaina. Most of it was filmed without government authorization on location in Cuba with Cuban actors—many of them non-professionals.

66 Pascal Fletcher, "Cuba insulta a la sede española," *El Nuevo Herald*, January 8, 2001.

67 Fidel Castro, *Fidel Castro: My Early Years*, (New York: Ocean Press, 1998), pp. 45-46.

68 See Schoeck, *op. cit.*, pp. 106-105.

69 Teresa Casuso said she heard rumors that Castro had been under electric-shock treatment. She also mentions that "the physician who attended him, a Dr. Soreghi, had studied 'brainwashing' in communist countries, and that, when he died suddenly of a heart attack, Raúl Castro appeared at his office and carried off his papers." See *Cuba and Castro* (New York: Random House, 1961), pp. 181-182.

70 Irving Peter Pflaum, *Tragic Island* (Englewood Cliffs, N.J.: Prentice-Hall, 1961), p. 15.

71 The editor was Carlota Caulfield, now a college professor in California. Fernando Aguado collaborated with the translation.

72 See, i.e., Paul M. Frick, *The Dysfunctional President* (New York: Birch Lane Press, 1995).

73 Victor Franco, *The Morning After* (New York: Praeger, 1963), p. 79.

74 Andres Oppenheimer, *Castro's Final Hour* (New York: Simon & Schuster, 1992), p. 294.

75 For this section I am relying heavily on Marcelo Fernández-Zayas, "El misterio de la salud de Fidel Castro: la conexión árabe." (Web document), as well as personal communications with Fernández-Zayas himself.

76 Victor Franco, *op. cit.*, p. 79. Neuroscientist Faraneh Vargha-Khadem, of the University College London Medical School, believes that some sociopathic behavior has its source in serious head injuries suffered in the person's early years. According to Vargha-Khadem, injuries that damaged a particular spot in the brain, just above the

eyes, "[T]urned the boys into walking time bombs, because the trouble didn't show until years after the injuries." The part of the brain in question is a small area in the orbital frontal cortex. Some researchers believe this region plays a big role in impulse control and judgment. It allows people to balance their needs and desires against morality and values. See Josh Fischman, "Seeds of a Sociopath. Violence in the Brain?" *U.S. News & World Report*, November 20, 2000, p. 82.

77 Ray Brennan, *Castro, Cuba and Justice* (Garden City, N.Y.: Doubleday, 1959), p. 53.

78 Fidel is famous for his long speeches. For almost forty years he has held the record for the longest speech delivered at the United Nations. No wonder Castro has turned Cuba into the most logocentric society in the world, where his words are everything and reality is nothing. As Anthony Daniels put it, "Havana is like Pompeii, and Castro is its Vesuvius. The lava of his words has poured over the city continuously for thirty years, preserving it from any form of change except decay." *Utopias Elsewhere* (New York: Crown, 1991), p. 154.

79 Carlos Alberto Montaner, "Cuba, verano del 2000," *El Nuevo Herald*, August 13, 2000.

80 Christopher Marquis, "Castro healthy, firmly in power, CIA chief says," *The Miami Herald*, December 6, 1997.

81 "Castro Taking Mystery Youth Medicine," *NewsMax.com*, May 2, 2001.

82 Carl Limbacher, "Castro Going Nuts," *NewsMax.com*, June 24, 2001.

83 Marc Frank, "Fidel Castro Nearly Faints, Then Recovers," *WorldNetDaily.com*, June 23, 2001.

84 Pablo Alfonso, "El desmayo de Castro revela su precaria salud," *El Nuevo Herald*, June 24, 2001.

85 Pablo Alfonso, "Castro puede haber sufrido una isquemia," *El Nuevo Herald*, June 24, 2001.

86 Teresa Casuso, *op. cit.*, pp. 168-169.

87 *Ibid.*, p. 169.

88 Exploitation and rage are some of the main characteristics of the narcissistic personality. See Dan Kiley, *The Peter Pan Syndrome* (New York: Avon, 1983), p. 131.

89 "I've been to a Marvelous Party," The *Wall Street Journal*, November 3, 1995, p. A-14.

90 Theodor Adorno and Max Horkheimer, *Dialectic of Enlightenment* (London: Verso, 1979), p. 235.

91 "Playboy Interview: Fidel Castro," *Playboy*, August 1985.

92 Carlos Franqui, *Vida, aventuras y desastres de un hombre llamado Castro*. (Barcelona: Planeta, 1988), p. 31; also in Conte Agüero, *Fidel*

Castro: psiquiatría y política (Mexico: Editorial Jus, 1968), p. 85.

93 Georgie Anne Geyer, *Guerrilla Prince* (Boston: Little, Brown and Company, 1991), p. 72.

94 Sandy Stokes, "Animal abuse often a precursor to human violence," *The San Francisco Examiner*, December 20, 1998, p. C-5.

95 Dariel (Benigno) Alarcón Ramírez, *Memorias de un soldado cubano* (Barcelona: Tusquets, 1997), p. 48.

96 Luis Conte Agüero, *op. cit.*, p. 18.

97 John Martino, *I Was Castro's Prisoner* (New York: Devin-Adair, 1963), p. 89 *passim*, quoted in Paul D. Bethel, *The Losers* (New Rochelle, N.Y.: Arlington House,1969), p. 192.

98 *Fidel Castro, vida y obra* (Havana: Editorial Lex, 1959), p. 263.

99 Jay Nordlinger, "Castro and 'His People,'" *National Review*, April 27, 2001.

100 "Castro Blasts 'Lackey' Powell," *CNSNews*, April 28, 2001.

101 The version of the Urrutia affair Castro told Frei Betto is totally disingenuous, see *Fidel and Religion* (New York: Simon and Schuster, 1987), p. 174.

102 Mireya Navarro, "Caribbean Unity? Bananas Are Getting in the Way." The *New York Times*, April 19, 1999, p. A4.

103 K. S. Karol, *Guerrillas in Power* (New York: Hill & Wang, 1970), p. 8.

104 This is a mental mechanism psychiatrists call projection. Since Castro is incapable of facing his own vices and weaknesses, he projects them unto others.

105 Hugh Thomas, *op. cit.*, p. 866.

106 Castro's speech at Céspedes Park was broadcasted by COBC radio on January 9, 1959.

107 Speech by Fidel Castro on January 8th, *Revolución*, 9 January 1959.

108 Speech by Fidel Castro, *Revolución*, 3, 4, & 5 January, 1959.

109 Frei Betto, *op. cit.*, p. 222.

110 "Playboy Interview: Fidel Castro," *Playboy*, August 1985.

111 A long time ago the Soviet intelligence services discovered that the polygraph (commonly known as lie detector) actually doesn't detect lies, but measures the fear of getting caught telling lies. So, they not only don't use the polygraph as a vetting tool, but teach their agents to hypnotize themselves to believe they are not telling lies, but the truth.

112 Carlos Franqui, *Diary of the Cuban Revolution* (New York: Viking, 1980), p. 6.

113 Jules Dubois, *Fidel Castro* (New York: Bobbs-Merrill, 1959), p. 15. However, "He has good timber," is a literal, but inaccurate transla-

tion of the Spanish idiomatic phrase *"tiene buena madera,"* roughly equivalent to "he has the right stuff."

114 Castro's letter to Melba Hernández, 17 April 1954, in Luis Conte Agüero, *Cartas del presidio* (Havana: Ed. Lex, 1959), p. 38.

115 Mireya Navarro, "Caribbean Unity? Bananas Are Getting in the Way,? the *New York Times*, April 19, 1999, p. A4.

116 Mark Falcoff, "How to Think about Cuban-American Relations," in Irving Louis Horowitz, ed., *Cuban Communism, Fifth Edition* (New Brunswick, N.J.: Transaction Books, 1984), p. 547.

117 Lazo, *Dagger in the Heart* (New York: Twin Circle, 1968), p. 182. For an insightful analysis of the deep roots of lying from a non-conventional perspective, see M. Scott Peck, *People of the Lie* (New York: Simon and Schuster, 1983).

118 Some people have observed that envious people never smile, except at the sight of someone else's troubles.

119 Hugh Thomas, *Cuba: The Pursuit of Freedom* (New York: Harper & Row, 1971), 822.

120 For example, a common joke running is Cuba is that Cubans and Americans actually have exactly the same rights: Americans can criticize the American President, and Cubans too! Another joke is that, in order to solve the present crisis, the Castro government only has to solve the Cuban people's three major problems: breakfast, lunch, and dinner.

121 Eduardo del Río (Rius), *Lástima de Cuba* (Mexico, D.F.: Grijalbo, 1994), pp. 232-234.

122 His friend Gabriel García Márquez reported that, "One Sunday, letting himself go, he finished off a good-sized lunch with 18 scoops of ice-cream." See "A Personal Portrait of Fidel," in *Fidel Castro, My Early Years* (New York: Ocean Press), p. 15.

123 Carlos Alberto Montaner, *Fidel Castro y la revolución cubana* (Madrid: Playor, 1983), p. 29.

124 Fred Ward, *Inside Cuba Today* (New York: Crown, 1978), p. 207.

125 Juan Vivés, *Los amos de Cuba* (Buenos Aires: Emecé, 1982), p. 299.

126 Peter Bourne, *Fidel: a Biography of Fidel Castro* (New York: Dodd, Mead & Company, 1986), p. 77; also in Jules Dubois, *op. cit.*, p. 31.

127 Carlos Franqui, *op. cit.*, p. 254.

128 Juan Abreu, "Las Vacas de Castro," *Diario Las Américas*, August 2, 1992.

129 Magda Martínez, "Las flores del naranjo," *Bohemia*, Year 76, No. 22 (June 9, 1984), p. 31.

130 Ernesto Betancourt, "The Revolution at Thirty: An Economic Assessment," in *The Cuban Revolution at Thirty*, Proceedings from a

conference by the Cuban American National Foundation, January 10, 1989, p. 11, 12.

131 Carlos Alberto Montaner, *Journey to the Heart of Cuba: Life as Fidel Castro* (New York: Algora, 2001), p. 164.

132 Herbert Matthews, *Revolution in Cuba* (New York: Scribner's, 1975), p. 307.

133 Carlos Franqui, *Vida, aventuras y desastres de un hombre llamado Castro* (Barcelona: Planeta, 1988), p. 29.

134 Frei Betto, *op. cit.*, p. 92.

135 Frei Betto, *op. cit.*, p. 95; for a pioneering article on Castro's weird fixation on cows, milk, and dairy products, see Servando González, "¿Milagro en La Habana?," *Mariel* , Year 1, Vol. 4 (1988), p. 10.

136 Jorge Edwards, *Persona non grata* (Barcelona: Barral Editores, 1973), pp. 274-275.

137 Carlos Franqui, *Family Portrait with Fidel* (New York: Random House, 1984), p. 118.

138 Otto Kernberg, "Borderline Personality Organization," *Journal of the American Psychoanalytical Association*, 15 (July 1967), pp. 641-685; Robert P. Knight, "Borderline States," in *Psychoanalytic Psychiatry and Psychology* (New York: 1954), pp. 97-109; and Eric Pfeiffer, "Borderline States," in *Diseases of the Nervous System*, (May 1974), p. 216.

139 Eric Fromm describes narcissism as "a state of experience in which only the person himself, *his* body, *his* needs, *his* feelings, *his* thoughts, *his* property, everything and everybody pertaining to him are experienced as fully real, while everybody and everything that does not from part of the person or is not the object of his needs is not interesting, is not fully real, is perceived only by intellectual recognition, while *affectively* without weight and color. *The Anatomy of Human Destructiveness* (New York: Fawcett, 1973), pp. 227-228. As I have shown above, Fidel Castro shows most of the typical symptoms of an extremely narcissistic individual described by Fromm: he is interested only in himself, *his* wishes, *his* ideas, *his* plans. For him the world is real only as far as it is the object of *his* desires and *his* schemes. Other people matter only as far as they serve him or can be used. He always knows everything better than anyone else.

Castro's extreme narcissism explains his utter lack of interest in anybody or anything, except what he sees of service to him, hence his cold remoteness from everybody, including his closest friends, his brothers, and even his children. His absolute narcissism is the reason for his almost absolute lack of love, tenderness, or empathy for anybody. In his long life one can not find a single person whom he sincerely calls his friend. This explains why it has been so easy for him to get rid of people like Camilo Cienfuegos, Ché Guevara, Arnaldo Ochoa or Tony the la Guardia, who mistakenly believed Fidel Castro was their friend.

140 Most authors who have written biographies of political leaders like Lincoln, Churchill, Kennedy, Khrushchev, Clinton, or even Mussolini, Franco or Perón, have found that the lives of these men have been a constant struggle against their dark side. Yet, their biographers have discovered that it is precisely that struggle which make them human, and therefore interesting to other people. See, i.e., David Maraniss, *The Clinton Enigma* (New York: Simon and Schuster, 1998), p. 17. In the case of leaders like Hitler, Stalin and Castro, however, their dark side is so overwhelmingly powerful that it is almost impossible to find any sign of internal struggle of the individual against it.

141 William E. Ratliff, *The Selling of Fidel Castro* (New Brunswick: Transaction Books, 1987), p. x.

142 Otto Kernberg, "Structural Derivatives of Object Relationships," *International Journal of Psycho-Analysis*, 47 (1966), p. 238.

143 See, Modesto Maidique, "Fidel's Plantation." *The Stanford Magazine*, Winter 1983, pp. 27-32.

144 After the deaths of Tony de la Guardia and José Abrahantes, many senior intelligence officers are frantically engrossing their spookers and planning for a post-Castro life. Spooker is spy lingo for an emergency stash: cash, gold bullion, diamonds, emeralds, several false IDs and passports, and perhaps an untraceable weapon. Many of them already have spookers secured abroad. Ileana de la Guardia, the daughter of Castro's personal assassin Tony de la Guardia, apparently found one of her father's spookers. She is now living the good life in Europe with the money her father stole from the Cuban people. Other members of the Cuban intelligence, however, have been less lucky than Ileana. Some of them are still looking for Abrahantes' spooker, which many believe amounts to several million dollars.

145 Luis Conte Agüero, *op. cit.*, p. 29.

146 Though lately most people in Cuba are convinced that the Maximum Leader has gone nuts, this is not the case. Actually, Fidel Castro has always been nuts; now it has become more evident.

147 Associated Press, "CIA Preparing Psychological Profile of Castro," The *San Francisco Chronicle*, March 7, 2000, p. A-12.

148 Juan O. Tamayo, "Preocupa a E.U. la siquis de Castro," *El Nuevo Herald*, March 4, 2000.

149 Pablo Alfonso, "Preocupa la psicología agresiva de Castro," *El Nuevo Herald*, February 4, 2001.

150 Charles W. Socarides, *Beyond Sexual Freedom*. (New York: Quadrangle, 1975), p. 101.

151 Crews, *Unauthorized Freud* (New York: Viking, 1998).

152 Ray Brennan, *Castro, Cuba and Justice* (New York: Doubleday, 1959), p. 43.

153 Robert E. Quirk, *Fidel Castro* (New York: W. W. Norton, 1993), p. 15.

154 *Ibid.*, p. 16. Effeminate homosexuals (*maricones*) have always occupied a special place in Fidel Castro's shit list, and calling somebody a *maricón* (faggot) is his ultimate verbal abuse. At least on two occasions, first to Panama's General Omar Torrijos, and several years later to Spain's Prime Minister Felipe González, he sent his special envoy, writer Gabriel García Márquez, to deliver a personal message to the target of his anger. The message was a very short one, and García Márquez delivered it *verbatim*: "*Dice Fidel que usted es un maricón.*" ("Fidel says that you are a faggot." See Norberto Fuentes, *Dulces guerreros cubanos* (Barcelona: Seix Barral, 1999) pp. 200-202.

155 Carlos Franqui, *op. cit.*, pp. 265, 304. The anecdote was corroborated by Norberto Fuentes. According to Fuentes a Cuban model and vedette known as Norka commented that Fidel was "*un mal palo del carajo*" (lit: "a fucking lousy fuck"), *Dulces guerreros cubanos* (Barcelona: Seix Barral, 1999), p. 136.

156 Carlos Franqui, *op. cit.*, p. 49.

157 García Márquez admitted that one of the things which draw his attention the first time he heard Fidel was "his terrible power of seduction," see Gabriel García Márquez, "Fidel Castro: El oficio de la palabra hablada," Prologue to Gianni Minà, *Habla Fidel* (Mexico: Edivision, 1968), p. 12.

158 *The Losers* (New Rochelle, New York: Arlington House, 1969), p. 31.

159 Paul Johnson, *Modern Times* (New York: Harper & Row, 1983), p. 628.

160 Carlos Alberto Montaner, *Fidel Castro y la revolución cubana* (Madrid: Playor, 1983), p. 26.

161 *Ibid.*, p. 26.

162 Luis Conte Agüero, *Fidel Castro: Psiquiatría y política* (Mexico, D. F.: Editorial Jus, 1968), p. 69, 89.

163 Kenneth N. Skoug, Jr., *Cuba as a Model and a Challenge*. Washington, D.C.: The Cuban American Foundation, 1984, 8.

164 For a controversial interpretation of Castro's Cuba see Innokenti Abramov, "Castro's Revolution: Gays in Power," http://home.earthlink.net/~lively/fidelgay.htm. Abramov makes an interesting distinction between gays and homosexuals. For a study of the role of gays in Nazi Germany, see Scott Lively and Kevin Abrams, *The Pink Swastika: Homosexuality in the Nazi Party*, Third Edition (Keiser, Or-

egon: Founders Publishing Corporation, 1997).

165 *The Prison Memoirs of Armando Valladares* (New York: Alfred Knopf, 1986), p. 358.

166 *Faces of Latin America* (London: Latin American Bureau, 1991), p. 144.

167 Allen Young, *Gays Under the Cuban Revolution* (San Francisco: Gray Fox Press, 1981); Dennis Altman, *The Homosexualization of America, the Americanization of the Homosexual* (New York: St. Martin's Press, 1982).

168 Herbert Matthews, *Revolution in Cuba* (New York: Scribner's, 1975), p. 333.

169 Carlos Franqui, *Vida, aventuras y desastres de un hombre llamado Castro* (Barcelona: Planeta, 1988), p. 388.

170 Franqui, *ibid.*, p. 388; for an in-depth analysis of the UMAPs, the critical literature on them, and the persecution of homosexuals in this period, see Jorge Dominguez, *Cuba: Order and Revolution* (Cambridge, Mass.: Belknap Press, 1978), pp. 357, 393.

171 (Barcelona: Montesinos, 1984).

172 The script of *Conducta Impropia* has been published in book form. See Néstor Almendros and Orlando Jiménez Leal, *Conducta impropia* (Madrid: Playor, 1984); for a criticism of *Conducta Impropia* see "¿Quién persiguió a Muchilanga?," in Servando González, *Observando, segunda edición* (San Francisco: El Gato Tuerto, 1986), pp. 74-76.

173 The ideological commitment to the dignity of work and labor, the celebration of work as a liberating experience and as a tool to unite the nation, and the vision of work as a source of joy and satisfaction with higher, ethical meaning, without the need for material incentives, is a characteristic common to most fascist regimes. See Mark Neocleous, *Fascism* (Minneapolis: University of Minnesota Press, 1997), 50.

174 Herbert Matthews, *Revolution in Cuba* (New York: Scribner's, 1975), p. 333.

175 See for example, Richard Mohr, "Policy, Ritual, Purity: Mandatory AIDS Testing," in Larry May and Shari Collins Sharratt, *Applied Ethics: A Multicultural Approach* (New Jersey: Prentice Hall, 1994), pp. 374-380.

176 July 3, 1997.

177 "Information on the Rise of Communism in Cuba," anibal @pipeline.com, (Internet document), May 12, 1996.

178 *El Nuevo Herald*, September 3, 1997.

179 "Revolution—For Internal Consumption Only," in Irving Louis Horowitz, ed., *Cuban Communism* (New Jersey: Transaction Books, 1970), p. 38.

180 For a list of blacks that left their mark in pre-Castro's Cuba, see

José Luis Fernández, "Lies and Accomplices—Accomplices and Lies," *Guaracabuya*, June 8, 2001.

181 Carlos Franqui, *Family Portrait with Fidel* (New York: Random House, 1984), p. 150.

182 Actually Fidel was a bastard son product of an extra-marital affair. He was born while Angel was still married to his previous wife. The whole story is explained in detail in the Epilogue.

183 Nathaniel Weyl, *Red Star Over Cuba* (New York: Hillman/MacFadden, 1961), p. 41.

184 Her name sometimes appears spelled "Argeta" or "Argota."

185 Mario Lazo, *Dagger in the Heart* (New York: Twin Circle, 1968), p. 112.

186 Marcelo Fernandez-Zayas, "Intelligence Report From Washington," February 10, 2001, wpais@cais.com.

187 Stephan Archer, "Castro Persecutes Blacks," *NewsMax.com*, May 9, 2000, www.newsmax.com/articles/?a=2000/5/9/210025.

188 Miriam Marquez, "Castro's U.S. dollar policy of haves, have-nots is pure racism," *The Orlando Sentinel*, Jan 15 1999.

189 See http://www.cubagob.cu.

190 Juan Benemelis and Melvin Mañón, *Juicio a Fidel* (Santo Domingo: Taller, 1990).

191 See, i.e., Joe Azbell, *The Riot Makers* (Montgomery, Al.: Oak Tree Books, 1968), p. 104-105. An interesting detail is that, like all revolutionary movements around the world which Castro has managed to penetrate, the Black Revolution ended in failure. Coincidence?

192 *Ibid.*, p. 102.

193 *Ibid.*, p. 106.

194 *International Herald Tribune*, June 26, 1969.

195 Nevertheless, some prominent american blacks still continue giving their support to the Cuban white slavemaster, notable among them Jesse Jackson and Al Sharpton. As their support for Castro in the Elián González case demonstrated, by helping Castro to enforce his non-written fugitive slave clause these people were actually backing an Underground Railroad in reverse. The fact indicates that their distaste for slavery is not ethically, but politically motivated. (The concept of Underground Railroad in reverse is from William Norman Grigg, "The Gospel According to Marx," *The New American*, March 13, 2000.)

196 Arthur Allen, "Long Time Gone. A black militant's exile in Castro's Cuba," *Salon Magazine*, http://www.salon1999.com/11/features/cuba1.html.

197 Guillermo Cabrera Infante, *Mea Cuba* (Barcelona: Plaza & Janés, 1992), pp. 37, 54. Also in Hugh Thomas, *op. cit.*, pp. 888, 1433.

198 Ron Howell, "Con el turismo se expande el racismo," *El Nuevo Herald*, May 18, 2001.

199 For a devastating critique of the American Left and its relations with Castro's racist government see Sidney Brinkley, "Racism in Cuba and The Failure of the American Left," *Blacklight online*, http://www.blacklightonline.com/cubaracism.html.

200 Jesús Arboleya, *The Cuban Counterrevolution* (Athens, Ohio: Ohio University Research Center for International Studies, 2000), p. 189.

201 Fidel married Mirtha Díaz-Balart in 1948. A year after they had a son, Fidelito. The marriage was not very successful, and they divorced a few years later. After 1959 Castro's personal life became one of the best kept secrets in Cuba. Though he never officially remarried, it is known that he has had several affairs and fathered many children. For the last fifteen years he has been living (nobody knows if they are actually married, but most people believe they are not) with Dalia Soto del Valle, a woman of very humble origins, whom he met when she was still a high school student (most of her relatives are in Miami). Currently the couple live in a mansion west of Havana, with their five sons: Alex, Alexander, Alexis, Antonio and Angel. Alejandro is Fidel's second given name, and he likes it so much he has given it to many of his sons. Alejandro is the name of choice of many members of the Ministerio del Interior and the Cuban intelligence services for naming their sons.

202 *Guerrilla Prince* (Boston: Little, Brown and Company, 1991), p. 71.

203 Further proof of this is that when Castro decided to attend the Summit of Chiefs of State of the European Union with Latin America and the Caribbean held in Rio de Janeiro on July 28-29, 1999, he expressly asked the manager of the Hotel Bahia Othon, where he was to be hosted during the meeting, to be served by Hedwigues Botello, 32 and Marinés Hanel, 31, two of the hotel's employees. Both women are fair-skinned blondes, the opposite of the typical Brazilian beauty. See "Castro pide ser atendido por 2 jóvenes brasileñas," *El Nuevo Herald*, June 23, 1999.

204 *Op. cit.* p. 21.

205 Michael Beschloss and Strobe Talbott, *At The Highest Levels: The Inside Story of the End of the Cold War* (New York: Little, Brown, and Company, 1993), p. 58.

206 "The Last Revolutionary," and interview with Dan Rather, *CBS*, July 19, 1996.

207 Alvaro Sanjurjo Torreón, "Fidel Castro, de extra a astro," *Números*, n. 314. The information appears in James Robert Parish and Gregory W. Mank, *The Best of MGM: The Golden Years 1928-1959* (Des

Moines, Iowa: Nostalgia Books, 1981), and in the CD-ROM *The Motion Picture Guide* (New York: Cine Books, 1996).

208 Even though Fidel received a generous monthly allowance from his parents, he was also a fast money-blower and used to borrow money from his classmates, first at Belén and later at the University of Havana. But, notwithstanding his prodigious memory, he always had difficulty in remembering to pay the money back. See, Carlos Franqui, *Vida, aventuras y desastres de un hombre llamado Castro* (Barcelona: Planeta, 1988), p. 36.

209 Frank Mankiewicz and Kirby Jones, *With Fidel* (New York: Ballantine, 1975), p. 13; also on the cover of *High Times*, March 1978.

210 Jorge I. Dominguez, "Cuban Foreign Policy," *Foreign Affairs* 57 (Fall 1978), p. 83. See also Jorge I. Dominguez, "Cuba as Superpower," *Cold War International History Project Electronic Bulletin*, Nos. 8-9 (Winter 1996-1997).

211 "Military Outcomes of the Cuban Revolution," in Irving Louis Horowitz, ed., *Cuban Communism, Fourth Edition* (New Brunswick: Transaction Books, 1981), p. 590.

212 This is why throughout this book I have consistently referred to "the Castro government" instead of "the Cuban government." As a matter of fact, there is no such thing as a "Cuban government" in today's Cuba. All acts of government in Castro's Cuba are expressions of the personal will of the Maximum Leader, Fidel Alejandro Castro Ruz.

213 He wants to keep his anonimity.

214 This I experienced myself first hand a long time ago, when I had a long conversation with Castro while he was having a late lunch at Vedado's restaurant Potin (it was in fact in Potin's kitchen). After he finished his lunch, Capt. José Abrahantes, then a young Captain in charge of Castro's personal security, came and cleaned Castro's beard, while he kept talking to me totally ignoring Abrahantes as if he was a non-person.

215 Dariel (Benigno) Alarcón Ramírez, *Memorias de un soldado cubano* (Barcelona: Tusquets, 1997), pp. 260-262.

216 *Ibid*, pp. 188-189.

217 *Ibid*, p. 267.

218 *Ibid*, pp. 271-272.

219 In this sense—and only in this sense—Secretary of State Colin Powell was right when he claimed that Castro has "done some good things for his people." Actually Castro has done also some good things for *his* cows, *his* chickens, *his* dogs and for most of the things he owns. As any feudal lord, Castro takes good care of *his* property—which now comprises the whole island of Cuba and its inhabitants. On

Powell's words see Jay Nordlinger, "Castro and 'His People,'" *National Review*, April 26, 2001. Nordlinger found Powell's words "alarming and repugnant."

On the other hand, Powell's words may be just the manifestation of a feeling prevalent among many American blacks. Apparently they have at the bottom of their hearts a soft spot for white slavemasters—hence their love for Fidel Castro. Perhaps this is a sort of atavic manifestation of the Stockholm syndrome.

220 For information about the Cuban slaves' diet see Manuel Moreno Fraginals, *El Ingenio*, Tomo I (La Habana: Editorial de Ciencias Sociales, 1978).

Chapter 7: Castroism: A Tropical Variety of Fascism?

1 New York *Herald Tribune*, December 7, 1961.

2 Mario Lazo, *Dagger in the Heart* (New York: Twin Circle, 1968), p. 248. We don't know for sure if St. George was a CIA officer acting under a journalist's cover or a *bona fide* journalist recruited by the CIA, but many people, including his own wife, had strong suspicions about his true job. It is known that Ché Guevara believed St. George was an FBI agent. In a series of articles about Guevara's guerrilla activities in Bolivia St. George is described as having done "a spell in the U.S. military intelligence service". See *Sunday Telegraph*, July 7, 1968.

3 Earl E. T. Smith, *The Fourth Floor* (New York: Random House, 1962), pp. 34-35.

4 Foy D. Kohler, "Cuba and the Soviet Problem in Latin America," in Jaime Suchlicki, ed.; *Cuba, Castro, and Revolution* (Coral Gables, Florida: University of Miami Press, 1972), p. 121.

5 William Benton, *The Voice of Latin America* (New York: Harper and Row, 1965), p. 83.

6 Foy D. Kohler, *op. cit.*, p. 121.

7 Robert J. Alexander, "Soviet and Communist Activities in Latin America," in DeVere E. Pentony, ed., *Red World in Tumult: Communist Foreign Policies* (San Francisco: Chandler, 1962), p. 240.

8 William Z. Foster, *Outline History of the Americas* (New York: International Publishers, 1951), p. 375.

9 It is standard diplomatic practice by most countries, particularly the powerful ones, to meddle with the internal politics of their host nations. But, if discovered, the issue is never brought to light unless, for some reason, the host country wants to create a diplomatic incident.

10 Robert Loving Allen, *Soviet Influence in Latin America* (Washington, D.C.: Public Affairs Press, 1959), p. 86.

11 The Cuban Communist party—the *true* one, not Castro's—changed its name three times. It was called *Partido Comunista de Cuba* when it was created in 1925; it changed its name to *Unión Revolucionaria Comunista* in 1940; and finally it became the *Partido Socialista Popular* in 1944. The Cuban communists, however, never used those names when talking among themselves. They just called it *"el Partido"* ("the Party").

12 Richard Pattee, "The Role of the Roman Catholic Church," in Robert Freeman Smith, ed., *Background to Revolution* (New York: Alfred A. Knopf, 1966), p. 110.

13 In one of those unexpected twists of destiny, Blas Roca's son, economist and former MiG fighter pilot Vladimiro Roca, became disenchanted with Castro's "communism" and is now one of the leading anti-Castro dissidents in Cuba. He was sentenced to five years in prison in March, 1999, after been in jail since July, 1997, with three other dissidents, for writing a civic manifesto titled "The Fatherland Belongs to Us All." At the time of this writing he was still doing time in an isolation cell in one of Castro's prisons.

14 Though largely ignored, there was also an attack against the military barracks in the city of Bayamo, also in Oriente province.

15 The *Daily Worker*, New York, August 5, 1953. It is revealing the Cuban Communists' repeated use of the word "putschist" —communist parlance for fascist—to criticize Castro's methods.

16 Dam's article, "El grupo 26 de julio en la cárcel," in *Bohemia*, July 8, 1956.

17 "¡Basta ya de mentiras!" ("Enough Lies!"), in *Bohemia*, July 15, 1956. Fidel's article is quoted in length in Rolando E. Bonachea and Nelson P. Valdés, eds., *Revolutionary Struggle, 1947-1958* (Cambridge, Massachusetts: The MIT Press, 1972), p. 323.

18 *Castroism, Theory and Practice* (New York: Praeger, 1965), p. 28.

19 "Cuba -'Long Live the Revolution'", *The New Republic*, November 3, 1962, p. 15.

Criticism of Castro's strange variety of "communism" did not stop after he assimilated the old pro-Soviet Cuban Communist party into his own "Communist" party in the mid sixties. In the mid seventies, two Cuban Marxist scholars, Ariel Hidalgo and Ricardo Bofill, discovered by themselves what the old Cuban Communists had always known, that Fidel Castro is anything but a Communist.

Hidalgo is a published author, known for his books on the history of Cuban socialism. One of his books, *Origins of the Workers' Movement and Socialist Thought in Cuba* (1976), earned the praise of the Cuban press and the revolutionary élite. But soon after, Hidalgo had second thoughts. By 1979 he was considered a political dissident. He was suspended from his teaching position at the Worker's College and barred from continuing his graduate studies at the University of Havana.

In 1981 Hidalgo was writing an essay about the Cuban political system when the State Security police got hold of a copy and arrested him. Fortunately, his sister managed to save a copy and smuggled it to the U.S. Hidalgo's essay is an attack from a Marxist point of view of the Cuban State under Castro. According to him it is the managerial class, the élite, and not the workers who control the Cuban State. Hidalgo's case in Carlos Ripoll, *Harnessing the Intellectuals* (Washington, D.C.: The Cuban American Foundation, 1985), pp. 38-41.

The other Marxist scholar, Dr. Ricardo Bofill was a member of the Castroist Cuban Communist Party and a professor of Marxist philosophy at the University of Havana until he was arrested in 1967 and later sentenced to twelve years in prison. His arrest came as a consequence of his association with a dissident group of Marxist professionals and intellectuals who were concerned about Castro's methods of implementing socialism in Cuba. Like Hidalgo, Bofill had serious doubts about Castro's Marxism and Cuba's Socialism.

20 Letter to Daniel (René Ramos Latour), Sierra Maestra, December 14, 1957, cited in Carlos Franqui, *Family Portrait with Fidel* (New York: Random House, 1984), p. 149.

21 *Ibid.*, pp. 152-153. *History Will Absolve Me* was in fact the heavily edited version of Fidel's self-defense speech at the trial for the attack on the Moncada garrison. The document circulated *samizdat* style all around the Island. Some people claim that the core of the document was not written by Castro himself, but by his university professor Dr. Jorge Mañach, then an anti-Batista in the closet. See, Guillermo Cabrera Infante, Introduction to Carlos Franqui, *Family Portrait with Fidel* (New York: Random House, 1984*)*, p. XIII. In the early 1980s, Mirta Aguirre, a member of the PSP opportunistically turned into a Castroist, made an unsuccessful attempt at trying to prove that *History Will Absolve Me* was Marxist-inspired. See, "El Leninismo en la Historia me absolverá," in *La revolución cubana* (Havana: Ministerio de Educación Superior, 1983), pp. 251-279.

22 The *New York Times*, March 28, 1982.

23 Andrew St. George's interview with Castro, *Look*, in April of 1958.

24 *The Early Fidel* (Seacaucus: Lyle Stuart, 1978), p. 118. Trying to prove his theory that Castro was a Marxist since his university days, Martin claims that Fidel was quite friendly with fellow students Leonel

Soto, Alfredo Guevara, Flavio Bravo and Luis Más Martín, all members of the Communist youth organization. But that conclusion is flawed, because it is also known that Fidel was quite friendly with some homosexuals at the university, and there is no hard evidence that he was a homosexual himself.

25 *Red Star Over Cuba* (New York: Hillman/Macfadden, 1961), pp. 73-85, 92-97.

26 *Cuba: The Pursuit of Freedom* (New York: Harper and Row, 1971), p. 829.

27 "The Impact of the Cuban Revolution," in Neal D. Houghton, ed., *Struggle Against History* (New York: Clarion, 1968), p. 135.

28 Claude Julien, *La Révolution Cubaine* (Paris: Maspero 1961), p. 166.

29 Daniel James, *Cuba: The First Soviet Satellite in the Americas* (New York: Avon, 1961), p. 29.

30 Franqui *op. cit.*, p. 153.

31 Andrés Valdespino quoting from *Carta Semanal* in a public polemic with Carlos Rafael Rodríguez, a PSP leader (*Bohemia*, June 26, 1960, p. 43). Rodríguez didn't challenge the assertion in his answer to Valdespino.

32 Though it was later denied, there is evidence that until late 1958 Castro did not consider guerrilla fighting as a fundamental method of struggle. Apparently his hopes when he landed in Oriente Province in 1956 were to prompt urban uprisings which could develop into an insurrection, but the very few that actually occurred were quickly crushed by Batista's army. Even then, Castro, who took not a single measure in the event of a prolonged guerrilla warfare in the Oriente mountains, still believed that Batista would be defeated by some kind of general strike or mass action—like Mussolini's March on Rome. But the Cuban people—especially the poor farmers and city workers—remained indifferent to his struggle.

33 Claude Julien, *La Révolution Cubaine* (Paris: Maspero, 1961), p. 81.

34 *Hoy*, La Habana, January 11, 1959.

35 Hugh Thomas *op. cit.*, p. 981.

36 "Note from K. Voroshilov to Manuel Urrutia, January 10, 1959", *Pravda*, January 11, 1959.

37 Edwin Leuwen, *Arms and Politics in Latin America* (New York: Praeger, 1961), p. 276.

38 Carlos Rafael Rodríguez to Herbert Matthews. See Herbert Matthews, *Fidel Castro* (New York: Simon & Schuster, 1969), p. 176.

39 *Guía del pensamiento político-económico de Fidel* (La Habana: Diario Libre, 1959, p. 48.

40 "Conclusiones del pleno del Comité Nacional del PSP, realizado en los días 25 al 28 de mayo de 1959", *Hoy*, June 7, 1959.

41 *Ibid.*

42 "El peor camino," *Hoy*, January 13, 1959.

43 The Cuban communists' distrust for Castro has been corroborated by sources behind the iron curtain. See, i.e., Markus Wolf, *A Man Without a Face: The Autobiography of Communism's Greatest Spymaster* (New York: Public Affairs,1997), pp. 343-344.

44 "The Cuban Revolution in Action," *World Marxist Review*, II, No. 8 (August, 1959), p. 17.

45 The *New York Times*, April 21, 1959.

46 *Revolución*, April 25, 1959; also in *Guía del pensamiento político-económico de Fidel* (La Habana: Diario Libre, 1959), p. 48.

47 *Time*, April 27, 1959.

48 *Hispanic American Report*, Vol. XII No. 4, 1959, p. 205.

49 *Revolución*, May 22, 1959.

50 Fidel's search for a third way, however, is not a new political phenomenon. A version of the third way is fascism—supposedly a halfway political system between the anarchy of capitalism and the prison-house of socialism. Fascism, allegedly the synthesis of all opposites, claims that it overcomes the artificial distinction between right and left. See Mark Neocleous, *Fascism* (Minneapolis: University of Minnesota Pres, 1977), p. 58. One may safely surmise that, putting his photographic memory to good use, Castro was just parroting one of the articles of Spanish fascist José Antonio Primo de Rivera's in which he summed up the position: fascism is neither right nor left. Primo de Rivera's article summing up the fascist position, "On the Occasion of the Foundation of the Spanish Falange," in Hugh Thomas, (ed.), *José Antonio Primo de Rivera: Selected Writings* (London: Jonathan Cape, 1972), pp. 53-54.

51 *Hoy*, June 30, 1959.

52 "Rubén Darío Rumbaut", *Bohemia*, January 1, 1961, p. 58.

53 Rumbaut's personal communication with the author, 10 January, 1999.

54 *Revolución*, May 22, 1959.

55 *Bohemia*, June 14, 1959.

56 Theodore Draper, *Castro's Revolution* (New York: Praeger, 1962), pp. 116-117.

57 Very soon the ever humorous Cuban people nicknamed Dorticós with an appropriate name: *"cucharita"*—teaspoon—a utensil that neither cuts nor punctures, signifying his lack of real power and decision-making in Castro's government. After long years of being a nonentity in Castro's shadow, Dorticós committed suicide in 1983. On

Dorticós death see Servando González, *Observando. Segunda edición* (San Francisco: El Gato Tuerto, 1986), pp. 76-78.

58 News Conference, December 10, *Department of State Bulletin*, December 28, 1959. p. 937.

59 The full text of Fidel's confession of Marxist faith was published in *Hoy*, December 2, 1961, and in the evening edition of *Revolución*, December 2, 1961. Usually Fidel's speeches first published in the evening edition of *Revolución* are reprinted the following day in the morning edition. For unknown reasons it was not done this time. There are several slightly different versions of the speech: the *Hoy* version, two versions published in the first and second edition of *Revolución*, one abridged version in *Bohemia* on December 10, and one in a pamphlet edition in *Obra Revolucionaria*.

60 Loree Wilkerson, *Fidel Castro's Political Programs from Reformism to Marxist Leninism* (Gainesville, Florida: University of Florida Press, 1965).p. 81. Wilkerson's is by far the best analysis of Fidel's "I am a Marxist" speech.

61 An illegal is an intelligence officer placed in a foreign country with false identity to operate independently from any of his embassies of consulates. Illegals are not covered by diplomatic immunity, therefore they normally operate under deep covers and use false documentation. A sleeper is an intelligence officer who has been implanted into a country under a false identity and has been living a normal life for a rather long amount of time, waiting to be roused into action. The main job of a sleeper is to wait, as unnoticed as possible, until he receives the wake up order, regardless of the length of time required.

62 *Editorial Research Reports* July 9, 1967.

63 *Op. cit.*, p. 1489.

64 Hugh Thomas, *op. cit.*, p. 946.

65 *Cahiers du Communisme* (January-February, 1959).

66 The *Times*, January 2, 1959.

67 *Revolución*, January 19, 1957.

68 John M. Kirk, "From Counterrevolution to *Modus Vivendi*: The Church in Cuba, 1959-84," in Sandor Halebsky and John M. Kirk, eds., *Cuba: Twenty-five Years of Revolution, 1959-1984* (New York: Praeger, 1985), p. 101.

69 Zacchi's interview in *Excelsior* quoted in Néstor Carbonell Cortina, palabras pronunciadas en Nueva York el 26 de julio del 2000 ante una selecta representación de la Iglesia.

70 Matthews, *op. cit.*, p. 330.

71 Armando Valladares, "ONU: Representante Vaticano favorece dictadura castrista," *Diario Las Américas*, October 26, 2000.

72 See, *Fides Agency*, "Cuba: Growing Government Intolerance and

Persecution Towards Catholics," November 25, 2000.

73 "La Santa Sede denuncia ante la ONU los efectos nefastos del embargo," *Agencia Zenith*, October 20, 2000.

74 New York: St. Martin's Press, 1995.

75 It seems that the Catholic Church's support for criminal dictatorships is not an exception, but rather the rule. Argentinean journalist and writer Jacobo Timerman observed that he is "from a country where almost all the Catholic Bishops supported and blessed the torturers and murderers of a military dictatorship, encouraged and justified them; a country where torturers and murderers were likewise Catholic." *Cuba: A Journey* (New York: Alfred A Knopf, 1990), p. 74

76 See, i.e., Humberto A. Pujals, "Cuba: Juan Pablo II habla, el *Granma* se complace, fieles católicos sufren," *El Nuevo Herald*, Julio 9, 2001. As early as 1986 I predicted the rapprochement between Castro and the Catholic Church. See my *Historia herética de la revolución fidelista* (San Francisco: El Gato Tuerto, 1986), p. 153. It turned out that my prediction was pretty accurate.

77 Was the Pope's visit to Cuba a Canossa in reverse? Many people have speculated about the true reasons behind the Pope's visit to Cuba, a visit that, as many expected, resulted in a total diplomatic triumph for Castro and meager gains for the Catholic Church and the Cuban Catholics. No one can be certain about why John Paul II took such a fateful step, but there are some clues pointing to an explanation. After realizing that the Jesuit order had been totally subverted under the control of a rebel anti-Catholic faction fighting for the creation of the New Man under the banners of Liberation Theology, the Pope decided to fight back. But very soon he realized not only that the Order had been transformed beyond all recovery, but that the rebel faction that had taken control over it had the strength and power he lacked.

Though in theory the Pope has the power to disband the Order, he knew he could not take such a drastic measure without risking the very destruction of the Church he was trying to avoid. Therefore, he decided to counterattack on the theological plane. To this effect, he relied on his ally, Joseph Cardinal Ratzinger, to produce, in 1984, an official *Instruction* to all Catholics condemning liberation theology in the strongest terms. But, to his surprise—and this gives us a measure of the arrogance and power of the rebel faction among the Jesuits—he found himself under the direct and open attack of the renegades. The culmination of this attack was a book, published in 1985 by Uruguayan renegade Jesuit Juan Luis Segundo. The title of the book, *Theology and the Church: A Response to Cardinal Ratzinger and a Warning to the Whole Church*, sets the tone of its outrageous content. Catholic scholar and orthodox Jesuit Malachi Martin wrote that Segundo's "purpose seems to be to put John Paul II on notice that if he as a Pope accepts and blesses Ratzinger's *Instruction* on the Theology of Liberation, then he as a pope will have trouble, much trouble." See *The Jesuits: The Society of Jesus and the Betrayal of the Catholic Church* (New York: Simon & Schuster, 1987), pp. 485-487.

There is the possibility that the true purpose of the Pope's untimely visit to Cuba was to placate, at least temporarily, the pro-Castro liberation theology Jesuits, while gaining some time to maneuver. The mysterious deaths of both John Paul I and Sixtus V, just after they had decided to fight the Jesuit rebel faction, indicate that taking Jesuits' threats lightly may prove to be extremely unhealthy.

78 Frei Betto, *Fidel and Religion* (New York: Simon and Schuster, 1987), p. 232.

79 Tad Szulc, *Fidel: A Critical Portrait* (New York: William Morrow, 1986), p. 38.

80 Frei Betto, *op. cit.*, p. 225. Probably he was not far from the truth. To have an idea of what a "communist" state organized by the new "Marxists" in the Catholic Church would be, see Padre J. Guadalupe Carney, *To Be a Revolutionary* (New York: Harper & Row, 1985). Father Carney is an American-born Jesuit priest who turned into a Castro-style revolutionary. Among other stupid things, Father Carney calls Ché Guevara "another Marxist saint, who gave his life for the poor guided by the Spirit of Jesus," p. 307.

81 Robert Rouquette, *Saint Ignace de Loyola* (Paris: Albin Michel, 1944), p. 44.

82 *Ibid.*, p. 44.

83 H. Boehmer, *Les Jesuites* (Paris: Armand Colin, 1910), p. 192.

84 A clue that perhaps this is the case is that author Eduardo Galeano, a staunch Fidelista, firmly believes that "In Hispanic America Jesuit missions developed along progressive lines," and describes in rosy colors the pillage and exploitation of the Guaraní by the Jesuits. See *Open Veins of latin America: Five Centuries of Pillage of a Continent* (New York: Monthly Review Press, 1973), p. 209.

85 H. Boehmer, *Ibid.*, p. 197.

86 Stealing and illegal killing of cattle has become so common in Castro's Cuba that the National Assembly voted to pass a law modifying the Penal Code to allow for stiff sanctions for this type of crime. According to *Granma*, in 1986 close to 17,000 head of cattle had been stolen and killed illegally. The number reached 48,656 in 1998. See Manuel David Orrio, "El cuchillo del matarife," *CubaNet* (www.cubanet.org), April 14, 1999. Also Pablo Alfonso, "En auge el cuatrerismo pese a drásticas penas," *El Nuevo Herald*, September 1, 1999.

87 Edmond Paris, *The Secret History of the Jesuits* (Chino, Calif.: Chick Publications, 1975), p. 68.

88 Himmler's closest confidant, Walter Schellenberg, wrote a pretty accurate picture of his boss' fascination with the Jesuits. "Himmler owned an extremely large and excellent library on the Jesuit Order and for years would sit up late studying the extensive literature. Thus he built up the SS organization according to the principles of the Jesuits. The *Spiritual Exercises* of Ignatius of Loyola served as the foundation; the supreme law was absolute obedience, the execution of any order whatsoever without any question. Himmler himself, as Reichsführer of the SS, was the general of the order. The structure of leadership was borrowed from the hierarchical order of the Catholic Church. He took over a medieval castle, the so-called Wevelsburg at Paderborn in Westphalia, and had it repaired so that it might serve as a kind of 'SS monastery.' Here the general of the order would hold a secret consistory once a year, attended by the top leadership of the order. They would take part in spiritual exercises and practice sessions in concentration." Walter Schellenberg, *The Labyrinth: Memoirs of Walter Schellenberg* (New York: Harper, 1956).

89 For an excellent analysis of the inner workings of the Jesuit "democracy", see Malachi Martin, *op. cit.*, pp. 228-229.

90 Rumors running in Cuba explain the new-found Castroist faith of Ortega and Céspedes in non-religious terms. According to the rumors, both men have a liking for young boys, and the efficient Cuban intelligence services are always on the look out for any type of weakness of the flesh. This perhaps also explains the sudden conversion to Castroism of many visitors to Cuba, including famous writers, politicians, and prestigious scholars. The MININT's vaults at Villa Maristas, the rumors claim, are full of incredible videos, most of them of American writers, scholars, religious leaders, and politicians, as well as people you frequently see on American tv and films, but playing quite different roles. It is also rumored that Castro keeps some of the tapes at his home for his personal enjoyment.

91 Carl Koch, FSC, *Creating a Christian LifeStyle* (Winona, MN: Saint Mary's Press, 1988), p. 341.

92 Poverty in Cuba after more than forty years of Castroism is so widespread, and the gap between the rich and the poor so wide, that the subject was included in the agenda of important matters to be discussed at the congress of the government-controlled *Central de Trabajadores de Cuba* (Central Workers' Union), the only union remaining in the country. See France Press Agency, "Piden atenuar las desigualdades en la sociedad cubana", *El Nuevo Herald*, November 7, 2000. Cuban workers' unions before Castro, some of them controlled

by the Communists, were probably the strongest in the American continent, the U.S. included.

A recent report, "Cuba: Facetas Sociales" ("Cuba: Social Highlights"), published by a prominent dissident group in Cuba, exposes the social failure of Castroism. "The Cuban citizen is a pariah in his own country, a third class person . . . Cubans are subject to "tourism apartheid," says the document. "Young people have lost all hope in their future, and they resort to alcohol, drugs and prostitution while their only hope is escaping the country." "The Cuban average salary of 232 Cuban pesos ($11 U.S. dollars), cannot provide for the very basic needs." "Social inequality is growing." See A. Cawthorne, Reuters, "Disidentes emiten un documento que fustiga duramente al régimen," *El Nuevo Herald*, November 18, 2000.

93 J. Meyerdorff, *The Orthodox Church and the Ecumenical Movement* (Geneva: WCC,1978), p. 320. Meyerdorff's words, motivated by the great temptation of a Christianity that identifies more and more with secular socialism, were directed at the World Council of Churches. Jesus rejected this identification unequivocally: "My kingdom is not of this world; if my kingdom were of this world, then would my servants fight . . ." (John 18:36)

94 "ONU: Representante Vaticano Favorece Dictadura Castrista", *Diario Las Americas*, October 26, 2000.

95 "La Santa Sede denuncia ante la ONU los efectos nefastos del embargo", *Agencia Zenit*, October 20, 2000.

96 Intelligence services try to be invisible to the outside world. In this, the Holy See's intelligence services (whose importance is evidenced by the fact that one of its four section leaders was Monsignor Giovanni Montini—later Pope Paul VI) are perhaps the best in the world. They are so invisible that are not mentioned in most books about intelligence and espionage, including dictionaries and encyclopedias. Though all Catholic orders gather intelligence for the Vatican, the Jesuits, with their sophisticated training, rigorous discipline and tight-knit organization, have always been among the best Vatican intelligence officers. (Sir Francis Walsingham, the father of the British intelligence services, became famous in the XVI century uncovering Jesuit priests acting as spies.) On may occasions, Jesuits have used their cover as missionaries to conduct secret diplomatic and intelligence missions as well as secret tasks for the secret police of Catholic states. To conduct their secret missions they have at times used plain clothing and pretended to be partisans of their enemies to infiltrate their ranks. As Sun Tzu pointed out a long time ago, deception and guile are more powerful tools than physical violence.

97 The fact that Reagan's Star Wars was actually an intelligence

hoax used to destroy the Soviet economy is explained in Alvin A. Snyder, *Warriors of Disinformation: American Propaganda, Soviet Lies, and the Winning of the Cold War* (New York: Arcade Publishing, 1995), pp. 120-125.

98 Richard J. Payne, *Opportunities and Dangers of Soviet -Cuban Expansion* (Albany, N.Y.: State University of New York Press, 1988), p. 9; also in W. Raymond Duncan, *The Soviet Union and Cuba* (New York: Praeger, 1985), p. 1.

According to some U.S. government estimates based on official Cuban and Soviet sources, from 1961 to 1983 the Soviets threw $34.290 billion U.S. dollars down into Castro's Cuban black hole. See U.S. Congress, *Cuba Faces the Economic Realities of the 1980s* (Washington, D.C.: U.S. Government Printing Office, 1982, p. 16; also Directorate of Intelligence, *The Cuban Economy: A Statistical Review*, Reference Aid ALA 84-10052 (Washington, D.C., June 1984).

99 Janette Habel, "Miser sur l'Église pour sauver la révolution cubaine?", subtitled "La religion comme solution", *Le Monde Diplomatique*, February. 22, 1997.

100 Recent information from Cuba tells of a secret document produced by Castro's "Communist" Party, informing about a program to counteract the activities of Christian organizations in Cuba. See, Pablo Alfonso, Ofensiva contra el auge religioso," *El Nuevo Herald*, June 17, 2001.

Though the source sees the document as evidence of a growing anti-religious attitude of the Castro government, it can be interpreted in other ways. Though Castro is not intrinsically against any religious manifestation *under his control*, he is not likely to tolerate any independent religious activity in the Island.

101 John Dorschner and Roberto Fabricio, *The Winds of December* (New York: Coward, McCann & Geoghegan, 1980), p. 35.

102 *Family Portrait with Fidel* (New York: Random House, 1984), p. 25.

103 Bartolomeo Maximiliano (Beny) Moré began his musical career singing on the streets of Havana as a street singer with his guitar and eventually became one of Cuba's most noted popular singers. He died in 1963 at the age of 44.

104 *Fidel Castro y la revolución cubana*. Madrid: Editorial Playor, 1983, 25-27.

105 "The Sozial-revolution Fidel Castros." (Manuscript. Sozial–forschungsstelle Dortmund, 1965).

106 "El transfondo revolucionario del sincretismo criollo," *Sondeos*, No. 86 (Cuernavaca, Mexico. Centro de Documentación de Cuernavaca (CIDOC), 1972), p. 29.

107 San Francisco: El Gato Tuerto, 1986.

108 *Encounters*, Vol I, Winter 1989.

109 Georgie Anne Geyer, *Guerrilla Prince* (Boston: Little, Brown & Co., 1991), p. 173.

110 *Ibid.*, p. 205.

111 Janet Farrar and Virginia Russell, *The Magical History of the Horse* (London: Robert Hale, 1992), p. 34.

112 *Ibid.*, p. 35.

113 Though most of the above information is obviously based on speculation, there seems to be a confirmed fact: dates have a special importance to Fidel Castro, because he is a believer in numerology. In his interview with Frei Betto, the Dominic mentions the fact that the number 26 seems to have had quite a bearing on Fidel's life. Castro's answer is revealing: "Well, I was born in 1926; that's true. I was 26 when I began the armed struggle, and I was born on the 13th, which is half of 26. Batista staged his coup d'état in 1952, which is twice 26. Now that I think of it, there may be something mystical about the number 26." Betto continues, "You were 26 when you began the struggle. The attack on the Moncada was won on the 26th of July, and it gave rise to the July 26th Movement." And Fidel proceeds, "And we landed in 1956, which is the round number of 30 plus 26." *Fidel: My Early Years* (New York: Ocean Press,1998), p. 32). Sources close to Castro claim that in several occasions he has made references to strange coincidences involving numbers and dates. For example, he has mentioned that his life seems to turn around the number 13. He was born on the 13th, and the year was 1926 (13+13); his entry into politics came at age 26 (13+13); the assault on the Moncada barracks took place on July 26 (13+13); and Celia Sánchez' funeral was held on June 13, 1981.

114 González-Whippler, *op. cit.*, p. 183. Another source in Cuba, a physician who was part of a team attending Castro, claims that Fidel used to drink daily glasses of bull's blood and also bathed in the blood.

115 See, Rafael Lara, "Fidel Castro and Cuba's Secret Societies, *Power Games*, www.inexplicata.com/samizdat/paranormal/power_games.html

116 *Castro's Daughter* (New York: St. Martin's Press, 1997, p. 7.

117 Andres Oppenheimer, *Castro's Final Hour* (New York : Simon & Schuster, 1992), p. 344.

118 Tad Szulc, *Fidel: A Critical Portrait* (New York: William Morrow, 1986), p. 469-70.

119 Oppenheimer, *op. cit*, p. 344 ; also in Tad Szulc, *op. cit.*, pp. 469-470.

120 Frei Betto, *Fidel and Religion* (New York: Simon and Schuster, 1987), p. 100, (emphasis added).

121 Rather is probably the most Castro-friendly among the Castro-friendly American journalists—and they are legion.

122 "The Last Revolutionary," an interview with Dan Rather, *CBS*, July 19, 1996 (emphasis added).

123 Ignacio Duarte, "Todos los santos y deidades le han virado las espaldas al tirano Castro." *Alerta* (Miami), (n. d.), pp. 10-14.

124 Andres Oppenheimer, *op. cit.*, p. 345.

125 Nelson P. Valdés, "La Cachita y el Ché: Patron Saints of Revolutionary Cuba," *Encounters*, Vol I, Winter 1989.

126 For an interesting compilation of articles appearing in the American press about Castro's drug trafficking activities, see The Cuban-American National Foundation, *Castro's Narcotic Trade*. (Washington, D.C.: The Cuban-American Foundation, Inc., 1983).

127 According to sources in Cuba, Castro's "official" babalawo is known as Enriquito, and he reports regularly to the MININT (Cuban State Security). See, Marcelo Fernández-Zayas, "Intelligence Report From Washington - 01112001," wpais@cais.com.

128 As I have mentioned over and over in this book, in the field of intelligence and espionage things are seldom as they seem. Therefore, there is a possibility that perhaps Castro's behavior in the Elián González case has a totally different explanation.

129 On the other hand, though it is true that most of the initial group of Cubans exiled in Florida were members of the Cuban oligarchy, the extended American view of the pro-Castro Cubans as progressive revolutionaries and the anti-Castro Cubans in Florida as right-wing reactionaries is a concoction created by Castro's intelligence services with the tacit complicity of the American main-stream media. As Holly Ackerman pointed out, "the political culture of Miami has been understudied and oversimplified, while the political culture in Cuba has been made sacred and is frozen in its 1959 colors. I contend that the political culture of exile has incorporated gradual but significant changes through democratization, while the political culture of the island has been imposed and maintained through repression. The surface appearance of consent and belief on the island is a veil. The monolithic image of Miami is a misconception," in "Searching for Middle Ground: Cuba's Chronic Dilemma," *Peace Magazine*, www.peacemagazine.org/9703/cuba-ha1.htm

130 Some keen observers have noticed the paradoxical fact that, perhaps unconsciously, some anti-Castro Cuban exiles adopt quasi-Marxist postures in their attacks on Castro. See, e.g., Ariel Hidalgo, "Un odio de amante despechado," *El Nuevo Herald*, 24 August 1999. But, as Italian Marxist ideologue Antonio Gramsci pointed out, there is not any essential difference between raw communism and raw capi-

talism. At heart both are essentially materialistic. Both value and define man based only on the material goods he produces and consumes. See Malachi Martin, *The Keys to This Blood* (New York: Simon & Schuster, 1990), p. 397-398. For an apparently contrarian view, but which essentially agrees with the above and asks capitalists to change their ethical values or perish, see George Gilder's excellent essay "The Soul of Silicon," *Forbes ASAP*, June 1, 1998, pp. 111-128.

On the other hand, visitors to Cuba report a new phenomenon. Contrary to Miami, where the name Fidel Castro is a mantra repeated over and over, Cubans in the Island, particularly the ones belonging to the new generations, rarely refer to Castro, not even indirectly by pulling an imaginary beard from their chins as they used to do. It seems as if they had agreed on totally ignoring the Cuban tyrant and, by eliminating Castro from their daily talk, they have erased him from their lives.

131 According to Alfonso Tarabocchia, of Florida's Dade County sheriff's intelligence unit, "The [Cuban] exile community has been penetrated to the fullest degree." See David Corn, *Blond Ghost* (New York: Simon and Schuster, 1994), p. 85. More recently, Juan O. Tamayo, a *Miami Herald* staff writer, reported that some people estimate Castro maintains about 300 trained intelligence officers in South Florida alone to spy on the Cuban exile community; see "Spies Among Us: Castro Agents Keep Eye on Exiles," *The Miami Herald*, April 11, 1999. Reports about Castro's espionage activities directed at penetrating anti-Castro organizations abound. See, for example, Mervin K. Sigale, "Castro's Spies Prowl Miami, Defector Says," *The Miami News*, Dec 18, 1971; "Dead 'Exile' Was My Spy, Castro Says," *The Miami Herald*, February 9, 1987; Liz Balmaseda, "Exile: I Was Mastermind of Mariel," *The Miami Herald*, July 31, 1989; "Cuba: Agents Leading the Anti-castro Opposition," *Intelligence Newsletter* # 28, July 10, 1992, http://www.indigo-net.com/intel.html; Tim Weiner, "Castro's Moles Dig Deep, Not Just Into Exiles," *The New York Times*, March 1, 1996; Charles Cotayo, "Supuestos espías nadaron entre un mar de organizaciones," *El Nuevo Herald*, September 16, 1998; Lucia Newman, "In Rare Admission, Castro Says Cuba has Dispatched Spies Across U.S.," *CNN*, October 20, 1998; Associated Press, "Cuban Museum a Tribute to Espionage," *The New York Times*, December 7, 1998; Juan O. Tamayo, "Witness: I Was Castro Spy in Foundation," *The Miami Herald*, March 12, 1999. See also Susana Lee, "Lo mejor de la misión: el regreso a Cuba," *Granma*, March 24, 2000, a detailed account in Castro's official newspaper of how the Castroist intelligence services has successfully penetrated most of the anti-Castro organizations in the U.S. For an account of how the Cuban intelligence launched a disinformation campaign against the Cuban

American National Foundation after the death of its chair Jorge Más Canosa, see Rui Ferreira, "Un presunto espía tuvo como tarea lanzar campaña contra la Fundación," *El Nuevo Herald*, December 22, 2000.

132 In his memoirs, *The Art of War*, written in 500 BC, Sun Tzu, a prominent Chinese general, advises: "If you know the enemy and know yourself, you need not fear a hundred battles. If you know yourself and not the enemy, for every victory you will suffer a defeat. If you know neither yourself nor the enemy, you are a fool and will meet defeat in every battle." Forty years of continued failures indicate that most anti-Castro Cuban exiles neither know themselves nor Fidel Castro.

133 A report issued on October 6, 1998, by Amnesty International, tells about extensive human-rights abuses in the U.S. criminal-justice system. The report is an exposé of police brutality, including prison beatings, deadly choke-holds, and policemen torturing suspects. The Amnesty report paints a grim picture of crowded and inhumane prisons, populated by inmates mostly members of minorities, where gay rape by other inmates and torture by officers are commonplace. See, "Abusive Behavior," *The Economist*, October 10, 1998. In late 1979 the U.S. was the subject of an international inquiry into human rights violations. After a comprehensive national investigation, including interviews with inmates and officials in prisons across the country, the commission's final report stated there was a "clear prima facia case" of human rights violations in American prisons. See, Nat Hentoff, "Seven International Jurists Journey to the Heart of Darkness," the *Village Voice*, December 9, 1978. The findings of the commission of jurists was largely unreported by the American mainstream media. Moreover, as in Castro's Cuba, there is a growing trend in American prisons of using inmates as a cheap source of labor. According to a report appearing in *The Nation* in January 29, 1996, "Since 1990, 30 states have legalized the contracting of prison labor to private companies." Human Rights Watch, the largest human rights organization in the U.S. who has been publishing every year Castro's human rights violations and condemning the Castro regime in the strongest terms, is also critical of human rights violations in the U.S.

A difference between human rights violations in the U.S. and in totalitarian countries, is that human rights violations in the U.S. are aired on prime time tv (i.e. COPS), but the American people are so anesthetized that they fail to see them. More recently, the anti-Castro exiles in Miami had a first-hand experience of human rights violations in the U.S. after witnessing the Gestapo-like abduction at gun point of Elián González by a government paramilitary group. I am still waiting, however, to read an article written by an anti-Castro exile living in the U.S. condemning human rights violations by the U.S. government. Perhaps it has never crossed their minds that their selective attitude towards human rights violations damages their credibility and their efforts to convincing others to join them in their condemnation of human rights violations by the Castroist government.

Granted, no one can even compare isolated cases of human rights violations in the U.S. with the ones systematically happening in countries like Cuba or the People's Republic of China. However, if the United States wants to keep a credible role as critic of human rights violations abroad, it should be more critical about that type of violations in its own territory. The battering rams crashing into children's bedrooms, the killing of dissidents (Castro calls them "counterrevolutionaries" and "CIA agents;" the U.S. government calls them "white separatists" and "cult members") by trigger-happy FBI snipers, and the fiery assault on a religious building by paramilitary forces are part of a disturbing trend that should have no place in a democratic America

134 This is the case, i.e., of Angela Davis, a strong critic of the abuses committed against black people in American prisons. But Ms. Davis, a Castro supporter and a frequent visitor to Cuba, has never raised her voice to condemn the abuses committed against black Cubans in Castro's prisons. Apparently she has never had the sensitivity to ask herself why, in a country where about 40 percent of the population is black, more than 85 percent of prison inmates belong to that racial group.

135 Jules Dubois *Fidel Castro* (New York: Bobbs-Merrill, 1959), pp. 14-15; also in Servando González, *Historia herética de la revolución fidelista* (San Francisco: Ediciones El Gato Tuerto, 1986), pp. 9-12.

136 Jesús Arboleya, *op. cit.*, p. 61.

137 Jaime Suchlicki, *Cuba: From Columbus to Castro* (New York: Scribner's, 1974), pp. 143.

138 *Bohemia Libre*, December 1961.

139 Daniel James, *Cuba: The First Soviet Satellite in the Americas* (New York: Avon, 1961), p. 34.

140 Peter G. Bourne, *Fidel: A Biography of Fidel Castro* (New York: Dodd, Mead & Company, 1986), p. 29.

141 Talent spotter: 1. An intelligence officer or operative whose function is to detect and assess individuals who might be of value for an intelligence service and potential recruits for intelligence work. 2. A deep-cover agent who recruits other agents to work against their own country or organization.

142 Agent: 1. One who is authorized or recruited, trained, controlled, and employed to obtain and report information from inside a target organization for intelligence or counterintelligence purposes.

Agents are the only members of the espionage system whose mission is actually spying. As a rule, intelligence services only rarely, if ever, employ fellow citizens as agents. The term, therefore, must never be confused with its lay use, as in "FBI agent" or "secret agent." In the interests of security, an agent acts independently from other agents and is under the control of a principal or a case officer. 2. Euphemism for a spy who is in your side.

143 Agents of influence: Suborned or ideologically committed people—not directly under control of an enemy intelligence organization, but willing to work for them—occupying positions within a country where they can affect policies or public opinion in favor of another country. Agents of influence usually are, or have access to, influential official and media leaders. Fidel Castro's intelligence services have mastered the art of recruitment of agents of influence, particularly among the American media stars and the intelligentsia.

144 Carlos Alberto Montaner, "¿Quiere Castro abandonar a los Soviéticos?" *La Estrella de Panamá*, February 22, 1985.

145 Daniel James, *op. cit.*, p. 31.

146 Theodore Draper, *Castroism, Theory and Practice*. New York: Praeger, 1965, 8.

147 The term fascist derives from the term *fasces*: bundles of elm or birch rods bound with red cord and carried by the lictors in ancient Rome in attendance upon magistrates. The tied rods symbolized unity and authority.

148 Luis Conte Agüero, *Cartas de presidio*. Havana: Editorial Lex, 1959), p. 60; Castro's leadership principle also mentioned in Theodore Draper, *op. cit.*, p. 9.

149 *Fascism: Past, Present, Future* (New York: Oxford University Press, 1996), pp. 34-35.

150 For a typical example of a fascist attack on capitalism see A. Grandi, *La futura civiltá del lavoro nel mondo* (Bologna: Stiassi and Tantini, 1941).

151 In a forthcoming book, *Fidel Castro Supermole: Walking Back the Cat in the Cuban Operation*, I will study in detail Castro's role in the Bogotazo.

152 Peter G. Bourne, *Fidel: A Biography of Fidel Castro* (New York: Dodd, Mead & Company, 1986), p. 46.

153 Jules Dubois, *Fidel Castro* (New York: Bobbs-Merrill, 1959), p. 83, and elsewhere. For a comparison of Castro's and Hitler's words in their own legal defense see "History Will Absolve Me," in F. Castro and R. Debray, *On Trial* (London: Lorringer, 1968), p. 40, and Konrad Heiden, *Der Führer* (Boston: Houghton Mifflin, 1944), p. 206. See also William Shirer, *The Rise and Fall of the Third Reich* (Greenwich, Conn.:

Fawcett, 1962), p. 118.

154 Hugh Thomas, *op. cit.*, p. 828.

155 On its issue of November 25, 1959, *El Libertario*, a publication of the Cuban anarchists, mentioned the fact that the newly created militia units resembled more Mussolini's "Fascist Combatini" or the Falangist "blue shirts," than the heroic French Maquis. See Carlos M. Estefanía, "Liquidación del socialismo libertario en Cuba: ¿final de una utopía?", *Revista Cuba Nuestra*, http://hem.passagen.se/cubanuestra. Soon after, *El Libertario* was banned.

156 See, Marta Rojas, "Manifestación de las antorchas por el centenario de José Martí," in Aldo Isidrón del Valle, Marta Rojas, Arturo Alape, *et al.*, *Antes del Moncada* (Havana: Editorial Pablo de la Torriente, 1986). pp. 119-126.

157 Daniel James, *op. cit.*, 55.

158 R. Hart Phillips, *The Cuban Dilemma* (New York: Ivan Obolensky, 1962), p. 18.

159 Mario Llerena, *The Unsuspected Revolution*, (Ithaca, N. Y.: Cornell Univ. Press, 1978), Chapter 5, note 7.

160 Lee Lockwood, *Castro's Cuba, Cuba's Fidel*. (New York: Macmillan, 1967), pp. 50, 52, 55.

161 Lee Lockwood, *Ibid.*, p. 57.

162 Franqui, *Family Portrait.*, p. 13; also in Lee Lockwood, *op. cit.*, pp. 7, 22.

163 U. S. Senate Internal Security Subcommittee, Hearings, *Communist Threat to the United States Through the Caribbean*, p. 544.

164 Daniel James, *op. cit.*, p. 34.

165 Festus Brotherson, Jr. Rapporteur, "Cuba: The New Regime of 1959 and Alternative Revolutionary Outcomes," in *José Martí and the Cuban Revolution Retraced, Proceedings of a Conference Held at the University of California,. Los Angeles, March 1-2, 1985*. (Los Angeles: UCLA Latin American Center Publication, 1986), p. 35.

166 I am making this fine distinction between fascism and communism not because I think communism is better than fascism, but just to emphasize the true nature of Castroism. Though the Soviet gulags were based on a different idea than the Nazi lagers, the results were pretty similar.

167 Paul D. Bethel, *The Losers* (New Rochelle, N.Y.: Arlington House, 1969), p. 116; Masetti a Peronist in David D. Burks, *Cuba Under Castro* (New York: Foreign Policy Association, 1964), p. 42. Masetti had been a member of the extreme right-wing and anti-semitic Nationalist Alliance, an armed band of Peronista thugs, disarmed and disbanded by the army after the fall of Perón in 1955. In 1961 Masetti left Prensa Latina and traveled to Bolivia where he created a small guerrilla group,

the People's Guerrilla Army, to invade Argentina. In April 1964, they had the first and only skirmish with the army and most of the guerrillas were killed. Masetti escaped into the jungle and never returned. Before the decimation of the group, however, Masetti had ordered the execution of three of its members for alleged disciplinary infractions. All of them were Jewish.

168 *The Militant*, April 17, 1961. For a relatively recent devastating attack on Castroism from a Marxist (of the Trotskyist type) point of view, see Bill Vann, "Castroism and the Politics of Petty-Bourgeois Nationalism," a lecture delivered in Sidney, Australia, on January 7, 1998, to the International Summer School on Marxism organized by the Australian Socialist Equality Party. The speech is available at the World Socialist Web Site at http://wsws.org/exhibits/castro.

169 Adam B. Ulam, *The Rivals* (New York: Penguin, 1976), p. 315.

170 Paul Seabury, *The Rise and Decline of the Cold War* (New York: Basic Books, 1967), p. 68.

171 Paul D. Bethel, *op. cit.*, p. 241.

172 *Ibid.*, p. 318.

173 *Ibid.*, p. 388.

174 See, i.e., Jean Cau, "Cuba a ses camps de mort," *Paris-Match*, June 12, 1971.

175 It seems, however, that though perhaps the incident at the Peruvian embassy triggered the Mariel boatlift, the exodus had been planned way in advance. Several months before the incident at the Peruvian embassy, rumors were running that the Castro government was readying the Marina Hemingway, a few miles east of Havana, for receiving boats from Florida with exiles to pick up their relatives in Cuba and bringing them to the U.S. after paying ransom. I remember approaching the Marina in the company of a friend, a Hungarian diplomat, and finding signs that it was closed to the public because of "construction works". The place was heavily guarded by Border Patrol forces. Moreover, there are other indications pointing to the fact that the boatlift was from the very beginning the implementation of Castro's secret plan. Napoleón Vilaboa, a Cuban exile which during the heyday of the Mariel boatlift was all over Little Havana radio, exhorting exiles to sail to Cuba and bring their relatives back, later revealed that he was a Castro agent. See Liz Balmaseda, "Exile: I Was Mastermind of Mariel," *The Miami Herald*, July 31, 1989.

176 See, Carlos Alberto Montaner, interview to Manuel Sánchez Pérez, *Diario Las Américas*, April 27, 1986, 5E. Montaner's perception is corroborated by this author's direct observation of the events in Cuba. For a first-hand description of the Mariel events, see Reinaldo Arenas, *Before Night Falls* (New York: Penguin, 1992), pp. 276-285. A

similar horrifying description is found in Alina Fernández, *Castro's Daughter* (New York: St. Martin's Press, 1998), 153-155. In a recent book Montaner adds more horrifying details by describing some of the actions of the Castroist gangsters in their harassment of the people leaving the Island. See *Journey to the Heart of Cuba: Life as Fidel Castro* (New York: Algora, 2001), pp. 131.

177 A. James Gregor, *The Fascist Persuasion in Radical Politics* (Princeton, N.J.: Princeton University Press, 1974), p. 302.

178 Alexander Torres Mega, *En las puertas del infierno cubano* (Montevideo: Flashes Culturales, 1990), p. 26-27.

179 Edwin Tetlow, *Eye on Cuba* (New York: Harcourt, Brace, 1966), p. 132. One of the identifying signs of the infamous CDRs was proudly displayed for many years at La Peña, an agitprop center in the People's Socialist Republic of Berkeley.

180 Juan Benemelis and Melvin Mañón, *Juicio a Fidel* (Santo Domingo: Taller, 1990), p. 187.

181 The idea of a "new man," athletic, virile, capable, laconic, persevering, wilful, full of life; a hero filled with self-denial and moved by moral rather than material incentives, appears in many works of fascist literature. See, i.e., Aldo Marinelli, quoted in Emilio Gentile, *Le Origini dell' Ideologia Fascista* (Bari: Laterza, 1974), p. 92; D. Begnac, *L'Arcangelo sindacalista: Filippo Corridoni* (Verona: Mondadori Edizione, 1943); also V. Rastelli, *Filippo Corridoni* (Rome: Conquiste d'Impero, 1940. History has shown, however, that when fascists talk about creating new men, as it is the case in Castro's Cuba, the practical result has been the treatment of some human beings as less than animals.

182 For a partial list and description of Cuban prisons and forced-labor camps see Alexander Torres Mega, *op. cit.*, pp. 101-102. See also "Cuba's Tropical 'Gulags'," a conversation with Armando Valladares, *The Miami Herald*, December 26, 1982; and Pierre Golendorf, *7 Años en Cuba: 38 meses en las prisiones de Fidel Castro* (Barcelona: Plaza y Janés, 1977). It is interesting to know that Ché Guevara, the beloved icon of the American Left, was the one who created the first concentration camp in Castro's Cuba. The camp was located in the Guanahacabibes peninsula, an inhospitable place near a mosquito-infested coast, in the Pinar del Río province, west of Havana.

183 "Within the Island of Bars," *CubaNet* (www.cubanet.org).

184 For information about torture and mistreatment of political prisoners in Castro's Cuba see *Sixth Report on the Situation of Political Prisoners in Cuba* (Washington, D.C.: OAS General Secretariat, 1979; *Amnistía Internacional, Informe 1982* (London: Publicationes Amnistía Internacional, 1982), pp. 113-114; *El presidio político en Cuba comunista* (Miami: Instituto Internacional de Cooperación y Solidaridad Cubana,

1983); "Political Imprisonment in Cuba," A Special Report from Amnesty International (Washington, D.C.: Cuban-American National Foundation, 1987); "Former Prisoners Tell of Torture in Cuban Jails," The *New York Times*, April 15, 1986; "Joy, Tears Greet 11 Cubans," *The Miami Herald*, September 16, 1986; Aryeh Neier, "Las víctimas de Castro," *Vuelta* 122 (January 1987), pp. 53-57. Contrasting with previously mentioned reports, the 1987 report about human rights in Cuba by the Institute for Policy Studies, depicting a rosy panorama of human rights in Castro's Cuba, is a shameless travesty of the truth. See, Institute of Policy Studies, "Human Rights in Cuba," in Philip Brenner et al, *The Cuba Reader* (New York: Grove Press,1989), pp. 241-247.

185 See Mark Neocleosus, *Fascism* (Minneapolis: University of Minnesota Press, 1997), 13.

186 *Ibid*.

187 *Ibid*., p. 23.

188 In his speeches Castro always mentions the Cuban *people*, never the Cuban workers or the Cuban proletariat.

189 See Ernst Nolte, *Three Faces of Fascism* (New York: Mentor, 1969), p. 269.

190 For a revealing study of the desperate situation of the Cuban workers under Castroist exploitation see Oscar Espinosa Chepe, "La situación de la clase obrera cubana y sus perspectivas," *Revista Desafíos* (La Habana), http://webstc.com/desafios/perspectivas.htm. For a recent denunciation by the World Federation of Workers of unions' persecution in Cuba see "Represión antisindical en Cuba, denuncia la Confederación Mundial del Trabajo," *Revista Desafíos*, http://webstc.com/desafios/denunciacmt.htm.

191 See Walter Laqueur, *Fascism: Past, Present, Future* (New York: Oxford University Press, 1996), p. 15.

192 Carl J. Friedrich and Zbigniew K. Brzezinski, *Totalitarian Dictatorship and Autocracy* (New York: Praeger, 1964), 60.

193 Herman Finer, *Mussolini's Italy*. (New York: 1935), 175-176.

194 John Guerassi, ed., *Venceremos! The Speeches and Writings of Ernesto Che Guevara* (New York: Macmillan, 1968), p. 422.

195 Regis Debray, *The Revolution Within the Revolution* (New York: Monthly Review Press, 1967).

196 Irving Louis Horowitz (ed.), Introduction to *Cuban Communism* (New Jersey: Transaction Books, 1970), p. 18.

197 James A. Gregor *op. cit.*, p. 310.

198 For an insightful analysis of the Castro-Debray foco theory as a Fascist construct see *ibid*., pp. 304-310.

199 Fidel Castro, *Palabras a los intelectuales* (Havana: Ediciones del Consejo Nacional de Cultura, 1961). Guillermo Cabrera Infante de-

scribed how, during one of the meetings, Castro gave a concrete expression to the well known Nazi metaphor when he grabbed his pistol and dropped it on the desk before his scared audience. *Mea Cuba* (Barcelona: Plaza & Janés, 1992), p. 85.

200 *Revolución*, August 17, 1962.

201 The term "amateur anti-Communists" was coined by deputy director of State Department Bureau of Intelligence and Research Thomas L. Hughes in a speech he gave in Minnesota on May 4, 1962. See Peter W. Rodman, *More Precious Than Peace* (New York: Charles Scribner's Sons, 1994), p. 108.

202 Some people have interpreted the recent rapprochement between Castro and the Church as a proof that he has fooled the Pope. But this can be decoded the other way around, as a further proof that he never fooled the Church. The recent history of the Vatican shows a visceral hatred for communism and everything Communist. Though it has proved to be very tolerant and friendly with fascist leaders, the Vatican would never accept any dealings with a Communist. Therefore, if the Catholic Church believes that an alliance with Castro is okay, that may be a strong indication that a Communist Castro is not. On the rapprochement between Castro and the Catholic Church see Armando Valladares, "El pedido de perdón que no hubo: la colaboración eclesiástica con el comunismo," *Diario Las Américas*, March 22, 2000.

203 On the socialist roots of fascism, see Ze'ev Sternhell, *The Birth of Fascist Ideology* (Princeton, N.J.: Yale University Press, 1994). For a word of caution against placing Hitler on the political Right wing, see Sebastian Haffner, *The Meaning of Hitler* (Cambridge, Mass.: Harvard University Press, 1979), 59-60, 75.

204 Georgie Anne Geyer, *Guerrilla Prince* (Boston: Little, Brown and Company, 1991), p. 391. See also Jim Guirard, "'Progressives' in Bed with a Fascist Fidel," *Guaracabuya*, http://www.amigospais-guaracabuya.org. There is, however, at least one scholar who considered Peronism a form of fascism of the left. See, Seymour Martin Lipset, *Political Man*, expanded edition (Baltimore: The Johns Hopkins University Press, 1981) p. 176.

205 Hugh Thomas, "The U.S. and Castro, 1959-1962," *American Heritage*, Vol. 29 No. 6 (October/November 1978), p. 34.

206 Hugh Thomas, *Cuba: The Pursuit of Freedom* (New York: Harper and Row, 1971), pp. 1490f.

207 *Bohemia*, January 31, 1960.

208 "Amnesty to Fidel Castro and His Followers in Jail," Speech by Majority Leader Rafael Díaz-Balart to the Chamber of Representatives, Cuban Capitol, May, 1955. (Emphasis added).

209 *Del socialismo al fascismo. Un español dentro de la revolución cubana, 1980-1996* (Madrid: Ediciones R, 1996).
210 "El Fascismo. Apuntes," *Diaspora(s)*, April 14, 1997, reproduced in *La Habana Elegante* (Segunda época), Internet Edition, No. 2, Summer of 1998.
211 Jesús Arboleya, *The Cuban Counterrevolution* (Athens, Ohio: Ohio University Center for International Studies), p. viii.
212 *Ibid.*, p. x.
213 Angelo Del Boca and Mario Giovana, *Fascism Today* (New York: Pantheon, 1969), p. 372. The idea of fascist leftist regimes is also in Seymour Martin Lipset, *Political Man: The Social Bases of Politics* (New York: Doubleday, 1960).
214 The insightful Georgie Anne Geyer saw this a long time ago. In an article appeared on July 8, 1983, in Caracas' *El Universal*, entitled "El fascismo reaparece bajo disfraz del comunismo en la América Central," she described in detail Castro's camouflaging strategy. Apparently President Reagan was not fooled either. In the same article Geyer quotes Reagan saying in Miami in 1981 that Castro was basically a Fascist.
215 The fact explains why Celia Sánchez, a zealous Fidelista but also a fervent anticommunist, was for many years Castro's closest associate and confident and never faced any ideological problems. However, though the fact that Celia was both an anticommunist and a lesbian was well known among Castro's inner circle, I have found it mentioned only in Norberto Fuentes, *Dulces guerreros cubanos* (Barcelona: Seix Barral, 1999), p. 138.
216 *Revolution in Cuba: An Essay in Understanding* (New York: Charles Scribner's Sons, 1975), p. 47-48.
217 For a detailed study of how the Jesuits turned from defenders into enemies of the Church and the Pope, see Malachi Martin, *The Jesuits* (New York: Simon and Schuster, 1987).
218 There is one person who seems to agree at least in part with me in my definition of Castro's ideology. Dr. Facundo Lima, a Cuban psychiatrist living in the U.S., told Georgie Anne Geyer that Castro "has substituted the religious practices of Jesuit teachers with his own brand of Marxism, his new religion." see Georgie Anne Geyer, "Castro: The 'Knowable' Dictator," in *The Cuban Revolution at Thirty*, Proceedings from a conference sponsored by the Cuban American National Foundation, Washington, D.C., January 10, 1989, p. 46.
219 Definition and background information about cults in Josh McDowell and Don Stewart, *Deceiver: What Cults Believe; How They Lure Followers* (San Bernardino, CA: Here's Life Publishers, 1992), pp. 14-15, 17-18

220 Ikeda, the wealthy leader of the powerful Soka Gakkai cult, visited Castro on June 25, 1996, and is in friendly terms with the Cuban tyrant.

221 As Alvin Toffler points out, however, "Even religions that insist on totalitarian control over every aspect of their own members' lives, but do not try to impose their control on nonmembers, may be compatible with democracy. What is *not* compatible are those religions (and political ideologies as well) that combine totalitarianism with universalism. Such movements are at war with any possible definition of democracy.' Such movements, Toffler adds, are "the agents of a new Dark Age." *Powershift* (New York: Bantam Books, 1991), p. 368.

222 The similarities of Castroism and cults have been overlooked by most authors, probably with the exception of José Barbeito in *Realidad y masificación: Reflexiones sobre la revolución cubana* (Caracas: Ediciones Nuevo Orden, 1964) p. 4. Mentions of Castroism as a cult are also in Irving Louis Horowitz' Introduction to *Cuban Communism, Fifth Edition* (New Brunswick, NJ: Transaction Books, 1984), p. 3; and Georgie Anne Geyer's "Castro: The 'Knowable' Dictator," in *The Cuban Revolution at Thirty*, Proceeding from a conference sponsored by the Cuban American National Foundation, Washington, D.C., January 10, 1989), p. 46.

223 Georgie Anne Geyer, *Guerrilla Prince* (Boston: Little, Brown and Company, 1991), p. 103.

224 Ray Brennan, *Castro, Cuba and Justice* (New York: Doubleday, 1959). p. 81.

225 The American embargo has helped Castro to maintain the isolation of the members of his cult.

226 "Domestic Sources of Foreign Policy," in Robert L. Pfaltzgraff, Jr., ed., *Politics and the International System, second edition* (Philadelphia: J.B. Lippincott, 1972), p. 402-403.

227 Any honest person who still doubts that communism produced more murders than fascism should read this book: Stephanie Courtois, Nicholas Werth, Jean-Louis Panné, *et al.*, *The Black Book of Communism: Crimes, Terror, Repression* (Boston: Harvard University Press, 1999). When it was published in France the book caused a major political and intellectual debate.

228 "Why We Fought," *National Review*, January 24, 2000.

229 Fuentes, *op. cit.*, p. 225.

230 "Meme" (pronounced to rhyme with "gene"); a neologism, coined by analogy to "gene," by the writer-zoologist Richard Dawkins in his book *The Selfish Gene* (New York: Oxford University Press, 1976). Dawkins defines a meme as a replicating information pattern that uses

minds to get itself copies into other minds, in a virus-like fashion.

The meme is the basic unit of replication and selection in the ideosphere. According to Dawkins, memes, like viruses of the mind, float about in the soup of human culture where they grow, replicate, mutate, compete, or become extinct. But, as Nazism and Marxism have proved, a meme does not need to be true to have a long life and exert a strong influence on many people.

231 In fact, Castroism's lack of principle and focus on action and power has been a source of inspiration for various American pressure groups, who have adopted many of its tactics.

232 The term "liberation theology" was coined by Gustavo Gutiérrez during a talk on the eve of the Latin American bishop's conference in Medellín, Colombia, in 1968. Ideologues of liberation theology describe it as "an interpretation of Christian faith out of the experience of the poor." Following this principle, priests help the poor organize themselves in *comunidades de base* ("grassroots communities," actually indoctrination centers). Once the poor are indoctrinated in the doctrine of envy and hate, they become vehicles for radical politics and a cannon fodder for guerrilla wars. The indoctrination process is called *concientización* (roughly translated as consciousness raising), a euphemism for brainwashing.

It is not a coincidence that it was during the Tricontinental Conference held in Havana in January 1966, just two years before the Medellín conference, when Castro made his pitch for anti-U.S. revolution. During the conference Castro promised that any anti-American revolutionary movement in the world could count on Cuba's unconditional help. The search for *conciencia revolucionaria* (revolutionary consciousness) was a major Castroist mantra during the 1960s. Similarly, it was not a coincidence that the Nicaraguan revolution, a direct result of Castro's activities in exporting his revolution, was a stronghold of liberation theology, and its government included several Catholic priests, best known among them the *franquista* (Spain's Franco sympathizer) Ernesto Cardenal.

233 One may more accurately talk about "factions," because the rebels among the Franciscans, Dominicans, Carmelites, Maryknolls, and lately the LaSallians, have joined forces with the Jesuit faction in their fight for the destruction of the Catholic Church as we know it.

234 According to the Church's own definition, the poor are "persons having a marginal existence, whose security depends on a menial job, of which the wages are insufficient to provide a minimum standard of living for their family." The definition, which probably describes less than ten percent of the Cuban population before Castro

grabbed power in 1959, now accurately portrays more than ninety percent of the Cubans living in the Island.

235 Perhaps some reader may think that I am using words too strong to describe the Castroist élite. As a proof that I am probably falling short of my target I recommend a close reading of Norberto Fuentes' book *Dulces guerreros cubanos* (Barcelona: Seix Barral, 1999), an intimate, at times revolting, look at the Castroist élite by an insider. David Horowitz accurately called Castro "the last great revolutionary gangster in the Soviet world." See Peter Collier and David Horowitz, *Deconstructing the Left: From Vietnam to the Persian Gulf* (Studio City, California: Second Thoughts, 1991), p. 76.

236 See, for example, Benigno E. Aguirre, "A Skeptical View of the Demise of Castroism," *Cuba in Transition, Vol. 3*, Proceedings of the Third Annual Meeting of the Association for the Cuban Economy, held at Florida International University, Miami, August 12-14, 1993.

237 Contrary to what some people may think, the concept of the American military-industrial complex is not Marxist-inspired. It was coined by President Eisenhower in his farewell speech to the nation.

238 For example, after Gary Powers' U-2 was shot over the Soviet Union—most likely the result of Pentagon-CIA sabotage—the price of shares of arms manufacturing companies rose sharply on the New York Stock Exchange, and government military-contract awards increased substantially. Just two months after the incident, the Eisenhower administration allocated the biggest military appropriations ever approved at that time, $48,300 million for fiscal 1960-61. See V. Cherniavsky, "U.S. Intelligence and the Monopolies," *International Affairs* (January 1965).

239 A long time ago I pioneered the concept of Fidel Castro as a benefactor of the American monopolies in my *Historia herética de la revolución fidelista* (San Francisco: El Gato Tuerto, 1986) pp. 138-139, 152. Many people at the time saw it either as a joke or a far-fetched idea. Now, however, it seems that some people are arriving at the same conclusion. See, for example, what Castro's daughter Alina Fernández wrote: "I left the [presidential] Palace with the bitter conviction that my conscience had been swindled, and that the Yankees were delighted to have Fidel ninety miles away, planting subversion in the rest of the world. As long as Fidel was there, the United States could always find employment for its blond, gum-chewing army, idle since Vietnam and Korea." *Castro's Daughter* (New York: St. Martin's Press, 1998), p. 129.

240 Apparently, a bold step in that direction has already been taken. See the report, Council on Foreign Relations, *U.S.-Cuban Relations in the 21st Century: A Follow-on Report* (New York: Council on Foreign

Relations, 2001). For a strong criticism of the Report see, Irving Louis Horowitz, "Humanitarian Capitulation: U.S.-Cuba Relations According to the Council on Foreign Relations," *Vital Speeches*, Vol. LXVII No. 11 (March 15, 2001).

Epilogue

1 Letter from Alice Walker to President Clinton in www.cubasolidarity.net/awalker.html.

2 I found it necessary to make the distinction because the usual portrayal of Castro in the American *liberal* media ranges from that of a Robin Hood to an angel.

3 As a historian myself, and having my own biases, it is likely that, consciously or unconsciously, in writing this book I selected the facts supporting my preconceived ideas while ignored the ones that do not fit. But the main difference between me and most "serious" historians is that I don't mislead the reader by concealing the trick under a cover of false detachment and impartiality.

4 I have to admit, however, that there are notable exceptions. While up to this moment there is not a single shred of evidence proving that there were strategic missiles or nuclear warheads in Cuba in 1962, most books and articles about the Cuban missile crises keep parroting the Kennedy administration's claims that the U-2 photographs provided hard evidence of the presence of nuclear missiles in Cuba. Of lately, they have added the far-fetched notion that the nuclear warheads for the missiles were already in Cuba and that the Soviet officers in the field had discretionary power to use them without further orders from Moscow. For a strongly contrarian view, see Servando González, "A missile is a Missile, is a Missile: A Semiological Analysis of Some Aspects of the Cuban Missile Crisis," *Sumeria*, www.sumeria.net/politics/amissile.html.

5 For a look at just a few of recent known crimes committed by the Castro government between 1980 and 1994, see Tim Brower, *Cuba: Between the Devil and the Deep Sea* (Washington, D.C.: The Cuban American National Foundation, [n. d.]).

6 Fidel Castro is basically a serial killer. Since an early age he is obsessed with killing, and has been dominated by his urge to kill—a compulsion he cannot control and probably does not want to. It seems that the only thing that gives him true pleasure is killing people. That explains why he has been systematically killing both his enemies and his friends. His *modus operandi* follows the pattern of most serial kill-

ers: most of the crimes he has committed are not haphazard or opportunistic, but carefully planned out in detail. Moreover, like most serial killers, it seems that he has never lost any sleep because of his crimes. The problem with Castro, like with many serial killers, is that even though they are monsters, they don't look like monsters, and that is precisely why they are so successful. As it happens with Fidel Castro, you *think* that you see him, but actually you are looking right *through* him. See John Douglas and Mark Olshaker, *Obsession* (New York: Scribner, 1998), p. 21. For a revealing look at the world of serial killers see also John Douglas and Mark Olshaker, *The Anatomy of Motive* (New York: Scribner, 1999); and Robert K. Ressler and Tom Shachtman, *Whoever Fights Monsters* (New York: St. Martin's Paperbacks, 1992). See also Stanton E. Samenow, *Inside the Criminal Mind* (New York: Times Books, 1984).

7 See, i.e., Ralph Rewes, "The Fall of the Cuban Reich," February 17, 2001, ruhig@gate.net.

8 It seems that the same forces that helped Fidel Castro grab power in Cuba in 1959 are already maneuvering to guarantee that Castroism remains in power after the death of the Maximum leader.

9 A good example of this is Eliseo Alberto [Diego], *Informe contra mí mismo* (Madrid: Alfaguara, 1996), an abject, self-justifying confession of collaboration with the worst aspects of the Castro regime by a person who, although fully conscious of the evil, choose not to oppose it.

10 *Guerrillas in Power* (New York: Hill & Wang, 1970), p. 8.

11 *Studies in Classic American Literature* (New York: Doubleday Anchor, 1951), p. 93.

12 That is, if one accept at face value that Castro is telling the truth about the things he claims he has tried to accomplish. For example, Dariel "Benigno" Alarcón Ramírez, one of Ché's closest men who was under his command in Cuba, Africa and Bolivia, now in exile in France, has strong doubts about Fidel's true intentions. According to Benigno, Castro intentionally sabotaged and betrayed not only Ché's guerrilla, but all of the Latin American guerrilla movements he claimed to be helping. That may explain why all of them, without exception, ended in failure. See Dariel Alarcón Ramírez "Benigno," *Memorias de un soldado cubano* (Barcelona: Tusquets, 1997), pp. 220-221, 223, 228.

13 Orlando Alomá, "In Fidel's Footsteps: A Tourist Views of Cuba," *The Miami Herald*, January 11, 1998.

14 *Cuba* (New York: Macmillan, 1964), p. 105. Matthews' friendliness toward Castro has been criticized by many people, included this author. It seems, however, that Matthews finally realized that, like many others, Castro used him as a tool to gain power. Matthews' late

works about Castro show his disappointment and perhaps his repentance for his role in the creation of the monster.

15 *Castro's Revolution: Myths and Realities* (New York: Praeger, 1962), p. 3.

16 If somebody sees my answers to Draper's questions as an effort to demonize Fidel Castro, so be it. I assume full responsibility. Fidel Castro has been so consistently angelized by leftists and liberals that a little demonization is in order, just to keep the balance. On the other hand, as M. Scott Peck pointed out, "while the evil people are still to be feared, they are also to be pitied. Forever fleeing the light of self-exposure and the voice of their own conscience, they are the most frightened of human beings. They live their lives in sheer terror," *People of the Lie* (New York: Simon and Schuster, 1983), p. 67. Far from a demonization, this book is an accurate, even compassionate analysis of Fidel Castro.

17 Carl Goldberg, *Speaking With The Devil: A Dialogue With Evil* (New York: Viking, 1996), p. 3.

18 *Op. cit.*, p. 4.

19 Typical of Castro's evil mind was his decision to send more than 15,000 hardened criminals and mental patients among the 125, 266 refugees escaping from Cuba during the 1980 Mariel boatlift. See Laurie Goering, "Mariel Refugees Fight for New Genesis. Cubans Who Arrived in Massive Boatlift Have Surmounted Stigma of 20 Years Ago," *The San Francisco Examiner*, May 21, 2000.

20 Arthur Allen, "Che and Diana: The Shocking Untold Story," *Salon*, October 14, 1997, http://www.salon.com/1997/10/14castro.html.

21 Peck, *op. cit.*, pp. 177, 241.

22 Peck, *op. cit.*, p. 222.

23 Jules Dubois, *Fidel Castro* (New York: Bobbs-Merrill, 1959), p. 145.

24 The warning signs are based on research made by various law-enforcement agencies, but several independent researches have arrived to very similar conclusions. See, i.e., Helen Smith, *The Scarred Heart: Understanding and Identifying Kids Who Kill* (Knoxville, Tennessee: Callisto Publishing, 2000).

25 *MSNBC* quiz on-line at http://www.msnbc.com/modules/quizzes/school_warning_signs.asp/.

26 Teresa Casuso, *Cuba and Castro* (New York: Random House, 1961), pp. 168-169.

27 One day a teacher at Belén expelled him from class for scuffling with another classmates. Fidel yelled in anger threatening the teacher: "I'm going to bring my gun." Nobody believed him, but a few min-

utes later he came back to the classroom brandishing a .45 pistol. See José D. Cabús, *Castro ante la historia* (Mexico: Editores Mexicanos Unidos, 1962), p. 24.

28 Another day he started a fist fight with Ramón Mestre, a classmate. But Mestre won, and the furious Fidel came back with this .45 pistol. Only the intervention of Father Larracea, who persuaded Fidel to give the pistol to him, saved Mestre. But now comes the most incredible thing. When Father Larracea persuaded him of the impropriety of his behavior, Fidel, in an act of repentance, went to his room again and came back with another .45 pistol he gave to the amazed Father Larracea. See Cabús, *op. cit.*, pp. 24-25.

29 *Ibid.*

30 Fidel himself told his biographer Carlos Franqui, ". . . I remember that whenever I disagreed with something the teacher said to me, or whenever I got mad, I would swear at her and immediately leave school, running as fast as I could. There was a kind of standing war between us and the teacher. Whenever we [Castro uses the royal "we" meaning "I"] would curse at the teacher, with dirty words we had picked up from the workers, we would get out of her way as fast as our feet could carry us." *Diary of the Cuban Revolution* (New York: Viking, 1980), p. 2.

31 "On Fridays a student was selected to lock the school's door. One day I was in charge and I left the door unlocked. Next day I came back with a group of classmates and entered the school. Once inside we destroyed desks, stole things and did lots of nasty things. It was never known who did it." See Carlos Franqui, *Vida, aventuras y desastres de un hombre llamado Castro* (Barcelona: Planeta, 1988), p. 23.

Helmut Schoeck points out that vandalism, defined in the criminal law as the senseless and malicious damage to, or destruction of, private or public property without any material gain to the perpetrator, is basically motivated by envy, *op. cit.*, p. 111. It seems that, as an adult, Fidel's acts of vandalism have extended to the whole Cuba and some parts of the world as well.

32 One day a Christian brother at the LaSalle school in Santiago dared to discipline Fidel while he was in line for lunch. According to Castro's own recollection, ". . . I turned on him, right then and there, threw a piece of bread at his head and started to hit him with my fists and bite him. I don't think I hurt the priest much, but the daring outburst became a historic event in school." See Carlos Franqui, *Diary of the Cuban Revolution* (New York: Viking, 1980), p. 4.

33 As Castro told his biographer Franqui, in order to convince her mother to send him back to a school in Santiago, "I appealed to her and told her I wanted to stay in school and that if I wasn't sent back,

I'd set fire to the house." See Franqui, *Diary of the Cuban Revolution* (New York: Viking, 1980), p. 5. Apparently Fidel's mother had learnt not to take her son's threats lightly, because soon after he was sent back to school.

34 The school used to issue three different types of report: a white one for students with good behavior, a red one for students with bad behavior, and a green one for students with very bad behavior. According to Castro himself, his behavior was so bad that the school stopped sending any type of report to his family. When the school finally contacted his father, he used to tell his friends that he had been told at the school that his son was the greatest ruffian they had ever known. See Carlos Franqui, *Vida, aventuras y desastres de un hombre llamado Castro* (Barcelona: Planeta, 1988), p. 29.

35 Georgie Anne Geyer, *Guerrilla Prince* (Boston: Little, Brown and Company, 1991), p. 72; also in Carlos Franqui, *Diary of the Cuban Revolution* (New York: Viking, 1980), p. 7.

36 There is no evidence that Fidel Castro had been sexually abused at his home in Birán or later when he attended Catholic boarding schools in Santiago and Havana. There is evidence, however, that Fidel was neglected. Angel Castro hated the sight of his son. He ignored him, would not talk to him, hold him or comfort him. Moreover, Angel's Birán estate was a violent place. Young Fidel witnessed the violence of Angel against his employees and members of his own family, and experienced Angel's verbal violence against him. The impact of this daily violence must have affected Fidel's developing brain. Pictures of Fidel during his early life consistently show a sad, angry boy, and later a sad, angry young man, never smiling or laughing.

Research has long shown that a lack of parental care and affection creates a multitude of dysfunctional behaviors in a social species. According to Dr. Bruce Perry, chief of psychiatry at Texas Children's Hospital in Houston, neglected children are generally difficult to handle. They tend to be withdrawn and anti-social with their parents and with other children. They usually have the lowest grades and test scores in elementary school, and the highest rates of school absences, grade repeats, and learning problems. They are usually inattentive, un–involved, overly passive at times, and anxious or impatient at other times. Neglected children don't laugh very much. They are very distant, have no friends, and have episodes of predatory and violent behavior. Usually they direct their anger toward young children or animals, and show very little remorse afterwards. (Perry's description of neglected children in Deborah Blum, "Attention Deficit," *Mother Jones*, January/February 1999, pp. 59-61.)

The description above is a very accurate picture of young Fidel

Castro at Birán and later at the schools he attended in Santiago de Cuba. This behavior continued after he moved to Havana to attend the Belén High School. Then, suddenly, his grades jumped as if by magic, and he became first in his class in almost every subject. The change, however, was not the result of a sudden change in his interest or increased motivation, but of the sudden apparition of his eidetic or photographic memory, perhaps as the result of a head trauma.

37 Carlos Franqui, *Diary of the Cuban Revolution* (New York: Viking, 1980), p. 7.

38 Cabús, *op. cit.*, p. 25.

39 There were two major gangs (or "action groups," as they were known) at the University of Havana at the time: the MSR (Movimiento Socialista Revolucionario), and the UIR (Unión Insurreccional Revolucionaria). As soon as Castro began attending the University he joined the UIR. See Herbert Matthews, *Revolution in Cuba* (New York: Charles Scribner's Sons, 1975), p. 45.

40 Luis Conte Agüero, *Fidel Castro: Psiquiatría y política* (Mexico, D.F.: Editorial Jus, 1968), p. 14.

41 Another indication of Castro's sick mind is the fact that he has told his biographers in detail about his reprehensible childhood escapades, and he seems to be proud of them.

42 *Salon*, May 12, 1999.

43 Like Castro, the Columbine killers Dylan Klebold and Eric Harris were actually planning a fascist *coup d'état*. In one of several videos they recorded while planning the massacre, Harris clearly expressed their goal, "We're going to kick-start a revolution,"—a revolution of the dispossessed. See Nancy Gibbs and Timothy Rocher, "The Columbine Tapes," *Time*, December 20, 1999, p. 42.

44 In his controversial book, *Inside the Criminal Mind* (New York: Times Books, 1984), Stanton E. Samenow points out that criminals alone—not inadequate parents, schools, bad neighborhoods, drugs or unemployment—are the cause of crime. And they commit crimes basically because they want to. Samenow believes that crime reside within the minds of criminals, and is not caused by social conditions. How a person behaves is determined largely by how he thinks, and criminals think differently. Since he was a small child at the Birán state, Fidel Castro began thinking differently.

45 The true role of the Jesuits in the creation of the monster needs to be thoroughly investigated, and is a fact the Cuban people should have in mind when, in a Cuba after Castro, the Jesuits would try to resume their educational endeavors as if nothing had happened.

46 It is also very disturbing that Fidel Castro, the monster next door, has been for more than forty years the darling of the American

liberals and the Left. Their love and admiration for Castro perhaps gives a clue about their true roles in the creation of the monsters next door who are killing children in our schools. See, Servando González, "The Real Makers of Lethal Weapons Are In Our Schools," *The New Australian*, No. 123 (12-20 June), 1999.

47 *Identity: Youth and Crisis* (New York: W.W. Norton, 1968), p. 75.

48 Frei Betto, *Fidel and Religion* (New York: Simon and Schuster, 1987), pp. 99-100. There is the possibility, however, that the children had something different in mind when they called Fidel "Jew." The surname Castro is common among the *marranos* (Jews who adopted the Catholic faith) in Galicia, Spain, the region where Angel Castro was born.

49 *Ibid.*, pp. 104-105.

50 In typical Castro fashion, Fidel enjoys disinforming the people about his bastard origins. See, i.e., Julio García "Domingo en Birán," *Granma*, 18 June, 1980, a report of Castro's impromptu visit to the Birán estate in 1980. According to the article, the reason for Castro's visit was to look at the preservation work done on the farm buildings. "First, the Commander in Chief made a brief visit to a former servants' house." Later, he visited a reconstruction of his parents house (the original house was destroyed during a fire on September 4, 1954, while Castro was in prison in Isle of Pines). Actually, the so-called "servants' house" was the one in which Fidel was born.

51 Priests discovered psychoanalysis many years before Freud.

52 Betto, *op. cit.*, pp. 101.

53 Berel Lang, *Act and Idea in the Nazi Genocide* (Chicago: University of Chicago Press, 1990); Erich Fromm, *The Heart of Man* (New York: Harper & Row, 1964); M. Scott Peck, *People of the Lie: The Hope for Healing Human Evil* (New York: Simon & Schuster, 1983); Ron Rosenbaum, *Explaining Hitler: The Search for the Origins of His Evil* (New York: Random House, 1998).

54 Dahmer is the infamous serial killer captured in 1991 after having killed no less than seventeen people during a twelve year period. Dahmer sexually assaulted his victims, mutilated them, and committed acts of necrophilia and cannibalism.

55 George Victor, *Hitler: The Pathology of Evil* (Washington, D.C.: Brassey's, 1998), p. 9.

56 Erikson, *op. cit.*, pp. 74-90.

57 Thomas, *op. cit.*, p. 804.

58 See, Ernesto Betancourt, "El aislamiento de Castro," *El Nuevo Herald*, May 8, 2001.

59 See Domingo Amuchástegui, "Cuban Intelligence and the October Crisis," in James G. Blight and David A. Welch, *Intelligence and the Cuban Missile Crisis* (London: Frank Cass, 1998), pp. 96-98. How-

ever, Amuchástegui's claims about his personal participation in the event are highly exaggerated. It seems likely that, though he had no direct participation in the events as he claims, he heard the story from some of his friends at high levels of the Castro government.

60 *Granma Digital Internacional*, 28 July, 1999 (emphasis added).

61 "Cuba calls for sanctions against U.S. for 'genocidal' embargo," *Associated Press*, September 14, 1999.

62 Norberto Fuentes, *op. cit*, p. 117.

63 *Ibid.*, p. 118.

64 See, i. e., Manuel Cereijo, "Castro: A Threat to the Security of the United States, *InfoNews*, February 1999, InfoNews@ aol.com; Roberto Fabricio, "Ex oficial cubano confirma la posesión de armas bacteriológicas," *El Nuevo Herald*, July 12, 1999; Rui Ferreira, "El Comando Sur es un objetivo impor–tante para espías cubanos," *El Nuevo Herald*, December 29, 2000; Rui Ferreira, "Revelan plan de Cuba para infiltrar armas y agentes en E.U.," *El Nuevo Herald*, December 30, 2000; Rui Ferreira, "Papeles en manos federales inculpan a los cubanos. Podría confirmarse en corte que Castro ha querido trasladar a E. U. su pugna con Washington," *El Nuevo Herald*, January 3, 2001; Rui Ferreira, "Acepta un espía que fue entrenado para vigilar bases de E.U.," *El Nuevo Herald*, January 6, 2001. See also, Daniel James, "Castro Plan to Destabilize U.S. May Be Broadening: Defector Reveals Castro Plan to Destabilize the United States," *The Chicago Tribune*, August 23, 1981.

65 That is, if they are really what they claim to be. There is evidence that Castro's intelligence agents have infiltrated the anti-Castro Cubans and commonly act as *agent provocateurs* to help the Maximum leader fulfill his prophecies. Also, the role of Castroist agents of influence in the U.S. government and in many American non-government organizations is evident. One must keep in mind that in the convoluted world of intelligence and espionage things are often not what they seem.

66 I don't want anybody to misinterpret my criticism. I have the highest opinion and respect for Brothers to the Rescue, its humanitarian mission, and its leaders. But I sincerely believe that they have been extremely naïve in dealing with Castro. Proof of this is that they were easily penetrated by Castro's intelligence services.

67 See, "Senator Helms Proposes $100 million in U.S. Aid to Cuba," Reuters, May 12, 2001, *CubaNews*, http://64.21.33.164/CNews/y987/may98/15e.htm.

68 Rui Ferreira, "La disidencia recelosa por la Ley de la Solidaridad," *El Nuevo Herald*, May 18, 2001.

69 *Ibid*.

70 It seems that most anti-Castro Cubans are not aware of the turn

to the left America has experienced in the last 20 years. In the first place, American liberals and leftists actually love Castro because they think he *is* a Communist, therefore, it would be better to convince them that Castro *is not* a communist. Secondly, there is an extensive bibliography showing that, despite anti-communist rhetoric, the U.S. government and most large American corporations have secretly helped many Communist regimes to survive. See, i. e., Antony C. Sutton, *Western Technology and Soviet Economic Development*; 3 Vols. (Stanford, Calif.: Stanford University Press, 1968-1973); Antony C. Sutton, *National Suicide: Military Aid to the Soviet Union* (New Rochelle, N.Y.: Arlington House, 1973); Charles Ferry and Robert Pfaltz, eds., *Selling the Rope to Hang Capitalism?* (Washington, D.C.: Pergamon-B'assey, 1987).

71 Operation Boomerang in Domingo Amuchástegui, "Cuban Intelligence and the October Crisis," in James G. Blight and David A. Welch, *Intelligence and the Cuban Missile Crisis* (London: Frank Cass, 1998), p. 99. There is evidence that the plans for Operation Boomerang are still active.

72 M. Scott Peck, *People of the Lie* (New York: Simon & Schuster, 1983), pp. 186, 1888.

73 *Conducta impropia* (Conduct Unbecoming), a documentary film by Néstor Almendros and Orlando Jiménez Leal. The script of *Conducta Impropia* has been published in book form. See Néstor Almendros and Orlando Jiménez Leal, *Conducta impropia* (Madrid: Playor, 1984).

74 I have paraphrased Aldous Huxley words, see *The Devils of Loudun* (New York: Harper & Row, 1952), p. 192. A proof that one cannot fight evil with evil is that Castro has been for many years fighting against what he believes are the evil actions committed against him by the United States, and the result is that he has become even more evil in the process.

There is evidence, however, that not all the evil Castro ascribes to the U.S. is just the product of his imagination. A recent book by James Bamford, *Body of Secrets* (New York: Random House, 2001), tells about Operation Northwoods, the code name for a proposed series of sabotages, provocations and assassination attempts. The plan, detailed in a recently declassified Joint Chiefs of Staff document from 1961, outlined U.S. plans to covertly fabricate various pretexts that would justify an American invasion of Cuba. The plan included staging the assassination of Cubans living in the U.S., simulating an attack of the Guantánamo base, and blowing a U.S. ship in Cuban waters to create a "Remember the Maine" like incident. The document is available at the National Security Archives Web site at: www.nsarchive.

org/news/20010430.

Bamford believes that Operation Northwoods is perhaps the most corrupt plan ever created by the U.S. government. I fully concur. Moreover, the military men who created the anonymous document, consciously dishonored their uniforms, their branch of service, and their country.

75 I am thankful to Dr. Earl Nelson for reminding me of Nietzsche's warning.

76 I see as a grave error the efforts of some anti-Castroist Catholics in trying to involve the Church in the political battle against the Cuban tyrant. Apart from the constitutional violation of the separation between state and religion it involves, the most important mission of the Church should be the salvation of the soul of the Cuban Catholics, which has been under a frontal attack from Castroism for more than 40 years. On the other hand, perhaps the main battle of the Catholic Church nowadays is not the salvation of the Cuban's soul but the salvation of its own soul.

77 Malachi Martin, *The Jesuits* (New York: Simon & Schuster, 1987), p. 80.

78 *Associated Press*, 17 September, 1999.

79 A friend who read the manuscript told me this was a very scary book.

80 It seems that the only American friends Castro accept are the ones who have been compromised or co-opted by the Cuban intelligence services and are totally subservient to him.

81 Rui Ferreira, "Castro impedirá cualquier transición, afirma un ex agente de la CIA," *El Nuevo Herald*, 27 July 1999.

82 Raúl's appearance on tv in Sixto Martínez, "Raúl Castro llama a EU a negociar," *El Nuevo Herald*, January 6, 2001.

83 See, i.e., Vivian Sequera, "En vida de Castro, Cuba pide negociar," *El Nuevo Herald*, January 10, 2001; also Pablo Alfonso, "Granma corrige las palabras de Raúl Castro," *El Nuevo Herald*, January 10, 2001. Although *Granma* corrected some parts of Raúl's statements, the one about the normalization of relations while Castro was still alive remained unchanged.

84 See, Agence France Press, "Castro la emprende contra Jean Chrétien," *El Nuevo Herald*, April 27, 2001.

85 See, Pablo Alfonso, "Cuba con capacidad de amenaza cibernética," *El Nuevo Herald*, February 19, 2001.

86 George Gedda, "Preocupa a EU un ataque cibernético de Cuba," *El Nuevo Herald*, May 17, 2001.

87 Powell expressed his opinion about Castro when questioned by New York congressman Jose Serrano at a House Appropriations Sub-

committee hearing on April 26, 2001. It seems, however, that Mr. Powell is not alone. In a 1998 report approved by the entire U.S. intelligence community, the Defense Intelligence Agency concluded that "At present, Cuba does not pose a significant threat to the U. S. or to other countries in the region. Cuba has little motivation to engage in military activity beyond the defense of its territory and political system" See Defense Intelligence Agency, "The Cuban Threat to U.S. National Security," April 22, 1998. The report, however, seems based mostly on an analysis of conventional warfare capabilities than in intentions or capabilties for asymmetric warfare. Saying that "Cuba has no longer any functioning submarines in its inventory," is foolish, to say the least. The Cuban navy never had more than a few Soviet-made WWII diesel-powered submarines used mainly for training purposes. Moreover, the use of "Cuba" all over the document, without mentioning "Castro" is a strong indication that the whole report is flawed. As we have seen above in this book, Castro has a strong motivation to engage in military activity beyond the defense of the Cuban territory, and he has the capability and the will to do it.

88 As Richard Pipes pointed out, ". . . even the best-functioning intelligence service cannot be counted upon reliably to predict the actions of foreign powers: divining political intentions is far and away the most difficult aspect of intelligence work. This holds specially true of dictatorial regimes, with which U.S. intelligence is particularly concerned, because their decisions are in the hands of unstable and impulsive individuals subject to few if any external controls. It is hard to predict the behavior of unpredictable personalities." See "What to do About The CIA," in Neal Kozodoy, *What to do About . . . : A Collection of Essays from* Commentary *Magazine* (New York: Regan Books, 1995), p. 225.

Cold War assumptions that leaders of countries in possession of weapons of mass destruction are rational opponents who calculate the risks and benefits before using such force do not apply when these countries are ruled by messianic leaders with suicidal instincts.

89 Fulbright's memorandum to President Kennedy, March 30, 1961.

90 See, Jesús Hernández Cuéllar, "Lo peor del dragón está en la cola: Entrevista al escritor cubano Guillermo Cabrera Infante," *Contacto*, March 1997.

91 I still don't understand why people keep calling the strange phenomenon that took place in Cuba a "revolution." Revolution means change, but what happened in Cuba brought back the worst things of the past increased tenfold: exploitation, hunger, drugs, prostitution, corruption, cronyism, and the total capitulation to both the U.S. dollar and Spain's neo-colonialism. Instead of referring to it as the Cuban

revolution we should call it the Cuban regression.

92 Some of them probably written by the same authors who have been for more than forty years churning out book after book portraying a disingenuous, Castro-friendly history of Cuba.

93 Reading the history of Nazi Germany some people have asked themselves, if it happened in Germany, could it happen elsewhere; could it happen here in the U.S.? My answer is, yes. The fact that we were spared does not guarantee that it will not happen in the near future. Perhaps he/she is already among us and his/her eyes are targeted on the White House.

94 U.S. Department of State, *Cuba*, Inter-American Series No. 66, Washington, D.C., 1961, p. 1.

95 Typical of this line of reasoning is Sebastian Balfour's erroneous belief that "Events in Cuba can only be properly understood in the light of Cuban history." See *Castro*, second edition (London: Longman, 1995) p. ix.

96 For a detailed, in depth view of how the American popular culture had influenced Cuba in the pre-Castro years (and, to some extent, how the Cuban popular culture *has* influenced America), see Louis A. Pérez, Jr., *On Becoming Cuban* (Chapel Hill: The University of Carolina Press, 1999). Paradoxically, after forty-two years of "anti-Yankee" Castroism the mutual cultural influence is stronger than never before.

97 No serious study in the forties or fifties mentions Cuba as a potential candidate for an anti-American revolution. For example, a 1940 book by James Fred Rippy curiously titled *The Caribbean Danger Zone* (New York: G. P. Putnam's Sons), does not mention Cuba as a source of potential danger for the U.S. Probably the single exception is a tract written by Blas Roca, a senior member of the Partido Socialista Popular (the original Cuban communist party), titled *Los fundamentos del socialismo in Cuba* (The foundations of Socialism in Cuba). However, as I have shown above in this book, the Cuban communists were probably the most surprised with the victory of Castro's guerrilla and his conversion to "communism."

98 One of the few authors who agrees with me in this assertion is Adolfo Rivero Caro. See "Cuba: The Unnecessary Revolution," http://www.neoliberalismo.com/unnecessary.htm.

99 This is, for example, the opinion expressed by Mario Lazo in his *Dagger in the Heart* (New York: Twin Circle, 1970), pp. 73-108, and by Lowry Nelson in *Cuba: The Measure of a Revolution* (Minneapolis: University of Minnesota Press, 1972).

100 Lewis Mumford pointed out that the true sources of fascism are to be found "in the human soul, *not in economics*." Adding that, "In overwhelming pride, delight in cruelty, neurotic disintegration—in

this and not in the Treaty of Versailles or in the incompetence of the German Republic lies the explanation of Fascism." *Faith and Living* (New York: Harcourt, Brace & Co., 1940), p. 118.

101 Arturo García Hernández,"Entrevista con Norberto Fuentes," *La Jornada*, No. 279, October 16, 1994, p. 18.

102 Robert R. Reilly, "Culture of Vice," *National Review*, November 25, 1996, p. 60.

103 Thomas in Foreword to Mario Llerena, *The Unsuspected Revolution* (Ithaca, New York: Cornell University Press, 1978), p. 11.

104 Fitzgibbon, Andreski, Fagg, Ruiz and Tannenbaum quoted in Louis A. Pérez, Jr., *Cuba: Between Reform and Revolution*, second edition (New York: Oxford University Press, 1995), p. vii.

105 The fact that the Castroist revolution was solely the product of Castro's mind has been extensively documented, among other authors, by Andrés Suárez in his *Cuba: Castroism and Communism, 1959-1966* (Cambridge, Mass.: The M.I.T. Press, 1967), and succinctly expressed in Ernst Halperin's foreword to the same work. According to Halperin, "One man alone, Fidel Castro, is responsible for the course of events in Cuba," (p. viii). Suárez' findings, however, are in strong disagreement with modern sociological interpretations of history, held both by Marxist and non-Marxists historians, according to which historical events are not determined by individuals but by social forces. Though dubious even when applied to the French and Russian revolutions—Halperin affirms—in the case of Cuba, sociological interpretations of history are totally inapplicable. In the same fashion, Milton Himmelfarb dismissed all the grand theories about the causes of the holocaust in his controversial essay "No Hitler, No Holocaust," *Commentary*, March 1984, pp. 37-43. Himmelfarb believes, and I fully agree with him, that Hitler murdered the Jews not because any external reason compelled him to do it, but "because he wanted to."

On the other hand, one should not discard the possibility that, though the fertile soil was totally Castro's, the seed was wittingly or unwittingly planted by other people. This is an interesting subject of research for scholars.

106 Though Fidel has mentioned several times Raúl as his designated successor, the truth is that there is no provision in the Castroist Constitution in accordance with which a successor may be elected, or an institution possessing the unquestioned right and unquestioned power to produce one. Moreover, Raúl has many enemies among the high hierarchy of the Army and the MININT.

107 The confusion and chaos in the minutes after Castro fainted while giving a speech on June 23, 2001, was a short rehearsal of things to come. See Pablo Alfonso, "Dudan de la estabilidad del régimen

cubano," *El Nuevo Herald*, June 24, 2001.

108 Brazilian journalist Gonzalo Guimaraens compared Castro to Dr. Ox, an enigmatic character created by Jules Verne (*Une fantaisie du docteur Ox*, Amiens, 1872). Dr. Ox controlled the behavior of the inhabitants of the village of Quinquendone by releasing mysterious gases he produced in his lab. See "El doctor Ox, Cuba y Colombia," *Cubdest Servicio de Difusión*, January 25, 2001, cubdest@uol.com.br.

109 There is at least one historical precedent: As soon as their Jesuit masters abandoned the socialist experiment they had been developing for more than a century in Paraguay, the Guaraní Indians went back to their forest and returned to their traditional customs as if nothing had ever happened.

Some Cubans, in Cuba and abroad, fear that the death of Castro may bring something even worse to the country. Granted, after more than forty years of physical and moral destruction of the country and its people, the death of Castro will create difficult problems for Cuba, and their solution may not bring what many have in mind. But, as we have seen above in this book, nothing can be worse than Fidel Castro.

110 As 17th Century Spanish thinker and sage Baltasar Gracián pointed out, "Just as virtue is its own reward, vice is its own punishment. The person who races through a life of vice comes to a double quick end. The one who races through virtue never dies," *The Art of Wordly Wisdom: A Pocket Oracle*, translated by Christopher Maurer (New York: Doubleday, 1992), p. 51.

Afterword

1 *Dulces Guerreros Cubanos* (Barcelona: Seix Barral, 1999), p. 117.

2 Del Pino's forthcoming book quoted in Ernesto Betancourt, "Castro's Terrorist Connection," *No Castro.com*, October 2001, www.nocastro.com/Terrorism/castro-terrorist2.htm.

3 The main cause for the Sandinista takeover was not their military successes, but the fact that the U.S. retired its support to President Somoza. See, i. e., Anastasio Somoza, *Nicaragua Betrayed* (Boston: Western Islands, 1980). The process followed the same lines as the Castro takeover on Cuba in 1959. See, Fulgencio Batista, *Cuba Betrayed* (New York: Vantage Press, 1962). A cursory examination of the bibliography on the subject shows a long list of books accusing the U.S. of betraying its allies and selling them to the communists.

4 Quoted in Betancourt, *op. cit.*

5 See, i.e., John Barron, "Castro, Cocaine and the A-Bomb Connection," *Reader's Digest*, March 1990, p. 70; Harvey McGeorge, "Chemical Addiction," *Defense and Foreign Affairs*, April 1989, p. 17; and George Gedda, "U.S. Gen. Supports Some Cuba Ties," *Associated Press*, April 25, 1998. In his article, Gedda quotes the allegations made by Congressman Lincoln Díaz-Balart, that "Under the guise of genetic, biological and pharmaceutical research, Castro is developing a serious germs and chemical warfare capability."

In early 1998, the U.S. Department of Defense expressed similar concerns about Cuba's potential for creating biological weapons. The Defense Intelligence Agency assessment at the time was that "Cuba's current scientific facilities and expertise could support an offensive BW program in at least the research and development stage. Cuba's biotechnology industry is one of the most advanced in emerging countries and would be cabable of producing BW agents." See DIA, "The Cuban Threat to U.S. National Security," May 6, 1998. In a letter of transmittal of the document to Strom Thurmond, Chairman of the Armed Services Committee, dated May 6, 1998, Secretary of Defense William S. Cohen pointed out, "I remain concerned about Cuba's potential to develop and produce biological agents, given its biotechnology infra-estructure." See, DoD public affairs web site, www.defenselink.mil.

6 During an interview with CNN's Lucia Newman in 1998, Castro accused the U.S. of waging bacteriological warfare and terrorism against Cuba. See "CNN 1998 interview with Fidel Castro, 'Cuba has no need for spies,'" *Granma*, June 4, 2001

7 One of the most accepted definitions of terrorism is "the use of violence against civilians in order to terrorize and force them to exert pressure upon their government to accept the terrorist's demands." Though there are many definitions of terrorism, the use of violence against non-combatants (i.e., civilians), is a characteristic present in most of them.

8 Ernesto Betancourt, *op. cit.*

9 *Ibid*. For a comprehensive overview of Castro's terrorist activities, see, Eugene Pons, "Castro and Terrorism: A Chronology 1959-1967," Institute for Cuban & Cuban-American Studies, Occasional Paper Series, September 2001, with a Foreword by Jaime Suchlicki.

10 See, J. R. Nyquist,"Clinton's Sympathy for Marxist Terrorists," *WorldNetDaily.com*, September 27, 1999. Before leaving the White House, Presiden Clinton abused his presidential executive privilege by pardoning 11 FALN and 5 Macheteros terrorists doing time in U.S. prisons. Moreover, the Clinton administration pushed to get a U.S. visa for Castro's terrorism chief, Fernando García Bielsa, a high

ranking Cuban intelligence officer, who is suspected of being in charge of overseeing the terrorist activities of the FALN and the Macheteros. Bielsa is currently operating in the U.S. under a diplomatic cover as a senior official at the Cuban Interests Section in Washington, D.C. See J. Michael Waller, "A Visa for Castro's Terrorism Chief in Washington?," *Insight on the News Online*, September 24, 1999, www.insightmag.com.

11 Pons, *op.cit.*

12 The *Miami Herald*, November 11, 2000.

13 "Ayatollah Khomeini's grandson visits Cuba," *Granma Internacional Digital*, August 2, 2001, www.granma.cu/ingles/julio5/30ayat-i.html.

14 Mireya Castañeda, "The people of Cuba march for justice," *Granma Internacional Digital*, July 26, 2001, www.granma.cu/ingles/julio4/marcha-I.html, (emphasis added).

15. "Fidel meets with Portuguese authorities before returning from extensive tour," *Granma Internacional Digital*, www.granma.cu/ingles/mayo/21portu-i.html. Curiously, just a few hours after the September 11 terrorist attacks on the U.S., *Granma Internacional Digital* purged its databases of all the information related to Castro's links with the anti-American muslim world.

16 See, i.e., "Patterns of Global Terrorism: 1999," www.state.gov/www/global/terrorism/1999report/intro.html

17 *AFP*, May 10, 2001.

18 "Fidel Castro and the Ayatollah Khamanei," *Agency France Press*, May 10, 2001, www.neoliberalismo.com/iran_cuba.htm.

19 *Ibid*. Apparently Khamenei's sources of intelligence were very good, because a few weeks before the attack the Mossad informed the FBI and the CIA that it had picked up indications of a "large-scale target" in the U.S. and that Americans would be "very vulnerable." See Richard A. Serrano and John-Thor Dahlburg, "Officials Told of 'Major Assault' Plans," The *Los Angeles Times*, September 20, 2001. The use of the word "vulnerable" suggests that the Mossad picked it up from an intercepted message between anti-U.S. terrorists.

20 *Ibid*.

21 Nancy San Martin, "Cuba Sold to Iran Biotechnology that Can be Used to Make Biochemical Arms, Scientist Says," The *Miami Herald*, October 10, 2001.

22 U.S. Department of State Note: Iran, www.state.gov/r/pa/bgn/index.cfm?docid=5314.

23 "A Tribute to the Syrian Symbol of Struggle," *Granma Internacional Digital*, May 16, 2001, www.granma.cu/ingles/

mayo3/20siria-i.html.

24 "Fidel Visits the House Bombed by the United States, Causing the Death of Qadaffi's Daughter," *Granma Internacional Digital*, May 17, 2001, www.granma.cu/ingles/mayo3/2lilia-i.html.

25 Toby Westerman, "Bin Laden Using U.S. Radio Broadcasts?," *WorldNetDaily*, November 8, 2001, www.worldnetdaily.com/news/articles.asp?ARTICLE_ID=25242.

26 Sim Leoi Leoi, "Study of Religion Interests Castro," *The Star*, November 9, 2001, thestar.com.my/news/story.asp?file=/2001/5/13/nation/13011fi&sec=nation.

27 William F. Jasper, "The Enemy Within," *The New American*, November 19, 2001.

28 Since the mid-1970s, Castro has been accussing the U.S. of waging biological warfare against Cuba. In 1971 the island suffered a massive outbreak of African hog fever, which Castro claimed was caused by germs introduced by the CIA. Castro claimed that near 500,000 hogs had to be killed in an effort to stop the infection. See Warren Hinckle and William Turner, *Deadly Secrets* (New York: Thunder's Mouth Press, 1992), p. 349. In the same fashion, when hemorrhagic conjunctivitis appeared in Cuba in 1981, Castro rushed to accuse the U.S. of its introduction, see *Havana Domestic Service*, September 9, 1981.

On the other hand, Castro's allegations must be taken with caution. Given his propensity for projecting his evil ideas unto others, it is not far-fectched to think that probably Castro made these allegations to divert attention from his own activities.

29 The whole story is told in Ken Alibek, *Biohazard* (New York: Random House, 2000), pp. 273-277.

30 For many years, in more than 200 medical schools and mental hospitals, the CIA tested diseases and chemicals on American citizens without their knowledge. Other U.S. government agencies also released bacteriological warfare agents in many U.S. cities, inluding New York, Washington, D.C., and San Francisco, to evaluate the people's reaction to the attack. In San Francisco in 1950, after one of these tests, 11 people were hospitalized and one person died. Relatives of the deceased found out as a result of a lawsuit that between 1950 and 1969 the U.S. government had conducted no less than 300 open air biological attacks on the American people. In 1955 the CIA released the whopping cough virus in Palmetto, Florida, and at least 12 people died of the disease. In 1966 the Army dispensed a bacteria in the New York subway. In 1968, the CIA came close to poisoning the water supply of the FDA headquarters in Washington. During a 1977 congressional investigation, the Army

admitted conducting hundreds of open air experiments with toxic agents on unaware American citizens. See, Louis Wolf, "This side of Nuclear War: The Pentagon's Other Option," *Covert Action*, Number 17 (Summer, 1982), pp. 16-17; also, "Biological War Testing in 1953 by Army Probed," *San Francisco Examiner*, June 26, 1994.

31 See John Crewdson, "Cuba Link Sought in Spread of AIDS," The *Chicago Tribune*, January 31, 1988, p. 6.

32 *Ibid.*

33 Mark Fineman, "Trying Poison on Embargo of Cuba Caribbean: Pastors Visiting the Island Nation Hope to Bring Back Biorat, a Product to Kill Rodents, for U.S. Inner Cities," The *Los Angeles Times*, July 5, 2001.

34 Joseph Douglass and Neil Livingstone, *America the Vulnerable* (New York: D. C. Heath and Company, 1987), pp. 151-152.

35 *Dulces Guerreros Cubanos* (Barcelona: Seix Barral, 1999), p. 118.

36 The *Washington Post*, September 25, 2001, A10.

37 The *New York Press*, April 26 - May 2, 2000.

38 Michael McGuire, "U.S. Pressed to Remove Cuba from Terrorist-states List," The *Chicago Tribune*, September 28, 2001.

39 *Ibid.*

40 Wayne S. Smith and Anya K. Landau, "Keeping Things in Perspective: Cuba and the Question of International Terrorism," *Center for International Policy*, November 6, 2001, www.ciponline .org/cuba/ipr/keepingthingsinperspective.PDF. On-line in the CIP site there is another article, "Letter from Miami," written by Nita Rous Manitzas, a former Ford Foundation program advisor, which follows closely the arguments expressed in the Smith-Landau article. The most interesting thing about it is that the Manitzas' article is dated August 22, 2001, that is, *before* the terrorist attacks on U.S. territory.

41 This follows Castro's *modus operandi*. Keep in mind his comments to Jean Daniel after he received the news of the assassination of President Kennedy.

42 Smith and Landau, *op. cit.*

43 Which probably does not cover terrorist actions against the American people *from American territory.*

44 Smith and Landau, *op. cit.*

45 *Ibid.*

46 Fidel Castro, "Remarks by Dr. Fidel Castro Ruz, President of the Republic of Cuba, at the Round Table Discussion of the Most Recent Lies Spread by the United States Against Cuba," held in the Televisión Cubana Studios on June 19, 2001, www.iacenter.org/ castro_061901.htm.

47 Powell declaring at a House Appropriations Subcommittee hearing on April 26, 2001.

48 See, "U.S. Continues to Ignore Castro Terrorism," *Judicial Watch Press Release*, November 1, 2001, www.judicialwatch.org/press_release.asp?pr_id=1734. See also, Carl Limbacher, "U.S. Keeps Ignoring Castro's Terrorism," *NewsMax.com*, www.newsmax.com/showinside.shtml?a=2001/10/30/200338.

49 "U.S. Continues to Ignore Castro Terrorism," *Judicial Watch Press Release*, November 1, 2001, www.judicialwatch.org/press_release.asp?pr_id=1734.

50 Montes is a Defense Intelligence Agency senior analyst who was responsible for Cuban affairs. The detention of Montes constitutes a factual rebuttal of Castro's claim that "Cuba has no Need for Spies," as he told *CNN* during an interview with Lucia Newman on October 19, 1998. (See "*CNN* 1998 interview with Fidel Castro, 'Cuba has no need for spies,'" *Granma*, June 4, 2001).

51 It seems that, before her detention, Belén's star was on the rising. See, Tim Johnson, "Cuba Spy Suspect was Rising Into Senior Intelligence Ranks," The *Miami Herald*, September 29, 2001.

52 "U.S. Continues to Ignore Castro Terrorism," *Judicial Watch Press Release*, November 1, 2001, www.judicialwatch.org/press_release.asp?pr_id=1734.

53 Martin Arostegui, "Fidel May be Part of Terror Campaign," *Insight*, December 3, 2001.

54 *Ibid.*

55 *Ibid.*

56 Though "supermarket tabloid' has been used for many years as a derogatory term, it seems that the tabloids reivindicated themselves with their excellent coverage during the Washington scandal involving the mysterious desaparition of Chandra Levi, an aide to California Congressman Gary Condit.

57 See, "Anthrax: Is there a Castro Connection?," *The New Australian*, www.newaus.com.au/us290_anthrax_castro.html.

58 *Ibid.*

59 See, Christopher Ruddy, "Of Course It Was Weaponized," *NewsMax.com*, October 22, 2001, www.newsmax.com/archives/articles/2001/10/21/140757.shtml.

60. "What Does Dr. Weeks Believe?," *NewsMax.com*, October 25, 2001.

61 *Ibid.*

62 As I wrote above in this book, some years ago Castro bough three 10,000 RPM, high capacity centrifuges shielded against lethal agents. This type of centrifuges are an indispensable tool for

weaponizing bacteriological warfare agents, anthrax among them.

63 Wes Vernon, "Castro's Planes Fly Over U.S. Despite Terrorist Ties," *NewsMax.com* Wires, www.newsmax.com/archives/articles/2001/11/2/191844.shtml.

64 With the benefit of hindsight, it seems that it is probably not a coincidence that this is the organization for which Cuban spy Ana Belén Montes used to work for.

65 "Secretary Cohen, Casey Institute Symposia Agree: Castro's Cuba Remains an Asymmetric Threat," Press Release, May 7, 1998, *Publications of the Casey Institute of the Center for Security Policy*, No, 98-R 80.

66 *Ibid.*

67 "Summary of the William J. Casey Institute of the Center for Security Policy's Symposia on Vital U.S. Security Interests in Cuba," Press Coral Gables and West Palm Beach, 12 and 13 March, 1998, *Publications of the Casey Institute of the Center for Security Policy*, No, 98-R 80 (Attachment).

68 The Bush administration's betrayal of the Cuban-American community is not limited to the issue of Castro's terrorist activities. See, i.e., "Bush Abandons Pledge to Cuban-Americans to Toughen Law Against Castro," *Judicial Watch* Press release, July 18, 2001, www.judicialwatch.org/press_release.asp?pr_id=1404. As Judicial Watch Chairman Larry Klayman pointed out, "No amount of photo-op parties at the White House with Cuban-American leaders will mask the hard fact that President Bush thus far has talked a good game but taken a few, if any, actions to strengthen the American commitment to overthrow the illegal Castro government in Cuba. Sadly, the President's appeasement towards Castro is a bit like his approach to government corruption—all talk and no action."

69 See, "Cheney Announces 'Bush Doctrine'," *NewsMax.com*, October 18, 2001.

Bibliography

Books

Acuña, Juan Antonio. *Cuba: revolución traicionada.* Montevideo, Uruguay: Imp. Ed. Goes, 1962.
Aguilar, Alonso. *Latin America and the Alliance for Progress.* New York: Monthly Review Press, 1963.
Alape, Sergio. *El Bogotazo: memorias del olvido.* La Habana: Casa de las Américas, 1983.
Alarcón Ramírez, Dariel "Benigno." *Memorias de un Soldado Cubano: Vida y Muerte de la Revolución.* Barcelona: Tusquets, 1997.
Alexander, Robert J. *Communism in Latin America.* New Brunswick, N.J.: Rutgers University Press, 1957.
Allen, Robert Loring. *Soviet Influence in Latin America: The Role of Economic Relations.* Washington, D.C.: Public Affairs Press, 1959.
Artime, Manuel. *¡Traición!* Mexico, D.F.: Editorial Jus, 1960.
Alvarez Díaz, José R. *Un estudio sobre Cuba.* Coral Gables, Fla: University of Miami Press, 1963.
_____ *La trayectoria de Castro.* Miami, Fla.: Ed. AIP, 1964.
Andrew, Christopher M., and Oleg Gordievsky. *KGB: The Inside Story.* New York: Harper Collins, 1990.
Arcocha, Juan. *Fidel Castro en rompecabezas.* Madrid: Ediciones Erre, 1973.
Arnault, Jacques. *Cuba et le Marxisme.* Paris: Editions Sociales, 1963.

Baeza Flores, Alberto. *Las cadenas vienen desde lejos.* Mexico, D.F.: Editorial Letras, 1960.
Balfour, Sebastian. *Castro.* New York: Longman, 1995.
Barbeito, José. *Realidad y masificación: Reflexiones sobre la revolución cubana.* Caracas: Ediciones "Nuevo Orden", 1964.
Barron, John. *KGB: The Secret World of Soviet Secret Agents.* London: Corgi, 1975.

Bayard, James. *The Real Story on Cuba*. Derby, Conn.: Monarch, 1963.
Bender, Lynn Darrell. *The Politics of Hostility: Castro's Revolution and United States Policy*. Hato Rey, P. R.: Inter American University Press, 1975.
Bethel, Paul D. *The Losers*. New Rochelle, New York: Arlington House, 1969.
Betto, Fray. *Fidel y la religión. Conversaciones con Frei Betto*. Havana: Oficina de Publicaciones del Consejo de Estado, 1985.
Beyer, Don E. *Castro!* New York: Franklin Watts, 1993.
Blakey, G. Robert, and Richard N. Billings. *The Plot to Kill the President*. New York: Times Books, 1981.
Boca, Angelo Del, and Mario Giovana. *Fascism Today*. New York: Pantheon, 1969.
Bonachea, Ramón L., and Marta San Martín. *The Cuban Insurrection 1952-1959*. New Brunswick, N.J.: Transaction Books, 1974.
Bonachea, Rolando E, and Nelson P. Valdés, eds. *Revolutionary Struggle, 1947-1958*. Volume I of the Selected Works of Fidel Castro. Cambridge, Mass.: The MIT Press, 1972.
Bonsal, Philip W. *Cuba, Castro and the United States*. Pittsburgh. Penn.: University of Pittsburgh Press, 1971.
Bourne, Peter G. *Fidel: A Biography of Fidel Castro*. New York: Dodd, Mead & Company, 1986.
Breuer, William B. *Vendetta: Castro and the Kennedy Brothers*. New York: John Wiley, 1997.
Bugge, Brian K. *The Mystique of Conspiracy: Oswald, Castro and the CIA*. Staten Island, N.Y.: n.p., 1978.
Burks, David D. *Cuba Under Castro*. Headline Series # 165, Foreign Policy Association, New York, June 29, 1964.
Burner, David, and Thomas R. West. *The Torch is Passed: The Kennedy Brothers and American Liberalism*. New York: Atheneum, 1984.
Burns, James MacGregor. *John Kennedy: A Political Profile*. New York: Hartcourt, 1960.

Cabús, José D. *Castro ante la historia*. México, D. F.: Editores Mexicanos Unidos, [1963].
Carbonell, Nestor T. *And the Russians Stayed: The Sovietization of Cuba*. New York: William Morrow, 1989.
Castro, Fidel. *La historia me absolverá*. La Habana: Editorial Luz-Hilo, 1960.
_____ *Guía del pensamiento político de Fidel Castro*. La Habana: Diario Libre, 1960.
_____ *History Will Absolve Me*. New York: Lyle Stuart, 1961.

_____ *Television speech delivered on Nov. 1, 1962.* Peking: Foreign Languages, 1962.
_____ Interview with Lee Lockwood. *Playboy,* January 1967.
_____ *Revolutionary Struggle, 1947-1958.* Cambridge: MIT Press, 1972.
_____. *My Early Years.* New York: Ocean Press, 1998.
Casuso, Teresa. *Cuba and Castro.* New York: Random House, 1961.
Clark. Juan. *Cuba: mito y realidad.* Caracas: Saeta, 1990.
Conte Agüero, Luis. *Cartas del Presidio: Anticipo de una biografía de Fidel Castro.* La Habana: Editorial Lex, 1959.
_____ *Fidel Castro: Vida y obra.* La Habana: Editorial Lex, 1959.
_____ *Los dos rostros de Fidel Castro.* Mexico, D.F.: Editorial Jus, 1960.
_____ *Fidel Castro. Psiquiatría y Política.* Mexico, D.F.: Editorial Jus, 1968.
Conte, Ramón B. *Historia oculta de los crímenes de Fidel Castro.* Miami: n. p., 1995.
Crasweller, Robert D. *Cuba and the U.S.; The Tangled Relationship.* New York: Foreign Policy Association, 1971.
Cumerlato, Corinne and Denis Rousseau, *L'Ile du docteur Castro.* Paris: Editions Stock, 2000.

Daniel, James. *Cuba: The First Soviet Satellite in the Americas.* New York: Aron Books, 1961.
Daniels, Anthony. *The Wilder Shores of Marx.* London: Hutchinson, 1991.
Debray, Régis. *Revolution in the Revolution?* New York: Monthly Review Press, 1967.
Devlin, Kevin. *The Soviet-Cuban Confrontation: Economic Reality and Political Judo.* Research Department of Radio Free Europe, 1 April, 1968.
Dolgoff, Sam. *The Cuban Revolution: A Critical Perspective.* Montreal: Black Rose Books, 1977.
Donald, Aida DiPace, ed. *John F. Kennedy and the New Frontier.* New York: Hill and Wang, 1966.
Draper, Theodore. *Castro's Revolution: Myths and Realities.* New York: Frederick A. Praeger, 1962.
_____ *Castroism: Theory and Practice.* New York: Praeger, 1965.
Dubois, Jules. *Fidel Castro: Rebel, Liberator or Dictator?* Indianapolis: Bobbs-Merrill Co., 1959.
Dumont, René. *Cuba: Socialism and Development.* New York: Grove Press, 1970.
Duncan, W. Raymond, ed. *Soviet Policy in Developing Countries.*

Waltham, Mass.: Ginn-Blaisdell, 1970.
_____. *The Soviet Union and Cuba: Interests and Influence.* New York: Praeger, 1985.

Eckstein, Susan. *Back From the Future: Cuba Under Castro.* Princeton, N.J.: Princeton Univresity Press, 1994.
Edmonds, Robin. *Soviet Foreign Policy 1962-1973: The Paradox of Superpower.* London: Oxford University Press, 1975.
Epstein, Edward Jay. *Counterplot. Inquest. Legend. The Assassination Chronicles.* New York: Carroll & Graf, 1992.
Erisman, H. Michael. *Cuba's International Relations.* Boulder, Colorado: Westview Press, 1958.
Evans, Stanton M. *The Liberal Establishment.* New York: The Devin-Adair Co., 1965.

Facts on File. *Cuba, The U.S. and Russia, 1960-63.* New York: Facts on File, 1964.
Fagg, John Edwin. *Cuba, Haiti, & the Dominican Republic.* Englewood Cliffs, N.J.: Prentice-Hall, 1965.
Falk, Pamela. *Cuban Foreign Policy: Carribbean Tempest.* Lexington, Mass.: Lexington Books, 1986.
Farber, Samuel. *Revolution and Reaction in Cuba, 1933-1960.* Middletown, Connecticut: Wesleyan University Press, 1976.
Fiallo, Amalio. *Cuba: Una revolución reaccionaria.* Miami, Fla.: Revista Ideal, 1979.
Fitzsimmons, Louise. *The Kennedy Doctrine.* New York: Random House, 1972.
Furiati, Claudia. *ZR RIFLE: The Plot to Kill Kennedy and Castro.* Melbourne: Ocean Press, 1994.
Franco, Victor. *The Morning After.* New York: Frederick A. Praeger, 1963.
Franqui, Carlos. *Diario de la revolución cubana.* Barcelona: Ediciones Erre, 1976.
_____ *Family Portrait with Fidel.* New York: Random House, 1984.
_____ *Vida, aventuras y desastres de un hombre llamado Castro.* Barcelona: Editorial Planeta, 1988.
Fuentes, Norberto. *Dulces guerreros cubanos.* Barcelona: Seix Barral, 1999.

Gerassi, John. *The Great Fear in Latin America.* New York: Collier, 1965.
_____ *Fidel Castro.* Garden City, N.Y.: Doubleday and Company,

1973.
Geyer, Georgie Anne. *Guerrilla Prince.* Boston: Little, Brown and Co., 1991.
Giménez, Armando. *Sierra Maestra: La revolución de Fidel Castro.* Buenos Aires: Editorial Lautaro, 1959.
Goldenberg, Boris. *The Cuban Revolution and Latin America.* New York: Praeger, 1965.
Goldston, Robert. *The Cuban Revolution.* Indianapolis: Bobbs-Merrill, 1970.
Gonzalez, Servando. *Historia herética de la revolución fidelista.* San Francisco: Ediciones El Gato Tuerto, 1986.
_____ *Observando.* San Francisco: Ediciones El Gato Tuerto, 1986.
Gonzalez, Edward. *Cuba Under Castro: The Limits of Charisma.* Boston: Houghton Mifflin, 1974.
_____ *A Strategy for Dealing with Cuba in the 1980s.* Santa Monica, Calif.: RAND Corporation, 1982.
Goodsell, James Nelson, ed. *Fidel Castro's Personal Revolution in Cuba: 1959-1973.* New York: Knopf, 1975.
Gouré, Leon, and Morris Rothenberg. *Soviet Penetration in Latin America.* Miami: University of Miami Press, 1975.
Gregor, A. James. *The Fascist Persuasion in Radical Politics.* Princeton, N.J.: Princeton University Press, 1974.
Gregory, Oswald J., and Anthony J. Estrover, eds. *The Soviet Union and Latin America.* New York: Praeger, 1970.
Guilbert, Yves. *El "infidel" Castro.* Mexico D.F.: Plaza & Janés [1961].

Halberstam, David. *The Best and the Brightest.* New York: Random House, 1972.
Halperin, Maurice. *The Rise and Decline of Fidel Castro.* Berkeley: Univ. of California Press, 1972.
_____ *The Taming of Fidel Castro.* Berkeley: Univ. of Calif. Press, 1981.
Hansen, Joseph, ed. *Dynamics of the Cuban Revolution: The Trotskyst View.* New York: Pathfinder Press, 1978.
Hernández, Eugenio. *Cuban-Soviet Relations: Divergence and Convergence.* Washington: Georgetown Univ., Latin American Studies Program, 1980.
Hersh, Seymour. *The Dark Side of Camelot.* New York: Little Brown, 1997.
Hinckle, Warren. *The Fish is Red: the Story of the Secret War Against Castro.* New York: Times Books, 1980.
Horowitz, Irving Louis, ed. *Cuban Communism, 3d., ed.* New Brunswick, N.J.: Transaction Books, 1977.

Huberman, Leo, and Paul M. Sweezy. *Cuba: Anatomy of a Revolution.* New York: Monthly Review Press, 1961.
Hudson, Rex A. *Castro's Americas Department.* Washington, D. C.: The Cuban American National Foundation, 1988.
Hunt, Christopher. *Waiting for Fidel.* New York: Houghton Mifflin, 1997.

Jackson, D. Bruce. *Castro, the Kremlin and Communism in Latin America.* Baltimore, Md.: The Johns Hopkins University Press, 1969.
James, Daniel. *Red Design for the Americas.* New York: John Day Co., 1954.
_____ Cuba: *The First Soviet Satellite in the Americas.* New York: Aron Books, 1961.
Judson, Fred C. *Cuba and the Revolutionary Myth.* Boulder, Colorado: Westview Press, 1984.
Julien, Claude. *La révolution cubaine.* Paris: Julliard, 1961.

Karol, K. S. *Guerrillas in Power.* New York: Hill and Wang, 1970.
Krich, John. *A Totally Free Man: An Unauthorized Autobiography of Fidel Castro.* Berkeley: Creative Arts, 1981.

Langley, Lester D. *The Cuban Policy of the United States: A Brief History.* New York: John Wiley & Sons, 1968.
_____ *The United States, Cuba, and the Cold War: American Failure or Communist Conspiracy?* Lexington, Mass.: D. C. Heath, 1970.
_____. *Cuba: A Perennial Problem in American Foreign Policy.* St. Charles, Mo.: Forum, 1973.
Laqueur, Walter. *Fascism: Past, Present, Future.* New York: Oxford University Press, 1996.
Lazo, Mario. *Dagger in the Heart.* New York: Twin Circle Pub., 1968.
Levesque, Jacques. *The USSR and the Cuban Revolution: Soviet Ideological and Strategical Perspectives.* New York: Praeger Publishers, 1978.
Llerena, Mario. *The Unsuspected Revolution.* Ithaca, N. Y.: Cornell University Press, 1978.
Lockwood, Lee. *Castro's Cuba, Cuba's Fidel.* New York: Macmillan, 1967.
López-Fresquet, Rufo. *My 14 months with Castro.* Cleveland, Ohio: World Publishing Co., 1966.
Luque Escalona, Roberto. *Fidel: El juicio de la historia.* Mexico: Dante, 1990.

MacGaffey, Wyatt, and Clifford R. Barnett. *Twentieth-Century Cuba: The Background of the Castro Revolution*. New York: Doubleday & Co., 1965.
MacGaffey, Wyatt, and Clifford R. Barnett. *Cuba. Its people, its society, its culture*. New Haven, Conn.: Hraf Press, 1962.
Mankievicz, Frank, and Kirby Jones. *With Fidel: A Portrait of Castro and Cuba*. New York: Playboy Press, 1975.
Mañón, Melvin, and Juan Benemelis. *Juicio a Fidel*. Santo Domingo, Dominican Republic: Editora Taller, 1990.
Manrara, Luis V. *Cuba Disproves the Myth that Poverty is the Cause of Communism*. Miami: The Truth About Cuba Committee, 1963.
_____ *Betrayal Opened the Door to Russian Missiles in Red Cuba*. Miami: The Truth About Cuba Committee, 1968.
Martin, Lionel. *The Early Fidel: Roots of Castro's Communism*. Seacaucus, N.J.: Lyle Stuart, Inc., 1978.
Martin, Malachi. *The Jesuits. The Society of Jesus and the Betrayal of the Roman Catholic Church*. New York: Simon & Schuster, 1988.
Masur, Gerhard. *Nationalism in Latin America*. New York: The Macmillan Co., 1966.
Matthews, Herbert L. *The Cuban Story*. New York: George Braziller, 1961.
_____ *Cuba*. New York: Macmillan, 1964.
_____ *Fidel Castro: A Political Biography*. London: Penguin Press, 1969.
_____ *Revolution in Cuba*. New York: Scribners, 1975.
Meneses, Enrique. *Fidel Castro*. New York: Taplinger Pub. Co., 1960.
Mesa Lago, Carmelo. *Revolutionary Change in Cuba*. Pittsburgh: University of Pittsburgh Press, 1971.
Mezerik, A. G. *Cuba and the United States* (2 vols.) New York: International Review Service, 1963.
Milan, Rigoberto. *Farsa y Farsantes de Cuba Comunista*. Chicago, Il.: Ahora Printing, 1984.
Minà, Gianni. *Il racconto di Fidel*. Milan: Mondadori, 1988.
Montaner, Carlos Alberto. *Informe secreto sobre la revolución cubana*. Madrid: SEDMAY, 1976.
_____ *Fidel Castro y la revolución cubana*. Madrid: Editorial Playor, 1983.
Moore, Carlos. *Castro, the Blacks, and Africa*. Los Angeles: Center for Afro-American Studies, Univ. of Calif., 1988.
Morton, Ward M. *Castro as a Charismatic Hero*. Lawrence, Kansas: Center for Latin American Studies, University of Kansas, 1965.
Moscovit, Andrei. *Did Castro Kill Kennedy?* Washington, D.C: The

Cuban American National Foundation, 1998, n.d.
Movimiento 26 de julio. *Nuestra razón: Manifiesto Programa del Movimiento 26 de julio.* Reprinted in Enrique González Pedrero. *La revolución cubana.* Mexico, D.F.: Escuela Nacional de Ciencias Políticas y Sociales, 1959.
Movimiento 26 de julio. *Tesis Económica del Movimiento Revolucionario 26 de julio.* Reprinted in Fidel Castro, La revolución cubana: Escritos y discursos, edited by Gregorio Selser Buenos Aires: Editorial Palestra, 1960.

Nelson, Lowry. *Cuba: The Measure of a Revolution.* Minneapolis: University of Minnesota Press, 1972.
Newman, Philip C. *Cuba Before Castro, An Economic Appraisal.* Ridgewood, N.J.: Foreign Studies Institute, 1965.

Oppenheimer, Andres. *Castro's Final Hour.* New York: Simon and Schuster, 1992,
Oswald, J. Gregory, and Anthony J. Strover, eds. *The Soviet Union and Latin America.* New York: Praeger, 1970.

Pardo Llada, José. *Fidel: de los jesuítas al Moncada.* Bogotá: Plaza y Janés,1976.
_____ *Fidel y el "Ché."* Barcelona: Plaza y Janés, 1988.
Partido Socialista Popular. *Carta del Comité Nacional del Partido Socialista Popular al Movimiento 26 de julio.* La Habana: junio de 1957.
Patterson, Thomas G. *Contesting Castro.* New York: Oxford University Press, 1994.
Pérez-Stable, Marifeli. *The Cuban Revolution: Origins, Course, and Legacy.* New York: Oxford University Press, 1993.
Petit, Antoine G. *Castro, Debray contre le Marxisme-leninisme.* Paris: Laffont, 1968.
Pflaum, I. P. *Tragic Island.* Englewood Cliffs, N.J.: Prentice-Hall, 1961.
Phillips, R. Hart. *Cuba: Island of Paradox.* New York: McDowell, Obolensky, 1960.
_____ *The Cuban Dilemma.* New York: Ivan Obolensky, 1962.
Plank, John. *Cuba and the United States: Long Range Perspectives.* Washington, D.C.: The Brookings Institution, 1967.
Poppino, Rollie, E. *International Communism in Latin America.* London: Collier-Macmillan, 1964.
Popular Socialist Party of Cuba. *The Cuban Revolution.* New York: New Century Publisher, 1961.

Quirk, Robert E. *Fidel Castro*. New York: W.W. Norton, 1993.

Ratliff, William E. *Castroism and Communism in Latin America, 1959-1976*. Stanford, Calif.: Hoover Institution Press, 1976.
_____ *The Selling of Fidel Castro*. New Brunswick: Transaction Books, 1987.
Reason, Barbara, Margaret B. Myghisuddin and Bum-Joon Lee Park. *Cuba Since Castro: A Bibliography*. Washington, D.C.: American University; Special Operation research Office, 1962.
Reitan, Ruth. *The Rise and Decline of an Alliance: Cuba and African American Leaders in the 1960s*. East Lansing, MI: Michigan State University Press, 1999.
Rius (Eduardo del Río), *Lástima de Cuba: El grandioso fracaso de los hnos. Castro*. México, D.F.: Grijalbo, 1994.
Robbins, Carla Anne. *The Cuban Threat*. New York: McGraw-Hill, 1983.
Robin, G. *La crise de Cuba*. Paris: IFRI, Economica, 1984.
Rodríguez Morejón, Gerardo. *Fidel Castro; biografía*. Habana: P. Fernández, 1959.
Roig the Leuchsenring, Emilio. *Cuba no debe su independencia a los Estados Unidos*. La Habana: Ediciones La Tertulia, 1960.
_____ *Los Estados Unidos contra Cuba Libre*. Santiago de Cuba: Ed. Oriente, 1982.
Ruffin, Patricia. *Capitalism and Socialism in Cuba*. New York: St. Martin's Press, 1990.
Ruiz, Leovigildo. *Diario de una traición*. Miami: Florida Typesetting, 1965.
Ruiz, Ramón Eduardo. *Cuba: The Making of a Revolution*. New York: W. W. Norton, 1968.
Russo, Gus. *Live by the Sword*. Baltimore: Bancroft, 1998.

Sauvage, Leo. *Autopsie du Castrisme*. Paris: Flammarion, 1962.
Seers, D., ed. *Cuba, The Economic and Social Revolution*. Chapel Hill, N.C.: The Univ. of North Carolina Press, 1964.
Semidei, Manuela. *Les États-Unis et la révolution cubaine, 1959-1964*. Paris: Libraire A Colin, 1968.
_____, ed. *Kennedy et la révolution cubaine, un apprentissage politique?* Paris: Julliard, 1972.
Smith, Earl T. *The Fourth Floor*. New York: Random House, 1962.
Smith, Robert F. *What Happened in Cuba? A Documentary History*. New York: Twayne Publishers, 1963.
Sobel, Lester A., ed. *Cuba, The U. S. and Russia, 1960-1963*. New York: Facts on File, 1964.

Suárez, Andrés. Cuba: *Castroism and Communism, 1959-1966*. Cambridge, Mass.: M. I. T. Press, 1967.
Suchlicki, Jaime. *Castro, Cuba, and Revolution*. Coral Gables, Fla.: University of Floridda Press, 1972.
_____ *Cuba: Continuity and Change*. Miami: North-South Center for the Institute of Interamerican Studies, Univ. of Miami, 1986.
Sutherland, Elizabeth. *The Youngest Revolution*. New York: Dial Press, 1969.
Szulc, Tad. *The Winds of Revolution*. New York: Praeger, 1964.
_____ *Fidel: A Critical Portrait*. New York: William Morrow, 1986.

Taber, Robert. *M 26: The Biography of a Revolution*. New York: Lyle Stuart, 1961.
Tannenbaum, Frank. *Ten Keys to Latin America*. New York: Vintage, 1966.
Tetlow, Edwin. *Eye on Cuba*. New York: Hartcourt, Brace and World, 1966.
Thomas, Hugh. *Cuba: The Pursuit of Freedom*. New York: Harper and Row, 1971.
Thornton, Thomas P. *The Third World in Soviet Perspective*. Princeton, N.J.: Princeton Univ. Press, 1964.
Torres Ramírez, Blanca. *Las relaciones cubano-soviéticas (1959-1968)*. Mexico, D. F.: El Colegio de Mexico, 1969.
Triska, Jan F., ed. *Soviet Communism: Programs and Rules*. San Francisco: Chandler, 1962.
_____, and David D. Finley. *Soviet Foreign Policy*. New York: Macmillan, 1968.

United States Department of State. *Events in the United States-Cuban Relations: a Chronology, 1957-1963*. Washington, D.C.: U.S. Government Printing Office, 1963.

Vail, John J. *Fidel Castro*. New York: Chelsea House, 1986.
Valladares, Armando. *Against All Hope*. New York: Alfred A. Knopf, 1986.
Valkenier, Elizabeth Kridl. *The Soviet Union and the Third World: An Economic Bind*. New York: Praeger, 1984.

Walton, Richard J. *Cold War and Counter-Revolution: The Foreign Policy of John F. Kennedy*. New York: The Viking Press, 1972.
Weyl, Nathaniel. *Red Star Over Cuba*. New York: Devin-Adair, 1960.
Wilkerson, Loree. *Fidel Castro's Political Programs from Reformism to*

"Marxism-Leninism." Gainesvile, Fla.: Univ of Florida Press, 1965.
Williams, William Appleman. *The United States, Cuba and Castro.* New York: Monthly Review Press, 1962.

Young, Allen. *Gays Under the Cuban Revolution.* San Francisco: Grey Fox Press, 1981.

Zeitlin, Maurice, and Robert Scheer. *Cuba: Tragedy in Our Hemisphere.* New York: Grove Press, 1963.

Articles

Alexander, Robert J. "Soviet Communist Activities in Latin America." *Problems of Communism*, X, No. 1, (January-February, 1961).
_____ "Latin American Communism." *Soviet Survey*, August 1962.
_____ "Latin America and the Communist Bloc." *Current History*, Vol. 44, No. 258, February 1963.
_____ "Old Quarrels in Havana." *New Politics*, 33, Fall 1964.
Anderson, Jack. "What You Don't Know CAN Hurt You." *Parade*, August 11, 1985.
Anderson, Jack. "Double Agents in Cuba." *San Francisco Chronicle*, March 21, 1988.
Atwood, William. "The Tragedy of Fidel Castro." *Look*, Sept. 15, 1959.

Beals, Caleton. "Cuba's Revolution: The First Year." *The Christian Century* (March 9, 1960).
Berle, Jr., A.A. "The Cuban Crisis." *Foreign Affairs*, October 1960.
Bolton, Charles. "Cuba: Pivot to the Future." *The Nation*, 17 November, 1962.
Burks, David D. "Soviet Policy for Castro's Cuba." in John J. TePaske and Sydney Nettleton Fisher, eds., *Explosive Forces in Latin America.* Columbus, Ohio: Ohio State University Press, 1964.

Castro, Fidel. "Why We Fight." *Coronet* (February 1958).
_____ Television speech delivered on Nov. 1, 1962. Peking: Foreign Languages, 1962.
Castro, Juana. "My Brother Fidel." *Life*, August 28, 1964.

Casuso, Teresa. "Mi amigo Fidel Castro." *Humanismo* (Mexico) Jan-Feb. 1958.

Devlin, Kevin. "The Soviet-Cuban Confrontation: Economic Reality and Political Judo." Research Department of Radio Free Europe, 1 April, 1968.
_____ "The Castroist Challenge to Communism." in J. Gregory Oswald and Anthony J. Strovel, eds., *The Soviet Union and Latin America*. New York: Praeger, 1970.

Draper, Theodore. "The Runaway Revolution." *The Reporter* (May 12, 1960).
_____ "Castro and Communism," *The Reporter*, 17 January 1963.

Ellsberg, Daniel. "The Day Castro Almost Started World War III." *The New York Times*, October 31, 1987.

Enzensberger, Hans Magnus. "Portrait of a Party: Prehistory, Structure and Ideology of the P.C.C." in Ronald Radosh, ed., *The New Cuba: Paradoxes and Potentials*. New York: William Morrow and Co., Inc., 1970.

Erice, Michael with Emma and Lidia Castro. "Vida de Fidel Castro." *El Diario de Nueva York*, April 22 to May 1, 1957.

Geyer, Georgie Anne. "El fascismo reaparece bajo disfraz del comunismo en la América Central." *El Universal* (Caracas), viernes 8 de julio de 1983.

González, Servando."Una nueva modalidad de exilio." *El Miami Herald*, 30 de agosto de 1983.
_____ "Did the Horse Kill the Bishop? Political Chess in the Caribbean." *Unveiling*, Vol. II, No. 1 (September-November, 1984).
_____ "¿Milagro en La Habana?" *Mariel*, Año 1, Vol. 4, (1988).
_____ "Fidel Castro Supermole," *Sumeria*, 1996.
_____ "A Missile is a Missile is a Missile," *Guaracabuya*, 2000.

Gonzalez, Edward. "Relationship with the Soviet Union," in Carmelo Mesa-Lago , ed., *Revolutionary Change in Cuba*. Pittsburgh: Univ. of Pittsburgh Press, 1971.

Gouré, Leon, and Morris Rothenburg. "Latin America," in Kurt London, ed., *The Soviet Union in World Politics*. Boulder, Co.: Westview Press, 1980.

Guevara, Ernesto "Ché". "Notes for the Study of the Ideology of the Cuban Revolution," in *Ché Guevara Speaks*: Selected Speeches and Writings. New York: Merit Publishers, 1967.

Hart Phillips, Ruby. "Castro Gets the Bill." *The Reporter* (October 29, 1959).
Hersh, Seymour. "Was Castro Out of Control in 1962?" *The Washington Post*, October 11, 1987.

Johnston, James. "Did Cuba Murder JFK? A New Look at Some Old Puzzles. The CIA, Castro and Revenge." *The Washington Post*, November 19, 1989.

Kirkpatrick, Jeanne. "Is a stubborn Castro testing U.S. defenses?" *The Miami Herald*, March 31, 1991.
Kohler, Foy D. "Cuba and the Soviet Problem in Latin America." in Jaime Suchlicki, ed., *Cuba, Castro, and Revolution*. Coral Gables, Fl.: University of Miami Press, 1972.

Maidique, Modesto. "Fidel's Plantation." *The Stanford Magazine*, Winter 1983.
Martin, Harold H. "Can Castro Save Cuba?" *Saturday Evening Post* (August 1, 1959).
Martin, Joseph, and Phil Santora. "The Real Castro." *The New York Daily News*, March-April, 1960.
Matthews, Herbert. "Return to Cuba." *Hispanic-American Report*, Special Issue, Stanford, 1964.
Meyer, Karl. E. "Who Won What in Cuba." *The Reporter*, Feb. 5, 1958.
Moats, Alice-Leone. "The Strange Past of Fidel Castro." *National Review*, Aug. 24, 1957.
Montaner, Carlos Alberto. "¿Quiere Castro abandonar a los soviéticos?" *La Estrella de Panamá*, 22 de febrero de 1985.
Montoro, Adrian G. "Moscow Was Caught Between Cuba and U. S." *The New York Times*, November 17, 1987.
Murkland, Harry B. "Cuba: The Evolution of Revolution." *Current History* (March 1960).

Nixon, Richard M. "Cuba, Castro, and John F. Kennedy." *Reader's Digest*, November 1964.

Padula, Alfred. "Financing Castro's Revolution, 1956-1958." *Revista/Review Interamericana* 8 (Summer 1978).
Preston, Julia. "The Trial that Shook Cuba." *New York Review of Books*, 7 December 1989.

Ross, Stanley. "We Were Wrong About Castro." *American Weekly*, June 12, 1960.

Safford, Jeffrey J. "The Nixon-Castro Meeting of 19 April 1959." *Diplomatic History* 4 (Fall 1980)

St. George, Andrew. "A Visit With a Revolutionary." *Coronet* (February 1958).

_____ "Inside Cuba's Revolution." *Look* (February 4, 1958).

Suárez, Andrés. "Soviet Influence on the Internal Politics of Cuba." in Alvin Z. Rubinstein, ed., *Soviet and Chinese Influence in the Third World*. New York: Praeger, 1975.

Taber, Robert. "Castro's Cuba." *The Nation* (January 23, 1960).

Thomas, Hugh. "The Origins of the Cuban Revolution." in James N. Goodsell, ed., *Fidel Castro's Personal Revolution in Cuba: 1959-1973*. New York: Knopff, 1975.

Treaster, Joseph B. "Defecting General Says Cuba Has Plan to Raid Base in U.S. If Is Attacked." *The New York Times*, October 11, 1987.

Walters, Robert S. "Soviet Economic Aid to Cuba." in James N. Goodsell, ed., *Fidel Castro's Personal Revolution in Cuba: 1959-1973*. New York: Knopff, 1975.

Index

A
Abalkin, Leonid, 41-42
Abrahantes, Gen. José, 117, 144, 154, 178, 192, 196, 221
abortions, 309-310
Agee, Philip, 386
Agencia Latina, 280
Agramonte, Roberto, 244
agrarian reform, 77, 138, 150-151, 245
AIDS, 117, 145, 221-222
Air raids on Cuba, Castro-sponsored, 90-91
Alarcón Ramírez, Dariel (Benigno), 114, 230
Alarcón, Ricardo, 299, 321, 330, 339
Aldana, Carlos, 321, 341
Alekseev (Shitov), Aleksandr, 34, 40-41, 47, 57, 164-165, 338
Alemán, José, 121-122
Alibek, Ken, 41, 73
Allende, Beatriz, 117
Allende, Laura, 117
Allende, Salvador, 40
Alliance for Progress, 46
Almeida, Juan, 230
Almendros, Néstor, 221
Almodóvar, Pedro, 223
Althusser, Louis, 247
Amado Blanco, Luis, 252
Amin, Idi, 267

Anderson, Bibi, 223
Angleton, James J., 118
Angola, 93, 225
  Cuban military assistance to, 94, 143, 156, 165, 168, 225, 267-269, 340
anthrax, 72, 336, 338, 348
Antuña, Vicentina, 107
Arbenz, Jacobo, 235
Arcocha, Juan, 32
Arcos Bergnes, Sebastián, 115
Arenas, Reinaldo, 220
Argote, María, 224
Ariza, René, 323
Artime, Manuel, 116
Assad, Bashar al-, 337
asymmetric war, 325-326, 346, 350
Asman, David, 195
Atta, Mohamed, 348
Azcárate, Mons. Fernando, 254
Azcue, Eusebio, 120
Azpillaga, Maj. Floren-tino, 73-74

B
babalawos, 268-270
Bacon, Sir Francis, 32
Baliño, Carlos, 241
Batista, Fulgencio, 44, 76, 78, 79, 83, 87- 88, 107-109, 134, 136, 207, 228, 235, 237, 238

Castro and, 45, 49, 87, 90, 102, 107, 112, 127, 135, 173, 175, 201, 224, 228, 241,
  CIA officers and, 224
  Cuban communists and, 235, 237, 238-239, 242-243, 280
  Moncada attack and, 107, 238
Bay of Pigs, 11-12, 33, 36, 43, 48, 50, 68, 93, 100, 102, 116, 129, 162, 179, 250
Beatles, The, 220
Beatón, Maj. Manuel, 113
Belén School, 21, 43-44, 86, 88, 105, 112, 172-173, 188, 190, 206, 215-216, 218, 237, 271, 274-276
Bergier, Jacques, 22
Betancourt, Rómulo, 82, 110,
Bethel, Paul, 219,
Betto, Frei, 21, 85, 187-188, 204, 211, 254, 265, 316-317
Biaín, Father Ignacio, 252
Binet-Sangle, Charles, 189
Biorat, 340
Bin Laden, Osama, 348-349,
Black Muslims, 225
Black Panthers, 226
Blomquist, Walter, 44
Bofill, Ricardo, 412-413
Bogotazo, 37-38, 68, 86, 89, 106, 117, 228, 277
Bohemia (magazine), 107, 204, 238-239, 248, 322
Bonsal, Philip, 32-33
Bradlee, Ben, 119
Bravo, Estela, 140
Bravo, Flavio, 414
Brezhnev, Leonid, 41
Brothers to the Rescue, 94, 130, 199, 321-322, 343
Brown, Jerry, 36
Brown, Rap, 225
Buenavista Social Club, 147
Bush, George W.,
Bustillo, Carlos, 38

C

Cabell, Gen. C. P., 233-234
Cabrera Infante, Guillermo, 34, 326
Camilo Cienfuegos Military Academy, 390
Caral, Oscar Fernández, 112
Carbonell, Walterio, 115, 226,
Cardenal, Ernesto, 50
Carmichael, Stokely, 225
Cartier-Bresson, Henri, 203
Casaroli, Mons. Agostino, 253
Castañeda, Jorge, 127
Castro, Fr. Alberto de, 275
Castro, Angel
  life in Cuba, 271, 274
  alcoholism of, 189
  Fidel and, 224, 252, 271
Castro, Fidel (Fidel Alejandro Castro Ruz)
  Angel's alcoholism and, 189
  assassination plots against, 97, 99, 118, 357
  bacteriological warfare and, 41, 62, 64, 67, 71-75, 215, 321, 323, 325, 332-333, 336, 345
  bola de churre (nickname of), 173
  books read by, 43, 164-165, 189, 274
  cows and, 19, 209-212
  cruelty of, 196-197, 199, 213, 294, 309, 312
  charisma and, 29-30, 33, 52,

168, 261, 277
clairvoyance, powers of, 23, 43, 52
depression of, 188-189, 191, 328
doves and, 36, 265
envy and, 31-32, 86, 156, 172, 179, 181-183, 188, 195, 229,
evil eye and, 32, 181
exile in Mexico, 82, 86, 89, 202, 204, 218, 262-262, 278, 298
father and, See Castro, Angel.
financial situation of, 137
gangsterism, involvement in, 51, 111-113, 115, 126, 147, 170, 228, 321, 360, 430, 444
guns and, 38, 88, 106-107, 113, 196, 201
hatred of Americans, 78, 228, 319
health of, 188-193
alleged homosexuality of, 216-220
The Horse (nickname of), 231, 260-262, 267
humanist connections, 243, 246-247, 297, 300-303, 306
humor, lack of, 42, 176, 207-208
humiliation and, 69, 86, 87-88, 101, 126, 130, 166, 182, 187, 198-199, 213, 216, 332, 334, 338-339
ideology of, 19, 169, 179, 247, 251, 253, 274, 279, 290, 292-295, 314-317, 343, 360
illegitimacy of, 172, 331-332, 334
leadership principle and, 167, 276, 279, 281, 292-293, 296-297
Marxist claims, 18, 147, 165, 169, 230, 233, 240-241, 247, 249-251, 253, 255, 260, 266, 271, 276-277, 279-281, 287-288, 292-293, 295, 302-303
milk and, 208-212, 217, 404,
moral attitudes and convictions of, 69, 138, 154, 163, 167, 170, 204, 239, 293, 296, 304, 306, 323, 335, 342, 362, 385
necrophilic discourse, 55, 60, 65-66, 68, 175, 179, 325
nuclear weapons and, 20, 35, 52-65, 70, 74-75, 228, 304, 337, 357, 368-369, 374
oratorial style and skills of, 21, 32, 34, 36, 38, 68, 165-166, 175, 178-179, 202, 204, 207, 216, 292
photographic memory, 19, 88, 104, 164-165, 193, 247, 275, 338
physical appearance and personal traits of
beard, 38, 42, 48, 230, 361
eyes, 35, 42-43, 65, 101, 171, 195, 204
stinkiness of, 172-173
peophesies about, 43-44, 324, 338
in prison, 49, 89, 204, 247, 293, 394, 451
racism of, 130, 191, 223-227, 305, 372
Santería and, 261-270
sense of destiny of, 43, 50, 77, 81, 95, 167, 214, 264, 324
as serial killer, 196

television, political use of, 38, 166, 201
at the university, 44-45, 51, 88, 101, 106, 109, 111-112, 115, 126, 142, 164, 170-171, 173, 190, 215, 217, 226, 279, 281, 321, 324-325, 327-328, 344
vindictiveness of, 21, 70, 88-89, 97, 101, 198, 333, 342, 360,
women and, 168, 181, 206, 217-219, 227, 306, 315,
work and, 131, 138, 163-164, 174, 177
Castro Díaz-Balart, Fidel (Fidelito)
and nuclear weapons, 63, 64
fired by Fidel, 70
Castro, Manolo, 111
Castro Ruz, Juana, 70, 360
Castro Ruz, Raúl, 39, 45, 55, 72, 83, 113, 123, 198, 221, 339
Castro Soto del Valle, Antonio, 224
Casuso, Teresa, 23, 37, 47, 49, 68, 101, 189, 193-194
Catholic Church. See Roman Catholic Church
Central Intelligence Agency (CIA), 22, 32-33, 36, 47-48, 51-52, 75, 88, 97-100, 115, 118, 120-129, 131, 161, 191, 216, 224, 233, 276, 280, 282, 292, 299, 306, 338, 357, 361, 364, 367-368, 374, 377, 379, 384-386, 393
Cesaire, Aimée, 226
Céspedes, Mons. Carlos Manuel de, 257
Chávez, Hugo, 389
Chernobyl nuclear plant, 62, 64, 66
Chibás, Eduardo (Eddy), 45, 106, 239, 243, 279, 292
Chiari, Roberto, 110, 127
Childs, Morris, 120
Chirino, Raúl, 117
Chrétien, Jean, 127
Church, Senator Frank, 52
CIA, see Central Intelligence Agency
Cienfuegos (city of), 62
Cienfuegos, Maj. Camilo, 136, 178, 196, 249, 269, 344, 359
disappearance of, 113
Cienfuegos, Osmani, 178
Claret, Fr. Antonio María, 48
Clark, Ramsey, 96
Cleaver, Eldridge, 225
Cockburn, Alexander, 342
Cohen, William, 350
Colegio de Dolores, 16, 86, 172, 173, 196, 228, 274, 326
Committees for the Defense of the Revolution, 283
Communist Party of Cuba (Castro's), 39, 55, 61, 65, 154, 168, 180, 192, 224, 229, 230
Communist Party of Cuba (PSP), pro Soviet, 219, 234, 235-246, 248, 251
Batista and, 235, 237-238, 239
Castro and, 239, 241-243
Communist Party of the Soviet Union, 59,
concentration camps, see prisons in Cuba
Conte Agüero, Luis, 88, 112, 139, 182, 199, 215, 276, 359

Convivio (secret society), 275
Cooder, Ry, 147
Cortázar, Julio, 34
Council on Foreign Relations, 156
Cowley, Col. Fermín, 112
Cruz, Celia, 344
Cruz Varela, María Elena, 283
Cuba
  economy of,
  before Castro, 133-135
  during Batista, 134
  Soviet Union and, 133, 143, 148, 156, 175, 259
  U.S. and, 133-135
Cuban American National Foundation, 115, 117, 285-286,
Cuban missile crisis, 11-12, 16, 19, 41, 54-55, 61, 75, 99-101, 114, 199, 272
Cugat, Xavier, 228
Curbelo, Merejo, 142
Curbelo, Maj. Raúl, 142

D

Daily Worker (newspaper), 54,
Dam, Luis, 239
Daniel, Jean, 101, 118, 125, 128
Debray, Regis, 34, 219, 290-291,
Déjoie, Louis, 110
Diario de la Marina (newspaper), 275
Díaz-Balart, Mirtha, 138, 227-228,
Díaz-Balart, Rafael, 293
Díaz Lanz, Maj. Pedro Luis, 89
Diem, Ngo Dinh, 120
Dinerstein, Herbert S., 19
Dixon, Jeanne, 98, 131
Dominican Republic, 106, 109, 110, 127, 198, 202, 207, 236
  See also Trujillo, Rafael.
Dorticós, Osvaldo, 50-51, 102, 143, 221, 230, 249
Draper, Theodore, 15, 18, 24, 25, 78, 239, 276, 323, 361
Dubois, Jules, 43, 241
Dulles, Allen, 48, 98, 240
Durán, Rubén, 120
Duvalier, François (Papa Doc), 110, 127

E

Echeverría, José Antonio, 107-108
Edwards, Jorge, 211
Ellsberg, Daniel, 58-59
Engels, Friedrich, 165
Erikson, Erik, 330, 334
Escalante, Aníbal, 244, 247
Escalante, Gen. Fabián, 99, 283
espionage, see intelligence and espionage
Esterline, John, 33
exiles (Cuban) in U.S., 38, 48, 109, 121, 145, 147, 157, 206, 233, 251, 271, 272-273, 282, 319, 335-336,
  Catholic Church and, 258-259
  Cuban intelligence and, 272, 292

F

Farrakhan, Louis, 226
Fast Action Brigades, 283
Feltrinelli, Giangiaccomo, 34
Fernández Revuelta, Alina, 264,
Fernández Caral, Oscar, 112
Fernández, Jesús M., 141
Fernández, Pablo Armando, 210

Fernández-Zayas, Marcelo, 190
Figueres, José, 83-84, 248
Fitzgerald, Desmond, 97
Fonda, Jane, 36
Forbes (magazine), 137
Fort Gulich, 75
Franco, Francisco, 275
Frank, Waldo, 38
Franqui, Carlos, 19, 21, 43, 46, 50-51, 58, 70, 132, 156, 184, 196-197, 205, 211212, 218, 240-241, 261
Frunze military academy, 269
Fuentes, Carlos, 31
Fuente, José de la, 336
Fuentes, Norberto, 141, 178, 315, 333, 335, 342

G

Gadea, Hilda, 117
Gainer, James R., 35
Gaitán, Jorge Eliécer, 106, 127, 277
Galeano, Eduardo, 418
Gallegos, Rómulo, 360
Gamonal, Alfredo, 114
Gandhi, Mahatma, 52
García Márquez, Gabriel, 34, 184, 219, 227, 362
García Orellana, José, 56
Garvey, Mike, 39
Gaulle, Charles de, 52
Geyer, Georgie Anne, 18, 23, 32-33, 38, 70, 162, 196, 227, 262, 292, 293, 298
Ginsberg, Allen, 217
globalism, 310, 317
Gómez Abad, José, 56
Gómez, Leonel, 11
González, Elián, 117, 169, 192, 216, 270-271, 309

Gorbachev, Mikhail, 41, 191, 227, 304, 338
Granma (yacht), 37, 109, 117, 241, 262-263, 298
Granma (newspaper), 70, 115, 186, 216, 284
Grau San Martin, Ramón, 105, 127, 132
Gregor, A. James, 290
Grenada, 30, 62, 267, 332, 338
GRU (Glavnoye Razvedyvatelnoye Upravieniye), 40,
Guantánamo Naval Base, 142, 333,
Guaraní Indians, 256
Guardia, Col. Antonio (Tony) de la, 190, 196, 231, 268-269, 315, 333
Guardia, Ernesto de la, 108
Guardia, Patricio de la, 268-269, 315
Guerra, Eutimio, 49
Guevara, Alfredo, 106-107, 217-219
Guevara, Hilda, 117
Guevara, Ernesto (Ché), 76, 108, 110, 113, 137, 168, 193, 248, 256, 263, 280, 290-291, 297, 319
and Castro, 178, 196, 219, 240, 249, 269, 316, 344
creates myth of reactive revolution, 77, 79
death of, 114,
definition of Castroism, 293
"foco" guerilla theory, 291
and "New Man", 293
nuclear missiles and, 53-55,
as saint, 297

H

Habanazo, 38
Habel, Janette, 260
Halperin, Ernst, 112
Halperin, Maurice, 43
Hart, Armando, 219,
hate speech, 342
Havel, Vaclav, 22, 127, 340
Helms-Burton Law, 336
Helms, Jesse, 336
Helms, Richard, 97, 100, 120
Hemingway, Ernest, 360
Hernández, Melba, 206, 209, 217, 219
Herter, Christian, 250
Himmler, Heinrich, 256-257
Hitler, Adolf, 22-23, 52, 66, 70, 85, 162, 166, 179, 220, 275, 277-278, 280, 284, 288, 292, 296, 303, 304,
Hoffman, Abie, 219
Homestead AFB (Florida), 62
homosexuals, 217-223, 340
Hoover, J. Edgard, 98, 119, 120,
Horowitz, Irving Louis, 229, 290
Howard, Lisa, 117
Hoy (Cuban Communist's newspaper), 235
Hunt, Christopher, 438
Hunt, Howard, 129
Hussein, Saddam, 72, 116

I

Ikeda, Daisaku, 296
Ilich Sánchez, Carlos (The Jackal),
Intelligence and espionage, terms of
  agent, 17, 40, 62, 67, 91, 100, 121-126, 129, 147, 228, 276, 282
  agent of influence, 276
  appraisal of information, see evaluation of information
  Bulgarian treatment, 116
  Comprehensive Personality Profile, 161-162
  control, 40
  disinformation, 17, 21-22, 99, 118, 128, 147, 205, 254, 272, 292, 294
  elint, 100
  espionage, 17, 88, 91, 216, 255, 272,
  evaluation of information, 250,
  illegal, 250
  legend, 250
  mokrie dela, see wet affairs
  need-to-know, 129
  plausible denial, 129
  sleeper, 250
  spooker, 405
  spy, 52, 98
  tradecraft, 17, 40
  wet affairs, 126
Isle of Pines, prison on, 37, 204

J

Jane's Defence Weekly (magazine), 67
Jehovah's Witnesses, 220, 223
Jesuits,
  assassination and, 105
  and Castro, 113, 169, 172, 184, 206, 253, 255-257, 274-276, 302
  and education, 302, 329
  influence on Castro, 21, 83, 86
  and liberation theology, 302

in Paraguay, 256
tyrannicide and, 105
ultramontanism and, 255
Jiménez Leal, Orlando, 221
Johnson, Lyndon B., 96, 272
Jones, Jim, 22, 39, 52, 296-297
Jones, Kirby, 42, 103, 118
Judicial Watch, 346-347
Julien, Claude, 242
Juraguá nuclear plant, 62, 64, 70

K
Kaiser, Rev. Konrad, 311
Kalinin, Maj. Gen Yuri, 73
Karamessines, John, 97
Karol, K. S., 203, 308
Kelly, Clarence, 120
Kennedy, John F., 52
  Alliance for Progress and, 46
  assassination of, 96-105, 118-131
  Castro and, 77, 87,
  and Cuban missile crisis, 17, 59
Kennedy, Michael, 35
Kennedy, Robert F., 35
Kennedy Jr., Robert F.,
KGB (Komitet Gosudarstvennoy Bezopasnosti), 22, 34, 40, 57, 114, 140, 161, 276, 286
Khamenei, Ayatollah Ali, 336
Khomenei, Ayatollah, 334
Khrushchev, Nikita S. 102, 235, 245
  Castro and, 41-42, 60, 174, 259
  Cuban missile crisis, 48, 54-57, 59, 75, 99-101, 193, 228
  Kennedy assassination, 98
Kissinger, Henry, 100, 299

Koresh, David, 296
Kornbluh, Peter, 99
Kudryavtsev, Sergei, 40

L
Lage, Carlos, 148, 184, 344
Lago, Armando, 312, 442
Landau, Saul, 34
LaSalle school, Santiago de Cuba, 274
Latell, Brian, 324
Latin America, 61, 106, 133, 134, 136-137, 151, 156, 220, 257, 288, 290, 341-342
  Castro and, 20, 30, 33, 60, 84, 94, 102, 110, 133, 157, 198, 214, 255, 267, 271, 285, 291
  Soviet Union and, 234-236
  U.S. and, 46, 275, 319
Lavie, Jean Baptiste, 43-44
Law, Cardinal Bernad, 254
Leal Spengler, Eusebio, 155,
Leante, César, 362
Lechuga, Carlos, 99
Le Monde (newspaper), 55
Le Monde Diplomatique (newspaper), 260
Lenin, Vladimir I., 165
Lesnick, Max, 107
Levin, Gerald, 35
liberation theology, 206, 309
Liberty City (Florida), 67
Llerena, Mario, 278
Llorente, Fr. Armando, 43, 275
Lojendio, Juan Pablo de, 201
López Fresquet, Rufo, 68, 80, 87
López, Gilberto, 123
Lorenz, Marie (Marita), 51
Lorié, Maj. Ricardo, 83
Loyola, St. Ignatius, 255, 257,
Lumumba, Patrice, 128

M

Maciques, Abraham, 144
McGovern, Senator George S., 34, 52, 56, 103, 118, 129-130
McKeown, Robert (Dick), 121
McNamara, Robert S., 34,
Mafia, 98, 120, 122, 128, 131, 144, 156
   efforts to assassinate Castro and, 121, 122, 126
Maidique, Modesto, 18
Maine (battleship), 78, 89, 93,
Malcolm X, 225
Malmierca, Isidoro, 221
Mankiewicz, Frank, 42, 103, 118
Manson, Charles (Charlie), 22, 52, 296
Mañach, Jorge, 413
Maradona, Diego, 436
Marambio, Max, 148
Mariana, Father Juan, 105
Mariel boatlift, 12, 227, 267, 282-283, 339-340
Marinello, Juan, 237
Maritain, Jacques, 247
Martí, José, 33, 85, 181, 200, 266, 319
Martin, Lionel, 81, 240
Martínez Páez, José, 219
Martínez Villena, Rubén, 241
Martino, John, 198
Martino, Archbishop Renato, 254
Marx, Karl, 165
Marxism, 317, 443
   Castro and, 278, 165, 240, 250-251, 274, 279-280, 294-295, 297
Más Canosa, Jorge, 115, 117
Masetti, Jorge Ricardo, 280
Masferrer, Rolando, 112, 116
Matos, Huber, 113, 136, 178, 249, 269
Matthews, Herbert L., 18, 22, 29, 34, 40, 59, 70, 76-77, 81, 83, 101, 136-137, 148, 204, 211, 220, 233, 234, 253
Mayor, Federico, 34-35
Medellín drug cartel, 63
Mella, Julio Antonio, 241
Menendez, Robert, 347
Mestre, Ramón, 88
Meyerdorff, John, 258
Michaux, Lewis, 225
Mikoyan, Anastas, 40-41
Milanés, Pablo, 210
militia, Cuban, 47, 76, 90, 93, 125, 235, 274, 277-278
Mills, C. Wright, 77,
Miret, Pedro, 37
misery specialists, 183, 186
missile gap, 379
missiles (Castro's) in Cuba, 61-62
missiles (Soviet) in Cuba, 17, 41, 48, 54-59, 75, 193, 228, 357, 368
Miyar Barruecos, José (Chomy), 314
Moncada barracks, Santiago de Cuba,
   attack on, 37-38, 44-45, 49, 84, 105, 107, 110, 138, 166, 179, 192, 199, 200, 204, 206, 209, 216, 218, 230, 237-238, 240-242, 252, 255, 277, 279, 293, 298
Monje, Mario, 114,
Montaner, Carlos Alberto, 70, 115-116, 219, 261
Montoro, Adrián, 59
Moon, Sun Myung, 296

Morais, Fernando, 62
Moré, Beny, 261
Morejón Almagro, Leonel, 116
Morejón, Nancy, 226
Morgan, Maj. William, 197-198
Mother Jones (magazine), 34
Muñoz Unsaín, Alfredo, 329
Mussolini, Benito, 20, 275, 277-279, 281, 283-284, 288-289, 291, 293-294

N

Naranjo, José Alberto (Pepín), 301
Naranjo, Maj. Cristino, 113
Nasser, Gamal Abdel, 237
Nelson, Lowry, 85
New man
  Castro's, 138, 285, 293, 295, 298
  Fascist, 284
Newton, Huey, 225
Nietzsche, Friedrich, 30, 306, 323
Nixon, Richard, 42, 81, 94
Nkrumah, Kwame, 237
Nogueras, Luis Rogelio (Wichy), 117
Novikov, Alexei, 140
Nuccio, Richard, 338
Nuclear Non-Proliferation Treaty, 60
Nuevo Herald, El (newspaper), 72, 115,
Núñez Jiménez, Antonio, 107

O

Ochoa, Gen. Arnaldo, 144, 154, 168, 170, 178, 190, 196, 231, 268-269
Oltulski, Enrique, 208

Oppenheimer, Andres, 23, 34, 39, 65, 261
Oro, Juan, 65
Ortega, Cardinal Jaime, 257, 260,
Orwell, George, 44
Ospina Pérez, Mariano, 106
Oswald, Lee Harvey, 98, 118, 120-121, 123

P

Padilla, Heberto, 154
Paglia, Camille, 329
País, Frank, 113, 178, 196, 263, 344
Pardo Llada, José, 45-46, 106-107, 275
Pastors for Peace, 149, 340
Patrick, Vincent, 74
Pavlov, Yuri, 41
Pauwels, Louis, 22
Pazos, Felipe, 80, 87, 249
Pazos, Javier Felipe, 240
Peck, M. Scott, 309-310, 318
Pérez, Faustino, 47, 249
Pérez, Jorge, 222
Pérez Serantes, Bishop Enrique, 252
Perón, Evita, 52
Perón, Juan Domingo, 20, 106, 275, 277, 280, 290, 293-294
Petronas twin towers, 337
Phillips, Ruby Hart, 38, 88-89
Pino Díaz, Gen. Rafael del, 62, 332,
Pino, Capt. Onelio, 117
Pinochet, Augusto, 270, 314
Pino Siero, Rafael del, 89, 106, 117, 279
Piñeiro Losada, Manuel, 114-115, 221
Piñera, Virgilio, 24, 117

Pogo (Walter Kelly), 272
Pons, Alfredo, 183
Powell, Colin, 199, 325, 346
Prío Socarrás, Carlos, 45-46, 106-107, 127, 241
Primo de Rivera, José Antonio, 275
prisons in Cuba, 116, 153, 198, 220, 221, 222-223, 254, 256, 282-283, 285-287, 305, 312, 314
PSP, see Communist Party of Cuba (PSP),
Puebla, Carlos, 184

Q

Qaddafi, Muammar al-, 337
Quevedo, Miguel Angel, 322
Quincena, La (Catholic Newspaper), 252

R

Rasco, José Ignacio, 276
Rather, Dan, 63, 206, 227-228, 265,
Ray, Manuel, 249
Reagan, Ronald, 127, 259
Revolución (M-26-7's newspaper), 19
Revuelta, Naty, 227
Roa, Raúl, 48
Roa Kourí, Raúl, 61
Roca, Blas, 238-239, 245
Rodríguez, Ana, 254
Rodríguez, Carlos Rafael, 242, 244, 275
Rodrígues Cruz, René, 114
Rodríguez Díaz, Humberto, 110
Rodríguez Llompart, Héctor, 149
Rodríguez Menier, Juan Antonio, 59, 63
Rodríguez, Silvio, 210
Roman Catholic Church, 166, 182, 288, 292, 311, 331
  and Castro, 252-255, 257-260, 317
Romero, Archbishop Oscar, 257
Roosevelt, Franklin D., 16, 69, 86, 88, 130, 228, 332, 334
Rosenbaum, Ron, 23
Ruby, Jack, 121-122
Russia. See Soviet Union.
Ruz, Lina, 215, 331
Ryan, Chuck, 39

S

St. George, Andrew, 233, 240
Salinger, Pierre, 120
Sánchez, Irma, 142
Sánchez Manduley, Celia, 81-82, 139, 153, 266
  death of, 188, 266, 422
  relations with Castro, 173, 200, 217, 219
  Santería and, 264, 266
Sánchez, Osvaldo, 114,
Sánchez Ramírez, Ilich ("Carlos," "the Jackal"), 334
Santamaría, Haydée, 209, 219, 308
Santería, 259-271, 303
Santiesteban Casanova, Roberto, 56
Sardiñas, Father Guillermo, 252
Sarría, Lieut. Pedro Manuel, 49
Sartre, Jean-Paul, 34, 77-78, 133
Sawyer, Diane, 35
Schellemberg, Walter, 419
Schlesinger Jr., Arthur M., 36, 119, 340-341,
Schweiker, Richard, 98

Seabury, Paul, 281
Seal, Bobby, 225
Seko, Mobutu Sese, 150
Serrano, Jose, 455
Sevareid, Eric, 37
Shafik, Ahmed, 190
Shitov, Aleksandr, see Alekseev, Aleksandr
Sierra Maestra mountains, 18, 39, 44, 46, 48-50, 76, 81, 84, 88,
Smith, Earl T., 69
Smith, Howard K., 96
Smith, Robert F., 84
Smith, Wayne S., 34, 344-345
Sohm, Rudolf, 30
Somoza, Luis, 109
Sorí Marín, Maj. Humberto, 197
Soto del Valle, Dalia, 224
Soto, Hernando de, 151
Sorensen, Ted, 100-101, 119
Soviet Union, 41, 59, 245, 290, 308, 317, 333
    and Castro, 20, 40, 61, 62, 96, 114, 206, 251, 259, 273, 304, 343
    and Cuba, 84, 243-244
    economic and military aid to Cuba, 74, 133, 143, 148, 156, 175, 259
    and Latin America, 234-236
    Soviet missile bases in Cuba (1962), 56-57, 59, 304
SS (Schutzstaffel), 200, 257, 290
Stalin, Joseph V., 20, 70, 234, 265, 277
Stone, I. F., 203
student congress, Bogotá, 106
Suárez, Andrés, 15
Suárez, Carlos Andrés, 51
Sukarno, 237

Sun (newspaper)
Szulc, Tad, 34-35, 37, 40-41, 45-47, 49, 57, 107, 128, 162, 254,

T

Tass (Soviet press agency), 40
terrorism, 20, 56, 156, 185, 325, 333-336, 338, 342-349
Terrorist organizations,
    ETA (Basque), 334
    FAL (Puerto Rico), 334
    FARC (Colombia), 334
    IRA (Irish), 334
    Macheteros (Puerto Rico), 334
    MIR (Chile), 334
    Montoneros, (Argentine), 334
    MRTA (Tupac Amaru, Peru), 334
    Weathermen (U.S.), 334
Terry, Héctor, 191,
Tetlow, Edwin, 32,
Theresa hotel, 225,
Thomas, Hugh, 15, 18, 83, 97, 105, 241, 250-251, 277, 292-293,
Thurmond, Strom, 350
torture, 44, 116, 196, 220, 282, 286
Touré, Sékou, 237,
Touze, Vincent, 55
Trafficante, Jr., Santos, 121
Tricontinental Conference, 141, 289, 304, 333-334
Trujillo, Rafael L., 106, 109, 120, 127-128
Turner, Ted, 34, 36
26th of July Movement, 113, 218, 240-241, 246, 249, 251, 264

U

Ubre Blanca, 210
UIR (Unión Insurrecional

Revolucionaria), 112
UMAPs (Military Units to Help Production), 220-222
United Nations Organization, 38, 48, 61, 68, 76, 99, 203, 206, 225
United States of America
　Castro visits to the, 35-36, 46, 68, 80, 87, 107, 193-195, 203, 206, 246
　Castro's hatred toward, 19, 70, 75, 85-87, 183, 228,
　embargo on Cuba, 68, 95, 144, 152, 185, 206, 302, 306,
　military-industrial complex, 98
　as pulverizer, 69-70
　as world policeman, 95
University of Havana, 44-45, 51, 88, 101, 106, 109, 111-112, 115, 126, 142, 154, 164, 170, 173, 190, 215, 217, 221, 226, 279, 294,
Urrutia Lleó, Manuel, 38, 79, 178, 201, 245, 249,
U-2 (spy plane), 57

V

Valdés, Maj. Ramiro, 46, 84, 114, 221
Valladares, Armando, 220, 258
Vallejo, René, 266,
Vance, Cyrus, 94
Venereo, Evaristo, 88
Vera, Maj. Aldo, 116
Verde Olivo (newspaper), 54
Vietnam, 67, 71, 114, 128, 153, 3
Vivés, Juan, 61
Voisin, André, 43

W

Walker, Lucius, 340
Wallace, Mike, 206
Walters, Barbara, 35
Warren Commission, 97-98, 103, 119-120
Warren, Earl, 97-98
Weber, Max, 29-30
Weeks, Byron, 349
Wenders, Win, 147
Williams, Robert F., 225
Wilson, Thomas, 339,
World Trade Center, 337

X

X, Malcolm, 225

Y

Yanes Pelletier, Capt. Jesús, 49
Yeltsin, Boris, 191
Young, Allen, 220

Z

Zacchi, Mons. Cesare, 252-253
Zig-Zag (newspaper), 207-208
Zuckerman, Mortimer, 35, 53, 195

About the Author

Servando González is a Cuban-born American writer. He received his training as a historian at the University of Havana. He has written books, essays, articles, and multimedia on contemporary Cuban history, intelligence and espionage, political satire, semiotics, hypertext, and art history.

From 1959 to 1963 Servando was a political officer in the Cuban Army. As such he participated in the Bay of Pigs operation, the Cuban missile crisis, the massive anti-guerrilla actions in the Escambray mountains, and other important military operations. Also, on two occasions, in 1960 and in 1964, he had the opportunity of engaging in long conversations with Castro.

In 1964 Servando joined the Cuban Chamber of Commerce, where he was the editor of the international publications *Cuba Foreign Trade* and *Cuba Economic News*, of worldwide distribution. While holding these jobs, he was teaching part-time art history at the National School of Art, and Semiotics at the Institute of Industrial Design—a short-lived Cuban version of the Bauhaus. Later he was appointed Assistant Director for Educational Technology at the Institute of Foreign Trade, an innovative institution pioneering the most advanced learning technologies.

Though Servando was never part of the Castroist *nomenklatura*, for some time he had the opportunity of moving within the high circles of the Castro government as a technocrat, specializing in educational technology—the fad of the moment among the Castroist élite. In that capacity, in the mid-seventies he was an advisor to Raúl León Torras, President of the National Bank of Cuba, and to Dr. José Rivero Muñiz, Cuban Minister of Public Health. For a short period of time he was an advisor to Antonio Enrique Lussón, Cuban Minister of Transportation. He also provided advice on such subjects to Marcelo Fernández Font, Cuban Minister of Foreign Trade.

He left Cuba in 1981. Since then he has lived in Zürich, Miami, New York, San Francisco, New Orleans, Mobile (Alabama), and Hot Springs (Arkansas). He is currently residing again in the San Francisco Bay Area. While in New York, Servando wrote his twice-a-week byline, "Observando," for *El Diario/La Prensa*, one of the most read hispanic newspapers in the U.S.

Servando is the author of *Historia herética de la revolución fidelista* (San Francisco: El Gato Tuerto, 1986); *Observando* (San Francisco: El Gato Tuerto, 1986). His articles have been published in important magazines, newspapers and Web publications in the U.S. and abroad.

Servando is an Apple Macintosh certified multimedia developer, and has authored many computer programs, among them: *Hypertext for Beginners, Popol Vuh: An Interactive Text/Graphics Adventure, The Riddle of the Swastika: A Study in Symbolism,* and *How to Create Your Own Personal Intelligence Agency.* He has created dozens of Internet sites for himself and for others. Among them: *CastroMania: The Fidel Watch, FAQs About Fidel Castro, Tyrant Aficionado, The Swastika and the Nazis,* and *Memoirs of a Computer Heretic,* most of them available on the Web.

www.ingramcontent.com/pod-product-compliance
Lightning Source LLC
Chambersburg PA
CBHW031227290426
44109CB00012B/190